CHILDREN AND YOUTH WITH AUTISM SPECTRUM DISORDER (ASD)

CHILDREN AND YOUTH WITH AUTISM SPECTRUM DISORDER (ASD)

Recent Advances and Innovations in Assessment, Education, and Intervention

EDITED BY

JAMES K. LUISELLI

OXFORD
UNIVERSITY PRESS

10-21-15
GB
$69.00

OXFORD
UNIVERSITY PRESS

Oxford University Press is a department of the University of
Oxford. It furthers the University's objective of excellence in research,
scholarship, and education by publishing worldwide.

Oxford   New York
Auckland   Cape Town   Dar es Salaam   Hong Kong   Karachi
Kuala Lumpur   Madrid   Melbourne   Mexico City   Nairobi
New Delhi   Shanghai   Taipei   Toronto

With offices in
Argentina   Austria   Brazil   Chile   Czech Republic   France   Greece
Guatemala   Hungary   Italy   Japan   Poland   Portugal   Singapore
South Korea   Switzerland   Thailand   Turkey   Ukraine   Vietnam

Oxford is a registered trademark of Oxford University Press
in the UK and certain other countries.

Published in the United States of America by
Oxford University Press
198 Madison Avenue, New York, NY 10016

Library of Congress Cataloging-in-Publication Data
Children and youth with autism spectrum disorder (ASD): recent advances and innovations
in assessment, education, and intervention / edited by James K. Luiselli.
    pages cm
    Includes index.
    ISBN 978-0-19-994157-5
1. Autism spectrum disorders in children.   2. Children with autism spectrum disorders—Rehabitation.
    3. Autistic children—Education.   I. Luiselli, James K., editor of compilation.
    RJ506.A9C447 2014
    618.92'85882—dc23
    2013035309

1 3 5 7 9 8 6 4 2
Printed in the United States of America
on acid-free paper

CONTENTS

PREFACE

There have been many developments in educational and intervention practices for children and youth with autism spectrum disorder (ASD). Indeed, ASD is a relatively new diagnostic label that reflects the variability and differentiation of symptomatology among children and youth commonly described as having autistic disorder, high-functioning autism (HFA), and Asperger syndrome. Current best practices have emerged from decades of evidence-based research, research-to-practice translation of empirically supported procedures, and consensus-driven recommendations from multiple disciplines. In consequence, practitioners have many educational and intervention choices for children and youth with ASD—what is critical is that these options are informed by empirical outcomes that have been replicated in experimental trials (group and single-case) and disseminated to professionals and researchers alike.

Children and Youth With Autism Spectrum Disorder (ASD): Recent Advances and Innovations in Assessment, Education, and Intervention features chapters by acknowledged experts on topics that demand attention by the professional and academic community. The title reflects current convention in viewing autism along a continuum of presenting symptoms and also alerts readers that the book's content embraces both children and adolescents with ASD. Section I, *Diagnosis, Assessment, and Measurement*, includes chapters about diagnostic screening and assessment instruments, comorbidity among children and youth with ASD, and conducting outcome measurement. Section II concerns *Evidence-Based Practices* and has chapters that address computer-based instruction, naturalistic approaches for teaching social skills, and

early intensive behavioral intervention (EIBI). In Section III, *Health and Development*, the chapters cover self-management training, pivotal response treatment (PRT), and evaluating and improving intervention integrity by care providers. Section III also examines critical developmental and quality-of-life concerns related to feeding, sleeping, and physical exercise. Finally, Section IV, *Additional Topics*, focuses on mindfulness caregiving and support, cognitive-behavioral therapy (CBT), and behavioral family intervention.

My hope is that *Children and Youth With Autism Spectrum Disorder (ASD): Recent Advances and Innovations in Assessment, Education, and Intervention* serves as a state-of-the-art resource that documents the most recent advances in evidence-based and empirically supported approaches toward diagnosis, education, treatment, and program development. Readers will discover emerging topics that now warrant detailed analysis (e.g., computer-based instruction, self-management, cognitive-behavioral therapy, mindfulness caregiving, physical exercise), as well as the latest findings and innovations for well-established methods (e.g., social skills training, early intensive behavioral intervention, feeding interventions). Also, my intent is that the book reaches both professionals who teach, educate, and treat children and youth with ASD, and academic faculty who teach at the undergraduate and graduate level, conduct research, and supervise students within clinical psychology, special education, and child development.

I am indebted once again to Oxford University Press for supporting the book and making the publication process such an enjoyable experience. My acknowledgments extend to both people and places that for many reasons became prominent during the 2 years it took to bring out the book. Thank you, Dr. Ingolf Tuerk and staff at St. Elizabeth's Medical Center for everything and more. To my late friend Billy Bostic, I am so happy that we were able to recapture old times—may you rest in peace. I also owe thanks to another long lost friend, Dr. Van Westervelt. And my gratitude goes to Team 7A coaches and players of Concord-Carlisle Youth Lacrosse, Middlesex School, The Skating Club of Boston, and the New England Stars, Assabet Valley Patriots, and New England Canucks hockey programs. Finally, I dedicate this book to my wife, Dr. Tracy Evans Luiselli, our daughter Gabrielle, and our son Thomas: how lucky I am to have this family and experience the love and wisdom that surround me.

ABOUT THE EDITOR

James K. Luiselli, Ed.D., ABPP, BCBA-D, is a clinical psychologist and Senior Vice President of Applied Research, Clinical Training, and Peer Review at May Institute, a private human services and behavioral health care organization serving children, adolescents, and adults with developmental disabilities, traumatic brain injury, psychiatric disorders, and medically compromised conditions. He also maintains a private practice in educational, clinical, and behavioral consultation.

Dr. Luiselli is a licensed psychologist, certified health service provider, diplomat in behavioral psychology from The American Board of Professional Psychology (ABPP), and Board Certified Behavior Analyst (BCBA-D). He has held academic appointments at Harvard Medical School, Northeastern University, and Indiana State University. Within May Institute he is Director of Training for the Predoctoral Internship and Postdoctoral Fellowship Programs in Clinical Psychology and the Director of the Program of Professional Continuing Education.

Dr. Luiselli is active in clinical treatment, consultation, and research. In 1996 he was ranked by the Association for Advancement of Behavior Therapy (AABT) as one of the top 50 most published authors in the behavior analysis and therapy literature for the period 1974 through 1994. The journal *Research in Developmental Disabilities* (2000) listed him as the eighth most published researcher in the developmental disabilities field from 1979 through 1999. He has authored more than 300 publications, including the books *Behavioral Medicine and Developmental Disabilities* (Springer-Verlag), *Self-Injurious Behavior: Analysis, Assessment, and Treatment* (Springer-Verlag), *Antecedent Control: Innovative Approaches to Behavioral Support* (Paul H. Brookes), *Behavior Psychology in the Schools: Innovations in Evaluation, Support,* and *Consultation* (The Haworth Press), *Antecedent Assessment and Intervention: Supporting Children and Adults with Developmental Disabilities in Community Settings* (Paul H. Brookes), *Effective Practices for Children With Autism: Educational and Behavior Support Interventions That Work* (Oxford University Press), *Teaching and Behavior Support for Children and Adults With Autism Spectrum Disorder: A Practitioner's Guide* (Oxford University Press), *Behavioral Sport Psychology: Evidence-Based Approaches to Performance Enhancement* (Springer), *The Handbook of High-Risk Challenging Behaviors in People With Intellectual and Developmental Disabilities* (Paul H. Brookes), and *The Handbook of Crisis Intervention and Developmental Disabilities* (Springer).

Dr. Luiselli has been the Senior Editor of special-topic journal issues published in *Behavior Modification, Mental Health Aspects of Developmental Disabilities, Child & Family Behavior Therapy, Journal of Developmental and Physical Disabilities,* and *International Journal of Behavioral Consultation & Therapy*. He is an Associate Editor for *Journal of Child & Family Studies* and was previously a Contributing Editor for the *Habilitative Mental Healthcare Newsletter*, Editor-in-Chief of *International Journal of Behavioral Consultation and Therapy*, and Associate Editor for *Education and Treatment of Children*. He is a Contributing Writer for *The New England Psychologist*, reviews books for *Metapsychology Online Reviews*, and serves on the Board of Editors of six peer-reviewed journals, including *Journal of Positive Behavior Interventions, Behavior Modification, Clinical Case Studies,* and *Mindfulness*. He has been a national Expert Consensus Panel member for the Treatment of Psychiatric and Behavioral Problems in Mental Retardation for the guideline series published by *The American Journal on Mental Retardation*.

CONTRIBUTORS

Jonathan Baker
Southern Illinois University

Jennifer S. Beighley
Department of Psychology
Louisiana State University

Tonya Davis
Baylor University

Florence D. DiGennaro Reed
Department of Applied Behavioral Science
University of Kansas, Lawrence

Mark R. Dixon
Southern Illinois University

V. Mark Durand
University of South Florida St. Petersburg

Summer Gainey
Department of Special Education and The
Meadows Center for Preventing Educational Risk
The University of Texas at Austin

Peter A. Girolami
Pediatric Feeding Disorders Program
The Kennedy Krieger Institute
The Johns Hopkins University School of Medicine

Evelyn R. Gould
Center for Autism and Related Disorders, Inc.

Leigh Grannan
Southern Illinois University

Charles S. Gulotta
Pediatric Feeding Disorders Program
The Johns Hopkins University School of Medicine
The Kennedy Krieger Institute

Nicole M. Hanney
Auburn University

Debora Kagohara
School of Educational Psychology
Victoria University of Wellington, New Zealand

Brittany Lynn Koegel
University of California at Santa Barbara

Lynn Kern Koegel
University of California at Santa Barbara

Robert L. Koegel
University of California at Santa Barbara

Rajinder Koul
Department of Speech, Language and Hearing
Sciences
Texas Tech University Health Sciences Center

Giulio E. Lancioni
Department of Neuroscience and Sense Organs
University of Bari, Italy

Russell Lang
Texas State University

Linda A. LeBlanc
Trumpet Behavioral Health

James K. Luiselli
May Institute

Johnny L. Matson
Department of Psychology
Louisiana State University

Anna C. May
Department of Psychology
Louisiana State University

Autumn McKeel
Southern Illinois University

Laura Moum
Queens College and The Graduate Center
City University of New York

Josh Nadeau
Departments of Pediatrics, Psychiatry and
Behavioral Neurosciences
University of South Florida

Adel C. Najdowski
Center for Autism and Related Disorders, Inc.

Nicole Neil
Queens College and The Graduate Center
City University of New York

Mark F. O'Reilly
Department of Special Education and The
Meadows Center for Preventing Educational Risk
The University of Texas at Austin

Natalie A. Parks
Trumpet Behavioral Health

Robert C. Pennington
College of Education and Human Development
University of Louisville

Parimala Raghavendra
Disability & Community Inclusion
School of Medicine
Flinders University, Australia

Sathiyaprakash Ramdoss
Department of Special Education and
Communication Disorders
New Mexico State University

Derek D. Reed
Department of Applied Behavioral Science
University of Kansas

Ruth Anne Rehfeldt
Southern Illinois University

Mandy Risploi
Texas A&M University at College Station

Ralf W. Schlosser
Department of Speech-Language Pathology and
Audiology, and Department of Counseling and
Applied Educational Psychology
Northeastern University and Center for
Communication Enhancement
Boston Children's Hospital

Robert R. Selles
Departments of Psychology and Pediatrics
University of South Florida

Howard Shane
Center for Communication Enhancement
Department of Otolaryngology and
Communication Enhancement
Boston Children's Hospital and Department of
Communication Sciences and Disorders
MGH Institute for Health Professions and
Department of Otology and Laryngology
Harvard Medical School

Jeff Sigafoos
School of Educational Psychology
Victoria University of Wellington, New Zealand

Angela D. Adkins Singh
American Health and Wellness Institute
Long Beach, CA

Ashvind N. Adkins Singh
American Health and Wellness Institute
Long Beach, CA

Judy Singh
ONE Research Institute, Raleigh, NC

Nirbhay N. Singh
Department of Psychiatry and Health Behavior,
Medical College of Georgia
Georgia Regents University, Augusta, GA

Audrey Sorrells
Department of Special Education and The
Meadows Center for Preventing Educational Risk
The University of Texas at Austin

Eric A. Storch
Departments of Pediatrics, Psychology, Psychiatry
and Behavioral Neurosciences
University of South Florida

Peter Sturmey
Queens College and The Graduate Center
City University of New York

Danielle Ung
Departments of Psychology and Pediatrics
University of South Florida

Ty W. Vernon
University of California at Santa Barbara

Lindsey W. Williams
Department of Psychology
Louisiana State University

Alan S. W. Winton
Massey University, New Zealand

SECTION I

Diagnosis, Assessment, and Measurement

1

Conducting Diagnostic Screening and Assessment

JOHNNY L. MATSON, JENNIFER S. BEIGHLEY,
LINDSEY W. WILLIAMS, AND ANNA C. MAY

Screening and diagnosis for children and youth with autism spectrum disorder (ASD) is a core construct in service provision for persons with ASD. The diagnosis is tied to funding sources and service provision. The rapidly developing knowledge further underscores the importance of employing systematic, reliable, and valid methods. (See treatment chapters in this book.) Many of these interventions are geared to children as young as 2 years. Therefore, early evaluation is also a critical approach. And, while the disorder is generally viewed as neurodevelopmental in origin, diagnosis is best accomplished with standardized tests, developmental history, and clinical interview (Matson, 2007). Rates of this most serious of childhood disorders are approximately 110 per 10,000, with similar symptoms and prevalence seen worldwide (Fujiwara, Okuyama, & Funahashi, 2011).

A substantial body of literature is developing on early intervention with applied behavior analysis (Eikeseth, 2009; Rogers & Vismara, 2008). What has been concluded is that these operant-based methods result in marked improvements in core symptoms of the disorder. Granpeesheh, Dixon, Tarbox, Kaplan, and Wilke (2009) found that an increase in treatment hours and a decrease in the child's age predicted an increase in skills that are learned. They also concluded that there is no point of diminishing returns. Researchers have focused on starting intensive interventions at an early age. Ospina et al. (2008) reviewed a number of these treatment studies and found the median age of the children treated was 62 months. Additionally, access to state programs and insurance coverage is linked to a diagnosis of ASD. Service provision, then, is based on early recognition and diagnosis.

Early diagnosis is impeded by a number of factors. Fujiwara et al. (2011) discuss a number of these. Among the points they note are reluctance of some parents to express concerns, failure to be provided prompt assessment and diagnosis, and failure of parents or professionals to identify "red flags." Researchers have found, for example, that pediatricians take 15.5 months (average) to refer for a diagnosis (Shevell, Majnemer, Rosenbaum, & Abrahamowicz, 2001). Additionally, Moh and Magiati (2012) underscore the important point that the entire diagnostic process can be very stressful. Notably, studies in the United States and Canada found that four to five professionals had to be consulted before an accurate diagnosis could be made (Goin-Kochel, Mackintosh, & Myers, 2006; Mandell, Novak, & Zubritsky, 2005; Siklos & Kerns, 2007). In addition to the stress associated with duration of the assessment(s), having a positive relationship with the professional, including seeing the parent(s), taking their concerns seriously, and explaining the process adequately were all important factors. Obtaining information on practical steps to take after the diagnosis with respect to service provision was also highly valued.

Early parent concerns are well documented. Ninety-three percent of parents noted worry about their child's development before 24 months of age (DeGiacomo & Fombonne, 1998). Having said that, ASD is believed to be present at birth (Baghdadli, Picot, Pasca, Pry, & Aussilloux, 2003). No biological markers exist; thus, behavioral observation and standardized tests are the accepted methods of differential diagnosis (Matson, Nebel-Schwalm, & Matson, 2007). However, even for persons with identifiable genetic causes such as Down syndrome, the heterogeneity in individual strengths and weakness makes the systematic evaluation of symptom presentation with standardized tests and behavioral observations essential.

One of the richest methods of obtaining information to assist in early diagnosis is parent observations. Kishore and Basu (2011), for example, reported that in India, mothers had concerns by 2.28 years of age, fully 6 years before a final diagnosis was made. Specific behaviors mothers noted were speech regression, loss of motor skills, poor visual tracking, and a lack of joint attention. A French study divided parents into groups based on the age at which they noticed signs of ASD (Guinchat et al., 2012). They identified (a) an early awareness group, including motor problems and passivity (14 months); (b) a later group, including emotional, hyperactivity, and sleep problems (15 months); and (c) an older group with communication problems, poor social interactions, and "autistic" behaviors. Similarly, Dewrang and Sandberg (2010) noted that parents are well aware of problems very early on, such as difficulties with food selectivity, sleep, and social activities. Additionally, Twyman, Maxim, Leet, and Ultmann (2009) observed social development problems at 19–25 months as particularly important for obtaining early diagnosis. Finally, Saint-Georges et al. (2010) conducted an interesting review of 18 studies and 317 films of the first 2 years of life. Factors that helped differentiate children who were later diagnosed with ASD from other children who had another developmental disability were less looking at others, failure to respond to their name, less eye contact, and fewer positive facial expressions.

Several challenges face professionals who are focused on early diagnosis of ASD. However, intensive and rapid efforts to develop methods and procedures to provide reliable and valid methods are under way. The purpose of this chapter is to provide an overview of this extensive literature. Additionally, an evaluation of the current status of these developments will be covered.

MAJOR TOPICS AND CONCERNS

We have discussed the importance of early diagnosis and the difficulty and time lags that have been endemic in efforts to arrive at an accurate diagnosis. The solution to this problem is, first, to develop methods and procedures to ensure an accurate diagnosis. Second, a critical factor is implementing methods to disseminate this information to parents and professionals.

A commonly used term in the fields of mental health is a "gold standard" (Matson, Beighley, & Turygin, 2012). This concept can apply to intervention or assessment, but in the case of the present review, it applies to methods and procedures for early diagnosis. Various researchers have made claims that a particular test is the gold standard for the field. However, these claims are premature on at least two grounds. First, for papers where such assertions appear, no direct test of different assessments has occurred to validate these conclusions. Second, the population is so heterogeneous that it is unlikely that any given test will prove to be "all things for all people." Factors such as intellectual functioning and the age when a diagnosable set of symptoms appears can vary widely from 1 year old, to around 2 years old when autistic regression (sudden loss of acquired skills) may occur, to 8–10 years of age in the case of Asperger syndrome. Thus, it is unlikely that any one test will emerge as the best substantiated method for all persons with ASD. And yet scales specifically designed for and normed on children 1 to 3 years of age will function as the primary diagnostic instruments for most people with ASD. In addition to diagnosis, tests to assess progress across the life span will be needed to measure the core symptoms of communication, social skills, and rituals and stereotypies. High-rate, co-occurring problems such as challenging behaviors and psychopathology will also need to be evaluated.

Real-world economics are also of great concern. Thus, measures need to be sufficiently brief so that the system is not overwhelmed. Conversely, the period of time for conducting the evaluation needs to be sufficiently long so that adequate data are collected to make a reliable and valid diagnosis while providing enough information to initiate an effective and comprehensive treatment plan. The assessment will likely vary in time, a good deal, from case to case. In some instances, where the person is on "the fence" for a diagnosis, more than one session and one test may be advisable. Similarly, where multiple co-occurring problems are evident, a more complex assessment process will be warranted. Many cases will provide a clear diagnosis with minimal co-occurring problems. These assessments will be much quicker.

A structured observation of and attempt to elicit core symptoms is essential. Also, collecting historical data on developmental milestones, socialization and communication, and the use of normed, standardized tests is also necessary. Where the clinician and parent data correlate highly, additional evaluation may be unnecessary. However, in some instances, parent data will appear to over- or underreport symptoms substantially. When that occurs, assessing other caregivers (another parent, grandparent, teacher) may be advisable.

Osborne, McHugh, Saunders, and Reed (2008) address an often overlooked but very important issue: the effects of early diagnosis on the parents. They found that early diagnosis increased parental stress, and they argue that this could negatively impact the child with respect to behavior problems and treatment outcomes. These findings underscore the importance of assisting parents in finding and accessing services and obtaining financial support. Additionally, where this stress produces serious emotional reactions, psychological counseling may also be in order.

The fifth edition of the *Diagnostic and Statistical Manual of Mental Disorders* (*DSM-5*) will be out shortly. The new definition of ASD is a major departure from the current diagnosis, collapsing social and communication into one core feature with a second core feature of restrictive behavior. The algorithm for meeting the criteria is much more stringent. Additionally, Asperger syndrome and pervasive developmental disorder-not otherwise specified (PDD-NOS) are collapsed into autism, while childhood disintegrative disorder and Rett syndrome are dropped off the spectrum entirely.

Researchers have looked at prevalence rates of ASD when comparing *DSM-IV-TR* criteria to proposed *DSM-5* criteria. In several studies, diagnosing based on the proposed *DSM-5* criteria led to a decrease in the number of children who would meet criteria for ASD. Similar results have been shown across all age ranges. Researchers comparing individuals with ASD using *DSM-IV-TR* criteria to *DMS-5* criteria have found that 35%–50% of children, adolescents, and adults who were diagnosed with ASD according to *DSM-IV-TR* no longer meet criteria under the proposed *DSM-5* (Matson, Belva, Horovitz, Kozlowski, & Bamburg, 2012; Matson, Kozlowski, Hattier, Horovitz, & Sipes, 2012; McPartland, Reichow, & Volkmar, 2012; Worley & Matson, 2012). Worley and Matson (2012) diagnosed 130 children with autism using *DSM-IV-TR* criteria. When *DSM-5* criteria were applied, the rate of autism declined 40%. McPartland, Reichow, and Volkmar (2012) evaluated a sample of 933 children and adults

who were included in the *DSM-IV* field trials and also found a 40% decline in prevalence of autism with *DSM-5*. Matson, Kozlowski, et al. (2012) compared *DSM* diagnoses for 2,721 children aged 17–36 months who were at risk for a developmental disability. The number of children decreased from 795 to 415 toddlers with the new criteria, a 47.79% decrease in young children with autism. Matson, Belva, et al. (2012) found that the number of adults diagnosed using proposed *DSM-5* criteria declined 36.53% as compared to *DSM-IV-TR* and individuals diagnosed under proposed *DSM-5* criteria showed more ASD symptomotology. Gibbs, Aldridge, Chandler, Witzlsperger, and Smith (2012) compared diagnostic outcome for 132 children and found 26 no longer met ASD criteria under the proposed *DSM-5*.

Many individuals failing to meet the proposed ASD criteria fell under the PDD-NOS category according to *DSM-IV-TR* criteria. In addition, researchers demonstrated in both children and adolescents that proposed *DSM-5* criteria captures a more impaired population as compared to those identified by the *DSM-IV-TR* criteria as ASD (Matson, Belva et al., 2012; Turygin, Matson, Beighley, & Adams, 2013). Concerning validity, while Frazier et al. (2012) suggest proposed *DSM-5* criteria for ASD had superior specificity, sensitivity was lower compared to the *DSM-IV-TR*. Though the proposed *DSM-5* may show a reduction in false positives, more children with ASD are not being identified with the new criteria; they found as many as 12% of ASD individuals will be missed, particularly females. The authors suggest relaxing the *DSM-5* criteria because results showed that by requiring one less symptom, sensitivity was increased with minimal reduction to specificity. Matson, Hattier, and Williams (2012) found similar results, relaxing proposed *DSM-5* criteria two different ways (both with fewer required symptoms than *DSM-5* permits), which led to more toddlers diagnosed with ASD as compared to the number when using currently proposed *DSM-5* criteria, thus increasing sensitivity. McPartland et al. (2012) also found similar results; specificity in the proposed *DSM-5* was found to be improved over *DSM-IV-TR*, but sensitivity was decreased in all areas, particularly for those with Asperger disorder and PDD-NOS. These data are very concerning and will have many unintended consequences for service eligibility and service provision.

EFFECTIVE
ASSESSMENT METHODS

When screening and assessing for ASD, it is important to keep in mind the three core features that characterize ASD: deficits in social skills, verbal and nonverbal communication problems, and repetitive behaviors or interests (Chowdhury, Benson, & Hillier, 2010; Duffy & Healy, 2011; Fodstad, Matson, Hess, & Neal, 2009; Matson, 2007; Matson & Biosjoli, 2007; Matson, Carlisle, & Bamburg, 1998; Sipes, Matson, Worley, & Kozlowski, 2011). Social skills deficits involve problems understanding as well as responding to social information (Dawson, Meltzoff, Osterling, Rinaldi, & Brown, 1998). These deficits include problems with (a) social imitation (Dawson et al., 1998; Hobson & Lee, 1999; Loveland et al., 1994), (b) joint attention (Baron-Cohen et al., 1996; Mundy, Sigman, Ungerer, & Sherman, 1986; Osterling & Dawson, 1994), (c) orienting to social stimuli (Osterling & Dawson, 1994; Ruffman, Garnham, & Rideout, 2001), (d) face perception (Boucher & Lewis, 1992; Hauk, Fein, Maltby, Waterhouse, & Feinstein, 1999; Tantam, Monaghan, Nicholson, & Stirling, 1989; Teunisse & DeGelder, 1994), (e) emotional perception and expression (Bormann-Kischkel, Vilsmeier, & Baude, 1995; Kasari, Sigman, Yirmiya, & Mundy, 1993; Loveland et al., 1994; Weeks & Hobson, 1987), and (f) symbolic play (Amato, Barrow, & Domingo, 1999; Baron-Cohen et al., 1996; Riguet, Taylor, Benaroya, & Klein, 1981; Ungerer, 1989; Wing, 1978). Communication deficits are characterized by delayed and problematic language development (Chawarska, Klin, Paul, & Volkmar, 2007; Paul, Chawarska, Cicchetti, & Volkmar, 2008; Wetherby, Watt, Morgan, & Shumway, 2007), including deficits such as immediate or delayed echolalia, abnormal prosody, and pronoun reversal (Cantwell, Baker, Rutter, & Mawhood, 1989; Kanner, 1943). Delays can also be seen in the semantic aspects of language (Tager-Flusberg, 1999) and language comprehension (Paul, Fischer, & Cohen, 1988). Repetitive behaviors and interests are invariant motor movements, as well as higher level behaviors such as insistence on routines and circumscribed interests (Turner, 1999). Examples of repetitive behaviors include stereotyped movements (e.g., rocking), toe walking, arm/hand/finger flapping, and whirling (Volkmar, Cohen, & Paul, 1986). Elaborate routines can involve complex motor movements, repeated rearrangement and organization of toys, or insistence

that the same routine be followed daily, while circumscribed interests include memorization of facts about a specific topic of interest (Klinger, Dawson, & Renner, 2003). Because these three core features characterize ASD, screening and assessment procedures should focus on determining whether deficits and excesses are exhibited in each area, across settings as well as across informants.

Currently, the criteria that are widely used by researchers and clinicians in North America and Europe are found in the *DSM-IV-TR* and the *International Classification of Diseases-10 (ICD-10)*, which have largely overlapping criteria (Sponheim, 1996). In addition, practitioners agree that an interview of parents about early developmental milestones and symptoms of ASD, as well as direct observation of the child, is necessary using psychometrically sound instruments (Filipek et al., 1999; Volkmar, Cook Jr., Pomeroy, Realmuto, & Tanguay, 1999). Guidelines for practice have been laid out by the American Academy of Neurology (Filipek et al., 2000), the American Academy of Child and Adolescent Psychiatry (Volkmar et al., 1999), and a multidisciplinary panel representing professional societies (Filipek et al., 1999), which describe Level 1 screening and Level 2 evaluation practices (Ozonoff, Goodlin-Jones, & Solomon, 2005).

Characteristics of tests and rating scales, including psychometric properties and pragmatic considerations, must be appraised when choosing a test (Matson, 2007). Specifically, reliability and validity should be evaluated in the test of choice. There are several types of reliability that may be appropriate for a given instrument, including test-retest, interrater, internal consistency, split-half, and inter-item. For instruments that measure more than one construct as determined from a factor analysis, internal consistency, split-half, and inter-item may be appropriate for items within each factor. Validity of a scale should also be considered, including the face validity of items, divergent validity, content validity, construct validity, and predictive validity. In addition to sound psychometric properties necessary in an appropriate scale, pragmatically, it is important to consider the feasibility of a test. Some factors that are critical to evaluate include the time and effort it takes to administer, score, and interpret; environmental and specialized equipment needs; the training or expertise needed to administer; the cost of the measure; the willingness of practitioners to use the test; and the willingness of informants to complete the test.

Further, practitioners should understand that an assessment which may be appropriate for one individual may not be appropriate for another. Specificity of many otherwise psychometrically sound measures may be affected by the overlap of ASD with other developmental disabilities (DDs), especially intellectual disability (ID) and language disorders (Coonrod & Stone, 2005; Eaves, Wingert, & Ho, 2006), and particularly at young ages. For example, the *Autism Diagnostic Observation Schedule* (*ADOS*; Lord, Rutter, DiLavore, & Risi, 1999) is one of the most widely used and well-researched assessment tools, and according to the authors it is psychometrically sound for ASD diagnosis in children as young as 12 months of age. However, the authors acknowledge this measure may overidentify ASD in young children with ID (Lord & Corsello, 2005). Accordingly, even when using evidence-based and psychometrically sound measures, the clinician must take care to consider all factors and choose assessments fitting to the individual's age, goals, cognitive abilities, and developmental level of the areas being assessed.

Screenings and Early Detection

We reiterate that diagnosing ASD at a young age is critical for access to services and early interventions. Early intensive behavioral interventions have been shown to increase the likelihood of more positive outcomes such as gains in IQ and/or adaptive behavior (Reichow & Wolery, 2009; Virués-Ortega, 2010). Early detection can also give the family access to information and assistance in all areas of life. Governmental screening and service programs screen infants and toddlers for possible DDs and provide services to families with infants and toddlers with DDs. These services can include assistive technology, audiology, health services, medical services, occupational therapy services, physical therapy services, psychological services, and more.

It is important when screening and assessing for ASD to determine whether the child is delayed in developmental milestones. For example, the Centers for Disease Control (CDC) indicates that by the end of age 12 months a child should be able to respond to simple verbal requests, imitate words, and stand momentarily without support. By the end of 24 months a child should be able to use two- to four-word sentences and simple phrases as well as walk alone. The CDC recommends having a child assessed for a DD if he or she cannot use two-word

sentences, say at least 15 words, imitate actions or words, walk, or follow simple instructions by 18 to 24 months or if the child experiences a dramatic loss of skills at this age. The CDC and the World Health Organization have released detailed reports on important milestones and recommendations of what to watch for at each age (CDC, 2012).

It is also necessary to screen and assess at-risk populations, for example, infants and toddlers who have been delayed in previous developmental milestones and siblings of those already diagnosed with ASD. Family members of children with ASD are at a higher risk for acquiring these disorders than the general population, suggesting a strong genetic influence (Bailey et al., 1995; Dawson et al., 2007; Folstein & Rutter, 1977, 1988; Landa et al., 1992; Paul, Fuerst, Ramsay, Chawarska, & Klin, 2011; Piven, Palmer, Jacobi, Childress, & Arndt, 1997; Santangelo, Folstein, & Tager-Flusberg, 1999). Thus, infant and toddler siblings of those diagnosed with ASD should be continually monitored.

When assessing for ASD, it is important to conduct interviews with those who spend the most time with the child and can provide information about the child's behavior in response to many different stimuli in different settings across development. These interviews are often conducted with the parents, other primary caregivers, and/or teachers. When conducting these interviews, it is also necessary to determine whether the child is delayed or is experiencing deficits in the three core features of ASD.

Often an unstructured interview is utilized in the beginning to determine problem areas and symptoms as well as to get a thorough developmental history. Follow-up structured interviews may be utilized, as they reduce the role of judgment and clinician error that can occur in an unstructured interview. Structured interviews use clear, specific criteria as a guide to determine the presence or absence of a diagnosis. These criteria are formulated into questions delivered in an interview format.

Observational Methods

Observational methods for assessing ASD can be implemented in the clinic/office, the child's natural environment (e.g., home), and school/daycare if applicable. During the observation, the child should be provided opportunities to play alone as well as interact with others such as clinicians, parents, family members, other caregivers, teachers, and peers. All three core features should be assessed during the observation session(s). Observational instruments are tools that can guide the clinician in what to look for or try to elicit during an observation to determine whether the core features are present and where/when the behaviors and symptoms occur. Some of the well-researched measures showing good psychometric properties are described next as well as newer measures showing promise in the literature.

One semistructured observation/interactive assessment that is widely used is the *Autism Diagnostic Observation Schedule-Generic* (*ADOS-G*; Lord et al., 2000), a revision of the *Autism Diagnostic Observation Schedule* (*ADOS*; Lord et al., 1989; Lord, Rutter, DiLavore, & Risi, 2002) that was combined with the *Pre-Linguistic Autism Diagnostic Observation Schedule* (*PL-ADOS*; DiLavore, Lord, & Rutter, 1995). The *ADOS-G* has four modules, each taking 30 minutes to administer, graded according to language and developmental level, and it can be administered across a wide range of ages and abilities. To administer the *ADOS-G* for research purposes, examiners are required to attend a training course and demonstrate interrater reliability. Authors of the *ADOS-G* reported adequate to excellent test-retest reliability for the modules. In a validity study, the authors reported that individuals with autistic disorder were correctly classified 95% of the time, typically developing individuals were correctly classified 92% of the time, and 33% of those with PDD-NOS were classified correctly with 53% of those with PDD-NOS classified with autistic disorder.

The *Autism Spectrum Disorders–Observation for Children* (*ASD-OC*; Neal, Matson, & Hattier, in press) is a new measure with 39 items created to assess children ages 1–15 years and is one part of the *Autism Spectrum Disorders-Diagnosis for Children* (*ASD-DC*; Matson & González, 2007b), a battery for assessing ASD in children. An examiner creates a play session with the child consisting of varying activities dependent on the age and developmental level of the child, cooperation of the child, and clinical judgment. Example probes are provided (e.g., looks when name is called, asks for help, makes eye contact, imitates facial expressions and pretend play). Items are rated on a scale from 0 to 2 (0, no impairment; 1, mild impairment; 2, severe impairment compared to same-age peers). The authors found that the *ASD-OC* has good to excellent interrater reliability and excellent internal consistency ($\alpha = 0.96$). Strong convergent validity was established with the *Childhood Autism Rating Scale* (*CARS*), and

moderate divergent validity was found using the daily living domain of the *Vineland Adaptive Behavior Scales, Second Edition* (*VABS-II*). Investigation of criterion-related validity found that the *ASD-OC* differentiates children with and without ASD and is able to predict group membership.

The *Childhood Autism Rating Scale* (*CARS*; Schopler, Reichier, & Renner, 1988) is classified as a rating scale but contains observational information. The measure consists of a 15-item structured observation of a variety of behaviors (i.e., relating to people; imitation; emotional response; body use; object use; adaptation to change; visual response; listening response; taste, smell, and touch response and use; fear/nervousness; verbal communication, nonverbal communication; activity level; level and consistency of intellectual response; and general impressions) and can be used with children over the age of 2 years as well as adults. The measure may be completed using observation, behavioral records, caregiver report, or some combination thereof, as long as each type of information is consistently used for each of the 15 items. The *CARS* takes approximately 30 minutes to administer, and following the observation, items are scored as 1 (normal when compared with others of the same age), 2 (mildly abnormal), 3 (moderately abnormal), or 4 (severely abnormal). Cutoffs include three categories, Nonautistic, Mildly to Moderately Autistic, and Moderately to Severely Autistic, and are reported for children and adolescents/adults separately. The *CARS* is more time efficient and requires less training than some other observational measures. Internal consistency is reported to be excellent with $\alpha = 0.94$, and interrater reliability is good. The test-retest reliability investigation resulted in a weighted kappa value of 0.64 (Schopler, Reichier, & Renner, 1988). Regarding convergence with the *ADI-R*, diagnostic agreement between the two scales was found to be only 66.7% when cutoff scores for both scales were used; the *CARS* more frequently classified cases of autism correctly (Saemunden, Magnusson, Smari, & Sigurdardottir, 2003). Another study found that the *CARS* identified 100% of children with autistic disorder using a sample of 65 children with and without ASD, though individuals with Asperger disorder and PDD-NOS were not correctly identified (Rellini et al., 2004).

The *Pre-Linguistic Autism Diagnosis Observation Schedule* (*PL-ADOS*; DiLavore et al., 1995) is a 30-minute, semistructured observation measure for assessing core symptoms in children under age 6 years. Substantial training is required for reliable administration of the measure. Parents may be involved to help the child engage with the prompts provided. The measure includes 12 standardized social and communicative interactions such as use of toys during free play, responding to name using a mechanical animal or car, anticipation of routine using bubble gun and balloons, turn taking with a toy drum, requesting during snack, and adaptation to strange situations when separated and reunited with caregiver. Each behavior is rated as 0 (no abnormality), 1 (neither clearly typical nor clearly indicative of autism), or 2 (definite abnormality), and six overall ratings are given at the end of the session. A major limitation of this study is in regard to use with children with verbal skills. Using the cutoffs suggested, all children with verbal abilities were misdiagnosed (DiLavore et al., 1995).

Another observational measure, the *Behavior Observation Scale* (*BOS*; Freeman & Schroth, 1984), assesses for the presence of 67 behaviors via a one-way mirror occurring across 3 days during 30-minute sessions. During these sessions, the examiner records whether the behavior occurred regularly, twice, once, or not at all during two baseline conditions, one interactive play condition, and several conditions where the child is presented with stimuli, though the examiner does not engage the child. The authors reported good interrater reliability for 60 of the behaviors. Further, the authors found that the *BOS* was better able to distinguish those with autistic disorder from those without autistic disorder when participants had IQs above 70 (Freeman & Schroth, 1984). Another limitation of the measure is the extensive amount of training necessary to conduct the observation, including the memorization of the coding system (Worley & Matson, 2011).

Rating Scales

Informant reports and rating scales offer the advantage of efficiency, a reasonable consideration in clinical settings in facilities with limited resources and professionals without time to administer and score lengthy, detailed measures. Psychometrically sound and parsimonious rating scales and report measures are valuable tools to assist in diagnosis and case formulation without demanding a great deal of time to score or administer. These measures may be particularly helpful in the interest of garnering more information about a child in a short amount of time,

as these measures generally take only a few minutes to complete and may be completed by the caregiver while the clinician is working with the individual or sent to parents or teachers to complete at their convenience. Some of the most well-researched scales are discussed next; however, a more complete list of measures can be found in an article by Matson, Nebel-Schwalm, and Matson (2007).

One of the best of the early diagnostic measures, the *Baby and Infant Screen for Children with aUtIsm Traits* (*BISCUIT*; Matson, Boisjoli, & Wilkins, 2007) is a well-researched measure for use with infants and toddlers aged 17–37 months. The *BISCUIT* is a comprehensive screening battery that begins with a brief demographic questionnaire. Part 1 of the battery assesses for the symptoms of ASD with 62 items. Informants rate the infant or toddler by making comparisons against typically developing, same-age peers and then score each item on a three-point scale (0 = no different from same-age peers, no impairment; 1 = somewhat different, mild impairment; 2 = very different, severe impairment). Part 2 of the battery measures comorbid psychopathology (e.g., obsessive-compulsive disorder, attention-deficit/hyperactivity disorder [ADHD], eating problems) using a similar format. Fifty-seven items are included with a similar three-point response scale. Finally, Part 3 of the BISCUIT includes 15 items measuring problem behavior common in individuals with ASD such as aggression, self-injury, disruption, and stereotypical behaviors. Cutoff scores are provided for Part 1, so that total score falls into one of three categories: Probably ASD/Autistic Disorder, Possible ASD/PDD-NOS, and No ASD/Atypical Development. Similar norms and cutoffs are available for Parts 2 and 3 as well. Comparison of the *BISCUIT* and the *M-CHAT* found specificity and sensitivity for the *M-CHAT* at 87.5% and 71.1%, respectively; specificity for the *BISCUIT* was 86.6% with sensitivity of 93.4% (Matson et al., 2009). Five critical items were identified using a study with 2,168 at-risk infants (LoVullo & Matson, 2012) that, when compared with Part 1, demonstrated comparable accuracy in diagnoses. These five items have been suggested to be used as a screener prior to implementing the entire battery (Matson, Fodstad et al., 2009). Psychometric properties, including reliability and validity of the BISCUIT, have been well established (Matson & Tureck, 2012). Factor structure was examined using a sample of 1,287 children; results supported the concept of three core symptoms of autism (i.e., communication, socialization, and stereotyped repetitive behavior; Matson, Boisjoli et al., 2011).

The *Checklist for Autism in Toddlers* (*CHAT*; Baron-Cohen et al., 2000) was created as a screener for use by pediatricians and health care providers during the 18-month wellness visit. The first section of the measure consists of nine questions asked of the caregiver and the second section is composed of behavioral observations made by the physician or health care provider. The authors reported excellent test-retest reliability in those with high and low risk and good test-retest reliability in medium-risk toddlers. High specificity was found though sensitivity was low.

The *Modified Checklist for Autism in Toddlers* (*M-CHAT*; Robins, Fein, Barton, & Green, 2001), based on the *CHAT*, is a 23-item parent report measure designed to screen toddlers aged 2 years in approximately 5–10 minutes. The measure adds 12 additional questions to the 9 questions asked of parents in the *CHAT* and was validated on an American sample versus the British research sample used for validation of the *CHAT*. The authors found internal consistency to be adequate (α = 0.85 for the entire measure and 0.83 for critical items) and reported the *M-CHAT* to have slightly higher predictive validity compared to the *CHAT* (Robins et al., 2001).

The *Autism Spectrum Disorders-Diagnosis for Children* (*ASD-DC*; Matson & González, 2007b) is a 40-item caregiver report measure used for differential diagnosis with children 2–16 years of age. This test takes between 10 and 15 minutes to administer and is part of a larger battery that also measures comorbid psychopathology and challenging behaviors (Matson, Gonzalez, Wilkins, & Rivet, 2007). High correlation of items was found with the items and *DSM-IV-TR* and *ICD-10* criteria. Reliability of the measure was established using a sample of 207 caregivers; the *ASD-DC* was found to have good interrater reliability, excellent test-retest reliability, and excellent internal consistency (Matson, Gonzalez, et al., 2007). Cutoffs place scores into categories including typical development, atypical development, Asperger disorder, PDD-NOS, and autistic disorder (Matson, Gonzalez, & Wilkins, 2009). In a study on convergent validity with the *ADI-R*, the *ASD-DC* correctly identified 73% of those with an ASD and 67% of controls, while the ADI-R correctly identified 46% of those with an ASD and 100% of controls (Matson, Hess, Mahan, & Fodstad, 2010).

Convergent validity was also established with the *CARS*. For the *ASD-DC*, 76.5% of children with ASD and 95% of children without ASD were correctly identified, while 58.8% of children with an ASD and 85.0% of children without an ASD were correctly identified using the *CARS* (Matson, Mahan, Hess, Fodstad, & Neal, 2010).

Another well-researched, frequently used interview-based measure for use with children is the *Autism Diagnostic Interview-Revised* (*ADI-R*; Lord, Rutter, & LeCouteur, 1994; Rutter, LeCouteur, & Lord, 2003). The *ADI-R* is a revision of the original measure published in 1989 (LeCouteur, Rutter, Lord, & Rios, 1989). It is administered by trained clinicians to primary caregivers of individuals 18 months of age through adulthood, though the individual being assessed must have a mental age of at least 20 months or an IQ of at least 20 (Cox et al., 1999; Lord, 1995). However, Charman et al. (2005) reported that an ADI-R diagnosis of autism at age 3 years, but not age 2 years, predicted diagnostic outcome at age 7 years, which suggests that the ADI-R is not appropriate for those between the ages of 18 through 36 months. The research version takes 3 hours to administer, while the short version (only those items used in the diagnostic algorithm are given) takes approximately 90 minutes. The *ADI-R* is a comprehensive, semistructured interview. If the measure is used for research purposes, a 3-day training seminar is required. The interview consists of 93 questions related to current behavior as well as developmental history and is linked to *DSM-IV-TR* criteria. The measure can be used to diagnose autism only, as cutoffs for diagnosing Asperger disorder and PDD-NOS are not provided; however, information is reported to be helpful in diagnosing other ASDs. Psychometric properties are reported in the manual (Lord et al., 1994). Authors report good interrater reliability and adequate test-retest reliability after a period of 2–5 months, though only six families were included in that study, which according to standard psychometric procedures would be too small of a sample to make that assertion. Good validity was established by the authors using *ICD-10* and *DSM-IV* criteria. Concurrent validity was established using the Social Communication Questionnaire, a rating scale designed as a short version of the *ADI-R* (Bishop & Norbury, 2002). Good internal consistency, face validity, discriminant validity, and construct validity was established in a study with 292 families (Tadevosyan-Leyfer et al., 2003).

The *ADI-R* was not shown to have good sensitivity to mild ASD such as Asperger disorder and PDD-NOS in children until they are around 4 years of age (Cox et al., 1999; Lord, 1995).

The *Gilliam Autism Rating Scale*, second edition (*GARS-2*; Gilliam, 2008) is a revision of the original scale (Gilliam, 1995) and consists of 42 items that are completed by parents in approximately 5–10 minutes and is often used for screening purposes. In addition to a total score, three scales are included related to the three core features. The *GARS-2* has norm-referenced scores and the authors report good internal consistency and differential validity (Gilliam, 2008). More research is available for the original version, which includes the finding that children with autism consistently score lower on the *GARS* than on other commonly used measures (Mazefsky & Oswald, 2006; Sikora, Hall, Hartley, Gerrard-Morris, & Cagle, 2008; South et al., 2002). Additional research is necessary to determine whether this is the case for the current version.

Another commonly used instrument is the *Autism Spectrum Rating Scale* (*ASRS*; Goldstein & Naglieri, 2009), which measures behaviors characteristic of ASD observed over the past month. Versions of this scale are available for ages 2–6 years and 7–18 years, with three empirically derived scales measuring self-regulation, social/communication, and stereotypical behaviors. The ASRS items correspond with *DSM-IV-TR* symptoms of autistic disorder, Asperger disorder, and PDD-NOS, and thus can be useful in differential diagnosis. Reliability of these scales, as reported by the authors, ranges from 0.85 to 0.95.

The *Social Communication Questionnaire* (*SCQ*; Rutter, Bailey, & Lord, 2003), formerly named the *Autism Screening Questionnaire* (Berument, Rutter, Lord, Pickles, & Bailey, 1999), can be administered to children as young as age 4 years through adulthood, and it takes between 10 and 12 minutes to complete. The *SCQ* is based on the *ADI-R*, with a briefer, yes/no format that can be completed by the parent. The measure is available in two forms: Lifetime and Current Behavior. The measure is useful as an alternative to the *ADI-R* for screening purposes (using the Lifetime form) or when tracking changes of ASD symptoms over time (using the Current Behavior form). This measure has shown promise in screening preschool-aged children (Lee, David, Rusyniak, Landa, & Newschaffer, 2007). The authors reported a sensitivity of 0.85 and specificity of 0.75.

The *Autism Spectrum Screening Questionnaire* (*ASSQ*; Ehlers, Gillberg, & Wing, 1999) is a 29-item checklist intended to screen for Asperger disorder as well as high-functioning autism. However, the measure does not differentiate between the disorders. Standardized directions enable informants to complete the measure independently in approximately 10 minutes. Authors report high internal consistency and good validity.

Assessing Asperger Disorder

The proposed version of the *DSM-5* intends to collapse autistic disorder, Asperger disorder, and PDD-NOS into one diagnostic category of ASD, although symptoms of ASD in individuals currently labeled as having Asperger disorder will remain important to identify. Measures found to successfully screen and assess for Asperger disorder are discussed next.

The *Asperger Syndrome Diagnostic Scale* (*ASDS*; Myles et al., 2001) is a rating scale completed by informants in approximately 10 minutes, for use with children and youth age 5–18 years for the purpose of diagnosing, monitoring behavior, and generating IEP goals. The *ASDS* consists of 50 items and results in five subscales, including language, social, maladaptive, cognitive, and sensorimotor. Scores also result in an Asperger Syndrome Quotient (ASQ), having a mean of 100 and a standard deviation of 15.

The *Childhood Asperger Syndrome Test* (*CAST*; Scott et al., 2002) is one of a handful of scales designed specifically to screen for Asperger disorder. A 37-item questionnaire completed by caregivers or teachers of children aged 4–11 years, the *CAST* can be completed in a short amount of time. Each item is rated as either present or absent, and 31 of the items contribute to a total score. The authors established cutoff scores that appeared to have adequate sensitivity in identifying those with Asperger disorder in nonclinical samples.

Another scale, the *Gilliam Asperger's Disorder Scale* (*GADS*; Gilliam, 2003), is also a relatively brief parent or teacher scale. The *GADS* was designed as a diagnostic aid for use with individuals aged 3–22 years and takes 5–10 minutes to complete. The scale targets social interactions, restricted patterns, cognitive patterns, and pragmatic skills. Scoring of this scale also results in an Asperger Syndrome Quotient with a mean of 100 and a standard deviation of 15. Though frequently used, this scale needs more psychometric evaluation, as test-retest reliability estimates were based on only 10 individuals and interrater reliability was evaluated using 16 participants. Further, internal consistency was not found to be at the standard accepted level (less than 0.90; Campbell, 2005).

The *Krug Asperger's Disorder Index* (*KADI*; Krug & Arick, 2003) is a 32-item scale for use with individuals between the ages of 6 and 21 years. The authors state that the scale is for use as a screener as well as a tool helpful in the generation of IEP goals. Scoring results in an overall score generated from two sections. A sufficiently high score on section one (11 items) signifies that the additional items should be completed. The authors suggest that section two be used to distinguish between Asperger disorder and high-functioning autistic disorder, though it should be recalled that this instrument was created to screen rather than to diagnose (Nellis, n.d.).

Intellectual Assessment

Though estimates vary, recent studies have found that approximately half of individuals with ASD have ID (Chakrabarti & Fombonne, 2001). In general, the *Stanford-Binet*, fifth edition (*SB5*; Roid, 2003) is often used when assessing for ID in those with DD due to a broader range of possible scores than many other cognitive tests (Nebel-Schwalm & Matson, 2008). The *SB5* can be administered to individuals between the ages of 2 and 85 years; it takes between 45 and 75 minutes to administer. Given the language difficulties that are prevalent in the ASD population, when assessing individuals with limited verbal skills, nonverbal tests such as the *Peabody Picture Vocabulary Test*, fourth edition (*PPVT-IV*; Dunn & Dunn, 2007), *Leiter International Performance Scale-Revised* (*Leiter-R*; Roid & Miller, 1997), or *Test of Nonverbal Intelligence* (*TONI-3*; Brown, Sherbenou, & Johnson, 2007) are frequently used. The *Leiter-R* can be used in children aged 2–20 years who do not communicate verbally or those with severely impaired language skills. Other scales used include the *Mullen Scales of Early Learning* (*MSEL*; Mullen, 1995), *Differential Ability Scales*, second edition (*DAS-II*; Elliott, 2007), *Wechsler Intelligence Scale for Children*, fourth edition (*WISC-IV*; Wechsler, 2003), and *Bayley Scales of Infant Development*, second edition (*BSID-II*; Bayley, 1993).

Adaptive Behavior

The most widely used measure of adaptive skills is the *Vineland Adaptive Behavior Scales*, second edition (*VABS-II*; Sparrow, Cicchetti, & Balla, 2005), available in both interview and rating forms. The *VABS-II* takes approximately 20–60 minutes to complete and asks caregivers to answer questions about adaptive skills in the areas of communication, social interactions, daily living skills, and maladaptive behaviors. Age equivalents are also generated. The *VABS-II* was normed on those from birth through age 18 years, though it can be administered to adults.

The *Adaptive Behavior Assessment System*, second edition (*ABAS-II*; Harrison & Oakland, 2003) measures the frequency of behaviors in the following areas: communication, community use, functional academics (or preacademics), home/school living, motor, health and safety, leisure, self-care, self-direction, social, and work (if the individual is employed). These areas provide conceptual (communication and academic skills), social (interpersonal skills and social competence), and practical (independent and daily living skills) composite adaptive scores; each domain offers a mean score of 100 with a standard deviation of 15. One advantage of this measure is that it is available in five forms for assessing individuals from birth to 89 years of age. Caregiver, teacher, and adult forms are available. The adult form can be completed via self-report or by a family member or other person familiar with the individual. Each item has a box to indicate whether the informant guessed or estimated performance on the item, thus allowing the clinician to determine whether the respondent is a suitable rater. The authors report good reliability of composite scores ($r \geq 0.92$) between teacher and caregiver report in the standardization sample. Because this measure is available for such a wide age range, it is useful in evaluating changes in behavioral functioning over time. However, while individuals with ASD were included in the standardization sample, there are currently no published studies using this measure in an ASD-only sample.

Other parent/caregiver behavior report measures available for use across the life span include the *Scales of Independent Behavior-Revised* (*SIB-R*; Bruininks, Woodcock, Weatherman, & Hill, 1996) and the *Adaptive Behavior Scale* (*ABS*; Lambert, Nihira, & Leland, 1993).

BEST PRACTICE RECOMMENDATIONS
The Evaluation Process

The purpose of an initial ASD evaluation is to determine the presence and severity of an ASD and possible comorbid disorders, inform future intervention and treatment planning, and provide a baseline to evaluate treatment efficacy. To conduct a thorough evaluation, a multimethod, multi-informant approach is generally accepted as best practice, including (a) a diagnostic interview with both the parents and child; (b) rating scales completed by the child, parent, and teachers; (c) informal interviews with the parents, child, and teachers; and (d) observations in both the clinic and school setting (Comer & Kendall, 2004; Silverman & Ollendick, 2005). Researchers largely concur that assessment instruments should not be used alone; rather, clinical observation, diagnostic criteria, and team collaboration should be incorporated alongside results of scales and measures (Matson et al., 2007).

Silverman and Ollendick (2005) have outlined guidelines for a comprehensive evidence-based assessment of children with anxiety; however, these guidelines outline best practice for assessment of all childhood disorders. Ozonoff, Goodlin-Jones, and Solomon (2005) build on these guidelines and indicate specific procedures for the assessment of ASD. First, interviews (unstructured, structured, semistructured) are administered to gain developmental and medical history and to determine the existence of a clinically significant disorder, then rating scales administered to multiple informants across several settings (e.g., home and school) are utilized to determine the amount, type, and severity of symptoms. Diagnostic observation instruments are used across multiple settings to allow the clinician to see firsthand the symptoms reported (Filipek et al., 1999, 2000; Ozonoff et al., 2005; Volkmar et al., 1999). The National Research Council (2001) recommends that complete evaluations include assessment of adaptive behavior, communication and language, cognitive and academic assessment, developmental history, and a medical screening to discern comorbid or contributing factors. With the ASD population, a neuropsychological assessment is sometimes in order (Ozonoff et al., 2005).

It is common to find discrepancies between and among multiple informants on a child's behavior (Achenbach, McConaughy, & Howell, 1987; De Los Reyes & Kazdin, 2009; De Los Reyes et al., 2011; Johnson & Wang, 2008; Perrin, Lewkowicz, & Young, 2000). The finding that when multiple informants report on behavior in the same setting they tend to agree more does not indicate that discrepant reports are unreliable; rather, discrepant reports are generally due to observations of how a child acts differently in various settings (Achenbach et al., 1987). The variation in reports thus gives valuable information on where problematic behaviors occur, the function of these behaviors, and if they are exhibited in multiple settings (De Los Reyes, 2011; De Los Reyes, Henry, Tolan, & Wakschlag, 2009; Hartley, Zakriski, & Wright, 2011). When doing an assessment, it is important to gain information from multiple informants who interact with the child in different situations. These informants should include parents, teachers, and other caregivers such as family members who assist in childcare, as well as the child, if possible. By gathering information from different informants, the clinician gains different perspectives and can determine whether the behavior is happening across all settings or in one particular setting.

ASD diagnoses made at age 3 years are generally stable (Charman & Baird, 2002; Turner, Stone, Pozdol, & Coonrod, 2006). Milder ASD symptom presentation, which may be present in those diagnosed with PDD-NOS or Asperger syndrome, may be more difficult to identify in young children (Matson, Nebel-Schwalm, & Matson, 2007). In such cases where it is difficult to determine whether symptom severity is to the degree to warrant a diagnosis or if there is a pervasive nature to the deficits, the clinician should consider Rule-Out diagnoses. This approach allows the child access to services such as early intervention programs, while avoiding giving an incorrect diagnosis, which may be less likely to be re-evaluated in an appropriate amount of time. The dangers of a child being misdiagnosed or not being re-evaluated after receiving a Rule-Out diagnosis are significant, particularly at a young age. Pursuing treatment for the wrong diagnosis would lead to misappropriation of valuable time and resources. Researchers have noted cases of PDD-NOS misdiagnosed as ADHD (Clark, Feehan, Tinline, & Vostanis, 1999); in such cases individuals are likely to miss out on the opportunity for the most appropriate early intervention services. Of course, another developmental disability or disorder misdiagnosed as an ASD would also lead to unnecessary stress for parents and less effective treatment for the child. A Rule-Out diagnosis should be accompanied by a recommendation to be re-evaluated after a period of time (e.g., a year), when deficits or delays are likely to be more pronounced and a more accurate diagnosis can be rendered.

During diagnostic evaluations, recommendations provided in the report can be as important as the actual diagnosis. With access to services often delayed for various reasons, the recommendations section of the diagnostic evaluation can provide parents with invaluable strategies to begin immediately, and it may also reduce parental stress by providing direction until more extensive resources can be accessed. For example, recommendations may include strategies for behavior management, specific types of treatments or resources to pursue, and recommendations for appropriate follow-up evaluation as necessary.

Differential Diagnosis and Co-occurring Conditions

At present, much research on differential diagnosis has centered on differentiating autism from other autism spectrum disorders, primarily focused on differentiating autism from PDD-NOS and Asperger disorder. However, it is worth noting that no specific diagnostic criteria exist for PDD-NOS in the *DSM-IV-TR*, and the disorder is at present largely defined as atypical or mild autistic symptoms (Matson & Boisjoli, 2007; Matson, Nebel-Schwalm, & Matson, 2007; Tidmarsh & Volkmar, 2003). Standardized measures, including the *CHAT*, have shown utility in differentially diagnosing between children with ASD from those without ASD, as well as differentiating autism versus PDD-NOS in children as young as 18 months (Baron-Cohen et al., 2000; Stone, Coonrod, & Ousley, 2000).

Another important consideration in differential diagnosis is that many of the professionals whom parents are likely to first consult in seeking a diagnosis (e.g., pediatricians, general practitioners, social workers, school teachers or counselors, clinical psychologists) may lack familiarity with the widely varying clinical presentation of ASD in children, particularly if comorbid conditions exist. ASD symptomatology can be heterogeneous between individuals of the same age. For example, children and youth with low IQ may manifest social impairment by a lack of interest in peers, whereas those with higher IQ may desire social interaction but exhibit traits that make it difficult to develop desired relationships. Similarly, children with low IQ may manifest repetitive behaviors in the form of motor stereotypies, while those with higher IQ are likely to manifest this trait in preoccupation with certain subjects and resistance to changes of routine (Corbett, Carmean, & Fein, 2009). The use of psychometrically sound measures may not only improve differential diagnosis but also serve to further educate professionals

about the clinical presentation of ASD (Matson, Nebel-Schwalm, & Matson, 2007). The reconfiguration of diagnostic criteria with the *DSM-5* will inevitably require researchers to invest considerable time and resources into investigating differential diagnosis and re-evaluating commonly used measures in order to re-establish convergent and divergent validity, particularly with the proposed new diagnostic category of social communication disorder, which at present is lacking in research. Though not categorized as an ASD, the proposed category includes many symptoms of or similar to ASD as defined under the *DSM-IV-TR*, thus confounding the current research on differential diagnosis. Clinicians are urged to bear these issues in mind as definitions of and research into the disorders continue to evolve.

Common symptoms associated with ASD have some overlap with other developmental disabilities. In assessing whether developmental problems represent an ASD or another developmental disability, the clinician should assess for discrepancies between the individual's overall developmental level and social/communication skills. A significant discrepancy between these measures lends support toward an ASD; however, if no discrepancy between developmental and social abilities is apparent, the clinician should more carefully consider the possibility of other DDs (Lord, 1995; Trillingsgaard, Sorensen, Nemec, & Jorgensen, 2005; Ventola et al., 2007).

ASD and specific language impairment (SLI) share some features of language and social behavior in common, supporting a common etiology for these distinct developmental disorders (Leyfer, Tager-Flusberg, Dowd, Tomblin, & Folstein, 2008). Individuals with autism, however, are more likely to exhibit pragmatic language impairment. In a study of children with SLI and those with ASD, Pickles and colleagues (2009) found that language loss and broad regression were largely limited to individuals with ASD, with 1% of children diagnosed with SLI and 15% of children with ASD having experienced language loss. Loss was even more likely in children with autism and was less frequent when language development was delayed. One study comparing children and adolescents with autism to those with an SLI noted that although both groups commonly exhibit attention impairments, the nature of the impairments may differ. The researchers concluded those with autism primarily exhibited deficits in executive functioning, whereas those with SLI exhibited deficits in auditory sustained attention and auditory selective attention as well as executive functioning (Noterdaeme, Amorosa, Mildenberger, Sitter, & Minow, 2001). The *Autistic Behavioural Indicators Instrument* (*ABII*; Ward & Gilmore, 2010) has indicated utility in differentiating young children with ASD from those with SLI, making this a measure worthy of further research.

Social abilities may be used to differentiate ASD from other developmental disabilities. On measures of social abilities in the *VABS-II* using individuals matched for chronological age, gender, and IQ, those with autism obtained lower scores in interpersonal skills than those with Down syndrome (Rodrigue, Morgan, & Geffken, 1991) or other DDs (Volkmar et al., 1987). A review by Ward and Gilmore (2010) found social attention behaviors, particularly in social orienting and joint attention, can be used to discriminate children with ASD from those with ID, DD, language delays, and Down syndrome. Indicators included orienting eye gaze toward objects rather than people, fewer attempts to initiate or respond to bids of joint attention with primary caregivers, and displays of positive affect to nonsocial stimuli with neutral responses to social stimuli (Ward & Gilmore, 2010).

Individuals with ID and those with ASD often exhibit similar symptoms, such as self-injurious behaviors and stereotypies (Matson & Minshawi, 2006), somewhat complicating differential diagnosis. Estimates of cognitive functioning can be difficult when comorbid language delays exist, also common in individuals with ASD or ID. It is commonly believed that individuals with ASD are characterized by a higher nonverbal IQ than verbal IQ (Lincoln, Hansel, & Quirmbach, 2007), with strengths in nonverbal visual-spatial tasks (Ghaziuddin & Mountain-Kimchi, 2004; Ozonoff, South, & Miller, 2000). However, research indicates that discrepancies in verbal and nonverbal IQ are related to both age and IQ; children with ASD and an IQ above 80 often show an even pattern of verbal and nonverbal ability by 7 years of age and those with IQ scores below 80 often show similar verbal and nonverbal scores by 10 years of age (Mayes & Calhoun, 2003). Individuals with Asperger syndrome may evince higher verbal IQ than nonverbal IQ (Ghaziuddin & Mountain-Kimchi, 2004; Joseph, Tager-Flusberg, & Lord, 2002, p. 216). Thus, although it is not uncommon for persons with ASD to have an uneven cognitive profile (Klin, Salnier, Tsatsanis, & Volkmar, 2005), no single IQ profile is indicative of an ASD diagnosis versus another DD. It is vital to obtain an accurate measure of cognitive and adaptive skills in differentiating between ID alone and ASD with comorbid ID. In order for a child to receive a diagnosis of ASD, social and communication delays must be greater than expected given the child's developmental level.

As discussed in chapter 2 of this book, individuals with ASD exhibit high rates of ADHD symptoms, and researchers have noted cases of PDD-NOS misdiagnosed as ADHD (Clark et al., 1999). Individuals with ASD often exhibit the ability to sustain attention for preferred activities but diminished ability to selectively attend to nonpreferred stimuli; many individuals also have difficulty switching attention from one stimulus to another (Courchesne et al., 1994; Garretson, Fein, & Waterhouse, 1990). In order to obtain an accurate evaluation of abilities during diagnosis, it is critical to provide adequate incentives for good performance in order to gain a true estimate of the individual's capacity for sustained attention. Visual checklists, sticker charts or reward systems, or incorporating preferred subjects or activities into the evaluation can be helpful.

Individuals with ASD present with a high rate of co-occurring disorders, including sleep disorders, epilepsy, gastrointestinal dysfunction, mood disorders, motor impairment, and aggressive or self-injurious behaviors (Maski, Jeste, & Spence, 2011; Ming, Brimacombe, Chaaban, Zimerman-Bier, & Wagner, 2008). Gastrointestinal problems are exacerbated by feeding issues and food selectivity, which are common in individual with ASD. Autism is very common in individuals with Fragile X syndrome, though rate estimates vary widely; this syndrome can be confirmed by genetic testing. Tuberous sclerosis has been reported in 1%–4% of children with autism (Zafeiriou, Ververi, & Vargiami, 2007).

Based on available research, ID appears to be the most prevalent co-occurring disorder in persons with ASD (Matson & Boisjoli, 2007). Recent studies suggest a prevalence rate of mental retardation of 40% to 71% in individuals with autistic disorder (see Fombonne, 2005, for a review). For those with PDD-NOS or Asperger disorder, estimates range from 6% to 49% (Fombonne, 2005). Self-injury correlates highly with both ASD and ID (Matson & Boisjoli, 2007); it stands to reason that an individual with both of these conditions should also be evaluated for self-injurious behaviors and functions of these behaviors. For more information about problematic behaviors, the clinician can do a functional analysis (Iwata, Dorsey, Slifer, Bauman, & Richman, 1982, 1994) to determine the antecedents and consequences of challenging or self-injurious behaviors that often co-occur with ASD (Love, Carr, & LeBlanc, 2009; Matson & Nebel-Schwalm, 2007; McClintock, Hall, & Oliver, 2003; Reese, Richman, Zarcone, & Zarcone, 2003). The *Questions About Behavioral Functioning* (*QABF*; Matson & Vollmer, 1995) is a brief caregiver report that can be useful to this effect.

Seizure disorders have been estimated to affect 11% to 39% of individuals with ASD (Ballaban-Gil & Tuchman, 2000). Lower IQ scores are often associated with co-occurring medical conditions, including seizure disorders (Mouridsen, Rich, & Isager, 2011). Epilepsy is not limited to those with ID, however; a review of the literature discerned that the rate of epilepsy in persons with ASD and normal IQ remains higher than the general population (Spence & Schneider, 2009). Evaluating, differentially diagnosing, and treating feeding problems, sleep disorders, ADHD, and mood disorders are topics covered more extensively elsewhere in this book, but during the diagnostic evaluation the clinician should be aware of how these potential co-occurring disorders might affect clinical presentation and behaviors.

Two large studies found over 70% of children with ASD met diagnostic criteria for a comorbid emotional or behavioral disorder (Leyfer et al., 2006; Tonge & Einfeld, 2003), and comorbid Axis I disorders are not limited to those with higher IQ (Kozlowski, Matson, Sipes, Hattier, & Bamburg, 2011). Co-occurring disorders may have an atypical presentation in individuals with ASD or ID. For example, symptoms of anxiety may include insistence on sameness or obsessive questioning (Deprey & Ozonoff, 2009). Leyfer and colleagues posit that bipolar disorder is relatively uncommon in individuals with ASD, although superficially behaviors may suggest episodes of mania. Notably, children with ASD often exhibit overreactive emotions, laugh for no apparent reason, or describe favorite topics in an overly excited manner. They may engage in dangerous activities, but as Leyfer et al. point out, the reasons behind these behaviors are very different in someone with ASD only versus someone with bipolar disorder. Someone with ASD may engage in dangerous activities simply because the person does not understand that the activity is unsafe, or the person may not comprehend the cause and effect of the behavior. The authors conclude that the best way to identify comorbid mood disorders is by comparison relative to baseline behavior. Decreases in adaptive functioning, loss of interest in a favorite topic or activity, and increase in maladaptive behaviors may indicate comorbid depression (Stewart, Barnard, Pearson, Hasan, & O'Brien, 2006). Though some symptoms such as avoiding eye contact may be common to both ASD and mood disorders, differential diagnosis may be easily made by reviewing developmental history. Individuals with depression alone are unlikely to have exhibited the long-term social and behavioral deficits common to ASD. Newman and Ghaziuddin (2008) found high rates of definite (29.7%) and probable (54.0%) comorbid psychiatric disorder in individuals with Asperger disorder convicted of violent crime. Palermo (2004) reported that the presence of psychopathology in individuals with PDDs may increase their risk of legal trouble and may precipitate hospital admission. The authors argue for the importance of early diagnosis and treatment of ASD and co-occurring psychiatric conditions.

Measures that have been used to measure psychopathology in persons with ASD include the *Child Behavior Checklist* (*CBCL*; Achenbach & Rescorla, 2001), *Behavior Assessment System for Children*, second edition (*BASC-2*; Reynolds & Kamphaus, 2004), and *Nisonger Child Behavior Rating Form* (*NCBF*; Aman, Tasse, Rojahn, & Hammer, 1996). The *Children's Yale-Brown Obsessive Compulsive Scale for Pervasive Developmental Disorders* (*CYBOCS-PDD*; McDougle et al., 2005; Scahill et al., 2006) includes a severity scale for repetitive and ritualistic behaviors to assist in differentiating whether symptoms are more closely associated with OCD or ASD; nonetheless, differential diagnosis is complicated by overlap of symptoms. Measures specifically intended to assess psychopathology in persons with ASD include the *Autism Spectrum Disorders-Comorbidity-Child Version* (*ASD-C-C*; Matson, González, 2007a) and *Autism Spectrum Disorders-Comorbidity-Adult Version* (*ASD-C-A*; Matson, Terlonge, & González, 2006a). Measures developed to assess for psychopathology in persons with ID include the Assessment for *Dual Diagnosis* (*ADD*; Matson, 1997) and *Diagnostic Assessment for the Severely Handicapped, Revised* (*DASH-II*; Matson, 1995).

Individuals with ASD are also more likely than the general population to be diagnosed with a tic disorder (Canitano & Vivanti, 2007). Critically, stereotypies should not be confused with tics. Clinicians trying to determine differential diagnosis can be aided by noting that stereotypies include movements that are rhythmical rather than spasmodic; they tend to involve the hands, fingers, or whole body rather than face, neck, arms, and shoulders; are less variable over time; and unlike people with tics, those with stereotypies are unlikely to be distressed by the behaviors (Lainhart, 1999).

Special Considerations in Testing

In assessing IQ in individuals suspected of ASD, the clinician must take care to obtain an accurate measure of cognitive ability. Characteristics of ASD include problems with attention, social interaction, and receptive and expressive language, which are all skills required during the administration of most standardized IQ tests. The clinician may consider the supplemental use of nonverbal tests or those that do not require speed or complex motor skills (National Research Council, 2001). Accommodations within the testing session may include having the examiner position the side of the table against a wall, position himself behind or beside rather than directly across from the child, having a parent or assistant sit next to the child, or conducting testing on the floor (Klinger, O'Kelley, & Mussey, 2009). Because many children with ASD become upset with changes in routine, having a visual schedule can reduce anxiety and improve attention during the session. If a child is distracted by special interests such as trains, these items can be incorporated into the schedule and break times. Klinger and colleagues (2009) recommend a "social routine" to further reduce anxiety in which the examiner keeps verbal instruction to a minimum and uses the same phrases such as "Time to work. Look" before presenting new items and "Good working" after each response. Koegel, Koegel, and Smith (1997) found significant improvements in IQ when testing sessions were modified, noting that unless the session is adapted to the child's specific needs, the session "becomes one of assessing motivation, attention, or compliance more than of assessing language or intelligence" (Koegel et al., 1997, p. 241). Akshoomoff (2006) recommends allowing parents to observe testing in order to provide feedback about whether the child is performing his or her best.

According to the National Research Council (2001), approximately 10% of children with ASD exhibit "splinter skills" of significant strength compared to other skills or to same-age peers; even individuals

with ASD who do not possess such unusual strengths often display wide variations in cognitive abilities. It is important for the evaluator to bear in mind that an average IQ score may misrepresent an individual's abilities by overestimating ability in the child's weakest areas and underestimating ability in other areas even within the same domain (such as Verbal IQ) (Klin, Saulnier, Tsatsanis, & Volkmar, 2005). Such results should be reported carefully in the evaluation.

In conclusion, ASD is a serious, lifelong condition. However, research has shown that early intervention can provide a critical advantage in skill development for those with the disorder. Interventions and funding are tied to diagnosis, and the need for accurate and timely evaluations cannot be underestimated. Though the disorder is considered neurodevelopmental in origin, at present diagnosis is made through the use of standardized measures, developmental history, and clinical interviews. The clinician must take care to avoid misdiagnosis with conditions having overlapping symptomatology and should also carefully assess for the presence of comorbid disorders and challenging behavior which may need to be treated concurrently with ASD. Though early diagnosis and evaluation for comorbid conditions can be challenging, intensive and rapid efforts to develop reliable methods have yielded useful measures and guidelines to facilitate the process.

REFERENCES

Achenbach, T. M., McConaughy, S. H., & Howell, C. T. (1987). Child/adolescent behavioral and emotional problems: Implications of cross-informant correlations for situational specificity. *Psychology Bulletin, 101,* 213–232.

Achenbach, T. M., & Rescorla, L. A. (2001). *Manual for the ASEBA school-age forms and profiles.* Burlington: University of Vermont, Research Center for Children, Youth, and Families.

Akshoomoff, N. (2006). Use of the Mullen Scales of Early Learning for the assessment of young children with autism spectrum disorders. *Child Neuropsychology, 12,* 269–277.

Aman, M. G., Tasse, M. J., Rojahn, J., & Hammer, D., (1996). The Nisonger CBRF: A child behavior rating form for children with developmental disabilities. *Research in Developmental Disabilities, 17,* 41–57.

Amato, J., Barrow, M., & Domingo, R. (1999). Symbolic play behavior in very young verbal and nonverbal children with autism. *Infant-Toddler Intervention, 9,* 185–194.

Baghdadli, A., Picot, M. C., Pascal, C., Pry, R., & Aussilloux, C. (2003). Relationship between age of recognition of first disturbances and severity of young children with autism. *European Journal of Child and Adolescent Psychiatry, 12,* 122–127.

Bailey, A., Le Couteur, A., Gottesman, I., Bolton, P., Simonoff, E., Yuzda, E., & Rutter, M. (1995). Autism as a strongly genetic disorder: Evidence from a British twin study. *Psychological Medicine, 25,* 63–77.

Ballaban-Gil, K., & Tuchman, R. (2000). Epilepsy and epileptiform EEG: Association with autism and language disorders. *Mental Retardation and Developmental Disabilities Research Reviews, 6,* 300–308.

Baron-Cohen, S., Cox, A., Baird, G., Swettenham, J., Nightingale, N., Morgan, K.,…Charman, T. (1996). Psychological markers in the detection of autism in infancy in a large population. *British Journal of Psychiatry, 168,* 158–163.

Baron-Cohen, S., Wheelwright, S., Cox, A., Baird, G., Charman, T., Swettenham, J.,…Doehring, P. (2000). The early identification of autism: The Checklist for Autism in Toddlers (CHAT). *Journal of the Royal Society of Medicine, 93,* 521–525.

Bayley, N. (1993). *Bayley Scales of Infant Development* (2nd ed.). San Antonio, TX: The Psychological Corporation.

Berument, S. K., Rutter, M., Lord, C., Pickles, A., & Bailey, A. (1999). Autism screening questionnaire: Diagnostic validity. *British Journal of Psychiatry, 175,* 444–451.

Bishop, D. V. M., & Norbury, C. F. (2002). Exploring the borderlands of autistic disorder and specific language impairment: A study using standardized diagnostic instruments. *Journal of Child Psychology and Psychiatry, 43,* 917–929.

Bormann-Kischkel, C., Vilsmeier, M., & Baude, B. (1995). The development of emotional concepts in autism. *Journal of Child Psychology and Psychiatry, 36,* 1245–1259.

Boucher, J., & Lewis, V. (1992). Unfamiliar face recognition in relatively able autistic children. *Journal of Child Psychology and Psychiatry, 33,* 843–859.

Brown, L., Sherbenou, R. J., & Johnson, S. K. (1997). *Test of non-verbal intelligence* (3rd ed.). Austin, TX: Pro-Ed.

Bruininks, R. H., Woodcock, R. W., Weatherman, R. F., & Hill, B. K. (1996). *Scales of independent behavior—revised.* Chicago, IL: Riverside.

Campbell, J. M. (2005). Diagnostic assessment of Asperger's disorder: A review of five third-party rating scales. *Journal of Autism and Developmental Disorders, 35,* 25–35.

Canitano, R., & Vivanti, G. (2007). Tics and Tourette syndrome in autism spectrum disorders: II. Developmental epidemiology. *Journal of the American Academy of Child and Adolescent Psychiatry, 45,* 8–25.

Cantwell, D. P., Baker, L., Rutter, M., & Mawhood, L. (1989). Infantile autism and developmental receptive dysphasia: A comparative follow-up into middle childhood. *Journal of Autism and Developmental Disorders, 19,* 19–31.

Centers for Disease Control and Prevention. (2012, July 5). *Learn the signs. Act early: Developmental milestones.* Retrieved August 2012, from http://www.cdc.gov/ncbddd/actearly/milestones/.

Chakrabarti, S., & Fombonne, E. (2001). Pervasive developmental disorders in preschool children. *Journal of the American Medical Association, 285,* 3093–3099.

Charman, T., & Baird, G. (2002). Practitioner review: Diagnosis of autism spectrum disorder in 2—and 3-year-old children. *Journal of Child Psychology and Psychiatry, 43,* 289–305.

Charman, T., Taylor, E., Drew, A., Cockerill, H., Brown J. A., & Baird, G. (2005). Outcome at 7 years of children diagnosed with autism at age 2: Predictive validity of assessments conducted at 2 and 3 years of age and pattern of symptom change over time. *Journal of Child Psychology and Psychiatry, 46,* 500–513.

Chawarska, K., Klin, A., Paul, R., & Volkmar, F. (2007). Autism spectrum disorder in the second year: Stability and change in syndrome expression. *Journal of Child Psychology and Psychiatry, 48,* 128–138.

Chowdhury, M., Benson, B. A., & Hillier, A. (2010). Changes in restricted repetitive behaviors with age: A study of high-functioning adults with autism spectrum disorders. *Research in Autism Spectrum Disorders, 4,* 210–216.

Clark, T., Feehan, C., Tinline, C., & Vostanis, P. (1999). Autistic symptoms in children with attention deficit hyperactivity disorder. *European Child and Adolescent Psychiatry, 8,* 50–55.

Comer, J. S., & Kendall, P. C. (2004). A symptom-level examination of parent-child agreement in the diagnosis of anxious youth. *Journal of the American Academy of Child and Adolescent Psychiatry, 43,* 878–886.

Coonrod, E. E, & Stone, W. L., (2005). Screening for autism in young children. In F. R. Volkmar, R. Paul., A. Klin, & D. Cohen (Eds.), *Handbook of autism and pervasive developmental disorders* (3rd ed., Vol. 2, pp. 707–729). Hoboken, NJ: Wiley.

Corbett, B. A., Carmean, V., & Fein, D. (2009). Assessment of neuropsychological functioning in autism spectrum disorders. In S. Goldstein, J. A. Naglieri, & S. Ozonoff (Eds.), *Assessment of autism spectrum disorders* (pp. 253–289). New York, NY: Guilford Press.

Courchesne, E., Townsend, J., Akshoomoff, N. A., Saitoh, O., Yeung-Courchesne, R., Lincoln, A. J.,…Lau, L. (1994). Impairment in shifting attention in autistic and cerebellar patients. *Behavioral Neuroscience, 108,* 848–865.

Cox, A., Klein, K., Charman, T., Baird, G., Baron-Cohen, S., Swettenham, J.,…Wheelwright, S. (1999), Autism spectrum disorders at 20 and 42 months of age: Stability of clinical and ADI-R diagnosis. *Journal of Child Psychology and Psychiatry, 40,* 719–732.

Dawson, G., Estes, A., Munson, J., Schellenberg, G., Bernier, R., & Abbott, R. (2007). Quantitative assessment of autism symptom-related traits in probands and parents: Broader Phenotype Autism Symptom Scale. *Journal of Autism and Developmental Disorders, 37,* 523–536.

Dawson, G., Meltzoff, A. N., Osterlin, J., Rinaldi, J., & Brown, E. (1998). Children with autism fail to orient to naturally occurring social stimuli. *Journal of Autism and Developmental Disorders, 28,* 479–485.

De Giacomo, A., & Fombonne, E. (1998). Parental recognition of developmental abnormalities in autism. *European Journal of Child and Adolescent Psychiatry, 7,* 131–136.

De Los Reyes, A. (2011). Introduction to the special section: More than measurement error: Discovering meaning behind informant discrepancies in clinical assessments of children and adolescents. *Journal of Clinical Child and Adolescent Psychology, 40,* 1–9.

De Los Reyes, A., Henry, D. B., Tolan, P. T., & Wakschlag, L. S. (2009). Linking informant discrepancies to observed variations in young children's disruptive behavior. *Journal of Abnormal Child Psychology, 37,* 637–652.

De Los Reyes, A., & Kazdin, A. E. (2009). Identifying evidence-based interventions for children and adolescents using the range of possible changes model: A meta-analytic illustration. *Behavior Modification, 33,* 583–617.

De Los Reyes, A., Youngstrom, E. A., Pabon, S. C., Youngstrom, J. K., Feeny, N. C., & Findling, R. L. (2011). Internal consistency and associated characteristics of informant discrepancies in clinic referred youth's age 11 to 17 years. *Journal of Clinical Child and Adolescent Psychology, 40,* 36–53.

Deprey, L., & Ozonoff, S. (2009). Assessment of comorbid psychiatric conditions in autism spectrum disorders. In S. Goldstein, J. A. Naglieri, & S. Ozonoff (Eds.), *Assessment of autism spectrum disorders* (pp. 290–317). New York, NY: Guilford Press.

Dewrang, P., & Sandberg, A. D. (2010). Parental retrospective assessment of development and behavior in Asperger syndrome during the first 2 years of life. *Research in Autism Spectrum Disorders, 4,* 461–473.

DiLavore, P. C., Lord, C., & Rutter, M. (1995). The pre-linguistic Autism Diagnostic Observation Schedule. *Journal of Autism and Developmental Disorders, 25,* 355–379.

Duffy, C., & Healy, O. (2011). Spontaneous communication in autism spectrum disorder: A review of topographies and intervention. *Research in Autism Spectrum Disorders, 5,* 977–983.

Dunn, L. M., & Dunn, D. M. (2007). *Peabody Picture Vocabulary Test* (4th ed.). Bloomington, MN: Pearson Assessments.

Dunn, W. (1999). *Short sensory profile.* San Antonio, TX: The Psychological Corporation.

Eaves, L. C., Wingert, H., & Ho, H. H. (2006). Screening for autism: Agreement with diagnosis. *Autism, 10,* 229–242.

Ehlers, S., Gillberg, C., & Wing, L. (1999). A screening questionnaire for Asperger syndrome and other high-functioning autism spectrum disorders in school age children. *Journal of Autism and Developmental Disorders, 29,* 129–141.

Eikeseth, S. (2009). Outcome of comprehensive psycho-educational interventions for young children with autism. *Research in Developmental Disabilities, 30,* 158–178.

Elliott, C. D. (2007). *Differential Ability Scales* (2nd ed.). San Antonio, TX: The Psychological Corporation.

Filipek, P. A., Accardo, P. L, Ashwal, S., Baranek, G. T., Cook, E. H., Jr., Dawson, G.,…Volkmar, F. R. (2000). Practice parameter: Screening and diagnosis of autism. *Neurology, 55,* 468–479.

Filipek, P. A., Accardo, P. J., Baranek, G. T., Cook, E. H., Jr., Dawson, G., Gordon, B.,…Volkmar, F. R. (1999). The screening and diagnosis of autistic spectrum disorders. *Journal of Autism and Developmental Disorders, 29,* 439–484.

Fodstad, J. C., Matson, J. L., Hess, J. A., & Neal, D. (2009). Social and communication behaviours in infants and toddlers with autism and pervasive developmental disorder-not otherwise specified. *Developmental Neurorehabilitation, 12,* 152–157.

Folstein, S., & Rutter, M. (1977). Infantile autism: A genetic study of 21 twin pairs. *Journal of Child Psychology and Psychiatry, 18,* 297–321.

Folstein, S. E., & Rutter, M. L. (1988). Autism: Familial aggregation and genetic implications. *Journal of Autism and Developmental Disorders, 18,* 3–30.

Fombonne, E. (2005). Epidemiological studies of pervasive developmental disorders. In F. R. Volkmar, R. Paul, A. Klin, & D. Cohen (Eds.), *Handbook of autism and pervasive developmental disorders. Vol. 1: Diagnosis, development, neurobiology, and behavior* (3d ed., pp. 42–69). Hoboken, NJ: Wiley.

Frazier, T. W., Youngstrom, E. A., Speer, L., Embacher, R., Law, P. Constantino, J.,…Eng, C. (2012). Validation of proposed *DSM-5* criteria for autism spectrum disorder. *Journal of the American Academy of Child and Adolescent Psychiatry, 51,* 28–40.

Freeman, B. J., & Schroth, P. C. (1984). The development of the behavioral observation system (BOS) for autism. *Behavioral Assessment, 6,* 177–187.

Fujiwara, T., Okuyama, M., & Funahashi, K. (2011). Factors influencing time lag between first parental concern and first visit to child psychiatric services in children with autism spectrum disorders in Japan. *Research in Autism Spectrum Disorders, 5,* 584–591.

Garretson, H. B., Fein, D., & Waterhouse, L., (1990). Sustained attention in children with autism. *Journal of Autism and Developmental Disorders, 20,* 101–114.

Ghaziuddin, M., & Mountain-Kimchi, K. (2004). Defining the intellectual profile of asperger syndrome: Comparison with high-functioning autism.

Journal of Autism and Developmental Disorders, 34, 279–284.

Gibbs, V., Aldridge, F., Chandler, F., Witzlsperger, E., & Smith, K. (2012). Brief report: An exploratory study comparing diagnostic outcomes for autism spectrum disorder under *DSM-IV-TR* with the proposed *DSM-5* revision. *Journal of Autism and Developmental Disorders.* 42(8), 1750–1756. doi:10.1007/s10803-012-1560-6.

Gilliam, J. E. (1995). *Gilliam Autism Rating Scale.* Austin, TX: PRO-ED.

Gilliam, J. E. (2003). *Gilliam Asperger Disorder Scale.* Austin, TX: PRO-ED.

Gilliam, J. E. (2008). *Gilliam Asperger Disorder Scale* (2nd ed.). Austin, TX: PRO-ED.

Goin-Kochel, R., Mackintosh, V., & Myers, B. (2006). How many doctors does it take to make an autism spectrum diagnosis? *Autism: The International Journal of Research and Practice, 10,* 439–451.

Goldstein, S., & Naglieri, J. A. (2009). *Autism Spectrum Rating Scale.* Toronto, ON: Multihealth Systems.

Granpeesheh, D., Dixon, D. R., Tarbox, J., Kaplan, A. M., & Wilke, A. E. (2009). The effects of age and treatment intensity on behavioral intervention outcomes for children with autism spectrum disorders. *Research in Autism Spectrum Disorders, 3,* 1014–1022.

Guinchat, V., Chamak, B., Bonniau, B., Bodeau, N., Perisse, D., Cohen, D., & Danion, A. (2012). Very early signs of autism reported by parents include many concerns not specific to autism criteria. *Research in Autism Spectrum Disorders, 6,* 589–601.

Harrison, P. L., & Oakland, T. (2003). *Adaptive behavior assessment system* (2nd ed.). San Antonio, TX: The Psychological Corporation.

Hartley, A. G., Zakriski, A. L., & Wright, J. C. (2011). Probing the depths of discrepancies: Contextual influences on divergence and convergence. *Journal of Clinical Child and Adolescent Psychology, 40,* 54–66.

Hauk, M., Fein, D., Maltby, N., Waterhouse, L., & Feinstein, C. (1999). Memory for faces in children with autism. *Child Neuropsychology, 4,* 187–198.

Hobson, R. P., & Lee, A. (1999). Imitation and identification in autism. *Journal of Child Psychology and Psychiatry, 40,* 649–659.

Iwata, B. A., Dorsey, M. F., Slifer, K. J., Bauman, K. E., & Richman, G. S. (1994). Toward a functional analysis of self-injury. *Journal of Applied Behavior Analysis, 27,* 197–209. (reprinted from *Analysis and Intervention in Developmental Disabilities, 2,* 3–20, 1982)

Johnson, S. B., & Wang, C. (2008). Why do adolescents say they are less healthy than their parents think they are? The importance of mental health varies by social class in a nationally representative sample. *Pediatrics, 121,* 307–313.

Joseph, R. M., Tager-Flusberg, H., & Lord, C. (2002). Cognitive profiles and social-communicative functioning in children with autism spectrum disorder. *Journal of Child Psychology and Psychiatry, 43,* 807–821.

Kanner, L. (1943). Autistic disturbances of affective contact. *Nervous Child, 2,* 217–250.

Kasari, C., Sigman, M., Yirmiya, N., & Mundy, P. (1993). Affective development and communication in children with autism. In A. P. Kaiser & D. B. Gray (Eds.), *Enhancing children's communication. Research foundations for intervention* (pp. 201–222). Baltimore, MD: Paul H. Brookes.

Kishore, M. T., & Basu, A. (2011). Early concerns of mothers of children later diagnosed with autism: Implications for early identification. *Research in Autism Spectrum Disorders, 5,* 157–163.

Klin, A., Salnier, C., Tsatsanis, K., & Volkmar, F. R. (2005). Clinical evaluation in autism spectrum disorders: Psychological assessment within a transdisciplinary framework. In F. R. Volkmar, R. Paul, A. Klin, & D. Cohen (Eds.), *Handbook of autism and pervasive developmental disorders* (3d ed., Vol. 2, pp. 772–798). Hoboken, NJ: Wiley.

Klinger, L. G., Dawson, G., & Renner, P. (2003). Autistic disorder. In E. J. Mash & R. A. Barkley (Eds.), *Child psychopathology, second edition* (pp. 409–454). New York, NY: Guilford Press.

Klinger, L. G., O'Kelley, S. E., & Mussey, J. L. (2009). Assessment of intellectual functioning in autism spectrum disorders. In S. Goldstein, J. A. Naglieri, & S. Ozonoff (Eds.). *Assessment of autism spectrum disorders* (pp. 209–251). New York, NY: Guilford Press.

Koegel, L. K., Koegel, R. L., & Smith, A. (1997). Variables related to differences in standardized test outcomes for children with autism. *Journal of Autism and Developmental Disorders, 27,* 233–243.

Kozlowski, A. M., Matson, J. L., Sipes, M., Hattier, M. A., & Bamburg, J. W. (2011). The relationship between psychopathology symptom clusters and the presence of comorbid psychopathology in individuals with severe and profound intellectual disability. *Research in Developmental Disabilities, 32,* 1610–1614.

Krug, D. A., & Arick, J. (2003). *Krug Asperger Disorder Index.* Austin, TX: Pro-Ed.

Lainhart, J. E. (1999). Psychiatric problems in individuals with autism, their parents and siblings. *International Review of Psychiatry, 11,* 28–298.

Lambert, N., Nihira, K., & Leland, H. (1993). *Adaptive Behavior Scale: School.* Austin, TX: Pro-Ed.

Landa, R., Piven, J., Wzorek, M., Gayle, J., Chase, G., & Folstein, S. (1992). Social language use in parents of autistic individuals. *Psychological Medicine, 22,* 245–254.

Le Couteur, A., Rutter, M., Lord, C., & Rios, P. (1989). Autism diagnostic interview: A standardized investigatory-based instrument. *Journal of Autism and Developmental disorders, 19,* 363–387.

Lee, L-C., David, A. B., Rusyniak, J., Landa, R., & Newschaffer, C. J. (2007). Performance of the Social Communication Questionnaire in children receiving preschool special education services. *Research in Autism Spectrum Disorders, 1,* 126–138.

Leyfer, O. T., Folstein, S. E., Bacalman, S., Davis, N. O., Dinh, E., Morgan, J., ...Lainhart, J. E. (2006). Comorbid psychiatric disorders in children with autism: Interview development and rates of disorders. *Journal of Autism and Developmental Disorders, 36,* 849–861.

Leyfer, O. T., Tager-Flusberg, H., Dowd, M., Tomblin, J. B., & Folstein, S. E. (2008). Overlap between autism and specific language impairment: Comparison of Autism Diagnostic Interview and Autism Diagnostic Observation Schedule scores. *Autism Research, 1,* 284–296.

Lincoln, A. J., Hansel, E., & Quirmbach, L., (2007). Assessing intellectual abilities of children and adolescents with autism and related disorders. In S. R. Smith & L. Handler (Eds.), *The clinical assessment of children and adolescents: A practitioner's handbook* (pp. 527–544). Mahwah, NJ: Erlbaum.

Lord, C. (1995). Follow-up of two-year-olds referred for possible autism. *Journal of Child Psychology and Psychiatry, 36,* 1365–1382.

Lord, C., & Corsello, C. (2005). Diagnostic instruments in autistic spectrum disorders. In F. R. Volkmar, R. Paul, A. Klin, & D. Cohen (Eds.), *Handbook of autism and pervasive developmental disorders* (3rd ed., Vol. 2, pp. 730–771). Hoboken, NJ: Wiley.

Lord, C., Risi, S., Lambrecht, L., Cook, E. H., Levanthal, B. L., DiLavore, P. C., ...Rutter, M. (2000). The Autism Diagnostic Observation Schedule-Generic: A standard measure of social and communication deficits associated with the spectrum of autism. *Journal of Autism and Developmental Disorders, 30,* 205–223.

Lord, C., Rutter, M., DiLavore, P., & Risi, S. (1999). *Autism Diagnostic Observation Schedule—WPS edition.* Los Angeles, CA: Western Psychological Services.

Lord, C., Rutter, M., DiLavore, P. C., & Risi, S. (2002). *Autism Diagnostic Observation Schedule manual.* Los Angeles, CA: Western Psychological Services.

Lord, C., Rutter, J. M., Goode, S., Heemsbergen, S., Jordon, J., Mawhood, L., ...Schopler, E. (1989). Autism Diagnostic Observation Schedule: A standardized observation of communicative and social behavior. *Journal of Autism and Developmental Disorders, 19,* 185–212.

Lord, C., Rutter, M., & LeCouteur, A. (1994). Autism Diagnostic Interview-revised: A revised version of a diagnostic interview for caregivers of individuals with possible pervasive developmental disorders. *Journal of Autism and Developmental Disorders, 24,* 659–685.

LoVollu, S. V., & Matson, J. L. (2012). Development of a critical item algorithm for the Baby and Infant Screen for Children with aUtIsm Traits. *Research in Autism Spectrum Disorders, 6,* 378–384.

Love, J. R., Carr, J. E., & LeBlanc, L. A. (2009). Functional assessment of challenging behavior in children with autism spectrum disorders: A summary of 32 outpatient cases. *Journal of Autism and Developmental Disorders, 39,* 363–372.

Loveland, K. A., Tunali-Kotoski, B., Pearson, D. A., Brelsford, K. A., Ortegon, J., & Chen, R. (1994). Imitation and expression of facial affect in autism. *Development and Psychopathology, 6,* 433–444.

Mandell, D. S., Novak, M. M., & Zubritsky, C. D. (2005). Factors associated with age of diagnosis among children with autism spectrum disorders. *Pediatrics, 116,* 1480–1486.

Maski, K. P., Jeste, S. S., & Spence, S. J. (2011). Common neurological co-morbidities in autism spectrum disorders. *Current Opinion in Pediatrics, 23,* 609–615.

Matson, J. L. (1995). *Diagnostic assessment for the severely handicapped revised (DASH-II).* Baton Rouge, LA: Disability Consultants.

Matson, J. L. (1997). *Assessment for dual diagnosis (ADD).* Baton Rouge, LA: Disability Consultants.

Matson, J. L. (2007). Current status of differential diagnosis for children with autism spectrum disorders. *Research in Developmental Disabilities, 28,* 109–118.

Matson, J. L., Beighley, J., & Turygin, N. (2012). Autism diagnosis and screening: Factors to consider in differential diagnosis. *Research in Autism Spectrum Disorders, 6,* 19–24.

Matson, J. L., Belva, B. C., Horovitz, M., & Bamburg, J. (2012). Comparing symptoms of autism spectrum disorders in a developmentally disabled adult population using the current *DSM-IV-TR* diagnostic criteria and the proposed *DSM-5* diagnostic criteria. *Journal of Developmental and Physical Disabilities, 24,* 403–414.

Matson, J. L., & Boisjoli, J. (2007). Differential diagnosis of PDD-NOS in children. *Research in Autism Spectrum Disorders, 1,* 75–84.

Matson, J. L., Boisjoli, J. A., Hess, J. A., & Wilkins, J. (2011). Comorbid psychopathology factor structure on the Baby and Infant Screen for Children with aUtIsm Traits-Part 2 (BISCUIT-Part 2). *Research in Autism Spectrum Disorders, 5,* 426–432.

Matson, J. L., Boisjoli, J. A., & Wilkins, J. (2007). *Baby and Infant Screen for Children with aUtIsm Traits (BISCUIT).* Baton Rouge, LA: Disability Consultants.

Matson, J. L., Carlisle, C. B., & Bamburg, J. W. (1998). The convergent validity of the Matson Evaluation of Social Skills for Individuals with Severe Retardation (MESSIER). *Research in Developmental Disabilities, 19,* 493–500.

Matson, J. L., Fodstad, J. C., Mahan, S., & Sevin, J. A. (2009). Cutoffs, norms, and patterns of comorbid difficulties in children with an ASD on the Baby and Infant Screen for Children with aUtIsm Traits (BISCUIT-Part 2). *Research in Autism Spectrum Disorders, 3,* 977–988.

Matson, J. L., & González, M. L. (2007a). *Autism spectrum disorders—comorbidity—child version.* Baton Rouge, LA: Disability Consultants.

Matson, J. L., & González, M. L. (2007b). *Autism spectrum disorders—diagnosis for children*. Baton Rouge, LA: Disability Consultants.

Matson, J. L., Gonzalez, M., & Wilkins, J. (2009). Validity study of the Autism Spectrum Disorders-Diagnostic for Children (ASD-DC). *Research in Autism Spectrum Disorders, 3*, 196–206.

Matson, J. L., Gonzalez, M. L., Wilkins, J., & Rivet, T. T. (2007). Reliability of the Autism Spectrum Disorder-Diagnostic for Children (ASD-DC). *Research in Autism Spectrum Disorders, 2*, 533–545.

Matson, J. L., Hattier, M. A., & Williams, L. W. (2012). How does relaxing the algorithm for autism affect DSM-V prevalence rates? *Journal of Autism and Developmental Disorders, 42*, 1549–1556.

Matson, J. L., Hess, J. A., Mahan, S., & Fodstad, J. C. (2010). Convergent validity of the Autism Spectrum Disorder Diagnostic for Children (ASD-DC) and Autism Diagnostic Interview-revised (ADI-R). *Research in Autism Spectrum Disorders, 4*, 741–745.

Matson, J. L., Kozlowski, A. M., Hattier, M. A., Horovitz, M., & Sipes, M. (2012). DSM-IV versus *DSM-5* diagnostic criteria for toddlers with autism. *Developmental Neurorehabilitation, 15*, 185–190.

Matson, J. L., Mahan, S., Hess, J. A., Fodstad, J. C., & Neal, D. (2010). Convergent validity of the Autism Spectrum Disorder Diagnostic for Children (ASD-DC) and Childhood Autism Rating Scales (CARS). *Research in Autism Spectrum Disorders, 4*, 633–638.

Matson, J. L., & Minshawi, N. F. (2006). *Early intervention for autism spectrum disorders: A critical analysis*. Oxford, UK: Elsevier Science.

Matson, J. L., & Nebel-Schwalm, M. (2007). Assessing challenging behaviors in children with autism spectrum disorders: A review. *Research in Developmental Disabilities, 28*, 567–579.

Matson, J. L., Nebel-Schwalm, M., & Matson, M. L. (2007). A review of methodological issues in the differential diagnosis of autism spectrum disorders in children. *Research in Autism Spectrum Disorders, 1*, 38–54.

Matson, J. L., Terlonge, C., & González, M. L. (2006a). *Autism spectrum disorders – comorbidity—adult version*. Baton Rouge, LA: Disability Consultants.

Matson, J. L., Terlonge, C., & González, M. L. (2006b). *Autism spectrum disorders-diagnosis (ASD-D)*. Baton Rouge, LA: Disability Consultants.

Matson, J. L., & Tureck, K. (2012). Early diagnosis of autism: Current status of the Baby and Infant Screen for Children with aUtIsm Traits (BISCUIT – Parts 1, 2, and 3). *Research in Autism Spectrum Disorders, 6*, 1135–1141.

Matson, J. L., & Vollmer, T. (1995). *Questions about behavioral function (QABF)*. Baton Rouge, LA: Disability Consultants.

Matson, J. L., Wilkins, J., Boisjoli, J. A., & Smith, K. R. (2008). The validity of the Autism Spectrum Disorders-Diagnosis for Intellectually Disabled Adults (ASD-DA). *Research in Developmental Disabilities, 29*, 537–546.

Matson, J. L., Wilkins, J., Sharp, B., Knight, C., Sevin, J. A., & Boisjoli, J. A. (2009). Sensitivity and specificity of the Baby and Infant Screen for Children with aUtIsm Traits (BISCUIT): Validity and cutoff scores for autism and PDD-NOS in toddlers. *Research in Autism Spectrum Disorders, 4*, 924–930.

Mayes, S. D., & Calhoun, S. L., (2003). Analysis of the WISC-III, Stanford-Binet: IV, and academic achievement test scores in children with autism. *Journal of Autism and Developmental Disorders, 33*, 329–341.

Mazefsky, C., & Oswald, D. (2006). The discriminative ability and diagnostic utility of the ADOS-G, ADI-R, and GARS for children in a clinical setting. *Autism, 10*, 533–549.

McClintock, K., Hall, S., & Oliver, C. (2003). Risk markers associated with challenging behaviors in people with intellectual disabilities: A meta-analytic study. *Journal of Intellectual Disability Research, 47*, 405–416.

McDougle, C. J., Scahill, L., Aman, M. G., McCracken, J. Tl, Tierney, E., Davies, M.,…Vitiello, B. (2005). Risperidone for the core symptom domains of autism: Results from the study by the Autism Network of the Research Units on Pediatric Psychopharmacology. *American Journal of Psychiatry, 162*, 1142–1148.

McPartland, J. C., Reichow, B., & Volkmar, F. R. (2012). Sensitivity and specificity of proposed *DSM-5* diagnostic criteria for autism spectrum disorder. *Journal of the American Academy of Child and Adolescent Psychiatry, 51*, 368–383.

Ming, X., Brimacombe, M., Chaaban, J., Zimmerman-Bier, B., & Wagner, G. C. (2008). Autism spectrum disorders: Concurrent clinical disorders. *Journal of Child Neurology, 23*, 6–13.

Moh, T. A., & Magiati, I. (2012). Factors associated with parental stress and satisfaction during the process of diagnosis of children with autism spectrum disorders. *Research in Autism Spectrum Disorders, 6*, 293–303.

Mouridsen, S. E., Rich, B., & Isager, T. (2011). A longitudinal study of epilepsy and other central nervous system diseases in individuals with and without a history of infantile autism. *Brain and Development, 33*, 361–366.

Mullen, E. M. (1995). *Mullen Scales of Early Learning*. Circle Pines, MN: American Guidance Services.

Mundy, P., Sigman, M., Ungerer, J., & Sherman, T. (1986). Defining the social deficits of autism: The contribution of nonverbal communication measures. *Journal of Child Psychology and Psychiatry, 27*, 657–669.

Myles, B., Bock, S., & Simpson, R. (2001). *Asperger Syndrome Diagnostic Scale*. Austin, TX: Pro-Ed.

National Research Council. (2001). *Educating children with autism*. (Committee on Educational Interventions of Children with Autism, C. Lord, & J. P. McGee, Eds.). Washington, DC: National Academy Press.

Neal, D., Matson, J. L., & Hattier, M. A. (in press). Validity of the Autism Spectrum Disorder—Observation for Children (ASD-OC). *Journal of Mental Health Research in Intellectual Disabilities.*

Nebel-Schwalm, M. S., & Matson, J. L. (2008). Differential diagnosis. In L. Matson (Ed)., *Clinical assessment and intervention for autism spectrum disorders* (pp. 91–119). Oxford, UK: Elsevier.

Nellis, L. M. (n.d.) [Review of the Krug Asperger's Disorder Index]. In *The sixteenth mental measurements yearbook*. Retrieved August 2012, from EBSCOHost Mental Measurements Yearbook database.

Newman, S. S., & Ghaziuddin, M. (2008). Violent crime in Asperger syndrome: The role of psychiatric comorbidity. *Journal of Autism and Developmental Disorders, 38,* 1848–1852.

Noterdaeme, M., Amorosa, H., Mildenberger, K., Sitter, S., & Minow, F. (2001). Evaluation of attention problems in children with autism and children with a specific language disorder. *European Child and Adolescent Psychiatry, 10,* 58–66.

Osborne, L. A., McHugh, L., Saunders, J., & Reed, P. (2008). A possible contra-indication for early diagnosis of autistic spectrum conditions: Impact on parenting stress. *Research in Autism Spectrum Disorders, 2,* 707–715.

Ospina, M. B., Seida, J., Clark, B., Karkhaneh, M., Hartling, L., Tjosvold, L.,...Smith, V. (2008). Behavioural and developmental interventions for autism spectrum disorder: A clinical systematic review. *Plos ONE, 3,* 1–32. doi:10.1371/journal.pone.0003755.

Osterling, J., & Dawson, G. (1994). Early recognition of children with autism: A study of first birthday home videotapes. *Journal of Autism and Developmental Disorders, 24,* 247–257.

Ozonoff, S., Goodlin-Jones, B. L., & Solomon, M. (2005). Evidence-based assessment of autism spectrum disorders in children and adolescents. *Journal of Clinical Child and Adolescent Psychology, 34,* 523–540.

Ozonoff, S., South, M., & Miller, J. N. (2000). DSM-IV defined Asperger syndrome: Cognitive, behavioral and early history differentiation from high-functioning autism. *Autism, 4,* 29–46.

Palermo, M. T. (2004). Pervasive developmental disorders, psychiatric comorbidities, and the law. *International Journal of Offender Therapy and Comparative Criminology, 48,* 40–80.

Paul, R., Chawarska, K., Cicchetti, D., & Volkmar, F. (2008). Language outcomes of toddlers with autism spectrum disorders: A two year follow-up. *Autism, 1,* 97–107.

Paul, R., Fischer, M. L., & Cohen, D. J. (1988). Brief report: Sentence comprehension strategies in children with autism and specific language disorders. *Journal of Autism and Developmental Disorders, 18,* 669–677.

Paul, R., Fuerst, Y., Ramsay, G., Chawarska, K., & Klin, A. (2011). Out of the mouths of babes: Vocal production

in infant siblings of children with ASD. *Journal of Child Psychology and Psychiatry, 52,* 588–598.

Perrin, E. C., Lewkowicz, C., & Young, M. H. (2000). Shared vision: Concordance among fathers, mothers, and pediatricians about unmet needs of children with chronic health conditions. *Pediatrics, 105,* 277–285.

Pickles, A., Simonoff, E., Conti-Ramsden, G., Falcaro, M., Simkin, Z., Charman, T., Chandler, S.,...Baird, G. (2009). Loss of language in early development of autism and specific language impairment. *Journal of Child Psychology and Psychiatry and Allied Disciplines, 50,* 843–852.

Piven, J., Palmer, P., Jacobi, D., Childress, D., & Arndt, S. (1997). Broader autism phenotype: Evidence from a family history study of multiple-incidence autism families. *American Journal of Psychiatry, 154,* 185–190.

Reese, R. M., Richman, D. M., Zarcone, J., & Zarcone, T. (2003). Individualizing functional assessments for children with autism: The contribution of perseverative behavior and sensory disturbances to disruptive behavior. *Focus on Autism and Other Developmental Disabilities, 18,* 87–92.

Reichow, B., & Wolery, M. (2009). Comprehensive synthesis of early intensive behavioral interventions for young children with autism based on the UCLA Young Autism Project model. *Journal of Autism and Developmental Disorders, 39,* 23–41.

Rellini, E., Tortolani, D., Trillo, S., Carbone, S., & Montecchi, F. (2004). Childhood Autism Rating Scale (CARS) and Autism Behavior Checklist (ABC) correspondence and conflicts with DSM-IV criteria in diagnosis of autism. *Brain Dysfunction, 4,* 308–319.

Reynolds, C. R., & Kamphaus, R. W. (2004). *Behavior assessment system for children* (2nd ed.). Circle Pines, MN: AGS.

Riguet, C., Taylor, N., Benaroya, S., & Klein, L. (1981). Symbolic play in autistic, Down's and normal children of equivalent mental age. *Journal of Autism and Developmental Disorders, 11,* 439–448.

Robins, D. L., Fein, D., Barton, M. L., & Green, J. A. (2001). The Modified Checklist for Autism in Toddlers: An initial study investigating the early detection of autism and pervasive developmental disorders. *Journal of Autism and Developmental Disorders, 31,* 131–144.

Rodrigue, J. R., Morgan, S. B., & Gefken, G. R. (1991). A comparative evaluation of adaptive behavior in children and adolescents with autism, Down syndrome, and normal development. *Journal of Autism and Developmental Disorders, 21,* 187–196.

Rogers, S. J., & Vismara, L. A. (2008). Evidence-based comprehensive treatments for early autism. *Journal of Clinical Child and Adolescent Psychology, 37,* 8–38.

Roid, G. H. (2003). *Stanford-Binet Intelligence Scales* (5th ed.). Itsaca, IL: Riverside.

Roid, G. H., & Miller, L. J. (1997). *Leiter International Performance Scale—Revised: Examiner's manual.* Wood Dale, IL: Stoelting.

Ruffman, T., Garnham, W., & Rideout, P. (2001). Social understanding in autism: Eye gaze as a measure of core insights. *Journal of Child Psychology and Psychiatry, 42,* 1083–1094.

Rutter, M., Bailey, A., & Lord, C. (2003). *Social Communication Questionnaire.* Los Angeles, CA: Western Psychological Services.

Rutter, M., LeCouteur, A., & Lord, C. (2003). *Autism Diagnostic Interview-Revised manual.* Los Angeles, CA: Western Psychological Services.

Saemunden, E., Magnusson, P., Smari, J., & Sigurdardottir, S. (2003). Autism Diagnostic Interview-Revised and the Childhood Autism Rating Scale: Convergence and discrepancy in diagnosing autism. *Journal of Autism and Developmental Disorders, 33,* 319–328.

Saint-Georges, C., Cassel, R. S., Cohen, D., Chetouani, M., Laznik, M. C., Maestro, S., & Muratori, F. (2010). What studies of family home movies can teach us about autistic infants: A literature review. *Research in Autism Spectrum Disorders, 4,* 355–366.

Santangelo, S. L., Folstein, S. E., & Tager-Flusberg, H. (1999). Autism: A genetic perspective. In H. Tager-Flusberg (Ed.), *Neurodevelopmental disorders* (pp. 431–447). Cambridge, MA: The MIT Press.

Scahill, L., McDougle, C., J., Williams, S. K., Dimitropoulos, A., Aman, A. G., McCracken, J. T.,...Research Units on Pediatric Psychopharmacology Autism Network. (2006). The Children's Yale-Brown Obsessive Compulsive Scales modified for pervasive developmental disorders. *Journal of the American Academy of Child and Adolescent Psychiatry, 45,* 114–1123.

Schopler, E., Reichler, R., & Renner, B. (1988). *The Childhood Autism Rating Scale (CARS).* Los Angeles, CA: Western Psychological Services.

Scott, F. J., Baron-Cohen, S., Bolton, P., & Brayne, C. (2002). The CAST (Childhood Asperger Syndrome Test): Preliminary development of a UK screen for mainstream primary-school-age children. *Autism, 6,* 9–31.

Shevell, M., Majnemer, A., Rosenbaum, P., & Abrahamowicz, M. (2001). Profile of referrals for early childhood developmental delay to ambulatory subspecialty clinics. *Journal of Child Neurology, 16,* 645–650.

Siklos, S., & Kerns, K. A. (2007). Assessing the diagnostic experiences of a small sample of parents of children with autism spectrum disorders. *Research in Developmental Disabilities, 28,* 9–22.

Sikora, D. M., Hall, T. A., Hartley, S. L., Gerrard-Morris, A. E., & Cagle, S. (2008). Does parent report of behavior differ across ADOS-G classifications: Analysis of scores from the CBCL and GARS. *Journal of Autism and Developmental Disorders, 38,* 440–448.

Silverman, W., & Ollendick, T. H. (2005). Evidence-based assessment of anxiety and its disorders in children and adolescents. *Journal of Clinical Child and Adolescent Psychology, 34,* 380–411.

Sipes, M., Matson, J. L., Worley, J. A., & Kozlowski, A. M. (2011). Gender differences in symptoms of autism spectrum disorders in toddlers. *Research in Autism Spectrum Disorders, 5,* 1465–1470.

South, M., Williams, B. J., McMahon, W. M., Owley, T., Filipek, P. A., Shernoff, E.,...Ozonoff, S. (2002). Utility of the Gilliam Autism Rating Scale in research and clinical populations. *Journal of Autism and Developmental Disorders, 32,* 593–599.

Sparrow, S. S., Cicchetti, D. V., & Balla, D. A. (2005). *Vineland Adaptive Behavior Scales, Second Edition (Vineland-II).* Circle Pines, MN: American Guidance Service.

Spence, S. J., & Schneider, M. T. (2009). The role of epilepsy and epileptiform EEGs in autism spectrum disorders. *Pediatric Research, 65,* 599–606.

Sponheim, E. (1996). Changing criteria of autistic disorders: A comparison of ICD-10 research criteria and DSM-IV with DSM-III-R, CARS, and ABC. *Journal of Autism and Developmental Disorders, 26,* 513–525.

Stewart, M. E., Barnard, L., Pearson, J., Hasan, R., & O'Brien, G. (2006). Presentation of depression in autism and Asperger syndrome: A review. *Autism, 100,* 103–116.

Stone, W. L., Coonrod, E. E., & Ousley, O. Y. (2000). Brief report: Screening Tool for Autism in Two-year-olds (STAT): Development and preliminary data. *Journal of Autism and Developmental Disorders, 30,* 607–612.

Tadevosyan-Leyfer, O., Dowd, M., Mankoski, R., Winklosky, B., Putnam, S., McGrath, L.,...Folstein, S. E. (2003). A principal of components analysis of the Autism Diagnostic Interview-Revised. *Journal of the American Academy of Child and Adolescent Psychiatry, 42,* 864–872.

Tager-Flusberg, H. (1999). A psychological approach to understanding the social and language impairments in autism. *International Review of Psychiatry, 11,* 325–334.

Tantam, D., Monaghan, L., Nicholson, J., & Stirling, J. (1989). Autistic children's ability to interpret faces: A research note. *Journal of Child Psychology and Psychiatry, 30,* 623–630.

Teunisse, J., & DeGelder, B. (1994). Do autistics have a generalized face processing deficit? *International Journal of Neuroscience, 77,* 1–10.

Tidmarsh, L., & Volkmar, F. R., (2003). Diagnosis and epidemiology of autism spectrum disorders. *Canadian Journal of Psychiatry, 48,* 517–525.

Tonge, B., & Einfeld, S. (2003). Psychopathology and intellectual disability: The Australian Child to Adult Longitudinal Study. In L. M. Glidden (Ed.), *International review of research in mental retardation* (Vol. 26, pp. 61–91). San Diego, CA: Academic Press.

Trillingsgaard, A., Sorensen, E. U., Nemec, G., & Jorgensen, M. (2005). What distinguishes autism spectrum disorders from other developmental disorders before the age of four years? *European Journal of Child and Adolescent Psychiatry, 14,* 65–72.

Turner, L. M., Stone, W. L., Pozdol, S. L., & Coonrod, E. E. (2006). Follow-up of children with autism spectrum disorders from age 2 to age 9. *Autism, 10,* 243–265.

Turner, M. (1999). Annotation: Repetitive behavior in autism: A review of psychological research. *Journal of Child Psychology and Psychiatry, 40,* 839–849.

Turygin, N., Matson, J. L., Beighley, J., & Adams, H. (2013). The effect of DSM-5 criteria on the developmental quotient in toddlers diagnosed with autism spectrum disorder. *Developmental Neurorehabilitation, 16*(1), 38–43.

Twyman, K. A., Maxim, R. A., Leet, T. L., & Ultmann, M. H. (2009). Parents' developmental concerns and age variance at diagnosis of children with autism spectrum disorder. *Research in Autism Spectrum Disorders, 3,* 489–495.

Ungerer, J. (1989). The early development of autistic children: Implications for defining primary deficits. In G. Dawson (Ed.), *Autism: Nature, diagnosis, and treatment* (pp. 75–91). New York, NY: Guilford Press.

Ventola, P., Kleinman, J., Pandey, J., Wilson, L., Esser, E., Boorstein, H., ... Fein, D. (2007). Differentiating between autism spectrum disorders and other developmental disabilities in children who failed a screening instrument for ASD. *Journal of Autism and Developmental Disorders, 37*(3), 425–436.

Virués-Ortega, J. (2010). Applied behavior analytic intervention for autism in early childhood: Meta-analysis, meta-regression and dose-response meta-analysis of multiple outcomes. *Clinical Psychology Review, 30,* 387–399.

Volkmar, F. R., Cohen, D. J., & Paul, R. (1986). An evaluation of DSM-III criteria for infantile autism. *Journal of the American Academy of Child Psychiatry, 25,* 190–197.

Volkmar, F. R., Cook, E. H., Jr., Pomeroy, J., Realmuto, G., & Tanguay, P. (1999). Practice parameters for the assessment and treatment of children, adolescents, and adults with autism and other pervasive developmental disorders. *Journal of the American Academy of Child and Adolescent Psychiatry, 38,* 32S–54S.

Volkmar, F. R., Sparrow, S. S., Gourgreau, D., Cicchetti, D. V., Paul, R., & Cohen, D. J. (1987). Social deficits in autism: An operational approach using the Vineland Adaptive Behavior Scales. *Journal of the American Academy of Child and Adolescent Psychiatry, 26,* 156–161.

Ward, S. L., & Gilmore, L. (2010). The Autistic Behavioural Indicators Instrument (ABII): Development and instrument utility in discriminating autistic disorder from speech and language impairment and typical development. *Research in Autism Spectrum Disorders, 4,* 28–42.

Wechsler, D. (2003). *Wechsler Intelligence Scale for Children* (4th ed.). San Antonio, TX: The Psychological Corporation.

Weeks, S. J., & Hobson, R. P. (1987). The salience of facial expression for autistic children. *Journal of Child Psychology and Psychiatry, 28,* 137–152.

Wetherby, A., Watt, N., Morgan, L., & Shumway, S. (2007). Social communication profiles of children with autism spectrum disorders in the second year of life. *Journal of Autism and Developmental Disorders, 37,* 960–975.

Wing, L. (1978). Social, behavioral, and cognitive characteristics: An epidemiological approach. In M. Rutter & E. Schopler (Eds.), *Autism: A reappraisal of concepts and treatment* (pp. 91–110). New York, NY: Plenum Press.

Worley, J. A., & Matson, J. L. (2011). Diagnostic instruments for core features of ASD. In J. L. Matson & P. Sturmey (Eds.), *International handbook of autism and pervasive developmental disorders.* New York, NY: Springer.

Worley, J. A., & Matson, J. L. (2012). Comparing symptoms of autism spectrum disorders using the current DSM-IV-TR diagnostic criteria and the proposed DSM-V diagnostic criteria. *Research in Autism Spectrum Disorders, 6,* 965–970.

Zafeiriou, D. I., Ververi, A., & Vargiami, E. (2007). Childhood autism and associated comorbidities. *Brain and Development, 29,* 257–272.

2

Comorbidity Among Children and Youth With Autism Spectrum Disorder

NICOLE NEIL, LAURA MOUM, AND PETER STURMEY

The *Diagnostic and Statistical Manual for Mental Disorders* (*DSM-5*) defines a psychiatric disorder as " characterized by significant dysfunction in an individual's cognitions, emotions, or behaviors that reflects a disturbance in the psychological, biological, or developmental processes underlying mental functioning" (American Psychiatric Association [APA], 2013). Comorbidity is two or more forms of psychopathology within the same person (Matson & Nebel-Schwalm, 2007; Simonoff et al., 2009). The *DSM-5* does not identify systematic standards for dual diagnosis (Hyrb, Kirkhart, & Talbert, 2007); nonetheless, one common interpretation is that a secondary diagnosis requires symptom presentation that meets diagnostic standards without assumptions of causality (Coghill & Seth, 2011). Others have required that the so-called secondary condition is sufficiently significant that it requires treatment in addition to the so-called primary condition. Although comorbid psychiatric disorders have been thoroughly investigated in typically developing youth, much less research has been dedicated toward comorbid psychiatric disorders occurring with autism spectrum disorder (ASD) (Matson & Nebel-Schwalm, 2007).

Evaluating comorbidity in people with ASD presents several challenges. First, many symptoms of psychopathology overlap with symptoms of ASD. For example, *DSM-IV* defined repetitious behavior as a symptom of both ASD and stereotypic behavior disorder. A second challenge is diagnostic overshadowing (Ghaziuddin & Ghaziuddin, 1992; Long, Wood, & Holmes, 2000; Matson & Nebel-Schwalm, 2007; Simonoff et al., 2008; Xenitidis, Paliokosta, Maltezos, & Pappas, 2007), which refers to a phenomenon in which a second disorder is not recognized because the diagnostician attributes the problem to the first disorder. For example, some clinicians might not diagnose attention-deficit/hyperactivity disorder (ADHD) in a child with ASD because they incorrectly attributed the symptoms of ADHD to ASD. Third, the heterogeneous nature of ASD symptomology complicates distinguishability of core ASD symptoms from symptoms of comorbid disorders (Matson & Nebel-Schwalm, 2007; Mazefsky & Oswald, 2012). As a result, psychiatric symptoms may be overlooked and attributed to the variability of ASD symptoms. Fourth, the presence of intellectual disability (ID), which is frequent in ASD (Long, Wood, & Holmes, 2000; Matson & Nebel-Schwalm, 2007; Simonoff et al., 2008), often complicates diagnosing other disorders. Notably, Lord and Volkmar (2002) estimated that between 26% and 80% of individuals with ASD also met criteria for ID. Fifth, psychopathology symptoms may have different overt manifestations in children with ASD than children without ASD (Ghaziuddin & Ghaziuddin, 1992; Matson & Nebel-Schwalm, 2007). Thus, children with ASD often have difficulty recognizing and articulating psychiatric symptoms, and they also may lack the ability to accurately respond to questions about symptomology (Gjevik, Elevik, Fjaeran-Granum, & Sponheim, 2011; Helverschou, Bakken, & Martinsen, 2009). Finally, because systematic methods of identifying and treating comorbid psychiatric disorders across the spectrum are lacking (Matson & Nebel-Schwalm, 2007), there is a need for professional standards of comorbid identification and diagnosis. Currently, diagnoses and treatments are based on clinical opinion; thus, accurate recognition of comorbidity in children and youth with ASD is challenging.

Prompt and accurate recognition of comorbidity has significant treatment implications. Early diagnosis and intensive intervention have substantial effects on cognitive ability, adaptive behavior such as social and communication skills, and psychopathology manifested by repetitive actions and obsessional features (Ben Itzchak, Lahat, Burgin, & Ditza Zachor, 2008). Ben Itzchak et al. (2008) noted that comorbid psychiatric disorders can cause significant impairments in learning and may contribute to significant challenging behavior (Leyfer et al., 2006). Thus, early treatment of comorbid diagnoses may improve early intervention techniques and associated gains. A second benefit of identifying comorbid disorders is that it can inform treatment planning (Leyfer et al., 2006). Also, availability of funding and service provision are based on type and severity of diagnosis. For example, Tsakanikos, Costello, Holt, Sturmey, and Bouras (2007) found that externalizing disorders, such as aggression, pestering staff, and hyperactivity, placed adults with ASD at risk for prescription of antipsychotic medication: More effective psychosocial interventions might prevent exposure to these risks. Finally, as comorbid psychiatric disorders are recognized and distinguished, researchers can focus on developing specific diagnostic tools, appropriate treatments, and effective psychopharmacology (Leyfer et al., 2006). Thus, recognition of comorbid disorders can affect the child's developmental trajectory, the quantity and quality of child services, and has also resulted in controversy regarding comorbid psychiatric disorders (Gjevik et al., 2011; Simonoff et al., 2009).

This chapter begins by examining the current status of research related to comorbidity in children and youth with ASD. We then examine current issues in research, diagnosis, and treatment of three common comorbid psychiatric disorders: ADHD, obsessive-compulsive disorder (OCD), and other related anxiety disorders. We selected these comorbid disorders because they are common in children and youth with ASD and have significant treatment and service delivery implications. For each of these three disorders, we discuss prevalence, issues of diagnosis, treatment options, and evidence-based practices regarding comorbid psychiatric disorders in children with ASD.

CURRENT STATUS OF RESEARCH

Substantial progress has been made over the past 30 years with regard to dual diagnosis and ID; however, the field of comorbidity and ASD is still in its infancy, reflecting the recent increased interest in ASD. Children with ASD present with more psychiatric disorders than other children (Gadow, DeVincent, Pomeroy, & Azizian, 2005). For example, Evans, Canavera, Kleinpeter, Maccubbin, and Taga (2005) found that children with ASD had more medical, animal, and situation phobias than children with other disabilities and typically developing peers; however, accurate prevalence rates for these disorders are unknown and of dubious accuracy. To illustrate, the reported prevalence rate for ADHD among children with ASD has ranged from 14% to 78% (Gargaro, Rinehart, Bradshaw, Tonge, & Sheppard, 2011). In the next sections we will review some current research issues related to assessment, symptom presentation, and individual and environmental factors related to comorbid disorders in children and youth with ASD.

Assessment Methods

There are several reasons for misunderstanding the relationship between ASD and comorbid psychopathology. One of the main reasons has been a lack of standardized assessment tools. While the most common method of assessing psychiatric symptoms among individuals with ASD is clinical judgment along with the *DSM-IV-TR* criteria (4th ed., text revision; *DSM-IV-TR*; APA, 2000), several researchers have responded to the call for tools designed specifically for those with ASD. Recently, different structured caregiver interviews have been designed specifically for the assessment of comorbid psychiatric symptoms among children with ASD such as the *Autism Comorbidity Interview–Present and Lifetime Version* (Leyfer et al., 2006), a modification of the *Kiddie Schedule for Affective Disorders and Schizophrenia* (Kaufman, Birmaher, & Breut, 1997), and the *Baby and Infant Screen for Children with Autism Traits* (Matson, Wilkins et al., 2009). There are also several questionnaires to assess comorbidity among adults and children with ASD. These include the *Autism Spectrum Disorder–Comorbid for Children* scale (Matson, LoVullo, Rivet, & Boisjoli, 2009), which is completed by parents, and the *Autism Spectrum Disorders—Comorbid for Adults* (Lovullo & Matson, 2009; Matson & Boisjoli, 2008), which is completed by an informant. A comprehensive review of research on these tools is beyond the scope of this chapter; however, most research on these new assessments has reported on internal consistency, development of cutoff scores, and factor validity. While the development of these tools represents an important step for the diagnosis of psychopathology in individuals with ASD, they still require further validation and independent replication. Further, they can be time intensive and require trained interviewers to administer them. Caution should also be exercised when using tools developed for typically developing individuals because the validity of these tools has not yet been established for individuals with ASD (Leyfer et al., 2006). Clearly, future research should continue to examine how to appropriately modify these tools for use with this population.

Symptom Presentation

Along with developing tools to assess comorbidity in individuals with ASD there is a need to delineate the relationship among challenging behavior, mental health, and atypical symptom presentation of disorders in children with ASD. Some professionals have suggested that challenging behavior may be a symptom of psychiatric disorder in children and youth with ASD; this is sometimes referred to as a "behavioral equivalent" (Sturmey, Laud, Cooper, Matson, & Fodstad, 2010). In individuals with ID, Deb, Thomas, and Bright (2001) found associations between the use of psychotropic medication, including antipsychotic, antidepressant, and antiepileptic medication, and rate of challenging behavior. Moss et al. (2000) also found associations between challenging behavior and psychiatric symptoms in individuals with ID; however, limited research has addressed how symptoms of particular psychiatric disorders manifest in individuals with ASD. If challenging behavior can be recognized as an atypical symptom of a comorbid psychiatric disorder, treatments can be tailored to address that atypical presentation of a comorbid disorder and diagnosis of a comorbid disorder could also permit medical insurance coverage for such treatment.

Mental health disorders may present differently in people with ASD than the general population. For example, Russell, Mataix-Cols, Anson, and Murphy (2005) compared symptomatology in adults with high-functioning ASD, and Asperger syndrome with OCD to adults who had OCD only. They found that, although both groups of adults had similar frequencies of OCD symptoms, adults with ASD were less likely to report somatic obsessions and repetitive rituals than the OCD-only group. Further, although 50% of the group with ASD and OCD reported at least moderate interference with daily functioning from OCD symptoms, the OCD-only group reported more severe symptoms.

Symptoms of mental health disorders may also manifest differently in individuals with ASD and those with ID. Severity of ID and ASD may mask or alter mental health symptomology presentation. For example, depressed persons with mild ID show similar symptom profiles to people in the general population with major depression (Matson, 1986; Matson, Barrett, & Helsel, 1988), yet individuals with severe ID may display somewhat different psychopathology symptom profiles, particularly lack of verbal behavior. We caution, however, that evidence on this point with people with ID is mixed and not all the data support this possibility (Sturmey et al., 2010; Tsiouris, Mann, Patti, & Sturmey, 2004).

Individual and Environmental Factors

Studies are needed to explore the relationship between individual and environmental factors that influence development of psychiatric disorders in children and youth with ASD because these factors may have a significant impact on an individual with ASD's vulnerability or resilience to developing particular disorders. Individual factors may include genetics, cognitive profiles, diagnosis (i.e., autism, Asperger's disorder, or pervasive-developmental disorder not otherwise specified), and self-management skills for coping with stress and aversive events. For environmental factors, research can explore relationships between community placements, stress, parenting styles, and mental health symptomology. A better understanding of the factors that influence development of comorbid disorder in children with ASD will not only aid in tailoring interventions but also hasten development of prevention techniques.

ATTENTION-DEFICIT/ HYPERACTIVITY DISORDER

ADHD consists of behavioral patterns of inattention and motor activity that result in social, educational, and other performance difficulties. The *DSM-IV* identified three subtypes of ADHD, which are determined by symptom presentation (APA, 2000). Predominantly inattentive type (PI) symptoms include difficulty in focusing and paying attention, missing important details, difficulty with organization, forgetfulness, and high levels of distractibility. Predominantly hyperactive-impulsive type (PH) symptoms include hyperactivity, such as fidgetiness, inability to participate in quiet activities, excessive talking, and constant physical movement, and impulsivity, including difficulty waiting turns and frequent interruption or intrusion. A combined type (C) diagnosis is given when symptoms of both PI and PH co-occur. In all diagnostic types, symptoms must be present and debilitating in two or more environments and many symptoms must appear before age 7 years.

ADHD is one of the most commonly diagnosed childhood psychiatric disorders with an average of 9% of all American children receiving a diagnosis before age 17 years (National Center for Health Statistics, 2011). Prevalence statistics of ADHD among children with ASD, however, are variable, with reported prevalence as low as 14% and as high as 78% (Gargaro et al., 2011). Such variable measures may be due to the ongoing debate about the presence of ADHD in individuals with ASD (Mayes & Calhoun, 2007; Mayes, Calhoun, Mayes, & Molitoris, 2012). Three central factors of this discussion are (1) differentiation of core symptoms of ASD and ADHD, (2) diagnostic practices and criterion for ADHD in persons with ASD, and (3) application and adaptation of evidence-based treatment methods to treat ADHD in persons with ASD.

Overlapping Symptoms of Autism Spectrum Disorder and Attention-Deficit/Hyperactivity Disorder

Many problems arising from ADHD appear similar to core symptoms of ASD, including impairments in social interactions, poor communication, and restricted and stereotyped interests and behavior patterns (American Psychiatric Association, 2000; Gadow et al., 2005; Hartley & Sikora, 2009; Mayes et al., 2012; Simonoff et al., 2008). ADHD and ASD also have common comorbid issues considered secondary to the primary diagnosis such as association with executive functioning deficits (Corbett, Constantine, Hendren, Rocke, & Ozonoff, 2009); learning disabilities and low processing speed (Mayes & Calhoun, 2007); deficits in attention, motor control, and perception (Sturm, Fernell, & Gillberg, 2004); early language delays (Hagberg, Miniscalco, & Gillberg, 2010); sleep disorders (Mayes, Calhoun, Bixler, & Vgontzas, 2009; Tsai, Chiang, Lee, Gau, Lee, Fan, Wu, & Chiu, 2012); fewer social relationships than same age peers (Hartley & Sikora, 2009);

disruptive behavior problems (American Psychiatric Association, 2000; Gadow et al., 2005; Mayes & Calhoun, 2011; Mayes & Calhoun, 2012); and difficulty adapting to change (American Psychological Association, 2012; Mayes et al., 2012).

Some researchers have argued that, because ASD encompasses so many features of ADHD, it is unnecessary to identify ADHD after an ASD diagnosis; rather, they argue that children diagnosed with ADHD should be screened for autism (Mayes et al., 2012). In fact, high-functioning ASD has often been first misdiagnosed as ADHD (Matson & Boisjoli, 2007). Other researchers, however, have identified distinctions between ASD with and without ADHD. For example, ADHD frequently, but not always, occurs in people diagnosed with ASD. Simonoff, Pickles, Charman, Chandler, Loucas, and Baird (2008) used standardized assessments in a population-derived sample of children with ASD and found that 28.2% of the sample also met diagnostic criterion for ADHD. Frazier et al. (2001) compared the psychiatric and behavioral symptoms in 165 consecutively referred children with possible ADHD, ASD, and comorbid diagnoses. They found that ADHD symptoms were similar regardless of presence or absence of secondary diagnosis, as were ASD symptoms regardless of the presence or absence of ADHD symptoms. They also found that children diagnosed with comorbid ASD/ADHD had higher rates of hospitalization, psychopharmacological treatment, and psychological treatment than children diagnosed with ASD alone. In a retrospective chart review, Goldstein and Schwebach (2004) replicated these findings and also found that children with comorbid ASD and ADHD demonstrated a similar degree and severity of ADHD symptoms as children without ASD. Furthermore, children with comorbid diagnoses did not have statistically significant differences in impairment than children diagnosed with ASD alone; however, the dually diagnosed children experienced more daily life difficulties than children diagnosed with ASD alone.

There is also genetic and neuroimaging support for comorbid diagnoses that may explain high rates of dual diagnosis. Family and twin studies provide preliminary evidence that ADHD and ASD originate from partly similar familial and genetic factors (Rommelse, Franke, Geurts, Hartman, & Buitelaar, 2010). Neuroimaging research has identified that the frontostriatal regions are implicated in both ASD and ADHD, and both disorders are associated with disruption to both resting and active brain networks (Gargaro et al., 2011). Genetic and neuroimaging research are in their infancy, but both have promising implications for future developments in dual diagnosis.

Assessment

DSM-IV lists pervasive developmental disorders (PDD) as exclusion criterion for an ADHD diagnosis, meaning a diagnosis of ADHD cannot be made if ASD is present (American Psychiatric Association, 2000). The *DSM-5*, published in May 2013, is currently planning to eliminate the PDD exclusion criterion (APA, 2013) in light of research, which was discussed earlier, and because of overlapping treatment evidence, which is discussed next. Because of *DSM*'s restrictions, research on comorbidity diagnostic methods has been limited (Frazier, 2011; Gadow, 2005; Gargaro et al., 2011; Sinzig, 2008, 2009), and clinical standards for dual diagnosis have yet to be defined.

Comorbid ASD and ADHD have previously been identified using clinical opinion, *DSM-IV* criteria questionnaires, and other related tools (Frazier, 2001; Gadow, 2005; Sinzig, 2008, 2009). Because ASD and ADHD symptoms can vary significantly within patients, many practitioners rely on symptom presentation alone without regard to causality (Coghill & Seth, 2011). With the *DSM-5* changes, it is hopeful that reliable and valid assessments for ADHD presentation in ASD will be developed.

Treatments

Psychopharmacology has long been the most popular treatment for ADHD in typically developing children. Multiple formulations of stimulant medications have been widely used since the 1970s and there are extensive databases supporting their efficacy (Daughton & Kratochvil, 2009). And yet these medications have not been indicated by the Food and Drug Administration as treatments for comorbid ASD and ADHD. Of concern, many available psychotropic medications have been used to treat ADHD symptoms in children and youth with ASD (King & Bostic, 2005).

Handen, Johnson, and Lubetsksy (2000) conducted a small-scale, crossover, double-blind trial of methylphenidate with 13 children aged 5–11 years with autism and ADHD. Eight of 13 participants had a 50% reduction on the Conner's hyperactivity index, and there were other positive changes for some psychometric measures of behavior. This study was limited because of the small number of participants, use of multiple statistical tests, and lack of social validity data.

Jahromi et al. (2009) reported the effects of methylphenidate on 33 children (29 boys), aged 5–13 years, with ASD and ADHD in a crossover placebo trial. Prior to the trial proper participants received placebo and low, medium, and high doses of methylphenidate for 2 days each day, and, based on blind ratings, children were assigned to their best dose during the crossover trial. Dependent variables were observational measures of child behavior taken during semistructured tasks such as cleanup tasks. Jahromi et al. observed several positive effects where the optimal dose of methylphenidate was superior to placebo on some measures, such as joint attention and reduction of negative affect during a task with divided attention, but had no effects on other measures, such as compliance with parental instructions. One potential limitation of this study is that it included many statistical tests with correction for repeated testing and did not report data on social validity or individual data.

Patel and Curtis (2007) combined typical behavioral and educational treatments with environmental and dietary limitations and chelation in a sample of 10 children. Although they found decreased ratings of ADHD symptoms, the study was not double blind and it is unclear which component of the package was responsible for behavior change if any did in fact occur.

The potential benefits of stimulant medication have to be weighed against its costs. Negative side effects include social withdrawal, irritability tics, sleep disturbance, anxiousness, gastrointestinal problems, appetite changes, sedation, and headache (Handen, Johnson & Lubetsky, 2000; Nickels et al., 2008). These negative side effects do not occur with psychosocial treatments. If used, stimulant medications should be introduced at low doses and behavioral side effects be closely observed (Aman, 2008; Rowles & Findling, 2010).

While both behavioral and psychosocial treatments have demonstrated efficacy for children with ASD and children with ADHD, there are very few studies that directly address ADHD concurrently with ASD (Brookman-Frazee, Stahmer, Baker-Ericzen, & Tsai, 2006; Kasari & Lawton, 2010).

Research on therapies specific to ADHD and ASD is needed. For example, future research might evaluate treatment that integrates behavioral and pharmacological treatments. Research could do this by comparing of best choice pharmacological and best choice behavioral and combined best choice treatments; such studies would substantially improve treatment options available for children with comorbid ASD and ADHD.

OBSESSIVE-COMPULSIVE DISORDER

OCD is a neurodevelopmental challenge that affects 2%–3% of children and adolescents (Freeman et al., 2006). For an individual to be diagnosed with OCD, he or she must report intrusive thoughts, impulses, or images that produce anxiety (i.e., obsessions), and repetitive behaviors that are carried out to reduce anxiety (i.e., compulsions). Obsessive and/or compulsive symptoms must cause marked distress, take more than 1 hour a day, and/or significantly interfere with the person's daily activities or relationships. In adults, obsessive and compulsive thoughts and behaviors are generally recognized as senseless, excessive (i.e., ego dystonic), or unreasonable (i.e., insight). In children, however, this criterion does not apply, as children may lack sufficient cognitive awareness to make this judgment (APA, 2000).

The limited communication skills that are characteristic of individuals with ASD, especially regarding internal states (Baron-Cohen et al., 1999; Gadow et al., 2005; Gillott, Furniss, & Walter, 2001), make it difficult to differentiate OCD from other repetitive behaviors. Several studies, however, indicate that the prevalence of OCD among individuals with ASD is higher than typically developing peers. Across six studies, the mean prevalence was 11.02% (range 1.47.%–37.2%) of individuals meeting criteria for comorbid OCD (De Bruin, Ferdinand, Meester, de Nijs, & Verheij, 2007; Ghaziuddin, Tsai, & Ghaziuddin, 1992; Gjevik, Eldevik, Fjaeran-Granum, & Sponheim, 2011; Leyfer et al., 2006; Muris, Steerneman, Merckelbach, Holdrinet, & Meester, 1998; Russell et al., 2005), with higher functioning (IQ > 70) adults potentially being more vulnerable to developing the disorder (Russell et al., 2005). It is difficult to draw confident conclusions about the individual characteristics that affect vulnerability to developing OCD among individuals with ASD given the varying assessment methods, informants, and diagnostic criteria across studies.

Overlapping Symptoms

Several authors have discussed the importance and difficulty of differentiating between the repetitive behaviors of autism and OCD behaviors (Fischer-Terworth & Probst, 2009; Hollander, 2009). There are repetitive behaviors that are a part of the clinical picture of autism that may resemble OCD symptoms, including excessive involvement in circumscribed special interests, engagement in compulsive rituals, stereotyped and repetitive motor mannerisms, and insistence on sameness. Although these repetitive behaviors and OCD are similar, individuals with ASD may not experience distress associated with their rigid beliefs and may not perform their rituals to alleviate anxiety (Ruta, Mugno, D'Arrigo, Vitiello, & Mazzone, 2010) as typically developing adults with OCD do. Fischer-Terworth and Probst (2009) have even suggested that these behaviors may be enjoyable for some individuals with ASD. On the other hand, some rituals in ASD resemble symptoms of OCD, and interrupting the routines is associated with subsequent distress (Fischer-Terworth & Probst, 2009). It may be that the function of related challenging behavior might be access to ritual or related material and termination of interruption. Insistence on sameness behavior (e.g., sitting in the same seat) also resembles typical OCD-related "just right" behaviors. In the absence of clear obsessions, it can be challenging to make the distinction between behaviors representing OCD and those of ASD.

A small number of studies have investigated the presence of specific OCD symptoms in individuals with ASD. Studies that have compared individuals with OCD to individuals with ASD and OCD have found few qualitative differences between the symptoms displayed using the *Children's Yale-Brown Obsessive Compulsive Scale* (CY-BOCS; Goodman, Price, Rasmussen, Riddle, & Rapoport, 1986) and the *Yale-Brown Obsessive-Compulsive Scale* (Y-BOCS; Goodman et al., 1989) for children and adults, respectively (Mack et al., 2010; Russell et al., 2005). When individuals with ASD without a formal diagnosis of OCD are compared to those with OCD, children with ASD are less likely to report contamination, aggressive obsessions, and checking compulsions (Ruta et al., 2010). Adults with ASD and OCD have also reported more ordering and hoarding compulsions than adults with OCD but no ASD (McDougle et al., 1995).

Assessment

The goal during assessment is to distinguish between behaviors that are representative of ASD and behaviors that constitute comorbid diagnosis of OCD. One approach to making this distinction is to identify the presence of obsessions. The *DSM-IV* defines obsessions as recurrent, persistent thoughts, impulses, or images that are experienced as intrusive and inappropriate and that cause anxiety or distress. Individuals with ASD identify obsessions, although at lower frequencies than those without ASD (McDougle et al., 1995; Russell et al., 2005; Zandt, Prior, & Kyrios, 2009). Diagnostic differentiation based on obsessions can also be obscured by the individual's communication impairments, emotion recognition deficits (Leyfer et al., 2006), comorbid ID, and having caregivers as informants.

Similarly, the degree to which symptoms cause distress, are unwanted, or cause interference may be used to differentiate OCD symptoms and ASD symptoms from one another (Mack et al., 2010; Russell et al., 2005). For the same reason that obsessions may be problematic to assess, the degree of distress and discomfort is also difficult to identify in many individuals with ASD. While these obsessions and the report of distress and interference are defining features of OCD in adults without ASD, the criterion that symptoms must be recognized as unwanted or senseless does not apply to children with OCD, according to the *DSM-IV*.

Acknowledging the difficulties with OCD diagnosis, a secondary diagnosis of OCD may not be useful (Zandt et al., 2007). While *DSM-IV* notes that the symptoms of OCD are distinct from the repetitive behaviors of ASD, this distinction has yet to be empirically determined. Note, for example, that research has not incorporated functional analysis to identify the maintaining variables of compulsions in individuals with ASD. Thus, the adoption of functional analysis techniques in the investigation of compulsions in individuals with ASD may provide useful information in not only determining treatment but also decreasing the reliance on self-report of obsessions, distress, and interference. Functional analysis of these behaviors may reveal that for some individuals, socially mediated consequences and not relief from obsessions may be the maintaining variable. For those individuals who are able to describe obsessions, distress, and interference, a differential diagnosis may be useful in accessing evidence-based treatments for OCD.

Treatment

There is limited research on treatment for a specific comorbid diagnosis of OCD, and most studies have included individuals with general anxiety disorders or repetitive behaviors of unknown significance. Primary areas of treatment include cognitive behavioral therapy (CBT), applied behavior analysis (ABA), and psychopharmacology.

CBT techniques are modified or enhanced to meet the cognitive, social, and linguistic abilities of the child with ASD (Reaven & Hepburn, 2003; Wood et al., 2009). CBT for OCD consists of psychoeducation, cognitive training, exposure and response prevention (ERP), and frequently, parent training. Psychoeducation and cognitive training involve educating the child to recognize OCD symptom-provoking situations, associated emotions, and effective response strategies (Sofronoff, Attwood, & Hinton, 2005; Sze & Wood, 2007) by using social stories (Ooi et al., 2008; Sofronoff et al., 2005), cartoon strips, group discussions (Sofronoff et al., 2005), role playing, or workbook activities (Sofronoff et al., 2005). Response strategies include self-talk (Sze & Wood, 2007), setting goals, and anxiety management techniques (Ooi et al., 2008) and are often taught in conjunction with ERP.

There are two popular ERP procedures: (1) gradually exposing the person from low to high anxiety-provoking situations while preventing compulsive behavior (Reaven & Hepburn, 2003; Wood et al., 2009) and (2) gradually increasing the amount of time between onset of anxiety-provoking situation and opportunity to engage in OCD behavior (El-Ghohoury & Krackow, 2011). In addition to child training, parents can be taught to implement positive reinforcement strategies in real-life situations (Reaven & Hepburn, 2003; Sofronoff et al., 2005; Wood et al., 2009). We advise, however, that although CBT can be an effective treatment for comorbid OCD and ASD, the components of CBT have not been tested in isolation and thus it is unknown which components are most effective.

Applied behavior analysis (ABA) focuses on behavior–environment relationships, functional assessment, and assessment-derived intervention. For example, Marchant, Howlin, Yule, and Rutter (1974) discussed an effective procedure for reducing object attachment in two children with ASD. They gradually reduced object size of a belt and blanket while increasing reinforcing activities in the object's absence. Sigafoos, Payne, O'Reilly, and Lancioni (2009) reduced the obsessive rearranging of objects in an academic setting by offering choices and attention prior to the usual behavior onset. Handen,

Apolito, and Seltzer (1984) decreased the frequency of obsessive question asking by giving token prizes for gradually declining frequency of asking questions. These studies illustrate just some ABA interventions that are applicable with children and youth who have ASD and OCD or OCD-like behavior.

We present two studies that demonstrate the critical role of functional assessment in treatment formulation. First, Kuhn, Hardesty, and Sweeney (2009) conducted a functional analysis followed by functional communication training to treat aggressive behavior related to being blocked from throwing away nontrash items in a 16-year-old boy with autism. Aggression received contingent consequences in a multielement design with five conditions: toy play, social attention, tangible, demand, and ignore (Iwata, Dorsey, Slifer, Bauman, & Richman, 1994). Following low undifferentiated rates of aggression across all five conditions, Kuhn et al. (2009) conducted a second functional analysis, with the same participant, which compared contingent access to throwing away nontrash items for aggressive behaviors to noncontingent access using an ABAB design. They found that when blocked from placing nontrash items in the waste bin, aggression was more frequent when it produced contingent access to throwing away nontrash items than when provided noncontingently. Using these results, they then trained the child to ask, "Is this trash," before clearing items and significantly reduced aggressive behavior related to being blocked from throwing away nontrash items.

The second study on functional assessment, by Rodriguez, Thompson, Schlichenmeyer, and Stocco (2012), used functional analysis methodology with three children who had ASD and displayed compulsive arranging, ordering, completeness, and washing/cleaning behaviors. The functional analysis showed the highest rates of compulsive behaviors during no-interaction conditions for two children and undifferentiated rates for the third child. A follow-up analysis comparing additional conditions was conducted for two of the children, which suggested that automatic reinforcement maintained the compulsive behaviors of all three children. Treatment using response blocking combined with access to stimuli that permitted appropriate forms of the behavior reduced the target behaviors to zero levels for all three children.

Psychopharmacological treatments for children with comorbid ASD and repetitive behaviors and/

or compulsions have mixed findings (Mohiuddin & Ghaziuddin, 2012). While therapeutic effects of antipsychotics, serotonin selective reuptake inhibitors (SSRIs), and other psychotropic medications have been observed, mild to severe side effects have included significant weight gain, irritability, self-injury, aggression, urinary retention, fatigue, tremors, and serotonin syndrome. One recent study has identified a small but significant effect of SSRIs on repetitive behaviors in *published studies* attributable to selective publication bias toward positive results (Carrasco, Volkmar, & Bloch, 2012). Therefore, psychopharmacological treatments for comorbid ASD and OCD should not be endorsed until reliable and accurate research is forthcoming.

OTHER ANXIETY DISORDERS

In this section we use the term "other anxiety disorders" to refer to generalized anxiety disorder, panic disorder, phobic disorder, and separation anxiety disorder. According to proposed revisions in the *DSM-5*, anxiety disorders categorize many disorders where the primary feature is abnormal or inappropriate anxiety or worry (APA, 2012). The context for heightened anxiety may be a person separating from significant others where there is strong attachment (separation anxiety), social situations (social phobia), daily activities or events (e.g., family, health, finances, and school/work difficulties; GAD), or specific objects and situations related to flying, heights, animals, receiving an injection, and seeing blood (specific phobia).

Children and youth with ASDs are at greater risk for anxiety in comparison to non-ASD clinic samples and nonclinic samples (Gadow et al., 2005; Gillott et al., 2001; Sofronoff, Attwood, & Hinton, 2005; Tantam, 2000). Children with high-functioning autism (HFA; those who are verbally fluent and possess an IQ >70) or who have Asperger syndrome are also more vulnerable to developing anxiety than typically developing children and children with low-functioning autism (Gadow et al., 2005). These findings may be due to higher cognitive and linguistic abilities that lend to verbalizing obsessions, thoughts, or beliefs required for the diagnosis of anxiety disorders (Fischer-Terwerth & Probst, 2009).

Between 11% and 84% of children with ASD experience some degree of impairing anxiety (White, Oswald, Ollendick, & Scahill, 2009), with simple phobias, GAD, separation anxiety disorder, and social phobia being most common (White et al., 2009). Anxiety can affect quality of life, stress levels, family functioning, and peer acceptance, and may contribute to severe behavior challenges and alter the effectiveness of educational interventions (Brenton, Tonge, & Einfeld, 2006; Howlin, 1998; Kim, Szatmari, Bryson, Streiner, & Wilson, 2000; Reaven & Hepburn, 2003). Left untreated, anxiety may lead to problems such as self-injury, depression, suicide, drug abuse, and social avoidance (Tantam, 2000). For these reasons, research into the nature, assessment, and treatment of anxiety should be seen as a major priority.

Overlapping Symptoms

Despite indications that individuals with ASD frequently experience anxiety symptoms, few individuals are actually diagnosed with anxiety disorders due to a common belief that these symptoms are captured by the ASD diagnosis itself. Clinicians often have difficulty determining if symptoms, like social avoidance, should be considered as a distinct diagnosis or as part of ASD. For example, the DSM-IV describes "excessive fearfulness in response to harmless objects" as an associated feature of ASD (APA, 2000), while insistence on sameness behaviors may result in anxiety, tension, and emotional upset when interrupted (Fischer-Terworth & Probst, 2009). Others have argued that routines in individuals have a negative reinforcement function by reducing anxiety when performed (Bodfish, Symons, Parker, & Lewis, 2000). The social disabilities associated with ASD may also lead to the development of social anxiety. Some individuals with ASD are aware of their social deficits, which may exacerbate social fears, particularly for youth with high-functioning autism (Attwood, 2000; Bellini 2004; Chamberlain, Kasari, & Rotheram-Fuller, 2007). Poor social skills may lead an individual to experience anxiety related to social interactions. On the other hand, high social anxiety may predispose individuals with ASD to avoid initiating social interactions, limiting their ability to develop and master social skills (Bellini, 2004).

Few studies have looked at differences in symptom presentation for individuals with ASD, but it appears that anxiety symptoms among individuals with ASD are similar to those in non-ASD samples (Weisbrot, Gadow, DeVincent, & Pomeroy, 2005). Individuals who worry both covertly (e.g., ruminating) and overtly, for example, actively avoiding social interaction with peers (Gillott et al., 2001), may

lack insight about the connection between social deficits and anxiety (Russell & Sofronoff, 2005). Furthermore, presentation of symptoms may be affected greatly by age and cognitive functioning, with older, higher functioning individuals having more anxiety symptoms (Weisbrot et al., 2005).

Assessment

Most studies investigating prevalence of anxiety among individuals with ASD have relied exclusively on parent—or combinations of parent—and other or self-report measures (Bellini, 2004; Gadow et al., 2005; Lecavalier, 2006). Some of the most commonly used semistructured interviews are the Anxiety Disorders Interview Schedule for DSM-IV Child and Parent Version (ADIS-C/P; Albano & Silverman, 1996), the Schedule for Affective Disorders and Schizophrenia for School-Aged Children (K-SADS-PL; Kaufman et al., 1997), and other measures of anxiety such as the Multidimensional Anxiety Scale for Children (March et al., 1999), the Psychometric Properties of the Screen for Child Anxiety Related Emotional Disorders (Birmaher et al., 1999), and Spence Children's Anxiety Scale (Spence, 1998). A handful of studies have used self-reported or informant-based assessment to identify the rate of anxiety symptoms and disorders in ASD (Gadow et al., 2005; Kim et al., 2000; Melfsen, Walitza, & Warnke, 2006). This reliance on caregiver report to assess anxiety symptoms is likely due to the impaired communication and cognitive abilities among individuals with ASD. Unfortunately, correspondence between parent-and self-report is low (Mazefsky, Kao, & Oswald, 2011).

Information obtained via interviews should be considered preliminary measures of anxiety and should be followed by direct observation that validates these measures. Researchers and practitioners should focus on the stimuli (e.g., needles, spiders) or classes of stimuli (e.g., social stimuli) that produce anxious behaviors. Using behavioral observation to identify anxiety must be done with caution because individuals with ASD may show behavioral signs of anxiety, like avoidance or negative emotional behaviors, during nonpreferred situations rather than during feared situations. Presence of avoidance and negative emotional behaviors should be considered along with the intensity of the emotional response and the continued display of fearful responses after removal of the stimulus (Jennett & Hagopian, 2008). Functional analysis may help to differentiate feared stimuli from nonpreferred stimuli by iden- tifying sources of reinforcement for behaviors. Nonpreferred stimuli may elicit avoidance because of the lack of necessary skills to complete tasks, or insufficient reinforcement to maintain the target behavior, while negative emotional behaviors may arise because of competing sources of reinforcement.

Treatment

Intervention studies for anxiety in ASD have con- sisted of three approaches: pharmacological, CBT, and ABA. Pharmacological interventions are rep- resented largely through uncontrolled case stud- ies showing preliminary evidence for the SSRIs, sertaline (Bhardwaj, Agarwal, & Sitholey, 2005; Ozbayrak, 1997), fluvoxamine (Kauffmann, Vance, Pumariega, & Miller, 2001), buspirone (Buitelaar, van der Gaag, & van der Hoeven, 1998), and dex- tromethorpan (Woodard, Groden, Goodwin, Shanower, & Bianco, 2005), notwithstanding that none of these studies contained adequate control groups or placebo-controlled protocols.

Researchers have also investigated CBT for indi- viduals with ASD displaying separation anxiety, spe- cific phobia, social phobia, panic disorder, and GAD (Chalfant, Rapee, & Carroll, 2006; Sofronoff et al., 2005; Wood et al., 2009). CBT for anxiety typically includes the following behavioral treatment compo- nents: (1) psychoeduction, which teaches awareness of anxiety symptoms and their origin; (2) creating a stimulus hierarchy of situations or stimuli from least to most anxiety producing; (3) training coping skills (e.g., relaxation techniques), and (4) exposure ther- apy. Cognitive elements of CBT include retrained thinking and patterns of attribution.

There have been several randomized controlled trials (RCTs) of modified CBT. The modifications have included high parental involvement, positive reinforcement, a simplified cognitive component, incorporation of a child's perseverative interests, emphasis on the use of visuals, role playing, and emphasis on direct instruction of social skills (Chalfant et al., 2006; Reaven et al., 2009; Sofronoff & Attwood, 2003; Sofronoff, Attwood, & Hinton; 2005; Sze & Wood, 2007; Wood et al., 2009). Three RCTs reported decreased anxiety on parent, teacher, and child self-reports compared to waitlist con- trols (Chalfant et al., 2007; Sofronoff et al., 2005; Wood et al., 2009). Children aged 7 to 12, with high-functioning autism and Asperger syndrome were included in these programs, and many of the

children no longer met criteria for any anxiety disor- der following intervention.

For individuals with ASD and an anxiety disorder without ID, treatment has been primarily behavioral, though much less evidence is available. A systematic review suggests that behavioral approaches includ- ing contingent reinforcement and graduated expo- sure are effective for individuals with ASD and ID. Indeed, graduated exposure and reinforcement for treatment of phobic avoidance have been established as "empirically supported" in this population (Jennett & Hagopian, 2008). Along with contingent reinforce- ment and graduated exposure, prompting, modeling, and distracting stimuli may aid in intervention. We suggest that behavioral interventions may be better suited for individuals with ASD and an ID over CBT techniques because they rely less on participants' abil- ity to communicate and more on establishing new con- tingencies of reinforcement for approach responses, or behavior that is incompatible with anxiety.

PRACTICE RECOMMENDATIONS AND CONCLUSIONS

Assessment and Diagnosis

In summary, comorbid conditions such as ADHD, OCD, and other anxiety disorders are common in children and youth with ASD. If not addressed, these disorders will seriously affect them, their family members, and other caregivers. Left untreated, there will be increased yet avoidable costs, especially when services are ineffective or not provided.

The first step for professionals and parents is to obtain accurate, comprehensive, efficient diag- nosis of those comorbid conditions. This objective requires diagnostic tools, including interviews, psy- chometric instruments, and observational protocols that are reliable, valid, efficient, readily usable, and available to practitioners. A start has been made on this endeavor, but researchers and practitioners need to establish other assessment protocols, perhaps involving initial screening measures with follow-up, detailed assessments if the screening results indicate that other psychopathology is present.

The forthcoming *DSM-5* will have substantial changes in diagnostic criteria for ASD and other dis- orders related to this chapter. The proposed *DSM-5* criteria merge autistic disorder, Asperger disorder, pervasive developmental disorder not otherwise specified (PDDNOS), and childhood disintegra- tive disorder into one diagnosis, autism spectrum disorder. It further introduces a new disorder, social communication disorder. In *DSM-IV* symptoms were organized into the domains of (a) qualitative impairments in social interaction, (b) qualitative impairments in communication, and (c) restricted repetitive and stereotyped patterns of behavior, interests, and activities (APA, 2000). The proposed *DSM-5* criteria use only two domains, persistent deficits in social communication and social interaction across contexts, not accounted for by general developmental delays, and restricted, repetitive patterns of behavior, interests, or activities. This reorganization of symptoms is based on factor analytic studies that have suggested that ASD symptoms are better conceived of as two, rather than three dimensions (Shuster et al., as cited in Taheri & Perry, 2012). *DSM-5* reduces the number of ASD symptoms from 12 in *DSM-IV* but requires that all three symptoms of "persistent deficits in social communication and social interaction across contexts" are present. These three symptoms include deficits in social-emotional reciprocity, nonverbal communicative behaviors, and in "developing and maintaining relationships, appropriate to developmental level (beyond those with caregivers)" (APA, 2013). To meet *DSM-5* criterion B, two of four symptoms must be met, which include "1. Stereotyped or repetitive speech, motor movements, or use of objects...2. Excessive adherence to routines, ritualized patterns of verbal or nonverbal behavior, or excessive resistance to change...3. Highly restricted, fixated interests that are abnormal in intensity or focus...[and] 4. Hyper—or hypo-reactivity to sensory input or unusual interest in sensory aspects of environment" (APA, 2011). These proposed criteria require that a greater proportion of symptoms must be met for a diagnosis of ASD to be made in *DSM-5* than in *DSM-IV*.

These changes in *DSM* criteria for ASD are not trivial and likely will reduce the number of children diagnosed with ASD. For example, Taheri and Perry (2012) applied both *DSM-IV* and *DSM-5* diagnostic criteria to a sample of 131 children aged 2–12 years previously diagnosed with autistic disorder or PDDNOS. They found that 91% of children diagnosed with *DSM-IV* autistic disorder and only 17% of children with diagnosed with *DSM-IV* PDDNOS were diagnosed with *DSM-5* autistic disorder. Multiple independent studies have now reported similar reductions in the numbers of children diagnosed with autism spectrum disorders with *DSM-5*

criteria (Gibbs, Aldridge, Chandler, Witzlsperger, & Smith, 2012; Matson, Belva, Horovitz, & Bamberg, 2012; Mattila et al., 2011; McPartland, Reichow, & Volkmar, 2012). Ritvo (2012) called for postponement of *DSM-5* criteria for ASD because there is not yet adequate research to evaluate these criteria for ASD. Furthermore, research has not evaluated communication disorder, children and youth who no longer meet *DSM-5* criteria for ASD will lose necessary services, clinicians and researchers worldwide will have to be retrained, and parents will be faced with additional challenges.

DSM-5 will also change criteria for other disorders that are commonly comorbid with ASD. Since these criteria are not yet finalized and the changes in each disorder's diagnostic criteria may vary from minor to substantial revisions, it is difficult to anticipate at this time what these changes will do to comorbidity prevalence in children and youth with ASD.

FUTURE TREATMENT AND RESEARCH

There is now a very large database of evidence-based psychotherapies (Sturmey & Hersen, 2012a, 2012b) and evidence-based treatments are now the hallmark of ethical and economically viable psychotherapies (Sturmey, in press). Yet treatment of comorbid conditions raises a classical objection to evidence-based practice, namely do the results of outcome research, often conducted with participants with a single disorder, generalize to people with more than one disorder simultaneously (O'Donohue & Lilienfeld, 2012). Ultimately, this is an empirical question, which research has not yet addressed extensively. What empirical evidence there is supports the hypothesis that evidence-based treatments are effective in limited populations and sometimes generalize to clients with multiple disorders and typical service settings (Clark, 2011; Clark et al., 2009; O'Donohue & Lilienfeld, 2012). One potentially useful consideration is extending functional assessment and analysis of comorbid conditions (Rodriguez et al., 2012). Future research should expand this and practitioners can begin to incorporate functional assessment and analysis into their routine practice.

Pharmacology continues to be the most commonly applied treatment for comorbid conditions in children and youth with ASD, despite the weakness or absence of research supporting its use and significant risk of short-term and long-term negative side effects when used in young children over an extended time during the developmental period. For example, although the FDA approved risperidone for treatment of ASD, this medication is associated with significant weight gain (Hellings, Zarcone, Crandall, Wallace, & Schroeder, 2004; Tarricone, Gozzi, Serretti, Grieco, & Berardi, 2010). The cumulative effects of weight gain during the life span may be both dangerous and expensive and can result in long-term negative health consequences such as early-onset diabetes. Other potential side effects deserve further scrutiny.

Concerning future research, assessment instruments for comorbidity need further development and refinement, especially for validity and efficiency of screening. Also, although behavioral interventions show promise in the treatment of comorbidity, there has been insufficient research on functional assessment and analysis, notwithstanding some recent demonstrations (Kuhn, Hardesty, & Sweeney, 2009; Rodriguez et al., 2012). Additionally, since some forms of pharmacological treatment such as methylphenidate for ADHD for children and youth with ASD also show promise, it would be useful to compare the effectiveness and social validity of pharmacological and function-based behavioral interventions.

REFERENCES

Albano, & Silverman, W. (1996). *Anxiety disorders interview schedule for DSM-IV: Parent version.* San Antonio, TX: Graywing.

Aman, M. G., Farmer, C. A., Hollway, J., & Arnold, L. E. (2008). Treatment of inattention, overactivity, and impulsiveness in autism spectrum disorders. *Child and Adolescent Psychiatric Clinic of North America, 17,* 713–738.

American Psychiatric Association. (2000). *Diagnostic and statistical manual of mental disorders* (4th ed., text rev.). Washington, DC: Author.

American Psychiatric Association. (2013). *Diagnostic and statistical manual of mental disorders* (5th ed.). Washington, DC: Author.

American Psychological Association. (2012). *ADHD.* Retrieved August 6, 2012 from http://www.apa.org/topics/adhd/index.aspx.

Attwood T. (2000). Strategies for improving the social integration of children with Asperger syndrome. *Autism, 4,* 85–100.

Baron-Cohen, S., Ring, H. A., Wheelright, S., Bullmore, E. T., Brammer, M. J., Simmons, A., & Williams, S. C. (1999). Social intelligence in the normal and autistic brain: An fMRI study. *European Journal of Neuroscience, 11,* 1891–1898.

Bellini, S. (2006). The development of social anxiety in adolescents with autism spectrum disorders. *Focus on Autism and Other Developmental Disabilities, 21,* 138–145.

Ben Itzchak, E., Lahat, E., Burgin, R., & Ditza Zachor, A. (2008). Cognitive, behavior and intervention outcome in young children with autism. *Research in Developmental Disabilities, 29,* 447–458.

Bhardwaj, A., Agarwal, V., & Sitholey, P. (2005). Asperger's disorder with co-morbid separation anxiety disorder: A case report. *Journal of Autism and Developmental Disorders, 35,* 135–136.

Birmaher, B., Brent, D., Chiappetta, L., Bridge, J., Monga, S., & Baugher, M. (1999). Psychometric properties of the Screen for Child Anxiety Related Emotional Disorders (SCARED): A replication study. *Journal of the American Academy of Child and Adolescent Psychiatry, 38,* 1230–1236.

Bodfish, J. W., Symons, F. J., Parker, D. E., & Lewis, M. H. (2000). Varieties of repetitive behavior in autism: Comparisons to mental retardation. *Journal of Autism and Developmental Disorders, 30,* 237–243.

Brenton, A. V., Tonge, B. J., & Einfeld, S. L. (2006). Psychopathology in children and adolescents with autism compared to young people with intellectual disability. *Journal of Autism and Developmental Disorders, 36,* 863–870.

Brookman-Frazee, L., Stahmer, A., Baker-Ericzen, M. J., & Tsai, K. (2006). Parenting interventions for children with autism spectrum and disruptive behavior disorders: Opportunities for cross-fertilization. *Clinical Child and Family Psychology Review, 9,* 181–200.

Buitelaar, J. K., van der Gaag, J., & van der Hoeven, J. (1998). Buspirone in the management of anxiety and irritability in children with pervasive developmental disorders: Results of an open-label study. *Journal of Clinical Psychiatry, 59,* 56–59.

Carrasco, M., Volkmar, F. R., & Bloch, M. H. (2012). Pharmacologic treatment of repetitive behaviors in autism spectrum disorders: Evidence of publication bias. *Pediatrics, 129,* 1301–1310.

Chalfant, A., Rapee, R., & Carroll, L. (2006). Treating anxiety disorders in children with high-functioning autism spectrum disorders: A controlled trial. *Journal of Autism and Developmental Disorders, 37,* 1842–1857.

Chamberlain, B., Kasari, C., & Rotheram-Fuller, E. (2007). Involvement or isolation? The social networks of children with autism in regular classrooms. *Journal of Autism and Developmental Disorders, 37,* 230–242.

Clark, D. M. (2011). Implementing NICE guidelines for the psychological treatment of depression and anxiety disorders: The IAPT experience. *International Review of Psychiatry, 23,* 318–327.

Clark, D. M., Layard, R., Smithies, R., Richards, D. A., Suckling, R., & Wright, B. (2009). Improving access to psychological therapy: Initial evaluation of two UK demonstration sites. *Behaviour, Research and Therapy, 47,* 910–920.

Coghill, D., & Seth, S. (2011). Do the diagnostic criteria for ADHD need to change? Comments on the preliminary proposals of the DSM-5 ADHD and disruptive behaviors committee. *European Child and Adolescent Psychiatry, 20,* 75–81.

Corbett, B. A., Constantine, L. J., Hendren, R., Rocke, D., & Ozonoff, S. (2009). Examining executive functioning in children with autism spectrum disorder, attention deficit hyperactivity disorder and typical development. *Psychiatry Research, 166,* 210–222.

Daughton, J. M., & Kratochvil, C. J. (2009). Review of ADHD pharmacotherapies: Advantages, disadvantages, and clinical pearls. *Psychopharmacology Perspectives, 48,* 240–248.

de Bruin, E. I., Ferdinand, R. F., Meester, S., Nijs, P. F. A., & Verheij, F. (2007). High rates of psychiatric co-morbidity in PDD-NOS. *Journal of Autism and Developmental Disorders, 37,* 877–886.

Deb, S., Thomas, M., & Bright, C. (2001). Mental disorder in adults with intellectual disability. I: Prevalence of functional psychiatric illness among a community-based population aged between 16 and 64 years. *Journal of Intellectual Disability Research, 45,* 495–505.

El-Ghohoury, N. H., & Krackow, E. (2011). A developmental-behavioral approach to outpatient psychotherapy with children with autism spectrum disorders. *Journal of Contemporary Psychotherapy, 41,* 11–17.

Evans, D. W., Canavera, K., Kleinpeter, F. L., Maccubbin, E., & Taga, K. (2005). The fears, phobias and anxieties of children with autism spectrum disorders and Down syndrome: Comparisons with developmentally and chronologically age matched children. *Child Psychiatry and Human Development, 36,* 3–26

Fischer-Terworth, C., & Probst, P. (2009). Obsessive-compulsive phenomena and symptoms in Asperger's disorder and high-functioning autism: An evaluative literature review. *Life Span and Disability, 7,* 5–27.

Frazier, J. A., Biederman, J., Bellordre, C. A., Garfield, S. B., Geller, D. A., Coffey, B. J., & Faaraone, S. V. (2001). Should the diagnosis of attention-deficit/hyperactivity disorder be considered in children with pervasive developmental disorder? *Journal of Attention Disorders, 4,* 203–211.

Freeman, J. B., Choate-Summers, M. L., Moore, P. S., Garcia, A. M., Sapyta, J. J., Leonard, H. L., & Franklin, M. E. (2006). Cognitive behavioral treatment for young children with obsessive-compulsive disorder. *Biological Psychiatry, 17,* 337–343.

Gadow, K. D., Devincent, C. J., Pomeroy, J., & Azizian, A. (2005). Comparison of DSM-IV symptoms in elementary school-age children with PDD versus clinic and community samples. *Autism, 9,* 392–415.

Gargaro, B. A., Rinehart, N. J., Bradshaw, J. L., Tonge, B. J., & Sheppard, D. M. (2011). Autism and ADHD: How far have we come in the comorbidity debate? *Neuroscience and Biobehavioral Reviews, 35,* 1081–1088.

Ghaziuddin, M., Tsai, L., & Ghaziuddin, N. (1992). Comorbidity of autistic disorder in children and adolescents. *European Child and Adolescent Psychiatry, 1,* 209–213.

Gibbs, V., Aldridge, F., Chandler, F., Witzlsperger, E., & Smith, K. (2012). Brief report: An exploratory study comparing diagnostic outcomes for autism spectrum disorders under the DSM-IV-TR and the proposed DSM-5 revision. *Journal of Autism and Developmental Disorders, 42,* 1750–56.

Gillott, A., Furniss, F., & Walter, A. (2001). Anxiety in high-functioning children with autism. *Autism, 5,* 277.

Gjevik, E., Eldevik, S. Fjaeran-Granum, T., & Sponheim, E. (2011). Kiddie-SADS reveals high rates of DSM-IV disorders in children and adolescents with austim spectrum disorders. *Journal of Autism and Developmental Disorders, 41,* 761–769.

Goldstein, S., & Schwebach, A. J. (2004). The comorbidity of pervasive developmental disorder and attention deficit hyperactivity disorder: Results of a retrospective chart review. *Journal of Autism and Developmental Disorders, 34,* 329–339.

Goodman, W. K., Price, L. H., Rasmussen, S. A., Riddle, M. A., & Rapoport, J. L. (1986). *Children's Yale-Brown Obsessive Compulsive Scale (CY-BOCS).* Bethesda, MD: National Institutes of Mental Health.

Goodman, W. K., Price, L. H., Rasmussen, S. A., Mazure, C., Delgado, P., Heninger, G. R., & Charney, D. S. (1989). The Yale–Brown Obsessive Compulsive Scale: II. Validity. *Archives of General Psychiatry, 46,* 1012–1016.

Hagsberg, B. S., Miniscalco, C., & Gillberg, C. (2010). Clinic attenders with autism or attention-deficit/hyperactivity disorder: Cognitive profile at school age and its relationship to preschool indicators of language delay. *Research in Developmental Disabilities, 31,* 1–8.

Handen, B. L., Apolito, P. M., & Seltzer, G. B. (1984). Use of differential reinforcement of low rates of behavior to decrease repetitive speech in an autistic adolescent. *Journal of Behavioral Theory and Experimental Psychiatry, 15,* 359–364.

Handen, B. L., Johnson, C. R., & Lubetsky, M. (2000). Efficacy of methylphenidate among children with autism and symptoms of attention-deficit hyperactivity disorder. *Journal of Autism and Developmental Disorders, 30,* 245–255.

Hartley, S. L., & Sikora, D. M. (2009). Which DSM-IV-TR criteria best differentiate high-functioning autism spectrum disorder from ADHD and anxiety disorders in older children? *Autism, 13,* 485–509.

Hellings, J. A., Zarcone, J. R., Crandall, K., Wallace, D., Schroeder, S. R. (2004). Weight gain in a controlled study of risperidone in children, adolescents and adults with mental retardation and autism. *Journal of Child and Adolescent Psychopharmacology, 11,* 229–238.

Helverschou, S. B., Bakken, T. L., & Martinsen, H. (2009). The psychopathology in autism checklist (PAC): A pilot study. *Research in Autism Disorders, 3,* 179–195.

Hollander, E., Wang, A. T., Braun, A., & Marsh, L. (2009). Neurological considerations: Autism and Parkinson's disease. *Psychiatry Research, 170,* 43–51.

Howlin, P. (1998). Psychological and educational treatments for autism. *Journal of Child Psychology and Psychiatry and Allied Disciplines, 39,* 307–322.

Hyrb, K., Kirkhart, R., & Talbert, R. (2007). A call for standardized definition of dual diagnosis. *Psychiatry, 4,* 15–16.

Iwata, B. A., Dorsey, M. F., Slifer, K. J., Bauman, K. E., & Richman, G. S. (1994). Toward a functional analysis of self-injury. *Journal of Applied Behaviour Analysis, 27*(2), 197–209.

Jahromi, L. B., Kasari, C. L., McCracken, J. T., Yee, L., Aman, M. G., McDougle, C. J., ...Posey, D. J. (2009). Positive effects of methylphenidate on social communication and self-regulation in children with pervasive developmental disorders and hyperactivity. *Journal of Autism and Developmental Disorders, 39,* 395–404.

Jennett, H. K., & Hagopian, L. P. (2008). Review identifying empirically supported treatments for phobic avoidance in individuals with intellectual disabilities. *Behavior Therapy, 39,* 151–161.

Kasari, C., & Lawton, K. (2010). New directions in behavioral treatment of autism spectrum disorders. *Current Opinion in Neurology, 23,* 137–143.

Kauffmann, C., Vance, H., Pumariega, A. J., & Miller, B. (2001). Fluvoxamine treatment of a child with severe PDD: A single case study. *Psychiatry: Interpersonal and Biological Processes, 64,* 268–277.

Kaufman, J., Birmaher, B., & Breut, D. (1997). Schedule for affective disorders and schizophrenia for school age children present and lifetime version (K-SADS-PL): Initial reliability and validity data. *Journal of the American Academy of Child and Adolescent Psychiatry, 36,* 83–93.

Kim, J., Szatmari, P., Bryson, S., Streiner, D., & Wilson, F. (2000). The prevalence of anxiety and mood problems among children with autism and Asperger syndrome. *Autism, 4,* 117–132.

King, B. H., & Bostic, J. Q. (2005). An update on pharmacologic treatments for autism spectrum disorders. *Child and Adolescent Psychiatric Clinics of North America, 17,* 713–738.

Kuhn, D. E., Hardesty, S. L., & Sweeney, N. M. (2009). Assessment and treatment of excessive straightening and destructive behavior in an adolescent diagnosed with autism. *Journal of Applied Behavior Analysis, 42,* 355–360.

Leyfer, O., Folstein, S., Bacalman, S., Davis, N., Dinh, E., Morgan, J., ...Lainhart, J. E. (2006). Comorbid psychiatric disorders in children with autism: Interview development and rates of disorders. *Journal of Autism and Developmental Disorders, 36,* 849–861.

Long, K., Wood, H., & Holmes, N. (2000). Presentation, assessment and treatment of depression in a young woman with learning disability and autism. *British Journal of Learning Disabilities, 28,* 102–108.

Lord, C., & Volkmar F. (2002). Genetics of childhood disorders: XLII. Autism part 1: Diagnosis and assessment in autistic spectrum disorders. *Journal of the America Academy of Child and Adolescent Psychiatry, 41,* 1134–1136.

Lovullo, S. V., & Matson, J. L. (2009). Comorbid psychopathology in adults with autism spectrum disorders and intellectual disabilities. *Research in Developmental Disabilities, 30,* 1288–1296.

Mack, H., Fullana, M., Russell, A., Mataix-Cols, D., Nakatani, E., & Heyman, I. (2010). Obsessions and compulsions in children with Asperger's syndrome or high-functioning autism: A case-control study. *Australian and New Zealand Journal of Psychiatry, 44,* 1082–1088.

March, J. S. (1999). *Multidimensional Anxiety Scale for Children manual.* North Tonawanda, NY: Multi-Health Systems.

Marchant, R., Howlin, P., Yule, W., & Rutter, M. (1974). Graded change in the treatment of the behaviour of autistic children. *Journal of Child Psychology and Psychiatry, 15,* 221–227.

Matson, J. L. (1986). Treatment outcome research for depression in mentally retarded children and youth: Methodological issues. *Psychopharmacology Bulletin, 22,* 1081–1085.

Matson, J. L., Barrett, R. P., & Helsel, W. J. (1988). Depression in mentally retarded children. *Research in Developmental Disabilities, 9,* 39–46.

Matson, J. L., Belva, B. C., Horovitz, M., & Bamberg, J. W. (2012). Comparing the symptoms of autism spectrum disorders in a developmentally disabled adult population using the current DSM-IV-TR diagnostic criteria and the proposed DSM-5 diagnostic criteria. *Journal of Developmental and Physical Disabilities, 24,* 403–417.

Matson, J. L., & Boisjoli, J. A. (2007). Differential diagnosis of PDDNOS in children. *Research in Autism Spectrum Disorders, 1,* 75–84.

Matson, J. L., & Boisjoli, J. A. (2008). Autism spectrum disorders in adults with intellectual disability and comorbid psychopathology: Scale development and reliability of the ASD-CA. *Research in Autism Spectrum Disorders, 2,* 276–287.

Matson, J. L., Kozlowski1, A. K., Hattier, M. A., Horovitz, M., & Sipes, M. (2012). DSM-IV vs DSM-5 diagnostic criteria for toddlers with autism. *Developmental Neurorehabilitation, 15,* 185–190.

Matson, J. L., LoVullo, S. V., Rivet, T. T., & Boisjoli, J. A. (2009). Validity of the autism spectrum disorder-comorbid for children (ASD-CC). *Research in Autism Spectrum Disorders, 3,* 345–357.

Matson, J. L., & Nebel-Schwalm, M. S. (2007). Comorbid psychopathology with autism spectrum disorder in children: An overview. *Research in Developmental Disabilities, 28,* 341–352.

Matson, J. L., Wilkins, J., Sevin, J. A., Knight, C., Boisjoli, J. A., & Sharp, B. (2009). Reliability and item content of the Baby and Infant Screen for Children with aUtIsm Traits (BISCUIT): Parts 1, 2, and 3. *Research in Autism Spectrum Disorders, 3,* 336–344.

Mattila, M., Kielinen, M., Linna, S-L., Jussila, K., Ebeling, H., Bloigu, R., ... Moilanen, I. (2011). Autism spectrum disorders according to DSM-IV-TR and comparison with DSM-5 draft criteria: An epidemiological study. *Journal of the American Academy of Child and Adolescent Psychiatry, 50,* 583–592.

Mayes, S. D., & Calhoun, S. L. (2007). Learning, attention, writing, and processing speed in typical children and children with ADHD, autism, anxiety, depression, and oppositional-defiant disorder. *Child Neuropsychology, 13,* 469–493.

Mayes, S. D., Calhoun, S., Bixler, E. O., & Vgontzas, A. N. (2009). Sleep problems in children with autism, ADHD, anxiety, depression, acquired brain injury, and typical development. *Sleep Medicine Clinics, 4*(1), 19-25.

Mayes, S. D., Calhoun, S. L., Mayes, R. D., & Molitoris, S. (2012). Autism and ADHD: Overlapping and discriminating symptoms. *Research in Autism Spectrum Disorders, 6,* 277–285.

Mazefsky, C. A., Kao, J., & Oswald, D. P. (2011). Preliminary evidence suggesting caution in the use of psychiatric self-report measures with adolescents with high-functioning autism spectrum disorders. *Research in Autism Spectrum Disorders, 5,* 164–174.

Mazefsky, C. A., Oswald, D. P. (2012). ASD, a psychiatric disorder, or both? Psychiatric diagnoses in adolescents with high-functioning ASD. *Journal of Clinical Child and Adolescent Psychology, 41,* 1–8.

McDougle, C. J., Kresch, B. A., Goodman, W. K., Naylor, S. T., Volkmar, F. R., Cohen, D. J., & Price, L. H. (1995). A case-controlled study of repetitive thoughts and behavior in adults with autistic disorder and obsessive-compulsive disorder. *American Journal of Psychiatry, 152,* 772–777.

McPartland, J. C., Reichow, B., & Volkmar, F. R. (2012). Sensitivity and specificity of proposed DSM-5 diagnostic criteria for Autism Spectrum Disorder. *Journal of the American Academy of Child and Adolescent Psychiatry, 51,* 368–383.

Melfsen, S., Walitza, S., & Warnke, A. (2006). The extent of social anxiety in combination with mental disorders. *European Child and Adolescent Psychiatry, 15,* 111–117.

Mohiuddin, S., & Ghaziuddin, M. (2012). Psychopharmacology of autism spectrum disorders: A selective review. *Autism, 16,* 1–10.

Moss S., Emerson E., Kiernan C., Turner S., Hatton C., & Alborz A. (2000). Psychiatric symptoms in adults with learning disability and challenging behaviour. *British Journal of Psychiatry, 177,* 452–456.

Muris, P., Steerneman, P., Merkelbach, H., Holdrient, L., & Meester, C. (1998). Co-morbid anxiety disorders symptoms in children with pervasive developmental disorders. *Journal of Anxiety Disorders, 12,* 387–393.

National Center for Health Statistics. (2011). *Attention deficit hyperactivity disorder among children aged 5-17 years in the United States, 1998-2009.* Retrieved August 4, 2012 from http://198.246.124.20/nchs/data/databriefs/db70.pdf.

Nickels, K. C., Katusic, S. K., Colligan, R. C., Weaver, A. L., Voigt, R. G., & Barbaresi, W. J. (2008). Stimulant medication treatment of target behaviors in children with autism: A population-based study. *Journal of Developmental and Behavioral Pediatrics, 29,* 75–81.

O'Donohue & Lilienfeld. (2012). Professional issues in evidence-based practice. In P. Sturmey & M. Hersen, (Eds.), *Handbook of evidence-based practice in clinical psychology. Vol. 2: Adults* (pp. 51–72). Hoboken, NJ: Wiley.

Ooi, Y. P., Lam, C. M., Sung, M., Tan, W. T. S., Goh, T. J., Fung, D. S. S., Pathy, P.,..., Chua, A. (2008). Effects of cognitive-behavioural therapy on anxiety for children with high-functioning autistic spectrum disorders. *Singapore Medical Journal, 49,* 215–220.

Ozbayrak, K. R. (1997). Sertraline in PDD. *Journal of the American Academy of Child and Adolescent Psychiatry, 36,* 7–8.

Patel, K., & Curtis, L. T. (2007). A comprehensive approach to treating autism and attention-deficit hyperactivity disorder: A prepilot study. *Journal of Alternative and Complimentary Medicine, 13,* 1091–1097.

Reaven, J. A., Blakeley-Smith, A., Nichols, S., Dasari, M., Flanigan, E., & Hepburn, S. (2009). Cognitive-behavioral group treatment for anxiety symptoms in children with high-functioning autism spectrum disorders: A pilot study. *Focus on Autism and Other Developmental Disabilities, 24,* 27–37.

Reaven, J., & Hepburn, S. (2003). Cognitive-behavioral treatment of obsessive-compulsive disorder in a child with Asperger syndrome. *Autism, 7,* 145–164.

Ritvo, E. R. (2012). Postponing the proposed changes in DSM 5 for autistic spectrum disorders until new scientific evidence supports them. *Journal of Autism and Developmental Disorders, 42,* 2021–2022.

Rodriguez, N. M., Thompson, R. H., Schlichenmeyer, K., & Stocco, C. S. (2012). Functional analysis and treatment of arranging and ordering by individuals with an autism spectrum disorder. *Journal of Applied Behavior Analysis, 45,* 1–22.

Rommelse, N. N., Franke, B., Geurts, H. M., Hartman, C. A., & Buitelaar, J. K. (2010). Shared heritability of attention-deficit/hyperactivity disorder and autism spectrum disorder. *European Child and Adolescent Psychiatry, 19,* 281–295.

Rowles, B. M., & Findling, R. L. (2010). Review of pharmacotherapy options for the treatment of attention-deficit/hyperactivity disorder (ADHD) and ADHD-like symptoms in children and adolescents with developmental disorders. *Developmental Disabilities Research Reviews, 16,* 273–282.

Russell, A. J., Mataix-Cols, D., Anson, M., & Murphy, D. (2005). Obsessions and compulsions in Asperger syndrome and high-functioning autism. *British Journal of Psychiatry, 186*, 525–528.

Russell, E., & Sofronoff, K. (2005). Anxiety and social worries in children with Asperger syndrome. *Australian and New Zealand Journal of Psychiatry, 39*, 633–638.

Ruta, L., Mugno, D., D'Arrigo, V. G., Vitiello, B., & Mazzone, L. (2010). Obsessive-compulsive traits in children and adolescents with Asperger syndrome. *European Child and Adolescent Psychiatry, 19*, 17–24.

Shuster, J., Perery, A., Bebko, J., & Toplak, M. E. (2012). Review of factor analytic studies examining symptoms of Autism Spectrum Disorders. Cited in Taheri & Perry (2012).

Sigafoos, J., Green, V. A., Payne, D., O'Reilly, M. F., & Lancioni, G. E. (2009). A classroom-based antecedent intervention reduces obsessive-repetitive behavior in an adolescent with autism. *Clinical Case Studies, 8*, 3–13.

Simonoff, E., Pickles, A., Charman, T., Chandler, S., Loucas, T., & Baird, G. (2008). Psychiatric disorders in children with autism spectrum disorders: Prevalence, comorbidity, and associated factors in a population-derived sample. *Journal of the American Academy of Child and Adolescent Psychiatry, 47*, 921–929.

Sofronoff, K., Atwood, T., & Hinton, S. (2005). A randomised control trial of a CBT intervention for anxiety in children with Asperger syndrome. *Journal of Child Psychology and Psychiatry, 46*, 1152–1160.

Spence, S. H. (1997). The Spence Children's Anxiety Scale. In I. Sclare (Ed.), *Child psychology portfolio* (pp. xx–xx). Windsor, ON: NFER-Nelson.

Sturm, H., Fernell, E., & Gillberg, C. (2004). Autism spectrum disorders in children with normal intellectual levels: Associated impairments and subgroups. *Developmental Medicine and Child Neuropsychology, 6*, 444–447.

Sturmey, P. (in press). Evidence-based practice in clinical psychology. *Boletim Contexto.*

Sturmey, P., & Hersen, M. (2012a). *Handbook of evidence-based practice. Vol. 1: Children and adolescents.* Hoboken, NJ: Wiley.

Sturmey, P., & Hersen, M. (2012b). *Handbook of evidence-based practice. Vol. 2: Adults.* Hoboken, NJ: Wiley.

Sturmey, P., Laud, R. B., Cooper, C. L., Matson, J. L., & Fodstad, C. L. (2010). Challenging behaviors should not be considered depressive equivalents in individuals with intellectual disabilities. II. A replication study. *Research in Developmental Disabilities, 31*, 1008–1016.

Sze, K. M., & Wood, J. J. (2009). Cognitive behavioral treatment of comorbid anxiety disorders and social difficulties in children with high-functioning autism: A case report. *Journal of Contemporary Psychotherapy, 37*, 133–143.

Tantam, D. (2000). Psychological disorder in adolescents and adults with Asperger syndrome. *Autism, 4*, 47–62.

Taheri, A., & Perry, A. (2012). Exploring the proposed DSM-5 criteria in a clinical sample. *Journal of Autism and Developmental Disorders, 42*, 1810–1817.

Tarricone, I., Ferrari Gozzi, B., Serretti, A., Grieco, D., & Berardi, D. (2010). Weight gain in antipsychotic naïve patients: A review and metaanalysis. *Psychological Medicine, 40*, 187–200.

Tsai, F., Chiang, H., Lee, C., Shur-Fen Gau, S., Lee, W-T., Fan, P., ... Chiu, Y. (2012). Sleep problems in children with autism, attention-deficit hyperactivity disorder, and epilepsy. *Research in Autism Spectrum Disorders, 6*, 413–421.

Tsakanikos, E., Costello, H., Holt, G., Bouras, N., Sturmey, P., & Newton, T. (2006). Psychopathology in adults with autism and intellectual disability. *Journal of Autism and Developmental Disorders, 36*(8), 1123-1129.

Tsiouris, J. A., Mann, R., Patti, P. J., & Sturmey, P. (2004). Symptoms of depression and challenging behaviours in people with intellectual disability: a Bayesian analysis. *Journal of Intellectual and Developmental Disability, 29*(1), 65-69.

Weisbrot, D. M., Gadow K. D., DeVincent, C. J., & Pomeroy, J. (2005). The presentation of anxiety in children with pervasive developmental disorders. *Journal of Child and Adolescent Psychopharmacology, 15*, 477–496.

White, S. W., Oswald, D., Ollendick, T., & Scahill, L. (2009). Anxiety in children and adolescents with autism spectrum disorders. *Clinical Psychology Review, 29*, 216–229.

Wood, J. J., Drahota, A., Sze, K., Har, K., Chiu, A., & Langer, D. A. (2009). Cognitive behavior therapy for anxiety disorders in children with autism spectrum disorders: A randomized, controlled trial. *Journal of Child Psychology and Psychiatry, 50*, 224–234.

Woodard, C., Groden, J., Goodwin, M., Shanower, C., & Bianco, J. (2005). The treatment of the behavioral sequelae of autism with dextromethorphan: A case report. *Journal of Autism and Developmental Disorders, 35*, 515–518.

Xenitidis, K., Paliokosta, E., Maltezos, S., & Pappas, V. (2007). Assessment of mental health problems in people with autism. *Advances in Mental Health and Learning Disabilities, 1*, 15–22.

Zandt, F., Prior, M., & Kyrios, M. (2007). Repetitive behaviour in children with high functioning autism and obsessive compulsive disorder. *Journal of Autism and Developmental Disorders, 37*, 251–259

Zandt, F., Prior, M., & Kyrios, M. (2009). Similarities and differences between children and adolescents with autism spectrum disorder and those with obsessive compulsive disorder. *Autism, 13*, 43–57.

3

Progress and Outcome Measurement

RUTH ANNE REHFELDT, JONATHAN BAKER, AND LEIGH GRANNAN

The National Professional Development Center on Autism Spectrum Disorders has identified the majority of the evidence-based interventions for persons with autism spectrum disorder (ASD) as falling under the rubric of applied behavior analysis (ABA). However, despite the overwhelming compilation of research indicating ABA as the only effective treatment for the disorder, nonvalidated interventions proliferate in the autism community, and information on such treatments is widely available to parents and professionals. For example, Long (2006) identified 5,290,000 Web sites on interventions for autism, many of which included unauthenticated treatment claims. The wide accessibility of such material confuses parents and professionals alike. To illustrate, physicians are not always well prepared to draw inferences about a treatment's efficacy before making recommendations to families: Golnik and Ireland (2009) found that over 50% of physicians surveyed from the American Medical Association encouraged families to explore complementary alternative medicine (CAM) for their children, with multivitamins, fatty acids, and melatonin ranking among the most recommended of CAM treatments for the disorder. Likewise, Hanson et al. (2007) found that 74% of parents of children with autism surveyed reported using CAM, presumably under physician recommendation. Unfortunately, these results suggest that practitioners and professionals, seemingly trained in the scientific method, may be no more skilled at discriminating between effective treatments and unauthenticated treatment claims than parents who lack such training.

Myers and Johnson (2007) formulated a list of points that practitioners and families should consider when exploring different treatment options, including (a) whether the treatment is based on overly simplified scientific theories, (b) is proclaimed to be effective for multiple conditions, (c) is suggested to result in a dramatic improvement, (d) is based upon anecdotal data rather than carefully designed studies, (e) lacks support in the published scientific literature, and (f) is purported to have no side effects (p. 1173). Ideally, physicians and practitioners should act on the best interests of their patients and clients, and facilitate families' allocation of time, energy, and financial resources to interventions that are of known efficacy. Clearly, however, a gap exists between what is now well documented in the scientific literature and the knowledge base of practicing professionals.

The behavior analytic community has a responsibility to ensure that parents and professionals are not only informed about effective treatments but also adhere to the recommendations of Myers and Johnson (2007). Odom et al. (2003) reported that those researchers who employed single-subject research methodology have contributed greatly to the identification of evidence-based practices for young children with autism. For these authors, the criteria for determining that an intervention is evidence based include the number of replications of the intervention, the type of design, evidence for improvement in behavior over time, and an assessment of treatment fidelity and social validity of the procedures employed. Thus, the interpretation of experimental design logic to parents and professionals seems to be an important responsibility for behavior analysts.

Further obscuring the conundrum is the fact that although a practitioner may claim to practice within the ABA framework, he or she may not possess the competencies to implement the treatment with fidelity and adequately evaluate clients' progress. Not all clients will progress at the same rate, and practitioners, although sharing credentials in common, may vary greatly in their own skills and experiences. The ability to ascertain a client's progress and make treatment decisions accordingly are critical skills for a behavior analyst. Not only does the Behavior Analysis Certification Board (BACB)'s Guidelines for Responsible Conduct for Behavior Analysts (2010) state that it is unethical to employ treatment strategies for which there is no empirical support, the board also mandates that behavior analysts continuously monitor the efficacy of their ongoing interventions and make modifications if a clients' goals are not attained. Thus, recognizing effective interventions from the large field of treatments currently being disseminated is an important ethical obligation, but so too is the objective evaluation and monitoring of treatment progress. Utilizing valid and reliable measures of behavior change is paramount to meeting the second of these two obligations.

The purposes of this chapter are to (1) provide an overview of the process known as behavioral assessment, utilized by behavior analysts to objectively evaluate their clients' progress in ABA treatment; and (2) outline the use of single-subject methodology for evaluating the efficacy of a particular intervention. To this end, we will explore representative studies from the published literature on behavioral interventions for persons with autism and how a study's measurement system and design contribute to conclusions regarding evidence for the particular intervention's efficacy.

BEHAVIORAL ASSESSMENT

Given the cost of behavior analytic services and the high demand for them, behavior analysts must know that their efforts are yielding important benefits for their clients. If not, valuable time and resources are wasted. Mayer, Sulzer-Azaroff, and Wallace (2012) advise that behavior analysts collect and report some reproducible measure to convince others that their intervention is producing meaningful changes in behavior. In the past some professionals may have chosen the less effortful approach by basing important decisions about a client's progress on subjective impressions. However, given the growing demand for human service professionals to be accountable for the services they deliver, today many human service professionals are expected to produce objective measures of their client's response to treatment. Mayer et al. (2012) define behavioral assessment as the process of validly and reliably observing, measuring, and recording behavior, such that scientifically and ethically sound decisions about a client or

student's placement in services can be made. The authors characterize a strong measurement system as one with sensitive, objective, reliable, and valid measures (Mayer, Sulzer-Azaroff, & Wallace, 2012, p. 107). A sensitive measure is one that reflects subtle yet meaningful changes in the behavior targeted for intervention. An objective measure is one that is free from one's personal biases or interpretations and includes a clear operational definition of the target behavior (Mayer et al., 2012, p. 108). A reliable measure is one that is repeatable or remains otherwise consistent regardless of who conducts the measurements and on what occasions. In other words, two or more independent observers must obtain the same results. Finally, a measure that is valid is one that measures what it claims to measure, and not some other related or unrelated aspect of behavior.

Mayer et al. (2012) point out that although a measure of behavior may be reliable or repeatable, there is no guarantee that the measure is valid or measures what the investigators intended for it to measure. Two observers may agree on the time a student spends studying 100% of the time, but if they claim to be measuring the student's academic performance, time spent studying does not necessarily reflect the latter, so their measures are not valid. Simply the process of being observed has been shown to affect how people behave, as many clients behave differently when they know their behavior is being observed and recorded. Reactivity, therefore, may affect the validity of one's measures. For this reason many behavior analysts allow for a period of adaptation when conducting direct observations of behavior, allowing time for the client's reactivity to subside (Mayer et al., p. 109).

Measuring and Recording Dimensions of Behavior

In light of the expectation that behavior analysts utilize objective, reliable, and valid measurement systems, there are useful techniques for measuring and recording behavior (Mayer et al., 2012).

Permanent Products

Certain behaviors leave physical evidence or a product that endures permanently after the individual has stopped engaging in the behavior. Permanent product recording is an observational method that assesses the results or outcomes of a behavior of interest. Clothes folded, math worksheets completed, and litter collected are all products of specific behaviors that might be of clinical interest. Permanent product recording is convenient because the behavior analyst does not have to actually observe the behavior as it occurs. In addition to saving time for the behavior analyst, reactivity is also minimized (Mayer et al., 2012). Dorminy, Luscre, and Gast (2009) used permanent product recording in a self-monitoring intervention that was designed to increase organizational skills of fourth- and fifth-grade students with autism. Students were taught to arrange study materials in a file box containing hanging file folders and to record and report their accuracy. The authors recorded the percentage of assignments filed in the appropriate folder for each subject. During baseline, students filed as few as 45% of the items correctly, but their performance increased to 70%–100% of items filed correctly during the intervention. Batchelder, McLaughlin, Weber, Derby, and Gow (2009) also used permanent product recording to measure handwriting while evaluating the effects of hand-over-hand and dot-to-dot tracing procedures in improving the handwriting of a 14-year-old student with autism. Investigators counted the number of letters written correctly on a worksheet at the end of each session and found that the number of correct letters increased substantially with instruction. These studies illustrate the ease with which permanent products can be collected in a variety of academic situations. However, permanent product recording may not lend itself well to recording improvements in language and social skills, as neither social nor linguistic behaviors leave products.

Event Recording

Many behaviors that are targeted in interventions for persons with autism may be considered transitory, meaning they are brief, temporary, and can be counted as they come and go. Event or frequency recording is typically used to measure such fleeting behavior (Mayer et al., 2012). This approach involves simply counting how often a specific behavior occurs during a designated time interval. For measures to be valid, event recording is typically used for behaviors that have a clear beginning and end (otherwise the count would be obscured) and for behaviors that do not occur at such a high frequency that they are impossible to record (Mayer et al., 2012). Consider that event or frequency recording is used to record the number of instructional trials to achieve mastery and the percentage of trials performed correctly per session. It may also be used to report the number or

percentage of steps performed correctly on a task analysis when teaching a chained task. Finally, if the time during which observations are collected varies from one recording instance to the next, Mayer et al. (2012) recommend that frequency data be reported as rate, that is, number of responses per unit time (Mayer et al., 2012).

Hagopian, Kuhn, and Strother (2009) used event recording to measure the number of inappropriate comments and instances of touching others displayed per hour by an adolescent with pervasive developmental disorder. Inappropriate comments included interrupting others while they were talking or abruptly changing the topic of conversation; inappropriate touching was defined as touching others anywhere on their body without permission. Because results from an experimental functional analysis showed the behaviors to be attention maintained, an intervention consisting of a differential-reinforcement-of-low-rate-behavior (DRL) schedule with corrective feedback was implemented for inappropriate comments. The intervention reduced inappropriate comments, and inappropriate touching and appropriate comments improved without direct intervention. Keintz, Miguel, Kao, and Finn (2011) provide another example of event recording in a study that examined the effects of conditional discrimination instructional procedures in establishing stimulus equivalence relations between coins and their names and values in preschool-age children with autism. The dependent measure on test trials was percentage of correct responses per nine-trial block for several skill areas indicative of equivalence class formation, including selecting the printed value when given a coin's dictated name, selecting the correct coin when given its printed and dictated value, stating the names of coins when given the coin or its dictated value, and stating a coin's value when given its name or printed value. All participants had increased percentage of correct responses on posttest probes, but only some met the criterion for equivalence class formation of eight of nine correct responses on all posttest probes (Keintz, Miguel, Kao, & Finn, 2011).

Ayres, Maguire, and McClimon (2009) and Jerome, Frantino, and Sturmey (2007) evaluated the efficacy of instructional procedures for teaching chained tasks to individuals with autism and recorded the percentage or number of steps performed correctly in a task analysis. Ayres et al. (2009) showed that computer-based video modeling produced

100% task mastery in three, 7- to 9-year-old children with autism. Using a task analysis of requisite skills, Jerome et al. (2007) showed that errorless teaching and backward chaining were effective in teaching adults with autism and intellectual disabilities to use the Internet.

While relying on the number or percentage of correct responses as the primary measure for inferring treatment progress is common in behavioral intervention, many behavior analysts believe that rate, or the number of correct responses per unit time, is a more meaningful measure of progress. Fluency, defined as responding accurately, quickly, and without hesitation (Binder, 1996), has grown in popularity as a treatment measure for individuals with autism (Weiss, 2001). Weiss (2001) points out that many individuals with autism experience disfluencies due to poor muscle coordination, resulting in reduced opportunities for academic instruction. Kubina, Morrison, and Lee (2002) note that relying exclusively on percentage correct measures can inaccurately reflect progress: For example, a child who completes 10 trials with 100% accuracy in 1 minute is a more fluent learner than a child who completes 10 trials with 100% accuracy in 5 minutes. Clearly, although each student performed with 100% accuracy, it would be a mistake to move both students forward in the curriculum (Kubina, Morrison, & Lee, 2002).

Duration Recording

Behavior analysts use duration recording when the amount of time in which an individual engages in some behavior is important. Time on task, time engaged with play materials, and time spent socially interacting with one's peers are all examples of situations in which knowing the duration of the target behavior may be important. Anglesea, Hock, and Taylor (2008) used duration recording when treating rapid eating in three adolescents with autism. The intervention consisted of teaching participants to set a vibrating pager that repeated vibrations at designated time intervals during eating. Vibration intervals were determined by dividing the duration required for a typically developing adult to consume the food by the number of bites taken by the participant during baseline. This criterion established how many bites participants would have to take, at how many seconds, to consume each food item in nearly the same amount of time required for a typically developing adult. The primary dependent measure

was the total number of seconds of eating time for participants to consume the target food. The data collector scored eating time from the second the teacher presented the food until the participant swallowed the last bite using a digital timer.

Latency Recording

Latency recording is similar to duration recording except that the observer records how long after the presentation of some stimulus, such as instructions, it takes an individual to demonstrate the target response. Latency recording is typically used to record behavior when the time it takes to initiate some response is a source of concern. It is important, for example, for a student to answer questions rapidly so that other opportunities for instruction are not missed (Donohue, Casey, Bicard, & Bicard, 2012). Donohue et al. (2012) delivered preferred stimuli contingent upon responding to instructions with gradually decreasing response latencies in a 17-year-old man with autism. Specifically, the experimenters gradually decreased the latency required for reinforcement from an average of 4.6 seconds to an average of 2.4 seconds following questions such as "What is your name?" (Donohue et al., 2012). Tiger, Bouxsein, and Fisher (2007) used a similar procedure with a man with Asperger syndrome across two tasks, question answering and stating answers to math problems. To decrease latency for responding to questions regarding personal information, the authors decreased the criterion for reinforcement during each session by 10% from the mean latency in the previous session. Differential reinforcement of short latencies was effective in reducing latency to fewer than 5 seconds during the final intervention phase. In a second study, math problems were divided into three difficulty levels: easy (problems the participant could answer quickly and correctly but inconsistently did so), medium (problems the participant could answer correctly requiring more time), and difficult (problems that participants could not do independently and often sought help with after a long delay). Explicit contingencies were required for the three types of problems due to generalization of responding in the medium problem condition following decreasing the criterion for reinforcement in responding for the easy and difficult problems. In the easy problem condition, reducing the mean latency for problem completion was targeted. In the medium problem condition, correct completion regardless of time was the focus of intervention, and in the difficult problem condition, reducing the mean latency for responding "I don't know" was the focus. Following intervention, mean response latencies decreased from 35.9 seconds for easy problems and 81.0 seconds for difficult problems to 2.1 seconds for easy and 2.9 seconds for difficult problems. Following differential reinforcement for correct responding to medium problems, mean correct responding increased from 22% to 93%, while the treatment effects for the easy and difficult problems were maintained.

Interval Time Sampling

This recording method measures target behaviors that are continuous or have no clear onset or offset. Time-sampling systems are also used to record behaviors that occur too frequently to be able to capture all instances with event recording. Time sampling involves estimating how often a target behavior occurs by periodically observing and recording its occurrence. With interval time sampling, the observer divides the observation session into time intervals of equal lengths and records the behavior as occurring or not occurring during each time interval. The percentage of intervals during which the behavior occurred is then calculated at the end of each session (Mayer et al., 2012). In whole-interval time sampling, the behavior must be emitted throughout the entire interval for it to be scored as occurring, and in partial-interval time sampling, the behavior must occur at least once during any part of the interval for it to be scored as occurring. Momentary time sampling requires that the behavior occurs at the moment the interval ends for it to be scored as occurring (Mayer et al., 2012). Because interval recording systems produce only estimates of a target behavior's occurrence, behavior analysts must give careful attention to which recording system is appropriate for a given target behavior, and also to the size of their sampling intervals (Mayer et al., 2012). Greatly over- or underestimating the occurrence of a target behavior would be problematic for inferring that a client was making progress toward attaining his or her treatment goals. Mayer et al. (2012) suggest selecting the most conservative time sampling procedure. Because data collected using whole-interval recording may underestimate the actual occurrence of behavior, whole-interval recording is often used with interventions designed to increase behavior. Because data collected using partial-interval recording may overestimate the occurrence of clinically relevant instances of behavior, partial-interval recording is often used with interventions designed to decrease behavior. Momentary time sampling can both over- and underestimate the occurrences of a target behavior, leading Mayer et al. (2012) to advise using relatively short recording intervals for frequent observations.

Miguel, Clark, Tereshko, and Ahearn (2009) used partial-interval recording to record vocal stereotypy: any instance of audible, noncontextual or nonfunctional speech with sustained vowel sounds, varying pitches of a sound, and spit swooshing. Functional analysis results showed that the behavior was maintained by automatic reinforcement. During the functional analysis, the percentage of 1-second intervals with vocal stereotypy was recorded per 5-minute session time. The authors found that an intervention consisting of response interruption and redirection, which involved the experimenter interrupting instances of vocal stereotypy by removing any task items and presenting mastered vocal imitation tasks, was more effective at reducing the percentage of intervals with stereotypy than sertraline, a commonly prescribed selective serotonin reuptake inhibitor, in a 4-year-old boy with autism. Sidener, Carr, and Firth (2005) also used partial-interval recording to record stereotypy in two 6-year-old girls with autism. These investigators targeted scratching, defined as movement of the fingertips or fingernails across a surface without using the same fingers to grasp the items. The percentage of intervals with toy engagement, defined as touching a toy without scratching it, was collected during a toy enrichment condition. All behaviors were recorded from videotape using noncontinuous partial-interval recording with 10-second intervals and 5 seconds recording time between intervals (Sidener, Carr, & Firth, 2005).

Machalicek et al. (2009) reported an intervention consisting of picture activity schedules and correspondence training to reduce challenging behaviors and increase play during outdoor recess for three school-age children with autism. The intervention featured graduated guidance to teach participants how to follow an activity schedule consisting of pictures of playground activities. The investigators collected data on challenging behavior, including self-stimulatory behaviors, screaming, pica, and stereotypic responses on the playground such as manipulating small rocks, and on play behavior, defined as engaging in behavior appropriate to the play activity specified in the activity schedule. Play was measured using 10-second whole-interval recording. The percentage of 10-second intervals with play during baseline was near zero levels for all participants, and mean scores for play during the intervention were 73%, 92%, and 59%, for the three participants, respectively.

Watanabe and Sturmey (2003) used momentary time sampling to record on-task behavior in adult workers with autism participating in a community vocational rehabilitation program. The intervention allowed participants the opportunity to sequence the order of tasks assigned to them by supervisors in their activity schedules. Momentary time sampling was chosen for ease of recording on-task behavior among multiple participants. During the intervention condition, participants were instructed to "make today's schedule" and were given a schedule sheet and a list of nine activities. Participants wrote the names of the tasks in empty columns to make the day's activity schedule. On-task behavior was recorded using 1-minute momentary time sampling during a 30-minute observation period, and the percentage of on-task and off-task behavior was calculated by dividing the number of scored intervals by the total number of intervals. On-task behavior increased to 50%–100% of intervals relative to baseline levels as a function of the simple choice-making intervention. Ulke-Kurkcuoglu and Kircaali-Iftar (2010) reported similar results with children with autism in a simple choice-making intervention on on-task behavior. In this study, participants could choose between different activities or task materials. Sessions were videotaped and videos were analyzed daily to collect 15-second momentary time-sampling data for each session. On-task behavior was substantially higher in a choice versus no-choice condition, but the type of choice participants were given (materials versus tasks) was not shown to matter for increasing on-task behavior.

Reliability of Dependent Measures

As behavior analysts strive to draw valid inferences about the relationship between their intervention and a client's behavior change, others must be confident in the reported treatment outcomes reported as well. Nonetheless, it is difficult, if not impossible, to affirm the accuracy of data collected via direct observation (Hayes, Barlow, & Nelson-Gray, 1999). For this reason, the most common way of evaluating the quality of observational data is by interobserver agreement (IOA), which involves comparing data that are recorded simultaneously and independently by two observers. Consistency between observations suggests that the observers are interchangeable, and another individual trained to record in the same manner would obtain similar findings. While this result does not necessarily mean that the observation system is accurate, it does mean that the observation data are reliable (Hayes et al., 1999; Kazdin, 1977). For observation data that are collected continuously, such as frequency, duration, latency, and permanent product recording, IOA is calculated by dividing the smaller of the two scores obtained for a session by the larger of the two scores obtained for a session, and multiplying this ratio by 100. Note, however, that this formula may inflate percentage agreement for high rate behavior. Thus, many behavior analysts may artificially divide a period of observation into smaller recording intervals. For example, a 40-minute observation period could be divided into ten 4-minute observation periods, with IOA calculated for each smaller observation period, thereby providing a more stringent evaluation of reliability between the two observers (Hayes et al., 1999; Kazdin, 1977).

A percent agreement formula is primarily used for observation data collected using time-sampling procedures. Agreement refers to both observers agreeing on the occurrence or nonoccurrence of the behavior. For overall percent agreement, the behavior analyst sums agreement on the occurrence and nonoccurrence of behavior and divides the sum of agreements and disagreements, usually if the occurrence and nonoccurrence of the behavior is relatively equivalent. If the occurrence of the target behavior is relatively infrequent, it is best to calculate percent occurrence agreement, done by dividing the agreements on occurrence by the sum of the agreements on occurrence and disagreements. Finally, if agreement on nonoccurrence of behavior is important, as when one is attempting to reduce a behavior to near zero levels, percent agreement on nonoccurrence can be calculated by dividing the agreements on nonoccurrence by the sum of the agreements on nonoccurrence and disagreements (Hayes et al., 1999; Kazdin, 1977).

A behavior analyst can also calculate IOA by computing correlations with the data collected from the two observers. This approach can be used with frequency counts, latencies, and the percentage agreement methods previously described. The result is simply the product-moment correlation based on the paired scores provided by two observers for the sessions that are jointly observed (Hartmann, 1977).

Interobserver agreement scores of 80% or higher are considered sufficient levels of agreement between two observers (Hartmann, 1977) and typically reported as a mean and range across sessions. To enhance IOA, observers should be trained in a particular observation system before implementing it because training increases the likelihood that observers will adhere to the operational definitions of behavior and record accurately (Kazdin, 1977). Despite training, even the best clinicians may "drift" from the original behavior definitions, particularly with cumbersome or overly complex observation systems. Kazdin (1977) advises continuously training all observers together throughout an investigation, requiring observers to meet as a group, implementing periodic retraining of observers, and utilizing simple assessment systems that do not require observing too many behaviors at once. In addition, observers seem to produce higher IOA when they know that their agreement is being assessed. Taplin and Reid (1973) recommend further the conducting of random agreement checks and, of course, precisely defined target behaviors.

Treatment Integrity

Not only is evaluating the reliability of the dependent variable a priority when assessing treatment outcomes, so too is evaluating the integrity of the independent variable. Treatment integrity is defined as the degree to which the intervention or independent variable is implemented as originally intended (Peterson, Homer, & Wonderlich, 1982). If practitioners deviate from implementing an intervention from how it was originally intended, it will be impossible to draw valid conclusions about the intervention's efficacy. Surprisingly, Wheeler, Baggett, Fox, and Blevins (2006) found that only 11 of 60 published experimental studies on behavioral interventions conducted with children with autism between the years 1993 and 2003 included formal measures of treatment integrity. The studies that evaluated treatment integrity did so by requiring another observer to monitor sessions and sometimes videotaping sessions for subsequent review and monitoring. Another strategy is using a component checklist that sequences the steps for accurately implementing the intervention and provides a reference for delivering performance feedback. McIntyre, Gresham, DiGennaro, and Reed (2007) obtained similar findings, reporting that most studies published in

Journal of Applied Behavior Analysis in school settings between 1991 and 2005 included a clear specification of the dependent but not independent variable.

Gresham, Gansle, and Noell (1993) advise that clear, unambiguous, comprehensive operational definitions of all components of the intervention should be monitored and measured using an accuracy criterion: An observer records accurate and inaccurate implementation of each treatment component and calculates the percentage of treatment components implemented correctly. DiGennaro-Reed, Codding, Catania, and Maguire (2010) used video modeling and performance feedback to improve teachers' treatment integrity in implementing students' individual behavior intervention plans. A unique task analysis was devised for participants that allowed observers to score whether the clinician implemented each intervention component as intended. Task analyses were individualized for each student according to the function of problem behavior and included discrete steps for a combination of different treatment approaches, including functional communication training, differential reinforcement, escape extinction, and nonexclusionary time-out. Percent treatment integrity then was calculated by dividing the number of intervention steps implemented as written, by the total number of intervention steps implemented.

Social Validity

Another step toward evidence-based practice is a careful consideration of the variables that affect implementation of interventions and evaluation of their impact (Deitrich, 2008). To this end, Deitrich (2008) encourages consumers and their families to be involved in deciding what interventions get implemented. Social validity measures can inform researchers and practitioners about which interventions are most desirable for clients and their families. Measures of social validity can provide information on how acceptable or viable others find a particular intervention, as well as how likely others will be to implement it (Schwartz & Baer, 1991). Such information is important because although an intervention may be successful in producing clinically important changes in behavior, the intervention's success is irrelevant if people judge the intervention as too arduous, time consuming, or unpleasant to implement.

Social validity is typically accomplished by asking people other than the investigators to complete a questionnaire about acceptability of the intervention or program goals, methods, personnel, outcomes, and ease of integration within the client's day-to-day-life (Schwartz & Baer, 1991). Specifically, it should be questioned whether the goals of an intervention are relevant to desired lifestyle changes on part of the client; whether the intervention techniques are acceptable to clients and the community in terms of effort, time, and discomfort; and whether consumers or their families are satisfied with the intervention (Wolf, 1978). Consumers themselves, family members, and those who interact with consumers are relevant informants for social validity assessments. Carr, Austin, Britton, Kellum, and Bailey (1999) disappointingly found that treatment acceptability was evaluated in fewer than 13% of all articles published during the first 31 years of *Journal of Applied Behavior Analysis*, noting that studies conducted in naturalistic versus analog settings were more likely to include such measures.

Mavropoulou, Papadopoulou, and Kakana (2011) evaluated the efficacy of a variety of components of the TEACCH model in a classroom setting such as (a) presenting the components of a task as one unit, (b) providing visual instructions in a variety of forms (including pictures and text), and (c) limiting irrelevant features of tasks by using colors and large photographs. To evaluate social validity, the authors developed a 12-item questionnaire focusing upon the objectives, procedures, and outcomes of the TEACCH intervention. The survey required respondents to indicate their degree of endorsement with all questions, and it was completed before and after the intervention by four members of the school staff who were familiar with the students in the study. An example of a statement regarding intervention goals included, "My student cannot play independently." An example of a statement regarding treatment outcomes included, "My student can be taught to play independently." All respondents agreed that the instructional goals targeted in the study were important for the students, and following the intervention indicated that the students could be taught to play independently (Mavropoulou, Papadopoulou, & Kakana, 2011).

VISUAL INSPECTION AND INTERPRETATION OF SINGLE-SUBJECT DATA

Behavioral intervention data are typically portrayed in a simple line graph. Visually inspecting data allows clinicians and researchers to evaluate intervention effectiveness. Before implementing intervention, baseline or pretest data are collected and then compared to data collected during or following an intervention. In contrast to statistical analysis, visual inspection is a more subjective process. Some experts suggest peer review of data before judging intervention effectiveness, as even highly trained practitioners may disagree in evaluating data (Kazdin, 2011). Thorough examination of the data by trained clinicians and reviewers may decrease the likelihood of Type I (assuming an intervention was effective when in fact it was not) and Type II (assuming an intervention is not effective when it did produce a significant change) errors (Kazdin, 2011, p. 287). However, these errors are much more likely when visual inspection is used and are tied closely to how the data are presented. For example, depicted data that are aggregated or averaged for multiple sessions may be deceiving upon visual analysis, whereas conclusions about the effectiveness of an intervention may be quite clear in the instance that baseline data are zero, making moderate changes in the data more easily observed upon intervening. When performance across phases is not so contrasted, a clinician requires a set of criteria in order to make sound conclusions about the data (Kazdin, 2011, p. 293). For example, Grannan and Rehfeldt (2012) employed a multiple-probe design to assess the effects of multiple tact instruction and a match-to-sample procedure on intraverbal categorization responses in two children with autism. Because all baseline probes were zero for both participants, a clear result of the instructional protocol can be observed in posttest data in that participants listed from one to six category members on intraverbal probe test trials. If pretest data had been more variable and overlapped with posttest data points, visual analysis would have been more difficult. Likewise, Ulke-Kurkcuoglu and Kircaali-Iftar (2010) showed increased on-task behavior in four boys with autism when activity or material choice was provided. However, visual inspection was more difficult due to high percentages of on-task behavior during baseline phases for all participants. Kazdin (2011) outlines specific criteria to use in visual inspection of a line graph, namely changes in means across phases, changes in level, changes in trend, and changes in latency.

Changes in Means

When data are plotted across days or sessions, responding may vary significantly across observations, making it difficult for visual inspection to produce firm conclusions. To aide in inspection, it may be useful to observe the mean scores across phases. Although most published articles report the mean in the text of the article, line graphs may be supplemented by adding a straight line to each phase marking the mean of the data presented in each phase (Kazdin, 2011). As an illustration, Soares, Vannest, and Harrison (2009) employed an ABAB design to assess the effects of self-monitoring on task completion and self-injurious behavior. The authors included straight lines on the line graph depicting data on task completion across phases to supplement the reader's visual inspection of the data and reported that the mean percentage of task completion for baseline phases was 22% and 25% in contrast to 75% and 92% completion for intervention phases. For data that are particularly variable across sessions or days, a reader may also benefit from information about the range of the data points within each phase (Kazdin, 2011). In this instance visual inspection can be difficult and supplemented by indicating that the highest and lowest data points within each phase vary markedly. Watanabe and Sturmey (2003) assessed the effects of choice-making during activity schedules on the on-task behavior of adults with autism. Because the data were more variable across baseline and intervention phases, the authors supplemented data presented in a line graph with the mean on-task behavior and ranges for baseline and intervention phases for the three participants. The mean score for on-task behavior during baseline was 19.4% (range of 1.3% to 46.7%) and 50.8% (range of 36.7% to 73.3%) during the intervention phase for participant 1, 23.9% (0 to 63.3%) during baseline and 67.5% (28% to 90%) for participant 2, and 40.8% (1.7% to 76.7%) during baseline and 58.6% (35.3% to 70%) for participant 3.

Changes in Level

In addition to assessing the means for each phase, a clinician should be concerned with the change in the level of the data from one phase to the next. An intervention may be deemed to be particularly effective if there is a sharp contrast between the last data point of one phase and in the first data point of the subsequent phase. This immediate change, especially if drastic, can indicate that the intervention was likely the cause of the change in behavior, as opposed to the change resulting from typical fluctuations in performance across sessions or days (Kazdin, 2011). Changes in level must be replicated across a phase to further determine that the intervention was

specifically the cause. The clearest indication of an intervention's effectiveness can be observed when data are nonoverlapping across phases (Kazdin, 2011); in other words, the data collected for each phase do not share any values in common. For example, an intervention designed to decrease challenging behavior clearly can be deemed effective if all data points in intervention phases are drastically lower than all data points in baseline phases. Shabani et al. (2002) employed an ABAB design to demonstrate the effectiveness of using a tactile prompt (a pager) on increasing social initiations during free play with three children with autism. Data on the percentage of intervals in which participants verbally initiated interaction and responded to peers' initiations were depicted in a line graph, and a drastic change in level could be observed for three participants immediately following changes between baseline and intervention phases. In addition, the data for the participants appeared to be nonoverlapping across phases for all three participants. Specifically, during intervention phases when the tactile prompt was activated at least every 25 seconds to prompt participants to make a verbal response, initiations occurred in 72%, 71%, and 88% of intervals for the three participants compared to 0, 50%, and 25% of intervals on average during baseline phases.

Changes in Trend

As specified previously, changes in the level of data across phases must be consistent for the duration of a phase. Data may remain at the same level with moderate fluctuations, or it may be expected that performance continues to increase or a challenging behavior continues to decrease across sessions or days as an intervention continues. For example, intervention to increase augmentative and alternative communication (AAC) may decrease challenging behavior that is functionally equivalent. Charlop-Christy, Carpenter, Le, LeBlanc, and Kellet (2002) taught three children with autism to use the Picture Exchange Communication System (PECS) and measured effects on problem behavior and spontaneous speech. In addition to all three children acquiring the use of PECS, their vocalizations increased and challenging behavior decreased during intervention and follow-up phases. Because changes were moderate over time for some participants, the clinician is concerned with observing the trend of the data. Visual inspection of the trend of data may be aided by inclusion of a trend line, a straight line through the middle of most of the data points (Kazdin, 2011). In interventions designed to increase a skill, a clinician would be concerned with observing an upward trend in the data and for an intervention designed to decrease an inappropriate behavior, and a downward trend in the data should be observed. One exemplary study by Ingvarsson and Hollobough (2011) evaluated the effects of echoic versus tact prompts in increasing correct intraverbal responses in three participants with autism. Visual inspection of the data revealed a clear upward trend in the number of correct responses on test probes (e.g., "What animals says moo?" and "What do you sleep on?") in the intervention phases with both types of prompts. Participants did not respond to any questions correctly during baseline probes, with the exception of one correct response for one participant, and all participants quickly met criterion of four out of five correct answers on three consecutive sessions per condition. Fewer trials to criterion were needed for acquisition of intraverbal responses during the picture prompt condition for all three participants (56 trials to criterion during the picture prompt phase compared to 88 in the echoic prompt condition for participant 1, 63 versus 73 for participant 2, and 61 versus 100 trials to criterion for participant 3).

Changes in Latency

A final means by which behavioral data can be inspected is by examining the latency of the behavior change once an intervention has been started or stopped. In some instances one would expect change to be gradual; however, an immediate effect is often expected. A clinician can clearly determine that an intervention is likely the cause of change in data when the data quickly decrease or increase across sessions or days. A clear intervention effect could be observed via a line graph that includes a sharp decreasing trend or rapid continuous decrease in data for inappropriate behavior or a drastic increasing trend for skill acquisition or performance on a task (Kazdin, 2011). For example, Taylor and Hoch (2008) demonstrated the effects of baiting the environment with novel or atypical items (e.g., a doll hanging from a ceiling, an oversized balloon) on responses to joint attention bids with participants with autism. Participants were prompted to shift gaze and comment on the atypical items, and social praise was delivered following the child's correct responses. Upon visual inspection of the data, treatment increased percentage of correct

responses to joint attention bids out of opportunities presented on posttest probes for all children. In addition, training was conducted to increase the participants' initiations for joint attention using a prompt delay; however, one participant required the use of tangible reinforcers to increase initiations.

SINGLE-CASE RESEARCH DESIGN

Behavior analysts take a scientific approach to understanding, explaining, and predicting behavior change (Baer, Wolf, & Risley, 1968). In both research and clinical applications these objectives are achieved with single-case designs (Kazdin, 2011). In this section of the chapter, we describe how single-case designs are used to demonstrate empirical support for an intervention. We also describe different single-case designs and examples of how these designs have been used to demonstrate behavior change among individuals with ASD.

Single-Subject Design as a True Experimental Design

True experimental designs allow the researcher or clinician to make a definitive statement about "causal relationships between variables" (Martella, Nelson, &Marchand-Martella, 1999, p. 132). Chambless and Hollon (1998) note that empirical support for an approach can come only from true experimental designs. They argue that true experimental designs rule out "chance or confounding factors such as passage of time, the effects of psychological assessment, or the presence of different types of clients in various treatment conditions" (p. 7). That is, with true experimental designs, extraneous variables that could cause improvements but are not the result of the intervention can be confidently ruled out and the benefits that individuals receive can be contributed "to the effects of the treatment" (p. 7). They (in conjunction with two task forces) promote two types of research designs that constitute such controlled research (i.e., true experimental designs): randomized control trials (RCTs; which are less likely to be employed by behavior analysts due to the difficulty to evaluate individual effects) and single-subject research designs with proper controls. Chambless and Hollon (1998) begin their discussion about single-subject research designs by emphasizing that such designs can only be considered true experimental designs when a stable baseline has been established.

By employing a baseline condition in which a steady state of behavior is observed, the researcher begins to lay the groundwork for a scientific account of the determinants of behavior. As many researchers have stated, employing a baseline is the basis from which any statement of causality can be made (Baer, Wolf, & Risley, 1968; Chambless & Hollon, 1998; Johnston & Pennypacker, 2009; Martella et al., 1999; Sidman, 1960). Steady-state responding refers to the repeated measure of behavior until there is minimal variation among the data in a given condition (Johnston & Pennypacker, 2009). For example, a clinician may collect rate, duration, or magnitude data with the goal of changing the behavior along the given dimension. The clinician should continue to collect data in that condition (e.g., baseline) until it is possible to predict, with some degree of certainty, where the next data point might fall. As such, the more variable the responding over time (e.g., rates of 3 responses per minute, 20 responses per minute, and 10 responses per minute over three consecutive sessions), the longer the baseline should be because with highly variable data, it is more difficult to predict the next data point (e.g., any rate between 3 and 20 would be reasonable in the earlier example). In contrast, relatively stable data (e.g., rates of 7 responses per minute, 6 responses per minute, and 8 responses per minute over three consecutive sessions) more accurately predict behavior (e.g., a rate between 6 and 8 per minute would be expected in this scenario).

Although there are no universally accepted criteria for what level of behavior constitutes steady-state responding, Johnston and Pennypacker (2009) encourage researchers and clinicians to reference standards of the existing literature (i.e., how much stability exists in published studies on this behavior), the features of the response class (i.e., is this something that would be expected to vary from session to session or remain relatively stable), and the characteristics of control (i.e., how reasonable is it to rule out all sources of external influence on the data) when deciding how many data points are necessary.

Once baseline data achieve steady-state responding, it is possible to employ the baseline logic (Bailey & Burch, 2002), which is the essence of visual inspection for evaluating the relation between variables (i.e., the independent variable, which is the intervention, and dependent variable, which is the behavior being measured). A researcher or clinician employs the baseline logic when he or she assumes

that once steady-state responding has been observed, behavior would continue in a similar fashion if no intervention were put in place. That is, the variability (i.e., the range or bandwidth), trend (i.e., whether behavior is overall increasing, decreasing, or remaining the same), and the level (i.e., the mean of a data set) would remain the same. When an intervention is implemented and data do not fall along the path predicted by baseline data, the researcher or clinician has begun to show the impact of the independent variable. As with baseline, it is important to establish steady-state responding during intervention phases. Once steady-state responding during baseline and an intervention has been demonstrated, replication can begin.

In summary, single-subject designs are true experimental designs and allow for statements about functional relations between interventions and behavior. Such statements can be made when steady-state responding has been obtained during baseline, and the baseline logic is employed when evaluating an intervention. Finally, replication is key. In the following section, we describe several single-subject research designs, noting how baseline logic and replication occur within these designs, and provide examples of these designs in the published literature evaluating intervention efficacy in persons with autism.

Reversal Designs

Reversal designs (Johnston & Pennypacker, 2009) or withdrawal designs (Martella et al., 1999)[1] involve units of AB comparisons. The A condition constitutes the first of two conditions and B constitutes the second. Typically, the A condition is the control condition, that is, the condition in which the intervention (B condition) is not in place and to which the

---

[1] Martella et al. (1999) distinguish between reversal designs and withdrawal designs, noting that in a withdrawal design, the baseline condition consists of the lack of treatment, the intervention involves some treatment, and then that treatment is removed, resulting in a withdrawal of the treatment. They propose that the term *reversal designs*, on the other hand, should be saved for situations in which the contingencies for a behavior are reversed from one condition to the next. For example, reinforcing problem behavior while putting functionally communicative behavior on extinction during baseline, then reinforcing functionally communicative behavior and putting problem behavior on extinction during treatment.

intervention (B) condition will be compared. These conditions are then alternated once steady-state responding is observed in each. In general, the minimally accepted number of alternations is two, in which an A condition alternates with a B condition, which then alternates back to an A condition (i.e., an ABA design). In this scenario, the steady-state responding during the A condition is replicated. However, the change from A to B is shown only once and therefore the number of AB units should be two or more (i.e., ABAB design; Chambless & Hollon, 1998). In such a design, the steady-state responding of the A condition is replicated (i.e., *A*BA*B*), the steady-state responding of the B condition is replicated (i.e., A*B*A*B*), and the change from A to B is replicated (i.e., *AB AB*). Further replications might involve additional replications of conditions (ABABAB...) or determining the components of the intervention (B) that are responsible for the change. As such, following the ABAB comparison, the researcher might incorporate a modified B condition in which different variables are evaluated (e.g., ABABCBC; Johnston & Pennypacker, 2009).

There are many published studies utilizing ABAB reversal designs to evaluate interventions for individuals with autism spectrum disorders (e.g., Friedman & Luiselli, 2008; Koegel, Vernon, & Koegel, 2009; Leung & Wu, 1997; Mavropoulou, Papadooulou, & Kakana, 2011; Piazza et al., 1999). Piazza et al. (1999) utilized ABAB designs to evaluate both the efficacy of functional communication training (FCT) compared to baseline (the attention condition from the functional analysis) and the efficacy of FCT that incorporated praise compared to FCT that incorporated physical attention, with two boys diagnosed with autism spectrum disorders. In the first analysis, data on aggression and disruption per minute were collected until an increasing trend in data was present during baseline (i.e., steady-state responding), at which point an intervention of FCT with extinction was implemented and the rate of destructive responses reached zero levels. The condition was reversed back to baseline, at which point responding on an increasing trend, similar to the first baseline, was observed. Then, FCT with extinction was reintroduced and disruptive behaviors reached near zero levels again. The comparison of the different types of FCT was conducted in a similar fashion, in which steady-state responding was observed and the condition was reversed. This study provides an example for how an ABAB design can be used to provide evidence for a relation between the independent variable and the dependent variable.

Multielement Designs

Multielement designs are a variation on the reversal design in that a comparison of at least A to B is employed (Johnston & Pennypacker, 2009). However, instead of obtaining repeated measures in A before exposing the participant to the B condition, the conditions are rapidly (and often times randomly or quasi-randomly) alternated from session to session (e.g., session 1 = A, session 2 = B, session 3 = A, session 4 = A, session 5 = B, session 6 = A, session 7 = B, session 8 = B). Multielement designs are used when multiple approaches need to be evaluated in a relatively short time period. Unlike reversal designs, multielement designs, due to their rapid alternation, require discriminative stimuli to signal the change from one condition to the next (Bailey & Burch, 2002). Additionally, the interventions should be expected to have little to no carryover effect when changing from one condition to the next. As noted earlier, multielement designs typically involve a comparison of A to B, and the baseline logic can be applied in a multielement design similarly to a reversal design. That is, after repeated observations, a pattern of responding during the A condition (i.e., steady-state responding) is compared to the pattern of responding during the B condition. Additionally, the multielement design allows for numerous replications of the change from A to B and from B to A, as the conditions are rapidly alternated. Additional components can be added (e.g., C) and compared to the control condition (e.g., in an experimental functional analysis, the A condition or control condition is compared to the different test conditions). When the noncontrol conditions involve potential treatments, the multielement design is also called an alternating treatments design (Martella et al., 1999).

As noted earlier, multielement designs are common in experimental functional analyses but are also featured in treatment studies (e.g., Clark & Green, 2004, Devlin, Healy, Leader, & Hughes, 2011; Rispoli et al., 2011). Rispoli et al. (2011) provide an example of a relatively simple AB multielement design to evaluate presession exposure to tangible conditions and the impact on both challenging behavior and academic engagement among three boys with ASD. Rispoli et al. evaluated the impact of no presession exposure to preferred toys (A) and 20-minute exposure to preferred toys (B). The two conditions (A and B) were alternated each session (i.e., ABABABABABABAB). Steady-state responding occurred in both conditions, with presession exposure resulting in lower levels of challenging behavior and higher levels of academic behavior compared to no presession exposure. Each alternation from one condition to the next provided a replication of the previous change in responding (e.g., each change from A to B resulted in a decrease in challenging behavior and an increase in academic behavior). Devlin et al. (2011) also used the multielement design to the evaluate efficacy of a function-based behavioral intervention and sensory integration therapy (SIT) compared with baseline rates of challenging behavior among four boys diagnosed with ASD. The researchers collected baseline (A) data, then during phase 2, they presented the two interventions in a multielement design and used the intervention with largest, most stable decrease in challenging behavior in an extended final condition. It is important to note that the control condition data in Devlin et al. (2011) were obtained prior to the multielement design. To properly utilize baseline logic in this study, the authors compared the two interventions back to the control condition. That is, although two interventions were implemented, the appropriate comparison is back to the control condition, not between the two interventions.

Multiple-Baseline Designs

Although reversal and multielement designs provide robust demonstrations of the relation between variables, an underlying assumption for both designs is that the intervention can be reversed or withdrawn. Another assumption is that alternating between intervention and control condition will not harm a participant (Bailey & Burch, 2002). In instances where conditions cannot be reversed (e.g., when teaching a new skill) or when alternating between intervention and control condition would not be in the individual's best interest (e.g., interventions designed to reduce elopement from school or family), multiple-baseline designs can be used to evaluate the effects of an intervention.

Similar to reversal and multielement designs, multiple-baseline designs compare control conditions (A) to intervention conditions (B). However, the application of the baseline logic requires comparison data across participants, settings, and behaviors. For example, in a multiple-baseline design across participants, two or more participants experience a control condition (A). Once steady-state responding is observed, an intervention (B) is implemented for one participant, while the other participant remains in baseline. Ideally, the comparison in a multiple-baseline design occurs concurrently (i.e., baseline session 1 is obtained on the same day for the first participant as it is for the second participant). Next, assuming that responding for participant 1 in B is steady and responding for participant 2 in A is steady, participant 2 is moved to the B condition.

The baseline logic is applied to a multiple baseline across participants by comparing the steady-state responding for participant 1 during baseline (A) to the steady-state responding for participant 1 during intervention (B), resulting in the first AB comparison. At the same time, the responding of participant 1 (in B) is compared to the responding of participant 2 (who is still in A), resulting in a BA comparison. Once participant 2 is moved into the B condition, this allows for a comparison of the steady-state responding for participant 2 during baseline (A) to the steady-state responding during intervention (B), resulting in the second AB comparison. Thus, the multiple-baseline design results in two AB evaluations, an AA evaluation (participant 1 in baseline to participant 2 in baseline), a BB evaluation (participant 1 in treatment to participant 2 in treatment), and one BA evaluation (participant 1 in treatment to participant 2 in baseline). This is the same number of comparisons that are obtained in an ABAB reversal design (i.e., two AB evaluations, *AB AB*; an AA evaluation, *A*BA*B*; a BB evaluation, A*B*A*B*; and a BA evaluation, A*BA*B). However, the AA, BB, and BA evaluations in a multiple-baseline design are made between participants, settings, or behaviors, rather than within.

As noted earlier, the key assumption in reversal and multielement designs is that the independent variable can be withdrawn or reversed. In multiple-baseline designs, there is a different assumption: One leg of the multiple baseline can be impacted by introducing treatment in another. That is, if the design is across participants, a multiple baseline should only be used if there is a chance that intervening on one participant could impact another. When the participants are in different locations and do not interact with one another, it is unlikely that one could be affected by introducing the intervention on another (Johnston & Pennypacker, 2009). In this situation, it is inappropriate to apply the baseline logic described earlier, as it is not an appropriate comparison of conditions.

There are many research examples of multiple-baseline designs with individuals who have ASD (e.g., Carbone, Sweeney-Kerwin, Attansasio, & Kasper, 2010; Charlop-Christy, Carpenter, Le, LeBlanc, & Kellet, 2002; Miguel, Yang, Finn, & Ahearn, 2009; Whitcomb, Bass, & Luiselli, 2011; Williams, Perez-Gonzalez, & Vogt, 2003). Whitcomb et al. (2011) provide an eloquent example of a multiple-baseline design across behaviors when evaluating an early reading program (Headsprout®) for a child with autism. To reiterate, a multiple-baseline design should be utilized when there is a chance that reversing the intervention could cause unnecessary harm or if there is concern that the intervention cannot be reversed. In this case, the learning that occurred during exposure to Headsprout® could not be removed and therefore a multiple baseline across behaviors was an appropriate choice. Additionally, it was reasonable to believe that intervening on one word set using Headsprout® might impact other word sets, so the comparison across behaviors was also appropriate (Johnston & Pennypacker, 2009). Whitcomb et al. (2011) measured the percent reading accuracy for word sets and sampled four word sets each session. Once steady-state responding was observed in word set 1, the intervention was put in place for that word set only, while the remaining three sets remained in baseline. Next, the intervention was put in place for word set 2, such that word sets 1 and 2 were in intervention while word sets 3 and 4 were not. This continued until all word sets were in intervention. By utilizing four word sets, Whitcomb et al. (2011) were able to demonstrate four AB evaluations, six BA evaluations, four AA evaluations, and four BB evaluations, providing strong evidence for a functional relation between the variables of interest.

Multiple-baseline designs are well suited for evaluating educational and skill-building interventions. However, in some situations the repeated measures used in multiple-baseline designs present a threat to internal validity in the form of reactivity during baseline or practice effects (i.e., that the skill would develop as a result of repeated testing; Martella et al., 1999). A well-documented variation of the multiple-baseline design is the multiple-probe design, which involves fewer samples of the behavior during conditions but still adheres to the design components of a multiple-baseline design. Chan and O'Reilly (2008) employed a multiple-probe across behaviors design to evaluate a Social Stories™ treatment package. Chan and O'Reilly obtained three data points for the first behavior (inappropriate social interactions) before intervening. During that same time period, they obtained three data points on the percentage of opportunities of hand raising and one data point on the frequency of inappropriate vocalizations. During the initial evaluation of the intervention on inappropriate social interactions, which spanned four sessions, two more data points were collected on raising hand in baseline and only one more data point was obtained for inappropriate vocalizations in baseline. That is, data on the other two behaviors were probed, but not regularly assessed. During the initial evaluation of the intervention for raising hand, which spanned five sessions, four data points were obtained for inappropriate vocalizations in baseline. Thus, the investigators were still able to apply the baseline logic to evaluate the efficacy of the treatment, while minimizing repeated testing and data collection that may have impacted behavior.

Changing-Criteria Designs

In situations when behavior change should occur gradually, in a stepwise format, and it is unlikely that the terminal goal could be otherwise achieved, researchers and clinicians can implement a changing-criterion design. Changing-criterion designs are typically AB designs in which behavior changes systematically along some parameter during the B condition in which the researcher or clinician sets the criterion level of responding. If behavior matches this criterion and continues to do so as the researcher or clinician raises or lowers the criterion, evidence for the replication of the effect is obtained. Although changing-criteria designs are not common (Martella et al., 1999), there are examples of the design being used to evaluate interventions for individuals with ASD (Ganz & Flores, 2009; Gentry & Luiselli, 2008; O'Connor, Prieto, Hoffman, DeQuinzio, & Taylor, 2011; Schumacher & Rapp, 2011).

Gentry and Luiselli (2008) used a changing-criterion design to increase the number of bites taken by a boy diagnosed with ASD. During baseline (A), the boy did not take any bites of food. During the intervention (B), the boy spun a "Mystery Motivator" (a plastic game spinner with multiple sections, each with a number on it) and was instructed to eat as many bites as the number in the section that the spinner stopped on (e.g., if the spinner stopped on 2, he had to eat two bites from each section of the plate). If he responded compliantly, he was able to eat whatever else he wanted or leave to play a preselected activity. During the initial level of B, the criterion was set at 1 to 2 (the spinner had the numbers 1 and 2 in the sections) and the number of bites he consumed matched the number spun. That is, he typically took one or two bites, exceeding the number of bites observed in baseline. Over the next 36 sessions, the criterion gradually increased to 5 and 6 and the number of bites consumed matched the criteria. During the second intervention, the mystery motivator was removed and the boy was instructed to consume the number of bites that his mother put on the plate. Gentry and Luiselli (2008) added to the experimental control of the changing-criterion design by reducing the criterion back to 3 for this second intervention, even though the criterion had been 5 and 6 during the last phase of intervention I. Once again, the number of healthy bites consumed matched the criterion and reached the terminal goal.

Combination Designs

Each of the aforementioned designs can be used to demonstrate some level of relation between variables, and it is possible to combine these designs to provide even stronger evidence of relations. For example, Plavnick and Ferreri (2011) used a multiple-probe design with embedded multi-element designs to compare function-based and non-function-based video modeling for vocal mands across participants. For each participant, Plavnick and Ferreri (2011) used a multiple-probe design across behaviors combined with the multi-element design. As such, this combination design resulted in the three evaluations of AB, three evaluations of AA, three evaluations of BB, and three evaluations of BA that are inherent in a multiple-probe design with three legs. Additionally, within the three evaluations of AB, there was a within-behavior replication of the treatment effect when comparing the function-based intervention to baseline, as well as to the non-function-based intervention. The resulting combination design provided strong evidence for the relation between the change in the independent variable and the observed changes in the dependent variable.

Conclusion

Van Houten et al. (1988) recognized over 25 years ago that many individuals who would benefit from behavioral treatment were not receiving it, a conclusion that remains a concern in the current day.

Van Houten et al. (1988) further emphasize behavior analysts' professional obligation to make available the most effective treatment that the discipline can provide, which includes the delivery of treatment by a clinically competent behavior analyst, the obligation to use only those techniques that have been demonstrated by research to be effective, and continuously searching for the most optimal means of changing behavior. Implementing one's system of measurement according to the best practices outlined in this chapter is one component of this obligation, as is accurately employing and interpreting the efficacy of one's interventions using single-subject methodology. We hope this chapter provides some tools and resources for behavior analysts to be able to fulfill these ethical obligations, as well as the knowledge base to educate those outside of our discipline on best practices in ABA.

REFERENCES

Anglesea, M. M., Hoch, H., & Taylor, B. (2008). Reducing rapid eating in teenagers with autism: Use of a pager prompt. *Journal of Applied Behavior Analysis, 41,* 107–111.

Ayres, K. M., Maguire, A., & McClimon, D. (2009). Acquisition and generalization of chained tasks taught with computer based video instruction to children with autism. *Education and Training in Developmental Disabilities, 44,* 493–508.

Baer, D. M., Wolf, M. M., & Risley, T. R. (1968). Some current dimensions of applied behavior analysis. *Journal of Applied Behavior Analysis, 1,* 91–97.

Bailey, J. S., & Burch, M. R. (2002). *Research methods in applied behavior analysis.* Thousand Oaks, CA: Sage.

Batchelder, A., McLaughlin, T. F., Weber, K. P., Derby, K. M., & Gow, T. (2009). The effects of hand-over-hand and a dot-to-dot tracing procedure on teaching an autistic student to write his name. *Journal of Physical and Developmental Disabilities, 21,* 131–138.

Behavior Analysis Certification Board. (2010). *Guidelines for responsible conduct for behavior analysts.* Retrieved October 2012, from http://www.bacb.com/index.php?page=100165.

Binder, C. (1996). Behavioral fluency: Evolution of a new paradigm. *Behavior Analyst, 19,* 163–197.

Carbone, V. J., Sweeney-Kerwin, E. J., Attanasio, V., & Kasper, T. (2010). Increasing the vocal responses of children with autism and developmental disabilities using manual sign and training and prompt delay. *Journal of Applied Behavior Analysis, 43,* 705–709.

Carr, J. E., Austin, J. L., Britton, L. N., Kellum, K. K., & Bailey, J. S. (1999). As assessment of social validity trends in applied behavior analysis. *Behavior Interventions, 14*, 223–231.

Chambless, D. L., & Hollon, S. D. (1998). Defining empirically supported therapies. *Journal of Consulting and Clinical Psychology, 66*, 7–18.

Chan, J. M., & O'Reilly, M. F. (2008). A social stories intervention package for students with autism in inclusive classroom settings. *Journal of Applied Behavior Analysis, 41*, 405–409.

Charlop-Christy, M. H., Carpenter, M., Le, L., LeBlanc, L. A., & Kellet, K. (2002). Using the picture exchange communication system (PECS) with children with autism: Assessment of PECS acquisition, speech, social-communicative behavior, and problem behavior. *Journal of Applied Behavior Analysis, 35*, 213–231.

Clark, K. M., & Green, G. (2004). Comparison of two procedures for teaching dictated-words/symbol relations to learners with autism. *Journal of Applied Behavior Analysis, 37*, 503–507.

Digennaro-Reed, F. D., Codding, R., Catania, C. N., & Maguire, H. (2010). Effects of video modeling on treatment integrity of behavioral interventions. *Journal of Applied Behavior Analysis, 43*, 291–295.

Detrich, R. (2008). Evidence-based, empirically supported, or best practice? A guide for the scientist-practitioner. In J. K. Luiselli, D. C. Russo, W. P. Christian, & S. M. Wilczynski (Eds.), *Effective practices for children with autism* (pp. 3–25). New York, NY: Oxford University Press.

Devlin, S., Healy, O., Leader, G., & Hughes, B. M. (2011). Comparison of behavioral intervention and sensory-integration therapy in the treatment of challenging behavior. *Journal of Autism and Developmental Disorders, 41*, 1303–1320.

Donohue, M. M., Casey, L. B., Bicard, D. F., & Bicard, S. E. (2012). Effects of differential reinforcement of short latencies on response latency, task completion, and accuracy of an adolescent with autism. *Education and Training in Autism and Developmental Disabilities, 47*, 97–108.

Dorminy, K. P., Luscre, D., & Gast, D. L. (2009). Teaching organizational skills to children with high functioning autism and Asperger's syndrome. *Education and Training in Developmental Disabilities, 44*, 538–550.

Friedman, A., & Luiselli, J. K. (2008). Excessive daytime sleep: Behavioral assessment and intervention in a child with autism. *Behavior Modification, 32*, 548–555.

Ganz, J. B., & Flores, M. M. (2009). The effectiveness of direct instruction for teaching language to children with autism spectrum disorders: Identify materials. *Journal of Autism and Developmental Disorders, 39*, 75–83.

Gentry, J. A., & Luiselli, J. K. (2008). Treating a child's selective eating through parent implemented feeding intervention in the home setting. *Journal of Developmental and Physical Disabilities, 20*, 63–70.

Golnik, A. E., & Ireland, M. (2009). Complementary alternative medicine for children with autism: A physician's survey. *Journal of Autism and Developmental Disorders, 39*, 996–1005.

Grannan, L., & Rehfeldt, R. A. (2012). Emergent intraverbal responses via tact and match-to-sample instruction. *Journal of Applied Behavior Analysis, 45*, 601–605.

Gresham, F. M., Gansle, K. A., & Noell, G. H. (1993). Treatment integrity in applied behavior analysis with children. *Journal of Applied Behavior Analysis, 26*, 257–263.

Hagopian, L. P., Kuhn, D. E., & Strother, G. E. (2009). Targeting social skills deficits in an adolescent with pervasive developmental disorder. *Journal of Applied Behavior Analysis, 42*, 907–911.

Hanson, E., Kalish, L. A., Bunce, E., Curtis, C., McDaniel, S., Ware, J., & Petry, J. (2007). Use of complementary and alternative medicine among children diagnosed with autism spectrum disorder. *Journal of Autism and Developmental Disorders, 37*, 628–636.

Hartmann, D. P. (1977). Considerations in the choice of interobserver reliability estimates. *Journal of Applied Behavior Analysis, 10*, 103–116.

Hayes, S. C., Barlow, D. H., & Nelson-Gray, R. O. (1999). *The scientist practitioner: Research and accountability in the age of managed care* (2nd ed.). Needham Heights, MA: Allyn & Bacon.

Ingvarsson, E. T., & Hollobaugh, T. (2011). A comparison of prompting tactics to establish intraverbals in children with autism. *Journal of Applied Behavior Analysis, 44*, 659–664.

Jerome, J., Frantino, E. P., & Sturmey, P. (2007). The effects of errorless learning and backward chaining on the acquisition of internet skills in adults with developmental disabilities. *Journal of Applied Behavior Analysis, 40*, 185–189.

Johnston, J. M., & Pennypacker, H. S. (2009). *Strategies and tactics of behavioral research* (3rd ed.). New York, NY: Routledge.

Kazdin, A. E. (1977). Artifact, bias, and complexity of assessment: The abcs of reliability. *Journal of Applied Behavior Analysis, 10*, 141–150.

Kazdin, A. E. (2011). *Single-case research designs: Methods for clinical and applied settings.* (2nd ed.) New York, NY: Oxford University Press.

Keintz, K. S., Miguel, C. F., Kao, B., & Finn, H. E. (2011). Using conditional discrimination training to produce emergent relations between coins and their values in children with autism. *Journal of Applied Behavior Analysis, 44*, 909–913.

Koegel, R. L., Vernon, T. W., & Koegel, L. K. (2009). Improving social initiations in young children with autism using reinforcers with embedded social interactions. *Journal of Autism and Developmental Disorders, 39*, 1240–1251.

Kubina, R. M., Morrison, R., & Lee, D. L. (2002). Benefits of adding precision teaching to behavioral interventions for students with autism. *Behavioral Interventions, 17*, 233–246.

Long, E. S. (2006, February). *The National Standards Project: Promoting evidence-based education and treatment practices for autism.* Paper presented to the California Association for Behavior Analysis, Burlingame, CA.

Leung, J., & Wu, K. (1997). Teaching receptive naming of Chinese characters to children with autism by incorporating echolalia. *Journal of Applied Behavior Analysis, 30,* 59–68.

Machalicek, W., Shogren, K., Lang, R., Rispoli, M., O'Reilly, M. F., Franco, J. H., & Sigafoos, J. (2009). Increasing play and decreasing the challenging behavior of children with autism during recess with activity schedules and task correspondence training. *Research in Autism Spectrum Disorders, 3,* 547–555.

Martella, R. C., Nelson, J. R., & Marchand-Martella, N. E. (1999). *Research methods: Learning to become a critical research consumer.* Boston, MA: Allyn & Bacon.

Mavropoulou, S., Papadopoulou, E., & Kakana, D. (2011). Effects of task organization on the independent play of students with autism spectrum disorders. *Journal of Autism and Developmental Disorders, 41,* 913–925.

Mayer, G. R., Sulzer-Azaroff, B., & Wallace, M. (2012). *Behavior analysis for lasting change* (2nd ed.). Cornwall-on-Hudson, NY: Sloan.

McIntyre, L. L., Gresham, F. M., DiGennaro, F. D., & Reed, D. D. (2007). Treatment integrity of school-based interventions with children in the journal of applied behavior analysis. *Journal of Applied Behavior Analysis, 40,* 659–672.

Miguel, C. F., Clark, K., Tereshko, L., & Ahearn, W. H. (2009). The effects of response interruption and redirection and sertraline on vocal stereotypy. *Journal of Applied Behavior Analysis, 42,* 883–888.

Miguel, C. F., Yang, H. G., Finn, H. E., & Ahearn, W. H. (2009). Establishing derived textual control in activity schedules with children with autism. *Journal of Applied Behavior Analysis, 42,* 703–709.

Myers, S. M., & Johnson, C. P. (2007). Management of children with autism spectrum disorders. *Pediatrics, 120,* 1162–1182.

O'Connor, A. S., Prieto, J., Hoffmann, B., DeQuinzio, J. A., & Taylor, B. (2011). A stimulus control procedure to decrease motor and vocal stereotypy. *Behavioral Interventions, 26,* 231–242.

Odom, S. L., Brown, W. H., Frey, T., Karasu, N., Smith-Canter, L. L., & Strain, P. S. (2003). Evidence-based practices for young children with autism: Contributions for single-subject design research. *Focus on Autism and Other Developmental Disabilities, 18,* 166–175.

Peterson, L., Homer, A. L., & Wonderlich, S. A. (1982). The integrity of independent variables in behavior analysis. *Journal of Applied Behavior Analysis, 15,* 477–492.

Piazza, C. C., Bowman, L. G., Contrucci, S. A., Delia, M. D., Adelinis, J. D., & Goh, H. (1999). An evaluation of the properties of attention as reinforcement for destructive and appropriate behavior. *Journal of Applied Behavior Analysis, 32,* 437–449.

Plavnick, J. B., & Ferreri, S. J. (2011). Establishing verbal repertoires in children with autism using function-based video modeling. *Journal of Applied Behavior Analysis, 44,* 747–766.

Rispoli, M. J., O'Reilly, M. F., Sigafoos, J., Lang, R., Kang, S., Lancioni, G., & Parker, R. (2011). Effects of presession satiation on challenging behavior and academic engagement for children with autism during classroom instruction. *Education and Training in Autism and Developmental Disabilities, 46,* 607–618.

Schumacher, B. I., & Rapp, J. T. (2011). Increasing compliance with haircuts in a child with autism. *Behavioral Interventions, 26,* 67–75.

Schwartz, I. S., & Baer, D. (1991). Social validity assessments: Is current practice state of the art? *Journal of Applied Behavior Analysis, 24,* 189–204.

Shabani, D. B., Katz, R. C., Wilder, D. A., Beauchamp, K., Taylor, C. R., & Fischer, K. J. (2002). Increasing social initiations in children with autism: Effects of a tactile prompt. *Journal of Applied Behavior Analysis, 35,* 79–83.

Sidener, T. M., Carr, J. E., & Firth, A. M. (2005). Superimposition and withholding of edible consequences as treatment for automatically reinforced stereotypy. *Journal of Applied Behavior Analysis, 38,* 121–124.

Sidman, M. (1960). *Tactics of scientific research: Evaluating experimental design in psychology.* Boston, MA: Authors Cooperative.

Soares, D. A., Vannest, K. J., & Harrison, J. (2009). Computer aided self-monitoring to increase academic production and reduce self-injurious behavior in a child with autism. *Behavioral Interventions, 24,* 171–183.

Taplin, P. S., & Reid, J. B. (1973). Effects of instructional set and experimenter influence on observer reliability. *Child Development, 44,* 547–554.

Taylor, B. A., & Hoch, H. (2008). Teaching children with autism to respond to and initiate bids for joint attention. *Journal of Applied Behavior Analysis, 41,* 377–391.

Tiger, J. H., Bouxsein, K. J., & Fisher, W. W. (2007). Treating excessively slow responding of a young man with Asperger syndrome using differential reinforcement of short response latencies. *Journal of Applied Behavior Analysis, 40,* 559–563.

Ulke-Kurkcuoglu, B., & Kircaali-Iftar, G. (2010). A comparison of the effects of providing activity and material choice to children with autism spectrum disorders. *Journal of Applied Behavior Analysis, 43,* 717–721.

Van Houten, R., Axelrod, S., Bailey, J. S., Favell, J. E., Foxx, R. M., Iwata, B. A., & Lovaas, O. I. (1988). The right to effective behavioral treatment. *Journal of Applied Behavior Analysis, 21,* 381–384.

Watanabe, M., & Sturmey, P. (2003). The effect of choice-making opportunities during activity schedules on task engagement of adults with autism. *Journal of Autism and Developmental Disorders, 33,* 535–538.

Weiss, M. J. (2001). Expanding ABA intervention in intensive programs for children with autism: The inclusion of natural environment training and fluency based instruction. *Behavior Analyst Today, 2,* 182–186.

Wheeler, J. J., Baggett, B. A., Fox, J., & Blevins, L. (2006). Treatment integrity: A review of intervention studies conducted with children with autism. *Focus on Autism and Other Developmental Disabilities, 21,* 45–54.

Whitcomb, S. A., Bass, J. D., & Luiselli, J. K. (2011). Effects of computer-based early reading program (Headsprout®) on word list and text reading skills in a student with autism. *Journal of Developmental and Physical Disabilities, 23,* 491–499.

Williams, G., Perez-Gonzalez, L. A., & Vogt, K. (2003). The role of specific consequences in the maintenance of three types of questions. *Journal of Applied Behavior Analysis, 36,* 285–296.

Wolf, M. M. (1978). Social validity: The case for subjective measurement or how applied behavior analysis is finding its heart. *Journal of Applied Behavior Analysis, 11,* 203–214.

SECTION II

Evidence-Based Practices

4

Early Intensive Behavioral Intervention

Current Status and Future Directions

LINDA A. LEBLANC, NATALIE A. PARKS, AND NICOLE M. HANNEY

Early and intensive behavioral intervention (EIBI) is generally defined as comprehensive applied behavior analytic programming to target a broad range of skills critical to early childhood development. This approach to intervention with young children with autism is the only intervention to meet the stringent criteria for qualification as a well-established and efficacious intervention, according to the American Psychological Association's evaluation rubric for evaluating the level of empirical support for interventions (Eikeseth, 2009; Eldevik et al., 2009; Reichow & Wolery, 2009). This category requires multiple controlled trials of the intervention compared with various reasonable controls with clear evidence of the superiority of the target intervention (Chambliss & Hollon, 1998). Early intensive behavioral intervention is also the only intervention for autism that has been endorsed by the Surgeon General (US Department of Health and Human Services, 1999).

The purpose of EIBI is to increase intellectual (i.e., communication, cognitive, academic) skills and adaptive functioning (i.e., social skills, self-care skills, safety) and decrease the core autism spectrum disorder (ASD) symptoms and deficits to prepare children to learn from, and succeed in, typical home and school environments with the fewest possible supports (Green, 1996; Lovaas, 1987; Lovaas & Smith, 2003; McEachin, Smith, & Lovaas, 1993). These goals are achieved by creating a precise and sophisticated instructional environment for as many of the child's waking hours as possible, at the youngest age possible, to alter the developmental trajectory in all areas of functioning. Perhaps the most critical repertoires targeted are the learning-to-learn skills (e.g., imitation, following instructions, initiating interactions) that allow children to learn from more typical

environments in ways that are similar to their peers (Green, 1996; Lovaas & Smith, 2003). Large and sustained improvements in specific skills and in overall functioning increase the likelihood that a child will continue to be able to succeed throughout life with less intensive behavioral supports (McEachin et al., 1993).

Although various models of EIBI exist, they all share three primary characteristics: (a) intensive treatment delivery (e.g., 30–40 hours per week for 2 years); (b) a hierarchically organized curriculum that focuses on learning readiness, communication, social, and preacademic repertoires (e.g., Leaf & McEachin, 1999; Lovaas, 2002; Romanczyk, Lochshin, & Matey, 1996); and (c) use of teaching methods based on the principles of operant conditioning. Although multiple well-controlled investigations have been conducted on EIBI, the most well known is the initial investigation of the UCLA Young Autism Project conducted by Ivar Lovaas (1987). Lovaas compared data from a group of 19 children diagnosed with autism receiving 40 hours per week of services to two control groups receiving fewer hours and standard community care in their geographic area. The results showed that 47% of children who received 40 hours per week of EIBI services were placed in general education and on average had an IQ increase of 37 points. These children who achieved the "best outcome" status were successfully integrated into regular education environments with substantial reduction in readily apparent characteristics of autism. In addition to these best outcome cases, an additional 42% of the children in this EIBI group improved significantly and were placed in a less restrictive classroom environment and displayed increased IQ scores. These results were even more striking when compared to the two control groups in which there were no substantial changes in IQ, and only one child was placed into a general education classroom environment. This finding of substantial change for the intervention group and poorer outcomes for control groups has since been replicated several times by independent investigators (Cohen, Amerine-Dickens, & Smith, 2006; Howard, Sparkman, Cohen, Green, & Stanislaw, 2005; Reichow & Woolery, 2009; Sallows & Graupner, 2005), whereas no other treatment approach has been able to replicate the magnitude of these effects for children with ASD.

The publication of the landmark treatment outcome study (Lovaas, 1987) sparked substantial controversy in both behavioral and nonbehavioral professional communities. The study was criticized by behavioral psychologists for various deviations from standard randomized clinical trial methodologies (Gresham & MacMillan, 1988, 1997). For example, the lack of random assignment to treatment condition has been sharply criticized though sound arguments have been made about the ethical issues associated with random assignment to nontreatment control groups and the likelihood of pursuit of alternative treatments in such control groups (Smith & Lovaas, 1997). In addition, use of the term "recovery" from autism to describe the dramatic improvement in intellectual capabilities and characteristic language and social deficits proved to be a lightning rod for critics who have alternatively been criticized by researchers who suggest that the children in the original study must not have had autism at all. Additionally, autism advocates objected to the implication that autism is a condition from which one should recover. Subsequent popular press publications such as *Let Me Hear Your Voice* (Maurice, 1994) describe the transformation in functioning and life potential of individuals who were fortunate enough to receive sustained access to high-quality EIBI services. The dissemination of these outcomes has consistently driven legislative change, and as of 2013, the majority of states had adopted insurance reform legislation that funded the provision of behavioral intervention services for individuals with autism.

Although the empirical evidence for the effects of EIBI as a treatment for autism is substantially stronger than the evidence for any other intervention (see summary of reviews), the literature is consistently scrutinized by critics, and important research questions still need to be examined (Smith, 2013). In

this chapter we summarize the current evidence base for overall effectiveness and identify variables that appear to predict desirable outcomes. In addition, the chapter outlines important directions for future research and potential threats associated with misuse or misinterpretation of research findings.

IMPORTANT CONCERNS

Prior to examining the evidence base directly, it is important to acknowledge several critical issues that arise with interpretation and use of the data. Three of the most critical concerns will be explored here: research methodology mismatches, motivations for use of the data, and diversification of intervention models.

First, the evidence base for EIBI has been generated by behavior analysts primarily interested in the scientific application of learning theory. These scientists have a strong propensity to use single-case design methodologies to examine the effects of specific component variables and mechanisms of action for interventions (Smith, 2013). Single-case methodologies can offer a substantial degree of experimental control and great confidence about the extent to which the independent variable produced changes in the dependent variable (Kazdin, 2010). However, the vast majority of users and synthesizers of treatment outcome studies are unfamiliar with these methodologies and have a strong preference for randomized controlled trials as a gold standard for scientific investigation. Thus, the consumers of the evidence base share different scientific preferences and training from the creators of the evidence base (Smith, 2013).

The mismatch in preferred methodologies creates substantial disconnects in the interpretation of the findings and conclusions about the potential impact of EIBI. For example, an enormous number of studies document the effectiveness of specific teaching procedures incorporated in EIBI programming with comparisons of strategies for targeting specific skills. This formative evaluation research has been conducted using single-subject designs, and the results have been used to refine and improve EIBI practices to produce more robust generalization of skills and faster rates of acquisition in comparison to initial treatment procedures. However, external, independent reviewers of the literature who have not actually conducted any of this research have focused on summative evaluation research and do not identify this literature during searches or dismiss these studies from their syntheses due to the alternative research designs (Smith, 2013). In recent years, behavior analysts familiar with single-subject designs have crafted guidelines for evaluating the scientific merit of studies employing the designs, illustrating how to incorporate this research base into analyses with group design methodologies (Horner et al., 2005; Horner & Kratochwill, 2011). In addition, behavioral researchers have conducted meta-analyses of components of the behavioral literature on treatment of autism using various indices of the scale of effects, including standard effect sizes and the percentage of nonoverlapping data points (PND) (Bellini & Akullian, 2007; Reichow & Woolery, 2009; Tincani & Davis, 2011). Whether the standard is group design, randomized clinical trials, or quantitative analyses of single-subject design studies, there is strong evidence for the effects of EIBI and applied behavior analysis (ABA) for children with ASD.

Second, both the creators and the synthesizers of the evidence base always have some purpose for their analysis. For scientists, the motivation is often to examine the impact of a specific independent variable at large scale or to identify predictor variables that allow researchers to account for variance in outcomes. Our understanding of behavioral mechanisms of change is enhanced by knowing the factors contributing to variance. However, funders of services often have entirely different motivations for such analyses and are likely to interpret and use research findings in ways that are surprising and unintended by researchers. For example, Blue Cross Blue Shield commissioned their own evaluation of the evidence base for EIBI and concluded that there were no substantial effects of EIBI/ABA. This commissioned study has been introduced repeatedly as evidence against the effectiveness of EIBI in an effort to control mandatory expenditures of authorized benefits for their insured consumers. Third-party funders are likely eager to see studies of variables that would predict nonoptimal responsiveness to intervention and can be expected to use such findings to justify termination of services or refusal to pay for services for these individuals in spite of the benefits that are produced by intervention even for those who do not eventually achieve best outcome status.

As services have become more available, various approaches to therapy have been branded in the marketplace. Although these approaches are all essentially applied behavior analytic interventions,

the creators are motivated to distinguish their services from others and create proprietary terms for their products. This branding has led to a confusing array of terms being applied both in the scientific literature and in the professional market. For example, the term *discrete trial teaching or discrete trial training* (DTT) has often been used as a synonym for UCLA model programming (Lovaas, 2002). However, the first term refers specifically to the primary teaching procedure, while the second term (i.e., UCLA model) refers to the overall intervention approach, including the curriculum, preferred primary teaching procedure, and structured approach to supervision and training. Alternatively, models such as Pivotal Response Training have been copyrighted and popularized, giving the impression that they are separate from ABA or EIBI though they are based on the same principles of operant learning and use many of the same procedures identified in the behavioral literature such as incidental teaching and natural language paradigm (Koegel & Koegel, 2006). The creators of such approaches usually conduct the studies to evaluate the effectiveness of their proprietary interventions, which can lead to professional overattachment and concern about the effects of the intervention in broader application (Koegel, Koegel, Vernon, & Brookman-Frazee, 2010). Note these same concerns were raised about the application of UCLA model programming prior to the successful independent replication of the model—the same concerns are likely to arise with each new variation of EIBI (Gresham & MacMillan, 1988). The dissemination of these new proprietary models often precedes publication of carefully controlled studies comparing the model to the gold-standard UCLA program (Carr & Firth, 2006).

Third, the best outcomes with EIBI seem to be achieved when universities are involved in their creation and evaluation and when grant funding allows a level of rigor that may or may not be fully attainable in private-sector service delivery (Lovaas, 1987; McEachin et al., 1993; Sallows & Graupner, 2005). When less optimal models (i.e., parent training model; parent-directed in-home programs) have been examined, the outcomes have typically been less robust (Bibby, Eikeseth, Martin, Mudford, & Reeves, 2002; Smith, Wynn, & Groen, 2000). Better early screening procedures for autism and the enactment of legislation to mandate coverage of intervention services have created more demand for behavior analysts to deliver the services in virtually every corner of the United States (LeBlanc, Heinicke, & Baker, 2012). However, the university-based training programs have not been able to keep pace with the increasing demand, thereby creating the possibility of quality control issues in available programming and in university training models. This supply and demand imbalance could mean that services remain unavailable to many families or that the services that are available do not produce the impact that has been achieved and documented in the literature. The task facing the field at this point is detailed analysis of the existing literature, careful planning for the next wave of critical studies, and dissemination of the impacts of EIBI in a readily consumable format.

CURRENT STATUS OF THE EVIDENCE FOR EARLY AND INTENSIVE BEHAVIORAL INTERVENTION

Over the past 25 years, researches have continued to investigate EIBI services and several studies have replicated Lovaas's (1987) robust effects for children receiving EIBI services as compared to nontreatment groups. Based on comparison studies, systematic reviews, and meta-analyses, the results indicate that EIBI is still the most effective intervention for children with ASD. Within the past 10 years, several comparison studies of children receiving EIBI services and other treatment options have not only discussed outcome measures (e.g., increase in IQ, differences in language) but also specific predictor variables, namely age of child, intensity of services, amount of supervision, parental involvement, and types of effective reinforcers that could optimize treatment effects. See the summary of recent studies in EIBI for a description of several of these studies and the summary of reviews for information on several systematic reviews and meta-analyses.

Often times studies have compared those receiving EIBI services to those receiving a variety of other services. These services are typically referred to as "treatment as usual" or "eclectic intervention" and often include treatments like speech therapy, the TEACCH program, or sensory integration therapy. Remington et al. (2007) examined outcomes for 44 children approximately 3 years old diagnosed with autism who were either receiving EIBI services or treatment as usual from local service providers. The children in the EIBI group received home-based services for an average of 25.6 hours per week for a duration of 2 years. The services included both DTT and naturalistic teaching

strategies as well as inclusion of verbal behavior concepts. Those children in the comparison group most frequently received either speech therapy or programs implementing TEACCH principles and procedures. Results were that 26% of children in the EIBI group and 14% of children in the comparison group showed significant increase in IQ, respectively.

Eldevik, Jahr, Eikeseth, Hastings, and Hughes (2010) also compared outcomes for groups of children ranging in age from 2 to 6 years old who either received early behavioral intervention (EBI) services or eclectic interventions. The EBI group received services for an average of 10.3 hours per week (note: this volume of services would not be considered intensive) for an average of 12.1 months, whereas the eclectic intervention group received services for a similar duration per week and an average of 14.8 months. The EBI group received standard behavioral intervention services using the concepts of ABA, which included adequate staff training, experienced supervisors, parental involvement, and 1:1 teaching sessions. The eclectic intervention group received several intervention types, including alternative communication, ABA, sensory motor therapies, and TEACCH. All programming for this group was supervised by a special education teacher. The results also showed that those participants in the EBI group made significant gains in IQ and communication when compared to the eclectic group. There were not substantial differences between groups when adaptive behavior gains were evaluated.

Strauss and colleagues (2012) evaluated the outcomes of children who received EIBI services versus eclectic services. The EIBI services were implemented in both a preschool-type setting and in the home environment in which caregivers delivered services for 25 hours per week. These programs emphasized DTT sessions, as well as incidental and natural environment teaching, with programs developed from ABA and verbal behavior concepts. The EIBI services also included an intensive parent training program with weekly supervision meetings since those services in the home were parent mediated. Children in the eclectic intervention group received only 12 hours per week of a variety of programs such as speech and music therapy. The results showed that those children receiving EIBI services had significant decreases in the severity of core features of autism, especially in language production, as compared to the children in the eclectic intervention group. While both groups showed increases in receptive language skills and adaptive behavior skills, only those children in the EIBI group demonstrated significant increases in expressive language skills.

Eldevik, Hastings, Jahr, and Hughes (2012) compared outcomes for 31 children diagnosed with autism either receiving EIBI services or treatment as usual (speech therapy and TEACCH) from a local preschool service provider. After 2 years of intervention, the children receiving EIBI services showed significant increases in IQ, adaptive behaviors, and communication and social skills as compared with the treatment as usual group.

Overall, when EIBI services were compared to other eclectic treatments such as speech therapy, sensory integration therapy, and TEACCH, children showed more gains in communication and IQ scores than those who received these other treatments. In summary, EIBI services have been repeatedly shown to be effective and to result in better overall outcomes than other treatments. Each study differs slightly in the mode of implementation, the number of hours of therapy, and parental involvement, which makes it challenging to determine exactly which variables are most important when predicting outcomes.

Granpeesheh, Dixon, Tarbox, Kaplan, and Wilke (2009) investigated the intensity of EIBI services as a predictor of a child's number of acquired behavioral targets per month. All 245 children included in the analysis were diagnosed with either autism or PDD-NOS and ranged in age from 16 months to 12 years. These children received an average of 76.65 hours per month of EIBI services with a substantial range of 20.25 to 168.88 hours per month. The results were analyzed by parsing data into three age groups: (a) 2.00–5.15 years old, (b) 5.15–7.14 years old, and (c) 7.14–12.00 years old. Those children in the youngest age group showed a greater number of mastered targets while receiving less intense EIBI services as compared to children in the oldest age group receiving a similar amount of services. The children in the youngest group receiving more intense EIBI services (40 hours per week) mastered a greater number of targets compared to those who received less intensive services. However, the children in the oldest group averaged around the same number of mastered targets per month regardless of intensity of services. In general, the results showed that when services are provided at a younger age, more intensive services were associated with greater skill gains in the form of more behavioral acquisition targets mastered per month.

Luiselli, Cannon, Ellis, and Sisson (2000) investigated age as a predictor for overall outcomes. They examined outcomes for 16 children diagnosed with autism who began receiving home-based EIBI services either before or after the age of 3 years. Trained therapists implemented the services in the home environment using DTT and incidental teaching. No differences were found between the overall progress of children within both groups, as they improved significantly on measures of language and social domains after similar lengths of treatment. Thus, this study illustrates that children can make substantial gains even when services are not initiated at the youngest ages as long as the services are of reasonable intensity and duration.

Eikeseth, Hayward, Gale, Gitlesen, and Eldevik (2009) examined the effects of frequency of supervision on changes in IQ scores for 20 preschool-aged children diagnosed with autism receiving EIBI services. Each child's consultant conducted a team meeting with the child, tutors, and caregivers on average either every 3, 4, or 6 weeks, ranging from 2.9 hours to 7.8 hours per month. During the team meetings, the consultant reviewed the child's data and determined whether program modifications should be implemented. The directors of the EIBI program then provided supervision to the consultants. The children whose consultants delivered more frequent supervision showed a greater increase in IQ score between intake and follow-up measures. More frequent opportunities to review and make changes in programming may maximize the impact of intervention hours by ensuring ineffective strategies are altered more quickly and that new skills are introduced as rapidly as possible. The authors also indicated that there might be a ceiling at which a certain frequency or intensity of supervision corresponds with optimal effects for a child with no added benefit of increased frequency beyond that point. However, to date there have been no direct parametric evaluations of supervision provided at 1- or 2-week intervals, which are probably most common in professional practice. The optimal frequency and intensity of supervision might also be impacted by child characteristics, such as, IQ, age at intake, multiple diagnoses, and history with EIBI services. Additional factors, such as competency of tutors and parental involvement, might also contribute to the effectiveness of an optimal level of supervision.

Finally, Klintwall and Eikeseth (2012) investigated outcomes for 21 children diagnosed with autism ranging in age from 2.30 years to 4.11 years. These children received EIBI services from a clinic for an average of 20 hours per week. The results showed that there was a positive relation between treatment effects and the number of socially mediated reinforcers. This finding illustrates the importance of examining the impact of participant characteristics as well as intervention parameters, as there are likely interaction effects in the observed outcomes.

In summary, substantial research demonstrates the effectiveness of EIBI, but the results about various predictor variables are somewhat idiosyncratic. Various factors, including the intensity of services, the age of the child at the onset of services, level of parent involvement, intensity and timing of the supervision of programming, and participant characteristics such as the variety of socially mediated reinforcers, could all potentially be important determinants in the magnitude of treatment effects for children with autism. However, many of these findings have not been replicated and some of the findings contradict other findings. The specifics about many of these variables remain unknown and further research is necessary to ensure that we have fully explored the combined and interactive effects of these variables on treatment results.

PRACTICE
RECOMMENDATIONS

Based on the research literature to date, professionals delivering and supervising EIBI services should consider the following parameters when developing their programming: the intensity of services and supervision, the setting of the services, the implementers of the services, the criteria for existing services, and the selection and ordering of targets and teaching procedures. While EIBI programs have repeatedly proven effective as an evidence-based practice (Eldevik, Hastings, Jahr, & Hughes, 2012; Freeman, & Perry, 2010; Kovshoff, Hastings, & Remington, 2011; Luiselli, Cannon, Ellis, & Sisson, 2000; O'Connor & Healy, 2010; Reichow, 2012; Remington et al., 2007; Warren et al., 2011), relatively little research has evaluated specific practice standards, notwithstanding publication of federal and state guidelines about treatment for children with autism (Behavior Analyst Certification Board, 2012; California Department of Education, 1997; Missouri Autism Guidelines Initiative, 2010; National Autism Center, 2009). We highlight four of these guidelines next.

Determine Entry and Exit Criteria

Determine clear entrance and exit criteria for services prior to establishing your program with a consumer. First, determine the overall purpose of programming and whether the family is capable of engaging in EIBI services at a level that will facilitate effective outcomes. Ensure that the family is well informed about the nature and recommended intensity of services necessary to impact functioning significantly. The family should evaluate their options for time and financial investment and their willingness to fully engage as involved members of the treatment team prior to initiating services. Second, determine the critical skills and behavioral improvement that must be achieved for services to no longer be deemed necessary. One method to determine the target level of functioning for discharge is to compare the consumer's level of functioning with his or her typically developing peers with a goal of accelerating development until the child with autism "catches up" in developmental level based on standardized measures and observations within natural settings. Generally, once children are able to function independently in and learn from their natural settings, specific EIBI services may no longer be warranted though a lower intensity of services may be required to ensure that any achieved gains are maintained over time.

Exit criteria should also be set to determine whether services should continue when progress is slow or nonexistent. In these situations children may not be benefitting from the current services and alternatives may need to be explored. The alternatives might involve a change in programming with the same provider or a different model of services altogether. There is no experimental evidence at this time to guide setting these exit criteria. However, it is important to note that children who are continuing to gain skills are benefitting from programming even if they are not achieving gains at the level of the "best outcome" participants in the Lovaas (1987) study. When children are not progressing at a rate determined to be beneficial, consider several factors before deciding whether services should be discontinued. First, mastery criteria and data collection procedures should be reviewed to ensure that the data accurately reflect the child's progress. Second, the quality of intervention implementation should be evaluated to ensure that treatment is being delivered consistently and as programmed. Finally, consider whether the services are occurring at an insufficient intensity to produce improvements that might occur with more intensive services.

In addition to the general entrance and exit criteria for services, establish specific criteria for progressing through the selected EIBI curriculum. If the overall exit criterion is effective independent functioning in a general education kindergarten setting without supports, select a curriculum to target all necessary skills. Include objective criteria for progressing through the skill targets so that progress can be easily documented and measured throughout intervention prior to transition to the target setting. As data are collected to evaluate individual skills mastery, specify whether the skills must be evident during single naturalistic probes or perhaps in the context of intermixed teaching trials. Data collected during initial naturalistic probes are often referred to as discontinuous data because all performance opportunities are not captured, whereas continuous data include performance on all teaching trials. Targets may be mastered more quickly using discontinuous data collection methods; however, maintenance is stronger when continuous data collection procedures are used (Cummings & Carr, 2009; Lerman, Dettlinger, Fentress, & Lanagan, 2011).

Provide Services Early and Intensively

Intervention services should be intensive and initiated at the earliest age possible to produce the greatest chance of successful outcomes. Current research has repeatedly shown that those who receive 25–40 hours of intervention per week most often achieve the best outcomes (Howard et al., 2005; LeBlanc & Gillis, 2012; Lovaas & Smith, 2003; Reichow & Woolery, 2009; Sallows & Graupner, 2005; Smith et al., 2000). In addition, these services should be provided for 2–3 years and initiated at a young age (i.e., below the age of 3 years for onset of services) (Howlin, Magiati, & Charman, 2009; Luiselli et al., 2000). Therefore, optimal service delivery for EIBI would include therapy implementation for at least 25 hours per week for a span of 2–3 years to produce maximum impact (Behavior Analyst Certification Board, 2012; Eikeseth, 2009; Eldevik et al., 2009). Some funding agencies are reluctant to continue funding services when the trajectory of developmental change is not altered quickly enough to predict a best outcome result for a child (see 2013 changes to TriCARE model funding); however, the beneficial effects of behavior analysis are well documented for individuals with ASD even when provided outside

of the context of EIBI and when best outcomes are not attained (Roane, Fisher, Green, Mclannahan, & Taylor, 2010).

Research also suggests that more highly qualified and credentialed supervisors are associated with better outcomes for consumers than professional supervisors with lower credentials or parents who manage their own in-home services (Bibby et al., 2002; Reichow & Woolery, 2009). The existing best practice guidelines suggest that a board-certified behavior analyst should conduct supervision for at least 1–2 hours for every 10 hours of direct therapy (Behavior Analyst Certification Board, 2012). The BCBA credential requires a master's degree or higher (PhD for the BCBA-D credential), extensive supervised experience hours, and continuing education post certification. In addition, some specific models of service (e.g., pivotal response training) offer training endorsements for those who have completed specified activities in the specific intervention approach (http://www.prtcertification.com/ retrieved July 17, 2013).

Involve Parents and Implement Across Settings

Parents should be involved in intervention programming at all stages of planning and implementation (Luiselli, 2011). We note that parents can play a critical role in helping to select the full range of skills that are targeted in programming. Although the basic skill areas are often specified as part of a comprehensive curriculum (e.g., functional requests, receptive labels, social initiations), the individual targets in those areas (e.g., labeling a picture with "dog") should be selected with input from the family. When targets are directly applicable for the family's everyday life, the new skills may be more likely to be used in multiple settings, producing robust skill maintenance and generalization. Second, parents who learn to implement effective teaching strategies can create many more learning opportunities by applying those teaching skills throughout "nontherapy" hours and in a variety of contexts that therapists cannot enter or re-create. For example, a family who learns how to teach direction-following, attending, and imitation skills may be able to facilitate their child's success within their church community where therapists are typically not available or when therapy services have stopped. Finally, parents often struggle with problematic behavior exhibited by their children and parent training can teach parents to respond in ways that decrease problem behavior and prevent future occurrences of problem behavior (Koegel, Koegel, Kellegrew, & Mullen, 1996; Luiselli, 2011; Wacker et al., 2013). Parent training generally includes the general principles and specific procedures used in EIBI as well as optimal responses to prevent problem behavior of the child with autism or the child's siblings (Doyle, DeRosa, & Roane, 2013).

Family involvement in treatment is also important for the overall care of the child and well-being of the family. Because children receiving EIBI services frequently have comorbid concerns such as sleep, feeding, and medical problems, families often need other supports incorporated with their EIBI programming. Programming should focus on the family's daily routine and ways to structure normative activities. For example, many families alter dining schedules and diets because their child does not sit at the table to eat and resists new or nonpreferred foods that are introduced. These families can be supported with behavioral interventions that give them the opportunity to have positive family time with minimal problem behavior (Najdowski et al., 2010). Behavior analysts providing EIBI programming should never lose sight of the family's overall needs and stressors and should provide support as necessary to improve overall family functioning (Koegel et al., 1996).

Ensure Consistency Across People and Settings

As mentioned in the prior section, families must be involved in EIBI treatment in order to foster generalization and allow for implementation in a greater number of environments. It is also critical to incorporate multiple implementers of EIBI services in the home, center, or community-based integration settings. Treatment teams should include multiple therapists, and the mastery criteria for individual skill targets should be based on demonstration of skill fluency and independence with multiple people and potentially in multiple settings (e.g., structured, natural play). As more people are included in treatment implementation, it is important to ensure that these different people are implementing programming consistently for both skill acquisition and problem behavior programming.

We advise using behavioral skills training (BST), performance management procedures, and frequent communication to promote consistency across settings and implementers (LeBlanc, Gravina, & Carr,

2009; Parsons, Rollyson, & Reid, 2012; Seiverling, Pantelides, Ruiz, & Sturmey, 2010). Behavioral skills training refers to structured evidence-based procedures that include clear instructions and an explicit written program, live or video models of implementation of the procedures, and rehearsal and feedback of the procedures to a rigorous performance criterion (e.g., 100% accuracy on multiple successive implementations) (Seiverling et al., 2010). All implementers should experience the same training and should have a written program and simplified job aid as permanently available guides for implementing each program (Parsons et al., 2012). Procedural integrity of implementation should occur regularly following completion of training, and performance management procedures (e.g., feedback, goal setting, differential reinforcement) should be used to ensure ongoing accurate implementation (Gianoumis, Seiverling, & Sturmey, 2012; Seiverling et al., 2010). Finally, regular communication should occur between all treatment implementers to ensure swift detection and remediation of emerging stimulus control problems or problem behavior or other indicators of nonoptimal progress (LeBlanc et al., 2009).

SUMMARY AND CONCLUSIONS

There is a substantial literature to support the effectiveness of EIBI for children with autism (see Table 4.1). The original controlled outcome study created substantial excitement about the possibility of excellent and transformative outcomes for a large percentage of the participants (Lovaas, 1987). Despite initial criticisms and concerns that the original findings would not be replicable, several studies have since replicated the early findings. The recent literature on EIBI has focused on additional replications, identification of predicator variables for child outcomes, and evaluation of outcomes obtained with different intervention and supervisory models.

Several important findings have emerged from the current literature, and these findings should guide our design and execution of EIBI programming for children with autism. First, the best outcomes tend to be achieved when services are provided at an early age and intensively. In addition, more frequent supervision by highly qualified professionals is associated with better outcomes than less frequent supervision or supervision by those with lesser professional degrees or parents who manage their own in-home programming. Second, families can enhance the

TABLE 4.1 RECENT STUDIES IN EARLY AND INTENSIVE BEHAVIORAL
INTERVENTION (2000–2012)

Authors	Publication Year	Participants	Duration of Services	Predictor Variables	Outcomes and Findings
Luiselli, Cannon, Ellis, & Sisson	2000	16 children with autism	Under 3 years old: avg. 11.8 hours per week; 11.6 months. After 3 years old: avg. 15.6 hours per week; 7.12 months	Intensity and duration of services; age at intake of services before and after 3 years old	Significant improvements on language and social for both groups
Bibby, Eikeseth, Martin, Mudford, & Reeves	2002	45 children with autism	25–40 hours per week	Amount of home-based treatment or time at school; IQ and adaptive scores; age at intake of services	Significant increases across skill domains; learning rates higher than comparison group at follow-up
Eikeseth, Smith, Jahr, & Eldevik	2002	25 children with autism	Avg. 28.52 hours per week; 1 year	Age at intake of services (4–7 years old)	Significantly larger gains on standardized tests than comparison group
Howard, Sparkman, Cohen, Green, & Stanislaw	2005	61 children with autism	Under 3 years old: avg. 25–30 hours per week Over 3 years old: avg. 35–40 hours per week	N/A	Significant increases in IQ, communication, and adaptive behaviors as compared to eclectic treatments
Sallows & Graupner	2005	24 children with autism	Avg. 31–39; 4 years	Parent-directed; amount of supervision	Combined from both groups (clinic vs. parent directed), 48% in reg. education classrooms after treatment
Cohen, Amerine-Dickens, & Smith	2006	42 children with autism	35–40 hours per week;	N/A	6 children included in gen. education and 11 with supports after 3 years
Reed, Osborne, & Corness	2007	27 children with autism	avg. 30 hours per week	Intensity of services	Stronger gains in high-intensity group compared to low-intensity group
Remington, Hastings, Kovshoff, et al.	2007	44 children with autism	2 years; avg. 25.6 hours per week	Parental well-being	26% significant increase in IQ with only 14% in comparison group
Eikeseth, Hayward, Gale, Gitlesen, & Eldevik	2009	20 children with autism	N/A	Amount of supervision	Increase in supervision leads to more significant increases in child's IQ
Granpeesheh, Dixon, Tarbox, Kaplan, & Wilke	2009	245 children with autism	Avg. 20 hours or more per month	Age at intake of services; intensity of services	Decrease in age plus increase in treatment hours leads to increase in skills
Eldevik, Jahr, Eikeseth, Hastings & Hughes	2010	25 children with autism	Avg. 12.1 months; 10.3 hours per week	N/A	Significant increases in IQ, communication, and adaptive behaviors

(continued)

TABLE 4.1 CONTINUED

Authors	Publication Year	Participants	Duration of Services	Predictor Variables	Outcomes and Findings
Eldevik, Hastings, Jahr, & Hughes	2012	31 children with autism	At least 5 hours per week for 2 years	Age and IQ at intake; diagnosis other than autism spectrum disorder	Significant increases in IQ, communication, and social skills
Klintwall & Eikeseth	2012	21 children with autism	Avg. 20 hours per week	Age at intake; no. of socially mediated reinforcers	Positive correlation between number of socially mediated reinforcers and learning rate; negative correlation between number of automatic reinforcers and learning rate
Strauss, Vicari, Valeri, D'Elia, Arima, & Fava	2012	44 children with autism	25 hours per week	Parental involvement in treatment	Significant decreases in core symptoms and increases in expressive language

effects of EIBI programming if parental participation is encouraged from the outset with the expectation of skill development and treatment implementation in multiple settings. Incorporation of natural change agents in natural environments can enhance generalization and maintenance of treatment effects and lead to increased capacity for change beyond the delivery of EIBI services. Skill generalization is enhanced when multiple therapists and natural change agents implement programming. However, without consistent and effective implementation across intervention agents and settings the impact of EIBI services may be jeopardized. Thus, it is critical to actively plan for comprehensive training and performance management to ensure a high degree of consistency across all intervention settings and agents.

Although the current literature on EIBI gives us several important guidelines for practice, there is limited experimental literature that directly compares different models of EIBI (e.g., verbal behavior, UCLA model) in large-scale evaluations with long-term outcomes. Thus, it is unclear whether any of these models produce equally or superior effects independent of the other variables that have been found to predict outcomes. Future research should directly compare different models. Second, the findings of Smith et al. (2000) provided preliminary evidence that a measure of early learning such as rate of acquisition on specific skill sets predicted later outcomes

in EIBI. Unfortunately, the sample size was small and the findings need to be replicated in future studies. It is important that researchers evaluate whether this measure or any others that are being used to measure progress yearly or semiannually actually predict subsequent outcomes. Without strong evidence to indicate that measures are truly predictive of subsequent outcomes when the optimal dose of EIBI is delivered, services should not be truncated based on a lack of early progress on these measures. Finally, extensive research should be done to examine strategies for enhancing the effects of EIBI for those individuals who have historically been nonresponders and require additional and alternative procedures to enhance their learning and developmental gains.

REFERENCES

Behavior Analyst Certification Board. (2012). *Health plan coverage of applied behavior analysis treatment for autism spectrum disorder*. Retrieved July 2013, from http://www.bacb.com/index.php?page=100772.

Bellini, S., & Akullian J. (2007). A meta-analysis of video modeling and video self-modeling interventions for children and adolescents with autism spectrum disorders. *Exceptional Children, 73*, 264–287.

Bibby, P., Eikeseth, S., Martin, N. T., Mudford, O. C., & Reeves, D. (2002). Progress and outcomes for children with autism receiving parent-managed intensive interventions. *Research in Developmental Disabilities, 23*, 81–104.

California Department of Education. (1997). *Best practices for designing and delivering effective programs for individuals with autistic spectrum disorders.* Retrieved July 2013, from http://iier.isciii.es/autismo/pdf/aut_gcalif.pdf.

Carr, J. E., & Firth, A. (2006). The verbal behavior approach to early intensive behavioral intervention: A call for additional empirical support. *Journal of Early and Intensive Behavioral Intervention, 2,* 18–27.

Chambliss, D. L., & Hollon, S. D. (1998). Defining empirically supported therapies. *Journal of Consulting and Clinical Psychology, 66,* 7–18.

Cohen, H., Amerine-Dickens, M., & Smith, T. (2006). Early intensive behavioral treatment: Replication of the UCLA model in a community setting. *Developmental and Behavioral Pediatrics, 27,* 145–155.

Cummings, A. R., & Carr, J. E. (2009). Evaluating progress in behavioral programs for children with autism spectrum disorders via continuous and discontinuous measurement. *Journal of Applied Behavior Analysis, 42,* 57–71.

Doyle, N. M., DeRosa, N. M., & Roane, H. S. (2013). Development of a combined intervention to decrease problem behavior displayed by siblings with pervasive developmental disorder. *Journal of Developmental and Physical Disabilities, 25,* 91–104.

Eikeseth, S. (2009). Outcome of comprehensive psycho-educational interventions for young children with autism. *Research in Developmental Disabilities, 30,* 158–178.

Eikeseth, S., Hayward, D., Gale, C., Gitlesen, J., & Eldevik, S. (2009). Intensity of supervision and outcome for preschool aged children receiving early and intensive behavioral interventions: A preliminary study. *Research in Autism Spectrum Disorders, 3,* 67–73.

Eikeseth, S., Smith, T., Jahr, E., & Eldevik, S. (2002). Intensive behavioral at school for 4-to-7 year-old children with autism treatment. *Behavior Modification, 26,* 49–68.

Eldevik, S., Hastings, R. P., Hughes, J. C., Jahr, E., Eikeseth, S., & Cross, S. (2009). Meta-analysis of early intensive behavioral intervention for children with autism. *Journal of Clinical Child and Adolescent Psychology, 38,* 439–450.

Eldevik, S., Hastings, R. P., Jahr, E., & Hughes, J. C. (2012). Outcomes of behavioral intervention for children with autism in mainstream preschool settings. *Journal of Autism and Developmental Disorders, 42,* 210–220.

Eldevik, S., Jahr, E., Eikeseth, S., Hastings, R. P., & Hughes, C. J. (2010). Cognitive and behavior outcomes of behavioral intervention for young children with intellectual disability. *Behavior Modification, 34,* 16–34.

Freeman, N., & Perry, A. (2010). Outcomes of intensive behavioural intervention in the Toronto Preschool Autism Service. *Journal of Developmental Disabilities, 16,* 17–32.

Gianoumis, S., Seiverling, L., & Sturmey, P. (2012). The effects of behavior skills training on correct teacher implementation of natural language paradigm teaching skills and child behavior. *Behavioral Interventions, 27,* 57–74.

Granpeesheh, D., Dixon, D. R., Tarbox, J., Kaplan, A. M., & Wilke, A. E. (2009). The effects of age and treatment intensity on behavioral interventions outcomes for children with autism spectrum disorders. *Research in Autism Spectrum Disorders, 3,* 1014–1022.

Green, G. (1996). Early behavioral intervention for autism: what does the research tell us? In C. Maurice, G. Green, & S. Luce (Eds.), *Behavioral interventions for young children with autism: A manual for parents and professionals* (p. 29–44). Austin, TX: Pro-Ed.

Gresham, F. M., & MacMillan, D. L. (1988). Early intervention project: Can its claims be substantiated and its effects replicated? *Journal of Autism and Developmental Disorders, 28,* 5–13.

Gresham, F. M., & MacMillan, D. L. (1997). Autistic recovery? An analysis and critique of the empirical evidence on the Early Intervention Project. *Behavioral Disorders, 22,* 185–201.

Horner, R. H., Carr, E. G., Halle, J., McGee, G., Odom, S., & Wolery, M. (2005). The use of single-subject research to identify evidence-based practice in special education. *Council for Exceptional Children, 71,* 165–179.

Horner, R. H., & Kratochwill, T. R. (2011). Using single-case research to identify evidence-based practices. *Savage Controversies, 5,* 2–5.

Howard, J. S., Sparkman, C. R., Cohen, H. G., Green, G., & Stanislaw, H. (2005). A comparison of intensive behavior analytic and eclectic treatments for young children with autism. *Research in Developmental Disabilities, 26,* 359–383.

Howlin, P., Magiati, I., & Charman, T. (2009). Systematic review of early intensive behavioral interventions for children with autism. *American Association on Intellectual and Developmental Disabilities, 114,* 23–41.

Kazdin, A. E. (2010). *Single case research designs: Methods for clinical and applied settings* (2nd ed.). Oxford, UK: Oxford University Press.

Klintwall, L., & Eikeseth, S. (2012). Number and controllability of reinforcers as predictors of individual outcome for children with autism receiving early and intensive behavioral intervention: A preliminary study. *Research in Autism Spectrum Disorders, 6,* 493–499.

Koegel, L. K., Koegel, R. L., Kellegrew, D., Mullen, K. (1996). Parent education for prevention and reduction of severe problem behaviors. In L. K. Koegel, R. L. Koegel, & G. Dunlap (Eds.), *Positive behavioral support: Including people with difficult behavior in the community* (pp. 3–30). Baltimore, MD: Paul H. Brookes.

Koegel, R. L., & Koegel, L. K. (2006). *Pivotal response treatments for autism: Communication, social and academic development.* Baltimore, MD: Paul H. Brookes.

Koegel, R. L., Koegel, L. K., Vernon, T. W., & Brookman-Frazee, L. I. (2010). Empirically supported pivotal response treatment for autism spectrum disorders. In J. R. Weisz & A. E. Kazdin (Eds.), *Evidence-based psychotherapies for children and adolescents* (2nd ed., pp. 327–344). New York, NY: Guilford Press.

Kovshoff, H., Hastings, R., & Remington, B. (2011). Two-year outcomes for children with autism after the cessation of early intensive behavioral intervention. *Behavior Modification, 35*, 427–450.

Leaf, R., & McEachin, J. (1999). *A work in progress: Behavior management strategies and a curriculum for intensive behavioral treatment of autism.* New York, NY: DRL Books.

LeBlanc, L. A., & Gillis, J. M. (2012). Behavioral interventions for children with autism spectrum disorders. *Pediatric Clinics of North America, 59*, 147–164.

LeBlanc, L. A., Gravina, N., & Carr, J. E. (2009). Training issues unique to autism spectrum disorders. In J. Matson (Ed.), *Practitioner's guide to applied behavior analysis for children with autism spectrum disorders* (pp. 225–235). New York, NY: Springer.

LeBlanc, L. A., Heinicke, M. R., & Baker, J. C. (2012). Expanding the consumer base for behavior analytic services: Meeting the needs of consumers in the 21st century. *Behavior Analysis in Practice, 5*, 4–14

Lerman, D. C., Dettlinger, L. H., Fentress, G., & Lanagan, T. (2011). A comparison of methods for collecting data on performance during discrete trial teaching. *Behavior Analysis in Practice, 4*, 53–62.

Lovaas, O. I. (1987). Behavioral treatment and normal educational and intellectual functioning in young autistic children. *Journal of Consulting and Clinical Psychology, 55*, 3–9.

Lovaas, O. I. (2002). *Teaching individuals with developmental delays: Early intervention techniques.* Austin, TX: Pro-Ed.

Lovaas, O. I., & Smith, T. (2003). Early and intensive behavioral intervention in autism. In A. E. Kazdin & J. R. Weisz (Eds.), *Evidence-based psychotherapies for children and adolescents* (pp. 325–340). New York, NY: Guilford Press.

Luiselli, J. K. (2011). Training parents and other care providers. In J. K. Luiselli (Ed.), *Teaching and behavior support for children and adults with autism spectrum disorder: A practitioner's guide* (pp. 212–216). New York, NY: Oxford University Press.

Luiselli, J. K., Cannon, B., Ellis, J. T., & Sisson, R. W. (2000). Home-based behavioral intervention for young children with autism/pervasive developmental disorder: A preliminary evaluation of outcome in relation to child age and intensity of service delivery. *Autism, 4*, 426–438.

Maurice, C. (1994). *Let me hear your voice: A family's triumph over autism.* New York, NY: Random House.

McEachin, J., Smith, T., & Lovaas, O. I. (1993). Long-term outcome for children with autism who received early intensive behavioral treatment. *American Journal of Mental Retardation, 97*, 359–372.

Missouri Autism Guidelines Initiative. (2010). *Autism spectrum disorders: Best practice guidelines for screening, diagnosis, and assessment.* Retrieved July 2013, from http://www.autismguidelines.dmh.mo.gov/.

Najdowski, A. C., Wallace, M. D., Reagon, K., Penrod, B., Higbee, T. S., & Tarbox, J. (2010). Utilizing a home-based parent training approach in the treatment of food selectivity. *Behavioral Interventions, 25*, 89–107.

National Autism Center. (2009). *National Standards Report: The National Standards Project: Addressing the need for evidence-based practice guidelines for autism spectrum disorders.* Retrieved July 2011, from http://www.nationalautismcenter.org/pdf/NAC%20Standards%20Report.pdf.

O'Connor, A. B., & Healy, O. (2010). Long-term post-intensive behavioral intervention outcomes for five children with autism spectrum disorder. *Research in Autism Spectrum Disorders, 4*, 594–604.

Parsons, M. B., Rollyson, J. H., & Reid, D. H. (2012). Evidence-based staff training: A guide for practitioners. *Behavior Analysis in Practice, 5*, 2–11.

Reed, P., Osborne, L. A., & Corness, M. (2007). Brief report: Relative effectiveness of different home-based behavioral approaches to early teaching intervention. *Journal of Autism and Developmental Disorders, 37*, 1815–1821.

Reichow, B. (2012). Overview of meta-analyses on early intensive behavioral intervention for young children with autism spectrum disorders. *Journal of Autism and Developmental Disorders, 42*, 512–520.

Reichow, B., & Wolery, M. (2009). Comprehensive synthesis of early intensive behavioral interventions for young children with autism based on the UCLA young autism project model. *Journal of Autism and Developmental Disorders, 39*, 23–41.

Remington, B., Hastings, R. P., Kovshoff, H., Espinosa, F., Jahr, E., Brown, T., ... Ward, M. (2007). Early intensive behavioral intervention: Outcomes for children with autism and their parents after two years. *American Journal on Mental Retardation, 112*, 418–438.

Roane, H. S., Fisher, W. W., Green, G., McClannahan, L. E., & Taylor, B. A. (2010). *Behavior analysis in autism.* Lawrence, KS: Allen Press.

Romanczyk, R. G., Lockshin, S., & Matey, L. (1996). *Individualized goal selection curriculum.* (9th ed.). Apalachin, NY: CBTA.

Sallows, G. O., & Graupner, T. D. (2005). Intensive behavioral treatment for children with autism: Four year outcome and predictors. *American Journal on Mental Retardation, 110*, 417–438.

Seiverling, L., Pantelides, M., Ruiz, H. H., & Sturmey, P. (2010). The effect of behavioral skills training with general case training on staff chaining of child vocalizations within the natural language paradigm. *Behavioral Interventions, 25*, 53–75.

Smith, T. (2013). What is evidence-based behavior analysis? *Behavior Analyst, 36,* 7–34.

Smith, T., Groen, A. D., & Wynn, J. W. (2000). Randomized trial of intensive early intervention for children with pervasive developmental disorder. *American Journal of Mental Retardation, 105,* 269–285.

Smith, T., & Lovaas, O. I. (1997). The UCLA Young Autism Project: A reply to Gresham and MacMillan. *Behavioral Disorders, 22,* 202–218.

Strauss, K., Vicari, S., Valeri, G., D'Elia, L., Arima, S., & Fava, L. (2012). Parent inclusion in early intensive behavioral intervention: The influence of parental stress, parent treatment fidelity and parent-mediated generalization of behavior targets on child outcomes. *Research in Developmental Disabilities, 33,* 688–703.

Tincani, M., & Davis, K. (2011). Quantitative synthesis and component analysis of single-participant studies on the picture exchange communication system. *Remedial and Special Education, 32,* 458–470.

United States Department of Health and Human Services. (1999). *Mental health: A report of the surgeon general.* Rockville, MD: US Department of Health and Human Services, Substance Abuse and Mental Health Services Administration, Center for Mental Health Services, National Institutes of Health, National Institute of Mental Health.

Wacker, D. P., Lee, J. F., Dalmau, Y. C. P., Kopelman, T. G., Lindgren, S. D., Kuhle, J., ... Waldron, D. B. (2013). Conducting functional communication training via telehealth to reduce the problem behavior of young children with autism. *Journal of Developmental and Physical Disabilities, 25,* 35–48.

Warren, Z., McPheeters, M. L., Sathe, N., Foss-Feig, J. H., Glasser, A., & Veenstra-VanderWeele, J. (2011). A systematic review of early intensive intervention for autism spectrum disorders. *Pediatrics, 127,* e1303–e1311.

5

Computer-Based Instruction

JEFF SIGAFOOS, SATHIYAPRAKASH RAMDOSS, DEBORA KAGOHARA,
ROBERT C. PENNINGTON, GIULIO E. LANCIONI,
AND MARK F. O'REILLY

This chapter focuses on the use of computer-based instruction (CBI) for teaching persons with autism spectrum disorder (ASD). We begin by defining CBI and describing its application in general education settings. Next, we consider the potential benefits of CBI in educational interventions involving persons with ASD. This is followed by an overview of several priority issues and concerns about CBI in the education of persons with ASD. The bulk of the chapter is devoted to a summary of research on the use of CBI as an educational intervention for individuals with ASD. Our review considers the types of CBI systems that have been evaluated, the skills or behaviors that have been targeted for intervention, and the degree to which CBI has been successful as a teaching method for persons with ASD. The final section of this chapter outlines a number of practice implications and offers recommendations regarding the use of CBI for individuals with ASD.

DEFINING AND DESCRIBING COMPUTER-BASED INSTRUCTION

CBI (also referred to as computer-assisted instruction or computer-based teaching) generally refers to the use of personal computers and related devices (e.g., iPads®, iPods®) for instructional/educational purposes. Typically with CBI, computer software provides learners with access to instructional stimuli, opportunities to perform skills, and/or provision of feedback on performance. A variety of instructional stimuli across visual, auditory, and/or kinesthetic modalities have been presented during CBI, and learners have been required to perform computer-based tasks using different response topographies such as using a touch screen to select

icons, using speech to text software, and typing out words on the computer keyboard.

Researchers have demonstrated the effectiveness of CBI in teaching many skills in the areas of academic skills (Pennington, 2010; Ramdoss, Mulloy, et al., 2011), social and communication (Bosseler & Massaro, 2003; Ramdoss, Lang, et al., 2011; Ramdoss, Machalicek, et al., 2012), adaptive behavior (Ramdoss, Lang, et al., 2012), and organizational and vocational functioning (Kellems & Morningstar, 2012). Computers also have been used for assessment purposes, such as testing the extent to which an individual has mastered new skills or acquired new knowledge (Anohina, 2005). There are several general applications of CBI (Kagohara et al., 2013; Kulik, 1994; Lowe, 2004):

1. *Teach new knowledge/behaviors.* The most common form of CBI is presenting instructional materials that are intended to teach a person something new. For example, CBI might be used to present a series of matching to sample problems where the learner is prompted to select the correct match, with the computer program fading the prompt over successive opportunities.

2. *Drill and practice.* Another common application of CBI is to present material for the learner to practice and gain fluency. Programs presenting addition and subtraction problems might be one way to increase fluency in arithmetic.

3. *Stimulation.* In some cases the goal of CBI may be to teach the person to independently access age-appropriate stimulation. For example, children might be taught to operate an Apple iPad® to access

games and music videos (Kagohara et al., 2011). Many computer games also have the added benefit of promoting the acquisition of new skills (Tobias & Fletcher, 2011).

4. *Evaluate performance.* CBI has been used for testing and recording data of learner responses (e.g., ratio of correct to incorrect responses). Software-based data collection can help teachers save time and conduct formative assessments that can be used to evaluate and modify instruction. For example, computer-based spelling tests could reveal a consistent pattern of errors, which could then be addressed by a redesign of the computer-based instructional program.

5. *Compliment teacher-directed instruction.* CBI has been used to supplement, expand, and enhance teacher-directed instruction. For example, learners might work through a CBI program related to the causes of World War I, followed by participating in a teacher-directed discussion of these causes.

CBI is widely used in a range of education settings, including primary and secondary schools, colleges and universities, adult training centers, and special education classrooms (Inan, Lowther, Ross, & Strahl, 2010). Indeed, Lee and Vail (2005) noted that CBI is becoming more prevalent in general educational settings. Early reviews of CBI in these settings revealed that a variety of academic performances and skills have served as intervention targets (Kulik, 1994; Kulik & Kulik, 1991), namely reading, math, history, chemistry, and keyboard typing. Numerous additional studies support the effectiveness of CBI in general education (Greene, Moos, & Azevedo, 2011; Hall, Hughes, & Filbert, 2000; Johnson & Rubin, 2011; Molenaar, Roda, van Boxtel, & Sleegers, 2012). The results of these studies suggest that CBI is an effective educational approach. Possible reasons for the general efficacy of CBI are that it may enable learners to (a) work independently and at their own pace, (b) exert greater control over learning, and (c) receive immediate feedback (reinforcement and error correction).

Computer-Based Instruction for Individuals With Autism Spectrum Disorder

CBI also has been widely investigated for use in the education of individuals with ASD (Pennington,

2010; Ramdoss, Lang, et al., 2011, 2012; Ramdoss, Machalicek, et al., 2012; Ramdoss, Mulloy, et al., 2011). Researchers have offered several potential reasons and advantages for implementing CBI with this population. Bernard-Opitz, Ross, and Tuttas (1990), for example, noted that CBI may be an effective approach because individuals with ASD often have an interest in using computer technology and might thus be more motivated to participate in CBI, as compared to adult-directed instruction. In addition, unlike adult-directed instruction, CBI might be less aversive for people with ASD, due perhaps to the lack of social interaction and greater predictability. Furthermore, some individuals with ASD might prefer CBI compared to other methods of instruction. Mancil, Haydon, and Whitby (2009), for example, reported that three 6- to 9-year-old students with ASD preferred a computer-based Social Stories™ intervention (Gray, 1998) compared to the same intervention presented in print.

Related to these potential advantages, there are some data to suggest that individuals with ASD often respond better to instructional materials that are presented visually, rather than material presented via the auditory mode (Bondy & Frost, 1994). CBI can provide instructional material in visual or multimodal (auditory plus visual) formats. In addition, CBI can be customized to individual learner strengths and preferences using features such as dynamic visual displays and voice-over support via natural (recorded) or synthetic speech output. CBI also has the potential to accommodate or address learning and behavioral characteristics associated with ASD (Silver & Oaks, 2001), for example, stimulus overselectivity and executive functioning deficits or by providing instructional materials that highlight relevant stimuli for the learner to attend to and by removing distracting (irrelevant) stimuli.

However, several potential drawbacks to CBI for teaching persons with ASD also have been noted (Pennington, 2010). One potential concern, noted by Moore, McGrath, and Thorpe (2000), is that CBI may allow individuals to opt out of social interaction and thus restrict their social development. Potential barriers to the use of CBI are that, at least initially, CBI is likely to be more expensive to set up and more complicated to implement. Given these potential disadvantages and barriers, it would seem important to critically appraise the available evidence about CBI, beginning with a consideration of the priority concerns for the use of CBI in the education of persons with ASD.

PRIORITY CONCERNS

Priority concerns related to the use CBI for educating persons with ASD can be conceptualized in terms of three areas. The first concern is the extent to which CBI can be successfully applied for improving the academic, social, and communication skills deficits associated with ASD. The second concern is the extent to which individuals with ASD can be successfully taught to operate CBI systems for accessing instruction via CBI. And the third concern is identification of critical issues or questions about the design, delivery, and evaluation of CBI.

Educational Priorities for Individuals With Autism Spectrum Disorder

There are numerous behavioral and curriculum areas that CBI could be directed toward. Lovaas (2003) described some of the behavioral deficits or delays associated with ASD and recommended these as the targets for educational intervention, including (a) communication and social skills, (b) attention to relevant stimuli during instruction, (c) emotional expression, (d) play skills, and (e) self-care routines (e.g., dressing, toileting). Vocational and community living skills are also likely to be important treatment priorities for many individuals with ASD. Numerous behavioral excesses such as aggression, tantrums, self-injury, and ritualistic/stereotyped movements also are common intervention priorities due to their high prevalence among individuals with ASD (Luiselli, 2012). Educational priorities reported by parents of children with ASD include (a) making friends and playing with peers, (b) personal (e.g., cautious of strangers) and pedestrian safety, (c) social skills, (d) responding to questions, (e) writing, and (f) listening to the teacher (Pituch et al., 2010). The value of CBI for individuals with ASD would therefore seem dependent on the extent to which it can successfully address the aforementioned deficits, excesses, and parent priorities.

Prerequisites for Computer-Based Instruction

Successful use of CBI within educational programs for persons with ASD requires a reliable and efficient way of accessing the instructional material (software) delivered via the computer. This means that the person must be able to operate the computer and access instructional materials and software. Accordingly, the person must learn how to (a) turn on the computer, (b) login, and (c) navigate to the required applications and files. Some individuals might also need to learn how to control and operate a mouse, use word processing and other software programs, and enter numbers, letters, words, or sentences via the computer keyboard. In some cases, the computer-based instructional program may require a high degree of literacy skills.

Relevant here then are studies that have aimed to teach persons to operate computers and related devices. Indeed, several studies have focused on teaching persons with ASD to operate computers and related devices to access instructional materials/educational software or preferred stimuli (Achmadi et al., 2012; Kagohara, 2011; Kagohara et al., 2011, 2013). The results suggest that well-established systematic instructional procedures, such as response prompting, prompt fading, error correction, and differential reinforcement (Duker, Didden, & Sigafoos, 2004), can be used to teach persons with ASD and other developmental disabilities how to operate computers and related devices (e.g., iPads®, iPods®). Thus, in some cases, direct instruction by a teacher or therapist might be necessary to develop the prerequisite skills for using CBI.

There has been some research on using technology-assisted instructional procedures, such as computer-delivered video prompting, to teach individuals with ASD and related developmental disabilities to use computers (Kagohara, 2011; Kagohara, Sigafoos, Achmadi, O'Reilly, & Lancioni, 2012; Zisimopoulos, Sigafoos, & Koutromanos, 2011). For example, Kagohara (2011) developed an instructional video to teach three students with developmental disabilities how to operate an iPod® to access entertainment video. The instructional video was delivered on the same iPod® that the students then operated to access and watch the entertainment videos. This raises the intriguing possibility that computers and video instruction might be used to teach the prerequisite skills necessary for participating in CBI. For example, teachers might embed video clips on computer desktops that are designed to guide students through the completion of educational tasks.

Priorities in the Design, Delivery, and Evaluation of Computer-Based Instruction

CBI is an approach to teaching that is intended to promote learning and address related educational objectives (e.g., building fluency through drill and practice, evaluating performance). An important priority for evaluating CBI is thus to determine whether the computer-based intervention has been designed according to empirically validated learning and assessment principles. Research has demonstrated that teaching procedures based on the principles of applied behavior analysis (ABA) are consistently associated with successful educational outcomes for individuals with ASD (Duker et al., 2004; Lovaas, 2003; Sturmey & Fitzer, 2007). These procedures/principles include (a) task analysis, (b) targeting objective and measurable responses, (c) reinforcement, (d) prompting and prompt fading, (e) stimulus control, (f) shaping and chaining, (g) discrimination training, and (h) generalization programming. Kulik (1994) noted several common features of CBI interventions, derived from Skinner (1968), that would seem consistent with these principles, including (a) presenting instructional material in sequences of small, manageable steps (i.e., programmed instruction or task analysis), (b) requiring learner responding at each step, and (c) immediate feedback (e.g., reinforcement or error correction) for each learner response. The success of CBI may therefore depend on how well these procedures/principles are incorporated into the design of instructional materials and delivered via the computer system. For example, feedback for correct responses should be reinforcing (e.g., fanfare and advancement to the next frame in the sequence), whereas feedback for errors should be informative and corrective, but not reinforcing.

A final priority when evaluating CBI is empirical research that provides a convincing demonstration that CBI has led to new learning and/or improved adaptive behavior functioning. To this end, several questions could be asked about CBI for persons with ASD:

1. What types of skills/knowledge/behaviors have been successfully taught/improved using CBI?
2. Do these skills/knowledge/behaviors relate to the core deficits/excess and parental priorities associated with ASD?
3. What instructional materials or software programs have been used? Are these programs readily available or easily reproduced?
4. How successful was the intervention for its intended purpose? Were there any negative or positive side effects?
5. Was the CBI efficient in terms of training time?
6. How does CBI compare to other methods of education for individuals with ASD?
7. What are the critical components of effective CBI?

These questions should be kept in mind when reviewing research studies that have evaluated the use of CBI for teaching persons with ASD.

RESEARCH FINDINGS
As noted previously, research has evaluated the effects of CBI for educating individuals with ASD. Indeed, several systematic reviews have synthesized this literature (Pennington, 2010; Ramdoss, Lang, et al., 2011, 2012; Ramdoss, Machalicek, et al., 2012; Ramdoss, Mulloy, et al., 2011). To assist professionals in appraising the evidence about CBI for individuals with ASD, this section summarizes these systematic reviews, including providing details on specific illustrative studies.

The systematic reviews have been divided into four groups based on the skill or behavior that was targeted for improvement; Specifically: (a) daily and community living skills, (b) communication skills, (c) social-emotional functioning, and (d) academic/literacy skills.

Computer-Based Instruction for Daily and Community Living Skills
Ramdoss, Lang, et al. (2012) conducted a systematic review of studies evaluating CBI for improving daily livings skills of individuals with intellectual disabilities. Their systematic search of electronic databases and journals identified 11 studies meeting three inclusion criteria: (a) evaluated a CBI intervention, (b) had at least one participant with a developmental disability, and (c) focused on teaching daily living skills (e.g., hygiene, dressing, shopping). These 11 studies, published between 2002 and 2010, included a total of 42 participants ranging from 7 to 58 years of age (*M* = 19 years). Of the 42 participants, only 5 had an ASD diagnosis. These five participants came from three separate studies (Ayres, Maguire, & McClimon, 2009; Hutcherson, Langone, Ayres, & Clees, 2004; Mechling & O'Brien, 2010).

First, Ayres et al. (2009) used CBI to teach meal preparation and table setting to two boys and one girl (aged 7 to 9 years) with autism. IQ and developmental ratings suggested the children functioned in the moderate range of [intellectual] disability. The CBI consisted of a computer with a two-button mouse. The instructional software was a program called *I Can—Daily Living and Community Skills* (Sandbox Learning Company, undated). The software presented a video simulation of the environment for setting a table, making soup, and making a sandwich and required children to respond by moving images around the environment (e.g., using the mouse to move utensils to the proper table setting). Prior to participating in CBI, the children were repeatedly tested in vivo. Correct responses during this baseline phase were generally in the 11% to 34% correct range. The children then received CBI until they reached a 90% criterion in the simulated environment. Subsequently, their in vivo performance was again tested and showed an increase from the previous baseline levels (79% to 100% correct). These results provide evidence that reaching criteria with CBI was responsible for improved performance in vivo. However, this conclusion is tentative because performance by one child increased during baseline. Still, the results suggest that this commercially available software program, which could be seen as providing an interactive virtual learning environment, holds promise for teaching meal related skills to relatively young children with autism and moderate intellectual disability.

Second, Hutcherson et al. (2004) used CBI to teach four students to select items at a grocery store. The students were 14 to 16 years of age and had IQ scores from 36 to 54. One of the four students (Brad) was diagnosed with autism. The students used a computer (Windows 95 or higher) and *Project SHOP*, a software program presenting photographs of numerous grocery items (e.g., cereals, canned soup, frozen pizza) and a virtual shopping cart. A cartoon character delivered instructions and feedback. The CBI task involved clicking on specific screen items (e.g., a particular can of soup) that corresponded to items on the student's hard-copy shopping list. Generalization probes were conducted in grocery stores. The results suggested that acquisition of correct matching with CBI generalized to correct item selection in the grocery store. However, three of the children, including Brad, were able to make some correct selections prior to CBI. Still, there was evidence of generalization from the virtual (CBI) environment to the actual community grocery store.

Third, Mechling and O'Brien (2010) used CBI to teach three young adults (19 and 20 years old) to

press the stop button to indicate that they wanted to exit the bus at the next (correct) stop. Their IQ scores were 52, 46, and 70 with the latter participant, Michael, diagnosed with pervasive developmental disorder not otherwise specified. CBI, consisting of *PowerPoint* and Windows *MovieMaker* presentations, was delivered on a laptop with a touch screen. Participants watched the CBI presentation that showed a picture of the destination and a video of the bus route. Computer voice output instructed participants to use the touch screen to press the stop button on the bus. The CBI presentation lasted 10 minutes and participants received this intervention three times per day and 2 to 3 days per week. None of the participants performed correctly on a real bus prior to CBI. After reaching 100% correct with CBI, participants were then able to correctly respond when riding a real bus in the community. These results represent an impressive level of generalization following CBI.

Overall, the results of these three studies suggest that CBI is promising for teaching daily and community living skills to individuals with ASD notwithstanding the small number of studies and participants. Still, the promising results suggest that CBI involving simulated environments may be a useful way of reducing the amount and intensity of in vivo training. This use of CBI might be indicated when teaching community-based skills because it could reduce the amount of direct instruction that is required in community settings and also when community instruction would be intrusive or stigmatizing.

Computer-Based Instruction for Communication Skills

There is an important difference between using a computer (or speech-generating device) to communicate and using CBI to teach communication skills. The former has been widely studied in persons with ASD and shown to be an effective alternative for individuals who fail to acquire speech (van der Meer & Rispoli, 2010). With these studies, the communication skills were generally taught using adult-delivered instruction. In the latter case, however, CBI is used to teach the person one or more communication skills, whether those skills are expressed via speech, manual signs, picture-based systems, or with a computer-based, speech-generating device.

Ten studies of the latter type were reviewed by Ramdoss, Lang, et al. (2011) following a systematic search for studies that (a) had at least one participant with an ASD diagnosis, (b) focused on teaching expressive or receptive language skills, and (c) used CBI as the main intervention procedure. These 10 studies, published between 1993 and 2006, included a total of 70 participants ranging from 3 to 14 years of age (M = 8 years). Of the 70 participants, 54 were male and 16 were female. Most of these 70 participants appeared to have what might be referred to as mild to moderate autism symptoms with a minority probably having autism plus intellectual disability.

The communication skills targeted for CBI in these studies included (a) vocal imitation of syllables, words, or sentences; (b) receptive identification of words or pictures; (c) matching words to pictures; (d) decreasing echolalia; and (e) increasing spontaneous utterances, such as answering questions, requesting objects, commenting, and greeting others. Most of the studies targeted more than one communication skill, for example, teaching participants to answer questions, request objects, and comment on the environment. The studies also generally concentrated on teaching receptive communication (pointing to named object) or expressive speech, rather than the use of augmentative and alternative communication modes.

In terms of hardware, most of these 10 studies used desktop or laptop computers. The desktop setups included monitor, keyboard, and mouse. The associated instructional materials or software programs were those developed specifically by the researchers for the study, as well as three commercially available programs (i.e., *PowerPoint, HyperStudio,* and *Baldi/Timo*). Three studies are summarized here to illustrate the range of computer-based applications that have been used in teaching communication skills to persons with ASD.

First, Coleman-Martin, Heller, Cihak, and Irvine (2005) used CBI to increase language in a 12-year-old girl with autism. The child appeared to have moderate autism based on the authors' description of her adaptive behavior. The CBI system used a Windows PC computer, which presented *PowerPoint* slides and corresponding speech output. The slides showed a target word, while the computer program spoke the word and instructed the child to say it. The number of words said correctly by the child increased with CBI, suggesting its effectiveness as a language teaching method.

Second, Simpson, Langone, and Ayres (2004) used video and CBI to increase spontaneous verbal greetings to peers in four 5- to 6-year-old children with mild to moderate autism. The CBI setup made use of a PowerMac computer and *HyperStudio* software. The software was arranged to present written instructions, synthesized speech, and video examples of how to greet peers. With CBI, all of the children's greetings to peers increased and within 24 (45-minute) sessions of CBI. These positive results suggest that CBI was effective in teaching a socially oriented and expressive communication skill that is often deficient in children with ASD.

Third, Hetzroni and Shalem (2005) used CBI to teach six children with autism and moderate intellectual disability (aged 10 to 13 years) to recognize printed words. The printed words were those associated with logos of food items. The PC-based computer program presented a seven-step fading procedure in which the logo gradually changed to the printed word. The results showed that CBI was effective in teaching the participants to transition from logo to printed word equivalents. The results also showed that most of the participants maintained a high level performance with identifying printed words and this performance generalized to a different setting.

In line with the generally positive results of these three studies, Ramdoss, Lang, et al. (2011) noted that the overall results from the studies they reviewed were generally positive. Specifically, in the 10 studies they reviewed, CBI was associated with improvement in the targeted communication skills for the majority of participants. However, many of these studies had design limitations that make their findings tentative. Thus, at the present time, CBI is perhaps best viewed as a promising, but not yet well-established, approach for improving communication skills of individuals with ASD. Another limitation of the evidence base was that only three readily available software programs were evaluated across these studies (i.e., *HyperStudio, PowerPoint,* and *Baldi/Timo*) and only one of these (i.e., *Baldi/Timo*) is explicitly intended for communication intervention.

Computer-Based Instruction for Social and Emotional Skills

Social and emotional skills are responses or behaviors that establish and maintain a social interaction (Ramdoss, Machalicek et al., 2012). This definition entails responses such as maintaining an appropriate amount of eye contact, understanding the feelings and thoughts of others, recognizing emotions and facial expressions, and responding to nonverbal cues. Ramdoss, Machalicek, et al. (2012) identified 11 studies that evaluated the effects of CBI for improving these types of social and emotional skills in individuals with ASD.

These 11 studies, published between 1996 and 2010, included a total of 330 participants. Sample sizes of individual studies ranged from 4 to 79 ($M = 28$), and the participants ranged from 4 to 52 years of age ($M = 13.5$ years). Most participants (70%) were male and had an ASD diagnosis and apparently mild-to-moderate deficits in adaptive behavior functioning. About one-third of the participants ($n = 118$) were diagnosed with high-functioning autism or Asperger syndrome.

The social skills targeted for intervention with CBI included (a) initiating and maintaining conversations, (b) peer interaction, and (c) generating a solution to a social problem, such as negotiating a turn on the playground slide. The majority of studies targeting emotional skills focused on using CBI to teach participants to recognize emotions in facial expressions or voices. One study focused on developing correct responses in false-belief tasks (Swettenham, 1996).

The hardware used in these studies mainly consisted of desktop and laptop computers. The instructional materials and software programs included a mix of researcher-developed and commercially available programs. The commercially available programs included *Mind Reader—The Interactive Guide to Emotions; Emotion Trainer*; and *Let's Face It!* Three studies are summarized here to illustrate the range of computer-based applications that have been used in teaching social and emotional skills to persons with ASD.

First, Silver and Oakes (2001) examined the use of CBI for teaching individuals with ASD to identify emotions and predict the responses of others. The multimedia software program *Emotion Trainer* presented pictures of a face, a scene, or an object with a sentence describing the situation and asking questions (e.g., Carol wants a pizza but gets a beef burger. How does Carol feel?). The target response was to identify the feelings of the characters in the scene. Twenty-two participants (aged 10 to 18 years) were randomly assigned to the experimental or control group. The experimental group received 10, 30-minute sessions of CBI, while the control group had no instruction. The results suggested that CBI was effective in that posttest scores for the experimental group were higher than those for the control

group. In addition, the number of times the computer program was used was positively correlated with gains in the posttest.

Second, Bernard-Opitz, Sriram, and Nakhoda-Sapuan (2001) provided CBI to eight children with mild to moderate ASD (six boys and two girls, aged 5 to 8 years) and eight typically developing children (five boys and three girls, all 4 years old). CBI was used to teach the children to solve social problems. For example, the computer software program presented animations of conflict scenarios (two children fighting to use the playground slide) and several animated response options (e.g., a child making a polite request versus having a tantrum). When children generated a socially appropriate response, a favorable outcome for the scenario was shown (e.g., the child making a polite request then gets his turn on the slide). The results showed that CBI was associated with improvements in generating appropriate solutions for the children with ASD, although the gains for some children were modest and, as a group, they provided fewer novel responses than the typically developing children. While the results suggest value in using dynamic animations within CBI, generalization to in vivo conflict scenarios was not assessed. One important question then is whether the children would use the appropriate solutions learned from CBI when confronted with similar conflict scenarios in the home, school, or community.

Third, Tanaka et al. (2010) used CBI to teach several facial recognition skills, such as recognizing changes in facial expressions when facial features were presented in isolation or with a whole face. The study involved 79 individuals (62 males and 17 females) with ASD (mean age 10 to 11 years). Participants were randomly assigned to an active treatment group ($n = 27$) or a waitlist control ($n = 37$). CBI, involving a series of seven computer games, was used for about 100 minutes per week until 20 hours had been logged. The software program (*Let's Face It!*) presented images for participants to recognize and included animated graphics. Scores were awarded for correct responses. Results showed that participants in the active treatment group performed better on recognition of mouth and eye features, suggesting the CBI program was effective in teaching certain types of facial recognition skills to children with ASD. However, Ramdoss, Machalicek, et al. (2012) noted that evidence for an intervention effect across the range of skills tested (e.g., recognizing changes in facial dimensions, immediate memory for faces, and matching faces to facial expression) was neither compelling nor conclusive.

The results of studies on CBI for teaching social and emotional skills are mixed. While some studies reported positive results, other studies did not show CBI to be successful. Still, because teaching social and emotional skills using other (adult-directed) interventions have proven rather difficult (Ramdoss, Machalicek, et al., 2012), the mixed results across these 11 studies suggest the CBI does have some potential for enhancing social and emotional skills of individuals with ASD.

Computer-Based Instruction for Academic/Literacy Skills

Two reviews have covered studies evaluating CBI for teaching academic and literacy skills to individuals with ASD. In the first, Pennington (2010) identified 15 studies meeting four criteria: (a) included at least one participant with ASD; (b) involved CBI as the main independent variable; (c) CBI focused on teaching or improving an academic skill, such as reading, writing, or math; and (d) CBI was evaluated using a recognized experimental or quasi-experimental design. The 15 studies, published between 1997 and 2007, involved a total of 52 participants, comprising 40 males and 12 females. These individuals ranged from 3 to 17 years of age with most (90%) aged less than 13 years. Specific diagnoses of the participants included autism ($n = 45$), Rett syndrome ($n = 3$), Asperger syndrome ($n = 3$), and pervasive developmental disorder-not otherwise specified ($n = 1$).

Six classes of academic skills were targeted for CBI in these 15 studies: (a) reading, (b) matching to sample, (c) decoding skills, (d) spelling, (e) sentence construction, and (f) essay writing. The technology used for teaching these skills included similar types of hardware used in other studies (e.g., desktop computers) and portable text-to-speech processors (i.e., LightWRITER). As in previous research, most ($n = 9$) studies made use of researcher-developed instructional materials or software, but the remaining studies adopted commercially available software, such as PowerPoint.

For example, Schlosser and Blischak (2004) examined the effects of computer-generated print and speech output for teaching spelling to four children with autism (aged 8 to 12 years). The computer system was a LightWRITER. The device was programmed to present print and speech feedback, and the children used it to try to spell the words.

Participants were exposed to speech and print, print-only, and speech-only output (feedback) conditions. The results showed that spelling improved as a function of CBI. Indeed, the children learned under each of the three output conditions, but some participants reached criterion faster when presented with print output, while others learned faster with speech output. There did not appear to be any disadvantage to using print plus speech output.

In the second review, Ramdoss, Mulloy, et al. (2011) focused only on studies that used CBI to teach literacy skills to individuals with ASD. Literacy, in this case, included (a) decoding, (b) comprehension, (c) writing, (d) reading, and (e) spelling. Twelve studies were identified, published between 1995 and 2010, which included a total of 94 participants (15% female) from 3 to 21 years of age ($M = 9.6$ years). Most participants were considered to have mild to moderate symptoms of autism based on the descriptions provided by researchers. Desktop and laptop computers were used as hardware and a range of software products were evaluated, including (a) Delta Messages, (b) Alpha program, (c) Teach Town, (d) PowerPoint, and (e) Illuminatus.

For example, Basil and Reyes (2003) used CBI with two children with ASD (8 and 14 years old). The target skills were (a) reading letters, syllables, words, and sentences; (b) writing sentences; and (c) reading comprehension. They presented CBI on an Apple Mac computer via Delta Messages software. The software presented an animated cartoon and the children were instructed to construct a sentence describing the cartoon by selecting words. The software provided feedback through animation and digitized speech output. CBI was provided across 24 sessions with each session lasting 30 minutes. With this amount of CBI, only one child showed gains in sentence construction, reading letters, and reading comprehension. While this child's improvements were probably due to CBI, the mixed results suggest that not all children are likely to benefit from this level of exposure to the program.

Two related studies used commercially available adaptive writing programs (i.e., Clicker5™, Pixwriter™) to improve the story-writing skills of four boys with ASD (Pennington, Ault, & Schuster, 2011; Pennington, Stenhoff, Gibson, & Ballou, 2012). In both investigations, the researchers used simultaneous prompting (Gibson & Schuster, 1992) to teach participants to select words from an array to create simple stories. During instruction, the software provided auditory feedback after the selection of each word and the completion of the story. All four participants acquired story construction responses, but interestingly, they also demonstrated at least some generalization across untrained responses topographies (i.e., handwriting, speaking).

Another illustrative study, by Yamamoto and Miya (1999), investigated CBI to improve the academic skills in three boys with autism. The target skills were (a) sentence construction, (b) particle choice, and (c) verbal production of constructed sentences. During CBI, the software showed a picture of a person doing an action and provided a description of the picture. The boys then practiced selecting descriptive words for the picture from a word bank. Fanfare sound was used as positive feedback for correct responses. The results indicated substantial improvement on sentence construction, particle choice, and verbal production tasks for all three participants.

In terms of overall efficacy, Pennington (2010) concluded that the studies he reviewed showed CBI to be an effective approach for teaching the range of targeted academic skills. However, Ramdoss, Mulloy, et al.'s (2011) review showed more inconsistent results when CBI was applied to literacy skills. Because of these mixed findings, design limitations among these two sets of studies (e.g., none of Pennington's group studies included control groups), and the relatively small number of studies for teaching any given academic skill, CBI does not yet qualify as an evidence-based procedure for teaching general academic and literacy skills. Still, the fact that a majority of participants in these studies showed improvements that were most likely due to CBI suggests it is a promising educational intervention for the academic/literacy domain.

PRACTICE RECOMMENDATIONS

The studies and systematic reviews summarized in this chapter reported generally positive results. Indeed, most of the participants in these studies showed improvements that were most likely attributable to their use of CBI. However, due to mixed results and compromised designs, CBI does not yet seem to meet the criteria for classifying it as a well-established educational intervention for individuals with ASD (Horner et al., 2005). Instead, at the present time, CBI is perhaps best viewed as a promising educational intervention. Still, given that data showing its promise

have been generated from numerous independent studies, we feel confident in recommending CBI as an educational intervention for individuals with ASD. The promising data in support of CBI point to several practice implications and recommendations.

Hardware Recommendations

Both (PC- and Apple-based) desktop and laptop computers can present CBI to children, adolescents, and adults with ASD. In most studies to date, the CBI materials or software was accessed via a keyboard or mouse. Thus, to enable learners to concentrate on learning from CBI, it would seem important to first ensure learners gain fluency in using a computer mouse and keyboard. Indeed, given the ubiquity of computers in society, development of computer literacy and operational skills would seem important in their own right, regardless of whether CBI was to become a major component of the person's educational program.

One potential limitation of providing CBI on a desktop computer is restricting learning to a particular location. Laptop computers, being more portable, may be recommended for enabling learning to occur across multiple settings. This could be an advantage for accessing "just-in-time" instruction. For example, a child might quickly run through a CBI program on how to enter a peer group, just prior to attempting this on the playground.

Similarly, devices such as iPods®, iPads®, and android-based tablets may offer even greater portability and flexibility for accessing CBI. Such devices might also be more intuitive for learners to operate because educational materials or software is accessed via a touch screen, thus bypassing the need for mouse, track pad, or keyboard skills. Kagohara et al. (2013) reviewed 15 studies that focused on teaching individuals with ASD to operate iPods®, iPads®, and related devices. Their summary suggested that individuals with ASD can be taught to successfully operate such devices for (a) checking the spelling of words, (b) requesting preferred stimuli, (c) participating in vocabulary-building activities, (d) completing vocational tasks, and (e) accessing music and entertainment videos. We anticipate that iPods®, iPads®, and related devices will become more prevalent in CBI for individuals with and without ASD. If our prediction is correct, it would seem timely to investigate procedures for promoting effective use of such devices in the educational programs of individuals with ASD.

Software Recommendations

The studies and reviews summarized in this chapter evaluated different instructional materials or software programs. This is encouraging because it suggests there is considerable vitality with respect to educational software research and development. However, most of the studies to date have evaluated researcher-generated, rather than commercially available, software. While researchers might be very willing to share their software, an increase in commercially available software would likely help to increase access to user-friendly educational software. Even most of the commercial software evaluated to date (e.g., *Illuminatus, PowerPoint*) is not aimed explicitly at CBI and would thus seem to require parents, teachers, or therapists to design and upload custom-made instructional materials. While such tasks might be familiar to many, ensuring that the resulting instructional materials contain the components of effective CBI (e.g., a logical and progressive sequence of material, instructional prompts that are effectively faded, and provision of reinforcing and corrective feedback) may prove more difficult.

One recommendation with respect to software is to source programs for CBI that have been evaluated and shown to be effective in research involving individuals with ASD. The research reviewed in this chapter and by others (Pennington, 2010; Ramdoss, Lang, et al., 2011, 2012; Ramdoss, Machalicek, et al., 2012; Ramdoss, Mulloy, et al., 2011) provides numerous examples of effective instructional materials and software programs for use in CBI involving individuals with ASD (see also Whitcomb, Bass, & Luiselli, 2011).

There are, however, a growing number of software programs and applications (apps) being developed. Schuler, Levine, and Ree (2012) provided an analysis of educationally oriented applications from Apple's App store that could be used in CBI. There are also numerous new apps that are intended to teach communication, social, and academic skills to individuals with ASD. Many of these apps would be compatible with a range of hardware and operating systems, including laptops, iPods®, iPads®, and related devices. The potential advantages of such apps are their relatively low cost, ease of access, and the fact that most are ready to use once they have been installed. Many apps can also be customized to suit individual need and ability. However, as noted by Pennington (2010) and Kagohara et al. (2013), very few of the current large number of commercially available and educationally oriented apps have been empirically validated via research. The need to do so is great because unproven programs might be ineffective or, worse, detrimental.

We do not, however, want to suggest that the large number of potentially promising educational software and apps should not be used until such time when researchers have been able to catch up with the market so to speak. Rather we recommend that parents, teachers, and therapists undertake their own evaluations to determine whether any such software program or app is effective. Along these lines, parents, teachers, and therapists might look for the following features in commercially available educational software and apps:

1. Is the aim or objective of the program clear? What specific skills, responses, or behaviors are targeted? Are these skills, responses, or behaviors objectively defined and measureable?
2. Are the skills, responses, or behaviors priority concerns for the individual?
3. Is it clear what the person is expected to do to use the app/educational software?
4. Does the person have the prerequisite skills to operate the hardware and access the software?
5. Does the program follow a logical progression (e.g., from easy to more difficult)?
6. Does the program include the type of prompts that the person can respond to and include in-built mechanisms for fading such prompts?
7. Does the program include consequences that are likely to reinforce correct responses and extinguish errors?
8. Does the individual appear to enjoy using the software and is there evidence that use of the program is producing learning?

Target Skills Recommendations

As suggested by our present review of research, CBI has been used with success to teach a variety of important skills to persons with ASD. For the purpose of this chapter, these skills were classified into four broad domains. While direct comparison across domains is problematic given the diversity of skills studied, CBI did appear to be more effective for teaching daily/community living skills and communication skills than social/emotional and academic/literacy skills. There are also many skills relevant to individuals with ASD that have not yet been targeted within a CBI environment, such as vocational skills, personal safety skills, and reduction of tantrums, self-injury, and repetitive/stereotyped behaviors. These and many other types of skills are not necessarily unteachable via CBI; it is just that this is currently uncharted territory. If target behaviors can be precisely specified and appropriate hardware/software programs interfaced, it is conceivable that a much wider range of target behaviors could be taught via CBI. In illustration, Burke, Andersen, Bowen, Howard, and Allen (2010) used a novel form of CBI with six participants with ASD (18 to 27 years of age) for addressing fire safety education. The researchers employed an Apple iPhone® as a cueing system. The iPhone® was connected to an iPod Touch® and programmed to remotely prompt participants through 63 fire safety steps. The results suggested that this cueing system was effective in teaching complex fire safety skills.

Recommendations for Designing Effective Computer-Based Instruction

The studies and reviews summarized in this chapter suggest that mere provision of a computer with educational software is not sufficient to ensure successful outcomes from CBI. Similar to person-implemented instruction (Duker et al., 2004), the success of CBI is perhaps most primarily determined by the effectiveness of the teaching procedures implemented (e.g., prompting hierarchy, reinforcement delivery, scaffolding techniques), which may depend on how well the software integrates these procedures into the overall instructional program. In addition to incorporating empirically validated instructional principles and procedures, it is recommended that CBI design consider the following points raised earlier in this chapter:

1. Presenting instructional material in sequences of small, manageable steps.
2. Requiring a response from the learner at each step.
3. Programming immediate feedback (e.g., reinforcement or error correction) for each learner response.

The amount of exposure to CBI may also be a critical variable affecting the success of CBI. Indeed, the studies on using CBI to improve social and emotional skills suggest a possible relation between frequency

with respect to the use of CBI and improved performance of individuals with ASD. Specifically, the results of studies conducted by Golan and Baron-Cohen (2006) and Silver and Oakes (2001) suggested that the magnitude of improvement in emotion recognition was positively correlated with number of times the programs were used.

In designing CBI, it would seem important to emphasize that CBI is perhaps best conceptualized as an intervention delivery system (Ramdoss, Lang, et al., 2011, 2012). Instructional programs are more likely to be practical if they are easily adaptable and provide opportunities for quick and effective customization. For example, a software program is more useful if the consequences are based on individual preferences.

Performance in the CBI environment, while important, is perhaps less critical to showing that CBI leads to changes in vivo. Thus, good CBI programs must be designed to promote generalization outside of the CBI environment. For example, computer-based instructional stimuli should share features of those in natural contexts and skills should be taught to a fluency that will ensure contact with reinforcers in the natural environment. Ultimately, educators will need to assess the performance of skills taught via CBI in real-world settings and reteach those skills that fail to generalize.

A final design consideration relates to the concern expressed by Moore et al. (2000) that CBI may reduce opportunities for social interaction and reciprocal communication and could even potentially lead to loss of social skills (Bernard-Opitz, Ross, & Tuttas, 1990). Pennington (2010) noted that this concern suggests the need to balance CBI with adult interaction by limiting the amount of CBI. While some children may prefer to use CBI over adult-directed instruction (Mancil et al., 2009), this preference will not necessarily hold for all children. We therefore recommend that individuals should be allowed to choose when and if to use CBI and other instruction procedures on at least some occasions. Allowing this degree of choice (self-determination) could be facilitated by a two-step process that involves teaching them to use CBI and creating opportunities for choosing whether to use CBI or some other learning approach.

Recommendations for Computer-Based Instruction Access

A relevant practical implication of the promising results obtained with CBI for individuals with ASD is that there might be an increased application of

CBI in the educational settings of these individuals. CBI may become more widely prescribed because of the purported advantages it might have over other instructional approaches. When these potential advantages are bolstered by additional empirical demonstrations of successful use, it is likely that CBI will become more widely recommended. There might thus be an increasing need for CBI competence among parents, teachers, and clinicians, including competence related to designing and implementing CBI.

Recommendations for Future Research

There are few studies into the relative efficacy of CBI versus adult-directed instruction for individuals with ASD. Bernard-Opitz, Sriram, and Sapuan, (1999), for example, compared CBI to adult-directed instruction for teaching vocal imitation to 10 children with severe autism. They found CBI was more effective. Given the paucity of such studies, however, the relative efficacy of CBI versus adult-directed instruction is an obvious question that warrants further research.

Even if CBI is shown to be more effective than adult-directed instruction, a critical test is whether what is learned during CBI generalizes to other contexts. There have been few such direct tests, even though the probability of generalization appeared relatively higher for daily living skills and lower for social and emotional skills in the studies reviewed for this chapter. Generalization for social and emotional skills might be a problem given that individuals with ASD seem to experience difficulties identifying subtle social cues in vivo (Golan & Baron-Cohen, 2006). This problem might be overcome by using upgraded CBI with virtual technology. Future studies might therefore aim to establish the effectiveness of virtual-technology-based instruction for promoting generalization of social and emotional skills in individuals with ASD.

CONCLUSION

CBI is a promising educational intervention for individuals with ASD and there are studies showing it can be successful for teaching a range of daily living and community skills, communication, social-emotional, and academic/literacy skills. Successful use of CBI appears to hinge on the quality of software and the instructional materials provided and the amount of access to CBI.

ACKNOWLEDGMENTS

Support for writing this chapter was provided, in part, from the New Zealand Government through the Marsden Fund Council, administered by the Royal Society of New Zealand; and by Victoria University of Wellington.

REFERENCES

Achmadi, D., Kagohara, D. M., van der Meer, L., O'Reilly, M. F., Lancioni, G. E., Sutherland, D., ... Sigafoos, J. (2012). Teaching advanced operation of an iPod-based speech-generating device to two students with autism spectrum disorders. *Research in Autism Spectrum Disorders, 6*, 1258–1264.

Anohina, A. (2005). Analysis of the terminology used in the field of virtual learning. *Journal of Educational Technology and Society, 8*, 91–102.

Ayres, K. M., Maguire, A., & McClimon, D. (2009). Acquisition and generalization of chained tasks taught with computer-based video instruction to children with autism. *Education and Training in Developmental Disabilities, 44*, 493–508.

Basil, C., & Reyes, S. (2003). Acquisition of literacy skills by children with severe disability. *Child Language Teaching and Therapy, 19*, 27–45.

Bernard-Opitz, V., Ross, K., & Tuttas, M. (1990). Computer-assisted instruction for autistic children. *Annals of the Academy of Medicine, 19*, 611–616.

Bernard-Opitz, V., Sriram, N., & Nakhoda-Sapuan, S. (2001). Enhancing social problem solving in children with autism and normal children through computer-assisted instruction. *Journal of Autism and Developmental Disorders, 31*, 377–384.

Bernard-Opitz, V., Sriram, N., & Sapuan, S. (1999). Enhancing vocal imitations in children with autism using the IBM Speechviewer. *Autism, 3*, 131–147.

Bondy, A. S., & Frost, L. A. (1994). The picture exchange communication system. *Focus on Autism and Other Developmental Disabilities, 9*, 1–19.

Bosseler, A., & Massaro, D. W. (2003). Development and evaluation of a computer animated tutor for vocabulary and language learning in children with autism. *Journal of Autism and Developmental Disorders, 6*, 653–672.

Burke, R. V., Andersen, M. N., Bowen, S. L., Howard, M. R., & Allen, K. D. (2010). Evaluation of two instruction methods to increase employment options for young adults with autism spectrum disorders. *Research in Developmental Disabilities, 31*, 1223–1233.

Coleman-Martin, M., Heller, K., Cihak, D., & Irvine, K. (2005). Using computer-assisted instruction and the nonverbal reading approach to teach word identification. *Focus on Autism and Other Developmental Disabilities, 20*, 80–90.

Duker, P., Didden, R., & Sigafoos, J. (2004). *One-to-one training: Instructional procedures for learners with developmental disabilities.* Austin, TX: Pro-ed.

Gibson, A. N., & Schuster, J. W. (1992). The use of simultaneous prompting for teaching expressive work recognition to preschool children. *Topics in early Childhood Special Education, 12,* 247–267.

Golan, O., & Baron-Cohen, S. (2006). Systemizing empathy: Teaching adults with Asperger syndrome or high-functioning autism to recognize complex emotions using interactive multimedia. *Development and Psychopathology, 18,* 591–617.

Gray, C. A. (1998). Social stories and comic strip conversations with students with Asperger syndrome and high-functioning autism. In E. Schopler, G. B. Mesibov, & L. J. Kunce (Eds.), *Asperger syndrome or high-functioning autism?* (pp. 167–198). New York, NY: Plenum.

Greene, J. A., Moos, D. C., & Azevedo, R. (2011). Self-regulated learning with computer-based learning environments. *New Directions for Teaching and Learning, 126,* 107–115.

Hall, T. E., Hughes, C. A., & Filbert, M. (2000). Computer assisted instruction in reading for students with learning disabilities: A research synthesis. *Education and Treatment of Children, 23,* 173–194.

Hetzroni, O. E., & Shalem, U. (2005). From logos to orthographic symbols: A multilevel fading computer program for teaching nonverbal children with autism. *Focus on Autism and Other Developmental Disabilities, 20,* 201–212.

Horner, R. H., Carr, E. G., Halle, J. W., McGee, G., Odom, S., & Wolery, M. (2005). The use of single-subject research to identify evidence-based practice in special education. *Exceptional Children, 71,* 165–179.

Hutcherson, K., Langone, J., Ayres, K., & Clees, T. (2004). Computer assisted instruction to teach item selection in grocery stores: An assessment of acquisition and generalization. *Journal of Special Education Technology, 19,* 33–42.

Inan, F. A., Lowther, D. L., Ross, S. M., & Strahl, D. (2010). Patterns of classroom activities during students' use of computers: Relations between instructional strategies and computer applications. *Teaching and Teacher Education, 26,* 540–546.

Johnson, D. A., & Rubin, S. (2011). Effectiveness of interactive computer-based instruction: A review of studies published between 1995 and 2007. *Journal of Organizational Behavior Management, 31,* 55–94.

Kagohara, D. M. (2011). Three students with developmental disabilities learn to operate an iPod to access age-appropriate entertainment videos. *Journal of Behavioral Education, 20,* 33–43.

Kagohara, D. M., Sigafoos, J., Achmadi, D., O'Reilly, M. F., & Lancioni, G. E. (2012). Teaching children with autism spectrum disorders to check the spelling of words. *Research in Autism Spectrum Disorders, 6,* 304–310.

Kagohara, D. M., Sigafoos, J., Achmadi, D., van der Meer, L., O'Reilly, M. F., & Lancioni, G. E. (2011). Teaching students with developmental disabilities to operate an iPod Touch to listen to music. *Research in Developmental Disabilities, 32,* 2987–2992.

Kagohara, D., van der Meer, L., Ramdoss, S., O'Reilly, M. F., Lancioni, G. E., Davis, T. N., ... Sigafoos, J. (2013). Using iPods® and iPads® in teaching programs for individuals with developmental disabilities: A systematic review. *Research in Developmental Disabilities, 34,* 147–156.

Kellems, R. O., & Morningstar, M. E. (2012). Using video modeling delivered through iPods to teach vocational tasks to young adults with autism spectrum disorders. *Career Development and Transition for Exceptional Individuals, 35,* 1–13.

Kulik, J. A. (1994). Meta-analytic studies of findings on computer-based instruction. In E. L. Baker & H. F. O'Neil, Jr. (Eds.), *Technology assessment in education and training* (pp. 9–33). Hillsdale, NJ: Erlbaum.

Kulik, C. C., & Kulik, J. A. (1991). Effectiveness of computer-based instruction: An updated analysis. *Computers in Human Behavior, 7,* 75–94.

Lee, Y., & Vail, C. (2005). Computer-based reading instruction for young children with disabilities. *Journal of Special Education Technology, 20,* 5–17.

Lovaas, O. I. (2003). *Teaching individuals with developmental delay: Basic intervention techniques.* Austin, TX: Pro-ed.

Lowe, J. S. (2004). *A theory of effective computer-based instruction for adults* (Unpublished doctoral dissertation, Louisiana State University, Baton Rouge, LA). Retrieved September 2013, from http://etd.lsu.edu/docs/available/etd-04132004-172352/unrestricted/Lowe_dis.pdf.

Luiselli, J. K. (Ed.). (2012). *The handbook of high-risk challenging behaviors in people with intellectual and developmental disabilities.* Baltimore, MD: Paul H. Brookes.

Mancil, G. R., Haydon, T., & Whitby, P. (2009). Differentiated effects of paper and computer-assisted Social Stories™ on inappropriate behavior in children with autism. *Focus on Autism and Other Developmental Disabilities, 24,* 205–215.

Mechling, L., & O'Brien, E. (2010). Computer-based video instruction to teach students with intellectual disabilities to use public bus transportation. *Education and Training in Autism and Developmental Disabilities, 45,* 230–241.

Molenaar, I., Roda, C., van Boxtel, C., & Sleegers, P. (2012). Dynamic scaffolding of socially regulated learning in a computer-based learning environment. *Computers and Education, 59,* 515–523.

Moore, D., McGrath, P., & Thorpe, J. (2000). Computer-aided learning for people with autism: A framework for research and development. *Innovations in Education and Training Internationally, 37,* 218–228.

Pennington, R., Ault, M. J., & Schuster, J. W. (2011). Using response prompting and assistive technology to teach story-writing to students with autism. *Assistive Technology Outcomes and Benefits, 7,* 24–38.

Pennington, R., Stenhoff, D. M., Gibson, J., & Ballou, K. (2012). Using simultaneous prompting to teach story writing to a student with autism. *Education and Treatment of Children, 35,* 389–406.

Pennington, R. C. (2010). Computer-assisted instruction for teaching academic skills to students with autism spectrum disorders: A review of the literature. *Focus on Autism and Other Developmental Disabilities, 25,* 239–248.

Pituch, K. A., Green, V. A., Didden, R., Lang, R., O'Reilly, M. F., Lancioni, G. E., & Sigafoos, J. (2010). Parent reported treatment priorities for children with autism spectrum disorders. *Research in Autism Spectrum Disorders, 5,* 135–143.

Ramdoss, S., Lang, R., Fragale, C., Britt, C., O'Reilly, M., Sigafoos, J., ... Lancioni, G. E. (2012). Use of computer-based interventions to promote daily living skills in individuals with intellectual disabilities: A systematic review. *Journal of Developmental and Physical Disabilities, 24,* 197–215.

Ramdoss, S., Lang, R., Mulloy, A., Franco, J., O'Reilly, M., Didden, R., & Lancioni, G. (2011). Use of computer-based intervention to teach communication skills to children with autism spectrum disorders: A systematic review. *Journal of Behavioral Education, 20,* 55–76.

Ramdoss, S., Machalicek, W., Rispoli, M., Mulloy, A., Lang, R., & O'Reilly, M. (2012). Computer-based interventions to improve social and emotional skills in individuals with autism spectrum disorders: A systematic review. *Developmental Neurorehabilitation, 15,* 119–135.

Ramdoss, S., Mulloy, A., Lang, R., O'Reilly, M., Sigafoos, J., Lancioni, G., ... El Zein, F. (2011). Use of computer-based interventions to improve literacy skills in students with autism spectrum disorders: A systematic review. *Research in Autism Spectrum Disorders, 5,* 1306–1318.

Schlosser, R. W., & Blischak, D. M. (2004). Effects of speech and print feedback on spelling by children with autism. *Journal of Speech, Language, and Hearing Research, 47,* 848–862.

Shuler, C., Levine, A., & Ree, J. (2012). *iLearn II: An analysis of the education category of Apple's App Store.* New York, NY: The Joan Ganz Cooney Centre at Sesame Workshop.

Silver, M., & Oakes, P. (2001). Evaluation of a new computer intervention to teach people with autism or Asperger syndrome to recognize and predict emotions in others. *Autism, 5,* 299–316.

Simpson, A., Lagone, J., & Syers, K. M. (2004). Embedded video and computer-based instruction to improve social skills for students with autism. *Education and Training in Developmental Disabilities, 39,* 240–252.

Skinner, B. F. (1968). *The technology of teaching.* Englewood Cliffs, NJ: Prentice-Hall.

Sturmey, P., & Fitzer, A. (Eds.). (2007). *Autism spectrum disorders: Applied behavior analysis, evidence, and practice.* Austin, TX: Pro-ed.

Swettenham, J. (1996). Can children with autism be taught to understand false belief using computers? *Journal of Child Psychology and Psychiatry and Allied Disciplines, 37,* 157–165.

Tanaka, J. W., Wolf, J. M., Klaiman, C., Koenig, K., Cockburn, J., Herlihy, L., ... Schultz, R. T. (2010). Using computerized games to teach face recognition skills to children with autism spectrum disorder: The Let's Face It! program. *Journal of Child Psychology and Psychiatry, 51,* 944–952.

Tobias, S., & Fletcher, J. D. (2011). *Computer games and instruction.* Charlotte, NC: Information Age.

van der Meer, L., & Rispoli, M. (2010). Communication interventions involving speech-generating devices for children with autism: A review of the literature. *Developmental Neurorehabilitation, 13,* 294–306.

Whitcomb, S. A., Bass, J. D., & Luiselli, J. K. (2011). Effects of a computer-based reading program (Headsprout) on word list and text reading skills in a student with autism. *Journal of Developmental and Physical Disabilities, 23,* 491–499.

Yamamoto, J., & Miya, T. (1999). Acquisition and transfer of sentence construction in autistic students: Analysis of computer-based teaching. *Research in Developmental Disabilities, 20,* 355–377.

Zisimopoulos, D., Sigafoos, J., & Koutromanos, G. (2011). Using video prompting and constant time delay to teach an internet search basic skill to students with intellectual disabilities. *Education and Training in Autism and Developmental Disabilities, 46,* 238–250.

6

Naturalistic Approaches to Social Skills Training and Development

MARK F. O'REILLY, AUDREY SORRELLS, SUMMER GAINEY,
JEFF SIGAFOOS, GIULIO E. LANCIONI, RUSSELL LANG,
MANDY RISPLOI, AND TONYA DAVIS

Individuals with autism spectrum disorder (ASD) suffer from poor social skills (Flynn & Healy, 2012; National Research Council, 2001), a defining characteristic across all levels of severity on the spectrum. For many individuals with ASD, both language and cognitive abilities may remain intact, leaving social skills the predominant difficulty. Consequently, social skills intervention should be an absolute priority with the ASD population.

It is important to differentiate between social skills and other forms of communication skills such as those addressed in Chapter 7. Communication deficits such as language delay, mutism, and echolalia are common among the ASD population and are the focus of much intervention. All communication intervention involves a social component because it is fundamentally designed to teach the person with ASD to share information with a partner. To reduce any confusion between communication and social skills intervention techniques, this chapter will focus on a selective review of evidence-based interventions designed to teach social skills to individuals with ASD who already possess relatively sophisticated language and communication skills (high-functioning autism [HFA] and Asperger syndrome). While some of the social skill strategies described in this chapter (e.g., modeling and reinforcement) might be viable interventions for persons with more severe levels of this disorder, other interventions will require relatively intact cognitive and language skills (e.g., social stories, social problem solving).

Before any discussion of intervention strategies, it is necessary to provide the reader with a clear definition of social skills. One of the difficulties when reviewing the intervention literature with this population is a general lack of consensus on what constitutes social skills. Some researchers will describe very discrete and observable behaviors such as initiating a conversation. Other researchers describe relatively complicated cognitive and behavioral dynamics such as identifying and interpreting social cues followed by reacting appropriately to such cues. A viable definition of social skills should try to incorporate the complex and discrete phenomena that constitute skilled social behavior. For example, social skills incorporate both verbal and nonverbal behaviors that are necessary for successful social exchange and interpersonal communication but also specific behaviors such as initiating an interaction ("Would you like a coffee?"), responding to an initiation ("Yes, please. Thank you"), and terminating an interaction ("No thanks. I've had two cups already this morning"). Social skills also involve cognitive and behavioral phenomena such as accurately interpreting a social context, behaving appropriately according to such context, and evaluating one's behavior in the light of the responses of others. In other words, social skills involve a complex cognitive behavioral interplay that is contextually influenced.

Our definition of social skills would seem to match the complex deficits in social skills exhibited by the ASD population as described in the *Diagnostic and Statistical Manual of Mental Disorders* (*DSM-IV-TR*) (American Psychiatric Association, 2000). According to the *DSM-IV-TR*, social skills deficits include impairment in nonverbal behavior to regulate ongoing social interactions. Persons with ASD can experience difficulties with eye contact, using appropriate facial expressions, and body posture and gestures during social interactions. There is a lack of motivation to share experiences or interests with others. Conversely, persons with ASD have difficulty relating to social and emotional states of others (social reciprocity).

These social deficits are evident at initial diagnosis. Parents often report that their child seems to want to play on his or her own. These children do not respond to initiations from other same-age children and do not initiate interactions with peers. They tend to prefer isolate activities. These patterns occur in familiar social settings (family gatherings) and during situations with unfamiliar peers (playing at the local park). These deficits can become more acute as the child grows older and enters school. Children who are high functioning on the spectrum are generally included in the regular classroom. This social aloofness is often combined with intense interests in specific items (e.g., dinosaurs, trains) and can lead to rejection, ridicule, and bullying. As these children grow older, they become painfully aware of their own social ineptitudes. Many of these children are motivated to fit in, to belong to a peer network, to have friends. Mental health issues are not uncommon for these children because they may suffer from depression and social anxiety. In our clinical practice many of these children receive a combination of mental health counseling and social skills training. Note, too, that social deficits are not confined to early childhood and the school years. Many adults with HFA and Asperger syndrome have little social support, experience mental health issues, and are underemployed or unemployed. There is a clear need for effective and comprehensive social skills interventions for this population across the life span. Optimally, intervention should start at an early age with the goal that social deficits will be remediated eventually. However, it is clear that individuals with this diagnosis experience social deficits at all ages. Consequently, effective interventions should be available for all ages (young children, school age, and adults).

In this chapter we provide a selective overview of several social skills intervention strategies that can be used to teach skills to persons with HFA and Asperger syndrome. Each of these social skills strategies has been empirically researched with several studies published in reputable peer-reviewed academic journals. The strategies reviewed include modeling and reinforcement, peer tutoring, social scripts, social problem solving, and social skills training groups. We chose these strategies for review because they may be optimal for different age ranges and contexts. Modeling and reinforcement may be relatively simple strategies that parents could use with a young child. Peer tutoring and social scripts are relatively easily incorporated within a school curriculum. Social problem solving and social skills training groups might be more appropriate for adolescents and adults.

SELECTING SOCIAL SKILLS FOR TRAINING

Before discussing the various social skill intervention strategies, it is important to briefly address procedures for selecting social skills for intervention. In fact, social skills that are selected for intervention may to some degree drive the type of intervention to be used with the person. As we emphasized previously, social skills deficits are typically multifaceted, involving behavioral and cognitive components, and manifest themselves differently across various social contexts.

Practitioners and parents should have a clear picture of the variety of social skills deficits across all relevant social contexts for an individual. While several social skills questionnaires exist (e.g., Matson, Rotatori, & Helsel, 1983), we suggest using an informal assessment approach. Informal assessment generally involves direct observation of the person across real-world contexts where social skills are deemed to be problematic. Direct observations can be conducted by parents, teachers, or therapists. It may be prudent to interview older children and adults about the social difficulties they experience across different social contexts, as direct observation may be embarrassing or stigmatizing.

Social skills priorities may differ across various cultural groups (Rivera & Rogers-Adkinson, 1997). Working with culturally diverse groups may influence such factors as the social behaviors targeted and contexts in which skills are assessed. Certain social behaviors such as making eye contact and being assertive, while valued in Anglo-American culture, may be interpreted as aggressive and offensive in other cultures. In our experience some culturally diverse families need a period to establish a trusting relationship with the therapist before the family allows access to the home environment. This distrust may stem from a history of abuse and neglect on the part of health care and education systems of culturally diverse groups in the United States (Gourdine, Baffour, & Teasley, 2011).

We recommend that observations be conducted in home, school, community, and work environments (depending on the age of the person). A list of social difficulties can then be compiled and prioritized. Those social deficits that produce the greatest barriers to inclusion should be addressed initially. Once social skills have been prioritized, they need to be described in clear and objective language to allow measurement prior to, during, and following intervention. These clearly described social skills also become the focus of the intervention, which should only be deemed effective if it produces observable change in these social skills within real-world contexts.

SOCIAL SKILLS INTERVENTION STRATEGIES

We discuss five social skills intervention strategies, including modeling and reinforcement, peer tutoring, social scripts, social problem solving, and social skills training groups. Some of the intervention components will overlap across these social skills interventions. For example, all of the intervention strategies will involve some form of modeling of social skills or reinforcement of appropriate behavior. However, each of these interventions has distinctive properties as detailed next.

Modeling and Reinforcement

This is one of the earliest social skills intervention strategies documented in the literature and has been widely researched. In fact, Matson, Matson, and Rivet (2007) in their scholarly review of social skills intervention strategies reported over 30 published studies evaluating modeling and reinforcement. This is a relatively simple strategy that can be adapted in many ways to fit the instructional situation. In essence, the strategy involves several components: (a) the target social skill is demonstrated or modeled for the person, (b) the person then practices the skill, (c) corrective feedback and repeated practice occurs if the person does not perform the skill correctly, and (d) reinforcement in the form of praise or edibles is presented to support appropriate performance of the social skills. We highlight that parents and teachers can be easily taught to use this strategy within situations where the skill is expected to occur. For example, a parent may model appropriate social etiquette (e.g., "Can I watch TV now please?") in the target environment (TV room at home). When the child repeats the model

correctly, the parent permits access to the TV and provides verbal praise. Teaching the social skill in the criterion environment (where it is expected to occur) can help overcome the difficulties with generalization of skills often seen with this population. These strategies could also be used easily with young children in school settings. For example, a teacher could model initiations, responses, and participation requests for students with ASD. Systematic feedback (corrective or positive) could be delivered based on student performance. Additionally, the strategies could be used in an inclusive manner for all young children in a classroom so that students with ASD would not be singled out or stigmatized. As children get older, it may be appropriate to use such interventions in a more private situation at schools (e.g., a resource classroom). However, difficulties with generalization of skills to criterion environments are then inevitable.

A brief review of two empirical studies will serve to illustrate the research on modeling and reinforcement as an intervention technique (Apple, Billingsley, & Schwartz, 2005; Maoine & Mirenda, 2006). Apple et al. (2005) taught two 5-year-old boys with HFA to deliver compliments to peers during free time at an integrated preschool setting. Compliments were selected based on parent interview and observation of children of similar age in other preschool or kindergarten classrooms. The target behaviors included such compliments as "Neat," "Cool," "I like your...," and "You have a nice...". A series of video vignettes were made to demonstrate the appropriate use of the target behaviors. Each child individually watched the videos in a private room and then immediately returned to a 15-minute free-play period in his or her classroom. Peer confederates solicited the targeted behaviors by showing the children toys/items and prompting them to "Look!" Spontaneous compliments were also measured. Video models combined with reinforcement (opportunity to select item from pool of reinforcers) increased compliments by both children. The intervention was evaluated using a multiple baseline across participants design (Kennedy, 2005) and demonstrated that the positive changes in social skills occurred for both children with the introduction of the modeling plus reinforcement intervention. Another point worth mentioning about this study is that the authors used video models as part of their instructional protocol. In recent years we see an increased use of computer-based video instruction to teach a variety of skills to persons with ASD (DiGennaro Reed, Hyman, & Hirst, 2011).

In a second example of this type of intervention, Maione and Mirenda (2006) taught peer-directed social language skills to a 5-year-old child with ASD. This study was conducted in the child's home with peers (a boy and girl around the same age as the target child). The child was taught such interaction skills as comments, initiations, responding, questions, and acknowledgments. These skills were taught using a series of video vignettes in which adults modeled appropriate skills during three play activities. The three play activities were selected based on the child's preference for these activities and included Play Doh, toy cars, and toy house with figurines. The mother was involved in implementing the video modeling intervention. The intervention also included video feedback (the child observed his or her own performance with peers) and prompting (child is encouraged to engage in interactions during peer play). The effectiveness of these interventions was evaluated using a multiple baseline design across the three different play activities. Overall, the results were generally positive, as the child demonstrated the social skills more frequently. Additionally untrained social skills also seemed to increase as a function of the intervention. We suggest that this study is an instructive example of how such interventions can be incorporated into a natural setting, the child's home, while involving the mother and featuring preferred play activities with regular peers.

Peer Tutoring

Peer tutoring is another social skills intervention strategy that has been researched extensively (Bass & Mulick, 2007). Matson et al. (2007) in their review of social skills interventions for children with ASD reported a total of 20 empirical studies of this intervention. In another recent review, Chan et al. (2009) reported that 42 studies employed peer tutoring to teach a variety of academic, social, and leisure skills to children with ASD. Peer tutoring is an intervention strategy whereby peers (e.g., classmates) are taught to implement instructional procedures to facilitate social skills for children with ASD. This intervention strategy has been predominantly investigated in school settings with younger children. This strategy has been described as a practical approach in schools settings given the natural abundance of same-aged peers (Chan et al., 2009).

Peers can assume different roles during social skill interventions such as modeling appropriate behaviors, implementing prompting procedures, and reinforcing targeted social skills. There are several potential advantages to peer tutoring as an intervention option in schools. First, there is an abundance of peers to act as intervention agents. Accordingly, implementing intervention is not limited to teachers or therapists, thereby increasing potential access to the intervention by students with ASD. Second, the very nature of peer intervention may foster inclusion in peer social networks in the school. As peers with and without disabilities interact, reciprocal skills may increase because students without disabilities learn to comfortably interact with children who have ASD and children with ASD become more proficient with social skills. In other words, children with and without disabilities may gain in social competence and thus a more inclusive school community may emerge. Third, children with ASD may have an opportunity to practice social skills across multiple partners, settings, and times. These opportunities should foster not only acquisition but also generalization and maintenance of social skills (Stokes & Baer, 1977).

Peer tutoring may also have some potential disadvantages and possible limitations (Chan et al., 2009; Matson et al., 2007). For example, training peers to implement an intervention and monitoring peer interactions and progress for the child with ASD is a relatively complicated skill set for a teacher to implement. Furthermore, not all teachers might be up to this task, especially for children with HFA or Asperger syndrome who are placed in regular classrooms. It is our experience that regular teachers get little or no training on instruction of students with special needs. Hence, special education support may be required to regular classrooms should teachers decide to implement such strategies. Some teachers have also raised concerns about the possibility that peers may be missing out on the regular curriculum if they are involved in such interventions. However, such concerns seem unwarranted and could be rectified if the teacher involves peers in a judicious manner. For example, a peer could tutor for brief periods during the school day, or tutoring of social skills could occur during break and leisure times of the school schedule, thus mitigating the potential of deleterious schooling effects on the peers. Another limitation is that peer tutoring may necessitate structural changes to the class routine. This may warrant careful consideration and possible consultation with special education support teams, probably not a major issue with kindergarten and elementary-age children, but more pressing in later academic years as the curriculum becomes more regimented.

Two examples from the empirical literature illustrate these peer tutoring strategies (Chung et al., 2007; Gonzalez-Lopez & Kamps, 1997). Gonzalez-Lopez and Kamps (1997) studed 4 children with autism (ages 5–7 years) and 12 typically developing peers. Children with autism attended a special education segregated classroom while the peers attended either kindergarten or first-grade regular classrooms. Training sessions included a teacher, one child with autism, and three typical peers. Sessions were 20 minutes in length and were conducted three to four times per week in the special education classroom. Social skills were taught in the context of didactic play. Peers were taught a set of behavior management strategies such as giving easy instructions, demonstrating to others how to perform tasks and then physically prompting the appropriate skills, praising when the child is doing well, and ignoring inappropriate behavior. Children with autism were taught to greet peers (including saying "hello," asking friends to play, asking questions about toys), imitate and follow instructions, share and take turns, ask for help, and make requests. Social skills training groups were followed by free play activities during which teachers periodically prompted peer skills and social skills. The findings, evaluated in a reversal design, were that the quality and duration of appropriate social interactions increased and problem behavior (aggression and property destruction) decreased for three of the four children with ASD.

Chung et al. (2007) examined a peer tutoring intervention to teach social skills to four boys with HFA aged 6–7 years. Four regular peers ages 6–10 years participated. The social skills intervention occurred over 12 weeks with weekly 90-minute sessions. Peers were taught prior to the intervention and immediately prior to each session to prompt appropriate behavior, reinforce appropriate behavior, and encourage the children with HFA to ask questions. Social skills training sessions involved all eight children and each session involved a welcome, explanation of skills of the day, didactic teaching, practice, snack, video time, and wrap-up. Observations were conducted immediately following training in a free-play-style situation. Skills targeted during training and measured during posttraining included securing attention, initiating comments, and initiating requests. Inappropriate social skills were also measured and included inappropriate topic change,

unintelligible speech, and no response. Percentage of intervals with appropriate and inappropriate social skills was measured and individual participant pretest posttest designs were used to evaluate intervention effectiveness. Overall, the results seemed to indicate positive change in social skills for three of the four participants.

Social Stories

Social stories have become a popular intervention strategy with teachers and clinicians. In a recent review of social story interventions, Reynhout and Carter (2006) reported 16 studies (published articles and dissertations) that targeted different behaviors (self-help, academics, aggression) including social skills. The premise for social story interventions is that individuals with ASD have difficulty understanding social context and are unable to take the perspective of others (Attwood, 2000; Baron-Cohen, 1995). Effective social skills intervention must therefore teach them to understand the social context and to perform appropriately within that specific context. Thus, social stories promote the skills to interpret a particular social context in addition to the social skills needed to perform within that context. Also, social stories appear to be particularly suited for young children with basic reading skills and can be implemented in the home or school setting.

A social story is an individualized short story that is designed to clarify a specific social context, the perspectives of others in that context, and the social skills to be performed. In other words, a social story provides "information on what people in a given situation are doing, thinking, or feeling, the sequence of events, the identification of significant social cues and their meaning, and the script of what to do or say" (Attwood, 2000, p. 90). The guidelines for constructing a social story are specific and involve the use of *descriptive, directive, perspective,* and *affirmative* sentence types (see Gray & Garand, 1993). Descriptive sentences describe the situation in terms of relevant social cues, directive sentences specify an appropriate response on the part of the child with ASD, perspective sentences describe feelings and responses of those in the social situation, and affirmative sentences basically reinforce a shared value(s) among the group within that context. A ratio of these different sentence types is also recommended with two to five descriptive, perspective, or affirmative sentences to every directive sentence. Social stories should be tailored to the child's comprehension level and focus on the appropriate social skills to be performed and not the social difficulties experienced by the child in such contexts. Originally, social stories were presented solely in written format, but researchers have since presented social stories with pictures, through video modeling, and handheld computers (Kagohara et al., 2013). Social stories are usually taught using a combination of modeling, role play, and feedback by parents or teachers. During initial phases of training, students are examined on their comprehension of the social story following practice. The student may eventually be able to practice the social story independently.

Two empirical studies illustrate the social stories intervention strategy (Chan & O'Reilly, 2008; Sansosti & Powell-Smith, 2006). Chan and O'Reilly (2008) implemented a social stories intervention with two children (5 and 6 years old) with ASD who attended regular kindergarten classrooms at a public elementary school. Social story intervention was implemented in school prior to the school day. The children's social behavior was observed during circle time and center time on the same days as training. Classroom observation sessions (where social skills were measured) were 1 hour in length, while social story sessions were 10 to 20 minutes in length (depending on the number of social stories being practiced). Three social skills were targeted for each of the children: (a) social interactions such as standing too close to peers when initiating conversations and asking to play appropriately, (b) raising hand to answer questions during class, and (c) inappropriate vocalizations (comments irrelevant to the interaction). Experimental control was demonstrated using a multiple-baseline design across social skills for each student. The social stories intervention was staggered across each of the social skills for each student. Each of the social stories (three stories per participant) was presented in written format on a single piece of paper. The student could choose to read the story aloud, silently, or have the therapist read the story aloud. Next, a therapist asked three comprehension questions related to the story. If the student could not adequately answer the questions, he or she was required to read the story again and the questions were repeated. Finally, the therapist with an accomplice modeled the appropriate behavior and the student was then required to role-play the appropriate response. Verbal prompts were delivered when errors occurred and the student was praised

for correct responding. The intervention produced increases in appropriate social skills (e.g., social initiations) and decreases in inappropriate behavior. Maintenance probes in the classroom for up to 10 months following the intervention continued to show positive effects.

Sansosti and Powell-Smith (2006) implemented a social story intervention protocol with three elementary school children (ages 9–11 years) diagnosed with Asperger syndrome. Interventions occurred in each student's respective school setting during sport or leisure activities (courtyard, soccer field, gym area). Target behaviors included sportsmanship (respectful comments to teammates and opponents), maintaining conversations (specifically small talk during break periods), and joining in (appropriately entering into a sports game). The social story was included in a booklet form that the students could carry with them. During intervention students practiced the social story twice daily (before and after school) with a parent. Social skill observations took place during regular school periods in the locations identified earlier. Experimental control was demonstrated using a multiple baseline across participants design. Overall, the results showed benefits for two of the participants while a third participant did not show substantial gains in social skills.

Social Problem Solving

The value of using social problem-solving interventions to teach social skills to persons with disabilities has been proposed in the literature (Gumpel, 1994). Teaching social skills within the context of a broad problem-solving strategy is based on an understanding of social skills as a process involving social and cognitive components (McFall, 1982). The problem-solving understanding of social skills is compatible with our earlier definition of the social deficits experienced by persons with ASD, that is, failure to understand social context and hence experiencing difficulties regulating appropriate social behavior. While there has not been extensive research of problem-solving interventions with individuals with ASD, numerous rigorous research studies have examined this procedure with individuals diagnosed with intellectual disabilities (e.g., O'Reilly & Glynn, 1995; O'Reilly, Lancioni, & O'Kane, 2000; Park & Gaylord Ross, 1989). Although we did not conduct a formal review of social problem-solving studies, we did identify 10 published empirical studies examining social problem-solving techniques with individuals with intellectual disabilities. Because this body of work has produced positive results and is conducted with individuals with intellectual disabilities, we believe it might be worth examining such intervention protocol with individuals with ASD. In fact, our own research team has conducted many of these problem-solving studies and believes that several of the participants in these earlier studies would today be diagnosed with ASD.

Problem-solving interventions involve teaching social skills as part of a generic process of engaging in social interactions. The person is taught a set of behaviors to manage and monitor his or her own social skills in addition to teaching specific social skills themselves. In other words, social skills training is combined with self-monitoring and self-management training. Self-management of instruction has proven to be very effective in teaching durable repertoires to persons with ASD (see Chapter 8 for a detailed review of these strategies).

Problem-solving training involves teaching the person to ask and answer a series of questions in relation to the social context, to perform appropriate social behaviors, and finally, to examine the outcomes of the social interaction. The person is first taught to discriminate the salient social stimuli by asking himself or herself, "What's happening here?" The person should then accurately describe the social situation. Next, the person should make a decision about how he or she should behave, that is, by asking, "What should I do?" The person learns to generate a series of alternative action plans and then to choose the most appropriate interaction for the current context. At this point the person performs the overt social skills. Finally the person evaluates the social interaction by asking himself or herself, "What happened when I (description of how he or she behaved)?" The person is prompted to generate a description of the responses of other people in the social interaction and to evaluate whether these responses were positive or negative. This social process is taught using role play, modeling, and feedback. The training process can be intensive, often lasting up to an hour initially, but tapering in intensity as the participant becomes proficient at the skills. Training usually occurs in a setting removed from the environment in which the skills are to be performed (e.g., resource room in a school setting). This might not be an optimal strategy to use in elementary school settings (because of pull-out requirements for training) but might be adapted and taught at a class-wide level.

Several empirical studies have evaluated this problem-solving intervention procedure (O'Reilly & Glynn, 1995; O'Reilly, Lancioni, & Kierans, 2000; Park & Gaylord-Ross, 1989). Park and Gaylord-Ross (1989) taught three persons with intellectual disabilities appropriate social skills within a supported employment setting. Some of the social skills deficits exhibited by these workers were failure to initiate conversations with coworkers and unclear or off-topic conversations when they did initiate. The three workers learned to initiate, expand, and terminate conversations using the problem-solving procedure in a setting removed from the employment site. The appropriate social skills rapidly generalized to the employment site once participants acquired the problem-solving strategy. The problem-solving strategy was compared to a more traditional model of teaching social skills (role play of overt social behaviors only) and proved superior to the traditional model. Experimental control was demonstrated using combinations of multiple-baseline and reversal designs.

O'Reilly and Glynn (1995) taught two high school students to initiate appropriately with the classroom teacher during ongoing lessons. Both students were diagnosed with mild intellectual disabilities and were described as being socially withdrawn by their teachers. They did not respond to teacher questions, initiate appropriate questions, or interact with others in the schoolyard during breaks. Social skills training occurred in a resource room removed from the regular classroom. Fellow students were involved in the role plays, and portions of the class curriculum were used to train the initiation and responding skills. The students learned to initiate and respond using the problem-solving protocol and generalized the skills to the regular classroom context. Both students also began to initiate with peers in the schoolyard during breaks. This skill was not targeted as part of the problem-solving intervention and is therefore evidence of generalization of social skills to untrained contexts. Multiple-baseline designs were used in this study to evaluate the effects of the intervention.

In a final example, the problem-solving strategy was used to teach leisure social skills to four adults with moderate levels of intellectual disability (O'Reilly, Lancioni, & Kierans, 2000). These individuals were taught to order and pay for their own drink at a local bar. Prior to the intervention participants did not interact with bar staff and fellow patrons. Instead, residential staff accompanied the participants to the bar, ordered, and paid for the drinks. Participants were taught to use the problem-solving strategies to greet bar staff, order their drink, accept the drink, and pay for it appropriately. Problem-solving training occurred in the participants' group homes. All the participants quickly generalized the skills to the local bars and, as well, were also able to use the skills in different bars without further training. In addition, participants maintained the skills for 3 years following training.

Social Skills Training Groups

Social skills training groups is the final set of intervention strategies described in this chapter. Cappadocia and Weiss (2011) reported 10 published empirical studies in their review of the published literature. This form of intervention may best be suited to older adolescents and adults with HFS and Asperger syndrome, as it sometimes involves grouping of individuals with disabilities with a view to developing social support networks and disability awareness (through psychoeducational processes). The format, intensity, and skills targeted during group training can vary widely. In general, social skills groups are led by a trained therapist, consist of group sizes from 4 to 20 individuals with disabilities, and last for a predetermined number of sessions. The content of the therapy sessions typically involves modeling, role play, practice, and feedback of core social skills deficits such as initiating conversations, complimenting, and expanding conversations. Several group training programs have offered supplemental support and training for parents (e.g., Marriage, Gordon, & Brand, 1995). Such parent support strategies may foster generalization of social skills beyond the group training setting. Some training groups foster socialization beyond the therapy settings such as going to dinner and movies as part of the planned extracurricular activities of the group.

To some degree, these group interventions do not fit comfortably within a chapter that describes naturalistic approaches because they are conducted in a clinical environment removed from where these skills are expected to occur. For example, a group may role-play greeting a hostess at a restaurant but never practice such skills in vivo at a real restaurant. A plethora of research has demonstrated that persons with ASD fail to generalize skills across context without explicit training. It would seem critical to program for generalization as part of social skills training

groups. This might be accomplished by conducting some of the training and measurement of skill acquisition in real-world settings. Compounding this issue are the primary measures used in the majority of these studies—questionnaire and interviews with significant others. These forms of assessment may not accurately reflect behavioral changes in social skills. Very few of these studies have conducted observational assessments of social skills performance in real-world settings. Both the design and outcome measures of group social skill interventions make conclusions as to their effectiveness tentative at best.

Two examples of published empirical studies will illustrate social skills group interventions (Barnhill, Cook, Tebbenkamp, & Miles, 2002; Marriage, Gordon, & Brand, 1995). Barnhill et al. (2002) conducted a group social skills intervention for 8 weeks (1 hour per week) with 8 adolescents (12–17 years of age) with ASD. The first four meetings focused on appropriate prosody to express different emotions, followed by four meetings that addressed understanding the emotions of others through interpreting facial expressions. Instruction took the form of modeling, role play, lecture, and feedback. Recreational activities occurred after training sessions (e.g., dining out, bowling, movies, etc.). A pre- and postassessment found no significant changes in social skills. However, several of the participants reported that they had established friendships and had made contact with others from the group several months after the training ended.

Marriage et al. (1995) implemented an intervention with eight students with Asperger syndrome (ages 8 to 12 years), conducted over eight group sessions, that targeted simple greetings to managing conversations. Intervention strategies included role play, modeling, feedback, and video presentations. Parents attended an informal support group while their children attended social skills training but unfortunately did not report significant improvement in social skills for their children following the intervention.

PRACTICE RECOMMENDATIONS

In this section we present practice recommendations for research scientists and clinicians based on our review of the socials skills training literature with individuals who have HFA and Asperger syndrome. In our overview of practice recommendations for researchers, we emphasize some of the methodological limitations that are common in the social skills literature and make suggestions for future research. In the overview of practice recommendations for clinicians, we summarize best clinical practices in terms of assessment and social skills intervention.

Practice Recommendations for Researchers

As social skills difficulties are one of the predominant chronic deficits experienced by the ASD population, it is not surprising to see a large and developing body of research that targets treatment of these deficits. Matson et al. (2007) reported increasing numbers of treatment studies in the peer-reviewed literature between 1979 and 2001. Despite the large number of published treatment studies (as we reported earlier in the chapter), there is currently no clear consensus about best clinical practices. This lack of clinical consensus may in part be due to methodological weaknesses that are somewhat pervasive across the treatment literature, including, but not limited to, participant characteristics, experimental control, and robustness of treatment effects. Of course, the implication here is that future studies should try to address these limitations.

Matson et al. (2007) noted in their review that descriptions of participant characteristics are often unclear or lacking in social skills treatment studies. Participants are described in general diagnostic terms with no assessment data provided. Matson et al. (2007) recommend that assessments be conducted as a routine practice in treatment studies. Additionally, diagnosis should be multifaceted involving evidence-based assessment scales of ASD symptomatology and assessment of other possible salient variables such as mental health status and intellectual disability. It would be optimal to employ a general battery of assessment protocols across treatment studies. Comprehensive and common assessment batteries permit a clearer understanding of treatment-by-characteristic interaction effects. Additionally, assessment and intervention with culturally diverse groups are sadly underreported in the literature. Researchers should report ethnicity and sociodemographic data of participants.

A second limitation can be broadly defined in terms of methodological or experimental control difficulties. This limitation is particularly true of two bodies of research mentioned earlier: social stories

and social skills groups. The majority of social stories interventions have used single-case research designs (multiple-baseline designs across behaviors or participants) to examine the relationship between the treatment variable and changes in the targeted social skills. These designs are appropriate, rigorous, and usually implemented accurately. Dependent measures usually have strong face validity in these studies (measuring changes in targeted social skills in real-world settings). However, the results of many of the social stories interventions are not impressive. For example, there often is overlap between socials skills performance during baseline (prior to treatment) and during treatment, an indication that social story interventions are not effective. And yet social story interventions remain popular in the face of poor evidence to support their efficacy, something not uncommon in the field of ASD treatment (Lang et al., 2012; Mulloy et al., 2010). Experimental control might also be described as weak in the social skills group treatment studies described in this chapter. We have already mentioned that the dependent measures routinely used in social skills training groups (questionnaires and interviews) may not have strong face validity. Often the basic parameters of group design are violated (e.g., sample size is small, control groups not used), making interpretation of the results tenuous at best. Given such pervasive experimental faux pas, it is reasonable to suggest that the effectiveness of socials skills training groups with the ASD population has yet to be confirmed.

Finally, treatment robustness should be measured. An effective social skills treatment should produce socially significant changes in targeted skills that occur in all salient social environments and persist over time. Unfortunately, few studies combine these measures. It is important not only to show changes in social skills as a function of the intervention but to also show that social behavior is now within normal parameters of social performance. This can be accomplished by comparing posttreatment social skills with those of socially competent peers. Social skills should also be assessed across multiple real-world social contexts (generalization across settings) and not be confined to treatment settings alone. Finally, long-term assessment of social skills change should be measured. Often posttreatment assessment is performed for several weeks. Such posttreatment assessment should be extended to several months or even years.

Practice Recommendations for Clinicians

Despite methodological shortcomings in the research literature, it is possible to suggest some practice recommendations for clinicians. First, initial assessment of social skills deficits should be comprehensive and should include all relevant social environments such as home, school, work, and leisure contexts. Assessment should be culturally sensitive, implemented informally, and include direct observations in natural contexts and interviews with significant others and the person with HFA. However, caution should be exercised when conducting informal assessments (choosing whom to interview and where to observe) in order to reduce stigmatization of the person. Social skills should be identified and prioritized for instruction based on this informal observation process. The skills targeted for intervention should maximize the person's social inclusion in regular life settings. Targeted social skills should be measured on an ongoing basis prior to, during, and following intervention to assess the impact of the intervention.

Concerning interventions, they should be conducted regularly, approximately once or twice per week. With younger children intervention could be implemented almost continuously as part of the school and family context. Interventions can be conducted as part of the ongoing natural flow of everyday interactions such as teacher prompts during routine classroom activities, using one-to-one instruction (e.g., problem-solving techniques), or in small group instruction. Interventions should provide the opportunity to practice observable social behaviors. For older children observable behaviors plus the rules for social engagement should be practiced. Social rules should include teaching the person how to interpret the current social situation, to make decisions about the most appropriate social behaviors, to perform those behaviors accurately, and to evaluate the consequences of his or her behavior. These skills should be practiced using a combination of modeling, role play, and feedback. Some culturally diverse groups have traditionally experienced difficulty accessing such interventions (Gourdine, Baffour, & Teasley, 2011). Equitable spread of resources should be considered by systems such as school districts as they plan these services for the student population.

Finally, follow-up support should be provided. Typically, interventions may need to be implemented for extended periods, including ongoing social skills support. Such follow-up support should be combined with periodic assessment of social competence in real-world settings. Targeted social skills and interventions may need to be adjusted based upon new priorities in the person's social world. It also is beneficial to assess the social validity of interventions so that practitioners approve of them and are satisfied with the outcomes.

REFERENCES

Apple, A. L., Billingsley, F., & Schwartz, I. S. (2005). Effects of video modeling alone and with self-management on compliant-giving behavior of children with high-functioning autism spectrum disorders. *Journal of Positive Behavior Interventions, 7*, 33–46.

American Psychiatric Association. (2000). *Diagnostic and statistical manual of mental disorders* (4th ed., text rev.). Washington DC: Author.

Attwood, T. (2000). Strategies for improving the social integration of children with Asperger syndrome. *Autism, 4*, 58–100.

Barnhill, G. P., Cook, K. T., Tebbenkamp, K., & Myles, B. S. (2002). The effectiveness of social skills intervention targeting nonverbal communication for adolescents with Asperger syndrome and related pervasive developmental disorders. *Focus on Autism and Other Developmental Disabilities, 17*, 112–118.

Baron-Cohen, S. (1995). *Mindblindness: An essay on autism and theory of mind.* Cambridge, MA: MIT Press.

Bass, J. D., & Mulick, J. A. (2007). Social play skill enhancement of children with autism using peers and siblings as therapists. *Psychology in the Schools, 44*, 727–735.

Cappadocia, M. C., & Weiss, J. A. (2011). Review of social skills training groups for youth with Asperger syndrome and high functioning autism. *Research in Autism Spectrum Disorders, 5*, 70–78.

Chan, J., Lang, R., Rispoli, M., O'Reilly, M. F., Sigafoos, J., & Cole, H. (2009). Use of peer-mediated interventions in the treatment of autism spectrum disorders: A systematic review. *Research in Autism Spectrum Disorders, 3*, 876–889.

Chan, J., & O'Reilly, M. F. (2008). Using social stories plus modeling to teach social skills to students with autism in regular classrooms. *Journal of Applied Behavior Analysis, 41*, 405–409.

Chung, K. M., Reavis, S., Mosconi, M., Drewry, J., Matthews, T., & Tasse, M. (2007). Peer-mediated social skills training program for young children with high-functioning autism. *Research in Developmental Disabilities, 28*, 423–436.

DiGennaro Reed, F. D., Hyman, S. R., & Hirst, J. M. (2011). Applications of technology to teach social skills to children with autism. *Research in Autism Spectrum Disorders, 5*, 1003–1010.

Flynn, L., & Healy, O. (2012). A review of treatments for deficits in social skills and self-help skills in autism spectrum disorder. *Research in Autism Spectrum Disorders, 6*, 431–441.

Gonzalez-Lopez, A., & Kamps, D. M. (1997). Social skills training to increase social interactions between children with autism and their typical peers. *Focus on Autism and Other Developmental Disorders, 12*, 2–14.

Gourdine, R. M., Baffour, T. D., & Teasley, M. (2011). Autism and the African American community. *Social Work Public Health, 26*, 454–470.

Gray, C., & Garand, J. D., (1993). Social stories: Improving responses of students with autism with accurate social information. *Focus on Autistic Behavior, 8*, 1–10.

Gumpel, T. (1994). Social competence and social skills training for persons with mental retardation: An expansion of a behavioral paradigm. *Education and Training in Mental Retardation and Developmental Disabilities, 29*, 194–201.

Kagohara, D., van der Meer, L., Ramdoss, S., O'Reilly, M. F., Lancioni, G. E., Davis, T. N., … Sigafoos, J. (2013). Using iPods and iPads in teaching programs for individuals with developmental disabilities: A systematic review. *Research in Developmental Disabilities, 34*(1), 147–156.

Kennedy, C. H. (1995). *Single-case designs for educational research*. Boston, MA: Allyn and Bacon.

Lang, R., O'Reilly, M., Healy, O., Risploi, M., Lydon, H., Streusand, W., … Giebers, S. (2012). Sensory integration therapy for autism spectrum disorders: A systematic review. *Research in Autism Spectrum Disorders, 6*, 1004–1018.

Maione, L., & Mirenda, P. (2006). Effects of video modeling and video feedback on peer-directed social skills of a child with autism. *Journal of Positive Behavior Interventions, 8*, 106–118.

Marriage, K. J., Gordon, V., & Brand, L. (1995). A social skills group for boys with Asperger's syndrome. *Australian and New Zealand Journal of Psychiatry, 29*, 58–62.

Matson, J. L., Matson, M. L., & Rivet, T. (2007). Social skills treatments for children with autism spectrum disorders. *Behavior Modification, 31*, 682–707.

Matson, J. L., Rotatori, A. F., & Helsel, W. J. (1983). Development of a rating scale to measure social skills in children: The Matson Evaluation of Social Skills with Youngsters (MESSY). *Behavior Research and Therapy, 21*, 335–340.

McFall, R. (1982). A review and reformation of the concept of social skills. *Behavioral Assessment, 4*, 1–33.

Mulloy, A., Lang, R., O'Reilly, M. F., Sigafoos, J., Lancioni, G., & Rispoli, M. (2010). Gluten-free and casein-free diets in the treatment of autism spectrum disorders: A systematic review. *Research in Autism Spectrum Disorders, 4*, 328–339.

National Research Council. (2001). *Educating children with autism*. Washington, DC: National Academy Press.

O'Reilly, M. F., & Glynn, D. (1995). Using a process social skills training approach with adolescents with mild intellectual disabilities in a high school setting. *Education and Training in Mental Retardation and Developmental Disabilities, 30*, 187–198.

O'Reilly, M. F., Lancioni, G., & Kierans, I. (2000). Teaching leisure social skills to adults with moderate mental retardation: An analysis of acquisition, generalization, and maintenance. *Education and Training in Mental Retardation and Developmental Disabilities, 35*, 250–258.

O'Reilly, M. F., Lancioni, G., & O'Kane, N. (2000). Using a problem-solving approach to teach social skills to workers with brain injuries in supported employment settings. *Journal of Vocational Rehabilitation, 14*, 187–194.

Park, H., & Gaylord-Ross, R. (1989). A problem-solving approach to social skills training in employment settings with mentally retarded youth. *Journal of Applied Behavior Analysis, 29*, 263–290.

Reynhout, G., & Carter, M. (2006). Social stories for children with disabilities. *Journal of Autism and Developmental Disorders, 36*, 445–469.

Rivera, B., & Rogers-Adkinson, D. (1997). Culturally sensitive interventions: Social skills training with children and parents from culturally and linguistically diverse backgrounds. *Intervention in School and Clinic, 33*, 75–80.

Sansosti, F. J., & Powell-Smith, K. A. (2006). Using social stories to improve the social behavior of children with Asperger syndrome. *Journal of Positive Behavior Interventions, 8*, 43–57.

Stokes, T. F., & Baer, D. M. (1977). An implicit technology of generalization. *Journal of Applied Behavior Analysis, 10*, 349–367.

7

Augmentative and Alternative Communication

RALF W. SCHLOSSER, JEFF SIGAFOOS, HOWARD SHANE, RAJINDER KOUL, AND PARIMALA RAGHAVENDRA

Augmentative and alternative communication (AAC) is "a set of procedures and processes by which an individual's communication skills (i.e., production as well as comprehension) can be maximized for functional and effective communication" (American Speech-Language-Hearing Association, 2002, p. 4). This may entail the supplementing ("augmentative") or replacing ("alternative") of natural speech through aided symbols and means of transmission or unaided symbols and means of transmission (Beukelman & Mirenda, 2013; Lloyd, Fuller, & Arvidson, 1997). Aided symbols include picture communication symbols, line drawings, graphic systems (e.g., Blissymbols), traditional orthography, and tangible symbols. Aided symbols require some means of transmission such as a dedicated speech-generating device, a general consumer-level device (e.g., iPad), a nonelectronic communication board, or flashcards. An individual can point to or scan to a graphic symbol on a communication board or speech-generating device or general consumer-level device, or hand over (exchange) a symbol to a communication partner. Unaided symbols include manual signs, gestures, finger spelling, and facial expressions. Unlike aided symbols, unaided symbols only require the user's body for producing communication.

Autism spectrum disorder (ASD) is an umbrella term that, according to the *Diagnostic and Statistical Manual of Mental Disorder*, fifth edition (*DSM-5*; to be released in May 2013), includes a variety of conditions, including autism, Asperger syndrome, pervasive developmental disorders—not otherwise specified (PDD-NOS), and childhood disintegrative disorders. Among these subgroups, individuals with Asperger syndrome are not typically candidates for AAC, but all other subgroups might potentially benefit from AAC depending on their individual needs.

Hence, use of "individuals with ASD" in this chapter refers to all subgroups except Asperger syndrome.

Individuals with ASD often present with difficulties in the areas of speech, language, and communication. In fact, communication is one of the core deficits associated with ASD. Depending on the source consulted, it has been estimated that 25% to about 60% of children with autism fail to develop functional speech and remain essentially nonspeaking (Matson, Mahan, Kozlowski, & Shoemaker, 2010; Peeters & Gillberg, 1999; Prizant, 1996). At this point it is not known why some children with ASD do not develop functional speech. Clearly, it is important to investigate the reason(s) as to why children with ASD are not developing speech. Yet the fact that their speech is currently insufficient to meet their communication needs demands that they be provided with a means of communication that permits expressive use and/ or receptive understanding. In our opinion, it is critical that AAC strategies are not viewed as a last resort and only considered when it is evident that a child is unlikely to acquire functional speech. It is important, even for young children with little or no functional speech, who are receiving some type of speech-focused intervention (e.g., Paul, Campbell, Gilbert, & Tsiouri, 2012),[1] that they be introduced to AAC strategies at least until their speech becomes functional or for as long as necessary. AAC may help some children meet their communication needs as they struggle with speech on their way toward becoming a functional speaker. Being able to rely on AAC modes may allow some

---

[1] According to Paul et al. (2012), preschool children with little or no functional speech who show at least a modicum of joint attention skills should receive a speech-focused intervention.

children to experience communicative success and perhaps temporarily reduce the pressure to speak. This, in turn, may transform the sometimes observed low level of social motivation among these children (e.g., Paul, Chawarska, Fowler, Cicchetti, & Volkmar, 2007) into greater confidence to seek out communicative opportunities. Additionally, augmented input provided by communication partners may successfully circumvent the frequently observed difficulty among children with ASD to comprehend speech (e.g., Striefel, Bryan, & Aikins, 1974; Von Tetzchner et al., 2004).

The purpose of this chapter is to synthesize the research evidence related to four current key issues and priorities facing children and youth with ASD and little or no functional speech, including (a) natural speech production, (b) Picture Exchange Communication System (PECS), (c) augmented input, and (d) advances in technology. To do so, we will rely on existing systematic reviews rather than individual studies where systematic reviews are available. Systematic reviews strive to be rigorous and use scientific methods to reduce bias in the identification of studies, data extraction from studies, and synthesis of outcomes (Petticrew & Roberts, 2006). Additionally, we will consult appraisals of systematic reviews because systematic reviews are no panacea and vary greatly in quality (e.g., Schlosser, Wendt, & Sigafoos, 2007). For priority areas where systematic reviews are not available, we will strive to identify appraisals of individual studies. If such appraisals of individual studies are not available, we will go the individual studies themselves and perform our own appraisals. In the next section, we will introduce the four key issues related to children and youth with ASD using AAC.

PRIORITY CONCERNS: CHILDREN WITH AUTISM SPECTRUM DISORDER USING AUGMENTATIVE AND ALTERNATIVE COMMUNICATION

There are a myriad of issues that require consideration when implementing AAC assessments and interventions. Questions such as when to begin using AAC, what communication modes to teach, what symbols to select, and how to introduce AAC are clearly important. These issues have been addressed elsewhere and the interested reader may wish to consult these sources (e.g., Schlosser & Sigafoos, 2011;

Schlosser & Wendt, 2008). In this chapter we would like to focus on issues that we deem to be current priority concerns in the field.

The first issue relates to effects of AAC intervention on natural speech production. There has been some concern that AAC may possibly hinder speech development and production. Some professionals and researchers working in the AAC field are puzzled that this issue is still being debated when, in their minds, it should have been put to rest a long time ago (Balandin, 2009) given the field is now in its fifth decade (Zangari, Lloyd, & Vicker, 1994). Yet, since there are always new families beginning to explore AAC for the first time, this will continue to be an important topic to address. With the development and greater research emphasis on interventions to improve speech production in this population, parents are likely to ask even more questions about this issue. Hence, this concern will continue to grow in importance over the next decade.

The second issue pertains to the Picture Exchange Communication System (PECS) (Bondy & Frost, 1994), which continues to be extremely popular as an intervention package for beginning communicators with ASD and one of the most heavily studied treatment packages in the communication arena. For these reasons PECS deserves attention in this chapter.

Another priority concern centers on the comprehension difficulties of many children with ASD, and how AAC modalities and strategies might be leveraged to compensate for these difficulties with spoken language. Because the expressive difficulties of children with ASD who present with little or no functional speech are naturally more obvious, they tend to receive more empirical attention (e.g., Tager-Flusberg et al., 2009; Yoder & Stone, 2006a). Therein lies the danger that the less obvious aspect of comprehension is largely ignored (Sevcik, 2006). We will shed some light on this issue so that it is not forgotten and perhaps receives some renewed attention.

The advent of affordable general consumer-level hardware (e.g., the iPad) in combination with specialized communication software or general-purpose software, along with low-cost widely available peripheral devices (e.g., cameras), has paved the way for more opportunities for children with ASD as well as some new challenges (Shane et al., 2012). These will be discussed with an eye toward the future. In the next section we will review the research base for each of these identified priority areas.

REVIEW OF RESEARCH
Effects of Augmentative and Alternative Communication Intervention on Natural Speech Production

Recent guidelines for navigating evidence-based information sources suggest that it is preferred for stakeholders to seek out syntheses (also known as systematic reviews) of literature rather than individual studies (DiCenso, Bayley, & Haynes, 2009; Haynes, 2006; Schlosser, Raghavendra, & Sigafoos, 2013; Schlosser & Sigafoos, 2009). Using systematic reviews has the advantage that someone else has vetted the evidence for quality, aggregated the evidence, and derived some data-based conclusions. Also, one study awaits replication and often individual studies may produce contradictory findings that can be sorted out by looking at an entire body of studies. This allows stakeholders to rely on someone else's expertise and, at the same time, save valuable time that would have otherwise been spent identifying, analyzing, and interpreting individual studies.

Due to its continued importance for stakeholders such as parents, Schlosser and Wendt (2008) conducted a systematic review to determine the effects of AAC intervention on natural speech production in children with autism. The previously mentioned guidelines for navigating evidence-based information sources recommend that, instead of going to these systematic reviews directly, it is preferred for stakeholders to seek out *synopses* of these reviews. Synopses are appraisals of the reviews. Using synopses permits stakeholders to rely on someone else's expertise for determining whether the methods used and conclusions drawn in the systematic review are trustworthy.

Synopses of this systematic review are available from the EBP Compendium and the journal *Evidence-Based Communication Assessment and Intervention* (EBCAI). Appraisals from Evidence in Augmentative and Alternative Communication (EVIDAAC) and the Database of Abstracts of Reviews of Effects (DARE) are currently under way. The URLs for these sources are found in Appendix A.

The EBCAI appraisal was generally complimentary (e.g., "Thus, this review stands as an excellent model for those considering undertaking their own systematic reviews"; Balandin, 2009, p. 13). Balandin did question the lack of reported interrater agreement data for data extraction—saying that it is not sufficient to state that there were few disagreements without rendering the actual data. Further, Balandin

reiterated two limitations acknowledged by Schlosser and Wendt (2008): First, there is a possibility that the results were an artifact of publication bias (i.e., only studies with positive speech outcomes get published)—unpublished dissertations were sought out, but no effort was made to locate other unpublished papers. Second, the results may have been due to a language bias (only material written in English was included) and this possibility cannot be ruled out.

The second source that provided a synopsis of this review, the EBP Compendium, appraises reviews along five quality indicators, including whether (a) the review addresses a clearly focused question, (b) the criteria for inclusion of studies are provided, (c) the search strategy is described in sufficient detail for replication, (d) included studies are assessed for study quality, and (e) the quality assessments are reproducible. Each of these indicators is marked with a "yes" with the exception of the first one. Although we technically did not ask a question, our purpose statement seems clear (see Schlosser & Wendt, 2008, p. 212).

In sum, although this was not deemed a perfect review, the review represents a respectable effort and seems overall trustworthy. Although publication bias and language bias are not to be underestimated, we are not aware of any systematic review efforts in AAC that have successfully ruled out these biases. Hence, this review is a worthy effort for determining the effects of AAC intervention on speech production.

Using stringent criteria for inclusion, Schlosser and Wendt (2008) located and included nine single-case experimental design studies and two group studies involving a total of 98 participants. Results indicated that AAC intervention does not hinder speech production; in fact, there was no single study where a decline in speech production was evident. More important, the synthesis established that AAC intervention leads to increases in speech production, although the increases were of a rather modest nature. It is important that parents be informed of the expected degree of improvement to enable them to develop realistic expectations. This finding is consistent with the fact that AAC, as an intervention, is not primarily a speech-facilitation set of methods and therefore speech gains ought to be viewed as a bonus. Rather, AAC is primarily used to provide children with a means of communication—and an absence of gains in speech production should not be used to devalue AAC. Along these lines, AAC intervention does not preclude a child from using and learning speech either. It is considered best practice for communication partners to use natural speech together with other modes (i.e., augmented input) as they interact with the child (e.g., Wood, Lasker, Siegel-Causey, Beukelman, & Ball, 1998). Additionally, children using speech-generating devices and/or apps that speak are exposed continuously to digitized or synthetic speech as they access graphic symbols or visual scene displays.

The authors of the systematic review offered several directions for future research. For one, they called for better documentation of relevant characteristics that children bring to the task of learning to use AAC, including perceptual, speech (e.g., vocal imitation skills), and language skills. This could lead to a more fruitful examination of predictors of speech improvements. Future research should be designed to examine specific hypotheses related to AAC and speech production such as those summarized by Blischak, Lombardino, and Dyson (2003). For example, based on the principle of automatic reinforcement, manual signs presented together with spoken words linked to a reinforcer should not only result in the acquisition of the manual sign but also the spoken word. Another hypothesis argues that the immediate and consistent output provided by speech-generating devices may not only provide increased exposure to speech models but also enhance attention and imitation of speech. Studies are needed to examine these hypotheses.

Effects of the Picture Exchange Communication System

The Picture Exchange Communication System (PECS) is a manualized treatment for teaching requesting and commenting to beginning communicators with ASD and other developmental disabilities (Frost & Bondy, 2002). PECS consists of the following six phases: (a) make request through picture exchange, (b) persistence in initiating communication, (c) discrimination between symbols, (d) introduction of sentence structure, (e) answering questions with a request, and (f) commenting (see Frost & Bondy, 2002). Perhaps due to its popularity, a sizable body of research studies has been generated since 1994 when PECS was first introduced. A PsychINFO search for PECS evidence on December 18, 2012, using "Picture Exchange Communication System" as a free-text word in "titles" of studies along with the methodology constraint "empirical study" revealed 45 hits. It can be daunting to read and analyze that many

studies for stakeholders, especially for practitioners who have very little time away from teaching or providing speech-language services. Hence, using the previously described approach to navigating evidence-based information sources, we will look out for systematic reviews on this topic or, better yet, synopses of these reviews.

A proliferation of reviews about the effectiveness of the PECS method have been published over the last several years (Flippin, Reszka, & Watson, 2010; Fujino, 2009; Hart & Banda, 2010; Lancioni et al., 2007; Ostryn, Wolfe, & Rusch, 2008; Preston & Carter, 2009; Sulzer-Azaroff, Hoffmann, Horton, Bondy, & Frost, 2009; Tien, 2008; Tincani & Devis, 2011). On the one hand it is beneficial to have several systematic reviews to draw from—too often only a single systematic review is available. On the other hand, it can be daunting for stakeholders to make sense of several systematic reviews, to determine what we know, and which reviews to trust.

EBCAI has published synopses of five of the aforementioned reviews (Flippin et al., 2010; Hart & Banda, 2010; Preston & Carter, 2009; Sulzer-Azaroff et al., 2009; Ticani & Devis, 2011).[2] These synopses have been summarized along relevant appraisal aspects in Table 7.1. The reader may also wish to check the EBCAI appraisals against other appraisals such as EVIDAAC or the EBP Compendium, depending on availability.

Readers of this chapter are likely interested in PECS for children or adults with ASD. Hence, a first step is to determine which of the reviews specifically address this population. The synopses would reveal this in the title, the question stated, the study selection criteria, and/or the main results. Most of the reviews addressed participants with developmental disabilities, including individuals with autism (e.g., Hart & Banda, 2010; Preston & Carter, 2009; Sulzer-Azaroff et al., 2009; Tincani & Devis, 2011). One review by Preston and Carter (2009) provided autism-specific results for group designs only because all of the group studies happen to have included only participants with ASD. For single-case experimental designs, they provided a covariation analysis of diagnosis with outcomes and found that individuals with PDD-NOS

---

[2] Reviews by Lancioni et al. (2007), Ostryn et al. (2008), and Tien (2008) failed to meet basic quality criteria required for inclusion in EBCAI. The review by Fujino (2009) is published in Japanese.

TABLE 7.1 SYNOPSES OF PECS REVIEWS PUBLISHED IN EVIDENCE-BASED COMMUNICATION ASSESSMENT AND INTERVENTION

Appraisal Aspects	Synopses (and Original Reviews)				
	Beck (2009)—Synopsis of Sulzer-Azaroff et al. (2009)	Wendt & Boesch (2010)—Synopsis of Preston & Carter (2009)	Subramanian & Wendt (2010)—Synopsis of Hart & Banda (2010)	Raghavendra (2011)—Synopsis of Tincani & Devis (2011)	Simpson (2011)—Synopsis of Flippin et al. (2010)
Design	Systematic review	Systematic review and meta-analysis	Systematic review	Systematic review and meta-analysis	Systematic review and meta-analysis
Target population	Individuals with ASD or other developmental disabilities (see Main results, p. 137)	Individuals with ASD or other developmental disabilities (see Main results, p. 56)	Individuals with autism or developmental disabilities (see Study selection, p. 22)	Individuals with autism and other developmental disabilities (see Question) (p. 7)	Children with ASD (see title) (p. 3)
Appraisal summary	"the weaknesses evidenced in many of the studies reviewed and the potential source, selection, and scope biases within the review itself preclude the authors' ability to make a definitive statement about the effectiveness of the entire PECS protocol" (p. 140)	"is currently the most systematic research synthesis of the PECS literature (that we know about), there is still some room for improvement. These limitations are, however, for the most part not very dramatic in nature" (p. 58) "Overall, though, the authors provide an adequate review of the literature, with valid conclusions for clinical practice as well as future research directions" (p. 59)	"...while the review by Hart and Banda (2009) is timely, its results need to be viewed with caution due to some limitations regarding review methodology and analysis. Results can be regarded as preliminary but should not be used for clinical decision-making until confirmed by a more rigorous and valid, truly systematic review" (p. 25)	"...the review provides a quantitative value to the effectiveness of the PECS using an aggregated PND effect size showing it is moderately effective. This is useful information for practitioners who are considering implementing PECS. However, this applies only to Phases I to III with more research needed for higher phases and also whether using PECS increases the use of speech for communication across context and varying partners" (p. 10)	"the overall methodology, analysis procedures, and interpretation of results were generally appropriate and are judged by this reviewer to be reliable and trustworthy" (p. 4)
Search	"...searched four appropriate databases and also conducted hand searches of the reference section of articles found in their database searches" (p. 139)	No comments made	"...the search was limited to a relatively few—albeit perhaps the most relevant—databases..." (p. 24)	"The authors searched only three databases and hand-searched 6 journals" (p. 9) "Ancestry searches were not undertaken" (p. 9)	"The databases they searched and the related search protocol were first-rate. Thus, it is likely that they examined the relevant extant literature" (p. 4)

(continued)

TABLE 7.1 CONTINUED

Synopses (and Original Reviews)

Appraisal Aspects	Beck (2009)—Synopsis of Sulzer-Azaroff et al. (2009)	Wendt & Boesch (2010)—Synopsis of Preston & Carter (2009)	Subramanian & Wendt (2010)—Synopsis of Hart & Banda (2010)	Raghavendra (2011)—Synopsis of Tincani & Devis (2011)	Simpson (2011)—Synopsis of Flippin et al. (2010)
Study selection	"They did not, however, provide... any reliability measures on application of inclusion and exclusion criteria" (p. 138)	"The current authors did not restrict their review to purely experimental designs either, but studies are analyzed separately by categorizing into pre-experimental, group, and single-subject experimental designs" (p. 58) "By outlining their inclusion criteria..."	"A high degree of agreement (100% reported) increased the confidence in studies included in the review" (p. 24) Distinct, defined inclusion and exclusion criteria used in the review enable replicability, a feature of a systematic reviews (p. 24)	"Clear inclusion criteria are stated, and reasons for excluding 6 studies are also presented, providing the reader with confidence in the studies selected" (p. 9) "Inter-rater reliability has not been checked for selection of the appropriate articles" (p. 10)	"They also used acceptable criteria for narrowing studies for the meta-analysis..." (p. 4)
Publication bias	"They did not indicate, however, that they made an attempt to obtain unpublished studies, and so a publication bias cannot be ruled out" (p. 139)	"it would be nice to see inclusion of unpublished literature and an investigation of any potential publication bias in a meta analysis of PECS intervention studies" (p. 59)	No comment made, but only published studies were included	"The inclusion of only articles published in peer reviewed journals provides some rigor, but dissertations may contain high-quality research and conference presentations provide the latest research, so these should have been included in the search" (p. 9)	No comment made, but only published studies were included
Linguistic bias	"excluded three studies because none of them could read the language in which the studies were written [this language(s) was not specified]. Such an exclusion might have resulted in a geographical or linguistic source selection bias" (p. 139)	No comments were made, but only articles in English were included	"the search was limited to... English-language journal articles. While this is defensible, it may have meant that other relevant studies were not identified" (p. 24)	"The authors also did not provide limits on years or languages, and this information is important to examine any publication bias of including only English language articles" (p. 9)	No comments were made, but only articles in English were included

Data extraction	They did not, however, provide either a clear outline of the data extraction process or any reliability measures on application of inclusion and exclusion criteria or data extraction (p. 138)	"...providing coding categories, and conducting a sound inter-rater reliability calculation on some, but not all, of their data extraction" (p. 58)	"...To reduce bias, an integral part of a systematic review, the authors' calculation of Inter-rater Agreement is notable" (p. 24)	"Five out of 16 studies were coded and PNDs calculated separately by the first author and a graduate student, arriving at 100% demonstrating rigor in data extraction and coding" (p. 9)	No comments were made
Quality assessment	"included only two quality assessment criteria: presence of data regarding reliability and procedural fidelity" (p. 136)	"Study quality assessment is addressed and carried out appropriately through a self-constructed scale (based on Horner et al., 2005) for single-subject experimental designs, but unfortunately lacking for group designs" (p. 58)	'..., but the review lacks a sound quality appraisal, using an accepted instrument or framework to assess the internal validity of included studies. The lack of quality appraisal reduces the confidence in the conclusions drawn from the reviewed literature in light of methodological weaknesses" (p. 25)	"A major concern are the limited quality criteria used in appraising whether the single-participant studies followed the strict requirements of such designs. They did not us any quality measures, which are fundamental as quality of each study contributes to the overall quality of the meta-analysis" (p. 10)	"The procedures used to evaluate and rate the quality of the studies that comprised the meta analysis were less impressive. In particular, the reasons for using adapted rating scales were unclear. Moreover, the outcome of relying on an adapted scale is a vetting protocol that lacks clarity. One might argue that the relatively unrefined nature of the existent PECS empirical literature (i.e., lack of consistent fidelity of treatment information, lack of attention to maintenance and generalization, and so forth) made it difficult for the researchers to use existing scales that provided exacting descriptors to evaluate the quality of research and thus mitigates this perceived weakness" (p. 4)

(continued)

TABLE 7.1 CONTINUED

Synopses (and Original Reviews)

Appraisal Aspects	Beck (2009)—Synopsis of Sulzer-Azaroff et al. (2009)	Wendt & Boesch (2010)—Synopsis of Preston & Carter (2009)	Subramanian & Wendt (2010)—Synopsis of Hart & Banda (2010)	Raghavendra (2011)—Synopsis of Tincani & Devis (2011)	Simpson (2011)—Synopsis of Flippin et al. (2010)
Effectiveness, synthesis, and aggregation	"systematic reviews of treatment efficacy studies must clearly state and report the "criteria used to arrive at judgments of effectiveness" (p. 147) for each study included in the review. Sulzer-Azaroff et al. did not report any such information but appear, instead, to take results of studies included in their review at face value" (p. 139).	"These authors also deserve praise for their attempt to implement an appropriate effect size metric for the most precise and reliable estimation of treatment effect" (p. 58) " ... The use of the PEM in general is questionable as this metric showed the poorest performance in accurately detecting treatment effect when compared to other non-parametric techniques... (p. 59)	"Statistical aggregates of effect size estimates across studies were not calculated, and further statistical analysis (e.g., investigations of the impact of any moderator variables on overall treatment effect) were not conducted; therefore, the use of the term "meta-analysis" is inadequate to describe the nature of this review" (p. 24) "While the authors mention the limitations of the PND metric, they did not address these limitations. Supplemental measures including... would solve some of the limitations of relying solely on the PND metric" (p. 24) "PND values were inappropriately aggregated for different dependent variables (for example, exchanges, speech, or problem behaviors) to calculate the overall effectiveness of PECS, therefore comparing "apples" and "oranges" (p. 25)	"The authors also undertook analysis of the impact of critical variables such as age and diagnosis on the PECS acquisition" (p. 9) "Further, these reviewers did not utilize conservative tests such as Bonferroni to correct errors due to multiple-hypothesis testing of selected variables" (p. 10)	"and they applied appropriate analysis methods" (p. 4) "One of the most valuable contributions of this article was discussion of three child—related characteristics that make a child with autism a good candidate for PECS: (a) poor joint attention, (b) strong object exploration tendencies, and (c) limited motor imitation. Methodologically, this element of the study was not particularly strong, although it was strengthened by interpretations of data in relation to other research " (p. 5)

or with features of autism made more progress with PECS than those with autism. They stated that the reasons for this finding are still unclear, speculating whether the PECS protocol might be better suited for the former group or whether they might do better with any treatment.

It appears that the systematic review and meta-analysis by Flippin et al. (2010) (focused on children under the age of 18 years) is the only review that focused exclusively on the ASD population. They included eight single-case experimental designs and three group designs, of which seven single-case experimental designs and one group study were, respectively, deemed of at least adequate quality and strong quality. Based on the better quality evidence, Flippin et al. concluded that PECS is a promising (not yet empirically supported) intervention for achieving communication outcomes (i.e., requests, initiations) in children with ASD. This conclusion is consistent with that of the National Standards Project (National Autism Center, 2009), which classified PECS as an emerging (not established) intervention. In terms of speech, Flippin et al. concluded that the findings are mixed, varied, and not convincing, based on one group study of strong quality and four single-case experimental designs of at least adequate quality. Commenting, although not targeted as an outcome in the review by Flippin et al. (2010), has not received much empirical attention as an outcome of PECS intervention. This may be due to the fact that most studies ended the intervention at Phase III (Raghavendra, 2011; Tincani & Devis, 2011).

An analysis of the overview of the synopses of systematic reviews presented in Table 7.1 indicates several avenues for planning and implementing future systematic reviews on PECS interventions. To begin with, the questions asked by systematic reviews need to be stated with at least the following components: the population targeted, the outcomes to be reviewed, and the intervention evaluated. In terms of the population, it would be useful if the reviews defined broad age categories (e.g., adults, children, youth, or individuals [to include all age categories]) alongside the diagnosis (e.g., ASD). Each of the reviews possibly suffered from a linguistic bias or at least this bias cannot be ruled out because only studies in English were included.[3] Using only studies

in English might be defensible when a particular intervention is only practiced in geographic regions that are English speaking or when it is common for a field for most of its researchers across the globe to routinely publish in English (Schlosser, Wendt, & Sigafoos, 2007). PECS, per its developers, is implemented worldwide and there are researchers in special education and speech-language pathology who do not publish in English. Therefore, it seems appropriate for future systematic reviews to include studies at least in the most important languages.

Additionally, the existing reviews cannot rule out publication bias because only published peer-reviewed studies were included. The phenomenon of publication bias suggests that published studies tend to overestimate the true effect of an intervention due to the tendency of journals to publish studies with positive outcomes (e.g., Schlosser et al., 2007). Hence, in order to establish a more accurate sense of an intervention's real effect, unpublished studies should be included as well. However, finding and including unpublished studies is not an easy task in the field of communication disorders and special education. Typically, researchers in the health sciences rely on trial registers to identify unpublished work because this is where researchers have registered studies that they are planning to undertake, some of which will be published and some will end up being unpublished. In the field of communication disorders and special education, trial registers are not regularly used. Still, there may be ways to at least follow up with conference presenters to determine availability of full papers. Also, unpublished dissertations can be easily searched for on PsychINFO and Proquest Digital Dissertation, while unpublished dissertations have undergone some scrutiny by the dissertation committee.

In terms of the search, a combination of several methods such as electronic databases, ancestry searches, and forward citation searches might enhance the likelihood that no relevant study is missed. Obviously, guarding against publication bias and linguistic bias should also influence where researchers search for relevant studies.

Study selection should not only provide concise criteria for inclusion (and exclusion as necessary) but also interrater agreement on the selection process. Not all of these reviews provided reliability data on this process. Data extraction, that is the systematic coding of information from the original studies, should include an upfront description of

[3] The review by Sulzer-Azaroff et al. (2009) included one study in Spanish, but there was not a systematic attempt to locate literature in languages other than English.

the data that will be coded from each study and whether this extraction occurred in a reliable manner for each of the categories retrieved, not just the calculation of effect sizes. Again, not all reviews offered such information. Part of data extraction is an assessment of the quality of the included studies; the reviews considered here ranged from an entire absence of such an appraisal, to a very restricted appraisal focused only on few considerations, to an appraisal of only one design type but not the other, to the use of self-made scales or scales that lack demonstrated validity. In terms of evaluation, synthesis, and aggregation, researchers need to be mindful to choose appropriate effect size indicators for single-case experimental designs, to rely on more than one metric, and to conduct covariation analyses of participant and study characteristics with outcomes. In addition to comparing the synopses of reviews, a comparison of the actual reviews might also be helpful to those planning future systematic reviews on interventions such as PECS. This is currently under way.

Research on Augmented Input to Aid Comprehension

The topics thus far have focused on interventions to increase the expressive communication skills of children with ASD. Yet many children with ASD also face difficulties with comprehension (Tager-Flusberg, 1981). Some children attend to only part of verbal cues (Striefel, Bryan, & Aikins, 1974) and others display a total absence of comprehension (Von Tetzchner et al., 2004). In our society where so much is driven by spoken communication, this can create barriers for children with ASD, especially those who have difficulty comprehending spoken language. The use of augmented input by communication partners might be an effective means for supplementing spoken language.

Augmented input refers to strategies to supplement the input provided to individuals using AAC during communication interaction or during AAC instruction via visuographic or unaided modes (Wood, Lasker, Siegel-Causey, Beukelman, & Ball, 1998). As such, augmented input may serve several purposes, including one that is clearly aimed at aiding comprehension by helping the child to receive information more accurately (i.e., by augmenting the message). Unfortunately, there is currently no systematic review available on the effects of using augmented input with children with ASD. Therefore, we will review individual studies. We chose to focus on studies involving

an aided visual mode (e.g., graphic/pictorial, or video) alongside speech to deliver instructions.

Pictorial Cues

Pictorial cues are one such form of visual augmented input. Pictorial cues depict objects involved in an activity or objects needed for carrying out a directive. Peterson, Bondy, Vincent, and Finnegan (2005), for example, compared the effectiveness of instructions provided in three modalities: (a) spoken only, (b) pictorial, and (c) spoken plus pictorial.[4] Unfortunately, an appraisal of this study is currently not available. The participating child in Peterson et al. (1995) needed to hand over an object from an array of three objects. Interestingly, both visual modalities (i.e., pictorial and spoken plus pictorial) were more effective than spoken only. While pictorial cues have some benefits over spoken cues (see Table 7.2) and therefore can be an effective form of augmented input for some children, these cues are not designed to show or imply the movement needed to carry out an activity or to follow a directive. Hence, they may not work for some children for whom the mere representation of the object is insufficient for knowing what to do with it. This leads us to static scene cues.

Static Scene Cues

Static scene cues are defined as "a complete visual scene that portrays, in pictorial form, a concept or command that is being presented simultaneously through spoken language" (Shane, 2006, p. 5). Figure 7.1 provides an example of a static scene cue for the directive "put the boy on the box."

Research on the effectiveness of static scene cues is beginning to emerge (Dauphin, Kinney, & Stromer, 2004; Mechling & Gustavson, 2008; Pierce & Schreibman, 1994). Appraisals of these studies are currently not available. Dauphin et al. (2004) used static scene cues to teach a young child with autism to "say" and "do." For the "doing" component, most relevant to comprehension, the child was taught how to make a figurine dinosaur hop. The static scene cues were effective for this child, although they were part of a larger treatment package. Mechling and Gustafson (2008) effectively used static scene cues (a picture of "scooping cookie dough") to teach six youth with ASD to follow cooking-related directives (e.g., "Scoop the dough"). During baseline the

---

[4] A second child received gestural input.

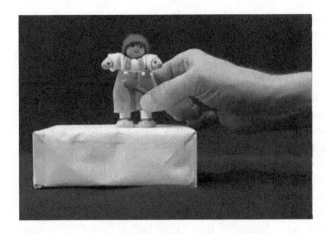

FIGURE 7.1. Static scene cue for the directive "put the boy on the box"

instructions were provided in spoken form. During intervention, the static scene cues were applied, and children's performance clearly rose above baseline levels. Finally, Pierce and Schreibman (1994) effectively used photographic static scene cues representing selected steps of a task-analyzed activity to teach three children with autism to complete daily living tasks. Undoubtedly, static scene cues are an improvement over pictorial cues because they provide a context of the activity relative to the isolated depiction of objects. Yet the movement or action is implied and this might be too abstract for some children with ASD. This implied movement is addressed by dynamic scene cues.

Dynamic Scene Cues

Dynamic scene cues are full-motion video clips that explicitly depict the action underlying an activity, directive, or concept (Shane & Weiss-Kapp, 2007). In Figure 7.2, a sequence of still shots illustrates the dynamic scene cue for the directive "Put the boy on the box." The reader may notice that the last still shot in the sequence is what became the static scene cue (Fig.7.1).

At this point there appear to be only two studies investigating dynamic scene cues with this population. The first one is the same study reviewed earlier by Mechling and Gustafson (2008) that compared instruction with dynamic scene cues with instruction involving static scene cues following a baseline of spoken cues. Although both static and dynamic scene cues were more effective than spoken cues, dynamic scene cues were more effective than static scene cues for each of the participants. Because the static scene cues were not derived from the dynamic scene cues, it is unclear whether the better outcomes for dynamic scene cues were due to the addition of movement or other documented differences between the conditions (see Schlosser, Laubscher et al., 2013). Recently, our research group compared three types of input modalities (spoken, static scene cues, and dynamic

FIGURE 7.2. Sequence of still frames illustrating the dynamic scene cue for the directive "put the boy on the box"

scene cues) in nine children with ASD and evaluated their performance in following directives such as "put the boy behind the box" (Schlosser, Laubscher et al., 2013). The children were presented with the target figurines and objects on the tabletop and had to place the agent relative to the object as indicated by the prepositional phrase. Unlike in the study by Mechling and Gustafson (2008), this study did not involve any instruction. Results indicated that both visual cues were more effective than the spoken cues. However, there were no significant differences between the static and dynamic scene cues. At this point it is unclear why no differences were found between static and dynamic scene cues (a finding that differs from Mechling and Gustafson, 2008). One hypothesis pertains to the presence of a ceiling effect that may have artificially curtailed performance. Because this area of research is still emerging, there are many more questions than answers at this point. For example, are there certain directives that bring out the best in dynamic scene cues? In other words, are dynamic scene cues required for certain kinds of instructions (whereas static scene cues might suffice for others)? Also, how can dynamic scene cues be used as a tool to teach understanding of static scene cues? Dynamic scene cues have much in common with video modeling, but then there are also important differences. For example, dynamic scene cues do not require a model, whereas video modeling does. Such differences make dynamic scene cues a worthwhile topic for future research.

Recent Advances of Technology

According to Shane and colleagues (2012), the escalating role of technology in society has provided opportunities for the development of new means of communication for children with ASD. Specifically, the growing use of handheld media devices along with applications stemming from a consumer-oriented delivery model has brought about a paradigm shift in AAC for children with ASD. Shane et al. (2012) proposed an organizational framework for describing traditional and emerging AAC technology, and highlighted how tools within the proposed framework may support a visual approach to everyday communication and improve language instruction. We will illustrate how various tools might bring about new opportunities, and we will emphasize the beginning research base on this topic.

New opportunities have arisen due to the widespread availability of general-purpose mobile platforms (e.g., Apple iPad™, Google Android™)

combined with specialized AAC applications ("apps") (Proloquo2go, MyTalk, AutisMate). Contemporary devices are small, low cost, easy to obtain and transport, readily available, and perhaps best of all, socially acceptable. In some cases, the combination of apps and general-purpose mobile platforms may serve as full AAC systems (like previously only dedicated AAC devices did). In other cases (e.g., Steps, First-Then, MyChoiceBoard, PicCalendar), these apps may support organization and enhance efficiency of simple functions such as choice making.

Prior to the availability of consumer-level, handheld alternatives (iPhone™, Blackberry Storm™, Android™, iPod touch™, iPad™), the use of static scene cues described in a previous section and graphic symbols required printing, laminating, and organizing that made it often difficult if not impractical for busy clinicians, teachers, and families. Dynamic scene cues are now easy to produce, store, and make available when needed. As Shane et al. (2012) stated, this "increases the ability of mentors and learners alike to quickly access scene cues 'just in time' to take full advantage of each communication opportunity" (p. 1231).

Research on Animation of Symbols

Recent advances in technology have also afforded a smoother execution of animation, which can be used to represent difficult-to-portray concepts and word classes such as verbs. By definition, verbs involve actions that consist of movement that may be difficult to represent via static graphic symbols. The widespread use of mobile technology affords the use of animation in natural environments. There are three studies examining the effects of animation with typically developing children (Mineo, Peischl, & Pennington, 2008; Schlosser, Shane, et al., 2012) and one study involving children with developmental disabilities (Fujisawa, Inoue, Yamana, & Hayashi, 2011). An appraisal is available only for the Fujisawa study since it is the only one focused on children with disabilities (Brock & Koul, 2011).

Fujisawa et al. (2011) included 16 participants with intellectual disabilities ranging developmentally from 3 years 2 months to 7 years 7 months on a Japanese standardized test. None of the participants had autism and all but one of the participants were able to speak in full sentences. Each of the participants received the experimental condition and the control condition. In the experimental condition the participants were first given a static symbol for a verb followed by an animated symbol if they made a mistake labeling the symbol. In the control condition, they received the static symbol but did not get the animated symbol. Results revealed that animation facilitated the correct labeling of static verb symbols. Brock and Koul (2011) raised some serious validity concerns, however, calling the results into question.

Mineo et al. (2008) reported that typically developing preschoolers identified symbols (specifically designed for this experiment) for actions more effectively when they were animated rather than static. Recently, the Autism Language Program of the Center for Communication Enhancement of Boston Children's Hospital has developed a set of over 110 verbs and prepositions (Autism Language Program Animated Graphics Set – ALP Animated Graphics Set) (for a description see Schlosser et al., 2011). In a study involving symbols for verbs and prepositions from the ALP Animated Graphics Set with typically developing preschoolers, (a) animated symbols were more guessable than static symbols; (b) animated verbs were named more accurately than static verbs but there was no difference for the prepositions; and (c) older children were more effective than younger children in guessing, naming, and identifying symbols (Schlosser, Shane et al., 2012). In a subsequent study using as of yet unpublished data, the symbols from the ALP Animated Graphics Set were compared to the Picture Communication Symbols (Mayer-Johnson©). Results replicated those of the previous experiment. Additionally, it was found that the symbols from the ALP Animated Graphics Set were guessed and identified more readily than the Picture Communication Symbols for prepositions. These studies offer benchmark data and set the stage for studies involving children with ASD (some of which are currently under way). Also, while the Fujisawa study presented with some methodological concerns, the underlying idea of using animation to teach the meaning of static symbols for verbs deserves research with children and youth with autism.

Research on General-Purpose Mobile Platforms

Research on the use of these handheld alternatives in AAC is just beginning. Obviously, it is too early for any systematic review to be available on this topic. Hence, individual studies will be reviewed. For example, Kagohara et al. (2012) successfully taught two youth with ASD to name pictures using an iPod (Study 1) and an iPad (Study 2). Both devices were equipped with Proloquo2Go™ software and afforded speech output. The adolescents were shown Google images (i.e., photographs) that they had to name using graphic symbols on the respective device. Students learned to name photographs in response to both open-ended (What do you see?) and closed-ended questions (What is this?). The intervention consisted of time delay, least-to-most prompting, and differential reinforcement.

In a related study, Achmadi et al. (2012) taught two students with ASD to request using an iPod with Proloquo2Go™. The requesting skill taught went beyond that in the Kagohara study in that it involved a two-step request, teaching the child to first make a general request using the broader category (e.g., snack) and following it up with a specific request (e.g., cookie) once the experimenter asked, "What type of snack do you want?" Subsequently, the two students were given an iPod that was in the off position and needed to be turned on or unlocked and the students needed to learn how to navigate to the correct page. The iPod was programmed across four pages. The first page was left blank and appeared when the device was turned off. The second page was a screensaver showing a picture of Earth once the home button was pressed to turn the device on. The second page had a slide bar that, when activated, unlocked the device, and opened page 3. This page showed two icons, one for SNACK and one for TOYS. If the student selected SNACK, the next page showed icons for COOKIE, LOLLY, and CHIPS. If the student selected TOYS, the next page featured icons for BOOK, CAR, and BALL. A multiple-probe design across participants was used to evaluate the intervention that consisted of response prompting, response fading, and differential reinforcement. Results indicated that both students were able to produce the two-step requests as well as the other operational competencies associated with using an iPod across multiple pages. While these results are promising, there are a few limitations to keep in mind. For one, the design involved only one replication since there were only two students involved. Typically, multiple-baseline designs lead to firmer conclusions if there are at least three or preferably more participants as part of the design (Horner et al., 2005). Second, the authors offered the requested items rather than having the student select the item from an array of items. Therefore, it is unclear whether the students demonstrated correspondence between "saying" (requesting) and "doing" (taking the requested object). Third, as acknowledged by the researchers, the students involved had previously had experience with the iPod using single-step requesting.

In a case study, Kagohara et al. (2010) describe an issue that can arise when teaching functional use of an iPod-based speech-generating device with Proloquo2Go™ software to an adolescent with autism. This adolescent was able to point to graphics on the device but pressed so hard that speech output could not be activated. The authors describe a behavioral intervention consisting of delayed prompting and differential reinforcement that allowed this individual to overcome this barrier to speech output activation. Results suggest that his continued use of too much force was maintained by continued reinforcement despite the lack of speech output activation.

Flores et al. (2012) compared the iPad with a nonelectronic communication system in terms of requesting in three elementary school students with autism and two students with other developmental disabilities. The nonelectronic communication system consisted of flashcards of PCS that were attached to a Velcro strip that was fixed onto the table at which the children worked. In both conditions, the students requested the same three snack items and one drink item during the snack activity. The symbols on the iPad platform were colored photographs. Additionally, some of the students had symbols for "I want" and "more" on their displays. The authors appear to have used an ABABA design whereby the A-phase represented the nonelectronic condition and the B-phase the iPad condition. Two of the children with ASD requested more during the iPad condition, whereas the third child showed more requesting during only one phase with the iPad; that is, the effect was not convincingly replicated.

While the authors acknowledged that this is a preliminary study, there are numerous unacknowledged flaws that render the outcomes questionable. For one, the ABABA design does not rule out order effects—the nonelectronic system always preceded the iPad condition. Second, using the same snack items in both conditions may have produced carryover effects that cannot be ruled out. For designs that permit more valid comparisons, the reader may wish to consult Schlosser (1999). Third, the researchers employed different types of symbols across the two conditions that may have by itself or in combination with the different platforms contributed to the results obtained. Fourth, the children did not have to select the items requested because the teacher handed the requested items to the child. In doing so, it is possible the child would have accepted any item, including those he or she did not request (see Schlosser & Sigafoos, 2002). Additionally, the authors acknowledged that the children had already mastered requesting with symbols prior to the onset of the study; hence, the study did not evaluate comparative effectiveness in teaching the acquisition of requesting. In sum, there are many unresolved methodological issues that call into question the validity of the yielded results.

These studies are important in that they aim to establish whether this general consumer-level mobile platform along with apps can be used effectively in their own right. Because the skills taught and tasks employed are those that could also be demonstrated with dedicated AAC devices, this growing research base is beginning to inform clinicians that these devices and apps can be used for the same kinds of purposes as dedicated AAC devices or, in some cases, nonelectronic low-tech AAC systems.

PRACTICE RECOMMENDATIONS AND DIRECTIONS FOR FUTURE RESEARCH

Selecting and Using Picture Exchange Communication System

For children with ASD who have not learned how to request through symbolic means (e.g., they might be using leading or unconventional gestures), PECS may be an appropriate intervention to select. PECS does offer promising evidence for its effectiveness in teaching children with ASD how to request by using graphic symbols. Before considering PECS for a child with ASD, clinicians should first determine whether a child can manage a pointing-based approach to requesting. Given that more sophisticated AAC systems would typically rely on pointing as a method of selection, it would help if the child did not need to transition from an exchange-based approach to a pointing-based approach in order to operate these systems. As far as identifying child characteristics to aid in the selection of PECS, Flippin et al. (2010) identified (a) poor joint attention, (b) strong object exploration tendencies, and (c) limited motor imitation as such characteristics. However, these did not grow out of a covariation analysis of pooled evidence. Rather, these were identified in individual studies, as pointed out by Simpson (2011). For instance, the proposition that children with strong object exploration tendencies and poor joint attention skills perform better with PECS than the comparison intervention (Prelinguistic Milieu Teaching) was based on an exploratory analysis (Yoder & Stone, 2006a, 2006b) with one sample of participants in a group study. Likewise, a few single-case experimental designs pointed to the potential pretreatment characteristics of poor joint attention (Charlop-Christy, Carpenter, Le, LeBlanc, & Kellet, 2002) and poor motor imitation (Charlop-Christy et al., 2002; Tincani, 2004). While these are important characteristics to pursue in future research, they do not yet present actionable evidence for practitioners. Moreover, PECS should not be used if the primary goal of intervention is to improve speech production. This conclusion is not only supported by the less than convincing evidence for this outcome but also because the aim of PECS, like other AAC approaches, is not to facilitate speech but to improve communication, as the developers have pointed out. Of course, it is a welcome bonus if speech does improve when implementing PECS. Finally, it is important to realize that while requesting is an important communicative function for beginning communicators to acquire, there are many other functions needed to become a competent communicator, including commenting, protesting and refusals, answering, and asking questions.

Using Augmented Input

The evidence base on the use of visual augmented input is very much in its infancy. In particular, potential effectiveness and efficiency differences between static scene cues and dynamic scene cues still need to be clarified before drawing any implications for practice. In the meantime, we are asking practitioners to be mindful of the potential pros and cons of these various cues (see Table 7.2) prior to making decisions on which ones to select for a particular child.

We do know, however, based on consistent findings across several studies, that there is a segment of the ASD population that experiences serious difficulties understanding spoken input. According to Schlosser, Laubscher et al. (2013), it is therefore problematic if spoken cues continue to be used as the primary or only mode of instruction for children with autism (Hall, McClannahan, & Krantz, 1995).

Selecting and Using Technology

In terms of animation, practice recommendations have to await the replication of the benchmark studies with typically developing children with children and youth with autism. Additionally, exploring the use of animation as an intervention for developing comprehension of static symbols would be a worthy direction for future research.

Due to the still emerging research base, evidence-based recommendations for the practice of selecting and using general consumer-level mobile platforms (with AAC apps or general consumer-level apps) seem premature. Yet we can state a word of caution and a plea for the use of established clinical processes: "caution must continue to be exercised to ensure that the dazzle of this impressive technology does not replace a methodical, clinical process that matches a person with communication assistance needs with the optimal communication technology available—a process that has come to be known as 'clinical feature matching'" (Shane et al., 2012, p. 1229). Likewise, practitioners must keep in mind that even with the best matched technology, there is still a need for a sound instructional approach to lead children and youth with ASD to become competent communicators using these devices.

Besides these rather preliminary and tempered practice recommendations, we can propose a few avenues for future research. The emerging body of research on general consumer-level mobile platforms has focused on the effectiveness of these platforms with AAC-specific software (currently limited to iPod/iPad with Proloquo2go) for teaching skills such as picture identification and requesting. These are skill areas that have been targeted with considerable success using dedicated AAC devices (e.g., Sigafoos, Drasgow, & Schlosser, 2003). As such, this body of work is beginning to demonstrate that these mobile platforms can be used as effectively as dedicated devices for the same kinds of purposes. This is important to know and work should continue in this vein while improving upon the methodological limitations described in the previous section.

At the same time, features that are potentially more effective than nonelectronic or dedicated devices have not been brought to bear in this research.[5] For example, the task involved in the Flores et al. (2012) study had both systems (iPad and nonelectronic flashcards) already made available to

---

[5] Likewise, there may be also some challenges that should be investigated; the work of Kagohara et al. (2010) is a case in point, but there may be others that need to be identified.

TABLE 7.2 SPOKEN AND AUGMENTED INPUT MODALITIES: DEFINITIONS, EXAMPLES, ADVANTAGES, AND DISADVANTAGES

Input Modalities	Definition and Sample Studies	Example	Advantages	Disadvantages
Spoken cues	The directive is communicated via spoken language by an instructor or a device. Goldstein & Brown (1989); West (2008)	"Put the boy behind the lamp" spoken by the instructor	Consistent with the predominant mode of communication in society Unaided; easy to use because no materials need to be created or chosen May facilitate verbal imitation	Transient; critical information might be missed Evoke a recall process Not understood (in part or entirely) May produce a higher error rate that could result in challenging behaviors or decrease in child motivation
Pictorial cues	Depict objects involved in an activity or objects needed for carrying out a directive. West (2008)		Nontransient/permanent; child can look away and return without loss of information Less instructor dependent Evoke a recognition process May produce fewer errors; this might result in less problem behaviors and better motivation Easy to generate and (re)use	Aided: require something external, are not as readily available (relative to spoken cues), requires planning Decontextualized representation (e.g., fails to show how an object is used in an activity) May discourage verbal imitation (relative to spoken cues)
Static scenes	"a complete visual scene that portrays, in pictorial form, a concept or command..." (Shane, 2006, p. 5). Mechling & Gustafson (2008); Schlosser et al. (2012)		Nontransient/permanent; child can look away and return without loss of information Less instructor dependent Evoke a recognition process May produce fewer errors; this might result in less problem behaviors and better motivation Easy to generate and (re)use Contextualized: May convey greater information (relative to pictorial cues) Contextualized: May trigger greater meaning of schematic or experiential content (relative to pictorial cues)	Aided: require something external, are not as readily available (relative to spoken cues), require planning May discourage verbal imitation (relative to spoken cues) Capture only a single moment and the action is implied (relative to dynamic scene cues)

| Dynamic scenes | Full motion video clips that explicitly depict the action underlying an activity, directive or concept (Shane & Weiss-Kapp, 2007). Mechling & Gustafson (2008); Schlosser et al. (2012) | Less instructor dependent
Evoke a recognition process
May produce fewer errors; this might result in less problem behaviors and better motivation
Easy to generate and (re)use
Contextualized: May convey greater information (relative to pictorial cues)
Contextualized: May trigger greater meaning of schematic or experiential content (relative to pictorial cues)
Actions and motions are captured and explicit (relative to static scene cues) | Aided: require something external, are not as readily available (relative to spoken cues), require planning
May discourage verbal imitation (relative to spoken cues)
Transient: critical information might be missed (relative to static scene cues) |

the child. Hence, differential portability, for example, was (intentionally) not brought to bear in the study. Yet portability is one of the potential advantages of iPods and iPads relative to many dedicated devices. Therefore, it is essential that we begin to elucidate what these devices and apps can do potentially more effectively than dedicated AAC devices or nonelectronic AAC systems, and design research studies to investigate these potential benefits. One such avenue for future research relates to recently developed technology by Boston Children's Hospital.

Boston Children's Hospital has created two communication apps that attempt to take advantage of the rich feature set offered by the iPad Mobile Platform. The first app, Symboltalk, allows for expressive communication using personalized topic displays arranged in a communication grid format. The app is unique, however, in that it allows an instructor (Mentor) to create a cue on an iPad (in the form of a static or dynamic scene cue or element cue [individual symbols]) and transmit that content to a user's (Learner's) iPad for interpretation. Accordingly, Symboltalk allows for a high-tech way to produce augmented input at the level in which the learner is processing information (i.e., as scene or element cues). The program is also unique in that the Mentor can retrieve content from the program's extensive symbol library through voice recognition as well as through traditional "type and search" search strategies. MSTARR (Multi-Sensory Transmission of Alerts Reminders and Rewards) is a complimentary/ companion app to Symboltalk. This program offers visual schedules and First-Then displays to assist with the understanding of daily routines and behavior management. Similar to Symboltalk, MSTARR content can be transmitted to a Learner's iPad platform. Furthermore MSTARR has time and trial reminders embedded into both First-Then and visual schedules displays.

Both MSTARR and Symboltalk apps offer features that never existed before in clinical practice, including retrieval of symbols through voice recognition and augmented input executed from the iPad platform of a Mentor to another in the possession of learner. While such features are technically feasible and captivating, the question remains as to whether they contribute to improved performance and, if so, in what ways. For example, will teachers provide more augmented input to their students with ASD because it is so much easier to retrieve symbols in real time through the use of the voice recognition feature (what we refer to as "Just in Time" or JITS) compared to dedicated AAC systems and/or

nonelectronic communication displays? Similarly, will students participate more in classroom activities now that activity-specific vocabulary can be made available "on the fly" (compared to the lesson planning necessary with dedicated AAC systems or nonelectronic displays)? With regard to MSTARR, containing embedded trials and a timer and various visual supports, are teachers going to provide more timely visual supports throughout the day? It has also been hypothesized that general consumer-level platforms are less stigmatizing than dedicated AAC systems (Shane et al., 2012). This might be particularly important in inclusive classroom or community settings, and calls for research into the effects of these technologies on the attitudes of peers as well as acceptance by families. These are some of the questions that tackle the differentiating features of these new apps on general-purpose mobile platforms.

CONCLUSIONS

In this chapter we have presented four issues that we deemed to be priority concerns in the field of AAC for children and youth with ASD, including (a) the effects of AAC intervention on natural speech production, (b) the effectiveness of PECS, (c) the effectiveness of augmented input, and (d) recent advances in technology such as general-purpose mobile platforms used in combination with AAC-specific apps. The research base for each of these priority concerns was synthesized, and subsequently practice recommendations or directions for future research were derived as appropriate.

ACKNOWLEDGMENTS
EVIDAAC, one of the information sources introduced in the paper, was funded by a grant from the National Institute on Disability and Rehabilitation Research (NIDRR), US Department of Education (H133G070150) to Ralf W. Schlosser. Also, part of the writing of this chapter was made possible with a grant from NIDRR ("Do animations facilitate symbol understanding in children with autism"), H133G100187. The authors, however, bear sole responsibility for the content of this paper and funding by NIDRR does not imply that the opinions expressed in this report are those of the agency.

REFERENCES
Achmadi, D., Kagohara, D. M., van der Meer, L., O'Reilly, M. F., Lancioni, G. E., Sutherland, D., ... Sigafoos, J. (2012). Teaching advanced operation of an iPod-based

speech-generating device to two students with autism spectrum disorders. *Research In Autism Spectrum Disorders, 6,* 1258–1264.

American Speech-Language-Hearing Association. (2002). *Augmentative and alternative communication: Knowledge and skills for service delivery.* Retrieved September 2013, from http://www.asha.org/policy.

Balandin, S. (2009). AAC intervention does not hinder natural speech production for children with autism, but natural speech gains tend to be small. *Evidence-Based Communication Assessment and Intervention, 3,* 11–14.

Beck, A. R. (2009). Research on the effectiveness of the Picture Exchange Communication System (PECS) has increased, but this review is not very systematic. *Evidence-Based Communication Assessment and Intervention, 3,* 136–140.

Beukelman, D. R., & Mirenda, P. (2013). *Augmentative and alternative communication: Supporting children and adults with complex communication needs* (4th ed.). Baltimore, MD: Paul H. Brookes.

Blischak, D. M., Lombardino, L. J., & Dyson, A. T. (2003). Use of speech-generating devices: In support of natural speech. *Augmentative and Alternative Communication, 19,* 29–35.

Bondy, A. S., & Frost, L. A. (1994). The Picture Exchange Communication System. *Focus on Autism and Other Developmental Disabilities, 9,* 1–19.

Brock, K. L., & Koul, R. (2011). Data suggest that animation assists individuals with intellectual disabilities to guess the meaning of action symbols, but internal validity concerns call these findings into question. *Evidence-Based Communication Assessment and Intervention, 5,* 159–162

Charlop-Christy, M. H., Carpenter, M., Le, L., LeBlanc, L. A., & Kellet, K. (2002). Using the Picture Exchange Communication System (PECS) with children with autism: Assessment of PECS acquisition, speech, social-communicative behavior, and problem behavior. *Journal of Applied Behavior Analysis, 35,* 213–231.

Dauphin, M., Kinney, E. M., & Stromer, R. (2004). Using video-enhanced activity schedules and matrix training to teach sociodramatic play to a child with autism. *Journal of Positive Behavior Interventions, 6,* 238–250.

DiCenso, A., Bayley, L., & Haynes, R. B. (2009). Accessing pre-appraised evidence: Fine-tuning the 5S model into a 6S model. *Evidence-Based Nursing, 12,* 99–101.

Flippin, M., Reszka, S., & Watson, L. R. (2010). Effectiveness of the Picture Exchange Communication System (PECS) on communication and speech for children with autism spectrum disorders: A meta-analysis. *American Journal of Speech-Language Pathology, 19,* 178–195.

Flores, M., Musgrove, K., Renner, S., Hinton, V., Strozier, S., Franklin, S., & Hil, D. (2012). A comparison of communication using the Apple iPad and a picture-based system. *Augmentative And Alternative Communication, 28,* 74–84.

Frost, L., & Bondy, A. (2002). *Picture Exchange Communication System training manual* (2nd ed.). Newark, DE: Pyramid Educational Consultants.

Fujino, H. (2009). Promotion of speech production through augmentative and alternative communication (AAC) based on the Picture Exchange Communication System (PECS): A review. *Japanese Journal of Special Education, 47,* 173–182.

Fujisawa, K., Inoue, T., Yamana, Y., & Hayashi, H. (2011). The effect of animation on learning action symbols by individuals with intellectual disabilities. *Augmentative and Alternative Communication, 27,* 53–60.

Goldstein, H., & Brown, W. H. (1989). Observational learning of receptive and expressive language by handicapped preschool children. *Education and Treatment of Children, 12,* 5–37.

Hall, L. J., McClannahan, L. E., & Krantz, P. J. (1995). Promoting independence in integrated classrooms by teaching aides to use activity schedules and decreased prompts. *Education and Training in Mental Retardation and Developmental Disabilities, 30,* 208–217.

Hart, S. L., & Banda, D. R. (2010). Picture exchange communication system with individuals with developmental disabilities: A meta-analysis of single subject studies. *Remedial and Special Education, 31,* 476–488.

Haynes, R. B. (2006). Of studies, syntheses, synopses, summaries, and systems: The 5S evolution of information services for evidence-based decision making. *ACP Journal Club, 145,* A8–A9.

Horner, R., Carr, E., Halle, J., McGee, G., Odom, S., & Wolery, M. (2005). The use of single subject research to identify evidence-based practice in special education. *Exceptional Children, 71,* 165–180.

Kagohara, D. M., van der Meer, L., Achmadi, D., Green, V. A., O'Reilly, M. F., Lancioni, G. E., ... Sigafoos, J. (2012). Teaching picture naming to two adolescents with autism spectrum disorders using systematic instruction and speech-generating devices. *Research in Autism Spectrum Disorders, 6,* 1224–1233,

Kagohara, D. M., van der Meer, L., Achmadi, D., Green, V. A., O'Reilly, M. F., Mulloy, A., ... Sigafoos, J. (2010). Behavioral intervention promotes successful use of an iPod-based communication device by an adolescent with autism. *Clinical Case Studies, 9,* 328–338.

Lancioni, G. E., O'Reilly, M. F., Cuvo, A. J., Singh, N. N., Sigafoos, J., & Didden, R. (2007). PECS and VOCAs to enable students with developmental disabilities to make requests: An overview of the literature. *Research in Developmental Disabilities, 28,* 468–488.

Lloyd, L. L., Fuller, D. R., & Arvidson, H. (1997). *Augmentative and alternative communication: A handbook of principles and practices.* Needham Heights, MA: Allyn & Bacon.

Matson, J. L., Mahan, S., Kozlowski, A. M., & Shoemaker, M. (2010). Developmental milestones in toddlers with autistic disorder, pervasive developmental disorder—not otherwise specified and atypical development. *Developmental Neurorehabilitation, 13,* 239–247.

Mechling, L. C., & Gustafson, M. (2008). Comparison of static picture and video prompting on the performance of cooking related tasks by students with autism. *Journal of Special Education Technology, 23,* 31–45.

Mineo, B. A., Peischl, D., & Pennington, C. (2008). Moving targets: The effect of animation on identification of action word representations. *Augmentative and Alternative Communication, 24,* 162–173.

National Autism Center. (2009). *National standards report.* Randolph, MA: Author.

Ostryn, C., Wolfe, P., & Rusch, F. (2008). A review and analysis of the Picture Exchange Communication System (PECS) for individuals with autism spectrum disorders using a paradigm of communication competence. *Research and Practice for Persons with Severe Disabilities, 33,* 13–24.

Paul, R., Campbell, D., Gilbert, K., & Tsiouri, I. (2012). Comparing spoken language treatments for minimally verbal preschoolers with autism spectrum disorders. *Journal of Autism and Developmental Disorders,* Epub ahead of print. doi:10.1007/s10803-012-1583-z

Paul, R., Chawarska, K., Fowler, C., Cicchetti, D., & Volkmar, F. (2007). Listen, my children and you shall hear: Auditory preferences in toddlers with ASD. *Journal of Speech, Language, and Hearing Research, 50,* 1350–1364.

Peeters, T., & Gillberg, C. (1999). *Autism: Medical and Educational Aspects.* London: Whurr.

Peterson, S. L., Bondy, A. S., Vincent, Y., & Finnegan, C. S. (1995). Effects of altering communicative input for students with autism and no speech: Two case studies. *Augmentative and Alternative Communication, 11,* 93–100.

Petticrew, M., & Roberts, H. (2006). *Systematic reviews in the social sciences: A practical guide.* Malden, MA: Blackwell.

Pierce, K. L., & Schreibman, L. (1994). Teaching daily living skills to children with autism in unsupervised settings through pictorial self-management. *Journal of Applied Behavior Analysis, 27,* 471–481.

Preston, D., & Carter, M. (2009). A review of the efficacy of the Picture Exchange Communication System intervention. *Journal of Autism and Developmental Disorders, 39,* 1471–1486.

Prizant, B. (1996). Brief report: Communication, language, social, and emotional development. *Journal of Autism and Developmental Disorders, 26,* 173–178.

Raghavendra, P. (2011). PECS promotes functional communication; however, more research is needed to investigate its efficacy in Phases IV to VI and its impact on speech and functional communication across contexts. *Evidence-Based Communication Assessment and Intervention, 5,* 7–10.

Schlosser, R. W. (1999). Comparative efficacy of interventions in augmentative and alternative communication. *Augmentative and Alternative Communication, 15,* 56–68.

Schlosser, R. W., Laubscher, E., Sorce, J., Koul, R., Flynn, S., Hotz, L., ... Shane, H. (2013). Implementing directives that involve preposition with children with autism: A comparison of spoken cues with two types of augmented input. *Augmentative and Alternative Communication, 29*(2), 132–145.

Schlosser, R. W., Raghavendra, P., & Sigafoos, J. (2013). Appraising systematic reviews: From navigating synopses of reviews to conducting one's own appraisal. In B. Cook, M. Tankersley, & T. J. Landrum (Eds.), *Advances in learning and behavioral disabilities* (pp. 45–64). Bingley, UK: Emerald..

Schlosser, R. W., Shane, H., Sorce, J., Koul, R., Bloomfield, E., Debrowski, L., ... Neff, A. (2012). Animation of graphic symbols representing verbs and prepositions: Effects on transparency, name agreement, and identification. *Journal of Speech, Language, and Hearing Research, 55,* 342–358.

Schlosser, R. W., Shane, H., Sorce, J., Koul, R., Bloomfield, E., & Hotz, L. (2011). Identifying performing and underperforming graphic symbols for verbs and prepositions in animated and static formats: A research note. *Augmentative and Alternative Communication, 27,* 205–214.

Schlosser, R. W., & Sigafoos, J. (2002). Selecting graphic symbols for an initial request lexicon: Integrative review. *Augmentative and Alternative Communication, 18,* 102–123.

Schlosser, R. W., & Sigafoos, J. (2009). Navigating evidence-based information sources in augmentative and alternative communication. *Augmentative and Alternative Communication, 25,* 225–235.

Schlosser, R. W., & Sigafoos, J. (2011). Augmentative and alternative communication. In J. K. Luiselli (Ed.), *Teaching and behavior support for children and adults with autism spectrum disorders: A "how to" practitioner's guide* (pp. 91–96). New York, NY: Oxford University Press.

Schlosser, R. W., & Wendt, O. (2008). Augmentative and alternative communication interventions for children with autism. In J. K. Luiselli, Dennis C. Russo, & Walter P. Christian (Eds.), *Effective practices for children with autism: Educational and behavior support interventions that work* (pp. 325–389). New York, NY: Oxford University Press.

Schlosser, R. W., Wendt, O., & Sigafoos, J. (2007). Not all systematic reviews are created equal: Considerations for appraisal. *Evidence-Based Communication Assessment and Intervention, 1,* 138–150.

Sevcik, R. A. (2006). Comprehension: an overlooked component in augmented language development. *Disability and Rehabilitation, 28,* 159–167.

Shane, H. C. (2006). Using visual scene displays to improve communication and communication instruction in persons with autism spectrum disorders. *Perspectives in Augmentative and Alternative Communication, 15,* 7–13.

Shane, H. C., Laubscher, E., Schlosser, R. W., Flynn, S., Sorce, J. F., & Abramson, J. (2012). Applying technology to visually support language and communication in individuals with ASD. *Journal of Autism and Developmental Disorders, 42,* 1228–1235.

Shane H. C., & Weiss-Kapp, S. (2007). *Visual language in autism.* San Diego, CA: Plural.

Sigafoos, J., Drasgow, E., & Schlosser, R. (2003). Strategies for beginning communicators. In R. W. Schlosser (Ed.), *The efficacy of augmentative and alternative communication: Toward evidence-based practice* (pp. 323–346). San Diego, CA: Academic Press.

Simpson, R. L. (2011). Meta-analysis supports Picture Exchange Communication System (PECS) as a promising method for improving communication skills of children with autism spectrum disorders. *Evidence-Based Communication Assessment and Intervention, 5,* 3–6.

Striefel, S., Bryan, K. S., & Aikins, D. A. (1974). Transfer of stimulus control from motor to verbal stimuli. *Journal of Applied Behavior Analysis, 7,* 123–135.

Subramanian, S., & Wendt, O. (2010). PECS has empirical support, but limitations in the systematic review process require this conclusion to be interpreted with caution. *Evidence-Based Communication Assessment and Intervention, 4,* 22–26.

Sulzer-Azaroff, B., Hoffmann, A. O., Horton, C. B., Bondy, A., & Frost, L. (2009). The Picture Exchange Communication System (PECS): What do the data say? *Focus on Autism and Other Developmental Disabilities, 24,* 89–103.

Tager-Flusberg, H. (1981). Sentence comprehension in autistic children. *Applied Psycholinguistics, 2*(1), 5–24.

Tager-Flusberg, H., Rogers, S., Cooper, J., Landa, R., Lord, C., Paul, R.,...Yoder, P. (2009). Defining spoken language benchmarks and selecting measures of expressive language development for young children with autism spectrum disorders. *Journal of Speech, Language, and Hearing Research, 52,* 643–652.

Tien, K-C. (2008). Effectiveness of the Picture Exchange Communication System as a functional communication intervention for individuals with autism spectrum disorders: A practice-based research synthesis. *Education and Training in Developmental Disabilities, 43,* 61–76.

Tincani, M. (2004). Comparing the Picture Exchange Communication System and sign language for children with autism. *Focus on Autism and Other Developmental Disabilities, 19,* 152–163.

Tincani, M., & Devis, K. (2011). Quantitative synthesis and component analysis of single-participant studies on the picture exchange communication system. *Remedial and Special Education, 32,* 458–470. doi:10.1177/0741932510362494.

Von Tetzchner, S. R., Øvreeide, K. D., Jørgensen, K. K., Ormhaug, B. M., Oxholm, B. B., & Warme, R. R. (2004). Acquisition of graphic communication by a young girl without comprehension of spoken language. *Disability and Rehabilitation, 26,* 1335–1346.

Wendt, O., & Boesch, M. (2010). Systematic review documents PECS effectiveness for exchange-based outcome variables, but effects on speech, social, or challenging behaviors remain unclear. *Evidence-Based Communication Assessment and Intervention, 4,* 55–61.

West, E. (2008). Effects of verbal cues versus pictorial cues on the transfer of stimulus control for children with autism. *Focus on Autism and Other Developmental Disabilities, 23,* 229–241.

Wood, L. A., Lasker, J., Siegel-Causey, E., Beukelman, D. R., & Ball, L. (1998). Input framework for augmentative and alternative communication. *Augmentative and Alternative Communication, 14,* 261–267.

Yoder, P., & Stone, W. L. (2006a). A randomized comparison of the effect of two prelinguistic communication interventions on the acquisition of spoken communication in preschoolers, with ASD. *Journal of Speech, Language, and Hearing Research, 49,* 698–711.

Yoder, P., & Stone, W. L. (2006b). Randomized comparison of two communication interventions for preschoolers with autism spectrum disorders. *Journal of Consulting and Clinical Psychology, 74,* 426–435.

Zangari, C., Lloyd, L. L., & Vicker, B. (1994). Augmentative and alternative communication: An historic perspective. *Augmentative and Alternative Communication, 10,* 27–59.

APPENDIX A

URLs for Sources of Synopses

Evidence-Based Information Source	URL
EBP Compendium	http://www.asha.org/members/ebp/compendium/
Evidence-Based Communication Assessment and Intervention (EBCAI)	http://www.psypress.com/ebcai
EVIDAAC—Evidence in Augmentative and Alternative Communication	http://www.evidaac.org
Database of Abstracts of Reviews of Effects (DARE)	http://www.crd.york.ac.uk/CRDWeb/AboutDare.asp

8

Self-Management and Self-Regulation

MARK R. DIXON AND AUTUMN MCKEEL

The term *self-management* has taken on many forms in both technical discussions and colloquial discourse. Perhaps the most commonly held understanding of self-management involves inference by which an individual can successfully direct his or her own activities toward a goal or achievement. The notion of *self* suggests internal control of the person that somehow becomes awakened and takes a charge toward a desired outcome. The term *management* implies one's ability to regulate a variety of courses of action and choose the most acceptable one. Most recently self-management has been discussed as interchangeable with executive functioning (Barkley, 1997), the latter concept holding considerable attention in the popular media and mainstream psychology (e.g., McEvoy, Rogers, & Pennington, 2006). It is the lack of an objective definition of the behavioral repertoire that is involved in, or responsible for, the outcome of "self-management" that creates confusion as to when an individual with autism spectrum disorder (ASD) might actually be displaying such behavior. When observers are defining the term differently and measuring it subjectively, there is little consensus on the behavioral mechanisms in place and the behavioral interventions that need to be adopted to eventually increase the person's self-management.

To understand the concept of self-management, one must initially adopt an objective definition of the parameters in which the term subsumes. Within the behavior analytic community, where there is great energy placed on the visible and measurable dimensions of a behavior, the term *self-management* needs to take on clear physical properties. While contemporary behavioral perspectives include the value of internal private events in their analysis, it is common for the thrust of the analysis to be placed on the physical dimensions of the response. In the case of self-management, undoubtedly there is thinking, perceiving, and planning involved within the skin or mind of the child with ASD. However, keeping the analysis of the outcome of such activity at the forefront will allow the caregiver to measure progress, or the lack thereof, to a greater degree than attempting to tap inside one's head to infer what has changed.

Self-management therefore can be defined as the allocation of responding to one alternative over other concurrently available options that may differ in size, quality, social significance, personal gain, delay, history, or abstracted psychological functions. As a result, we conclude that when a person with ASD is "self-managed," it is when that person has made a choice that yields a more optimal outcome on one or more of these dimensions than if an alternative choice was made. Examples of self-management abound within and beyond ASD. For example, when presented with a low-interest work task, the child with ASD is faced with the option of complying with the work demand or running from a caregiver. When the options to work on low preferred task and escape from low preferred task are presented, it seems almost logical why the child with ASD or even every one of us would opt for the escape. Yet what we have probably learned through the course of our development is "sometimes we have to work," "good work will eventually be valuable to us," and "please the teacher and do our work." Quantifying such utterances that control our behavior is challenging. It becomes even more so for children with ASD that possess limited or absent verbal repertoires, thus making it even more difficult to conceptualize how such processes are at work within their minds. As a result, we might conclude that if the child with ASD has a significant amount of cognitive disability, something as complex as self-management may not even be possible.

Educators are faced with considerable challenges in promoting self-management for children with ASD. The first question one may ask is whether the child possesses the basic skills necessary to self-manage. Next, the caregiver determines whether critical dimensions of the child's existing repertoire can be evoked under various conditions in which self-management is necessary. Third, the educator may have to enhance the environment using supplemental prompts to increase the chances of self-management occurring (e.g., pictures, video modeling, classroom rules). Finally, the educator may have to reinforce the child with ASD for successful self-management demonstrations. Complexity increases when there are vague definitions of what is expected from the child, poor agreement on the exhibitions of self-management, and when reinforcers for demonstration are delayed or probabilistic.

Although the task to produce self-managed behavior for the child with ASD is daunting, it is indeed possible. Once an objective measure of self-management is agreed upon and environmental contingencies are instated for fostering the repertoire, significant and meaningful changes can occur for the child. Perhaps one of the most important goals for any student with a disability is to foster a greater sense of independence and successful working in the world. To move in a positive direction toward such a goal, the caregiver must take meticulous efforts to maximize self-management.

It is a significant misconception for the educator to conclude that any child, regardless of disability, might not yet be ready for self-management—or worse, that self-management is too complex for a given child to understand and that teaching the skill should be postponed. The error is made, in part, because of the ambiguity of the term *self-management*, and that the child must have a sense of "self" prior to being able to manage the self. The error is compounded by a popular educational culture that endorses empty slogans such as "know yourself—grow yourself," "take a walk down self-control boulevard," and "who is managing your 'self' today." When the educator is faced with the critical dimensions of the behavioral repertoire that are in need of refinement, it is easy to see why objectives such as "staying on task," "keeping hands to oneself," and "seeking attention in socially appropriate ways" are the cornerstones of intervention plans. Unfortunately what has happened is that such caregivers have failed to realize that self-management is what truly underlies such desired outcomes.

PRIORITY CONCERNS

Priority Concern 1: *Challenging behavior for a child with ASD is the outcome of poor self-management.* The emission of a problem behavior that is considered a target for reduction or elimination is typically the result of poor self-management. When the child is presented with the choice between engaging in a problem behavior or engaging in a desired more optimal behavior, the allocation of responding comprising maladaptive behavior needs to be examined carefully. Consider a student who receives immediate attention from a teacher upon getting out of seat during independent work time in the classroom. When that student is instructed to stay in his seat but the teacher's attention is diverted, it is likely that out-of-seat behavior will increase. Other similar scenarios may occur in which sitting in seat yields the request to do more work, while getting out of seat produces the request to sit back in seat. The lower response effort of battling to get in/out of seat would be preferred to work/no work for a child wishing to escape from work itself.

Time and the delay to encounter certain consequences will work against an individual's ability to self-manage. There are several choices that a student with ASD will face that include options yielding immediate gains that compete with options yielding delayed gains. When everything else is held constant, there is an almost certain prediction that the child will select the option yielding the more immediate reinforcement. For example, if a student can scream to reduce her anxiety about an unplanned schedule change or, alternatively, breathe deeply, experience the change, and eventually reduce her anxiety, the caregiver can be sure that a scream is bound to occur. Probability of outcome will also impact the risk of maladaptive behavior. When a student with ASD is told to keep his hands to himself only to obtain a social praise statement at a less than 100% probability from the caregiver, it might be more reinforcing to poke the other student in line. While the chance of social praise is of value, its value is reduced by the less than predictable delivery.

Priority Concern 2: *Skill acquisition deficits in a child with ASD are due to ineffective self-management.* When we make claims that a child cannot manage her own behavior, it is typically concluded when certain skills have not been acquired within the repertoire. The child's inability to exhibit proper greetings, transition appropriately, speak at appropriate volumes, keep hands to self, and any other range of behaviors typically result in the conclusion that self-management is absent. However, instead of deducing a lack of self-management, the caregiver should be very specific about what behavior is desired and the degree to which it is lacking. Given that *self-management* is more of a blanket term which can encompass different behaviors, simply stating the child should "increase self-management" is an insufficient target to seek.

Priority Concern 3: *Self-management can be taught to a child with ASD regardless of disability level.* Self-management is comprised of many skills. Regardless of a child's ability, an individualized definition of self-management should be created. Once done, when coupled with individualized and preferred consequences for targeted behaviors, any child with ASD can increase his self-management. For the student who is nonverbal, self-management may consist of taking turns and keeping hands to self when other people have food. In the case of the student who is highly skilled but lacks social awareness,, self-management may consist of independent greetings to strangers and responding to questions asked by peers. Using this fluid conceptualization of self-management, it is easy to see how self-management is not an all-or-nothing outcome. Instead, self-management is a dynamic process that contains a wide variety of behaviors that we must define on the level of the child. And, as the child improves functioning capacity, the definition and requirements for self-management mature as well.

In conclusion, self-management will not be found within the pages of a sensory integration catalogue or via attendance at a workshop on the latest technological gadgets. Toys and magical devices cannot produce self-management in anyone. As caregivers, we may find ourselves needing to also self-manage our behavior. We often opt for the quick fix, the most salient solution, and the outcome that will take considerably less of our time. However, such responding will take us to the same limitations that are observed for our students with ASD. Instead, we must take a diligent and evidence-based approach to solving the self-management problem.

RESEARCH SUPPORT

In the most basic form, self-management is the choice to engage in a behavior that leads to more optimal consequences for the child with ASD. The optimal level of the choice is often constructed by us, as caregivers, and thus we seem a bit surprised when the child fails to respond according to our wishes. However, as one unpacks the various components of the consequences, as well as the preceding conditions that surround the choice, the unexpected failures to

self-manage seem a little less unexpected. Once we have identified the controlling factors that surround the response, simple modifications can often yield powerful results. The following factors immediately influence the effectiveness of a self-management system and must be carefully evaluated when developing respective strategies.

Delay

While we may believe that it is optimal to forgo eating candy at snack so we have enough room to eat our healthy lunch, the child with ASD more than likely will prefer the opposite. What we often fail to understand is the power of immediacy. We want good stuff, and we want it now. Therefore, the delay to reinforcement is an important concept to understand as a factor that can limit or promote self-management. Oftentimes, children are labeled with impulsive behaviors or poor choice-making abilities when they choose small, immediate reinforcers rather than waiting for a larger, more delayed reinforcer.

Early studies have examined this type of impulsive behavior with nonhuman organisms. Using basic experimental paradigms in which a small amount of food was available immediately and a larger amount of food following a short delay, results indicated that regardless of the size of the delayed reinforcer, the experimental subjects selected the suboptimal immediate reinforcer. However, preference reversed when delays to gain access to the larger reinforcer were eliminated. What was more perplexing is the consistency to select the larger reinforcer even when the delay to its access was gradually returned. Through the gradual introduction of a delay to reinforcement, preferences can be manipulated to the more optimal reinforcer, one that may be larger and has more benefits than choosing a smaller, more immediate reinforcer. Ferster (1953) illustrated how a progressively increasing delay of time to larger reinforcer could alter pigeons' choice for larger more optimal reinforcement. Subsequent work has explored the value of bridging the empty interval of time between choice and reinforcer presentation. When consequences are delayed, it appears that having something to do during that time can clearly improve an organism's preference for this response option. Grosch and Neuringer (1981) illustrated the effect with pigeons pecking at the opposite end of their experimental chamber while they waited to receive grain, and Dixon and Cummings (2001) extended the effect to children with ASD as they performed discrete trial training tasks prior to the delivery of a larger more optimal reinforcer.

The initial animal research showed how preference among response options could be altered when delays to reinforcement were present. Additional adaptation of these basic paradigms led to more applied human demonstrations. For example, Dixon, Rehfeldt, and Randich (2003) and Dixon et al. (1998) documented successful improvements in self-management of life skills and basic cognitive tasks in individuals with developmental disabilities. After evaluating the baseline levels of task completion, participants were asked to choose between a smaller immediate reinforcer and a larger yet delayed reinforcer. Such contingency arrangements yielded no self-management, as all participants selected the smaller reinforcer even though it was less optimal. However, when the researchers introduced gradual delays associated with the once drastically delayed reinforcer coupled by engaging in the basic tasks during the empty intervals of time, all participants showed improvements from their prior baseline rates of self-management. While these studies serve more as translational demonstrations of the power of self-management than actually changing considerable life practices for persons with ASD, they do suggest the technology is possible and should be explored in additional applied settings.

Quality

Reinforcer quality is another factor that impedes self-management. When the quality of the reinforcer is poor, at least from the perspective of the child with ASD, there is little reason to engage in any behavior to gain access to it. This effect is compounded when a higher quality reinforcer can be accessed for an alternative behavior. It may be standard for some teachers or caregivers to continuously give the same types of reinforcers to children for "good behavior." Although it may seem that all students would be motivated by receiving candy for appropriate behavior or a time-out for inappropriate behavior, it is unknown as to what will actually change behavior without first analyzing the child's preferences. A child in the classroom who is continuously attempting to get out of work by running out of the classroom may not sit and do his work for a long period of time to attain social attention or toy items. Rather, the child who is determined to escape the work will benefit most from a self-management program that provides reinforcement by taking planned breaks from the work he has

been attempting to get out of. This arrangement will not only motivate him to work longer but will also decrease the time spent on escaping the work.

Children show relative preference to various types of reinforcers, and these preferred reinforcers can be found based on their ranking during a preference assessment (Neef, Bicard, & Endo, 2001; Neef, Bicard, Endo, Coury, & Aman, 2005; Neef, Mace, & Shade, 1993). It is important to include potential reinforcers in the preference assessment and to utilize the high-quality reinforcers during high-effort tasks and the low-quality reinforcers for low-effort tasks. Examples of such functional reinforcers would include reinforcers related to attention, sensory stimulation, escape from demands, and tangible items. Attention-related reinforcers may include time with peers, time with teachers or staff, playing a game, or pubic display of good behavior. Sensory-related reinforcers may include toys that make noise, spin, and have different textures and visual features. Reinforcers related to escape from demands would include the ability to get out of work, skip a chore, or take a break. Tangible items include all material items such as small toys, food, or tokens. The quality of reinforcers differs with each child; thus, it is imperative that preference assessments categorize high-quality and low-quality preferences with each child. Also, because preferences do not always stay the same, it is beneficial to conduct the assessments often so the caregiver understands what motivates the child.

Probability

The probability of actually obtaining the reinforcer must also be considered when designing self-management programs. If the child believes he or she may only obtain a chance at a reinforcer, and not a guarantee, the probability of the positive behavior could also decrease. For example, a student could be informed that working hard all week (i.e., no targeted problem behaviors occurring) earns the chance to draw a ticket in the Friday prize party. However, if the prize party is designed such that only certain tickets win good prizes, and other tickets yield nothing (by chance), our student may be less inclined to work the following week under similar contingency arrangements. Essentially, working hard all week yielded a ticket that was redeemable for nothing. Thus, the positive behavior was placed on extinction. Low probability of reinforcement or reductions in probability tend to produce response declines (Dougherty & Chetek,

1994). To yield more optimal self-management, the caregiver should start with high-probability reinforcers, and once behavior is established under such conditions, gradually reduce the probabilities. Another strategy would be to establish contingencies whereby there are various probabilities for various reinforcing outcomes and avoiding the possibility of extinction altogether. Here we might yield better prizes for a few select number of ticket draws and smaller prizes for the remaining tickets. The notion of probability can extend far beyond lottery type arrangements and be used to regulate social and escape reinforcers as well. The unpredictability of reinforcement on these "random" reinforcement schedules has the possibility of yielding extremely high rates of self-managed behaviors.

Effort

The effort needed to engage in self-management should not be overlooked. When the choice between alternatives yields the same reinforcers but one choice requires more effort, most people will choose the lower effort behavior. A series of studies by Neef and colleagues have examined the various parameters of choice that are impacted by response effort. In Neef et al. (2005) easy, medium, and difficult math problems were presented to children and with reinforcer delay and quality held constant, all of them opted for the lower effort problems. When various other response/consequence dimensions were changed (i.e., low effort—low quality reinforcer; high effort—no delay), variations in responding occurred (Neef et al., 1993, 2001, 2005). It may be important to alter the high- and low-response effort demands to increase the on-task and self-managed behavior of the student with ASD. For example, if the child with ASD is having a difficult time completing math word problems, it would be beneficial to give him a low-response effort problem and gradually build up to the high-response effort problems. The skill building will establish a behavioral momentum that increases the child's contact with reinforcement for task completion.

Size

The magnitude of reinforcement has great influence over altering preference and managing behaviors, and it may include amount of reinforcers, as well as time given for access with a reinforcer. The magnitude of reinforcement can be evaluated in terms of managing behavior by altering the choices to be unequal or equal sizes. In a study that included three children diagnosed with autism, Hoch, McComas, Johnson, Faranda, and Guenther (2002) increased the magnitude and quality of reinforcement when the children played with peers. This resulted in more play with peers, as opposed to playing alone. The results also maintained when the magnitude and quality of the reinforcers were altered back to equal sizes for each play group. The results have great implications for the social validity in altering preferred behaviors in children who have ASD.

Changes in size can also occur while behavior remains constant. Dixon and Falcomata (2004) increased time spent on a difficult task by progressively increasing the magnitude of the larger, delayed reinforcer. In this study after initially avoiding a high-effort task, gradual delays to gain access to a larger reinforcer yielded more self-management in the participant. However, once a steady state of self-management was in place, the experimenters reduced the size of the reinforcer associated with the targeted behavior. Toward the end of the experiment, the size of the reinforcer was substantially reduced from initial levels. It appears from this study and others that perhaps size matters somewhat, but what is more important is a student's learning history with a given reinforcer and how that reinforcer may establish additional reinforcing relationships with once high-effort behaviors.

Instructions

Our ability to instruct students about how best to perform a given task or engage in a specific behavior allows us and them to forgo the endless trial and error that occurs in the world without such instructions. Rather than require students to experience repeated failures at self-management, we can simply tell them to "make sure to do the right thing and great stuff will happen to you in the future." Seemingly simple, such advice is readily given but minimally followed. When such advice is compounded by learning delays associated with ASD, the true power for instructions to govern behavior is weakened.

Although complex instructions are difficult to follow, other user-friendly approaches have been established within the autism community. Under the packaging of video and peer modeling, these methods create a series of multisensory instructional scripts to guide the child through various environments where self-management can be useful. For example, Marcus and Wilder (2009) demonstrated utility of both peer and self-video modeling to teach textual responses, with greater gains occurring for self-models. Additionally LeBlanc et al. (2003) were able to produce more effective perspective-taking when students with ASD were exposed to video modeling procedures. While caregivers can never instruct a child through every possible self-management challenge he will encounter, the more opportunities the student has to contact various instructions, observe the effects that come from engaging in the targeted behaviors, and use those experiences to develop self-instructions, the more effective that child will be in the real world. Bicard and Neef (2002) have also noted that instructions should be used in combination with other factors such as altering the magnitude or delay to reinforcement in order to produce optimal self-management. Because instructions alone only impact the antecedent side of the three-term contingency, consequences are also required.

Self-Instructions

Self-instructions can include any verbal mediation of words spoken. Self-instructions occur throughout the day, whether it is thinking what one has to do next, to speaking to peers, to even singing a song on the radio. For a child with ASD in the classroom, talking out loud through a task may have great benefits such as not getting too overwhelmed with a task. Instructions or rules that humans develop have been shown to alter behaviors. Mischel, Ebbeson, and Zeiss (1972) showed that implementing tasks that are incompatible with the behavior results in more optimal behavior management. For example, if the child were to sing or talk during a task, it is likely that she will decrease impulsive choice making. This adds more than just a delay to reinforcement; rather, the self-instructions distract the individual throughout the delay. In a similar study, Dixon, Binder, and Ghezzi (2000) showed effects of self-instructions, or verbal mediation, to fill the delay of time to reinforcement. All participants chose a larger, delayed reinforcer combined with a verbal activity during the delay as opposed to a smaller, more immediate reinforcer (with no verbal mediation). This was successful, regardless of the content of the instructions. This type of alteration is particularly effective in self-management strategies as it is very practical for children to use self-instructions during a wait time to reach reinforcement, whether it is aloud or silent. Many variations of this strategy could be practiced, including writing instructions as well. Another recent study by Faloon and Rehfeldt (2008) illustrated how complex tasks could be completed when self-rules

were taught to persons engaging in multistep life skills activities who failed to perform them prior to the self-instructional training procedures.

Associated Functions

Some self-management programs are most successful when the child is able to *derive* additional response–reinforcer relationships beyond the original caregiver-arranged contingencies. The ability to make these derived inferences about behavior and the related stimuli is at the heart of a problem-solving repertoire. What is of extreme value is how seemingly irrelevant characteristics of a response or stimuli may acquire associated functions and govern future behavior in powerful and predictable ways. For example, if a child is given a choice between a red and blue piece of identical type candy, that child may show a taste preference for the red one. The pairing of a relatively arbitrary stimulus feature (color) with a reinforcing function of taste may result in the color of red being preferred in other novel contexts. The red candy that tasted "better" from the child's perspective now may transfer to a "red" chair being the better chair to sit in instead of a blue chair when everything else remains constant.

In terms of self-management, the potential for associated stimulus functions is robust. After a caregiver detects or arranges for various stimuli to acquire associated functions, the caregiver may arrange conditions such that these functions enhance self-management. For example, knowing that our student from earlier prefers red candy, under demanding work conditions we may allow him access to red photocopied worksheets, picking a red pencil, or calling him by the nickname Reddy before we place the work demands on him. Other types of associated functions might include comparative (greater/smaller; bigger/smaller), coordination (I like Mike—Mike likes work—I should like work), and oppositions (Bobby does not eat beans—I don't like Bobby—I should eat beans). Caregivers should seek out a greater awareness of how stimuli and response functions emerge within their targeted child and capitalize on interventions based on these associations.

PRACTICE RECOMMENDATIONS
General Recommendations

To engage in successful implementation of self-management enhancing practices, caregivers should take a few preliminary cautions. First, a careful medical evaluation needs to be conducted prior to extensive behavioral intervention. If the child is displaying significant challenging behaviors or failing to acquire skills, one must first be confident that a biological condition has not changed for the child. This caution is particularly noteworthy when the child has limited or no verbal skills. Consider that prior seizure activity, earaches, brain tumors, digestive complications, and other aliments may be impeding progress. Thus, the more comprehensive a medical evaluation, the more you can be confident that the behavioral interventions recommended next will be successful at producing self-managed behavior. Second, the caregiver must obtain the necessary and proper consents to establish treatment of any sort. Within a school setting this may include child and parent consent to treatment, the school personnel, and even approval from certain school boards. It is often the case that when challenging behavior is at hand, swift interventions must be instated. While this is true, behavioral interventions should begin only after proper consents have been obtained. Third, caregivers should acquire formal baseline data before initiating intervention. In many clinical and school settings baseline data collection might be considered a luxury, but absent such information difficulties can arise when attempting to document effective behavioral change.

Various research designs can be adapted to the natural and practical world. We suggest that caregivers consider implementing multiple baselines across settings, alternating treatment designs when comparing interventions with a single student, and brief reversal designs to evaluate instructional and behavior support procedures. Such rigor in treatment implementation will require additional staff effort. However, this effort is rewarded with increased confidence that the treatments implemented truly changed behavior and that other factors such as time, seasons, medicine, or maturation were not responsible for observed differences in the student.

Recommendation 1: *Evaluate the context.* Perhaps the most important component to increasing self-management in a child with ASD is carefully examining the context in which the current behavior (or absence of a targeted behavior) is occurring. This evaluation must be more than a mere glance around the room or the completion of simplistic antecedent-behavior-consequence data sheets. Instead, the caregiver should attempt to discover the various choice points the child encounters and

reframe those choices to include the immediate and delayed consequences of each possible action. As discussed earlier, when certain consequences are delayed in time, they are discounted. If the optimal self-managed behavior we are hoping to see only yields powerful reinforcers after a delay in time (e.g., movie on "Fun Friday"), and the problematic non-self-managed behavior yields powerful reinforcers immediately (social attention from peers), we are facing an uphill battle with respect to change. The same could be true whereby the non-self-managed behavior produces high-quality reinforcers (escape from work task), while the self-managed behavior produces low-quality reinforcers (sticker on a sticker chart). Using the various techniques described in the literature, and outlined later, we can alter components of either the antecedent conditions or consequence conditions that surround the choice points. The goal here must be to examine the context surrounding the behavior and identify all of the potentially controlling consequences. The staff should look for these behavioral "crossroads" and map out how each course of action leads to various sets of consequences.

Recommendation 2: *Evaluate the potential for change.* There are many ways in which an individual child with ASD could learn to increase her self-management. However, such learning will vary based on factors such as age and functioning level of the child, commitment from staff and caregivers to implement the treatments with fidelity, financial resources needed to complete the intervention, and supports available outside of the treatment environment. For example, if the child is verbally competent, her repertoire may be more the product of her own self-rules and self-mediated reinforcement than simple contingency arrangements we may put in place during the day. A child who frequently says, "If I am not first in line, I will not get to the lunch room on time" may find the anxiety avoidance of lining up first to be more reinforcing than any amount of candy or stickers we introduce for "self-managed" behavior. Such a child will need to be exposed to more complex interventions that are matched for her level of functioning. Another evaluation may conclude that intensive self-managed protocols are successful at school, yet the home environment is fostering an opposite outcome. The cost/benefit of intensive interventions must be discussed with everyone involved to determine the overall chance of independent self-management.

Recommendation 3: *Tip the scale.* Once the context has been analyzed effectively and the potential for change determined, the caregiver should become one of tipping the scale that is balancing the two competing sets of reinforcing contingencies against each other. In the most basic form, if the child is obtaining 2 seconds of teacher attention immediately for throwing items, and no attention is given for keeping on task, the ratio of reinforcement/behavior for maladaptive throwing items is 2:1 and for self-managed work completion is 0:1. Here the scale needs to be tipped such that throwing items yields fewer reinforcers than work completion. If the behavior serves an attention function, then adding more frequent immediate attention for work completion is indicated. This scale-balancing philosophy can be adapted for even the most complex series of behaviors. For example, once we conclude that an escape function sustains the non-self-managed behavior of a child with ASD hitting peers, more escape needs to be programmed for an alternative self-managed behavior. The hitting may result in the student being sent to the office, having a discussion with the principal, and eventually being taken home from school that day. Our tipping of the scale may now strengthen self-management by delivering frequent access to short breaks, a trip to the ice-cream store on the way home from school, or even the radical consequence of immediate sending the student home. Also, if home is a reinforcer, we would want to explore the various components of that context which may be reinforcing (i.e., video games, 1:1 time with mom, low work demands, etc.) and attempt to replicate them in the school environment.

Recommendation 4: *Create autonomy.* The optimal implementation of self-management is when the child with ASD independently identifies the conditions in the environment that led to the various programmed contingency arrangements. Here the learner detects the various antecedent conditions in place, engages in the self-managed response, and contacts reinforcing consequences, thus continuing to strengthen the response in the future. The caregiver may initially attempt to promote autonomy using a variety of checklists, social stories, prompts, extra instructions, and descriptions of the programmed consequences. For example, when the child enters a high-risk context like Physical Education (PE) class, the caregiver may state, "*I know you like to run out of the room, but remember that if you don't, we will be going for an extra snack later today.*" Verbally bridging the delay in time from PE to snack may help the child detect the more optimal reinforcer that is soon to be had for self-managed compliance in PE and forgo the typical escape response. Another example may be when the caregiver fades the external monitoring of the student's performance of intervals of reading class when the student is responding in a socially appropriately manner. Initially the caregiver and the student may have concurrently tracked appropriate behavior, and as the student became more accurate in his own recording abilities, the teacher would find herself eliminating the redundancy of her data collection.

Specific Self-Management Practice Techniques

Alter Delays to Reinforcement

Research clearly shows that when delays to gain access to reinforcers are minimized, more responding will occur for this choice option. Caregivers should use whatever means necessary to eliminate unnecessary delays in time for providing consequences for good self-management. When delays are needed, they should be faded over the course of successful self-management attempts. In other words, when the student engages in initial self-managed behavior, staff should provide brief immediate reinforcers that over successive days and weeks could be titrated in delay. For example, if Mary is self-recording her transitions without a verbal outburst and such outbursts have declined after 2 days of the program, staff should not wait until the end of a week to deliver effective reinforcers to Mary. Instead, she may need intermediate reinforcers that can be contacted to strengthen the self-management attempts, and only after such contact, that the delays associated with the reinforcers begin to increase. When delays to gain access to more optimal reinforcement are impractical, caregivers should consider increasing the length of time needed to acquire the once immediate yet less optimal reinforcer. Consider the student who throws items across the room to gain attention from staff. If the larger delayed consequence of a social hour with staff at the end of the week is too far off, and bringing the social hour earlier in the week is impractical, withholding the attention for throwing the items, even for short amounts of time, will tend to weaken the student's preference for this poorly self-managed behavior.

Finally, caregivers should incorporate a series of self-tracking and monitoring protocols to encourage the student with ASD to understand that although reinforcement delay is apparent, the series of check-marks, acquired tokens, or crossed-out instructions on such forms signal the increasing availability of the delayed reinforcer. These visual and tangible stimuli will serve a discriminative function and may also acquire conditioned reinforcing properties. In other words, it is possible that checkmarks alone will become reinforcing to the student due to their repeated pairings with known yet delayed reinforcers.

Provide Distracting Activities

Caregivers should attempt to bridge empty intervals of time between self-managed behavior and pro-grammed reinforcement by incorporating interven-ing activities during such delay periods. It has been repeatedly shown in the literature that when a person has something to do, even if it is a low-probability activity, that he or she will be more apt at tolerat-ing delays often associated with reinforcers for self-management. Prior research has shown mini-mal difference between high- and low-effort tasks and that the type of task itself does not appear to make a difference on the child's overall ability to self-manage. Care should be taken to insure that the tasks are somewhat within the repertoire of the individual; otherwise task acquisition and delay tolerance will be competing against each other. Once the student has had experience with follow-ing caregiver-provided distracting activities, there should be an effort to promote the student's ability to seek out and engage in such distractors to further strengthen her own self-management. For example, when the child is being asked to make appropriate greetings to caregivers throughout the day and if five such greetings take place that she will be allowed to play on the computer at the end of the day, the child might seek out additional tasks and activities to bridge the empty intervals of time throughout the day between greetings. The transition of this contrived classroom assignment to an actual life skill may be greeting visitors at a local store (to earn an eventual paycheck at end of day) and organizing shopping carts or picking up trash between visitors (intervening/distracting activities).

Maximize Quality of Reinforcers

In order for the programmed consequences to have their greatest impact as reinforcers, the care-giver must take great efforts to improve the quality of those consequences delivered for self-managed behavior and reduce the quality delivered for non-self-managed behavior. When certain maladap-tive behaviors are emitted, we cannot simply ignore them. Some may be risky, others harmful, and even others dangerous. However, we can alter the quality of the consequences we provide. Instead of a long, drawn-out verbal reprimand for engaging in an unde-sirable behavior, we could simply do a brief redirect, perhaps even nonverbally. Or, when a time-out is necessary and functionally relevant, the least pre-ferred staff member by the child could implement the procedure. Even extreme cases of intervention such as physical restraint could contain high-quality interactions and reinforcers that the student does not experience at other times of the day. When self-managed behavior yields low-quality items such as stickers, tokens, or points and maladaptive behav-ior provides 3:1 attention, the quality distribution of available reinforcers is working against the caregivers. Interventions should be designed that include elimi-nation of social exchanges for maladaptive behavior, introducing escape or time-outs for self-managed behavior, intensive social time with staff, and func-tional reinforcers of higher quality than those found for aberrant behaviors.

Teach Self-Recording Techniques

One key component to self-management involves the student's ability to determine how well his behavior is matching up to what is expected by caregivers. When reinforcers are delayed, such self-discrimination and recording can serve a reinforcing fuction. Also, it serves as a discriminative stimulus that successive emissions of the self-managed response will lead to the programmed reinforcer. The self-recording may take the basic form of a check mark, tally mark, or smiley face. Other protocols may involve a journal log of successfully emitted self-management and how those instances are accumulating in such a way that they will produce the desired consequence. For example, a 10-year-old may create a journal entry each time she walked away from the classroom bully who makes insulting comments to her. The child with ASD may be taught to write down what hap-pened, how he responded, how he felt, and how the behavior of self-management will lead to desired consequences at the end of the week by getting a trip to the local toy store. Other forms of self-recording may involve voice recordings, video captures, or peers prompting the student to notice how well he just did in a certain setting or under certain stimulus conditions.

A problem that may arise with self-recording is that students may be prone to cheat by recording more instances of self-management than really occurred. The best way to minimize cheating is to make sure that you reinforce the child for self-recording, not just self-management. Smaller immediate reinforcers could be given for the student's correspondence of her own behavior with that of a caregiver who observed the same instance of behavior. Once firm correspondence is instilled, the subsequent recording of the caregiver could be eliminated. This too will allow for increased generalization of the self-recording and self-management repertoire.

Increase Instructions

While some students with ASD may not have the initial ability to understand instructions, they may benefit from modifications of such verbal descriptions to video and auditory format. The power of observational learning should not be underestimated. For example, if the student is having difficulty completing the series of steps involved in getting ready for school in the morning, he may watch a video of a peer or parent completing the steps and narrating through the activity. This alone may increase the probability of self-readiness in the future, even when no written instructions were presented to the child on what to do and when.

If the student is verbally sophisticated, adding instructions into the context is valuable as well. When delays to reinforcement are present, instruct the student of the consequences that will come. When the student is faced at a choice point of either to display an instant of self-management, the caregiver might instruct the student of the needed behaviors that should be emitted, just in case that the environmental cues are unclear. Also, it may be beneficial to instruct the student of the various consequences that will be accessed from either behavior option.

Move the Future Psychologically

At first glance this concept seems to fall outside the scope of a behavioral science. Moving the future can indeed be conceptualized behavior analytically. It is nothing more than the ability to discriminate and describe the consequences that are associated with a certain behavior even if those consequences are probabilistic, delayed, or only verbally defined. The "verbal definition" of consequences poses great challenges, yet it also can yield great outcomes. Consider

the following statement: "If you work very hard this week, you will get to attend the school Christmas party." For a student who is new to the school and has never been to such a party, the verbal description of such delayed events is weak at best. Here the caregiver must create a series of relations between the verbal statement "Christmas party" and other things already experienced by the child in his or her history. These other events must have reinforcing value, and thus such value may be transferred to the words used by the caregiver: "... Christmas party."

SUMMARY

In summary, the concept of self-management is not a unitary behavioral principle. Instead, it encompasses a variety of behavioral mechanisms and dimensions that include choice making, allocating responses based on available reinforcers, an increased conceptualization of the future, greater stimulus control, and self-recording/monitoring. As a result, self-management is often considered too vague to promote and too complex to expect from many students with ASD. However, there are a series of well-established behavioral practices that will allow for self-management to occur for the child. At a primary level, self-management may entail nothing more than the reallocation of responding in one risky, socially inappropriate situation. At a more robust level, however, self-management may be the embracing and evaluation of the various programmed reinforcers available immediately and in the future which occur based on any course of action. The ability to discriminate the choice points that are encountered throughout the day and allocate responses efficiently is the optimal goal of the self-managed child.

REFERENCES

Barkley, R. A. (1997). Behavioral inhibition, sustained attention, and executive functions. *Psychological Bulletin, 121*, 65–94.

Bicard, D. F., & Neef, N. A. (2002). Effects of strategic versus tactical instructions on adaption to changing contingencies to children with ADHD. *Journal of Applied Behavior Analysis, 35*, 375–389.

Dixon, M. R., Binder, L. M., & Ghezzi, P. M., (2000). A procedure to teach self-control to children with attention deficit hyperactivity disorder. *Journal of Applied Behavior Analysis, 33*, 233–237.

Dixon, M. R., & Cummings, A. (2001). Self-control in children with autism: Response allocation during delays to reinforcement. *Journal of Applied Behavior Analysis, 34*, 491–495.

Dixon, M. R., & Falcomata, T. S. (2004). Preference for progressive delays and concurrent physical therapy exercise in an adult with acquired brain injury. *Journal of Applied Behavior Analysis, 37,* 101–105.

Dixon, M. R., Rehfeldt, R. A., & Randich, L. (2003). Enhancing tolerance to delayed reinforcers: The role of intervening activities. *Journal of Applied Behavior Analysis, 36,* 263–266.

Dougherty D. M., & Chetek, D. R. (1994). Effects of social context, reinforcer probability, and reinforcer magnitude on humans' choices to compete or not to compete. *Journal of Experimental Analysis of Behavior, 62,* 133–148.

Falcomata, T. S., & Dixon, M. R. (2004). Enhancing physical therapy exercises in persons with acquired brain injury through a self-control training procedure. *European Journal of Behavior Analysis, 29,* 29–41.

Faloon, B., & Rehfeldt, R. A. (2008) The role of overt and covert self-rules in establishing a daily living skill in adults with mild developmental disabilities. *Journal of Applied Behavior Analysis, 41,* 393–404.

Ferster, C. B. (1953). Sustained behavior under delayed reinforcement. *Journal of Experimental Psychology, 45,* 218–224.

Grosch, J., & Neuringer, A. (1981). Self-control in pigeons under the Mischel paradigm. *Journal of the Experimental Analysis of Behavior, 35,* 3–21.

Hoch, H., McComas, J. J., Johnson, L., Faranda, N., & Guenther, S. L. (2002). The effects of magnitude and quality of reinforcement on choice responding during play activities. *Journal of Applied Behavior Analysis, 35,* 171–181.

LeBlanc, L. A., Coates, A. M., Daneshvar, S., Charlop-Christy, M. H., Morris, C., & Lancaster, B. M. (2003). Using video modeling and reinforcement to teach perspective-taking skills to children with autism. *Journal of Applied Behavior Analysis, 36,* 253–257.

Marcus, A., & Wilder, D. (2009). A comparison of peer video modeling and self video modeling to teach textual responses in children with autism. *Journal of Applied Behavior Analysis, 42,* 335–341.

McEvoy, R. E., Rogers, S. J., & Pennington, B. F. (2006). Executive function and social communication deficits in young autistic children. *Journal of Child Psychology and Psychiatry, 34,* 563–578.

Mischel, H. N., Ebbesen, E. B., & Zeiss, A. R. (1972). Cognitive and attentional mechanisms in delay of gratification. *Journal of Personality and Social Psychology, 16,* 204–218.

Neef, N. A., Bicard, D. F., & Endo, S. (2001). Assessment of impulsivity and the development of self-control in students with attention deficit hyperactivity disorder. *Journal of Applied Behavior Analysis, 34,* 397–408.

Neef, N. A., Bicard, D. F., Endo, S., Coury, D. L., & Aman, M. G. (2005). Evaluation of pharmacological treatment of impulsivity in children with attention deficit hyperactivity disorder. *Journal of Applied Behavior Analysis, 38,* 135–146.

Neef, N. A., Mace, F. C., & Shade, D. (1993). Impusivity in students with serious emotional disturbance: The interactive effects of reinforcer rate, delay, and quality. *Journal of Applied Behavior Analysis, 26,* 37–52.

9

Pivotal Response Treatment

LYNN KERN KOEGEL, BRITTANY LYNN KOEGEL,
ROBERT L. KOEGEL, AND TY W. VERNON

There have been many changes in the interventions for individuals with autism since Leo Kanner first described the disability seven decades ago (Kanner, 1943). Most notably, parents, who were once considered the cause of their child's autism (Bettleheim, 1967) and therefore excluded from the intervention (a theory that has long been debunked), are now considered an essential part of the treatment team (Ingersoll & Dvortcsak, 2006; Koegel & Koegel, 2012; Symon, 2001). Further, the children themselves, who were at one time considered "uneducable" and typically committed to institutions by adolescence, now benefit from an extensive body of empirically based interventions that address the core symptoms of the disability—socialization, communication, and restricted/repetitive interests and behaviors. These interventions have provided individuals diagnosed as having autism with the ethical and legal right to be educated and included in our society, a basic right afforded to other members of society.

This chapter will focus on empirically based interventions, namely applied behavior analysis (ABA), and will detail the procedures of pivotal response treatment (PRT), an outgrowth of the ABA procedures. To start, it is important to consider the importance of a continual and evolving iterative process of any "package" intervention. That is, PRT is a scientifically based approach that has evolved over the years based on the findings from hundreds of research studies. However, PRT continues to evolve as additional programmatic studies are conducted and findings are made. PRT was originally based upon the early discrete trial training (DTT) approach, a psychological approach that uses the application of ABA, to focus on the relationship of behavior to the environment using specific researched procedures. This approach uses observable data to guide goals and evaluate the effectiveness of the intervention, thereby excluding speculative (and possibly inaccurate) constructs, such as occurred with the early parental causation hypothesis. More specifically, the early work of Ivar Lovaas and colleagues (cf., Lovaas, Koegel, Simmons, & Long, 1973) was expanded upon to develop a more child-friendly approach that targeted motivation. Originally PRT was called the "natural language paradigm" (Koegel, O'Dell, & Koegel, 1987) because the motivational procedures were individually developed and researched, then packaged as a group, and first applied to communication to improve language use in children with autism. However, additional research showed that the motivational procedures could be effectively applied to a variety of other functional domains, including academics, disruptive behavior, social areas, and self-help skills, with more rapid and generalized gains when compared to a traditional ABA approach (Koegel, Koegel, & Surratt, 1992); thus, it was renamed "pivotal response treatment" (also known as pivotal response teaching, pivotal response training, and pivotal response therapy). The PRT approach is documented as one of the few effective and empirically based treatments for children with autism spectrum disorder (ASD; National Autism Center, 2008; National Research Council, 2001; Simpson, 2005).

PRIORITY CONCERNS

Several important principles underlie PRT. First, intervention is provided in the child's natural environment. This includes implementing intervention in the home and community, and including the children with autism in classrooms with typical children. Research has shown that natural settings, where individuals would participate if they did not have a disability, are critical for the most positive outcomes.

In fact, longitudinal research has proven that children included in regular education classrooms outperform their peers who are educated in segregated environments (Howard, Sparkman, Cohen, Green, & Stanislaw, 2005). In addition to school inclusion, parents are encouraged to enroll their children in extracurricular clubs, to take them to the grocery store and other community settings, and to engage in a variety of social events with their typical peers. Individualized PRT interventions are provided on an ongoing basis in these natural everyday environments (Koegel, Koegel, Hurley, & Frea, 1992; Pierce & Schreibman, 1997).

Second, and equally important, is parent participation. Coordination of goals and consistency of intervention procedures are critical for more rapid intervention gains (Dunlap, Koegel, & Kern, 1984) and the specific PRT procedures are taught to parents through a "practice with feedback" procedure wherein a parent educator observes parents working with their child and provides feedback regarding their use of the procedures. Parents are required to meet an 80% criterion on fidelity of implementation measures that are very specifically defined so that parents can quickly understand areas that they are implementing correctly and areas that would benefit from additional practice.

Finally, the approach focuses on "pivotal areas." Pivotal areas are targeted behaviors that, once learned, result in widespread improvements in a variety of symptoms of the disability. The focus on pivotal areas came about as a consequence of the labor and time intensiveness of the ABA approaches when individual behaviors were targeted. That is, children with autism experience many areas in need of remediation, and the early ABA interventions focused on targeting each and every area, which often required 40 or more hours a week of sitting the child at a table and drilling each behavior until an individual target behavior was learned. While the children progressed under this paradigm, progression was slow and many of the children engaged in disruptive behavior to avoid the teaching sessions. That led us to first focus on the pivotal area of "motivation" with the target goal of having active and enthusiastic learners.

Our early work on motivation was founded on principles of "learned helplessness," a construct that purports that when one does not experience a connection between behavior and its consequences on the environment, that individual ceases to act to change their environment over time. The early research in this area focused on inescapable punishment and found that after a period of time there is a failure to try and escape the aversive situation (Seligman & Maier, 1967). The problem of learned helplessness can also occur when noncontingent positive consequences are provided. That is, similar to noncontingent punishers, when a reinforcer is administered noncontingently and the child does not connect that positive consequence to the behavior emitted, learned helplessness can also occur. For children with autism, this situation may occur when a well-meaning adult provides repeated, unnecessary assistance to the child, whether it be getting dressed, communicating, or in social situations. The child then does not associate his or her attempts or responses with the environmental consequences and therefore may fail to respond in the future. This does not represent a lack of ability, but rather a lack of attempts. To this end, the first PRT discovery focused on improving the child's motivation to respond by emphasizing the connection between the child's behavior and the consequences of the behavior. Many studies provided the foundation for PRT that were eventually used in a package. The outcome of this research was the delineation of five components that were found to specifically improve motivation: (a) reinforcing attempts, (b) using natural reinforcers, (c) providing child choice, (d) interspersing maintenance and acquisition tasks, and (e) task variation. As can be noted, some of these procedures, such as reinforcing attempts and natural reinforcers, are applied to the consequences of a child's behavior. Child choice, interspersing maintenance tasks, and task variation can be conceptualized as antecedents that may be incorporated into the teaching procedures as motivating operations to increase the strength of the reinforcer.

MOTIVATION

Early studies focusing on improving a child with autism's motivation assessed whether contingencies could be manipulated to create a more responsive and active learner. For example, Koegel and Egel (1979) implemented a multiple-baseline design with three children with autism, wherein they looked at the enthusiasm of the children while attempting to, or completing, a fine motor task. This research showed that children who had low levels of responding or inconsistent responses tended to have inconsistent reinforcers for their attempts to respond (decreasing their motivation), but children who were reinforced for their attempts to respond ("Nice job," "Keep trying!") until they got the correct answer had increased levels of positive emotion and higher levels of responsiveness. Thus, by reinforcing attempts to respond, rather than relying on the previous ABA procedures that focused on a strict shaping paradigm wherein only responses that were equal to or better than the previous response were reinforced (Lovaas, 1977), the child's consistency of responses and enthusiasm improved, as rated on a Likert scale. Thus, by manipulating the consequences in the discrete trials, this study demonstrated the importance of motivation to respond to environmental stimuli as a key area for increasing task acquisition and child affect. Other similar research related to the delivery of reinforcers identified that reinforcing children's attempts, rather than using strict reinforcement criteria, was also effective for teaching communication (Koegel, O'Dell, & Dunlap, 1988). That is, early attempts at teaching expressive verbal communication only reinforced correct responses or responses that were better than the previous response (and did not reinforce attempts when they were incorrect). Specifically, when teaching phoneme discrimination and shaping phoneme production when a child was being taught first words, the child was required to produce a series of phonemes that were either close to the adult word or were closer to the adult word than the previous response. While somewhat effective, the intervention was so labor and time intensive that many children needed to be provided with hundreds or even many thousands of trials before they learned a single word (Lovaas, 1977). However, reinforcing clear attempts, no matter how distant they were from the final goal, improved motivation, speed of acquisition, and overall success in acquisition.

Additional research, also focused on consequences, showed that using natural reinforcers that were logically-related to the task itself, rather than an unrelated arbitrary reinforcer, improved the responsiveness of children with autism (Williams, Koegel, & Egel, 1981). Most of the ABA interventions in the 1980s used flash cards and edible reinforcers, and it is common to still see programs that use reinforcers that are unrelated to the child's behavior. The problem with such arbitrary response–reinforcer relationships is that they make it difficult for the child to learn the connection between responding and reinforcement. In contrast, if the reinforcer became a functional part of the activity, for example, a child got access to a toy after verbally requesting it (i.e., the reinforcer was inherently related to the child's response), the response–reinforcer contingency was emphasized. Williams, Koegel, and Egel (1981) used functional items, such as teaching children with autism the expressive verbal word "cup." Specifically, when the child requested a cup, an arbitrary reinforcer was handed to the child in one condition, or a cup filled with a small amount of juice provided as a natural reinforcer was given to the child in the other condition. The children who received the natural reinforcers dramatically outperformed the children in the group who were provided with an unrelated reinforcer, suggesting that specific intrinsic response–reinforcer relationships were a pivotal core deficit in autism.

In addition to efforts on understanding the role of contingencies, other studies focused on antecedent variables during instruction. For example, Dunlap and Koegel (1980) identified task variation as another key component to motivating children with autism. In this multiple-baseline study across participants, children exhibited a higher percentage of correct responding on an individual task when the interventionist frequently varied the task, rather than repeatedly "drilling" on a single task until the child reached criterion. Also, blind observers rated the children as more enthusiastic, more interested, happier, and better behaved during trials sessions where targeted tasks were varied.

In a related study also focused on antecedent manipulations, Dunlap (1984) found that interspersing "maintenance" or easy tasks that the child had previously mastered, with "acquisition" targeted tasks that the child had not yet learned, increased the child's responsiveness and correct responding. This study evaluated three different conditions: (a) one condition where there were only acquisition tasks targeting a single target behavior (until the child reached criterion) during the session, (b) another condition where 10 different acquisition tasks were presented during each session until the child reached criterion, and (c) another condition where a ratio of 50% maintenance and acquisition tasks were presented during the session. The children in the condition that included the maintenance tasks responded dramatically better than the children in the other two conditions, and naïve observers rated the attention and affect higher in the individuals in the condition that included maintenance tasks. Thus, when interspersing the previously acquired tasks, the children exhibited much faster acquisition and more positive affect.

Another line of research focused on antecedent manipulations related to curriculum issues. Specifically, Koegel, Dyer, and Bell (1987) found child selection of the stimulus materials and activities to be another key component in motivating children with ASD. In a multiple-baseline reversal design, children were either prompted to complete teacher-chosen tasks or complete a task of their own choice (with the same target behavior). The results showed that the children's social avoidance behaviors decreased when they were provided with choice. Many subsequent studies have emphasized the importance of child choice (or following the child's lead) as a curriculum strategy with children who have autism (Kaiser, Yoder, & Keetz, 1992).

Following the discoveries of these individual variables, Koegel, O'Dell, and Koegel (1987) found that by combining them as a package, individuals with ASD were able to learn communication faster and greater generalization occurred. Table 9.1 summarizes the differences between the more traditional DTT trial format and the PRT teaching format.

As noted earlier, the preliminary work began with communication (Koegel, O'Dell, & Koegel, 1987), but rapidly the motivational procedures were tested with other behaviors and were also found to be effective. For example, incorporating child choice, interspersing difficult and easy tasks, and providing natural rewards have been shown to decrease disruptive behavior and improve task engagement during academic activities, such as math and writing (Koegel, Singh, & Koegel, 2010). Specifically, in

a multiple-baseline design across participants, children engaged in schoolwork assigned by their teachers during baseline. These academic assignments were teacher-chosen worksheets without any individualization or motivational components, which resulted in considerable levels of disruptive behavior and low levels of academic engagement. During intervention the same goal was targeted, but the students could make choices, for example, selecting the topic of a writing assignment or favorite items to learn math concepts. To increase engagement, easy tasks were interspersed such as writing a single easy word with more difficult targeted spelling words or writing a sentence interspersed with writing a paragraph. After completing the assignment the students were allowed to engage in a favorite activity they had just written about or to play with a favorite toy they had just labeled and spelled. We suggest that incorporating these motivational strategies as an antecedent intervention can reduce the need for escape extinction procedures.

Furthermore, recent research has demonstrated that PRT can fundamentally alter the social interest and engagement of children with autism. In a study by Koegel, Vernon, and Koegel (2009), participants who demonstrated limited eye contact, neutral or low affect, and overall low social engagement took part in a novel social intervention using the principles of PRT. The participant children, however, were not completely devoid of engagement—they did, in fact, demonstrate strong levels of interest in specific nonsocial activities. Within

TABLE 9.1 COMPARISON OF DISCRETE TRIAL TRAINING AND PIVOTAL RESPONSE TREATMENT

	Discrete Trial Format	Pivotal Response Treatment
Stimulus items	Chosen by clinician Repeated until criterion is met	Chosen by child Varied every few trials Combination of maintenance and acquisition tasks
Interaction	Clinician holds up stimulus item Stimulus item is not functionally related to interaction	Clinician and child play with stimulus item Stimulus item is used functionally within the interaction
Environment	Teaching procedures take place in a structured setting	Teaching procedures take place in the context of naturally occurring activities
Response	Reinforce only correct responses	Reinforce reasonable attempts that are clear and goal oriented
Reinforcement	Arbitrary reinforcers (typically edibles) are provided after the child's response	Natural reinforcers are provided immediately after response

the intervention paradigm of the study, a traditional PRT antecedent-behavior-consequence teaching framework was used to target their communication skills. However, the natural reinforcer was modified to be social in nature. To accomplish this, the key components of the children's preexisting interests were used to develop a socially equivalent activity. For example, if a child enjoyed the vestibular reinforcement of jumping on a trampoline, the socially analogous natural reinforcer might involve jumping on the trampoline with the child following a verbal request. Likewise, a child requesting music would be naturally reinforced by an adult playfully singing a favorite tune, rather than being provided with the opportunity to listen to music alone. The study showed that embedding a social component into a natural reinforcer in the PRT sessions produced significant positive changes in the children's socialization, including strong levels of interest and engagement, which were directed toward a social partner instead of a nonsocial object. In other words, the participant children began to seek out and engage their social partners once social variables were incorporated into the reinforcer.

While the initial investigation of this approach consisted of a clinician-implemented social intervention, a follow-up research study evaluated the effectiveness of the procedures in the context of a parent education program. Specifically, the study assessed whether parents could be taught the same strength-based procedures (i.e., using their child's interests and incorporating social reinforcers) for increasing their children's interpersonal engagement (Vernon, Koegel, Dauterman, & Stolen, 2012). Within a parent education framework, mothers and fathers delivered PRT language-learning opportunities with social activities embedded into the reinforcers. Following the introduction of social reinforcement (again, incorporating their child's preexisting interests), robust positive changes were observed in eye contact, directed positive affect, and verbal initiations. Simultaneously, significant increases in the parents' positive affect and parent–child synchrony were noted. It appears, then, that PRT with embedded social reinforcers can improve social engagement between parents and their children. In essence, these parent–child dyads approximate back-and-forth exchanges that more closely resembled how a parent might interact with a typically developing child. Finally, generalization and follow-up behavioral data provided evidence that

parents continued to use these social intervention strategies when a clinician was not present (and even after the study had concluded), with continued high levels of child responsiveness and affect, adding to the evidence that PRT is a readily implementable and socially valid intervention model.

In summary, this research addresses the hypothesized deficits in social motivation exhibited in children with autism (Dawson, Meltzoff, Osterling, Rinaldi, & Brown, 1998; Dawson, Webb, & McPartland, 2005; Grelotti, Gauthier, & Schultz, 2002; Scott-Van Zeeland, Dapretto, Ghahremani, Poldrack, & Bookheimer, 2010). To successfully intervene in the face of such vulnerabilities, these children need exposure to social encounters of significant salience in order to successfully attract and maintain their often-fleeting attention. These recent studies, grounded in the PRT intervention model, operate from a strength-based perspective—recognizing that there are, in fact, existing stimuli (i.e., nonsocial objects and activities) that pique the interest and attention of children with ASD. By creating interactive versions of these nonsocial interests, empirical evidence suggests that children with autism will seek out, initiate toward, and remain engaged with parents and other social partners at a much higher level when socialization is embedded into the reinforcer. Such foundational interpersonal skills may be crucial for ultimately changing the social trajectories of children with autism, as it may reduce or eliminate the social avoidance frequently exhibited in individuals with ASD.

COLLATERAL IMPROVEMENTS WHEN MOTIVATION IS ADDRESSED

In addition to improved child outcomes when the motivational procedures of PRT were incorporated, studies found that parents had higher affect and lower levels of stress compared to DTT (Koegel, Bimbela, & Schreibman, 1996). Parents are critical to a child's progress, and procedures that are palatable and pleasing for the parents to implement are likely to be used regularly and frequently in comparison to interventions that are demanding or unsatisfying to implement. Further, research showed that children who were disruptive during DTT intervention were more attentive and exhibited lower levels of disruptive behavior during therapy sessions when the motivational components were incorporated

(Koegel, Koegel, & Surratt, 1992). Because children with autism were frequently punished for inappropriate and disruptive behaviors, often with painful consequences (Lovaas, 1977), these motivational procedures greatly improved the context of instruction for both the children and practitioners.

Initiations

In relation to communication, the PRT motivational procedures increased learning, but language samples of children with autism showed that most of them communicated for a limited number of functions, primarily requests and protests (Hurtig, Ensrud, & Tomblin, 1982; Wetherby & Prutting, 1984). Comparing verbal children with autism who had more positive long-term outcomes to verbal children with autism who had very poor long-term outcomes, Koegel, Koegel, Shoshan, and McNerney (1999) found that the children who exhibited initiations during their preschool years had better outcomes in adolescence and adulthood than children who did not initiate interactions even when verbal abilities were matched. This finding was independent of responding, as all of the children were able to verbally respond when an adult addressed them. Thus, this finding led to additional research focusing on whether initiations could be taught to children with autism who did not exhibit that function of communication, and if, consequently, they too would have better long-term outcomes. Following this initial finding that used archival data, a search of the literature indicated that a few studies had attempted to teach question-asking to individuals with autism, with the end goal of teaching "curiosity" that is frequent and common in the language and behavior of typically developing children. It is interesting that this general social interaction, including asking questions and sharing enjoyment with others, seems not to develop in children with ASD. Even early forms (before the onset of verbal communication) such as joint attention as a social way of seeking attention and information is depressed or absent in infants with ASD's first year of life. During a child's second year of life the primitive use of queries is evident in a typical language developer's first lexicon (Miller, 1981). Important initial attempts to teach social verbal initiations in the form of queries to children with ASD produced acquisition of questions in the clinic but poor generalization outside of this setting (Hung, 1977).

Understanding the importance of both incorporating motivation into the intervention and the long-term benefits of initiations, we focused our research on building motivation into teaching of initiations to increase generalized use of initiations across settings and people. With respect to the developmental order that questions are asked in typically developing children, the first query we targeted was "What's that?" with the end goal that this initiation would help the child learn new vocabulary words (Koegel, Camarata, Valdez-Menchaca, & Koegel, 1997). This question usually emerges with a typically developing child's first group of words (a primitive form of the question is used, which is produced as the single word "dat?" which is often emitted while pointing to items). Participants in the study did not use this form in their language samples during baseline. In order to improve the motivation for children to initiate the question, the child's favorite items were placed in an opaque bag and the child was prompted to ask, "What's that?" Once the child queried, a desired item was removed from the bag, labeled, and given to the child. After the child was asking a stable rate of questions, neutral items were systematically placed in the bag (beginning with every fourth item, then third, and so on), then the bag was gradually faded until the child was asking "What's that?" about many items. Vocabulary tests indicated that the children acquired large vocabularies as a direct consequence of the child-initiated questions. Further, the use of the question generalized across settings and people.

However, while the children began using the first question, there was no response generalization to other question types. Therefore, the intervention was continued, teaching additional queries. "Where" questions were taught by hiding a child's favorite items and prompting the child to ask, "Where is it?" Following the child's questions about the location, a preposition (such as "in" or "under" the box) was provided and the child could access the natural reinforcer by responding correctly to the adult's response to the child's question. Similarly, "Whose" questions were taught by prompting the child to ask, "Whose is it?" with favorite items or treats (Koegel, Koegel, Green-Hopkins, & Barnes, 2010). Following the query, the adult responded with "yours," prompting the child to reverse the pronoun and respond with "mine." The child was then given the opportunity to take the desired item, again providing a natural reinforcer. Once the child was responding correctly at a high rate, neutral items that belonged to the interventionist were interspersed with the highly desired items. In response to the neutral items the child was prompted to respond "yours" after the interventionist responded with "It's mine" or "mine". Likewise, possessive "s" endings were targeted with the same query (Whose is it?) by having parents bring in items specifically associated with a particular member of the family. Following the query, the owner was labeled with the possessive "s" ending (e.g., It's Mommy's), and the child could have access to the items.

Finally, Koegel, Carter, and Koegel (2003) expanded verb diversity and verb conjugation by teaching questions using pop-up books of the children's individual interest. Specifically, the tabs were manipulated and the children were prompted to ask, "What's happening?" The verb and –ing ending were modeled for the child, and after the child repeated the verb with the –ing ending, he or she was provided with an opportunity to manipulate the tab. A similar procedure was used for the past tense; however, the tab was manipulated briefly and then stopped. The child was then prompted to ask, "What happened?" and the verb with the past tense ending (or the irregular past tense) was modeled. Once the child repeated the verb using the past tense, the opportunity to manipulate the tab was provided. Other child initiations such as "help" and "look" were also taught using child choice activities or items and natural reinforcers.

Motivational procedures can be incorporated into teaching by, for example, putting desired items into a container with the lid screwed on tightly and prompting the child to ask for help. The prompt can be faded gradually and systematically until the child initiates asking for help. Similarly, "Look!" can be taught by prompting the child to say "Look!" about a favorite item or activity just before it is provided.

Because many collateral gains take place, we hypothesize that initiations are an important pivotal area. Once children with autism are using initiations, research shows that they are viewed as appearing more appropriate on normalcy scales (Koegel, Koegel, Shoshan, & McNerney, 1999). Interactions are more reciprocal, social interactions improve, and, importantly, children take an active role in the learning process (Doggett, Krasno, Koegel, & Koegel, 2012). Further, when child initiations are learned, disruptive behaviors decrease without needing direct intervention.

Self-Management

Self-management is an empirically validated intervention for individuals with ASD (National Standards Project, 2008). The procedures for teaching self-management include discriminating the occurrence or nonoccurrence of a target behavior, monitoring the target behavior, and obtaining a reinforcer when demonstrating the target behavior (or absence of the nondesired behavior). Some individuals can learn to self-administer rewards, thereby being completely independent. Like initiations, the advantage of self-management is that intervention can occur without support from a care provider.

Prior to the 1990s, self-management had been largely used with typically developing children and individuals with mild disabilities (Harris, 1986; Koegel, Koegel, & Ingham, 1986; Koegel, Koegel, Ingham, & Van Voy, 1988). However, effectiveness was also demonstrated with individuals with ASD. For example, Koegel and Koegel (1990) taught students to refrain from stereotypy by using alarming wristwatches to signal prescribed time intervals. This study showed that minimal one-on-one intervention was required, as the self-management could be programmed to occur in community and full-inclusion school settings in the absence of a treatment provider. In another study by Koegel, Koegel, Hurley, and Frea (1992), self-management was programmed to occur in community settings with elementary and middle school students. Specifically, the children were taught to respond to questions and to monitor their appropriate responses on wristcounters. Points were accumulated toward reinforcers. For all children, low levels of responsiveness that occurred in baseline improved during intervention to 80% to 100%, with generalization to new community settings without the presence of an interventionist. Furthermore, disruptive behaviors decreased. In a related study with three children who had autism, stereotypy and disruptive behaviors decreased and appropriate play improved through self-management training (Stahmer & Schreibman, 1992).

Notably, self-management may be an ideal intervention for adolescents when peers judge constant vigilance by a treatment provider as being unusual or age inappropriate. Self-management programs can also help students with autism when transitioning to new activities (Newman et al., 1995) and for social areas (Koegel & Frea, 1993). Additionally, self-management may be effective with children who have autism, are nonverbal or minimally verbal, and lack daily living skills (Pierce & Schreibman, 1994).

Overall, self-management procedures have been shown to be helpful in improving behaviors with verbal individuals with autism from preschool

(Reinecke, Newman, & Meinberg, 1999) through adulthood. While most of the publications have focused on verbal individuals, there is some suggestion that the procedures may be effective with nonverbal individuals if visual prompts (pictures) are used, as noted earlier. Because individuals who learn to self-manage their behavior also demonstrate positive improvements in untreated behaviors, self-management appears to be another influential pivotal area.

Empathy

Many people have suggested that individuals with autism lack empathy, but we argue that the absence or apparently low level of empathy may be more related to lack of practice with social conversation. Limited practice may be pervasive due to exclusionary practices imposed by society and because social interaction is often difficult and therefore not pleasurable for individuals with autism. Preliminary research suggests that we may be able to teach social conversation related to empathy that, once learned, improves other skills. For example, in a multiple-baseline design study with college students diagnosed with Asperger syndrome, Koegel, Ashbaugh, Koegel, Detar, and Register (in press) met weekly with college students to practice social conversation while supporting them in social activities on campus. Social conversation intervention was individualized but focused on appropriate question-asking, listening, nonverbal behaviors, and so on. Additionally, the students participated in interest-related clubs and events with a trained age-matched support person. The results indicated that following the social intervention the students' grade point averages improved, they reported increased levels of happiness, some secured jobs, and some began dating. Teaching appropriate question use as a way of expressing interest in a conversational partner can improve social communicative interactions among adolescents and young adults. Intervention may be implemented by having the participants engage in social conversation with similarly aged peers and then using video modeling to show instances of appropriate question-asking and segments that need improvement. On trials that need improvement, feedback can be provided and the target behavior of asking appropriate empathetic questions can be practiced and learned. Our research showed that participants' social conversation improved and they reported feeling more confident socially following

the intervention. Thus, while teaching empathy is not well researched with individuals diagnosed with ASD, preliminary research suggests that specific behaviors such as question-asking create a perceived interest and empathy by the conversational partner.

PRACTICE RECOMMENDATIONS

While PRT has its roots in ABA and DTT, PRT embraces more child-friendly, naturalistic procedures that have been evaluated extensively in applied research within school, home, clinic, and community settings. It is important to note that PRT is continually evolving and individualized, and is not a static, "one-size-fits-all" intervention. It is our hope that the field will continue to advance so that more pivotal behaviors will be discovered, thereby decreasing the need to address individual target behaviors and producing a greatly more effective and efficient intervention. To be specific, our approach embraces the idea that there are no "nonresponders"; there is just a shortage of interventions to address the needs of some children with autism. If a child is not responding to an intervention, it may very likely be an attention problem, and further research will be helpful for that child (Koegel, Shirotova, & Koegel, 2009).

As for practice recommendations, we have previously discussed the importance of motivational influences, teaching initiations, and teaching self-management skills. In addition, practitioners should record data routinely because research shows that data collection leads to greater child learning and response to intervention can be closely monitored. A baseline needs to be established and once intervention starts, regular data allow the interventionist to ascertain whether the child is responding to the intervention or if alterations or a different intervention altogether is warranted.

Typically, a combination of interventions, applied simultaneously, is most effective with children, youth, and adults who are diagnosed with ASD. Acquisition of target behaviors and general outcomes will be enhanced if these interventions are coordinated across settings and practitioners. Parent participation and parent–professional collaboration, in particular, have widespread positive effects because parents can train others with whom the individual with ASD interacts (Symon, 2001). And finally, but critically important, individuals with ASD should be included in natural education and community settings.

ACKNOWLEDGMENTS

Preparation of this manuscript and the research reported within were supported in part by generous donations from the Eli and Edythe L. Broad Center for Asperger's Research and by National Institutes of Health Research Grant No. DC010924 from the National Institute on Deafness and Other Communication Disorders. Robert L. Koegel and Lynn Kern Koegel are also partners in the private consulting firm Koegel Autism Consultants.

REFERENCES

Bettelheim, B. (1967). *The empty fortress: Infantile autism and the birth of the self.* New York, NY: The Free Press.

Dawson, G., Meltzoff, A. N., Osterling, J., Rinaldi, J., & Brown, E. (1998). Children with autism fail to orient to naturally occurring social stimuli. *Journal of Autism and Developmental Disorders, 28,* 6, 479–485. doi:10.1023/A:1026043926488.

Dawson, G., Webb, S. J., & McPartland, J. (2005). Understanding the nature of face processing impairment in autism: Insights from behavioral and electrophysiological studies. *Developmental Neuropsychology, 27*(3), 403–424. doi:10.1207/s15326942dn2703_6.

Doggett, R. A., A. M., Koegel, L. K., & Koegel, R. L. (2012). Acquisition of multiple questions in the context of social conversation in children with autism. *Journal of Autism and Developmental Disabilities, 43*(9), 2015–2025.

Dunlap, G. (1984). The influence of task variation and maintenance tasks on the learning and affect of autistic children. *Journal of Experimental Child Psychology, 37*(1), 41–64. doi:10.1016/0022-0965(84)90057-2.

Dunlap, G., & Koegel, R. L. (1980). Motivating autistic children through stimulus variation. *Journal of Applied Behavior Analysis, 13*(4), 619–627. doi:10.1901/jaba.1980.13-619.

Dunlap, G., Koegel, R. L., & Kern, L. (1984). Continuity of treatment: Toilet training in multiple community settings. *Journal of the Association for the Severely Handicapped, 9,* 134–141.

Grelotti, D. J., Gauthier, I., & Schultz, R. T. (2002). Social interest and the development of cortical face specialization: What autism teaches us about face processing. *Developmental Psychobiology. Special Issue: Converging method approach to the study of developmental science, 40*(3), 213–225. doi:10.1002/dev.10028.

Harris, K. R. (1986). Self-monitoring of attentional behavior versus self-monitoring of productivity: Effects on on-task behavior and academic response rate among learning disabled children. *Journal of Applied Behavior Analysis, 19,* 417–423.

Howard, J. S., Sparkman, C. R., Cohen, H. G., Green, G., & Stanislaw, H. (2005). A comparison of intensive behavior analytic and eclectic treatments for young children with autism. *Research in Developmental Disabilities, 26*(4), 359–383. doi:10.1016/j.ridd.2004.09.005.

Hung, D. W. (1977). Generalization of "curiosity" questioning behavior in autistic children. *Journal of Behavior Therapy and Experimental Psychiatry, 8*(3), 237–245. doi:10.1016/0005-7916(77)90061-1.

Hurtig, R., Ensrud, S., & Tomblin, J. B. (1982). The communicative function of question production in autistic children. *Journal of Autism and Developmental Disorders, 12*(1), 57–69. doi:10.1007/BF01531674.

Ingersoll, B., & Dvortcsak, A. (2006). Including parent training in the early childhood special education curriculum for children with autism spectrum disorders. *Journal of Positive Behavior Interventions, 8*(2), 79–87. doi:10.1177/10983007060080020601.

Kaiser, A. P., Yoder, P. J., & Keetz, A. (1992). Evaluating milieu teaching. In S. F. Warren & J. Reichle (Eds.), *Causes and effects in communication and language intervention* (Vol. 1, pp. 9–47). Baltimore, MD: Paul H. Brookes.

Kanner, L. (1943). Autistic disturbances of affective contact. *Nervous Child, 2,* 217–250.

Koegel, L. K. (2000). Interventions to facilitate communication in autism. *Journal of Autism and Developmental Disorders, 30*(5), 383–391. doi:10.1023/A:1005539220932.

Koegel, L. K., Ashbaugh, K., Koegel, R. L., Detar, W., & Regester, A. (in press). Increasing socialization in adults with Asperger's syndrome. *Psychology in the Schools.*

Koegel, L. K., Camarata, S., Valdez-Menchaca, M. C., & Koegel, R. L. (1997). Setting generalization of question-asking by children with autism. *American Journal on Mental Retardation, 102*(4), 346–357.

Koegel, L. K., Carter, C. M., & Koegel, R. L. (2003). Teaching children with autism self-initiations as a pivotal response. *Topics in Language Disorders, 23*(2), 134–145.

Koegel, L. K., Harrower, J. K., & Koegel, R. L. (1999). Support for children with developmental disabilities in full inclusion classrooms through self–management. *Journal of Positive Behavior Interventions, 1,* 26–34. doi:10.1177/109830079900100104.

Koegel, L. K., Koegel, R. L., Green-Hopkins, I., & Barnes, C. (2010). Brief report: Question-asking and collateral language acquisition in children with autism. *Journal of Autism and Developmental Disorders, 40*(4), 509–515. doi:10.1007/s10803-009-0896-z.

Koegel, L. K., Koegel, R. L., Hurley, C., & Frea, W. D. (1992). Improving social skills and disruptive behavior in children with autism through self-management. *Journal of Applied Behavior Analysis, 25*(2), 341–353. doi:10.1901/jaba.1992.25-341.

Koegel, L. K., Koegel, R. L., & Ingham, J. C. (1986). Programming rapid generalization of correct articulation through self-monitoring procedures. *Journal of Speech and Hearing Disorders, 51*(1), 24–32.

Koegel, L. K., Koegel, R. L., Shoshan, Y., & McNerney, E. (1999). Pivotal response intervention II: Preliminary long-term outcome data. *Research and Practice for Persons with Severe Disabilities, 24*(3), 186–198. doi:10.2511/rpsd.24.3.186.

Koegel, L. K., Singh, A., Koegel, R. L. (2010). Improving motivation for academics in children with autism. *Journal of Autism and Developmental Disorders, 40*(9), 1057–1066.

Koegel, R. L., Bimbela, A., & Schreibman, L. (1996). Collateral effects of parent training on family interactions. *Journal of Autism and Developmental Disorders, 26*(3), 347–359. doi:10.1007/BF02172479.

Koegel, R. L., Dyer, K., & Bell, L. K. (1987). The influence of child-preferred activities on autistic children's social behavior. *Journal of Applied Behavior Analysis, 20*(3), 243–252. doi:10.1901/jaba.1987.20-243.

Koegel, R. L., & Egel, A. L. (1979). Motivating autistic children. *Journal of Abnormal Psychology, 88*(4), 418–426. doi:10.1037/0021-843X.88.4.418.

Koegel, R. L., & Frea, W. D. (1993). Treatment of social behavior in autism through the modification of pivotal social skills. *Journal of Applied Behavior Analysis, 26*(3), 369–377. doi:10.1901/jaba.1993.26-369.

Koegel, R. L., & Koegel, L. K. (1990). Extended reductions in stereotypic behavior of students with autism through a self-management treatment package. *Journal of Applied Behavior Analysis, 23*(1), 119–127. doi:10.1901/jaba.1990.23-119.

Koegel, R. L. & Koegel, L. K. (2012). *The PRT Pocket Guide.* Baltimore, MD: Paul H. Brookes.

Koegel, R. L., Koegel, L. K., Ingham, J. C., & Van Voy, K. (1988). Within-clinic versus outside-of-clinic self-monitoring of articulation to promote generalization. *Journal of Speech and Hearing Disorders, 53*(4), 392–399.

Koegel, R. L., Koegel, L. K., & Surratt, A. (1992). Language intervention and disruptive behavior in preschool children with autism. *Journal of Autism and Developmental Disorders, 22*(2), 141–153. doi:10.1007/BF01058147x.

Koegel, R. L., & Mentis, M. (1985). Motivation in childhood autism: Can they or won't they? *Journal of Child Psychology and Psychiatry, 26*(2), 185–191. doi:10.1111/j.1469-7610.1985.tb02259.x.

Koegel, R., O'Dell, M., & Dunlap, G. (1988). Producing speech use in nonverbal autistic children by reinforcing attempts. *Journal of Autism and Developmental Disorders, 18*(4), 525–538. doi:10.1007/BF02211871.

Koegel, R. L., O'Dell, M. C., & Koegel, L. K. (1987). A natural language teaching paradigm for nonverbal autistic children. *Journal of Autism and Developmental Disorders, 17*(2), 187–200. doi:10.1007/BF01495055.

Koegel, R., Shirotova, L., & Koegel, L. (2009). Brief report: Using individualized orienting cues to facilitate first-word acquisition in non-responders with autism. *Journal of Autism and Developmental Disorders, 39*(11), 1587–1592. doi:10.1007/s10803-009-0765-9.

Koegel, R. L., Vernon, T. W., & Koegel, L. K. (2009). Improving social initiations in young children with autism using reinforcers with embedded social interactions. *Journal of Autism and Developmental Disorders, 39*(9), 1240–1251. doi: 10.1007/s10803-009-0732-5.

Lee, S. H., Simpson, R. L., & Shogren, K. A. (2007). Effects and implications of self-management for students with autism: A meta-analysis. *Focus on Autism and Other Developmental Disabilities, 22*(1), 2–13 doi:10.1177/10883576070220010101.

Lovaas, O. I. (1977). *The autistic child: Language development through behavior modification.* New York, NY: Irvington.

Lovaas, O. I., Koegel, R., Simmons, J. Q., & Long, J. S. (1973). Some generalization and follow-up measures on autistic children in behavior therapy. *Journal of Applied Behavior Analysis, 6*(1), 131–165. doi:10.1901/jaba.1973.6-131.

Miller, J. F. (1981). *Assessing language production in children: Experimental procedures.* Baltimore, MD: University Park Press.

National Autism Center. (2008). *National Standards Project.* Retrieved September 2013, from www.nationalautismcenter.org/about/national.php

National Research Council Committee on Educational Interventions for Children with Autism. (2001). *Educating children with autism.* Washington, DC: National Academy Press.

Newman, B., Buffington, D. M., O'Grady, M. A., McDonald, M. E., Paulson, & Hemmes. (1995). Self-management of schedule following in three teenagers with autism. *Behavioral Disorders, 20*(3), 190–196.

Pierce, K., & Schreibman, L. (1994). Teaching daily living skills to children with autism in unsupervised settings through pictorial self-management. *Journal of Applied Behavior Analysis, 27*(3), 471–481. doi:10.1901/jaba.1994.27-471.

Pierce, K., & Schreibman, L. (1997). Using peer trainers to promote social behavior in autism: Are they effective at enhancing multiple social modalities? *Focus on Autism and Other Developmental Disabilities, 12*(4), 207–218. doi:10.1177/108835769701200403.

Prizant, B. M. (1983). Language acquisition and communicative behavior in autism: Toward an understanding of the "whole" of it. *Journal of Speech and Hearing Disorders, 48*(3), 296–307.

Reinecke, D. R., Newman, B., & Meinberg, D. L. (1999). Self-management of sharing in three pre-schoolers with autism. *Education and Training in Mental Retardation and Developmental Disabilities, 34*(3), 312–17.

Scott-Van Zeeland, A. A., Dapretto, M., Ghahremani, D. G., Poldrack, R. A., & Bookheimer, S. Y. (2010). Reward processing in autism. *Autism Research, 3*(2), 53–67.

Seligman, M. E., & Maier, S. F. (1967). Failure to escape traumatic shock. *Journal of Experimental Psychology*, 74(1), 1–9. doi:10.1037/h0024514.

Shearer, D. D., Kohler, F. W., Buchan, K. A., & McCullough, K. M. (1996). Promoting independent interactions between preschoolers with autism and their nondisabled peers: An analysis of self-monitoring. *Early Education and Development*, 7(3), 205–220. doi:10.1207/s15566935eed0703_1.

Simpson, R. L. (2005). Evidence-based practices and students with autism spectrum disorders. *Focus on Autism and Other Developmental Disabilities*, 20(3), 140– 149. doi:10.1177/10883576050200030201.

Stahmer, A. C. (1999). Using pivotal response training to facilitate appropriate play in children with autistic spectrum disorders. *Child Language Teaching and Therapy*, 15(1), 29–40. doi:10.1191/026565999672332808.

Stahmer, A. C., & Schreibman, L. (1992). Teaching children with autism appropriate play in unsupervised environments using a self-management treatment package. *Journal of Applied Behavior Analysis*, 25(2), 447–459. doi:10.1901/jaba.1992.25–447.

Strain, P. S., Kohler, F. W., Storey, K., & Danko, C. D. (1994). Teaching preschoolers with autism to self-monitor their social interactions: An analysis of results in home and school settings. *Journal of Emotional and Behavioral Disorders*, 2(2), 78–88. doi:10.1177/106342669400200202.

Symon, J. B. (2001). Parent education for autism issues in providing services at a distance. *Journal of Positive Behavior Interventions*, 3(3), 160–174. doi:10.1177/109830070100300304.

Taylor, B. A., & Harris, S. L. (1995). Teaching children with autism to seek information: Acquisition of novel information and generalization of responding. *Journal of Applied Behavior Analysis*, 28(1), 3–14. doi: 10.1901/jaba.1995.28-3.

Vernon, T. W., Koegel, R. L., Dauterman, H., & Stolen, K. (2012). An early social engagement intervention for young children with autism and their parents. *Journal of Autism and Developmental Disorders*, 42(12), 2702–2717. doi: 10.1007/s10803-012-1535-7.

Wetherby, A. M. (1986). Ontogeny of communicative functions in autism. *Journal of Autism and Developmental Disorders*, 16(3), 295–316. doi:10.1007/BF01531661.

Wetherby, A. M., & Prutting, C. A. (1984). Profiles of communicative and cognitive–social abilities in autistic children. *Journal of Speech and Hearing Research*, 27(3), 364–377.

Williams, J. A., Koegel, R. L., & Egel, A. L. (1981). Response-reinforcer relationships and improved learning in autistic children. *Journal of Applied Behavior Analysis*, 14(1), 53–60. doi:10.1901/jaba.1981.14-53.

10

Evaluating and Improving Intervention Integrity

FLORENCE D. DIGENNARO REED AND DEREK D. REED

Recent prevalence estimates suggest that approximately 1 in 88 children have autism spectrum disorder (ASD), which reflects a 600% increase in the past two decades (Centers for Disease Control and Prevention, 2011). The individual and societal costs for treatment are staggering and grow exponentially as the prevalence increases. Latest reports indicate that, as a society, we spend $137 billion annually on direct and indirect expenses associated with ASD (Autism Speaks, n.d.b). Families spend an estimated $1.2 million caring for a loved one with ASD throughout their lifetime (Autism Speaks, n.d.a). Once a relatively rare disorder, ASD is now regarded as an urgent public health concern (Ganz, 2007). These figures suggest a need to provide high-quality, empirically supported intervention to promote independence and lifelong productivity of individuals with ASD (DiGennaro Reed, Hyman, & Hirst, 2011).

Fortunately, a diverse literature on empirically supported ASD interventions is available to guide the decision-making and treatment practices of interventionists and caregivers. Interventions based on the principles of applied behavior analysis have much empirical support (National Standards Project, 2009; New York State Department of Health, 1999) and are endorsed by the US Surgeon General (US Department of Health and Human Services, 1999), National Institutes of Health (Strock, 2004), the National Research Council (2001), and others (e.g., New York State Department of Health, 1999). Despite the availability of experienced interventionists and a published literature documenting the effectiveness of behavioral interventions, actual treatment practices often deviate from best practices. Sadly, knowledge about *what* interventions to implement, *when* to implement them, and for *whom* to implement is often not reflected in the quality of interventions provided (DiGennaro Reed, Hirst, &

Howard, 2013a; Jahr, 1998; Parsons, Reid, & Green, 1993; Reid & Green, 1990). That is, interventions are commonly implemented with less-than-ideal quality in applied settings. Deviations from prescribed intervention procedures constitute a violation in *intervention integrity*. Also known as *treatment integrity, procedural fidelity, implementation integrity,* and *instructional fidelity*, this construct refers to the degree to which behavioral interventions are implemented as designed (Gresham, 1989; Yeaton & Sechrest, 1981). A recent conceptualization of intervention integrity defines it as the "extent to which essential intervention components are delivered in a comprehensive and consistent manner by an interventionist trained to deliver the intervention" (Sanetti & Kratochwill, 2009a, p. 448). There has been a growing emphasis on intervention integrity measurement and evaluation as well as interventionist training in service delivery settings, in large part due to its relevance to ASD treatment effectiveness and sound clinical decision making.

RELEVANCE TO AUTISM SPECTRUM DISORDER EDUCATION AND INTERVENTION

The effectiveness of ASD treatment is mediated by intervention integrity in several ways. First, there is an emerging body of research documenting the importance of intervention integrity in treatment outcomes for individuals with and without disabilities. Across two studies, DiGennaro and colleagues demonstrated that student problem behavior is lower when educators implement function-based behavioral interventions with higher accuracy (DiGennaro, Martens, & Kleinmann, 2007; DiGennaro, Martens, & McIntyre, 2005). That is, as intervention integrity increased, student problem behavior decreased. Similarly, Dib and Sturmey (2007) improved the integrity with which teaching aides implemented discrete trial instruction and reported reductions in the levels of stereotypy for three children with ASD, even though problem behavior was not directly targeted. The results of these studies support the findings of Gresham, Gansle, Noell, Cohen, and Rosenblum (1993), who reported a significant correlation between intervention integrity and treatment effectiveness in their analysis of school-based behavioral interventions published between 1980 and 1990. Collectively, these results suggest that higher intervention integrity is associated with better treatment effects.

Researchers have also demonstrated a causal relation between intervention integrity and treatment outcomes (e.g., Northup, Fisher, Kahng, Harrell, & Kurtz, 1997; Rhymer, Evans-Hampton, McCurdy, & Watson, 2002). For example, Wilder, Atwell, and Wine (2006) experimentally manipulated the integrity of a three-step prompting procedure and examined the impact on child compliance. Using a multielement design, they omitted components of three-step prompting at 100%, 50%, and 0% integrity levels and showed a direct linear relation between intervention integrity level and compliance. Higher intervention integrity produced greater compliance; lower intervention integrity produced lower compliance. DiGennaro Reed, Reed, Baez, and Maguire (2011) adopted a similar parametric analysis to investigate whether systematic changes in intervention integrity impacted acquisition of a match-to-sample task during discrete-trial training for three children with autism. Their study manipulated reinforcement errors of commission (i.e., delivering reinforcement for incorrect matching responses) and extended the findings of Wilder and colleagues by demonstrating that skill acquisition of participating children was lower under conditions containing some (50%) or many (100%) errors of commission. It is important to note that consistent findings of a relation between integrity level and treatment outcome have not been produced across all studies investigating this phenomena. For example, Vollmer, Roane, Ringdahl, and Marcus (1999) demonstrated that differential reinforcement of alternative behavior effectively increased appropriate behavior and reduced inappropriate behavior for three individuals with mental retardation despite degradations in intervention integrity. Treatment efficacy was reduced only when intervention integrity errors provided a higher rate of reinforcement for inappropriate behavior than

appropriate behavior. Another study documented therapeutic outcomes of functional communication training despite integrity errors (Worsdell, Iwata, Hanley, Thompson, & Kahng, 2000). Although findings are mixed across studies and intervention protocols, a body of evidence exists to support the claim that the benefits of treatment may be compromised due to deteriorations in intervention integrity. Additional research is necessary to identify the conditions under which treatment outcomes are and are not negatively impacted by reductions in the integrity of an intervention.

The effectiveness of ASD treatment is also mitigated by intervention integrity as it pertains to clinical decision making (Vollmer, Sloman & St. Peter Pipkin, 2008). If interventionists cannot verify an intervention was implemented as intended, decisions about how best to proceed with treatment may be flawed. If intervention integrity is not assessed and desired treatment outcomes are not obtained, interventionists will be unable to evaluate whether a different intervention is necessary or the designed intervention—possibly an effective treatment—was poorly implemented. Thus, intervention integrity assessment allows interventionists and caregivers to draw valid conclusions about the effects of a treatment and informs subsequent decisions about treatment and training.

Finally, the relevance of intervention integrity to ASD education and intervention is elucidated in a recent class-action lawsuit brought to federal court as a result of delays students experienced in receiving special education services (*M.A. v. Newark Public Schools, New Jersey Department of Education* 344 F.3d 335). In addition to substantial delays to obtaining psychoeducational evaluations to determine eligibility for services, public school students with disabilities in Newark, New Jersey, did not receive the services to which they were entitled. The district was accused of delaying appropriate education and intervention for eligible students with disabilities, which violates the "free and appropriate education" clause of the Individuals with Disabilities Education Improvement Act (2004). Sadly, this situation is not unique; students with disabilities, including ASD, and their families have witnessed similar situations and been involved in countless lawsuits as a result of intervention integrity violations in the past 50 years. For example, in *Ferraro v. the Board of Education of the City of New York* 14 A.D.2d 815 (1961), the courts held educators and the school liable for neglect as a result of an injury stemming from peer-to-peer aggression/assault. The court ruled that the school was accountable because it failed to provide the necessary information and training to a substitute teacher who was unaware of the intervention procedures in place to prevent the assault. Gross omission of educational services and a lack of adherence to a program of service constitute an intervention integrity failure of the worst kind.

Priority Concerns

It seems clear that intervention integrity is a ubiquitous feature of all autism service delivery options. No matter one's experience with the term itself, issues of intervention integrity affect client outcomes in many ways and several decisions are necessary when designing, implementing, monitoring, and evaluating any form of ASD service delivery. These concerns consist of (a) how intervention integrity should be conceptualized; (b) the challenges and barriers associated with intervention integrity assessment; and (c) what levels of intervention integrity should be deemed acceptable.

Dimensions of Intervention Integrity

As described earlier, intervention integrity is a requisite concept whenever interventionists are interested in evaluating the effects of their services on the outcomes of their clients with ASD. Intervention integrity must therefore be understood as an empirical construct amenable to evaluation and modification. Sanetti and Kratochwill (2009a) proposed that intervention integrity is a multidimensional construct comprised of many component parts. In their review of the extant literature (through the year 2008), Sanetti and Kratochwill identified numerous conceptual models of intervention integrity, ranging from issues of "dosage" (Jones, Clarke, & Power, 2008) to a two-level model of service delivery comprised of consultative and treatment plan implementation (Noell, 2008). Central to most models (Dane & Schneider, 1998; Jones et al., 2008), however, were the following: (a) competence (the skill with which the interventionist implements the plan), (b) adherence (the degree to which the essential components of the intervention plan are followed), (c) exposure (the amount of intervention the client receives), (d) quality (qualitative aspects of intervention implementation, such as tone of voice during instructions or feedback), (e) participant responsiveness (the degree to which the client is engaged in the

intervention), and (f) program differentiation (the degree to which the intervention differs from baseline conditions). Sanetti and Kratochwill (2009a) therefore recommend that all six dimensions of intervention integrity be considered when designing a framework for interventionist training and monitoring intervention integrity.

Challenges and Barriers to Intervention Integrity Assessment

The multidimensional nature of intervention integrity presents numerous challenges and barriers to its assessment in applied settings. To sufficiently address the various concerns of intervention integrity, interventionists must prioritize valid and feasible approaches to its assessment. In a recent survey, Sanetti and DiGennaro Reed (2012) asked researchers interested in treatment outcomes to indicate the degree to which 30 possible impediments served as barriers to intervention integrity measurement (adapted from the Barriers to Treatment Integrity Implementation Survey [BTIIS]; Perepletchikova, Hilt, Chereji, & Kazdin, 2009). From these 30 items, six were identified as "strong barriers." The most significant barrier was the time required for adequate intervention integrity data collection and analysis. Another strong barrier was that intervention integrity measurement systems require added resources to ensure proper development and design. These features of intervention integrity data collection are necessary for producing reliable and valid accounts of interventionist implementation. A third strong barrier is the resource-intensive approaches to interventionist training—both monetary and time related—to proactively promote high levels of intervention integrity. The remaining three strong barriers were inconsistencies in the literature or vague standards, namely (a) definitions, (b) data collection standards, and (c) competence by interventionists. Other researchers have recommended that such barriers could potentially be overcome using explicit manualized systems (e.g., Gearing, El-Bassel, Ghesquiere, Gillies, & Ngeow, 2011) or using differential levels of measurement based on specific clinical needs (e.g., Perepletchikova, 2011). Unfortunately, field standards related to essential intervention integrity components or levels of measurements have yet to be developed. Collectively, the strong barriers identified by Sanetti and DiGennaro Reed highlight the concern that educational and clinical settings must find ways to overcome limited resources to ensure that intervention integrity is monitored and addressed. These findings suggest that resource-efficient procedures would greatly aid interventionists' delivery of services to individuals with ASD by circumventing the barriers described earlier.

Acceptable Levels of Intervention Integrity

Another barrier to intervention integrity data collection identified by Sanetti and DiGennaro Reed (2012) is that no standards exist on what levels of intervention integrity are deemed acceptable. This is concerning given our previous discussion that differential levels of integrity appear to be parametrically associated with differential gains in the affected learner (e.g., DiGennaro Reed et al., 2011; Wilder et al., 2006). Thus, a priority concern for interventionists working with individuals with ASD is whether perfect implementation of treatment/ teaching protocols is necessary to obtain acceptable gains. With recent economic downturns compromising resources in the educational and human service sectors, it may be difficult giving high-quality training and sufficient performance feedback to maintain acceptable integrity when implementing lesson plans or treatment protocols.

A growing literature has produced mixed results about acceptable levels of intervention integrity. For example, Groskreutz, Groskreutz, and Higbee (2011) demonstrated that one preschooler with ASD required 100% intervention integrity of a prompting procedure to learn appropriate toy play, while a second preschooler with ASD learned the skill with just 50% integrity. DiGennaro Reed and colleagues (2011) conducted a similar parametric evaluation of intervention integrity during discrete-trial training, showing that 50% intervention integrity was as detrimental as 0% integrity for two of three learners with ASD. A noteworthy difference between the Groskreutz et al. (2011) and DiGennaro Reed et al. (2011) studies is that intervention integrity in the former was defined by errors of omission (leaving out prompting steps), while the latter used errors of commission (providing incorrect feedback). More research is necessary to examine the differential effects of such errors on client outcomes.

Another important concern regarding acceptable levels of intervention integrity is the necessary amount required to affect change in problem behavior. As noted by Vollmer et al. (1999), it may be naïve to assume that interventionists will always

implement treatment plans with 100% integrity when faced with difficult, challenging problem behavior such as aggression or self-injury. Using a concurrent-operants design, Vollmer and colleagues varied the percentage of responses reinforced for both appropriate and inappropriate behavior within a differential reinforcement procedure to model the effects of perfect implementation, as well as varying degrees of intervention integrity, including complete degradation (i.e., 100% of inappropriate responses reinforced, 0% of appropriate). An intriguing finding was that the effects of perfect intervention integrity persisted even when subsequent sessions featured degradations in integrity levels; that is, following sessions featuring high intervention integrity, appropriate behavior still outnumbered problem behavior, despite the subsequent sessions featuring less-than-ideal integrity levels. These results have subsequently been reproduced in both translational and analog settings, using both undergraduate research participants and children with ASD (St. Peter Pipkin, Vollmer, & Sloman, 2010). Despite these strong empirical demonstrations, it is unknown what the effects of initially imperfect intervention integrity might be on subsequent sessions with either perfect or further degraded levels for treatment of problem behavior. It may be the case that a history of poor intervention integrity interferes with treatment success when integrity is improved to more acceptable levels, but research on this concern is scant.

EFFECTIVENESS AND EFFICACY OF ASSESSMENT AND INTERVENTION TECHNIQUES

An important feature of evidence-based practice or evidence-based education in the treatment of individuals with ASD is ensuring successful implementation of interventions that are efficacious and effective (http://www.winginstitute.org); that is, promoting intervention integrity. This is partially accomplished through high-quality interventionist training and support. We advocate a three-pronged approach to addressing intervention integrity: (1) adoption of behavioral skills training (BST) as an initial strategy to prevent intervention integrity violations, (2) ongoing assessment and monitoring of intervention integrity, and (3) follow-up support strategies to improve poor and/or maintain high intervention integrity. Because the majority of the staff or teacher training literature has evaluated the effects of *training packages* on performance (Roscoe & Fisher, 2008; Sarokoff & Sturmey, 2004; Sepler & Myers, 1978), and meta-analytic findings indicate that a combination of treatments may be more effective than a single treatment (van Oorsouw, Embregts, Bosman, & Jahoda, 2009), we recommend combining several empirically supported training and follow-up strategies.

Behavioral Skills Training

A robust body of literature supports BST to prepare interventionists for delivering services (DiGennaro et al., 2007; DiGennaro et al., 2005; Iwata et al., 2000; Lavie & Sturmey, 2002; Nigro-Bruzzi & Sturmey, 2010; Reid & Parsons, 1995; Roscoe & Fisher, 2008; Sarokoff & Sturmey, 2004). Also known as performance- and competency-based training (Reid, Parsons, & Green, 2011), BST consists of instructions, modeling, rehearsal or role play, and feedback until interventionists achieve criterion performance in either an analog/practice setting (Nigro-Bruzzi & Sturmey, 2010) or in the natural environment (Ricciardi, 2005). Once criteria are met, the interventionist is permitted to implement the intervention in the applied, real-world setting with less direct oversight and monitoring. Though the criterion performance required of interventionists varies across studies, we recommend requiring perfect or near perfect implementation of the intervention across multiple opportunities (e.g., 100% integrity across two practice sessions; 90% integrity or higher across three practice sessions) given that rehearsal often takes place under ideal conditions, which is rare in the applied setting.

Different training practices may be adopted within each of the components of BST. For example, modeling—which includes demonstration of correct performance followed by interventionist imitation—may take place in vivo with live demonstrations or with technology through video modeling. Both types of modeling have been shown to effectively produce desired performance (e.g., Catania, Almeida, Liu-Constant, & DiGennaro, 2009; Macurik, O'Kane, Malanga, & Reid, 2008; Nigro-Bruzzi & Sturmey, 2010; Sarokoff & Sturmey, 2004), though feedback is sometimes required to meet criterion performance when video modeling is used (DiGennaro Reed, Codding, Catania, & Maguire, 2010).

Although the procedures comprising BST can vary, we suggest the full package of instructions, modeling, rehearsal, and immediate feedback. Omitting any of these has the potential to negatively impact intervention integrity and, subsequently, treatment outcomes. For example, providing a high-quality model in vivo or via video may not produce robust changes in performance if the interventionist does not have the opportunity to practice the skill and receive feedback. Moreover, requiring the interventionist to implement the intervention with subsequent feedback may be challenging and potentially aversive if she or he has not had the opportunity to observe an experienced performer model the skill. The implications of previously summarized research are that intervention integrity errors *may* not negatively impact treatment outcomes so long as they occur following a period of high integrity (St. Peter Pipkin et al., 2010; Vollmer et al., 1999; Worsdell et al., 2000). Furthermore, treatment outcomes are at risk of being compromised if intervention integrity is low at the outset of treatment (DiGennaro Reed et al., 2011; Hirst, DiGennaro Reed, & Reed, 2013; Wilder et al., 2006). Thus, supervisors, staff trainers, and treatment providers are urged to provide BST before interventionists deliver services to their clients with ASD. Moreover, we advocate ongoing assessment and monitoring of intervention integrity to ensure quality intervention plan implementation in the applied setting for the reasons described earlier.

Intervention Integrity Assessment

Like other forms of behavioral assessment, intervention integrity measurement is intended to capture a sample of observations that generalize to the entire universe of intervention integrity levels; that is, the sample is inferred to be representative of all possible instances of intervention integrity (Cone, 1977). As discussed earlier in this chapter, the multidimensional nature of intervention integrity presents numerous considerations to those charged with ensuring reliable and valid measurement of this construct. Thus, to adequately assess intervention integrity, we propose adherence to Cone's behavioral assessment grid (1978) to balance the various dimensions of intervention integrity assessment; that is, the content (the type of integrity data collected), methods of measurement, and universes of generalization (differences across settings, time, raters, methods, etc.). The remainder of this section will broadly discuss assessment within this framework with specific attention to (a) self-assessment data, (b) permanent products versus direct observation techniques, (c) overt versus covert observations, and (d) scheduling of observations.

Self-Assessment

In most settings, intervention integrity is addressed within a consultative relationship. A consultant may be asked to observe degraded levels of integrity or invited to contribute to the plan from staff that suspect integrity failures may be occurring (either through direct observation or recognition of such concerns upon subpar client gains via outcome measurement). The consultant typically identifies the reasons for integrity failure and designs a remediation plan. According to Sanetti and Kratochwill (2009b), this process rarely involves the interventionists whom are expected to implement the intervention of question. To address this issue, Sanetti and Kratochwill developed the Treatment Integrity Planning Protocol (TIPP), a 17-item instrument that arrives at a three-stage planning and assessment procedure. During the first stage, the protocol guides the interventionist in treatment development of intervention steps, components, and contexts. During the second stage, the consultant works with the interventionist to plan for integrity assessment, taking into consideration the various idiosyncrasies of the treatment protocol, the client needs, and the constraints of the treatment setting. Finally, the third stage of the TIPP creates an interventionist self-assessment form, based off the outcomes from the first two stages of the process. In their empirical evaluation of the TIPP, Sanetti and Kratochwill reported significant improvements in intervention integrity, as measured by the TIPP and permanent products. The interventionists involved in the TIPP reported the process to be both acceptable and time efficient.

Despite the reported advantages of self-assessment via TIPP (Sanetti & Kratochwill, 2009b), other studies on self-assessment of intervention integrity have reported less-than-ideal results. For example, Wickstrom, Jones, LaFleur, and Witt (1998) described a study in which teachers serving as interventionists within a consultative framework were expected to follow a consultant-derived intervention plan, with integrity data collected via (a) self-assessment, (b) permanent products, and (c) direct observation. The researchers found that interventionists' self-assessment of integrity yielded a mean level of 54%. Researchers' direct observation of the interventionists' integrity was only 4%, documenting a dramatic and significant discrepancy. These data suggest that interventionists' self-assessment of integrity may be inflated compared to more rigorous forms of integrity assessment, such as direct observation. The literature on self-assessment remains sparse, so clinicians, consultants, and supervisors charged with measuring intervention integrity should be cautious when considering self-assessment. While it may be tempting to use self-assessment to reduce the need for independent observers of intervention integrity, the costs of possible invalid measures may grossly outweigh such benefits. Finally, it is noteworthy that the studies described previously (Sanetti & Kratochwill, 2009b; Wickstrom et al., 1998) did not involve individuals with ASD. Thus, the extent to which these findings generalize to the unique needs of interventions designed for individuals with ASD remains unknown.

Permanent Product Versus Direct Observation

Repeated empirical investigations have found that time is an important commodity for interventionists (e.g., Costenbader, Swartz, & Petrix, 1992; Elliott, 1988; DiGennaro et al., 2005), which is unsurprising given the increasing demands placed on such professionals due to economic downturns and budget cuts. Thus, asking interventionists to self-assess integrity levels may add responsibilities to an already strained list of job tasks for these staff. To circumvent increased workloads for interventionists, permanent products and/or direct observations are suitable replacements.

Permanent product recording consists of analyzing tangible behavioral outcomes associated with specific target responses such as completed token boards or checklists. By virtue of its ease and simplicity, researchers have considered permanent product recording an advantageous form of intervention integrity data collection (e.g., Noell, Duhon, Gatti, & Connell, 2002). Noell and colleagues described the successful use of permanent product records through daily student behavior record forms. In their study, teachers were interventionists treating typically developing elementary students' rates of problem behaviors (e.g., talking out in class, out-of-seat behaviors). The researchers calculated the number of observation periods within a day and the number of reward opportunities afforded by the consultant-formulated behavior intervention plan. The researchers created daily forms to serve as self-monitoring records for the target students to use throughout the school day. This allowed the researchers to determine whether the target students earned more rewards than what was programmed by the behavior plan and whether the interventionists agreed with the data on the self-monitoring forms throughout the day. These data were then compared to expected numbers of rewards and data variables collected. Discrepancies between the student and interventionist reports, as well as incorrect numbers of rewards provided given the schedules stipulated in the behavior plan, would indicate invalid permanent product records. Results suggested that permanent products were indeed reliable, valid, and efficient. Such procedures have been used in several similar studies to the same effect (e.g., Noell et al., 2002, 2005).

Despite the relative ease with which interventionists and consultants can use permanent products to assess intervention integrity, the results from the aforementioned study by Wickstrom et al. (1998) highlight potential drawbacks to this method. As discussed previously, Wickstrom and colleagues monitored intervention integrity using self-assessments, permanent products, and direct observation. Recall that self-assessment generated an average intervention integrity level of 54%, while direct observation was markedly lower at 4%. Levels of integrity assessed by permanent products—measured as the use of intervention stimulus products—generated the highest levels of integrity, with an average score of 62%; this suggests that permanent product assessments may grossly overestimate actual levels of intervention integrity. Thus, direct observation should be considered the gold standard of intervention integrity assessment because both qualitative and quantitative data can be generated through operational definitions of the treatment procedure.

In a recent review of practice recommendations for collecting intervention integrity data, only direct observation assessments are discussed, underscoring this form of assessment as a field standard for best practices (Vollmer et al., 2008). Vollmer and colleagues succinctly articulated many advantages to this form of assessment, highlighting the ability of direct observation to capture nuanced aspects of implementation integrity not possibly recorded by self-assessments or permanent products. These authors recommend that intervention protocols be

broken down into countable units (e.g., checklists) to help facilitate data counts during observations. Counts of correct implementation of procedural steps may then be divided by total number of opportunities to yield an overall percentage of integrity. Such data collection sessions should be relatively brief (approximately 10 minutes) and scheduled relatively infrequently; that is, data collection should be seen as a sample of the entire universe of possible observations (Cone, 1977), not a continuous procedure all day. When collecting direct observation data, Vollmer and colleagues suggested using separate counts for each major component of the behavior plan. This convention isolates where integrity errors are breaking down and facilitates ease of assessment. For example, percentage of implementation integrity could be generated for the following discrete trial training procedures: (a) presentation of task materials, (b) delivery of clear instructions and discriminative stimuli, (c) appropriate levels of prompting, (d) provision of feedback, and (e) interventionist recording of client outcomes at the conclusion of each trial. These five percentages of intervention integrity may then be aggregated into one summary percentage that captures overall level of integrity during the observation.

Overt Versus Covert Observations

When conducting direct observation assessments of intervention integrity, the mere presence of an observer may influence results. Known as *reactivity* (see Bloom, Fischer, & Orme, 1999), this effect on observation violates the assumption that the sample recorded is a valid indicator of integrity across all possible universes of observation (Cone, 1977). While the literature on reactivity in intervention integrity assessments is limited, two examples highlight the importance of considering whether overt (it is evident that the observer is watching the interventionist) or covert (the observer inconspicuously observers the interventionist) observations are to be used. Brackett, Reid, and Green (2007) reported differential levels of intervention integrity when supervisors were inconspicuously assessing staff. Specifically, more conspicuous measurement of intervention integrity generated greater fidelity to protocols, suggesting that conspicuous measurement may yield biased and invalid data that are not representative of typical performance. A second study on this topic, by Codding, Livanis, Pace, and Vaca (2008), reported no differential effects between overt and covert intervention integrity data collection, suggesting that these findings are mixed, awaiting further replications. Thus, the transparency of such measurement systems remains a pressing topic for empirical research. Professionals charged with recording intervention integrity levels for ASD service delivery should use their best clinical judgment when deciding on overt or covert observations, factoring in the nuances of their treatment setting (e.g., can video recording be conducted?), qualitative features of the interventionists being observed (i.e., do you suspect they will engage in reactivity based on professional histories and interactions?), and the complexity of the intervention protocol.

Scheduling Integrity Observations

In an effort to engage in best practices of autism service deliveries, many organizations and agencies proactively assign intervention integrity tasks to its interventionists. Planned observations are advantageous because they become part of an interventionist's typical list of job duties. As described by Reed, Fienup, Pace, and Luiselli (2010), a common approach to intervention integrity observation assignment is to require a particular number of observations to be completed within prescribed periods of time. This standard presents an additional concern, given that such schedules mimic schedule requirements often studied in experimental analyses of behavior (e.g., Ferster & Skinner, 1957). Reed and colleagues (2010) examined rates of intervention integrity observations and found that one human service setting's schedule of planned measurement mimicked those obtained in nonhuman experimental analyses, such that the observers scalloped their observations toward the end of the prescribed period of time. This effect may be problematic if the interventionists being observed learn to increase their levels of integrity toward the end of the observation periods. Given the research on overt and covert intervention integrity checks we described previously, these observations may not be valid indicators of integrity levels throughout the week or month.

Follow-Up Support Strategies

The goal of intervention integrity assessment is to not only determine whether interventions are implemented accurately and with high quality but to share these data with the interventionist and provide follow-up support as necessary. Despite evidence supporting BST to prepare interventionists for service-delivery and intervention implementation, follow-up support strategies are commonly required to ensure high intervention integrity. This requirement is a function of, but not limited to, (a) lack of contingencies that support continued intervention implementation despite the interventionist having the skills to do so (i.e., a performance deficit; Lentz, 1988); (b) inability to generalize skills demonstrated during the practice sessions to the applied setting (DiGennaro Reed, Hirst, & Howard, 2013a; Scheeler, 2008); (c) lack of resources to fully implement the intervention (i.e., time, cost, and labor demands; Sanetti & DiGennaro Reed, 2012); and (d) poor acceptance of the treatment procedures (Gresham, 1989). In the sections that follow, we summarize several follow-up support strategies shown to effectively improve or maintain high intervention integrity. Lengthier summaries of research-supported, effective training techniques are provided elsewhere (e.g., DiGennaro Reed & Codding, 2011; DiGennaro Reed, Hirst, & Howard, 2013b; Reid & Green, 1990). Readers are encouraged to consult these resources for specific details about the training and follow-up techniques themselves.

Performance Feedback

Feedback is a popular and widely studied procedure to improve employee performance (Alvero, Bucklin, & Austin, 2001) and is frequently adopted as a follow-up support strategy to improve intervention integrity (DiGennaro Reed & Codding, 2011; Gilligan, Luiselli, & Pace, 2007; Leblanc, Ricciardi, & Luiselli, 2005; Ricciardi, 2005). Performance feedback is defined as delivery of information regarding past performance that specifies how performance can be improved in the future (Daniels & Daniels, 2006; Prue & Fairbank, 1981). In a series of studies, Noell and colleagues improved teacher intervention integrity by delivering performance feedback during brief, daily meetings (e.g., Noell et al., 2000; Noell, Witt, Gilbertson, Ranier, & Freeland, 1997; Noell et al., 2005). Feedback consisted of showing graphic outcome (i.e., student performance) and process (i.e., intervention integrity) data to teachers. In addition, the classroom consultant discussed which intervention steps were missed or incorrectly implemented and how best to improve intervention integrity. Over time, the frequency of the feedback meetings decreased as teachers demonstrated high intervention integrity. Codding, Feinberg, Dunn, and Pace (2005) also documented the effectiveness of intermittent performance feedback delivered immediately to teachers following an observation conducted every 1–3 weeks. Intervention integrity of behavior support plans increased and maintained during follow-up observations. Sanetti, Luiselli, and Handler (2007) showed that verbal and graphic performance feedback was superior to verbal feedback alone for improving the intervention integrity of a behavior support plan implemented by a teaching team. In another practical application of feedback, Gilligan et al. (2007) improved the integrity of discrete trial instruction among paraprofessional staff instructing children with ASD. Their intervention consisted of a 5- to 8-minute meeting to identify the error, clarify the task, rehearse the procedure, and provide praise for intervention components implemented correctly on 90% of trials. The effects of this simple intervention maintained at a 3-month follow-up observation for one of the staff. In sum, these and other studies consistently document that performance feedback is a powerful behavior change strategy that effectively improves intervention integrity.

Performance feedback may be based on individual and group performance, presented publically or privately, and delivered in written, oral, graphic, and electronic formats (Alvero et al., 2001). Ricciardi (2005) recommended delivering feedback individually in a private location and as close to the observation session as possible. Although feedback has been shown to be effective when consultants have waited a period of time to deliver it to interventionists (e.g., Noell et al., 1997, 2000, 2005), others report that delayed feedback is less effective (Locke & Latham, 1990). Moreover, immediate feedback is preferred by interventionists (Reid & Parsons, 1996). Consultants should make every effort to deliver feedback *before* the next opportunity to implement the intervention to prevent continued intervention integrity errors. Moreover, meta-analytic findings indicate that performance feedback is most effective when it is used in combination with other support strategies comprised of antecedents to behavior (e.g., staff training, checklists, written objectives, or supervisory prompts) and consequences for behavior (e.g., reinforcement; Alvero et al., 2001).

Reinforcement

Reinforcement involves the contingent application of desired consequences (positive reinforcement) and termination or avoidance of undesired consequences (negative reinforcement), resulting in an increase in the future probability of the preceding behavior (Catania, 2007). Both positive and negative reinforcement have been used strategically as a follow-up strategy to promote high levels of intervention integrity. Within diverse organizations the types of positive reinforcement include money (e.g., Luiselli et al., 2009; Pommer & Streedback, 1974), privileges (e.g., parking space; Green, Reid, Perkins, & Gardner, 1991), vacation days or schedule changes (e.g., Iwata, Bailey, Brown, Foshee, & Alpern, 1976; Reid, Schuh-Wear, & Brannon, 1978), and other rewards (e.g., coupons or meals; Reid & Whitman, 1983). In many, if not all, of the performance feedback studies summarized previously, contingent praise was also used as a positive reinforcer to maintain correct performance of some aspect of an intervention. For example, Gilligan et al. (2007) delivered praise to paraprofessional staff for 90% or higher correct implementation of components of discrete trial intervention. In a survey of community agency supervisors, Parsons, Reid, and Crow (2003) reported findings from supervisors who indicated that positive feedback/interactions is the best strategy for motivating staff and that delivery of tangible rewards is one of the top five strategies.

Negative reinforcement may also be used to improve intervention integrity (e.g., Noell et al., 2000). Across two studies, DiGennaro and colleagues (2007, 2005) improved the integrity with which teachers implemented an intervention designed to address student problem behavior by implementing a treatment package involving negative reinforcement. The researchers used BST to train teachers to implement a function-based intervention and subsequently assessed intervention integrity in the classroom. Within several sessions teachers' integrity decreased to low levels at which time a meeting cancellation contingency was put in effect. Specifically, a meeting was scheduled after each observation session during which a directed rehearsal procedure was implemented (described later). Teachers were able to avoid meeting with the researchers and avoid the loss of time spent attending the meeting by implementing the intervention with 100% accuracy. That is, teachers were able to contact negative reinforcement in the form of avoiding the loss of time by demonstrating perfect intervention integrity. This package effectively improved intervention integrity for all teachers.

Directed Rehearsal

In directed rehearsal, an interventionist is asked to repeatedly practice a skill following a previous integrity error for that particular skill (Ward, Johnson, & Konukman, 1998). The effectiveness of this procedure was originally documented in two studies by Ward and colleagues (Ward, Smith, & Makasci, 1997; Ward et al., 1998). These researchers required preservice physical education teachers to practice missed or incorrectly implemented teaching steps 10 consecutive times during a meeting scheduled after an observation session. Integrity of the teaching procedure increased as a result of the directed rehearsal procedure. DiGennaro and colleagues (2005, 2007) also used directed rehearsal involving three practice opportunities, rather than 10, and showed improvements in teacher integrity. An advantage of using directed rehearsal is that it provides the interventionist with practice opportunities in a role-play scenario in areas requiring improvement.

PRACTICE RECOMMENDATIONS

In the remainder of this chapter, we present practice recommendations informed by the empirical literature and our own experiences. We encourage readers to proactively plan for intervention integrity failures because they can and will occur.

1. Promote investment and buy-in from interventionists by involving them in treatment plan conceptualization and integrity observation planning. Doing so enables consultants to gain better understanding of the intervention environment, learn about possible barriers to high intervention integrity, and develop more effective treatment procedures.

2. Be sure to develop written protocols with task analyses that clearly and succinctly outline the treatment procedure. The protocol will not only serve as instructions during initial training but can also be used to clarify the intervention procedures as a follow-up support strategy. Be transparent about the specific interventionist behaviors that will be observed and measured to reduce any anxiety about future integrity observations and to fully inform the interventionist about expected performance.

3. Avoid technical language in written protocols and training materials and instead rely on lay language that is more easily understood (Jarmolowicz et al., 2008).

4. Adopt a three-pronged approach to interventionist training and support that includes BST, ongoing assessment of interventionist integrity, and follow-up support.

5. Incorporate all BST procedures (instructions, modeling, rehearsal, immediate feedback) because omitting any of them may dramatically impact intervention integrity and, subsequently, treatment outcomes.

6. Expect reactivity and actively work to suppress its potential effects. When assessing intervention integrity, use inconspicuous direct observation whenever possible. In some environments it may be possible to compare intervention integrity percentages obtained during inconspicuous and conspicuous observations to determine whether reactivity is a concern for a particular interventionist.

7. Prioritize integrity observations for procedures with a high risk of integrity failure such as more complex treatments, treatments containing restrictive procedures, or treatments addressing severe and/or dangerous challenging behaviors.

8. Direct observations should be scheduled frequently and should be sampled throughout the day, across the week, and with unpredictable "check-ins." As interventionists show success with implementing the intervention, observations may be scheduled less often. However, we encourage brief, intermittent direct observations for even the most experienced and high-performing interventionists.

9. Assessment should be completed for each core component of the plan. Integrity percentages could be calculated for each component as well as one aggregate measure of gross intervention integrity.

10. Given its effectiveness, we advocate the frequent use of performance feedback. Feedback delivered in a respectful and positive manner tends to be better received even if it is corrective in nature. Be sure to provide corrective feedback with sensitivity

to the experience of the interventionist receiving this information given that some interventionists may be nervous about receiving feedback. Feedback meetings should be scheduled to allow adequate time for the interventionist to ask questions.

11. We encourage frequent use of praise and recognition so long as they are applied contingent on exemplary behavior. Although tangible items may also function as reinforcers for high intervention integrity, we caution readers against introducing them without carefully considering budget constraints and simple lottery systems and low- or no-cost rewards (e.g., flexible work schedule, extended lunch break, lottery for a gift card). Moreover, although a meeting cancellation contingency (i.e., negative reinforcement) has been shown to effectively improve intervention integrity, this follow-up strategy was packaged with other intervention procedures such as performance feedback, directed rehearsal, and BST. We do not know which aspect of the training package improved performance nor was meeting cancellation evaluated long term. The degree to which negative reinforcement in the form of a meeting cancellation contingency may interfere with the effectiveness of a consultant or supervisor over the long term is also unknown.

12. If intervention integrity remains low, despite following the aforementioned recommendations, the intervention likely requires more resources than the setting is able or willing to provide. It may also be the case that the intervention plan is overly complicated. In either situation, the plan will likely require modification.

REFERENCES

Alvero, A. M., Bucklin, B. R., & Austin, J. (2001). An objective review of the effectiveness and essential characteristics of performance feedback in organizational settings (1985-1998). *Journal of Organizational Behavior Management, 21,* 3–29. doi: 10.1300/J075v21n01_02.

Autism Speaks. (n.d.a). *Congress briefed on rising prevalence, cost of autism.* Retrieved June 2012, from http://www.autismspeaks.org/blog/2012/05/02/congress-briefed-rising-prevalence-cost-autism.

Autism Speaks. (n.d.b). *Facts about autism.* Retrieved June 2012, from http://www.autismspeaks.org/what-autism/facts-about-autism.

Bloom, M., Fischer, J., & Orme, J. G. (1999). *Evaluating practice: Guidelines for the accountable professional* (3rd ed.). Boston, MA: Allyn & Bacon.

Brackett, L., Reid, D. H., & Green, C. W. (2007). Effects of reactivity to observations on staff performance. *Journal of Applied Behavior Analysis, 40,* 191–195. doi: 10.1901/jaba.2007.112-05.

Catania, A. C. (2007) *Learning: Fourth interim edition.* Cornwall-on-Hudson, NY: Sloan.

Catania, C. N., Almeida, D., Liu-Constant, B., & DiGennaro Reed, F. D. (2009). Video modeling to train staff to implement discrete-trial instruction. *Journal of Applied Behavior Analysis, 42,* 387–392. doi: 10.1901/jaba.2009.42-387.

Centers for Disease Control and Prevention. *Facts about autism.* Retrieved September 2011, from http://www.cdc.gov/ncbddd/autism/facts.html.

Codding, R. S., Feinberg, A. B., Dunn, E. K., & Pace, G. M. (2005). Effects of immediate performance feedback on implementation of behavior support plans. *Journal of Applied Behavior Analysis, 38,* 205-219.

Codding, R. S., Livanis, A., Pace, G. M., & Vaca, L. (2008). Using performance feedback to improve treatment integrity of classwide behavior plans: An investigation of observer reactivity. *Journal of Applied Behavior Analysis, 41,* 417–422. doi: 10.1901/jaba.2008.41-417.

Cone, J. D. (1977). The relevance of reliability and validity for behavioral assessment. *Behavior Therapy, 8,* 411–426. doi: 10.1016/S0005-7894(77)80077-4.

Cone, J. D. (1978). The behavioral assessment grid (BAG): A conceptual framework and a taxonomy. *Behavior Therapy, 9,* 882–888. doi: 10.1016/S0005-7894(78)80020-3.

Costenbader, V., Swartz, J., & Petrix, L. (1992). Consultation in the schools: The relationship between preservice training, perception of consultative skills, and actual time spent in consultation. *School Psychology Review, 21,* 95–108.

Dane, A. V., & Schneider, B. H. (1998). Program integrity in primary and early secondary prevention: Are implementation effects out of control? *Clinical Psychology Review, 18,* 23–45. doi: 10.1016/S0272-7358(97)00043-3.

Daniels, A. C., & Daniels, J. E., (2006). *Performance management: Changing behavior that drives organizational effectiveness.* Atlanta, GA: Performance Management.

Dib, N., & Sturmey, P. (2007). Reducing student stereotypy by improving teachers' implementation of discrete-trial teaching. *Journal of Applied Behavior Analysis, 40,* 339–343. doi: 10.1901/jaba.2007.52-06.

DiGennaro, F. D., Martens, B. K., & Kleinmann, A. E. (2007). A comparison of performance feedback procedures on teachers' treatment implementation integrity and students' inappropriate behavior in special education classrooms. *Journal of Applied Behavior Analysis, 40,* 447–461. doi: 10.1901/jaba.2007.40-447.

DiGennaro, F. D., Martens, B. K., & McIntyre, L. L. (2005). Increasing treatment integrity through negative reinforcement: Effects on teacher and student behavior. *School Psychology Review, 34,* 220–231.

DiGennaro Reed, F. D., & Codding, R. S. (2011). Intervention integrity assessment. In J. Luiselli (Ed.), *Teaching and behavior support for children and adults with autism spectrum disorder: A "how to" practitioner's guide.* New York, NY: Oxford University Press.

DiGennaro Reed, F. D., Codding, R., Catania, C. N., & Maguire, H. (2010). Effects of video modeling on treatment integrity of behavioral interventions. *Journal of Applied Behavior Analysis, 43,* 291–295. doi: 10.1901/jaba.2010.43-291.

DiGennaro Reed, F. D., Hirst, J. M., & Howard, V. J. (2013a). Behavior analytic techniques to promote treatment integrity. In L. Hagermoser Sanetti & T. Kratochwill (Eds.), *Treatment integrity: Conceptual, methodological, and applied considerations for practitioners* (pp. 203–226). Alexandria, VA: APA Press.

DiGennaro Reed, F. D., Hirst, J. M., & Veronica, V. J. (2013b). Empirically supported staff selection, training, and management strategies. In D. D. Reed, F. D. DiGennaro Reed, & J. K. Luiselli (Eds.), *Handbook of crisis intervention for individuals with developmental disabilities* (pp. 71–85). New York, NY: Springer.

DiGennaro Reed, F. D., Hyman, S. R., & Hirst, J. M. (2011). Applications of technology to teach social skills to children with autism. *Research in Autism Spectrum Disorders, 5,* 1003–1010. doi: 10.1016/j.rasd.2011.01.022.

DiGennaro Reed, F. D., Reed, D. D., Baez, C. N., & Maguire, H. (2011). A parametric analysis of errors of commission during discrete-trial training. *Journal of Applied Behavior Analysis, 44,* 611–615. doi: 10.1901/jaba.2011.44-611.

Elliott, S. N. (1988). Acceptability of behavioral treatments in educational settings. In J. C. Witt, S. N. Elliott, & F. M. Gresham (Eds.), *Handbook of behavior therapy in education* (pp. 121–150). New York, NY: Plenum.

Ferster, C. B., & Skinner, B. F. (1957). *Schedules of reinforcement.* East Norwalk, CT: Appleton-Century-Crofts.

Ganz, M. L. (2007). The lifetime distribution of the incremental societal costs of autism. *Archives of Pediatrics and Adolescent Medicine, 161,* 343–349.

Gearing, R. E., El-Bassel, N., Ghesquiere, A., Baldwin, S., Gillies, J., & Ngeow, E. (2011). Major ingredients of fidelity: A review and scientific guide to improving quality of intervention research implementation. *Clinical Psychology Review, 31,* 79–88. doi: 10.1016/j.cpr.2010.09.007.

Gilligan, K. T., Luiselli, J. K., & Pace, G. M. (2007). Training paraprofessional staff to implement discrete

trial instruction: Evaluation of a practice performance feedback intervention. *Behavior Therapist, 30,* 63–66.

Green, C. W., Reid, D. H., Perkins, L. I., & Gardner, S. M. (1991). Increasing habilitative services for persons with profound handicaps: An application of structural analysis to staff management. *Journal of Applied Behavior Analysis, 24,* 459–471. doi: 10.1901/jaba.1991.24-459.

Gresham, F. M. (1989). Assessment of treatment integrity in school consultation and prereferral intervention. *School Psychology Review, 18,* 37–50.

Gresham, F. M., Gansle, K. A., & Noell, G. H. (1993). Treatment integrity in applied behavior analysis with children. *Journal of Applied Behavior Analysis, 26,* 257–263. doi: 10.1901/jaba.1993.26-257.

Groskreutz, N. C., Groskreutz, M. P., & Higbee, T. S. (2011). Effects of varied levels of treatment integrity on appropriate toy manipulation in children with autism. *Research in Autism Spectrum Disorders, 5,* 1358–1369. doi:10.1016/j.rasd.2011.01.018.

Hirst, J. M., DiGennaro Reed, F. D., & Reed, D. D. (2013). Effects of varying feedback accuracy on task acquisition. A computerized translational study. *Journal of Behavioral Education, 22,* 1-15 doi: 10.1007/s10864-012-9162-0.

Individuals with Disabilities Education Improvement Act of 2004, H.R. 1350, 108th Congress.

Iwata, B. A., Bailey, J. S., Brown, K. M., Foshee, T. J., & Alpern, M. A. (1976). A performance based lottery to improve residential care and training by institutional staff. *Journal of Applied Behavior Analysis, 9,* 417–431. doi: 10.1901/jaba.1976.9-417.

Iwata, B. A., Wallace, M. D., Kahng, S., Lindberg, J. S., Roscoe, E. M., Conners, J.,...Worsdell, A. S. (2000). Skill acquisition in the implementation of functional analysis methodology. *Journal of Applied Behavior Analysis, 33,* 181–194. doi: 10.1901/jaba.2000.33-181.

Jahr, E. (1998). Current issues in staff training. *Research in Developmental Disabilities, 19,* 73–87. doi: 10.1016/S0891-4222(97)00030-9.

Jarmolowicz, D. P., Kahng, S., Ingvarsson, E. T., Goysovich, R., Heggemeyer, R., Gregory, M. K., & Taylor, S. J. (2008). Effects of conversational versus technical language on treatment preference and integrity. *Intellectual and Developmental Disabilities, 46,* 190–199. doi: 10.1352/2008.46:190-199.

Jones, H. A., Clarke, A. T., & Power, T. J. (2008). Expanding the concept of intervention integrity: A multidimensional model of participant engagement. *In Balance, 23,* 4–5.

Lavie, T., & Sturmey, P. (2002). Training staff to conduct a paired-stimulus preference assessment. *Journal of Applied Behavior Analysis, 35,* 209–211. doi:v10.1901/jaba.2002.35-209.

Leblanc, M. P., Ricciardi, J. N., & Luiselli, J. K. (2005). Improving discrete trial instruction by paraprofessional staff through an abbreviated performance feedback intervention. *Education and Treatment of Children, 28,* 76–82.

Lentz, F. E., Jr. (1988). Effective reading interventions in the regular classroom. In J. L. Graden, J. E. Zins, & M. L. Curtis, (Eds.), *Alternative educational delivery systems: Enhancing instructional options for all students* (pp. 351–370). Washington, DC: National Association of School Psychologists.

Locke, E. A., & Latham, G. P. (1990). *Theory of goal setting and task performance.* Englewood Cliffs, NJ: Prentice Hall.

Luiselli, J. K., DiGennaro Reed, F. D., Christian, W. P., Markowski, A., Rue, H. C., St. Amand, C., & Ryan, C. J. (2009). Effects of an informational brochure, lottery-based financial incentive, and public posting on absenteeism of direct-care human services employees. *Behavior Modification, 33,* 175–181. doi: 10.1177/0145445508320624.

Macurik, K. M., O'Kane, N. P., Malanga, P., & Reid, D. H. (2008). Video training of support staff in intervention plans for challenging behavior: Comparison with live training. *Behavioral Interventions, 23,* 143–168. doi: 10.1002/bin.261.

National Research Council, Committee on Educational Interventions for Children with Autism, Division of Behavioral and Social Sciences and Education. (2001). *Educating children with autism.* Washington, DC: National Academy Press.

National Standards Project. (2009). *Evidence-based practice and autism in the schools: A guide to providing appropriate interventions to students with autism spectrum disorders.* Randolph, MA: National Autism Center.

New York State Department of Health. (1999). *Clinical practice guideline: Report of the recommendations. Autism/pervasive developmental disorders, assessment and intervention for young children (age 0-3 years).* Albany, NY: NYS Early Intervention Program.

Nigro-Bruzzi, D., & Sturmey, P. (2010). The effects of behavioral skills training on mand training by staff and unprompted vocal mands by children. *Journal of Applied Behavior Analysis, 43,* 757–761. doi: 10.1901/jaba.2010.43-757.

Noell, G. H. (2008). Research examining the relationships among consultation process, treatment integrity, and outcomes. In W. P. Erchul & S. M. Sheridan (Eds.), *Handbook of research in school consultation: Empirical foundations for the field* (pp. 315–334). Mahwah, NJ: Erlbaum.

Noell, G. H., Duhon, G. J., Gatti, S. L., & Connell, J. E. (2002). Consultation, follow-up, and implementation of behavior management interventions in general education. *School Psychology Review, 31,* 217–234.

Noell, G. H., Witt, J. C., Gilbertson, D. N., Ranier, D. D., & Freeland, J. T. (1997). Increasing teacher intervention implementation in general education settings through consultation and performance feedback. *School Psychology Quarterly, 12,* 77–88.

Noell, G. H., Witt, J. C., LaFleur, L. H., Mortensen, B. P., Ranier, D. D., & LeVelle, J. (2000). Increasing intervention implementation in general education following consultation: A comparison of two follow-up strategies. *Journal of Applied Behavior Analysis, 33,* 271–284. doi: 10.1901/jaba.2000.33-271.

Noell, G. H., Witt, J. C., Slider, N. J., Connell, J. E., Gatti, S. L., Williams, K. L.,…Duhon, G. J. (2005). Treatment implementation following behavioral consultation in schools: A comparison of three follow-up strategies. *School Psychology Review, 34,* 87–106.

Northup, J., Fisher, W., Kahng, S., Harrell, R., & Kurtz, P. (1997). An assessment of the necessary strength of behavioral treatments for severe behavior problems. *Journal of Developmental and Physical Disabilities, 9,* 1–16. doi: 10.1023/A:1024984526008.

Parsons, M. B., Reid, D. H., & Crow, R. E. (2003). Best and worst ways to motivate staff in community agencies: A brief survey of supervisors. *Mental Retardation, 41,* 96–102.

Parsons, M. B., Reid, D. H., & Green, C. W. (1993). Preparing direct service staff to teach people with severe disabilities: A comprehensive evaluation of an effective and acceptable training program. *Behavioral Residential Treatment, 8,* 163–186.

Perepletchikova, F. (2011). On the topic of treatment integrity. *Clinical Psychology: Science and Practice, 18,* 148–153. doi: 10.1111/j.1468-2850.2011.01246.x.

Perepletchikova, F., Hilt, L. M., Chereji, E., & Kazdin, A. E. (2009). Barriers to implementing treatment integrity procedures: Survey of treatment outcome researchers. *Journal of Consulting and Clinical Psychology, 77,* 212–218. doi: 10.1037/a0015232.

Pommer, D. A., & Streedback, D. (1974). Motivating staff performance in an operant learning program for children. *Journal of Applied Behavior Analysis, 7,* 217–221. doi: 10.1901/jaba.1974.7-217.

Power, T. J., Blom-Hoffman, J., Clarke, A. T., Riley-Tillman, T. C., Kellerher, C., & Manz, P. (2005). Reconceptualizing intervention integrity: A partnership-based framework for linking research with practice. *Psychology in the Schools, 42,* 495–507. doi: 10.1002/pits.20087.

Prue, D. M., & Fairbank, J. A. (1981). Performance feedback in organizational behavior management: A review. *Journal of Organizational Behavior Management, 3,* 1–16. doi: 10.1300/J075v03n01_01.

Reed, D. D., Fienup, D. M., Luiselli, J. K., & Pace, G. M. (2010). Performance improvement in behavioral health care: Collateral effects of planned integrity observations as an applied example of schedule-induced responding. *Behavior Modification, 34,* 367–385. doi: 10.1177/0145445510383524.

Reid, D. H., & Green, C. W. (1990). Staff training. In J. L. Matson (Ed.), *Handbook of behavior modification with the mentally retarded* (pp. 71–90). New York: Plenum Press.

Reid, D. H., & Parsons, M. B. (1995). *Motivating human service staff: Supervisory strategies for maximizing work effort and work enjoyment.* Morganton, NC: Habilitative Management Consultants.

Reid, D. H., & Parsons, M. B. (1996). A comparison of staff acceptability of immediate versus delayed verbal feedback in staff training. *Journal of Organizational Behavior Management, 16,* 35–47. doi: 10.1300/J075v16n02_03.

Reid, D. H., Parsons, M. B., & Green, C. W. (2011). *The supervisor training curriculum: Evidence-based ways to promote work quality and enjoyment among support staff.* Washington, DC: American Association on Intellectual and Developmental Disabilities.

Reid, D. H., Schuh-Wear, C. L., & Brannon, M. E. (1978). Use of a group contingency to decrease staff absenteeism in a state institution. *Behavior Modification, 2,* 251–266. doi: 10.1177/014544557822006.

Reid, D. H., & Whitman, T. L. (1983). Behavioral staff management in institutions. A critical review of effectiveness and acceptability. *Analysis and Interventions in Developmental Disabilities, 3,* 131–149. doi: 10.1016/0270-4684(83)90011-3.

Rhymer, K. N., Evans-Hampton, T. N., McCurdy, M., & Watson, T. S. (2002). Effects of varying levels of treatment integrity on toddler aggressive behavior. *Special Services in the Schools, 18,* 75–81. doi: 10.1300/J008v18n01_05.

Ricciardi, J. N. (2005). Achieving human service outcomes through competency-based training: A guide for managers. *Behavior Modification, 29,* 488–507. doi: 10.1177/0145445504273281.

Roscoe, E. M., & Fisher, W. W. (2008). Evaluation of an efficient method for training staff to implement stimulus preference assessments. *Journal of Applied Behavior Analysis, 41,* 249–254. doi: 10.1901/jaba.2008.41-249.

Sanetti, L. M. H., & DiGennaro Reed, F. D. (2012). Barriers to implementing treatment integrity procedures in school psychology research: Survey of treatment outcome researchers. *Assessment for Effective Intervention, 37,* 195–202. doi: 10.1177/1534508411432466.

Sanetti, L. M. H., & Kratochwill, T. R. (2009a). Toward developing a science of treatment integrity: Introduction to the special series. *School Psychology Review, 38,* 445–459. doi: 10.1037/a0015431.

Sanetti, L. M. H., & Kratochwill, T. R. (2009b). Treatment integrity assessment in the schools: An evaluation of the Treatment Integrity Planning Protocol. *School Psychology Quarterly, 24,* 24–35. doi: 10.1037/a0015431.

Sanetti, L. M. H., Luiselli, J. K., & Handler, M. W. (2007). Effects of verbal and graphic performance feedback on behavior support plan implementation in a public elementary school. *Behavior Modification, 31,* 454–465. doi: 10.1177/0145445506297583.

Sarokoff, R. A., & Sturmey, P. (2004). The effects of behavioral skills training of stall implementation of discrete-trial teaching. *Journal of Applied Behavior Analysis, 37,* 525–538. doi: 10.1901/jaba.2004.37-535.

Scheeler, M. C. (2008). Generalizing effective teaching skills: The missing link in teacher preparation. *Journal of Behavioral Education, 17,* 145–159. doi: 10.1007/s10864-007-9051-0.

Sepler, H. J., & Myers, S. L. (1978). The effectiveness of verbal instruction on teaching behavior-modification skills to nonprofessionals. *Journal of Applied Behavior Analysis, 11,* 198. doi: 10.1901/jaba.1978.11-198.

St. Peter Pipkin, C., Vollmer, T. R., & Sloman, K. N. (2010). Effects of treatment integrity failures during differential reinforcement of alternative behavior: A translational model. *Journal of Applied Behavior Analysis, 43,* 47–70. doi: 10.1901/jaba.2010.43-47.

Strock, M. (2004). *Autism spectrum disorders (pervasive developmental disorders)* [NIH Publication No. NIH-04-5511]. Bethesda, MD: National Institute of Mental Health, National Institutes of Health, US Department of Health and Human Services.

US Department of Health and Human Services. (1999). *Mental health: A report of the surgeon general.* Rockville, MD: US Department of Health and Human Services, Substance Abuse and Mental Health Services Administration, Center for Mental Health Services, National Institutes of Health, National Institute of Mental Health.

van Oorsouw, W. M. W. J., Embregts, P. J. C. M., Bosman, A. M. T., & Jahoda, A. (2009). Training staff serving clients with intellectual disabilities: A meta-analysis of aspects determining effectiveness. *Research in Developmental Disabilities, 30,* 503–511. doi:10.1016/j.ridd.2008.07.011.

Vollmer, T. R., Roane, H. S., Ringdahl, J. E., & Marcus, B. A. (1999). Evaluating treatment challenges with differential reinforcement of alternative behavior. *Journal of Applied Behavior Analysis, 32,* 9–23. doi: 10.1901/jaba.1999.32-9.

Vollmer, T. R., Sloman, K. N., & St. Peter Pipkin, C. (2008). Practical implications of data reliability and treatment integrity monitoring. *Behavior Analysis in Practice, 1*(2), 4–11.

Ward, P., Johnson, M., & Konukman, F. (1998). Directed rehearsal and preservice teachers' performance of instructional behaviors. *Journal of Behavioral Education, 8,* 369–380. doi: 10.1023/A:1022827415544.

Ward, P., Smith, S., & Makasci, K. (1997). Teacher training: Effects of directed rehearsal on the teaching skills of physical education majors. *Journal of Behavioral Education, 7,* 505–517. doi: 10.1023/A:1022863520165.

Wickstrom, K. F., Jones, K. M., LaFleur, L. H., & Witt, J. C. (1998). An analysis of treatment integrity in school-based behavioral consultation. *School Psychology Quarterly, 13,* 141–154.

Wilder, D. A., Atwell, J., & Wine, B. (2006). The effects of varying levels of treatment integrity on child compliance during treatment with a three-step prompting procedure. *Journal of Applied Behavior Analysis, 39,* 369–373. doi: 10.1901/jaba.2006.144-05.

Worsdell, A. S., Iwata, G. A., Hanley, G. P., Thompson, R. H., & Kahng, S. (2000). Effects of continuous and intermittent reinforcement for problem behavior during functional communication training. *Journal of* *Applied Behavior Analysis, 33,* 167–179. doi: 10.1901/jaba.2000.33-167.

Yeaton, W. H., & Sechrest, L. (1981). Critical dimensions in the choice and maintenance of successful treatments: Strength, integrity, and effectiveness. *Journal of Consulting and Clinical Psychology, 49,* 156–167. doi: 10.1037//0022-006X.49.2.156.

SECTION III

Health and Development

11

Food Selectivity and Refusal

CHARLES S. GULOTTA AND PETER A. GIROLAMI

Over the last decade the diagnosis of autism has been on the rise. In a report from Centers for Disease Control and Prevention (CDC) in 2009, the current estimate of autism spectrum disorder (ASD) in the population is 1 case per 110 individuals. Children with ASD often struggle with a range of issues, including impairments in social skills, communication patterns, and restricted and repetitive interests and behaviors (APA, 2000; Matson, Fodstad, & Dempsey, 2009). Similar to repetitive interests and behavior, food selectivity is an issue that parents of children with ASD report as a significant problem. Estimates of the prevalence rates of feeding issues in children with ASD range from 26% to 90% (Burklow, Phelps, Schultz, McConell, & Rudolph, 1998; Field, Garland, & Williams, 2003; Ledford & Gast, 2006).

Several explanations have been proposed as to why there are such high rates of feeding problems or food selectivity in children with ASD. The reasons often listed are core diagnostic symptoms of ASD such as perseveration, neophobia, rigidness to change, sensory impairments, and deficits in social compliance and communication (Ahearn, Castine, Nault, & Green, 2001; Ledford & Gast, 2006). The core characteristics of ASD are considered to be strongly heritable, although with a range of variability from one individual to the next (Ronald et al., 2006). Many of these core characteristics are not only resistant to change but can also be very damaging and problematic when it comes to socialization and functional communication (Matson & Fodstad, 2009). Attempting to redirect and stop these behaviors can often worsen the situation (Matson, Dixon, & Matson, 2005). Next we address several influences on food selectivity and refusal.

ENVIRONMENTAL VARIABLES

Environmental variables are often what maintain and strengthen food refusal or selectivity in children with ASD (Babbitt, Hoch, & Coe, 1994; Piazza et al., 2003). Specifically, when confronted with significant refusal behavior, parents will often provide attention to the refusal or remove food items and/or terminate a meal when the child refuses to eat. What may start out as an occasional rigid pattern is often inadvertently negatively and/or positively reinforced due to caregivers' attempts to reduce the amount of conflict and problem behavior that may arise during mealtime. Piazza et al. (2003) found that after conducting analog functional analyses of 12 individuals with various medical diagnoses and developmental disabilities (including ASD) that the majority of the participants (90%) were sensitive to negative reinforcement contingencies. They also found that 80% of the participants were likely to have multiple functions for their food refusal. Interestingly, the one participant who had a diagnosis of autism was the one individual that showed his food refusal was maintained by positive attention. By using a treatment that specifically provided attention contingent upon food consumption, the authors demonstrated marked improvement in the child's overall consumption. Although this study demonstrated that escape from food plays a primary role in food refusal for some children, it also provided evidence that some children may also be sensitive to multiple functions, particularly positive reinforcement (i.e., adult attention, access to preferred food) contingent on food refusal.

It is rare that children with ASD do not know how to eat food but rather the kind of food they will eat and how much they choose to eat are problem areas. For example, consumption among children with ASD is often restricted by texture (i.e., will only eat pureed foods and/or crunchy foods), food type (i.e., will only eat carbohydrates with limited or no amounts of proteins, fruits, and/or vegetables), and/or temperature (i.e., temperature of the food needs to be hot or cold). Sometimes they will only eat using the same utensil or drinking implement (i.e., will only use bottle instead of cup) (Ahearn et al., 2001; Schreck & Williams, 2006). Schreck, Williams, and Smith (2004) found when comparing age-matched controls to children with ASD, children with ASD were more likely to have food refusal, acceptance of a limited variety of texture and food types, as well as idiosyncratic meal time behavior such as only drinking from a bottle or a certain colored spoon or cup. Another study by Matson et al. (2009) examined children with ASD, atypically developing children, and typically developing children on several assessment instruments that focused on feeding issues. The authors found that children with ASD were more likely to have significant feeding issues compared to typically developing and atypically developing same-aged peers. The specific problem areas for children with ASD that the authors highlighted were that children with ASD preferred foods of a certain texture or smell, ate a limited variety of foods, exhibited higher rates of pica (i.e., eating things that are not food), ate food too quickly, and were more likely to overeat.

MEDICAL ISSUES

Bandini et al. (2010) compared children with ASD to typically developing children, 3–11 years old, on four domains of food selectivity: (1) level of refusal, (2) limited repertoire, (3) high-frequency single-food intake, and (4) nutritional differences based on a 3-day diet log. The authors found statistical differences between children with ASD and typically developing children, with ASD children being more likely to refuse foods at higher rates and more likely to have a narrow selection of food variety. They did not find differences between the groups on high-frequency single-food consumption. However, children with ASD were more likely to have nutritional deficiencies in fiber intake and Vitamins C and D. This finding supports Ibrahim, Voigt, Katusic, Weaver, and Barbaresi (2009), who examined children with ASD for increased risk of gastrointestinal issues. One finding of this study was that children with ASD were more likely to have issues with constipation (34%) and food selectivity (25%) versus 18% and 16% for control children, respectively. Constipation often stems from a low-fiber diet, which is also the diet that children with ASD prefer (Bandini et al., 2010; Kerwin, Eicher, & Gelsinger, 2005). This finding not only supports the potential negative medical effects

of food selectivity, but it also indirectly supports a biobehavioral explanation for food refusal and food selectivity in some children with ASD.

BIOBEHAVIORAL MODEL OF FOOD SELECTIVITY IN CHILDREN WITH AUTISM SPECTRUM DISORDER

Referencing Figure 11.1, children with ASD are already likely to be more restrictive and ritualistic in their food choices as a result of their diagnosis being complicated by other medical conditions such as constipation. As noted previously, studies indicate that children with ASD are more likely to eat a selective and low-fiber diet (Bandini et al., 2010). A low-fiber diet can cause constipation, producing stomach discomfort, pain, and lack of appetite, which can lead to even more food refusal. Backing down after attempting to persuade a constipated child may negatively reinforce food refusal. This biobehavioral model of food selectivity in children with ASD demonstrates a potential cycle of core characteristics of autism, medical issues that lead to physical discomfort, leading to food refusal, which then is inadvertently reinforced by caregivers, leading to greater food refusal and selectivity down the road.

ASSESSMENT OF FEEDING ISSUES IN CHILDREN WITH AUTISM SPECTRUM DISORDER

Although it is generally accepted that children diagnosed with ASD often have feeding problems, the severity (i.e., how debilitating the problem is to the child), actual topography (i.e., what the problem looks like), and the function (i.e., why the problem is occurring) vary from child to child (Kuhn, Girolami, & Gulotta, 2007; Laud, Girolami, Boscoe, & Gulotta, 2009). Accordingly, different measures and procedures have been developed to identify and assess problematic mealtime behavior, including indirect questionnaires (Lukens & Linscheid, 2008), interview strategies (O'Neill, Horner, Albin, Storey, & Sprague, 1990), direct observational (descriptive) procedures (Ahearn et al., 2001; Borrero, Woods, Borrero, Masler, & Lesser, 2010; Munk & Repp, 1994), and experimental manipulations (Najdowski, Wallace, Doney, & Ghezzi, 2003; Piazza et al., 2003). Assessments

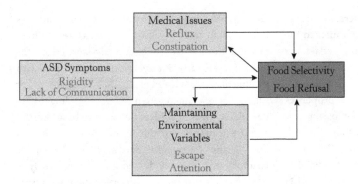

FIGURE 11.1. Food selectivity in children with autism spectrum disorder (ASD): a biobehavioral model for Assessment.

range from the more broad or nomothetic and norm-referenced measures like behavior problem checklists and surveys to more specific, or idiographic, functional assessments that can identify variables of special relevance for a child. This broad to narrow focus approach to assessment can aid in effectively identifying target behaviors and causal variables associated with the onset and maintenance of the behaviors (Hawkins, 1979; Nelson-Gray & Hayes, 1986).

Self-Report Measures to Identify Feeding Issues

The Children's Eating Behavior Inventory

The Children's Eating Behavior Inventory (CEBI) is a 40-item caregiver report measure intended to provide a more standardized assessment of eating and mealtime problems across a wide variety of children with medical and developmental disorders (Archer, Rosenbaum, & Streiner, 1991). The two scores derived from this measure include the (a) Total Eating Problems score, which measures the occurrence of 19 different eating behaviors through a 5-point rating scale, and the (b) Total Perceived Problems score, which asks caregivers to determine whether each behavior is a problem for the family (e.g., "My child chews food as expected for his/her age"). Test-retest reliability has been reported at .87 for the Total Eating Problem score and .84 for the percentage of items perceived to be a problem. Laud et al. (2009) used the CEBI as one of the measures in a treatment outcome study involving 46 children diagnosed with ASD and severe feeding problems referred for treatment at an interdisciplinary feeding disorders program. Significant improvement was observed from admission to discharge in the CEBI total eating problems scale and during direct observation of feeding behavior. Thus, the CEBI may be a useful tool to evaluate mealtime behavior problems in children with autism.

Screening Tool of Feeding Problems

The Screening Tool of Feeding Problems (STEP) was originally developed by Matson and Kuhn (2001) to aid mental health providers with identifying problematic mealtime behaviors for adults with intellectual disabilities. The STEP consists of 23 items, each targeting specific categories of feeding problems, including risks for aspiration, selectivity, feeding skills, food refusal–related behavior problems, and nutrition-related feeding problems (Kuhn & Matson, 2002). Professionals who have experience with a particular individual and have observed the individual exhibit problematic feeding behaviors fill out the form. The STEP has adequate psychometric properties, including test–retest reliability and inter-rater reliability of 0.72 and 0.71, respectively (as cited in Kuhn et al., 2007). In a recent case study, Koslowski et al. (2011) utilized the STEP and other direct methods of functional assessment to assess and treat a young child with ASD and severe food refusal. Taking into account that the original STEP was designed for adults with intellectual disability, Seiverling et al. (2011) evaluated its psychometric properties when administered to children attending a feeding disorders clinic. Eventually, Seiverling et al. developed the STEP-CHILD as a useful measure for assessing children's feeding problems.

Brief Autism Mealtime Behavior Inventory

Lukens and Linscheid (2008) developed the Brief Autism Mealtime Behavior Inventory (BAMBI), the first standardized measure of problematic feeding behavior specifically in young children diagnosed with ASD. The BAMBI is an 18-item questionnaire that parents complete using a 5-point Likert scale across several domains. When filling out the BAMBI, parents are asked to reference observations of mealtime behavior (e.g., cries and screams during mealtimes) during the last 6 months. Similar to the CEBI, parents rate whether the feeding behavior is a "problem." The BAMBI yields a total score and three subscales: Limited Variety, Food Refusal, and Features of Autism. The psychometric properties of the measure were conducted by comparing eating behavior of 68 children with ASD and 40 children without ASD, aged 3 to 11 years old. Reliability for this measure was .87 for test-retest reliability and .78 for interrated reliability. Sharp et al. (2013) administered the BAMBI as part of a multimethod assessment battery involving a standardized mealtime observation and a food preference inventory. They compared the results of the BAMBI with direct observations of mealtime behavior, food preference inventories, and dietary intake of children diagnosed with autism. Limited Variety subscale scores on the BAMBI were negatively correlated with direct observation of bite acceptance, positively correlated with problem behaviors during the meal, and positively associated with foods that had never been consumed on the food preference inventory, indicating that the BAMBI may be a good measure of mealtime difficulties. However, the lack of association between the scores on the Food Refusal subscale and problem behaviors observed during meal sessions reveals that the psychometric properties of the BAMBI need to be explored further (Sharp et al., 2013).

Food Inventories or Diet Records

Food preference inventories or diet records may also be helpful when screening for feeding problems and identifying foods to target during intervention. For example, in a study comparing food selectivity of children with ASD and typically developing children, Bandini et al. (2010) had parents complete a food frequency questionnaire and a 3-day food record. Teachers also recorded all food eaten during the school day. Similarly, Sharp, Jaquess, Morton, and Miles (2011) provided caregivers with a questionnaire including a 3-day food diary assessing all foods and drinks consumed. Caregivers also listed all fruits, meats, breads, cereals, vegetables, dairy, and sweets accepted regularly by their child. Perhaps the best use of food preference inventories is documenting long-term changes in dietary intake (Sharp et al., 2013)

Functional Assessment

By identifying the environmental variables associated with the onset and maintenance of problematic feeding behaviors, functional assessments such as indirect/informant self-report measures, direct observation, and experimental analysis are critical for designing effective interventions for children with feeding disorders (Kuhn et al., 2007). The method of functional assessment often varies depending on the complexity of the problem behavior to be addressed and the resources available to the professionals conducting the assessment. Piazza et al. (2003), for example, not only conducted a functional analysis of six participants but also observed them with their caregivers in a natural setting. Half the participants had identical maintaining variables for both functional analysis and the descriptive assessment of the participants' meal with their caregivers.

Interviews

Interviews are a good way to gather information about child behavior. Indeed, a first strategy for conducting a functional assessment of feeding problems is to talk to the people that have direct contact and experience with the individual and during mealtimes. The Functional Assessment Interview Form (FAIF; O'Neill et al., 1997) is such an instrument to identify target behaviors and potential functions of problematic feeding behavior (Girolami & Scotti, 2001). As an example, Kozlowski et al. (2011) interviewed the mother of a 9-year-old with ASD and found that information about behavioral function supported results of other function-based measures (like the QABF; see later).

Direct Observations

Many direct observation methods are available for identifying the influences on problematic feeding behavior. For example, in an assessment of the antecedent events associated with food refusal, Munk and Repp (1994) manipulated food types and textures (i.e., antecedents to feeding problem behavior) to determine which foods were associated with mealtime problems such as refusal and negative vocalizations. Ahearn et al. (2001) adapted Munk and Repp's direct assessment to measure food acceptance in children with ASD by classifying acceptance across different levels of acceptance (i.e., low: 30 or few bites; moderate: 31–60 bites; and high: 61 or more bites) based on the number of bites consumed. To assess food selectivity, Ahearn et al. analyzed acceptance within food groups. Results of this study corroborate and extend the findings of Munk and Repp by identifying individual patterns of food refusal, food type selectivity, and food texture selectivity across participants. Patel, Piazza, Santana, and Volkert (2002) also extended the Munk and Repp methodology by assessing food type and texture. They found that expulsion occurred more often with meats compared to other foods (fruits, vegetables, and starches) and that dropping the texture of meats (but not the other foods) decreased expulsion. Patel et al. (2002) speculated that the response effort associated with consuming meats may be higher than consuming other foods; thus, reducing texture may be an effective intervention.

Experimental (Functional) Analyses

A functional analysis involves the systematic manipulation of antecedent and consequent variables to determine their onset and maintenance of a problem behavior (Piazza et al., 2003). Najdowski et al. (2003) trained parents to conduct functional analysis and used the information to develop and implement treatment of a 5-year-old boy who had ASD and exhibited a variety of food refusal behavior, including throwing utensils, whining, and crying when presented with novel foods. The participant's regular diet consisted of crunchy snack foods and brand-specific french fries and chicken nuggets. The functional analysis consisted of four conditions: no interaction, attention, play, and escape. Mealtime problem behavior occurred most frequently in the escape condition, indicating that escape from food or other mealtime-related stimuli negatively reinforced problem behavior. An intervention consisting of an escape extinction procedure and differential reinforcement of alternative behavior was effective.

Functional analyses are often time consuming when compared to indirect measures such as interviews, questionnaires, and direct observations. However, a functional analysis is the most rigorous approach for confirming behavior–environment relationships. A functional analysis also eliminates subjectivity and bias that may influence indirect and descriptive assessment methods. As an illustration, some parents may purposely exaggerate or minimize problem behavior. Of course, inconsistent information will lead to ineffective intervention.

Self-Report Function-Based Questionnaire

Function-based questionnaires are another way to determine the variables maintaining problem behavior in people with developmental disabilities (Matson et al., 2005). The Questions About

Behavioral Function (QABF) (Matson &Vollmer, 1995) is a 25-item rating scale that identifies the functions of maladaptive behavior. Matson and colleagues (2005) found that participants with behavior problems (i.e., aggression and self-injury) during mealtime and with food refusal were more likely to demonstrate problem behavior maintained by escape than people who stole food, demonstrated pica, or demonstrated rumination. In contrast, people with pica and rumination were more likely to have automatically reinforced problem behavior than other problems. Similarly, those people showing food refusal were more likely than those in other groups to demonstrate higher scores on the Tangible scale, indicating that their behavior was maintained by tangible reinforcement.

In summary, interviews, questionnaires, and direct observations can provide important information about the potential antecedents, setting events, and consequences that can be targeted in a more formal functional analysis. These methods can also be viewed as a sufficient and reliable step in the identification of function and subsequent development of an intervention plan. When an intervention is not successful, more information would then be gathered, perhaps through functional analysis, to revise the understanding of the maintaining factors and the related intervention plan. Therefore, indirect assessments such as interviews or questionnaires may be a more appropriate first step in identifying the presence and possible function of a feeding problem. Nevertheless, when the function of mealtime problem behavior appears unclear, experimental analyses may be more helpful than indirect measures.

Medical Considerations and Treatment

There is currently an ongoing debate whether children with ASD have higher rates of gastrointestinal disease than typically developing children (Buie et al., 2010; Whitehouse, Maybery, Wray, & Hickey, 2011). However, recent research in this area has yielded inconclusive results because many studies were poorly controlled and reported anecdotal information (Buie et al., 2010). Despite this dilemma, many children with ASD do experience gastrointestinal difficulties, particularly when there is food refusal and selectivity. Some other medical conditions that exacerbate feeding disorders in children with ASD are constipation, gastroesophageal reflux, food allergies, and motility disorders (Laud et al., 2009; Molly & Manning-Courtney, 2003). Constipation, a common side effect of a low-fiber diet, is typically easily treated with laxatives (e.g., Miralax). Gastroesophageal reflux disease (GERD) can contribute to food refusal via pain associated with caustic gastric fluid in the esophagus (Furta et al., 2007). Fortunately GERD can be medically controlled with proton inhibitors (PPI) (e.g., Prilosec, Prevacid, Nexium) or H2 blockers (e.g., Zantac, Pepcide). Common food allergies in children are milk, egg, and peanuts (Wood, 2003), usually treated with an elimination diet once identified through radioallergosorbent tests (RASTs) and skin tests (Wood, 2003). While less common motility disorders can lead to vomiting and delayed emptying, medical therapies are somewhat limited but include smaller and more frequent meals during the day and promotility agents (e.g., erythromycin, Reglan).

TREATMENT OF FOOD REFUSAL AND SELECTIVITY IN CHILDREN WITH AUTISM SPECTRUM DISORDER

Consequence-Based Treatments

Many behavioral feeding interventions have relied on consequence-based procedures, either contingent on desirable eating responses or specific mealtime problems.

Escape Extinction

The majority of the empirical support for treating food selectivity/refusal in children with ASD comes from single-case studies employing specific behavioral contingencies. Although many feeding problems have been researched (rapid eating, pica, inadequate caloric intake), most studies have concerned food selectivity. As noted previously, the maintaining operant variable in food refusal or food selectivity is often negative reinforcement (Babbitt et al., 1994; Piazza et al., 2003). Accordingly, escape extinction (EE) has been a popular intervention (Ahearn, Kerwin, Eicher, Shantz, & Swearingin, 1996; Babbitt et al., 1994; Kozlowski et al., 2011; Piazza et al., 2003). One type of EE is *nonremoval of the spoon*, in which a caregiver presents a spoon of food to a child's lip and keeps it there or persists until the child opens his or her mouth and accepts the food. A second type of EE, *physical guidance*, has the caregiver apply gentle pressure on the child's mandibular joint as a prompt for the child to open his or her mouth and accept the food.

Escape Extinction Combined With Reinforcement

"Bursting," or increase in refusal behavior and possible appearance of collateral behaviors (i.e., expelling, vomiting, and packing) after initiating EE can be attenuated with positive reinforcement or noncontingent delivery of preferred stimuli. Piazza, Patel, Gulotta, Sevin, and Layer (2003), as an example, evaluated whether reinforcement alone without EE could increase food acceptance by three children who had food refusal. The study found that reinforcement alone was not effective in increasing food acceptance; however, it was effective in reducing overall collateral behaviors, such as disruptions, expulsions, and vomiting when combined with EE. In a replication and extension of this study, Reed et al. (2004) compared noncontingent reinforcement (NCR), NCR plus EE, and EE alone. The results were similar to the Piazza et al. (2003) study in that NCR alone did not increase food acceptance but reduced collateral refusal behaviors to lower levels than the no-reinforcement conditions.

Motivating Operations

Manipulating the relative states of satiation and deprivation (motivating operations) associated with preferred stimuli (Bachmeyer, 2009) is a strategy that offers some interesting potential in enhancing reinforcement-based strategies for treating food selectivity without having to implement EE. Levin and Carr (2001) examined four children with ASD and food selectivity across several treatment conditions in which they manipulated reinforcement for nonpreferred foods and the children's access to preferred foods prior to their meals with nonpreferred foods. The results of the study indicated that when a child was restricted from preferred foods prior to the meal with nonpreferred foods, the child was more likely to accept nonpreferred foods when reinforcement was provided for food acceptance in the meal. Bachmeyer (2010) replicated this study with a 2½-year-old girl with developmental delays and gastric tube dependence. Before meal sessions with noncontingent reinforcement for food acceptance, tube feedings were reduced by 50% of normal, full calorie requirements. This procedure increased the toddler's food acceptance of age-appropriate textured food and reduced her overall dependence on gastric tube feeds. It appears, then, that various motivating operations can enhance reinforcement procedures without EE.

Antecedent-Based Treatments

An antecedent-based approach to food selectivity and refusal is intended to prevent interfering behaviors and promote food acceptance independent of contingent consequence procedures.

Simultaneous Presentation

Simultaneous presentation consists of pairing a preferred food with a nonpreferred food. In the studies described next the researchers evaluated slightly different presentation formats. Piazza et al. (2002) studied three children with ASD by comparing contingent presentation of preferred food for consuming a nonpreferred food to simultaneous presentation of preferred food with nonpreferred food. In the simultaneous condition the nonpreferred food was often covered by a preferred food (e.g., a chip was placed on top of a piece of broccoli). For two of the three children, the simultaneous presentation worked more effectively when compared to contingent presentation (EE was not needed to achieve this effect). Unfortunately, the other child required EE to increase acceptance of a novel food. In another study, Ahearn (2003) had a child with ASD dip the nonpreferred food (i.e., vegetables) into a preferred condiment to increase acceptance. Finally, Buckley and Newchock (2005) examined a 9-year-old female with autism who packed and/or pocketed nonpreferred or new foods presented to her. To treat her packing, the authors ground a preferred food (i.e., cookies) into a nonpreferred food and were able to increase acceptance of nonpreferred food and reduce packing of the food. All three of these studies demonstrated that when a child with ASD accepts highly preferred foods, there are other potential treatment options available other than consequence-based behavioral treatments.

Behavioral Momentum

Behavioral momentum is usually characterized by high-probability instructional sequences where a series (i.e., usually 3 to 5) of high-p requests (i.e., tasks with a high probability of compliance, such as acceptance of an empty spoon) are followed by a low-p request (i.e., a task that is not likely to be complied with, such as acceptance of food on a spoon for a child with food refusal). Patel et al. (2007) used a high-p/low-p request sequence to increase food acceptance in a child with ASD by presenting an empty spoon to her three times (high-p request)

followed by a spoon containing nonpreferred food (low-p request). At discharge the child was eating four foods from each of the main food groups (i.e., protein, starch, fruit, and vegetable) all at age-appropriate portions. A notable difference in this study compared to a similar study by Dawson et al. (2003) was that the participant in Patel et al. engaged in passive refusal (refusal with no active behavior), whereas in the latter study, the participant engaged in active refusal. In Dawson et al. the authors did not find that behavioral momentum was effective in increasing food acceptance, but the participants in the Dawson et al. study engaged in active refusal (i.e., head turns, mouth covers, and disruptions).

Fading Procedures

Knox, Rue, Wildenger, Lamb, and Luiselli (2012) evaluated intervention with a 16-year-old youth with autism and long-standing food selectivity to increase acceptance of novel foods in a classroom setting. Teachers first presented small amounts of nonpreferred food with contingent verbal attention and delivery of preferred items following consumption. Through demand fading, the amount of food required for reinforcement was increased gradually to regular portion sizes.

Several studies have also looked at increasing the variety of liquids children with ASD will consume and how they will consume those liquids. Hagopian et al. (1996) faded liquid in a syringe to an open cup in a 12-year-old child with ASD. The authors employed backward chaining and fading components to shape swallowing to accepting liquid from a cup. Similarly, Luiselli, Ricciardia, and Gilligan (2005) treated a 4-year-old girl with ASD who would only drink a milk supplement, Pediasure®, and refused full-strength milk. The fading intervention slowly increased the concentration of milk to Pediasure® until the child was drinking 100% milk.

Group Outcome Studies

There is a paucity of research that has examined the overall short- and long-term outcomes of children with ASD and food selectivity in large group studies. Laud et al. (2009) conducted a 5-year chart review of 46 children with ASD, 3–12 years old, who were enrolled in a 6- to 8-week intensive, interdisciplinary feeding program. The researchers found significant improvements from admission to discharge for food acceptance, refusal behavior, and grams consumed. They also reported follow-up data from parents at intervals of 1–3 years and greater than 3 years from discharge. The parents reported gains across several feeding domains such as increased texture, greater variety, and less mealtime refusal behavior. The majority of parents also endorsed that they would recommend the program to other parents. Another finding was that 40% of parents reported that they no longer needed to implement the behavioral feeding protocol 3 years later.

In a recently published small group outcome study, Sharp, Jaquess, Morton, and Miles (2011) conducted a retrospective chart review of 13 children diagnosed with ASD and severe food selectivity who received behavioral intervention to improve feeding. The study reported increased variety of type and texture of food the children would eat, amounts of food eaten, as well as less refusal behavior. A self-report questionnaire administered to caregivers at the end of the treatment revealed high scores of satisfaction and acceptance of the treatment. A 17-month follow-up via phone and direct observation revealed good maintenance of the treatment gains in acceptance and increased variety of food consumptions.

CONCLUSION

Food selectivity and refusal are commonly identified problems in children with ASD. The biobehavioral model presented in this chapter provides a roadmap for assessment and treatment (see Fig. 11.2), given the complexity and multifactorial origins of these feeding problems. We emphasize that an interdisciplinary team approach will insure that the entire child's behavioral, social, and medical issues are assessed, thereby increasing the probability for a more favorable outcome.

In general there are three main factors to be considered when treating food selectivity in a child with ASD. First, the severity of the child's ASD symptoms could greatly affect a child's progress in increasing food variety and decreasing refusals. We suggest that children who had intense and frequent early intervention in the areas of functional communication and social skills are going to respond more favorably to behavioral treatments for their feeding issues. They should also have less problematic behaviors to manage outside and inside of the meal context. The second concern is resolving potential medical issues before implementing behavioral interventions. For example, a laxative to help with constipation or reflux medications to address eating-related pain highlight the contribution of medical care. As part of interdisciplinary and/or multidisciplinary feeding evaluation, a child with ASD and food selectivity should have a thorough medical examination to rule out any possible medical conditions such as constipation, structural swallowing issues, food allergies, and gastrointestinal issues (e.g., reflux, vomiting, Crohn disease, etc.). Finally, environmental contingencies play a major role in etiology and maintenance of most food selectivity issues in children with ASD. It is in this area that behavioral interventions can have a profound impact on changing the course of a child with ASD and severe food selectivity.

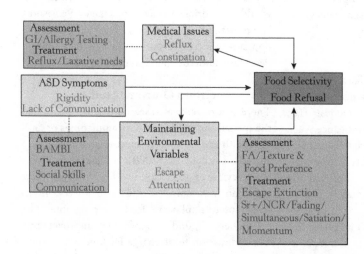

FIGURE 11.2. A Biobehavioral Model of Children with ASD in the Assessment and Treatment of Food Selectivity.

REFERENCES

Ahearn, W. H. (2003). Using simultaneous presentation to increase vegetable consumption in a mildly selective child with autism. *Journal of Applied Behavior Analysis, 36,* 361–365.

Ahearn, W. H., Castine, T., Nault, K., & Green, G. (2001). An assessment of food acceptance in children with autism or pervasive developmental disorder-not otherwise specified. *Journal of Autism and Developmental Disorders, 31,* 505–511.

Ahearn, W. H., Kerwin, M. E., Eicher, P. S., Shantz, J., & Swearingin, W. (1996). An alternating treatments comparison of two intensive interventions for food refusal. *Journal of Applied Behavior Analysis, 29,* 321–332.

American Psychiatric Association. (2000). *Diagnostic and statistical manual of mental disorders* (4th ed., text re.). Washington, DC: Author.

Archer, L. A., Rosenbaum, P. L., & Streiner, D. L. (1991). The Children's Eating Behavior Inventory: Reliability and validity results. *Journal of Pediatric Psychology, 16,* 629.

Babbitt, R. L., Hoch, T. A., & Coe, D. A. (1994). Behavioral feeding disorders. In D. N. Tuchman & R. S. Walter (Eds.). *Disorders of feeding and swallowing in infants and children.* (pp. 77–95) San Diego, CA: Singular.

Bachmeyer, M. H. (2009). Treatment of selective and inadequate food intake in children: a review and practical guide. *Behavior Analysis in Practice, 2,* 43–50.

Bachmeyer, M. H. (2010). An evaluation of motivating operations in the treatment of food refusal. Doctoral dissertation, University of Iowa, Iowa City, IA. Available at http://ir.uiowa.edu/etd/637.

Bandini, L. G., Anderson, S. E., Curtin, C., Cermak, S., Evans, E. W., Scampini, R.,...Must, A. (2010). Food selectivity in children with autism spectrum disorders and typically developing children. *Journal of Pediatrics, 157,* 259–264.

Borrero, C. S. W., Woods, J. N., Borrero, J. C., Masler, E. A., & Lesser, A. D. (2010). Descriptive analyses of pediatric food refusal and acceptance. *Journal of Applied Behavior Analysis, 43,* 71–88.

Buckley, S. D., & Newchok, D. K. (2005). An evaluation of simultaneous presentations and differential reinforcement with response cost to reduce packing. *Journal of Applied Behavior Analysis, 38,* 305–409.

Buie, T., Campbell, D. B., Fuchs III, G. J., Furta, G. T., Levy, J., Vandewater, J.,...Winter, H. (2010). Evaluation, diagnosis, and treatment of gastrointestinal disorder in individuals with ASDs: A consensus report. *Pediatrics, 125,* 1–18.

Burklow, K. A., Phelps, A. N., Schultz, J. R., McConell, K., & Rudolph, C. (1998). Classifying complex pediatric feeding disorders. *Journal of Pediatric Gastroenterology, 27,* 143–147.

Center for Disease and Prevention (CDC). (2009). Prevalence of autism spectrum disorder–Autism and developmental disabilities monitoring network. United States, 2006. *MMWR Surveillance Summaries, 58,* 1–20.

Dawson, J. E., Piazza, C. C., Sevin, B. M., Gulotta, C. S., Lerman, D., & Kelley, M. L. (2003). Use of the high-probability instructional sequence and escape extinction in a child with food refusal. *Journal of Applied Behavior Analysis, 36,* 105–108.

Field, D., Garland, M., & Williams, K. (2003). Correlates of specific childhood feeding problems. *Journal of Pediatrics and Child Health, 39,* 299–304.

Furta, G. T., Liacouras, C. A., Collins, M. H., Gupta, S. K., Justinich, C., Putnam, P. E.,...Rothenberg, M. E. (2007). Eosincopillic esophagitis in children and adults: A system review and consensus recommendations for diagnosis and treatment. *Gastroenterology, 133,* 1342–1363.

Girolami, P. A., & Scotti, J. R. (2001). Use of analogue functional analysis in the assessing the function of meal time behavior problems. *Education and Training in Mental Retardation and Developmental Disabilities, 36,* 207–223.

Hagopian, L. P., Farrell, D. A., & Amari, A. (1996). Treating total liquid refusal with backward chaining and fading. *Journal of Applied Behavior Analysis, 29,* 573–575.

Hawkins, R. P. (1979). The functions of assessment: implications for selection and development of devices for assessing repertoires in clinical, educational, and other settings. *Journal of Applied Behavior Analysis, 12,* 501–516.

Ibrahim, S. H., Voigt, R. G., Katusic, S. K., Weaver, A. L., & Barbaresi, W. J. (2009). Incidence of gastrointestinal symptoms in children with autism: A population-based study. *Pediatrics, 124,* 680–686.

Kerwin, M. E., Eicher, P. S., & Gelsinger, J. (2005). Parental report of eating problems and gastrointestinal symptoms in children with pervasive developmental disorders. *Children's Health Care, 34,* 217–234.

Knox, M., Rue, H. C., Wildenger, L., Lamb, K., & Luiselli, J. K. (2012). Intervention for food selectivity in a specialized school setting: Teacher implemented prompting, reinforcement, and demand fading for an adolescent student with Autism. *Education and Treatment of Children, 35,* 407–417.

Kozlowski, A. M., Matson, J. L., Fodstad, J. C., & Moree, B. N. (2011). Feeding therapy in a child with autistic disorder: Sequential food presentation. *Clinical Case Studies, 10,* 236–246.

Kuhn, D. E., Girolami, P. A., & Gulotta, C. S. (2007). Feeding disorders. In J. L. Matson (Ed.), Handbook of assessment in persons with intellectual disability (pp. 387–414) San Diego, CA: Elsevier.

Kuhn, D. E., & Matson, J. L. (2002). A validity study of the Screening Tool of Feeding Problems (STEP). *Journal of Intellectual and Developmental Disability, 27,* 161–167.

Laud, R. B., Girolami, P. A., Boscoe, J. H., & Gulotta, C. S. (2009). Treatment outcomes for severe feeding problems in children with autism spectrum disorder. *Behavior Modification, 33*, 520–536.

Ledford, J. L., & Gast, D. L. (2006). Feeding problems in children with autism spectrum disorders: A review. *Focus on Autism and Other Developmental Disabilities, 21*, 153–166.

Levin, L., & Carr, E. G. (2001). Food selectivity and problem behavior in children with developmental disabilities: Analysis and intervention. *Behavior Modification, 25*, 443–470.

Luiselli, J. K., Ricciardi, J. N., & Gilligan, K. (2005). Liquid fading to establish milk consumption by a child with autism. *Behavioral Interventions, 20*, 155–163.

Lukens, C. T., & Linscheid, T. R. (2008). Development and validation of an inventory to assess mealtime behavior problems in children with autism. *Journal of Autism and Developmental Disorders, 38*, 342–352.

Matson, J. L., & Fodstad, J. C. (2009). The treatment of food selectivity and other feeding problems in children with autism spectrum disorders. *Research in Autism Spectrum Disorders, 3*, 455–461.

Matson, J. L., & Kuhn D. E. (2001). Identifying feeding problems in mentally retarded person. Development and reliability of the Screening Tool of Feeding Problems (STEP). *Research in Developmental Disabilities, 22*, 165–172.

Matson, J. L., & Vollmer, T. R. (1995). *User's guide: Questions about behavioral function (QABF).* Los Angeles, CA: Scientific Publishers.

Matson, J. L., Dixon, D. R., Matson, M. L. (2005). Assessing and treating aggression in children and adolescents with developmental disabilities: A 20 year review. *Educational Psychology, 26*, 41–45.

Matson, J. L., Fodstad, J. C., & Dempsey, T. (2009). The relationship of children's feeding problems to core symptoms of autism and PDD-NOS. *Research in Autism Spectrum Disorders, 3*, 759–766.

Molly, C. A., & Manning-Courtney, P. (2003). Prevalance of chronic gasterintenstial symptoms in autism and autism specturm disorder. *Autism, 7*, 165–171.

Munk, D. D., & Repp, A. C. (1994). Behavioral assessment of feeding problems of individuals with severe disabilities. *Journal of Applied Behavior Analysis, 27*, 241–250.

Najdowski, A. C., Wallace, M. D., Doney, J. K., & Ghezzi, P. M. (2003). Parental assessment and treatment of food selectivity in natural settings. *Journal of Applied Behavior Analysis, 36*, 383–386.

Nelson-Gray, R. O, & Hayes, S. C. (1986). *Conceptual foundations of behavioral assessment.* New York, NY: Guilford Press.

O'Neill, R., Horner, R. H., Albin, R. W., Sprague, J. R., Storey, K., & Newton, J. S. (1997). *Functional assessment and program development for problem behavior: A practical handbook (2nd Ed.).* Pacific Grove, CA: Brooks/Co.

Patel, M. R., Piazza, C. C., Santana, C. M., & Volkert, V. M. (2002). An evaluation of food type and texture in the treatment of a feeding problem. *Journal of Applied Behavior Analysis, 35*, 183–186.

Patel, M., Reed, G. K., Piazza, C. C., Mueiller, M., Bachmeyer, M. H., & Layer, S. A. (2007). Use of a high-probability instructional sequence to increase compliance to feeding demand in the absence of escape extinction. *Behavioral Interventions, 22*, 305–310.

Piazza, C. C., Patel, M. R., Gulotta, C. S., Sevin, B. M., & Layer, S. A. (2003). On the relative contributions of positive reinforcement and escape extinction in the treatment of food refusal. *Journal of Applied Behavior Analysis, 36*, 309–324.

Piazza, C. C., Patel, M. R., Santana, C. M., Goh, H., Delia, M. D., & Lancaster, B. M. (2002). An evaluation of simultaneous and sequential presentation of preferred and non-preferred food to treat food selectivity. *Journal of Applied Behavior Analysis, 35*, 259–270.

Piazza, C. C., Fisher, W. W., Brown, K. A., Shore, B. A., Patel, M. R., Katz, R. M.,...Blakely-Smith, A. (2003). Functional analysis of inappropriate mealtime behaviors. *Journal of Applied Behavior Analysis, 36*(2), 187–204.

Reed, G. K., Piazza, C. C., Patel, M. R., Layer, S. A., Bachmeyer, M. H., Bethke, S. D., & Gutshall, K. A. (2004). On the relative contributions of non-contingent reinforcements and escape extinction in the treatment of food refusal. *Journal of Applied Behavior Analysis, 37*, 27–42.

Ronald, A., Happe, F., Bolton, P., Butcher, L. M., Price, T. S., Wheeelwright, S.,... Plomin, R. (2006). Genetic heterogeneity between the three components of the autism spectrum: A twin study. *Journal of American Academy of Child and Adolescent Psychiatry, 45*, 691–699.

Schreck, K. A., & Williams, K. (2006). Food preferences and factors influencing food selectivity for children with autism spectrum disorders. *Research in Developmental Disabilities, 27*, 353–363.

Schreck, K. A., Williams, K., & Smith, A. F. (2004). A comparison of eating behaviors between children with and without autism. *Journal of Autism and Developmental Disorders, 35*, 433–438.

Seiverling, L. J., Hendy, H. M., & Wiliams, K. E. (2011). Child and parent variables associated with texture problems in children's feeding. *Journal of Developmental and Physical Disabilities, 23*, 303–311.

Sharp, W. G., Jaquess, D. L., & Lukens, C. T. (2013). Multi-method assessment of feeding problems among children with autism spectrum disorders. *Research in Autism Spectrum Disorders, 7*, 56–65.

Sharp, W. G., Jaquess, D. L., Morton, J. F., & Miles, A. G. (2011). A retrospective chart review of dietary diversity and feeding behavior of children with autism spectrum disorder before and after admission to a day-treatment program. *Focus on Autism and Other Developmental Disabilities, 26*, 37–48.

Whitehouse, A. J. O., Maybery, M., Wray, J. A., & Hickey, M. (2011). No association between early gastrointestinal problems and autistic-like traits in the general population. *Developmental Medicine and Child Neurology, 5,* 457–462.

Williams, K. E., Gibbons, B. G., & Schreck, K. A. (2005). Comparing selective eaters with and without developmental disabilities. *Journal of Developmental and Physical Disabilities, 17,* 299–309.

Wood, R. A. (2003). The natural history of food allergy. *Pediatrics, 111,* 1631–1637.

12

Sleep Problems

V. MARK DURAND

It is now manifestly clear that sleep is a vitally important biological activity necessary for proper mental and physical health. Experiencing inadequate amounts of sleep affects multiple systems in the body that can increase the risk of cardiovascular and metabolic disease (Barclay & Gregory, 2013). In addition, poor sleep impacts academic and behavioral performance in school (Bates, 2011) as well as overall emotional states (Berger, Miller, Seifer, Cares, & Lebourgeois, 2012). This chapter reviews the research on sleep among persons with autism spectrum disorder (ASD), including how inadequate amounts of sleep can impact the individual with ASD as well as the rest of the family, important information about assessing sleep difficulties, and evidence-based treatments for many of these difficulties. Reviewed next will be research on the nature of sleep and the more common sleep problems experienced by persons with ASD. An understanding of the basic biology behind sleep is important for identifying different sleep disorders as well as designing appropriate interventions.

SLEEP AND ITS DISORDERS

Sleep Cycles

The human brain has evolved to influence major systems to go through daily cycles, including changes in temperature, hormones, and sleep-wake cycles. When sleep patterns follow the typical cycle, we tend to be awake approximately 16 hours during the day and are asleep for 8 hours at night, although the number of hours asleep is higher in young children and lower among older adults (see Fig. 12.1). The range of sleep needs illustrated is considered just an average. Typically, a diagnosis of a sleep problem is not determined by the number of hours asleep *per se*, but by how sleep affects the individual at other times (i.e., daytime *sequela*). If, for example, a child

only sleeps 7 hours per night but is not difficult to awaken in the morning and does not appear sleepy during the day, then this would not be considered a problem. However, if a person sleep 10–12 hours per night but has trouble getting up in the morning and needs naps during the day, this would be considered problematic. I return to this type of sleep problem in the section on assessment and discuss possible causes and treatment implications.

During sleep the human brain goes through four distinctly different stages (Rowley & Badr, 2012). Three of these stages (labeled N1, N2, and N3) occur during what is referred to as non–rapid eye movement (NREM) sleep (Iber, Ancoli-Israel, Chesson, & Quan, 2007). Stage N1 sleep represents the brain's transitional period to deeper sleep where the person has some awareness of the external environment. If uninterrupted, the person transitions into stage N2 and then ultimately stage N3 sleep—the "deep" or "slow-wave" sleep. During this deep sleep stage the person is relatively unaware of the external environment and it can be extremely difficult to awaken someone in this stage of sleep. It is generally believed that stage N3 sleep plays a restorative role for the brain and provides energy conservation and the recuperation of nervous system functioning (Siegel, 2005).

After a period of time, the brain cycles out of deep sleep (stage N3) and moves into rapid eye movement (REM) sleep (Peigneux, Urbain, & Schmitz, 2012). It is this stage of sleep where, if awakened, people will often report dreams. During REM sleep one's limbs are paralyzed (or atonic)—a possible evolutionary development to prevent people from hurting themselves moving about during this period of brain activity. REM sleep may help with emotion regulation and may play a role in learning and memory (Maquet, 2001; Siegel, 2005). The brain repeats these cycles throughout the sleep period. Early in the

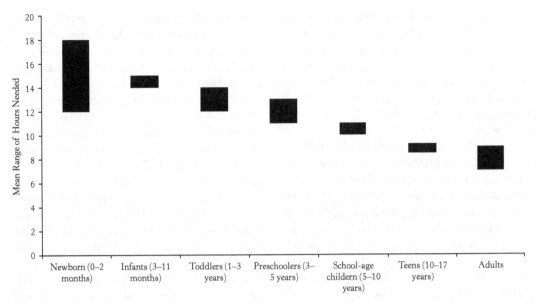

FIGURE 12.1.   Range of sleep needs by age.

Source: National Sleep Foundation, 2011

evening the brain spends more time during stages of NREM sleep and then as sleep duration increases, the length of time spent in REM sleep increases. However, in persons who are sleep deprived, they will tend to move more quickly to REM sleep—a possible sign of the importance of this stage of sleep to our health (Rowley & Badr, 2012). There are occasional points during the sleep phases where there are "partial awakenings"—times when an individual will wake up for a brief period of time. Young children will on average experience one or two of these events at night, and they increase as the person ages. Older adults will often have numerous partial wakings, which can lead to overall nonrestorative sleep. Typically the person has no memory of these events the next morning. These partial awakenings may play a role in the later development of night waking in children (Durand, 2014).

The brain's biological clock (the suprachiasmatic nucleus or SCN) is responsible for a variety of systems in the body, including the regulation of temperature, hormones, and our sleep cycles (Peigneux et al., 2012; Rowley & Badr, 2012). Under typical conditions the SCN will regulate the neurohormone melatonin to be released at night and will slow down its production in the morning—providing a 24-hour sleep-wake cycle. However, some individuals have disrupted sleep cycles—called circadian rhythm disorders—which results in their sleeping "at the wrong

times" (e.g., not falling asleep until 2:00 a.m. or waking up for the day at 4:00 a.m.). This is of particular importance in ASD because evidence suggests that this circadian cycle may be disrupted in this population and may account for the increased prevalence of sleep problems in this group (Glickman, 2010).

Prevalence of Sleep Problems in Autism Spectrum Disorder

Estimating the prevalence of sleep disorders in ASD is complicated by the use of nonstandardized definitions in most prevalence studies (Richdale & Schreck, 2009). In other words, research in this area typically does not rely on official diagnostic criteria such as those detailed in versions of the *Diagnostic and Statistical Manual of Mental Disorders*, fifth edition (*DSM-5*; American Psychiatric Association, 2013), *International Classification of Diseases*, 10th edition (*ICD-10*; World Health Organization, 1993), or *International Classification of Sleep Disorders–2* (*ICSD-2*; American Academy of Sleep Medicine, 2005). However, there are a large number of studies that, despite their use of varying definitions, concur on the increased prevalence of sleep problems in persons with ASD, usually as reported by family members (e.g., Couturier et al., 2005; Goldman, Richdale, Clemons, & Malow, 2012; Johnson, Giannotti, & Cortesi, 2009; Johnson & Malow, 2008; Richdale & Schreck, 2009).

The prevalence of sleep problems in the general population varies somewhat with age. Bedtime problems and night waking occur among almost 40% of infants and in 25% to 50% of preschoolers; bedtime resistance is observed in from 15% to 27% of school-aged children (Owens & Mindell, 2011). These percentages increase for children with special needs. For example, 25% to 50% of school-aged children and adolescents with attention-deficit/hyperactivity disorder (ADHD) display difficulty initiating and maintaining sleep (Cassoff, Wiebe, & Gruber, 2012). Research on the prevalence of sleep problems in children with ASD suggests an even higher range from 50% to 80% (Couturier et al., 2005; Krakowiak, Goolin-Jones, Hertz-Picciotto, Croen, & Hansen, 2008; Richdale & Schreck, 2009). In one longitudinal total population study on the prevalence of sleep problems in children with ASD, researchers found that chronic insomnia was more than 10 times higher than the rate observed among typically developing children (Sivertsen, Posserud, Gillberg, Lundervold, & Hysing, 2011). In addition, this and other studies tend to find that children with ASD develop more sleep problems as they grow older and they tend to continue to experience sleep problems over time. Conversely, the sleep problems of typically developing children often remit over time (e.g., Goldman, Richdale, Clemons, & Malow, 2012; Sivertsen et al., 2011).

The higher prevalence of sleep disorders observed among persons with ASD appears to be partly caused by the overlap of neurobiological influences on both sleep and ASD. For example, abnormalities in the GABA (an inhibitory neurotransmitter) and melatonin (a brain hormone) appear in both sleep disorders and ASD (Johnson & Malow, 2008). Disruptions in these systems can lead to poor quality sleep and changes in the circadian sleep-wake cycles, which can appear as resistance at bedtime and sleeping at other times during the day.

Sleep Problems in Autism Spectrum Disorder

The official diagnostic system for sleep disorders includes eight major categories: insomnia, sleep-related breathing disorders, hypersomnias of central origin (the inability to stay awake during the day, such as in narcolepsy), circadian rhythm sleep disorders (sleeping at the wrong times), parasomnias (abnormal events during sleep such as sleep terrors, sleepwalking), sleep-related movement disorders, isolated symptoms and normal variants, and other sleep disorders (American Academy of Sleep Medicine, 2005). Under those categories are typical problems experienced by children and adults (trouble falling asleep at night) as well as relatively rare sleep-related problems. Persons with ASD do not have unique sleep disorders compared to those without ASD, although as mentioned, the prevalence of their sleep problems is significantly higher. An extensive review of all of these sleep-related difficulties is beyond the scope of this chapter and therefore the focus here will be on the more common and routine sleep problems. This emphasis is consistent with the evidence-based intervention research with those with ASD (Turner & Johnson, 2013; Vriend, Corkum, Moon, & Smith, 2011). These sleep-related difficulties include bedtime disturbances, night waking, sleep schedule problems, nightmares, and sleep terrors.

Dyssomnias are disturbances in the amount, timing, or quality of sleep. The main problems reported among both young children and adolescents with ASD tend to be insomnia with prolonged sleep latency (time to fall asleep), disruption at bedtime, decreased sleep efficiency (decreased time asleep/time in bed), decreased total sleep time, and decreased sleep duration (Goldman et al., 2012; Richdale & Schreck, 2009). This includes disruptive or nondisruptive night waking. As will be seen in the section on assessment, understanding the contributing factors associated with these sleep problems is essential for designing an appropriate intervention plan. For example, the inability to fall asleep at night could be the result of a problem with the person's circadian rhythms. As previously described, evidence suggests that these cycles may be disrupted in many individuals with ASD and could contribute to their irregular sleep patterns (Glickman, 2010). However, the inability to fall asleep at night or frequent night waking could also be a function of poor sleep hygiene (Malow et al., 2009). Sleep hygiene refers to activities during the day that interfere with sleep and can include drinking caffeinated beverages too soon before sleep, watching television or working on a computer right before bedtime, and not having a regular bedtime routine. Some bedtime difficulties also resemble daytime challenging behaviors (called *behavioral insomnia*) that serve social functions such as a child wanting attention at bedtime or not wanting to stop playing a game to go to sleep (Durand, 2008). In addition, levels of anxiety may also be related to problems with sleep, although the direction of this effect (i.e., does anxiety lead to more problems with sleep or vice versa) is not yet clear (Rzepecka, McKenzie, McClure, & Murphy, 2011). I return to the reasons behind disrupted sleep in the section on assessment.

Although there is scant research on sleep-related breathing disorders (e.g., apnea) or on sleep-related movement disorders (e.g., restless leg syndrome) in ASD, they do appear to occur in this population at levels comparable to others without ASD (Williams, Sears, & Allard, 2004). It is important to assess for these types of sleep problems because they can reveal why someone might have a difficult time being awakened in the morning after what appears to be a good amount of sleep (Malow, McGrew, Harvey, Henderson, & Stone, 2006). Interrupted breathing or excessive limb movement during sleep can cause a person to awaken briefly without awareness numerous times throughout the night (partial wakings), and this disturbed sleep can cause waking in the morning to be difficult. A medical evaluation of nighttime breathing and limb movement problems is essential in order to improve sleep and avoid potentially dangerous outcomes, especially resulting from interrupted breathing.

Disturbances in arousal and sleep stage transition that intrudes into the sleep process are referred to as parasomnias. These include nightmares, sleep terrors, sleep talking (formally called "somniloquy"), and sleepwalking (formally called "somnambulism") (Durand, 2006; Durand & Christodulu, 2003). Although they may present themselves in a similar manner (e.g., child crying out after a period of sleep), nightmares need to be distinguished from sleep terrors because intervention differs for these two nighttime disturbances. Nightmares are disturbing dreams that awaken the sleeper. Because nightmares occur during REM sleep, the person is essentially paralyzed and not able to walk around or talk. The crying or screaming that occurs at this time is when the person awakens from the bad dream. In contrast, sleep terrors occur while the child is still asleep and usually begin with a piercing scream. The child is extremely upset, often sweating, and frequently has a rapid heartbeat. On the surface, sleep terrors appear to resemble nightmares because the child cries and appears frightened. However, sleep terrors occur during NREM sleep and therefore are not caused by frightening dreams (Durand, 2006). During sleep terrors, children are asleep and cannot

be easily awakened and comforted, as they can during a nightmare. Children typically do not remember sleep terror events the next morning despite their often dramatic effect on the observer. As can be seen in Figure 12.2, nightmares occur during REM (or dream) sleep while the other parasomnias are primarily observed during deeper stages of NREM sleep. There is conflicting evidence for the prevalence of parasomnias among children with ASD, although most studies in this area suggest that they may be more frequent in this population as well (Liu, Hubbard, Fabes, & Adam, 2006; Schreck & Mulick, 2000; Williams, Sears, & Allard, 2004). There is some evidence that this increased prevalence of parasomnias declines in adolescence for those with ASD (Goldman et al., 2012).

Impact of Disturbed Sleep on Persons With Autism Spectrum Disorder and Their Families

Chronic and seriously disturbed sleep has multiple negative consequences on the person affected. For example, there is emerging evidence that there is a relationship between specific sleep problems (i.e., sleep onset delay and sleep duration) and symptoms of ASD (Schreck, Mulick, & Smith, 2004; Tudor, Hoffman, & Sweeney, in press). One study found that sleep onset delay (taking longer than 15–20 minutes to fall asleep at bedtime) was a strong predictor of communication deficit, stereotyped behavior, and ASD severity (Tudor et al., in press). In addition, sleep problems appear to increase problem behaviors displayed by these individuals (e.g., Goldman et al., 2011; Henderson, Barry, Bader, & Jordan, 2011; Park et al., 2012). In one study, for example, more than 1,000 children with ASD (ages 4 to 10 years) were assessed for the presence of sleep difficulties as well as daytime behavior problems (Sikora, Johnson, Clemons, & Katz, 2012). This research found that children with ASD who also had sleep problems had more internalizing (e.g., anxiety) and externalizing (e.g., aggression, tantrums) behavior problems than children without sleep difficulties. Although there is as yet little research on the impact of sleep problems in those with ASD on learning and memory, research on typically developing individuals suggests that sleep disruption can negatively impact these important cognitive processes (Maquet, 2001; Peigneux et al., 2012).

In addition to the impact of poor sleep on individuals with ASD, research finds that these nighttime

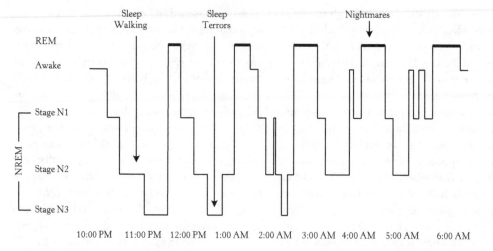

FIGURE 12.2. Sleep stages and associated sleep problems.

disruptions can also negatively impact family members. Research suggests that the disrupted sleep of children with ASD will, in turn, disrupt the sleep of other family members (Lopez-Wagner, Hoffman, Sweeney, Hodge, & Gilliam, 2008; Schreck et al., 2004). The challenges posed by a child with ASD during the day such as difficulties with mealtimes, transitions, and routines as well as the extra time required to assist with the child's needs can by itself result in significant stress on these families (Abbeduto et al., 2004; Dumas, Wolf, Fisman, & Culligan, 1991; Durand, Hieneman, Clarke, Wang, & Rinaldi, 2013). With difficulties at bedtime and/or frequent night waking, disrupted sleep creates significant strain to an already difficult home life. There appears to be a strong relationship between a child's poor sleep and maternal sleep, stress, and mental health. For example, one study found that mothers of children with ASD were more negatively affected by their child's poor sleep compared to mothers of children without ASD (Hodge, Hoffman, Sweeney, & Riggs, 2013). There appeared to be a direct effect of these nightly disruptions on mothers' well-being. This research suggests that improvements in child sleep should be a major priority for the child as well as for other members of the family.

ASSESSMENT OF SLEEP PROBLEMS

Initial screening for the presence of sleep problems can occur through the administration of one of several sleep questionnaires, including the Pediatric Sleep Questionnaire (Chervin, Hedger,

Dillon, & Pituch, 2000) and the Children's Sleep Habits Questionnaire (CSHQ) (Owens, Spirito, & McGuinn, 2000). This type of screening allows the clinician to determine the types of sleep problems that are occurring. For example the CSHQ asks whether a child falls asleep in own bed, falls asleep in others' bed, or needs parent in room to sleep. It also asks questions about sleep onset delay, for example, how long does the child take to fall asleep? As noted previously, most people fall asleep within 15 to 20 minutes of going to bed. Taking longer to fall asleep is assumed to be problematic. Other questions about sleep address sleep duration, sleep anxiety, night wakings, breathing problems, daytime sleepiness, and/or the presence of parasomnias.

Once the sleep problems are identified it is typically recommended that parents complete a sleep diary (see Fig. 12.3). The sleep diary is designed to help parents check the times at which the child is asleep and awake during the day and at night. A sleep diary yields useful information that can assist with assessing the sleep problem and designing an intervention plan. For example, in the sleep diary presented you can see that the child was asleep on Tuesday evening but awakened at 3:00 a.m., stayed awake until 7:00 a.m., and then took a nap from 7:00 a.m. to 11:00 a.m. The child then was awake from 11:00 a.m. until 10:00 p.m. On subsequent days the pattern is different with the child awakening at different times in the morning, sometimes as early as 2:00 a.m. or 4:00 a.m., sometimes falling back to sleep and then sometimes staying up the rest of the day.

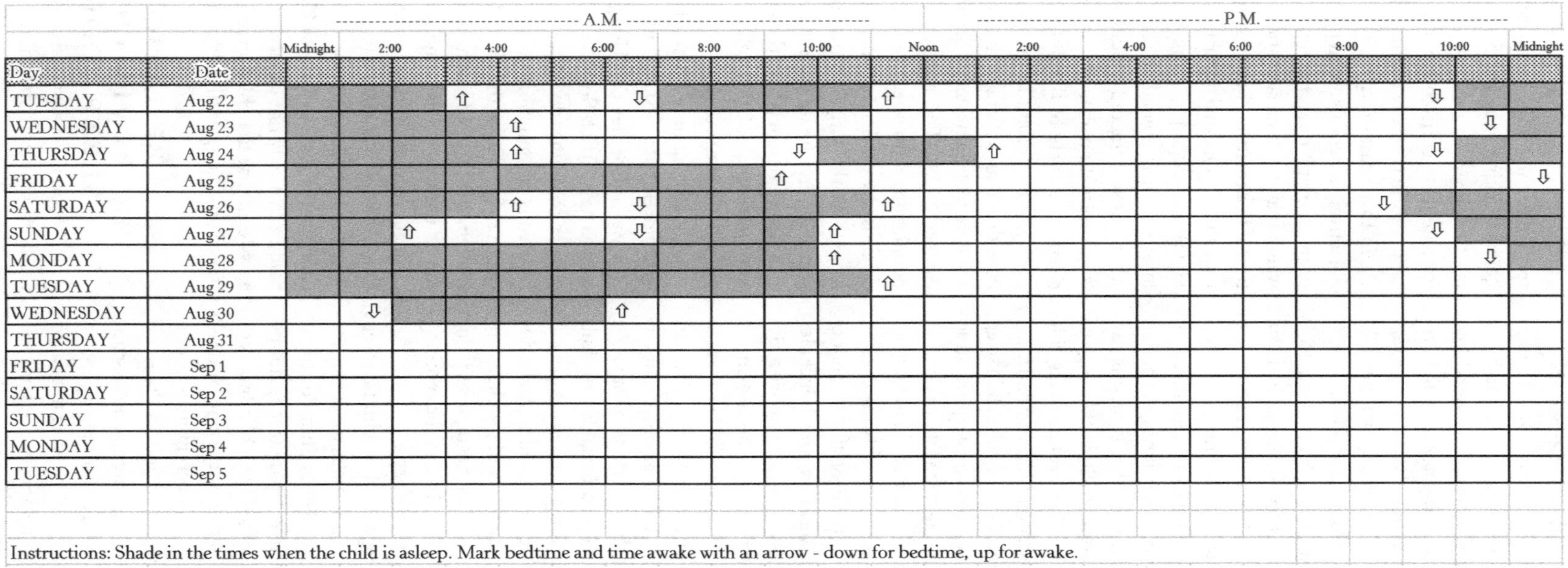

Instructions: Shade in the times when the child is asleep. Mark bedtime and time awake with an arrow - down for bedtime, up for awake.

FIGURE 12.3. Sleep diary.

We look for a number of things in this diary. For example, are bedtime problems associated with napping during the day? If the child is catching up on his or her sleep during the day, then he or she will not be tired and will have a difficult time falling asleep in the evening. Another pattern that is assessed is if there is a regular bedtime. Again, Figure 12.3 reveals that the child went to bed one night at 10:00 p.m., another night at 11:00 p.m., and once not until midnight. We would follow up with the family to see if there is a regular bedtime because regular bedtimes and bedtime routines are part of good sleep hygiene and can be important intervention strategies in and of themselves. In addition, the overall mean number of hours asleep during the period of the assessment is calculated so that clinicians can see if the person sleeps on average within the range of others his or her age (see Fig. 12.1). Additionally, this number is used if an intervention called *sleep restriction* is recommended since it requires having the child sleep only about 90% of his or her average sleep duration during each night. If there are questions about possible breathing problems during the evening, a formal sleep evaluation is always recommended. This involves an overnight sleep study at a sleep lab. Staff will conduct polysomnographic (PSG) evaluation, which includes assessment of airflow, leg movements, brainwave activity, eye movements, and heart activity. The assessment of airflow will be used to determine whether there is obstructed breathing during periods of sleep. This can be as simple as snoring or as serious as sleep apnea in which breathing ceases for short periods of time. As mentioned previously, interrupted breathing or limb movement problems during sleep can cause a person to wake up briefly, fall back to sleep, and typically not remember the incident. These types of problems are suspected when a parent describes having a very difficult time awakening his or her child in the morning despite having 8 or more hours of sleep.

Sometimes parental report of a child's sleep using a sleep diary may be incomplete, especially for children who have nondisruptive bedtime or night waking problems. For example, a parent may not be aware that a child is taking longer than 20 minutes to fall asleep at night if the child is not crying or does not get out of bed. In addition, a parent may not be aware that the child has awakened and has been up for some time in the evening if there is no disruption. In some children or youth with the Asperger's type of ASD, the individual might be lying in bed for some time perseverating about some favorite interest or worrying about something that happened that day

in school. For those on the Kanner's type end of the spectrum, children or youth can sometimes be found quietly rocking back and forth or even lightly banging their heads in order to self-soothe. It is difficult for parents to constantly monitor their child's sleep, especially in the early morning hours.

In these cases *actigraphy* can be a useful tool to objectively assess sleep. Actigraphy involves the use of an actigraph or an instrument resembling a wristwatch that contains sensors allowing for the collection of information about the movement of the limbs (Sadeh, 2011). After wearing the device for several nights, the actigraph is connected to a computer and information is uploaded about the periods of time when movement did or did not occur. Collecting this information can give a rough estimate of the sleep-wake cycle of the individual without actually having to be present in the room. It is important to note that at an actigraph does not always give a fully accurate picture of sleep (Sitnick, Goodlin-Jones, & Anders, 2008). This appears especially true among populations with special needs such as with those diagnosed with ASD (Sadeh, 2011). It is been estimated that the actigraph may under certain circumstances overestimate the total amount of sleep time and sleep efficiency (i.e., the amount of time asleep as a percentage of the time lying in bed). On the other hand, the actigraph can also underestimate the amount of sleep time. Finally, between 10% and 30% of children with ASD do not tolerate wearing the wristwatch-like device (Hodge, Parnell, Hoffman, & Sweeney, 2012). Because of these limitations, it is usually recommended that supplemental measures be used in conjunction with or instead of actigraphy (e.g., using video of the child during the sleep time) (Sadeh, 2011). In addition, there are now "apps" that can be used with smart phones to collect this rough estimate without having to directly touch the child. Once the app is installed (e.g., "Sleep Cycle" for the iPhone), it is turned on and can be slipped under the child's cover sheet and pillow. This can provide information that may not otherwise be accessible to parents (e.g., that the child awakened at 2:00 a.m. and stayed up quietly until 3:30 a.m.).

BEHAVIORAL INTERVENTIONS FOR SLEEP PROBLEMS

This section reviews research on interventions for sleep problems specific to the type of problem exhibited. The common sleep problems displayed by individuals with ASD include disruptive and non-disruptive problems at bedtime, disruptive and non-disruptive night waking, sleeping at the wrong times (circadian rhythm problems), as well as the parasomnias (sleepwalking, sleep talking, sleep terrors, and nightmares).

Sleep Hygiene

The first line of intervention for problems surrounding sleep is to assess and, when warranted, change the person's sleep hygiene (Vriend et al., 2011). As described previously, sleep hygiene refers to an assortment of behaviors and activities that can interfere with falling asleep at night and that can influence night waking or generally interrupt sleep patterns. A portion of children, youth, and adults with ASD can improve their sleep with just these changes in daytime habits (Durand, 2014, 2008; Malow et al., 2009). In addition, some intervention approaches combine changes in sleep hygiene with other behavioral methods to treat a variety of sleep problems (Adkins et al., 2012; Durand & Christodulu, 2004; Moon, Corkum, & Smith, 2011).

The first aspect of sleep hygiene assessed is if the person has a regular bedtime and a regular time to awaken in the morning. It appears that some individuals with disordered sleep may be sensitive to changes in these schedules and that by regularizing this pattern issues surrounding falling asleep, staying asleep, and even sleep quality may be improved (Souders et al., 2009). A second important aspect of sleep hygiene is having a regular bedtime routine. Maintaining a regular pattern of calming activities prior to bedtime for approximately 30 minutes can signal the brain that bedtime is coming and may assist with falling asleep at the same time each evening. These familiar activities include first washing up and brushing teeth, then changing into pajamas, then reading a favorite story, and so on.

Another recommendation to improve sleep hygiene is restricting activities in bed to those that are sleep related. In other words, getting dressed, listening to relaxing music, or reading a story are all calming actions that can relax the child and signal sleep. This recommendation relies on the principle of *stimulus control*—situations where a behavior (e.g., falling asleep) is triggered by the absence or (in this case) the presence or of some stimulus (e.g., the bed). If other activities like playing games occur in the bed, they may interfere with the bed being a signal only for sleep. For those who have difficulty falling asleep in their own bed, this suggestion is particularly important. Another sleep hygiene recommendation is to make sure that the person does not engage in excessive activity just before bedtime. This suggestion may relate to how our sleep-wake cycles are effected by temperature change because we tend to fall asleep as our temperature cools at night and we awaken in the morning as our temperature warms (Atkinson & Davenne, 2007). It may be that being very active just before bedtime increases body temperature artificially and extends the time to fall asleep. Finally, noise that can be heard in the bedroom, the amount of light in the room, and the room's temperature should all be assessed to determine whether these aspects of the sleep environment possibly contribute to sleep problems.

Once clinicians rule out sleep hygiene as an important influence on sleep disturbances, then the next steps are determining (1) which aspect of sleep needs to be addressed, (2) whether multiple sleep problems are involved and, if so, how to prioritize intervention, and (3) what type of intervention will fit best with the needs of the whole family. The first step is usually determined by parental interview and the assessments described previously. If it is determined that there are multiple concerns (e.g., short sleep duration and disruptive nighttime awaking), then the rule of thumb typically is to select that problem that most interferes with the individual's and the family's quality of life. One exception to this way of prioritizing sleep problems is if the choice is between intervention for bedtime disturbances and night awakening. Some data suggest that if intervention is initiated with bedtime disturbances first, night waking will sometimes resolve itself on its own (Mindell & Durand, 1993). The reverse, however, does not seem to be the case. Finally, the decision about the intervention and any modifications should take into account the needs of the whole family (Durand, 2014). A discussion of this process follows a review of the evidence base for interventions for specific sleep problems (Durand, 2008).

Bedtime Disturbances

Different intervention approaches have some empirical support for improving bedtime disturbances for individuals with ASD (see Table 12.1). The first documented use of a behavioral intervention for an individual with ASD was *standard extinction* for bedtime tantrums (Wolf et al., 1963). This case involved a case study of a 3½-year-old boy with ASD.

TABLE 12.1 BEHAVIORAL INTERVENTIONS FOR SLEEP PROBLEMS IN CHILDREN WITH AUTISM SPECTRUM DISORDER

Sleep Problem	Behavioral Intervention	Research Support	Description
Insomnia/bedtime disturbances	Standard extinction w/ mild punishment and bedtime routine	Wolf, Risley, & Mees, 1963	One child with ASD aged 3.5 years. Study conducted in an inpatient unit. Initial increase in problematic behaviors followed by improvements that were maintained at 6-month follow-up.
	Graduated extinction w/ bedtime routine	Durand, 1996	Two children (one male, one female) with ASD aged 2 and 12 years. Reduced sleep onset latency and bedtime disturbances
	Graduated extinction w/ social story, reinforcement chart, bedtime routine, tokens, and treats	Moore, 2004	One child aged 4 years with ASD, severe learning disabilities, and receptive language delay. Reduction in sleep onset latency and co-sleeping.
	Faded bedtime with response cost and a reward program, education, and sleep hygiene	Moon, Corkum, & Smith, 2011	Three children aged 8–9 years with ASD, reduction in sleep onset latency, small daytime behavior improvements, and parent satisfaction, improvements maintained at 12–week follow-up.
	Children randomly assigned to faded bedtime with response cost ($n = 3$) or bedtime scheduling ($n = 2$)	Piazza, Fisher, & Scherer, 1997	Five children aged 5–8 years with ASD, FBRC treatment yielded significantly greater reduction in disturbed sleep than bedtime scheduling. All children in FBRC group improved; one child in bedtime scheduling group displayed slight improvement, other child showed no improvement, FBRC was superior to bedtime scheduling.
	Sleep restriction and bedtime routine	Christodulu & Durand, 2004	One child aged 4 years with ASD. Number and duration of bedtime disturbances decreased.
	Sleep restriction and sleep hygiene	Durand & Christodulu, 2004	One child aged 4 years with ASD. Number and duration of bedtime disturbances and night waking decreased and child slept somewhat less after intervention.
	Behavioral parent training	Montgomery, Stores, & Wiggs, 2004	21 children aged 2–8 years with ASD. Face-to-face training and booklet-delivered behavioral treatment for sleep problems were equally effective.
	Controlled-release melatonin, singly and combined with cognitive-behavioral therapy	Cortesi, Giannotti, Sebastiani, Panunzi, & Valente, 2012	134 children aged 4–10 years with a diagnosis of autism. Combination of melatonin and CBT was most effective for reducing sleep onset delay and night waking; melatonin therapy alone was more effective than CBT in improving insomnia. Children in the treatment groups were able to initiate and maintain sleep more effectively than those in placebo group.
	4-page sleep education pamphlet for parents	Adkins et al., 2012	36 children aged 2–10 years with ASD. Results show no improvement with use of the sleep education pamphlet alone, although there was a very small improvement in sleep efficiency.

	Parent-based sleep education workshops	Reed et al., 2009	20 families having a child with autism aged 3–10 years. Measures of sleep improved in children and parents reported less daytime behavioral issues, overall parent satisfaction improved.
Night waking	Standard extinction w/ bedtime routines, visual supports, sticker charts, and parent education	Weiskop, Matthews, & Richdale, 2001	One child aged 4.5 with ASD. Co-sleeping and bedtime disturbances in addition to night waking. Study conducted by parent in home, improvements maintained at 12-month follow-up.
	Standard extinction w/ bedtime routines, visual supports, sticker charts, and parent education	Weiskop, Richdale, & Matthews, 2005	Five children with ASD (and five children with fragile X syndrome without ASD) between 3 and 7 years old. Co-sleeping and bedtime disturbances in addition to night waking. Studies conducted by parents in their homes; improvements were maintained at 12-month follow-up.
	Sleep restriction and bedtime routine	Christodulu & Durand, 2004	One child aged 4 years with ASD. Number and duration of night waking decreased.
Night waking along with self-injurious behaviors	Faded bedtime	DeLeon, Fisher, & Marhefka, 2004	4-year-old boy with ASD, study conducted in inpatient unit. Decreased number of night waking and frequency of SIB associated with night waking.
Sleep terrors	Scheduled awakening w/ parent education	Durand, 2002	Three children with ASD aged 3, 5, and 7.5 years. Scheduled awakenings reduced sleep terrors in all three children and total sleep time increased in 2/3 children.
Co-sleeping	Stimulus fading and parent education	Howlin, 1984	One 5-year-old with ASD resulted in overall decrease in sleep onset latency, night waking, and co-sleeping. Improvements in mothers self-report of mental health and marital relationship.
Co-sleeping and difficulty falling asleep, night waking, and early morning awakening	Stimulus fading w/ extinction, sleep hygiene visual supports, and rewards program	Reed et al., 2009	20 children aged 3–10 years with ASD, improvements in sleep habits, daytime behavior, and in total and many insomnia-related scores, night waking did not improve, reduced sleep onset latency was shown by actigraphy.
Disrupted sleep-wake cycle	Chronotherapy	Piazza, Hagopian, Hughes, & Fisher, 1997	One 8-year-old child with ASD, severe developmental delay, and food refusal. Age appropriate sleep time was achieved in 11 days and improvements were maintained at a 4-month follow-up.

Intervention began in a hospital setting (although eventually was transferred to home) and involved simply ignoring the tantrums of this boy and closing his door if he continued to tantrum (punishment). Although he eventually went to bed with less disruption over time, the researchers described his initial tantrums as significant ("The resulting tantrums were quite violent, one series totaling more than one hour," p. 189). From a practical point of view, most families are unable or unwilling to endure this type of disruption, which may account for why this approach is rarely recommended (Durand, 2014). A version of standard extinction, called *graduated extinction*, has been examined in several single-subject design studies (Durand, 1996; Moore, 2004). Graduated extinction involves spending increasingly longer amounts of time ignoring the cries and protestations of a child at bedtime. It is a variation of the typical approach of simply ignoring the crying, and it is an adaptation that many parents find more acceptable because they are able to check on their child periodically. However, the evidence base for this intervention is still emerging in the field of ASD.

An additional class of intervention for bedtime problems includes some version of modifying the child's sleep schedule. *Faded bedtime* creates a later bedtime for the person and if sleep does not occur, then the person is removed from the bed (Piazza & Fisher, 1991). If sleep occurs within a set period of time, then an earlier bedtime is attempted (faded). A related intervention is called *sleep restriction*, and it involves having the person sleep only about 90% of his or her average sleep time per day either by creating a later bedtime or an earlier time to awaken (Durand, 2008; 2014). Once the person is going to bed with limited disruption, the schedule is modified to approximate a typical schedule appropriate for the family.

Chronotherapy involves systematically delaying bedtime (e.g., 2 hours) each evening but allowing the person to be in bed for a typical amount of time (Piazza, Hagopian, Hughes, & Fisher, 1997). After several days the child is being put to bed during the day and kept awake at night. Eventually the goal is to move the schedule through the full cycle until bedtime is now at the desired time. What may be occurring in these treatments is that the bedtime (and sometimes the time to awaken) is modified so that the individual is more likely to be sleepy when it is time for bed, increasing the likelihood that a bedtime routine will be more successful in leading to sleep.

There is a slightly larger evidence base for using this general approach to improving bedtime problems (see Table 12.1). It is also important to point out that unlike extinction approaches, this type of intervention can be relatively errorless because the person is somewhat sleep deprived at bedtime and therefore he or she is less likely to create a significant disturbance. However, these interventions can be difficult for families to carry out at home—especially in the case of chronotherapy, which is usually implemented in a hospital setting.

Some group research is beginning to use a package of approaches, including aspects of sleep hygiene, graduated extinction, and sleep restriction (Cortesi, Giannotti, Sebastiani, Panunzi, & Valente, 2012; Montgomery, Stores, & Wiggs, 2004). For example, Adkins and colleagues (2012) evaluated the efficacy of providing parents with a pamphlet alone (the "Sleep Tool Kit," Autism Treatment Network, 2013) that incorporates all of these approaches but found no significant improvements in child sleep. Subsequent research by this research group that had sleep educators use this package with families appears to be more successful (B. A. Malow, personal communication, November 12, 2012). As I discuss in the "Practical Recommendations" section, the key to the success of any of these approaches may lie as much with a family's willingness and ability to carry out the technique as the specific intervention itself (Durand, 2008).

One aspect of bedtime problems that awaits further development is nondisruptive sleep-related events. Some individuals with ASD (e.g., Asperger's type) lie in bed but do not fall asleep for a considerable amount of time because they are perseverating on particular topics (see "Practical Recommendations" section). To date, there do not appear to be empirical outcome data suggesting appropriate intervention strategies for reducing this type of bedtime problem. Some form of faded bedtime or sleep restriction may be helpful in some cases. In addition, if anxiety is involved, it may be useful to add some form of soothing activities into the regular bedtime routine (Tikotzky & Sadeh, 2010).

Night Waking

The second major complaint by parents is frequent and/or disruptive night waking. Sometimes this results in the child sleeping in the parent's bed for the rest of the night. Interventions for night waking mirror work with bedtime problems. For example, one group addressed night waking across two studies using standard extinction (i.e., ignoring tantrums) and added good bedtime routines, visual supports, sticker charts, and parent education (Weiskop, Matthews, & Richdale, 2001; Weiskop, Richdale, & Matthews, 2005). They reported general improvements in night waking in the participants who completed the program. They also noted, however, that several families dropped out of intervention and speculated that standard extinction may have been too difficult for these families to implement (Weiskop et al., 2005, p. 103). One study looked at combining sleep restriction and sleep hygiene intervention and found improvements in night waking in the one participant in the study who had ASD (Christodulu & Durand, 2004). As can be seen, however, there remain few studies that have systematically studied the effects of behavioral intervention on night waking among persons with ASD.

Sleep Terrors

As described previously, sleep terrors are NREM events (i.e., not occurring during dreams) where the individual cries out, is extremely upset, and may talk and move about the house. Few studies exist on the use of behavioral interventions for this type of parasomnia. In one exception, and building on the research on sleep terrors among children without disabilities (Durand & Mindell, 1999), Durand (2002) used *scheduled awakening* to reduce the chronic and frequent sleep terrors observed in three children with ASD. Scheduled awakening involves lightly awakening the child by touching the arm or face until the child opens his or her eyes approximately 15–30 minutes prior to when he or she typically experiences the sleep terror. This technique is used for nighttime sleep interruptions (including regular night wakings) that occur at about the same time each night (Durand, 2014; Tikotzky & Sadeh, 2010). Durand (2002) showed that scheduled awakening significantly reduced sleep terrors across the three children and this reduction was maintained at a 12-month follow-up.

Nightmares

There does not appear to be any empirical evidence for treating nightmares in persons with ASD (Durand & Christodulu, 2003). The research with persons without ASD suggests that several cognitive-behavioral interventions may help reduce the frequency and intensity of nightmares (Augedal, Hansen, Kronhaug, Harvey, & Pallesen, 2013). One of the more frequently studied of these interventions is *imagery rehearsal therapy* (IRT) (Krakow & Zadra, 2006). This technique involves having the individual rehearse either verbally or by writing down alternative positive endings to unpleasant recurring nightmares. They then practice trying to become aware that their nightmare is just a dream, called *lucid dreaming*, and that they can change the outcome. Other techniques include exposing the person to the anxiety-provoking images while awake until they generate less distress (Augedal et al., 2013). These types of interventions may be useful to persons with ASD who are more verbal.

NONBEHAVIORAL INTERVENTIONS FOR SLEEP PROBLEMS

There are currently no medications that are approved by the Food and Drug Administration or that are regularly recommended by sleep medicine professionals for the treatment of insomnia in children with or without ASD (Cortesi et al., 2012). Despite this lack of support, as general practice most children and adolescents with ASD are routinely given some type of medication as prescribed by a pediatrician if their parents complain of poor sleep (Durand, 2014). These medications include Benadryl˚ (an over-the-counter allergy medication that causes drowsiness), clonidine (a blood pressure medication that is also used for ADHD and anxiety disorders), and chloral hydrate (a sedative) (Williams, Sears, & Allard, 2006). The concern about the routine administration of these medications is that over time an individual can begin to habituate to the medication, which would reduce its effectiveness and lead to a desire to increase the dosage. At the same time, if the medication is removed too abruptly, insomnia can return and initially may be more severe than previously observed—a phenomenon known as *rebound insomnia* (Kales, Scharf, & Kales, 1978). This too can cause concern and lead to reintroduction of the medication.

One pharmacological intervention that is receiving increased attention is the use of melatonin to improve sleep quality (Guénolé et al., 2011). Recall that melatonin is a naturally occurring hormone that is involved with the brain's circadian rhythm process and sleep. Some research suggests that the systems surrounding the production of melatonin may be disrupted in persons with ASD (Cortesi, Giannotti, Ivanenko, & Johnson, 2010). In addition to a number of small N studies, there are an increasing number of clinical trials (both "open label" and "blinded" studies) which suggest that melatonin can improve sleep in a majority of persons with ASD (e.g., Garstang & Wallis, 2006; Giannotti, Cortesi, Cerquiglini, & Bernabei, 2006). One study suggests that adding a behavioral intervention component can improve the effectiveness of using melatonin alone (Cortesi et al., 2012). It is important to point out that (1) not all individuals with ASD respond positively to melatonin, (2) many parents report that melatonin can lose its effectiveness over time, and (3) all studies show that once melatonin is removed the sleep problems return. And although no studies have yet to point out any short-term negative side effects from melatonin (Guénolé et al., 2011), there is as yet no information about chronic use on sleep and the melatonin system in the brain.

PRACTICAL RECOMMENDATIONS

Sleep Hygiene

Some of the recommendations for changing a person's sleep hygiene can pose challenges to families. For example, providing someone who has trouble with sleep with a regular bedtime and a regular time to awaken in the morning can sometimes be difficult to implement in most families. Although usually school or work schedules will dictate when a person goes to bed at night and awakens in the morning during the week, weekends can pose a problem for families. If a child has difficulty falling asleep at bedtime (e.g., 8:30 p.m.) and it is a Friday or Saturday night and the child resists, it is tempting for families to allow the child to stay up later since there are no early morning obligations. However, this arrangement can quickly change the child's sleep-wake pattern, moving the anticipation of bedtime later into the evening. On Sunday night the child may have already adjusted to a later bedtime and now it will be more difficult for him or her to fall asleep at the weekday bedtime. Although it is preferable to maintain the same bedtime (e.g., 8:30 p.m.) and awakening time (e.g., 6:00 a.m.) even through the weekend, many families resist this change. It means not only putting their child to bed early on the weekends but also waking them up early when the parent might want to "sleep in" as well. We typically try to negotiate some compromise

to this approach over the weekends. For example, rather than allowing a child or adolescent to sleep until 11:00 a.m. when their usual awakening time is 6:30 a.m., we try to come up with a time that is earlier but more palatable for the family's weekend activities (e.g., perhaps awakening the child at 8:30 a.m.). This way it can be easier to adapt to the changes needed during the week.

Another aspect of good sleep hygiene is having a regular bedtime routine of about 30 minutes prior to the desired sleep time. As described, this repeated pattern of activities can help signal the onset of sleep. However, in some who have ASD and are prone to rituals this can potentially lead to problems. If for some reason this bedtime routine is changed in any way (e.g., a lost favorite stuffed animal that was supposed to be lined up in a particular way before reading a story), it can cause extreme distress in these individuals. In these cases, we usually recommend that the bedtime pattern still be 30 minutes of bedtime-related activities but that the caregiver changes up the activities each night to avoid it becoming another highly restricted ritual.

It is also recommended that the person only engage in behaviors in bed that signal sleep. However, we sometimes find that individuals with Asperger's type ASD will sit in bed either at bedtime or after a night waking and ruminate on something that occurred that day (e.g., an argument with a classmate over the "right" way to play a game). Often these thoughts can be anxiety provoking and interfere with sleep. In any case where the person is in bed for more than 15–20 minutes without sleep it is recommended that the person get out of bed and sit in a chair or on the floor and engage in relaxing activities such as reading a favorite but soothing book, deep breathing exercises, or aromatherapy massage until the person appears drowsy and ready to sleep. At that point the person should get back in bed. We often make similar recommendations for family members whose sleep can be disturbed by their child's sleep problems. A common one is to ask adults not to look at the clock should they awaken in the middle of the night. Checking the time can lead to anxiety about falling back to sleep (e.g., Oh my gosh! It's 4:00 a.m. and if I don't fall back asleep soon I will only have had 4 hours of sleep!), which will keep them awake. We typically point out that even with a limited amount of sleep for a night people are able to function fine the next day and that they will tend to "catch up" on the sleep they will need over the next few nights.

I discussed earlier the sleep hygiene suggestion that the person with sleep problems not engage in vigorous activity just before bedtime. One way to take advantage of the relationship between temperature and sleep is to try to exercise in the late afternoon. What seems to impact sleep are large changes in temperature. So if you artificially raise someone's body temperature with exercise a few hours before bedtime, the cooling down after exercise may facilitate sleep onset several hours later.

Some children with ASD are particularly sensitive to noise. I have known children who awaken and come out of their room because they heard a candy wrapper being opened from the other side of the house. One recommendation that is made when noise inside or outside the home (e.g., neighbors, traffic, barking dog) is suspected as playing a role in interrupting sleep is to provide sound in the room to mask these interruptions. Called "white noise," this audible stimulus can come from commercially available products and even some apps exist for smart phones that can be helpful. Parents often report that their child prefers having a fan running in the room— not necessarily for the breeze but for the white noise that cancels out other interruptions. Temperature in the bedroom can also be a concern, but unless a child can communicate whether he or she is uncomfortable, it may be difficult to assess. We typically suggest that the family look at the child's covers or bed sheets to see if they are pushed off each morning to suggest the child is too warm.

A final sleep hygiene concern involves the ingestion of caffeine too close to bedtime. Caffeine is a naturally occurring chemical that acts as a stimulant to our brain. What most people do not realize is that caffeine stays in our system acting as a stimulant for up to 6 hours. Some are very sensitive to its effects, while others can fall asleep even after having two cups of coffee. It is important to be aware of foods and drinks that contain caffeine and to try to avoid them in the hours prior to bedtime. In addition to coffee, other common foods and drugs have sufficient caffeine to interfere with sleep. Tea contains less caffeine than drip coffee, but one cup has enough to keep you awake at night. Chocolate, especially the kind used in baking, contains caffeine, which means eating too many chocolate chip cookies before bed could contribute to bedtime problems. Many cola drinks have significant amount of caffeine—probably enough to keep most people awake if they drink 8 ounces or more before bedtime. More recently, "energy drinks"

have appeared in many forms, and these tend to contain various amounts of caffeine—sometimes more per ounce than coffee (McCusker, Goldberger, & Cone, 2006). Certain over-the-counter weight control drugs, diuretics (drugs designed to increase the discharge of urine), cold and allergy medicines, and even some pain relief drugs contain significant amounts of caffeine. Parents should check to see whether their child is consuming caffeine in significant quantities anywhere up to about 6 hours before the desired bedtime and, if so, try to find caffeine-free substitutions.

It may be helpful to point out two influences on sleep that, although may not be relevant to most children and youth, may be useful to parents. Although it can relax you at bedtime and help drive out thoughts that may interfere with your sleep, alcohol can also disrupt sleep during the night. This can lead to a particularly vicious cycle. Unfortunately, alcohol will interfere with getting restful sleep and tends to shorten the duration of sleep (Chaput, McNeil, Després, Bouchard, & Tremblay, 2012). Also, alcohol before sleep can also interfere with appetite such that you tend to eat more. In addition to a concern about alcohol, smoking (especially the nicotine in cigarette smoke) can also negatively impact sleep. Nicotine is a stimulant and can also, like alcohol, interfere with quality sleep (Cohrs et al., 2012; Jaehne et al., 2012).

Selecting the Intervention to Fit the Family

Experience suggests that families have different tolerances when it comes to problems surrounding sleep. For example, some parents are very sensitive to their child's distress and have a difficult time ignoring outbursts. On the other hand, other families are better able to listen to the cries of their child knowing that it will ultimately lead to better sleep. There are also differences in how families are able to implement some of the interventions that may require staying up later at night or waking earlier in the morning. To assess these different tolerances prior to suggesting an intervention, we routinely assess these factors with the "Selecting Sleep Interventions Questionnaire" (SSIQ) (see Table 12.2). The SSIQ asks questions about sensitivity to disruption by their child, willingness to change sleep schedules, and certain attitudinal barriers to intervention success. If parents report difficulty listening to the cries of their child, extinction-based interventions (e.g., graduate extinction) may not be successful and more "errorless"

TABLE 12.2 SELECTING SLEEP INTERVENTIONS QUESTIONNAIRE (SSIQ)

Disruption Tolerance

Does your child misbehave at bedtime or when waking up at night in a way that is too serious or upsetting to ignore? Yes No

Would it be difficult or impossible for you to listen to your child being upset for long periods of time (more than a few minutes)? Yes No

Do you find it too difficult to put your child back in bed once he or she gets up? Yes No

Scoring: If the parents answer "yes" to one or more of these questions, they may not be good candidates for using graduated extinction as an intervention for their child's sleep problems.

Schedule Tolerance

Are you, or another member of your family, willing to stay up later at night to put a sleep plan into action? Yes No

Are you, or another member of your family, willing to get up earlier in the morning to put a sleep plan into action? Yes No

Scoring: If the parents answer "no" to one or more of these questions, they may not be good candidates for scheduled awakenings or sleep restriction as interventions for their child's sleep problems.

Attitudinal Barriers

Do you feel emotionally unable to deal directly with your child's sleep problem? Yes No

Do you feel guilty making your child go to bed (or go back to bed) when he or she does not want to? Yes No

Do you think it would be emotionally damaging to your child if you tried to change the way he or she slept? Yes No

Scoring: If the parents answer "yes" to one or more of these questions, they may need cognitive-behavioral intervention to explore their attitudes about their ability or their child's ability to improve sleep.

Source: Reprinted from Durand, 2008.

interventions may be more appropriate (e.g., sleep restriction). Other parents report being unwilling to stay up late or wake up early to implement a plan. Often these families prefer the extinction-based interventions. Finally, new work is suggesting that some parents of children with ASD doubt their child's ability to improve sleep (e.g., "It's because he has autism") or their own ability to change their child's behavior (Durand, 2011). These attitudinal barriers can interfere with their ability to carry out any sleep intervention, and directly addressing these thoughts can improve treatment fidelity and child outcomes (Durand et al., 2013). Responses from the SSIQ can assist clinicians to tailor the intervention plan for the family.

SUMMARY

Sleep problems are highly prevalent in the ASD population and can seriously disrupt family life. In addition, there is some concern that disrupted sleep can exacerbate other problems faced by individuals with ASD. Assessing the nature of these sleep problems is essential for treatment planning and must comprehensively address the range of sleep-related difficulties. The intervention literature remains limited, although more recently there are more studies addressing this urgent need. Future work must address the broader range of sleep problems (e.g., nightmares, circadian rhythm problems) as well as

examine factors that will assist families to implement the interventions more effectively at home.

REFERENCES

Abbeduto, L., Seltzer, M. M., Shattuck, P., Krauss, M. W., Osmond, G., & Murphy, M. M. (2004). Psychological well-being and coping in mothers of youths with autism, Down syndrome, or fragile X syndrome. *American Journal on Mental Retardation, 109,* 237–254.

Adkins, K. W., Molloy, C., Weiss, S. K., Reynolds, A., Goldman, S. E., Burnette, C.,...Malow, B. A. (2012). Effects of a standardized pamphlet on insomnia in children with autism spectrum disorders. *Pediatrics, 130*(Suppl. 2), S139–S144. doi: 10.1542/peds.2012-0900K.

American Academy of Sleep Medicine. (2005). *The international classification of sleep disorders: Diagnostic and coding manual* (2nd ed.). Westchester, IL: American Academy of Sleep Medicine.

American Psychiatric Association. (2013). *Diagnostic and statistical manual of mental disorders (5th Edition).* Washington, D.C.: American Psychiatric Association.

Atkinson, G., & Davenne, D. (2007). Relationships between sleep, physical activity and human health. *Physiology and Behavior, 90*(2–3), 229–235. doi:http://dx.doi.org/10.1016/j.physbeh.2006.09.015.

Augedal, A. W., Hansen, K. S., Kronhaug, C. R., Harvey, A. G., & Pallesen, S. (2013). Randomized controlled trials of psychological and pharmacological treatments for nightmares: A meta-analysis. *Sleep Medicine Reviews, 17*(2), 143–152.

Autism Treatment Network. (2013). ATN/AIR-P sleep tool kit (parent booklet) Retrieved January 2013, from http://www.autismspeaks.org/science/resources-programs/autism-treatment-network/tools-you-can-use/sleep-tool-kit.

Barclay, N. L., & Gregory, A. M. (2013). Quantitative genetic research on sleep: A review of normal sleep, sleep disturbances and associated emotional, behavioural, and health-related difficulties. *Sleep Medicine Reviews*, *17*(1), 29–40. doi: 10.1016/j.smrv.2012.01.008.

Bates, E. (2011). Childrens sleep deficits and cognitive and behavioral adjustment. *Sleep and Development*, *1*(9), 133–165.

Berger, R. H., Miller, A. L., Seifer, R., Cares, S. R., & Lebourgeois, M. K. (2012). Acute sleep restriction effects on emotion responses in 30–to 36-month-old children. *Journal of Sleep Research*, *21*(3), 235–246. doi : 10.1111/j.1365-2869.2011.00962.x.

Cassoff, J., Wiebe, S., & Gruber, R. (2012). Sleep patterns and the risk for ADHD: A review. *Nature*, *4*, 73–80.

Chaput, J. P., McNeil, J., Després, J. P., Bouchard, C., & Tremblay, A. (2012). Short sleep duration is associated with greater alcohol consumption in adults. *Appetite*, *59*(3), 650–655.

Chervin, R. D., Hedger, K., Dillon, J. E., & Pituch, K. J. (2000). Pediatric sleep questionnaire (PSQ): Validity and reliability of scales for sleep-disordered breathing, snoring, sleepiness, and behavioral problems. *Sleep Medicine*, *1*(1), 21–32.

Christodulu, K. V., & Durand, V. M. (2004). Reducing bedtime disturbance and night waking using positive bedtime routines and sleep restriction. *Focus on Autism and Other Developmental Disabilities*, *19*(3), 130–139.

Cohrs, S., Rodenbeck, A., Riemann, D., Szagun, B., Jaehne, A., Brinkmeyer, J.,…Mobascher, A. (2012). Impaired sleep quality and sleep duration in smokers—results from the German Multicenter Study on Nicotine Dependence. *Addiction Biology*, ePub ahead of print. doi: 10.1111/j.1369-1600.2012.00487.x.

Cortesi, F., Giannotti, F., Ivanenko, A., & Johnson, K. P. (2010). Sleep in children with autistic spectrum disorder. *Sleep Medicine*, *11*(7), 659–664. doi: http://dx.doi.org/10.1016/j.sleep.2010.01.010.

Cortesi, F., Giannotti, F., Sebastiani, T., Panunzi, S., & Valente, D. (2012). Controlled-release melatonin, singly and combined with cognitive behavioural therapy, for persistent insomnia in children with autism spectrum disorders: A randomized placebo-controlled trial. *Journal of Sleep Research*, *21*(6), 700–709.

Couturier, J. L., Speechley, K. N., Steele, M., Norman, R., Stringer, B., & Nicolson, R. (2005). Parental perception of sleep problems in children of normal intelligence with pervasive developmental disorders: Prevalence, severity, and pattern. *Journal of the American Academy of Child and Adolescent Psychiatry*, *44*(8), 815–822.

DeLeon, I. G., Fisher, W. W., & Marhefka, J-M. (2004). Decreasing self-injurious behavior associated with awakening in a child with autism and developmental delays. *Behavioral Interventions*, *19*(2), 111–119. doi: 10.1002/bin.154.

Dumas, J., Wolf, L., Fisman, S., & Culligan, A. (1991). Parenting stress, child behavior problems, and dysphoria in parents of children with autism, Down syndrome, behavior disorders, and normal development. *Exceptionality*, *2*(2), 97–110.

Durand, V. M. (1996). Treatment of sleep disorders in children with developmental disabilities. *Journal of the Association for Persons with Severe Handicaps*, *21*(3), 114–122.

Durand, V. M. (2002). Treating sleep terrors in children with autism. *Journal of Positive Behavior Interventions*, *4*(2), 66–72. doi: 10.1177/109830070200400201.

Durand, V. M. (2006). Sleep terrors. In J. E. Fisher & W. T. O'Donohue (Eds.), *Practitioners guide to evidenced based psychotherapy* (pp. 654–660). New York, NY: Springer.

Durand, V. M. (2008). *When children don't sleep well: Interventions for pediatric sleep disorders: Therapist guide*. New York, NY: Oxford University Press.

Durand, V. M. (2011). *Optimistic parenting: Hope and help for you and your challenging child*. Baltimore, MD: Paul H. Brookes.

Durand, V. M. (2014). *Sleep better! A guide to improving sleep for children with special needs (revised edition)*. Baltimore, MD: Paul H. Brookes.

Durand, V. M., & Christodulu, K. V. (2003). Nightmares. In T. H. Ollendick & C. S. Schroeder (Eds.), *Encyclopedia of pediatric and child psychology* (pp. 412–413). New York, NY: Kluwer Academic/Plenum.

Durand, V. M., & Christodulu, K. V. (2004). Description of a sleep-restriction program to reduce bedtime disturbances and night waking. *Journal of Positive Behavior Interventions*, *6*(2), 83–91.

Durand, V. M., Hieneman, M., Clarke, S., Wang, M., & Rinaldi, M. (2013). Positive family intervention for severe challenging behavior I: A multi-site randomized clinical trial. *Journal of Positive Behavior Interventions*, *15*(3), 133-143.

Durand, V. M., & Mindell, J. A. (1999). Behavioral intervention for childhood sleep terrors. *Behavior Therapy*, *30*(4), 705–715.

Garstang, J., & Wallis, M. (2006). Randomized controlled trial of melatonin for children with autistic spectrum disorders and sleep problems. *Child: Care, Health and Development*, *32*(5), 585–589. doi: 10.1111/j.1365-2214.2006.00616.x.

Giannotti, F., Cortesi, F., Cerquiglini, A., & Bernabei, P. (2006). An open-label study of controlled-release melatonin in treatment of sleep disorders in children with autism. *Journal of Autism and Developmental Disorders*, 36(6), 741–752. doi: 10.1007/s10803-006-0116-z.

Glickman, G. (2010). Circadian rhythms and sleep in children with autism. *Neuroscience and Biobehavioral Reviews*, 34(5), 755–768.

Goldman, S. E., McGrew, S., Johnson, K. P., Richdale, A. L., Clemons, T., & Malow, B. A. (2011). Sleep is associated with problem behaviors in children and adolescents with autism spectrum disorders. *Research in Autism Spectrum Disorders*, 5(3), 1223–1229.

Goldman, S. E., Richdale, A., Clemons, T., & Malow, B. (2012). Parental sleep concerns in autism spectrum disorders: Variations from childhood to adolescence. *Journal of Autism and Developmental Disorders*, 42(4), 531–538. doi: 10.1007/s10803-011-1270-5.

Guénolé, F., Godbout, R., Nicolas, A., Franco, P., Claustrat, B., & Baleyte, J-M. (2011). Melatonin for disordered sleep in individuals with autism spectrum disorders: Systematic review and discussion. *Sleep Medicine Reviews*, 15(6), 379–387. doi: 10.1016/j.smrv.2011.02.001.

Henderson, J. A., Barry, T. D., Bader, S. H., & Jordan, S. S. (2011). The relation among sleep, routines, and externalizing behavior in children with an autism spectrum disorder. *Research in Autism Spectrum Disorders*, 5(2), 758–767. doi: 10.1016/j.rasd.2010.09.003.

Hodge, D., Hoffman, C., Sweeney, D., & Riggs, M. (2013). Relationship between children's sleep and mental health in mothers of children with and without autism. *Journal of Autism and Developmental Disorders*, 43(4), 956–963. doi: 10.1007/s10803-012-1639-0.

Hodge, D., Parnell, A. M. N., Hoffman, C. D., & Sweeney, D. P. (2012). Methods for assessing sleep in children with autism spectrum disorders: A review. *Research in Autism Spectrum Disorders*, 6(4), 1337–1344. doi: 10.1016/j.rasd.2012.05.009.

Howlin, P. (1984). A brief report on the elimination of long term sleeping problems in a 6-year-old autistic boy. *Behavioural psychotherapy*, 12(03), 257–260.

Iber, C., Ancoli-Israel, S., Chesson, A., & Quan, S. F. (2007). *The AASM manual for the scoring of sleep and associated events: Rules, terminology and technical specifications*. Westchester, IL: American Academy of Sleep Medicine.

Jaehne, A., Unbehaun, T., Feige, B., Lutz, U. C., Batra, A., & Riemann, D. (2012). How smoking affects sleep: A polysomnographical analysis. *Sleep Medicine*, 13(10), 1286–1292. doi: http://dx.doi.org/10.1016/j.sleep.2012.06.026.

Johnson, K. P., Giannotti, F., & Cortesi, F. (2009). Sleep patterns in autism spectrum disorders. *Child and Adolescent Psychiatric Clinics of North America*, 18(4), 917.

Johnson, K. P., & Malow, B. A. (2008). Sleep in children with autism spectrum disorders. *Current Treatment Options in Neurology*, 10(5), 350–359.

Kales, A., Scharf, M. B., & Kales, J. D. (1978). Rebound insomnia: A new clinical syndrome. *Science*, 201(4360), 1039.

Krakow, B., & Zadra, A. (2006). Clinical management of chronic nightmares: Imagery rehearsal therapy. *Behavioral Sleep Medicine*, 4(1), 45–70.

Krakowiak, P., Goolin-Jones, B., Hertz-Picciotto, I., Croen, L. A., & Hansen, R. L. (2008). Sleep problems in children with autism spectrum disorders, developmental delays, and typical development: A population-based study. *Journal of Sleep Research*, 17(2), 197–206.

Liu, X., Hubbard, J. A., Fabes, R. A., & Adam, J. B. (2006). Sleep disturbances and correlates of children with autism spectrum disorders. *Child Psychiatry and Human Development*, 37(2), 179–191.

Lopez-Wagner, M. C., Hoffman, C. D., Sweeney, D. P., Hodge, D., & Gilliam, J. E. (2008). Sleep problems of parents of typically developing children and parents of children with autism. *Journal of Genetic Psychology*, 169(3), 245–260.

Malow, B. A., Crowe, C., Henderson, L. M., McGrew, S. G., Wang, L., Song, Y., & Stone, W. L. (2009). A sleep habits questionnaire for children with autism spectrum disorders. *Journal of Child Neurology*, 24(1), 19–24. doi: 10.1177/0883073808321044.

Malow, B. A., McGrew, S. G., Harvey, M., Henderson, L. M., & Stone, W. L. (2006). Impact of treating sleep apnea in a child with autism spectrum disorder. *Pediatric Neurology*, 34(4), 325–328.

Maquet, P. (2001). The role of sleep in learning and memory. *Science*, 294(5544), 1048–1052.

McCusker, R. R., Goldberger, B. A., & Cone, E. J. (2006). Caffeine content of energy drinks, carbonated sodas, and other beverages. *Journal of Analytical Toxicology*, 30(2), 112–114. doi: 10.1093/jat/30.2.112.

Mindell, J. A., & Durand, V. M. (1993). Treatment of childhood sleep disorders: Generalization across disorders and effects on family members. *Journal of Pediatric Psychology*, 18, 731–750.

Montgomery, P., Stores, G., & Wiggs, L. (2004). The relative efficacy of two brief treatments for sleep problems in young learning disabled (mentally retarded) children: A randomised controlled trial. *Archives of Disease in Childhood*, 89(2), 125–130. doi: 10.1136/adc.2002.017202.

Moon, E. C., Corkum, P., & Smith, I. M. (2011). Case study: A case-series evaluation of a behavioral sleep intervention for three children with autism and primary insomnia. *Journal of Pediatric Psychology*, 36(1), 47–54.

Moore, P. S. (2004). The use of social stories in a psychology service for children with learning disabilities: A case study of a sleep problem. *British Journal of Learning Disabilities*, 32(3), 133–138. doi: 10.1111/j.1468-3156.2004.00278.x.

National Sleep Foundation. (2011). *How much sleep do we really need?* Retrieved January 2013, from http://www.sleepfoundation.org/article/how-sleep-works/how-much-sleep-do-we-really-need

Owens, J. A., & Mindell, J. A. (2011). Pediatric Insomnia. *Pediatric Clinics of North America, 58*(3), 555.

Owens, J. A., Spirito, A., & McGuinn, M. (2000). The Children's Sleep Habits Questionnaire (CSHQ): Psychometric properties of a survey instrument for school-aged children. *Sleep, 23*(8), 1043–1052.

Park, S., Cho, S-C., Cho, I. H., Kim, B-N., Kim, J-W., Shin, M-S.,... Yoo, H. J. (2012). Sleep problems and their correlates and comorbid psychopathology of children with autism spectrum disorders. *Research in Autism Spectrum Disorders, 6*(3), 1068–1072. doi: 10.1016/j.rasd.2012.02.004.

Peigneux, P., Urbain, C., & Schmitz, R. (2012). Sleep and the brain. In C. M. Morin & C. A. Espie (Eds.), *The Oxford handbook of sleep and sleep disorders* (pp. 11–37). New York, NY: Oxford University Press.

Piazza, C. C., & Fisher, W. W. (1991). Bedtime fading in the treatment of pediatric insomnia. *Journal of Behavior Therapy and Experimental Psychiatry, 22*(1), 53–56.

Piazza, C. C., Fisher, W. W., & Scherer, M. (1997). Treatment of multiple sleep problems in children with developmental disabilities: Faded bedtime with response cost versus bedtime scheduling. *Developmental Medicine and Child Neurology, 39*(6), 414–418.

Piazza, C. C., Hagopian, L. P., Hughes, C. R., & Fisher, W. W. (1997). Using chronotherapy to treat severe sleep problems: A case study. *American Journal on Mental Retardation, 102*(4), 358–366.

Reed, H. E., McGrew, S. G., Artibee, K., Surdkya, K., Goldman, S. E., Frank, K.,... Malow, B. A. (2009). Parent-based sleep education workshops in autism. *Journal of Child Neurology, 24*(8), 936–945.

Richdale, A. L., & Schreck, K. A. (2009). Sleep problems in autism spectrum disorders: Prevalence, nature, and possible biopsychosocial aetiologies. *Sleep Medicine Reviews, 13*(6), 403–411.

Rowley, J. A., & Badr, M. S. (2012). Normal sleep. In M. S. Badr (Ed.), *Essentials of sleep medicine* (pp. 1–15). New York, NY: Humana Press.

Rzepecka, H., McKenzie, K., McClure, I., & Murphy, S. (2011). Sleep, anxiety and challenging behaviour in children with intellectual disability and/or autism spectrum disorder. *Research in Developmental Disabilities, 32*(6), 2758–2766. doi: http://dx.doi.org/10.1016/j.ridd.2011.05.034.

Sadeh, A. (2011). The role and validity of actigraphy in sleep medicine: An update. *Sleep Medicine Reviews, 15*(4), 259–267.

Schreck, K. A., & Mulick, J. A. (2000). Parental report of sleep problems in children with autism. *Journal of Autism and Developmental Disorders, 30*(2), 127–135.

Schreck, K. A., Mulick, J. A., & Smith, A. F. (2004). Sleep problems as possible predictors of intensified symptoms of autism. *Research in Developmental Disabilities, 25*(1), 57–66.

Siegel, J. M. (2005). Clues to the functions of mammalian sleep. *Nature, 437*(7063), 1264–1271.

Sikora, D. M., Johnson, K. P., Clemons, T., & Katz, T. (2012). The relationship between sleep problems and daytime behavior in children of different ages with autism spectrum disorders. *Pediatrics, 130*(Suppl. 2), S83–S90. doi: 10.1542/peds.2012-0900F.

Sitnick, S. L., Goodlin-Jones, B. L., & Anders, T. F. (2008). The use of actigraphy to study sleep disorders in preschoolers: Some concerns about detection of nighttime awakenings. *Sleep, 31*(3), 395.

Sivertsen, B., Posserud, M-B., Gillberg, C., Lundervold, A. J., & Hysing, M. (2011). Sleep problems in children with autism spectrum problems: A longitudinal population-based study. *Autism, 16*(2), 139–150. doi: 10.1177/1362361311404255.

Souders, M. C., Mason, T. B. A., Valladares, O., Bucan, M., Levy, S. E., Mandell, D. S.,... Pinto-Martin, J. (2009). Sleep behaviors and sleep quality in children with autism spectrum disorders. *Sleep, 32*(12), 1566.

Tikotzky, L., & Sadeh, A. (2010). The role of cognitive–behavioral therapy in behavioral childhood insomnia. *Sleep Medicine, 11*(7), 686–691. doi: http://dx.doi.org/10.1016/j.sleep.2009.11.017.

Tudor, M. E., Hoffman, C. D., & Sweeney, D. P. (2012). Children with autism: Sleep problems and symptom severity. *Focus on Autism and Other Developmental Disabilities, 27*(4), 254-262. doi: 10.1177/1088357612457989

Turner, K. S., & Johnson, C. R. (2013). Behavioral interventions to address sleep disturbances in children with autism spectrum disorders: A review. *Topics in Early Childhood Special Education, 33*(3), 144-152.

Vriend, J. L., Corkum, P. V., Moon, E. C., & Smith, I. M. (2011). Behavioral interventions for sleep problems in children with autism spectrum disorders: Current findings and future directions. *Journal of Pediatric Psychology, 36*(9), 1017–1029. doi: 10.1093/jpepsy/jsr044.

Weiskop, S., Matthews, J., & Richdale, A. (2001). Treatment of sleep problems in a 5-year-old boy with autism using behavioural principles. *Autism, 5*(2), 209–221.

Weiskop, S., Richdale, A., & Matthews, J. (2005). Behavioural treatment to reduce sleep problems in children with autism or fragile X syndrome. *Developmental Medicine and Child Neurology, 47*(2), 94–104. doi: 10.1111/j.1469-8749.2005.tb01097.x.

Williams, G., Sears, L. L., & Allard, A. (2006). Parent perceptions of efficacy for strategies used to facilitate sleep in children with autism. *Journal of Developmental and Physical Disabilities, 18*(1), 25–33. doi: 10.1007/s10882-006-9003-y.

Williams, P. G., Sears, L. L., & Allard, A. M. (2004). Sleep problems in children with autism. *Journal of Sleep Research, 13*(3), 265–268.

Wolf, M., Risley, T., & Mees, H. (1963). Application of operant conditioning procedures to the behaviour problems of an autistic child. *Behaviour Research and Therapy, 1*(2), 305–312.

World Health Organization. (1993). *The ICD-10 classification of mental and behavioural disorders: Diagnostic criteria for research*. Geneva, Switzerland: World Health Organization.

13

Exercise, Physical Activity, and Sports

JAMES K. LUISELLI

There is ample evidence that many children and youth with autism spectrum disorder (ASD) and related developmental disabilities do not participate in or have sufficient opportunities for routine exercise and physical activity (Draheim, Williams, & McCubbin, 2002; Foley & McCubbin, 2009; Pitetti, Beets, & Combs, 2009; Rimmer & Rowland, 2008; Whitt-Glover, O'Neill, & Stettler, 2006). This situation is due, in part, to limited resources within service settings, including exercise and sports equipment, access to recreational areas, and few organized events (Howie et al., 2012). Effective intervention practices, as presented in this chapter, also have not been studied or disseminated enough to be adopted routinely by human services and habilitation-care organizations.

As a consequence of a sedentary lifestyle, people with developmental disabilities frequently experience health problems such as obesity, cardiovascular disease, and respiratory complications (De, Small, & Baur, 2008; Rimmer, Braddock, & Fujiura, 1993, 1994). Conversely, engaging in exercise and physical activity, even to moderate levels, can improve balance and flexibility (Yilmaz, Yanardag, Birkin, & Bumin, 2004), increase muscular endurance (Chanias, Reid, & Hoover, 1998), and reduce weight and body mass index (BMI) (Fleming, 2011). Furthermore, there is convincing evidence that regular exercise and moderate-to-vigorous physical activity (MVPA) are associated with fewer problem behaviors, better self-concept, and enhanced intellectual functioning (Elliot, Dobbin, Rose, & Soper, 1994; Gabler-Halle, Halle, & Chung, 1993; Rosenthal-Malek & Mitchell, 1997).

Parents and care providers of children and youth with developmental disabilities, including ASD, also acknowledge the benefits of exercise and physical activity. For example, in studying athletes participating in Special Olympics, researchers have reported

that parents consistently perceive desirable effects on socialization, health, self-esteem, and family functioning (Gibbons & Bushakra, 1989; Glidden, Bamberger, Draheim, & Kersh, 2011; Weiss, 2008). Similarly, in a survey at a residential facility for children and youth with ASD, Luiselli, Woods, Keary, and Parenteau (2013) found that care providers endorsed exercise and athletic pursuits for improving social skills, learning, mood, sleep, personal happiness, and general health. Thus, it appears that providing opportunities for exercise, physical activity, and sports has good acceptance and approval by community members.

This chapter reviews the contributions of applied behavior analysis (ABA) toward exercise, physical activity, and sports for health promotion and therapeutic intervention among children and youth with ASD. Exercise, of course, can be distinguished from general physical activity by virtue of the former being goal-directed behavior that is intended to improve health and fitness (Capersen, Powell, & Christenson, 1985). Physical activity itself encompasses many actions that do not qualify as exercise; however, as Cushing and Steele (2011) posited, gross measures of physical activity usually are a "proxy indicator" of exercise. Furthermore, the goal of increasing physical activity and energy expenditure, independent of formal exercise objectives, is desirable for many children and youth with ASD. Sports, in particular, offer an exercise and physical activity venue with accompanying socialization and peer building outlets.

As relatively few exercise, physical activity, and sports studies have dealt exclusively with an ASD population, in this chapter I have included examples and cited research that evaluated intervention with individuals who had other developmental disabilities diagnoses. Also, I describe research with adults as well as children and youth because many procedures and applications with demonstrated efficacy are warranted across the life span. The first section of the chapter outlines the types of exercise, physical activity, and sports that researchers have targeted and disseminated in the extant literature. Next, I look at the intervention methods commonly used with people who have developmental disabilities to address their exercise needs. This section also examines sports applications with special needs athletes. Of note, exercise has been implemented to reduce problem behaviors, which I discuss with reference to several studies. The chapter concludes with a summary of pertinent issues, practice recommendations, and directions for future research.

FOCUS OF EXERCISE AND PHYSICAL ACTIVITY IN DEVELOPMENTAL DISABILITIES

Several systematic reviews have identified characteristics of exercise and physical activity studies within different developmental disabilities populations. Among children and youth with ASD, Lang et al. (2010) located 18 studies that comprised 64 participants from 3 to 41 years old. The majority of studies (61%) concerned jogging or running followed by bike riding, weight training, roller skating, and water-based activities (swimming and water aerobics). All of the studies reported that exercise-promoting interventions were associated with meaningful life changes, most notably better physical fitness, increased activity engagement, improved academic performance, and fewer problem behaviors (aggression, self-injury, stereotypy).

In another survey of participants who had ASD, Sowa and Meulenbroek (2012) conducted a meta-analysis of 16 studies which encompassed 133 children and adults. The types of exercise and physical activity in these studies were jogging (38%), swimming (31%), horseback riding (13%), weight training (6%), and walking (6%). All studies revealed significant progress on the dependent measures, with individual versus group interventions yielding better results for motor and social skills.

Lancioni, Singh, O'Reilly et al. (2008) reviewed studies that evaluated treadmills and walkers with microswitches to facilitate locomotion of children with developmental disabilities. Of 26 studies, 81% featured treadmills with children who had cerebral palsy, Down syndrome, and Rett syndrome. The other studies incorporated walkers with microswitches that produced contingent stimulation for children with multiple handicapping conditions. This research documented generally positive effects, for example, improvement in measures of functional ambulation, walking endurance, walking velocity, and motor milestones.

A small body of research has targeted athletic performance of people with developmental disabilities within individual competition or team sports. Cameron and Cappello (1993) had an adaptive physical education (APE) instructor teach hurdle jumping to a young adult who was participating in Special Olympics. Luyben, Funk, Morgan, Clark, and Delulio (1986) trained three adults to execute a side-of-the-foot soccer pass. More recently, Luiselli, Duncan, Keary, Nelson, Parenteau, and Woods (2013) compared several coaching methods to improve 100-meter sprint times of two Special Olympics track athletes. These and related studies are described more fully in the following section of the chapter.

INTERVENTION METHODS

In their systematic review of exercise and physical activity studies with people who have ASD, Lang et al. (2011) commented about the intervention methods that were implemented. The most common methods were physical prompting, prompt fading, verbal reinforcement, modeling with verbal instructions, and edible reinforcement. Some of these methods, with modifications, are not unlike the procedures employed with typically developing youth, collegiate, and elite athletes (Luiselli, Woods, & Reed, 2011). However, there is little comparative research to suggest the superiority of specific methods.

Lang et al. (2011) also noted that although the majority of reviewed studies mentioned intervention methods, very few of them had sufficient detail and information to permit replication by practitioners. Indeed, they concluded that "Perhaps the most important area for future research involves the evaluation of different procedures used to teach or maintain exercise. Only one of the reviewed studies evaluated such a procedure directly... other studies described only briefly how exercise was taught" (p. 574).

In order to better understand the types of instructional methods for teaching exercise, physical activity, and sports to children and youth with ASD, I selected studies that targeted jogging/running, soccer, swimming, bike riding, and track. Typically, several methods are combined and only rarely is intervention based on a single procedure. Significantly, and before engaging in purposeful exercise, planned physical activity, and sports, children and youth with ASD should be cleared medically to rule out abnormalities or limitations which could be harmful or put them at risk. Additionally, qualified professionals and legal guardians should decide about the appropriateness of the selected exercise and physical activity relative to a person's quality of life and personal preferences.

Jogging/Running

Most studies had participants jog or run for 10–30 minutes on an outdoor track (Allison, Basile, & MacDonald, 1991), in a gymnasium (Rosenthal-Malek & Mitchell, 1997), and on the lawn in front of school (Celiberti, Bobo, Kelly, Harris, & Handleman, 1997). The dominant intervention method was having one or two adults jog/run with the participant while providing physical guidance, modeling, and verbal reinforcement. Another method incorporated musical games ("tag" and "follow the leader") to encourage continuous movement. Jogging was also performed on a treadmill (Ellliot, Dobin, Rose, & Soper, 1994). Unfortunately, and as noted previously, these studies did not explain explicitly how prompting and similar procedures were implemented and faded.

It should be recognized that in studying jogging and running, most investigators have been concerned about exercise as an antecedent intervention (Luiselli, 2008). That is, compared to a baseline condition (no exercise) or comparative movement condition (e.g., walking), participants either jogged or ran preceding a standardized activity to determine behavior-reducing effects on problems such as aggression, self-injury, and stereotypy (Allison et al., 1991; Celiberti et al., 1997; Elliot et al., 1994; Gordon, Handleman, & Harris, 1986; Levinson & Reid, 1993). In other cases the measure of interest has been compliance with academic demands, correct responses, and completed work tasks (Kern, Koegel, Dyer, Blew, & Fenton, 1982; Rostenthal-Malek & Mitchell, 1997). Summarizing this research, it appears that brief, vigorous exercise through jogging and running can increase desirable learning responses and decrease problem behaviors during an immediately or closely following instructional session.

The advantages of jogging and running are that they are easily taught, do not require special equipment, and can be adapted to most settings. Additionally, relatively moderate exertion is needed to produce meaningful health benefits. Of course, there may be constraints on scheduling exercise opportunities, particularly when the emphasis is on antecedent intervention to reduce problem behaviors. Other considerations are choosing reasonable distances and a pace that makes jogging and running a pleasurable experience.

Soccer

Luyben et al. (1986) published one of the few studies that addressed team sports for people with developmental disabilities. Three adults (24–52 years old) were included because they were able to follow simple commands, stand on one foot for 1 second while unsupported, and swing one foot with support. Additionally, the participants were responsive to social praise, complied with physical prompting, and did not have vision or hearing impairments. Having preintervention screening criteria for people with developmental disabilities is advisable but underreported in most of the exercise and physical activity research to date.

The behavior Luyben et al. (1986) measured was a side-of-the-foot soccer pass, task analyzed into nine steps: (1) get set, (2) look at the ball, (3) grab a supportive device (to facilitate balance), (4) step forward, (5) turn foot, (6) pick up foot, (7) look at the ball, (8) push foot, and (9) pass the ball. During daily sessions, a trainer interacted with the participants according to a prompt hierarchy that started with verbal instruction and a "strong physical prompt" (holding and positioning the body correctly) for each step. Gradually, physical prompts were faded to demonstration, gestures, and verbal cues from the trainer. Other stimuli such as the supportive device and visual markers (tape on the floor and passing targets) were also eliminated through fading. Finally, the trainer praised the participants when they executed each step correctly.

Using a multiple-baseline design across task analysis steps, Luyben et al. (1986) showed that each participant learned the side-of-the-foot soccer pass without prompting following 22–29 sessions. The participants also demonstrated the target skills during posttraining assessment. This study, then, was one of the first to describe effective application of a most-to-least prompting hierarchy using forward chaining for teaching an isolated athletic skill to people with developmental disabilities. The study was limited because training and follow-up sessions were not conducted on an actual soccer field. Also, although the participants acquired the passing skill, they were not taught to perform it with a peer or in the context of team play. Of course, conducting evaluation under naturalistic conditions remains a priority for applied research.

Swimming

Swimming as well as aquatic aerobic programs can be enjoyable recreational activities with health-promoting effects (Fragala-Pinkham, Haley, & O'Neill, 2008; Pan, 2010, 2011; Rogers, Hemmeter, & Wolery, 2010). Dowrick and Dove (1980) reported one of the earliest swimming studies among people with developmental disabilities, specifically three children (5–10 years old) who had spina bifida. Unfortunately, this publication did not specify each child's level of intellectual functioning. The investigators identified four categories of "swimming behavior" that were sequenced into a rating checklist comprised of 35 responses. The total number of responses each participant achieved during video-taped swim sessions served as the dependent measure. Following baseline assessment the participants watched brief segments of self-modeling videotapes in which they "performed behaviors superior to those previously observed on the checklist" (p. 53). Each participant watched his own self-modeling videotape three times each week preceding a swim session. As an extension of the training program, one of the three participants also watched additional videotapes that depicted him "performing more checklist behaviors than before" (p. 53).

Compared to baseline, all of the participants in Dowrick and Dove (1980) had moderate gains in the number of checklist behaviors achieved after exposure to the self-modeling videotapes. The greatest improvement was seen with the child who viewed more videotapes and those video tapes that featured a higher skill performance. Again, without knowing the participants' intellectual functioning, it is not possible to speculate whether an intervention method such as self-monitoring might produce similar effects with people who have developmental disabilities, including ASD. Furthermore, the time and equipment required to film, edit, and display videotapes may be prohibitive for most educational and habilitation settings notwithstanding recent technological advancements and easier procurement of photographic media.

A more recent study by Rogers et al. (2010) evaluated a constant time-delay prompting procedure for teaching foundational swimming skills to three children (10–12 years old) with autism. Skills performance was measured by assessing each child's demonstration of three behaviors: (a) a flutter kick, (b) front-crawl arm strokes, and (c) head turns to the side. In the context of a multiple-probe design, the constant time-delay prompting procedure was introduced sequentially each time the children acquired the previous behavior(s). This method of prompting was highly effective with the children and relatively easy to implement. Because prompting is relied on heavily when teaching exercise skills and physical activity to children and youth who have ASD, comparative research is essential for isolating the most successful methods, be they verbal, physical, or as with time-delay, modeling.

Bike Riding

Riding a bike is a versatile form of exercise and developmentally appropriate at all ages. Whereas many children learn to ride a bike with little or no instruction, Cameron, Shapiro, and Ansleigh (2005) described a rigorous training program with a 9-year-old boy who had Asperger syndrome. Before intervention he was unable to ride his bike and resisted his parents' persuasion to do so. During the first phase of intervention the bike was placed in a kinetic trainer so that it remained stationary and could be pedaled without it moving. At this phase the child was required to pedal for 5 minutes. During subsequent phases, with the bike still in the kinetic trainer, he had to pedal for 8, 10, 12, and 15 minutes, brake, and dismount. The bike was then removed from the kinetic trainer, the pedals were removed, and the child was expected to glide 7 meters on a slightly declining grassy slope. The last phase of intervention had the child ride the bike with pedal attached for 14 meters on the slop and then ride the bike for. 4 kilometers on the road in front of his house.

Cameron et al. (2005) used a changing criterion design to evaluate intervention, each criterion corresponding to one of the training phases. The results were that with few exceptions, the child successfully achieved the gradually increasing criteria, making only five errors, and reaching the terminal bike riding objective after 64 sessions. This study also had the child's parents grant him 1 minute access to a preferred activity for every minute he rode his bike per phase. The child continued to ride his bike independently 1 year post intervention. This study is a good example of gradually introducing response demands, with positive reinforcement, for building complex skill repertoires and simultaneously shifting performance from simulated to natural conditions.

Track

The focus of a study by Cameron and Cappello (1993) was teaching a 21-year-old man with Down syndrome and developmental delay to jump hurdles in preparation for a Special Olympics track event. Before the study he would not leap over a hurdle at any height despite previous attempts at establishing the skill through physical prompting, modeling, and positive reinforcement. The basis on intervention was stimulus shaping via an 11-step instructional program that was implemented by an adaptive physical education teacher. During individual sessions at a school gymnasium, the teacher first had the man leap over four hurdles that were flat on the floor and spaced 12 feet apart. In successive steps the hurdles were gradually raised off of the floor, reaching a terminal height of 12 inches. Other components of the program were conducting brief, presession practice trials, physically guiding the man by running with him hand in hand, and praising him noncontingently. The man acquired the hurdle jumping skill after 37 sessions and competed successfully in the Special Olympics event 6 months later.

Luiselli et al. (2013) also designed a study with the intent of supporting performance at a Special Olympics event. The participants were a 20-year-old male with pervasive developmental disorder and a 21-year-old male with pervasive developmental disorder–not otherwise specified and features of Asperger syndrome. The primary dependent measure was their time (in seconds) running a 100-meter sprint. Like previously described research, this study began with a task analysis of critical behaviors that comprised the athletic skill: (a) stand behind start line, (b) bend knees with one leg in front of the other, (c) look up with eyes facing finish line, (d) start running within 3 seconds of audile signal, (e) place feet in front of one another at rapid pace, (f) swing arms back and forth within 45-degree angle, (g) stay within lane throughout the sprint, and (h) run past finish line. Following a baseline phase the participants were coached to run faster through different combinations of goal setting (Ward & Carnes, 2002), performance feedback (Brobst & Ward, 2002), positive reinforcement (Stokes, Luiselli, & Reed, 2010), and video modeling (Boyer, Miltenberger, Batsche, & Fogel, 2009). The principal finding was that when compared to baseline, both participants averaged lower sprint times during intervention. Following intervention, they ran faster than their baseline average in competition at a regional Special Olympics event. This study did not isolate the optimal combination of intervention methods but did reveal a promising behavioral coaching model for application with athletes who have ASD.

SUMMARY

Although still emerging, there is a good body of work that endorses ABA as an effective discipline for addressing exercise, physical activity, and sports among children and youth with ASD. A synthesis of the extant literature reveals that most of the research has been devoted to skill acquisition—that is, teaching a person the behaviors that are necessary to exercise properly, become more active physically, or participate in an athletic pursuit. The emphasis has been on instructional methods that have been validated extensively by ABA professionals (Cooper, Heron, & Heward, 2007), namely prompting, prompt-fading, and positive reinforcement, and with few modifications, appear to translate exceptionally well to the exercise, physical activity, and sports arena.

The research literature also documents ABA applications for *supporting and maintaining* the exercise, physical activity, and sports skills that were taught through intensive instruction. Put simply, the prominent question is that if a child or youth with ASD learns an exercise routine, how do care providers ensure active and enduring participation? This concern is a *performance* objective that is commonly discussed by exercise adherence specialists (Cushing & Steele, 2011). Schools and community-based programs can play a vital role in this regard by organizing peer support groups, sports activities, and similar physical activity outlets for students with ASD. Strategies such as self-monitoring (Michie, Abraham, Whittington, McAteer, & Gupta, 2009) and automated Internet, e-mail, and mobile phone systems (Hurling et al., 2008) are additional adherence-building strategies, mostly studied with adults in the general population but worthy of exploration with other individuals.

A third dominant area, antecedent intervention, has produced good results notwithstanding the need for advanced inquiry into the processes that produce behavior change. For example, are the positive findings from antecedent exercise research attributable to nonspecific influences (e.g., fatigue) or identifiable physiological functions which affect attention and information processing? From an ABA perspective, antecedent exercise likely serves as a motivating operation (MO) by altering the reinforcing consequences of behaviors like aggression and self-injury (Friman & Hawkins, 2006). Nonetheless, practical applications of antecedent exercise are dependent on more rigorous study of its mechanisms of change.

Beyond health and therapeutic benefits, we should not dismiss the recreational pleasures from exercising routinely, among them mood enhancement and social stimulation. Indeed, as much as possible, exercise, physical activity, and sports should have a prominent place in the lives of children and youth with ASD, leading to an exercise-rich lifestyle that will extend into their adult years.

RECOMMENDATIONS AND FUTURE DIRECTIONS

Though not inclusive, this section of the chapter discusses several areas that have relevance for ABA practice and research. Specifically, I highlight measurement, motivation, intervention implementation, and natural setting research studies.

Measurement

Measurement priorities include quantifying the direct and indirect effects from exercise and physical activity. For example, in teaching a person with ASD to jog, it may be necessary to first isolate the component responses of arm placement, body alignment, eyes/head orientation, foot pronation, and similar biomechanical indices. In essence, these responses represent steps in a task analysis for training "jogging skill." Other measures would be the distance a person jogs and the respective time. Jogging also yields physiological measures of energy expenditure such as heart and respiration rate. And if programmed exercise has relevance for treating a health concern like obesity (Fleming, 2011), a person's weight and BMI would be measured.

Measurement through direct observation is fundamental to ABA and has been incorporated in studies of physical activity. As examples, there is the *Behaviors of Eating and Activity for Children's Health Evaluation System* (BEACHES; McKenzie et al., 1991) and the *Observation System for Recording Activity in Children* (OSRAC) within preschools

(OSRAC-P; McIver, Brown, Pfeiffer, Dowda, & Pate, 2009) and homes (OSRAC-H; Brown et al., 2009). McIver et al. (2009) suggested that observational measurement of physical activity has the advantages of assessing behavior in a person's day-to-day environment while simultaneously recording moment-to-moment fluctuations in relation to different contexts and settings. In other words, these observation and measurement systems are able "to describe the social and environmental circumstances associated with various amounts of physical activity" (McIver et al., 2009, p. 2). In turn, it should be possible to influence the types and levels of physical activity by manipulating structural characteristics of environments that were confirmed though observation.

However, direct observation and measurement of physical activity has potential drawbacks. Hustyi, Normand, and Larson (2011) compared activity data from the OSRAC-P with data recorded from pedometers that were worn by two typically developing but significantly overweight 4-year-old children. The OSRAC-P codes were quantified into three activity levels that corresponded to sedentary, light, and moderate-to-vigorous physical activity. These measures were matched against the pedometer recorded steps the children took during an outdoor recess period at a preschool. Although both measurement systems were generally congruent, Hustyi et al. (2011) raised the question of whether some situations might dictate one system over the other. For example, direct observation and measurement of walking and running might reveal the same high activity level but due to different stride lengths, variation in the number of steps taken. Accordingly, "Because pedometers are likely to underestimate activity, they might be preferable to direct measurement in some circumstances because they produce more conservative estimates of behavior and behavior change" (p. 638).

As for actigraphy, the ambulatory measurement of physical activity, Tryon (2011) wrote a comprehensive review of methods, devices, and respective advantages and disadvantages. Pedometers and digital step counters are relatively easy to use but cannot be worn for nonwalking and nonrunning exercise (e.g., swimming). Though variables such as a person's height and stride length can vary considerably, possibly yielding an inaccurate measure of activity level, Beets and Pitetti (2011) demonstrated that it is now possible to accurately measure MVPA with pedometry by referring to step frequency thresholds adjusted to a person's gender and height.

Actigraphs, described by Tryon (2011), are "small lightweight computerized accelerometer-based devices worn typically at the wrist, waist, and/or ankle that rapidly and simultaneously digitize movement in one, two, or three dimensions every 15, 30, or 60 seconds continuously 24-hours a day for as many days as memory allows" (p. 28). Activity level and other exercise-related indices such as sleep and circadian rhythms can be recorded by actigraphs with high resolution and comprise several personal fitness trainers that rely on wireless sensor technology.

It would seem, then, that simultaneous direct observation measurement and automated ambulatory monitoring would be the ideal combination for accurately quantifying exercise and physical activity. Certainly, the measurement methods will be dictated by the behaviors of interest, the relevant settings, and the requisite resources, including financial cost of purchasing devices. Some children and youth with ASD may also have difficulty tolerating and wearing a device, although with intervention, they can learn to do so (Richling et al., 2011). As mentioned, self-recording, which has been evaluated positively in behavioral sport psychology research (Luiselli et al., 2011), is another method that some children and youth with ASD could be taught to measure their exercise and physical activity.

Motivation

For most people, it is not easy to plan and maintain regularly scheduled exercise and physical activity. Some sources of motivation are improving one's health, alleviating stress, and enjoying competitive sports. Unfortunately, many children and youth with ASD do not recognize these attributes nor do they experience the exercise and athletic options that are available to typically developing peers. Therefore, service providers such as schools and community support agencies must develop sustainable recreational opportunities for this underserved population. Additional services are needed to educate parents about the salutary outcomes that exercise, physical activity, and sports can produce.

Virtually every study reviewed in this chapter included a positive reinforcement procedure to strengthen the skills that were taught to the participants during intervention. The reinforcers were many, encompassing tangible (primary) items such as food and secondary stimuli such as praise,

acknowledgement, and tokens. Selecting potential reinforcers to promote exercise, physical activity, and sports among children and youth with ASD should follow empirically supported practices of stimulus preference assessment (DeLeon & Iwata, 1996; Fisher et al., 1992). The objective is to confirm child and youth preferences by conducting one or more assessments preceding intervention—the results of assessment can then be tested through reinforcer evaluations. For a practical guide, readers should consult Tiger and Kliebert (2011) about how to implement different stimulus preference assessment methods with people who have ASD.

A rather intriguing approach to exercise motivation and reinforcement can be found in gaming technology called *exergaming* in which "video games or various auditory or visual stimuli are paired with different types of exercise equipment and activities, and the individual must engage in physical activity to play the game or produce the auditory or visual stimulation" (Fogel, Miltenberger, Graves, & Koehler, 2012, p. 592). *NintendoWii*®, for example, is a popular virtual sports exergame series. As it relates to exercise and physical activity, several studies have reported that children expend more energy with interactive video games as compared to sedentary video games (Graves, Stratton, Ridgers, & Cable, 2007; Lanningham-Foster et al., 2006). Fogel et al. (2010) also found that exergaming was associated with more minutes of physical activity and more minutes of opportunity for physical activity than a traditional physical education classroom. This research suggests that finding exergames that appeal to children and youth with ASD may be a fortuitous motivational strategy to support beneficial physical activity. Other exergaming research measures are the intensity of physical activity expended during play and preplay and postplay fitness ratings (Fogel et al., 2010).

Intervention Implementation

Teachers, therapists, parents, and other care providers are usually responsible for implementing ABA intervention. Among several practitioner concerns is having efficient methods for training care providers, supervising their implementation practices, and sustaining acquired skills over time. Notably, there is substantive research that endorses several effective procedures (LeBlanc, Gravina, & Carr, 2009; Reid, 2004). First, training is conducted optimally in vivo instead of simulated conditions that may only approximate "real-world" settings.

Simulated training, though sometimes necessary, assumes that learned skills will generalize to natural environments. Second, a professional who is doing the training should have simple, written, and easily understood protocols that define training objectives and the steps necessary to achieve them. Studies also support a three-component model in which a trainer (a) demonstrates the behaviors (skills) to be acquired, (b) has the care provider perform accordingly, and (c) delivers performance feedback through behavior-contingent praise and correction (Luiselli, 2011; Ricciardi, 2005). This approach to training is time efficient, can be adapted to most settings, and through relatively simple data collection, makes it possible to quickly evaluate training outcomes.

There appear to be several factors that can facilitate success with the preceding training model. One consistent finding is that performance feedback works best when it is immediate and not delayed. As care providers make progress, the trainer can gradually reduce how often feedback is provided. Performance feedback can also be presented verbally, visually, or both. For example, many care providers respond favorably when a trainer comments about their performance while simultaneously showing them respective data in the form of a graph or similar visual reference (DiGennaro Reed & Codding, 2011). Additionally, performance feedback may affect care providers differently if a trainer delivers it to one person at a time or to several people in a group. Therefore when training care providers to implement exercise, physical activity, and sports interventions with children and youth who have ASD, professionals should carefully select methods that fit with the unique characteristics of trainees.

The topic of intervention integrity is examined in a separate chapter of this book but is worth highlighting when training care providers. Arguably, it is not possible to properly evaluate intervention if care providers do not implement it accurately. Intervention integrity assessment involves a professional observing care providers implementing procedures that are delineated in a written plan. Next, the observer records procedures that were implemented accurately and inaccurately, producing a composite, intervention integrity score. The final step is giving care providers feedback about their performance by reinforcing accurately implemented procedures and correcting inaccurately implemented procedures. This description reveals that intervention integrity assessment has both a detection and training function. Put another way, such assessment pinpoints and corrects implementation errors, thereby improving procedural fidelity and the probability that intervention will have a positive outcome.

Acknowledging the time and effort that is required to train care providers and fortify their implementation integrity, it is also possible to affect physical activity advantageously through low-demand environmental modifications. Hustyi, Normand, Larson, and Morely (2012) measured physical activity levels of four, typically developing children (4 years old) when they had access to outdoor toys (soft baseballs, jump rope, hula hoop, throwing objects), could climb on fixed equipment (slides, monkey bars, stairs), or were able to play in an open space that had neither outdoor toys nor fixed equipment. Absent any additional intervention, all of the children had the highest measures of moderate-to-vigorous physical activity during the fixed equipment condition. Although Hustyi et al. (2012) was primarily an observational and not intervention study, the results suggest that stand-alone environmental changes can influence physical activity, making this strategy reasonable for children and youth with ASD at school, home, and the community.

Research

This chapter had many examples of single-case experimental methodology, a convention within ABA (Cooper, Heward, & Heron, 2007; Kazdin, 2011), that also has a rich tradition in behavioral sport psychology research (Luiselli & Reed, 2011; Martin, Thomson, & Regehr, 2004). The advantages of single-case designs are that they can be tailored to individual children and youth, measure the direct effects of intervention, and offer robust controls for internal validity. I have argued previously, in fact, that single-case designs are valuable and adaptable tools that sport psychology and athletic performance professionals should use to conduct applied research in their work as consultants and trainers (Luiselli, 2012). Behavior analysts, in particular, must continue to conduct high-quality single-case research with children and youth who have ASD in order to strengthen the external validity of recommended practices.

One agenda for future ABA research is evaluating novel, potentially promising intervention methods as well as comparing the effects of more established procedures. Video modeling, for example, is a validated approach for teaching communication and social skills to children and youth with ASD (Darden-Brunson, Green, & Goldstein, 2008) but has only rarely been examined in exercise, physical activity, and sports research with this population (Luiselli et al., 2012). For comparative research, the proper single-case design is the alternating treatments design (ATD), which measures the behavior-altering effects of two or more interventions (Barlow & Hayes, 1979). As an illustration, Osborne, Rudrud, and Zezoney (1990) studied curveball hitting proficiency of five college baseball players under baseline and two intervention conditions in an ATD. Before intervention, the players practiced hitting against a pitching machine that was adjusted to simulate a curveball thrown at a standard speed. The interventions consisted of marking the seams of baseballs with either ¼-inch or 1/8-inch orange stripes. Each of these marked-ball conditions was compared to the unmarked-baseball condition during two batting practice sessions each day. The ATD showed that curveball hitting proficiency improved with the marked-ball interventions. This study, although it did not concern children and youth with ASD, is a good example of how "treatments" in an ATD can actually be any number of conditions, contexts, or procedures that can be manipulated to compare the one(s) that are most effective. Several ATD studies are possible for exercise instruction and promotion, examples being a comparison of different measurement tactics, types of positive reinforcement, and prompting techniques to name just a few.

Finally, as ABA research into exercise, physical activity, and sports within ASD continues, it is essential that studies assess the social validity among those who receive and implement intervention (Wolf, 1978). For one, we should be interested in perceptions about intervention acceptability, namely are the objectives and procedures reasonable, consistent with prevailing norms, and life fulfilling? Studies should also assess the level of satisfaction with methods and outcomes. Importantly, social validity assessment informs professionals about intervention formulation and design beyond the direct effects of procedures. Making ABA intervention palatable to children and youth with ASD and their care providers will expand the breadth of exercise, physical activity, and sports options available to them, refine existing empirically supported practices, and produce healthier and more satisfying lives.

REFERENCES

Allison, D. B., Basile, V. C., & MacDonald, R. B. (1991). Brief report: Comparative effects of antecedent exercise and lorazepam on the aggressive behavior of an autistic man. *Journal of Autism and Developmental Disorders, 21,* 89–94.

Barlow, D. H., & Hayes, S. C. (1979). Alternating treatments design: One strategy for comparing the effects of two treatments in a single subject. *Journal of Applied Behavior Analysis, 12,* 199–210.

Beets, M. W., & Pitetti, K. H. (2011). Using pedometers to measure moderate-to-vigorous physical activity for youth with intellectual disability. *Disability and Health Journal, 4,* 46–51.

Boyer, E., Miltenberger, R. G., Batsche, C., & Fogel, V. (2009). Video modeling by experts with video feedback to enhance gymnastics skills. *Journal of Applied Behavior Analysis, 42,* 855–860.

Brobst, B., & Ward, P. (2002). Effects of public posting, goal setting, and oral feedback on the skills of female soccer players. *Journal of Applied Behavior Analysis, 35,* 247–257.

Brown, W. H., Pfeiffer, K. A., McIver, K. L., Dowda, M., Addy, C. L., & Pate, R. R. (2009). Social and environmental factors associated with preschoolers' nonsedentary physical activity. *Child Development, 80,* 45–58.

Cameron, M. J., & Cappello, M. J. (1993). "We'll cross that hurdle when we get to it": Teaching athletic performance within adaptive physical education. *Behavior Modification, 17,* 136–147.

Cameron, M. J., Shapiro, R. L., & Ainsleigh, S. A. (2005). Bicycle riding: Pedaling made possible through positive behavioral interventions. *Journal of Positive Behavior Interventions, 7,* 153–158.

Capersen, C. J., Powell, K. E., & Christenson, G. M. (1985). Physical activity, exercise, and physical fitness: Definitions and distinctions for health-related research. *Public Health Reports, 100,* 126–131.

Celiberti, D. A., Bobo, H. E., Kelly, K. S., Harris, S. L., & Handleman, J. S. (1997). The differential and temporal effects of antecedent exercise on the self-stimulatory behavior of a child with autism. *Research in Developmental Disabilities, 18,* 139–150.

Chanias, A. K., Reid, G., & Hoover, M. L. (1998). Exercise effects on health-related physical fitness of individuals with an intellectual disability: A meta-analysis. *Adaptive Physical Education Quarterly, 15,* 119–140.

Cooper, J. O., Heron, T. E., & Heward, W. L. (2007). *Applied behavior analysis* (2nd ed.). Upper Saddle River, NJ: Pearson Education.

Cushing, C. C., & Steele, R. G. (2011). Establishing and maintaining physical exercise. In J. K. Luiselli & D. D. Reed (Eds.), *Behavioral sport psychology: Evidence-based approaches to performance enhancement* (pp. 127–141). New York, NY: Springer.

Darden-Brunson, F., Green, A., & Goldstein, H. (2008). Video-based instruction for children with autism. In J. K. Luiselli, D. C. Russo, W. P. Christian, & S. Wilczynski (Eds.), *Effective practices for children with autism: Educational and behavior support interventions that work* (pp. 241–268). New York, NY: Oxford University Press.

De, S., Small, J., & Baur, L. A. (2008). Overweight and obesity among children with developmental disabilities. *Journal of Intellectual & Developmental Disability, 33,* 43–47.

DeLeon, I. G., & Iwata, B. A. (1996). Evaluation of a multiple-stimulus presentation format for assessing reinforcer preferences. *Journal of Applied Behavior Analysis, 29,* 519–533.

DiGennaro Reed, F. D., & Codding, R. S. (2011). Intervention integrity assessment. In J. K. Luiselli (Ed.), *Teaching and behavior support for children and adults with autism spectrum disorder: A practitioner's guide* (pp. 38–47). New York, NY: Oxford University Press.

Dowrick, P. W., & Dove, C. (1980). The use of self-modeling to improve the swimming performance of spina bifida children. *Journal of Applied Behavior Analysis, 13,* 51–56.

Draheim, C. C., Williams, D. P., & McCubbin, J. A. (2002). Prevalence of physical activity and recommended physical activity in community-based adults with mental retardation. *Mental Retardation, 40,* 436–444.

Elliot, R. O., Dobbin, A. R., Rose, G. D., & Soper, H. V. (1994). Vigorous, aerobic exercise versus general motor training activities: Effects of maladaptive and stereotypic behaviors of adults with both autism and mental retardation. *Journal of Autism and Developmental Disorders, 24,* 565–576.

Fisher, W., Piazza, C. C., Bowman, L. G., Hagopian, L. P., Owens, J. C., & Slevin, I. (1992). A comparison of two approaches for identifying reinforcers for persons with severe and profound disabilities. *Journal of Applied Behavior Analysis, 25,* 491–498.

Fleming, R. K. (2011). Obesity and weight regulation. In J. K. Luiselli (Ed.), *The handbook of high-risk challenging behaviors in people with intellectual and developmental disabilities* (pp. 195–205). Baltimore, MD: Paul H. Brookes.

Fogel, V. A., Miltenberger, R. G., Graves, R., & Koehler, S. (2010). The effects of exergaming on physical activity among inactive children in a physical education classroom. *Journal of Applied Behavior Analysis, 43,* 591–600.

Foley, J. T., & McCubbin, J. A. (2009). An exploratory study of after-school sedentary behavior of elementary school-age children with intellectual disability. *Journal of Intellectual and Developmental Disabilities, 34,* 3–9.

Fragala-Pinkham, M., Haley, S. M., & O'Neill, M. E. (2008). Group aquatic aerobic exercise for children with disabilities. *Developmental Medicine and Child Neurology, 50,* 822–827.

Friman, P. C., & Hawkins, R. O. (2006). Contribution of establishing operations to antecedent intervention. In J. K. Luiselli (Ed.), *Antecedent intervention: Innovative approaches to behavior support* (pp. 31–52). Baltimore, MD: Paul H. Brookes.

Gabler-Halle, D., Halle, J. W., & Chung, Y. B. (1993). The effects of aerobic exercise on psychological and behavioral variables of individuals with developmental disabilities: A critical review. *Research in Developmental Disabilities, 14,* 359–386.

Gibbons, S. L., & Bushakra, F. B. (1989). Effects of Special Olympics participation on the perceived competence and social acceptance of mentally retarded children. *Adaptive Physical Activity Quarterly, 6,* 40–51.

Glidden, L. M., Bamberger, K. T., Draheim, A. R., & Kersh, J. (2011). Parent and athlete perceptions of Special Olympics participation: Utility and danger of proxy responding. *Intellectual and Developmental Disabilities, 49,* 37–45.

Gordon, R., Handleman, J. S., & Harris, S. L. (1986). The effects of contingent versus non-contingent running on the out-of-seat behavior of an autistic boy. *Child and Family Behavior Therapy, 8,* 37–44.

Graves, L., Stratton, G., Ridgers, N. D., & Cable, N. T. (2007). Comparison of energy expenditure in adolescents when playing new generation and sedentary computer games: Cross sectional study. *British Medical Journal, 335,* 1282–1284.

Howie, E. K., Barnes, T. L., McDermott, S., Mann, J. R., Clarkson, J., & Meriwether, R. A. (2012). Availability of physical activity resources in the environment for adults with intellectual disabilities. *Disability and Health Journal, 5,* 41–48.

Hurling, R., Catt, M., De Boni, M., Fairley, B. W., Hurst, T., Murray, P.,...Sodhi, J. S. (2008). Using internet and mobile phone technology to deliver an automated physical activity program: Randomized controlled trial. *Journal of Medical Internet Research, 9,* 1–12.

Hustyi, K. M., Normand, M. P., & Larson, T. A. (2011). Behavioral assessment of physical activity in obese preschool children. *Journal of Applied Behavior Analysis, 44,* 635–639.

Hustyi, K. M., Normand, M. P., Larson, T. A., & Morley, A. J. (2012). The effect of outdoor activity context on physical activity in preschool children. *Journal of Applied Behavior Analysis, 45,* 401–405.

Kazdin, A. E. (2011). *Single-case research designs: Methods for clinical and applied settings.* New York, NY: Oxford University Press.

Kern, L., Koegel, R. L., Dyer, K., Blew, P. A., & Fenton, L. R. (1982). The effects of physical exercise on self-stimulation and appropriate responding in autistic children. *Journal of Autism and Developmental Disorders, 12,* 399–419.

Lancioni, G. E., Singh, N. N., O'Reilly, M. F., Sigafoos, J., Didden, R., Manfredi, F.,...Basili, G. (2009). Fostering locomotor behavior of children with developmental disabilities: An overview of studies using treadmills and walkers with microswitches. *Research in Developmental Disabilities, 30,* 308–322.

Lang, R., Koegel, L. K., Ashbaugh, K., Regester, A., Ence, W., & Smith, W. (2010). Physical exercise and individuals with autism spectrum disorders: A systematic review. *Research in Autism Spectrum Disorders, 4,* 565–576.

Lanningham-Foster, L., Jensen, T. B., Foster, R. C., Redmond, A. B., Walker, B. A., Heinz, D., & Levine, J. A. (2006). Energy expenditure of sedentary screen time compared with active screen time for children. *Pediatrics, 118,* 1831–1835.

LeBlanc, L. A., Gravina, N., & Carr, J. E. (2009). Training issues unique to autism spectrum disorders. In J. L. Matson (Ed.), *Applied behavior analysis for children with autism spectrum disorders* (pp. 225–235). New York, NY: Springer.

Levinson, L. J., & Reid, G. (1993). The effects of exercise intensity on stereotypic behaviors of individuals with autism. *Adaptive Physical Activity Quarterly, 10,* 255–268.

Luiselli, J. K. (2008). Antecedent (preventive) intervention. In J. K. Luiselli, D. C. Russo, W. P. Christian, & S. Wilczynski (Eds.), *Effective practices for children with autism: Educational and behavior support interventions that work* (pp. 393–412). New York, NY: Oxford University Press.

Luiselli, J. K. (2011). Training parents and other care providers. In J. K. Luiselli (Ed.), *Teaching and behavior support for children and adults with autism spectrum disorder: A practitioner's guide* (pp. 212–216). New York, NY: Oxford University Press.

Luiselli, J. K. (2012). Behavioral sport psychology consulting: A review of some practice concerns and recommendations. *Journal of Sport Psychology in Action, 3,* 41–51.

Luiselli, J. K., Duncan, N. G., Keary, P., Godbold Nelson, E., Parenteau, R. E., & Woods, K. E. (2013). Behavioral coaching of track athletes with developmental disabilities: Evaluation of Sprint performance during training and Special Olympics competition. *Journal of Clinical Sport Psychology, 7,* 264–274.

Luiselli, J. K., & Reed, D. D. (2011) (Eds.). *Behavioral sport psychology: Evidence-based approaches to performance enhancement.* New York, NY: Springer.

Luiselli, J. K., Woods, K. E., Keary, P., & Parenteau, R. E. (2013). Practitioner beliefs about athletic and health promoting activities for children and youth with intellectual and developmental disabilities: A social validation survey. *Journal of Developmental and Physical Disabilities* (in press).

Luiselli, J. K., Woods, K. E., & Reed, D. D. (2011). Review of sports performance research with youth, collegiate, and elite athletes. *Journal of Applied Behavior Analysis, 44,* 999–1002.

Luyben, P. D., Funk, D. M., Morgan, J. K., Clark, K. A., & Delulio, D. W. (1986). Team sports for the severely retarded: Training a side-of-the-foot soccer pass using a maximum-to-minimum prompt reduction strategy. *Journal of Applied Behavior Analysis, 19,* 431–436.

Martin, G. L., Thompson, K., & Regehr, K. (2004). Studies using single-subject designs in sport psychology: 30 years of research. *The Behavior Analyst, 27,* 123–140.

McIlver, K., Brown, W. H., Pfeiffer, K. A., Dowda, M., & Pate, R. R. (2009). Assessing children's physical activity in their homes: The observational system for recording physical activity in children-home. *Journal of Applied Behavior Analysis, 42,* 1–16.

McKenzie, T. L., Sallis, J. F., Nader, P. R., Patterson, T. L., Elder, J. P., Berry, C. C.,...Nelson, J. A. (1991). BEACHES: An observational system for assessing children's eating and physical activity behaviors and associated events. *Journal of Applied Behavior Analysis, 24,* 141–151.

Michie, S., Abraham, C., Whittington, C., McAteer, J., & Gupta, S. (2009). Effective techniques in healthy eating and physical activity interventions: A meta-regression. *Health Psychology, 28,* 690–701.

Osborne, K., Rudrud, E., & Zezoney, F. (1990). Improved curveball hitting through the enhancement of visual cues. *Journal of Applied Behavior Analysis, 23,* 371–377.

Pan, C. Y. (2010). Effects of water exercise swimming program on aquatic skills and social behaviors in children with autism spectrum disorders. *Autism, 14,* 9–28.

Pan, C. Y. (2011). The efficacy of an aquatic program on physical fitness and aquatic skills in children with and without autism spectrum disorders. *Research in Autism Spectrum Disorders, 5,* 657–665.

Pitetti, K. H., Beets, M. W., & Combs, C. (2009). Physical activity levels of children with intellectual disabilities during school. *Medical Science Sports and Exercise, 41,* 1580–1586.

Ricciardi, J. N. (2005). Achieving human service outcomes through competency-based training. *Behavior Modification, 29,* 488–507.

Richling, S. M., Rapp, J. T., Carroll, R. A., Smith, J. N., Nystedt, A., & Siewert, B. (2011). Using noncontingent reinforcement to increase compliance with wearing prescription prostheses. *Journal of Applied Behavior Analysis, 44,* 375–379.

Rimmer, J. H., Braddock, D., & Fujiura, G. (1993). Prevalence of obesity in adults with mental retardation: Implications for health promotion and disease prevention. *Mental Retardation, 31,* 105–110.

Rimmer, J. H., Braddock, D., & Fujiura, G. (1994). Cardiovascular disease risk factors in adults with mental retardation. *American Journal of Mental Retardation, 98,* 510–518.

Rimmer, J. A., & Rowland, J. L. (2008). Physical activity for youth with disabilities: A critical need in an underserved population. *Developmental Neurorehabilitation, 11,* 141–148.

Rogers, L., Hemmeter, M. L., & Wolery, M. (2010). Using a constant time delay procedure to teach foundational swimming skills to children with autism. *Topics in Early Childhood Special Education, 30,* 102–111.

Rosenthal-Malek, A., & Mitchell, S. (1997). Brief report: The effects of exercise on the self-stimulatory behaviors and positive responding of adolescents with autism. *Journal of Autism and Developmental Disorders*, 27, 193–202.

Sowa, M., & Meulenbroek, R. (2012). Effects of physical exercise on autism spectrum disorders: A meta-analysis. *Research in Autism Spectrum Disorders*, 6, 46–57.

Stokes, J. V., Luiselli, J. K., & Reed, D. D. (2010). A behavioral intervention for teaching tackling skills to high school football athletes. *Journal of Applied Behavior Analysis*, 43, 509–512.

Tiger, J. H., & Kliebert, M. L. (2011). Stimulus preference assessment. In J. K. Luiselli (Ed.), *Teaching and behavior support for children and adults with autism spectrum disorder: A practitioner's guide* (pp. 31–37). New York, NY: Oxford University Press.

Tryon, W. W. (2011). Actigraphy: The ambulatory measurement of physical activity. In J. K. Luiselli & D. D. Reed (Eds.), *Behavioral sport psychology: Evidence-based approaches to performance enhancement* (pp. 25–41). New York, NY: Springer.

Ward, P., & Carnes, M. (2002). Effects of posting self-set goals on collegiate football players' skill execution during practice and games. *Journal of Applied Behavior Analysis*, 35, 1–12.

Weiss, J. A. (2008). Role of Special Olympics for mothers of adult athletes with intellectual disabilities. *American Journal of Mental Retardation*, 113, 241–253.

Whitt-Glover, M. C., O'Neill, K. L., & Stettler, N. (2006). Physical activity patterns in children with and without Down syndrome. *Pediatric rehabilitation*, 9, 158–164.

Wolf, M. M. (1978). Social validity: The case for subjective measurement or how applied behavior analysis is finding its heart. *Journal of Applied Behavior Analysis*, 11, 203–214.

Yilmaz, I., Yanardag, M., Birkan, B. A., & Bumin, G. (2004). Effects of swimming training on physical fitness and water orientation in autism. *Pediatrics International*, 46, 624–626.

SECTION IV

Additional Topics

14

Mindful Caregiving and Support

NIRBHAY N. SINGH, GIULIO E. LANCIONI, ALAN S. W. WINTON, JUDY SINGH, ASHVIND N. ADKINS SINGH, AND ANGELA D. ADKINS SINGH

Mindfulness is a foundational practice in most of the world's wisdom traditions. As a concept and as a practice, mindfulness seems to have caught the imagination of social scientists in the West. Indeed, it is the emerging practice du jour across many disciplines, including education, medicine, neuroscience, politics, psychology, and management, among others. Furthermore, over the past 30 years, there has been an exponential growth in clinical research using mindfulness-based therapies to alleviate pain and suffering arising from a broad range of diseases and disorders (Williams & Kabat-Zinn, 2011). This proliferation of therapies that use some facet of mindfulness includes, among others, dialectical behavior therapy (DBT; Linehan, 1993), mindfulness-based stress reduction (MBSR; Kabat-Zinn, 1990), acceptance and commitment therapy (ACT; Hayes, Strosahl, & Wilson, 1999), mindfulness-based cognitive therapy (MBCT; Segal, Williams, & Teasdale, 2002), and mindfulness-based relapse prevention (MBRP; Bowen, Chawla, & Marlatt, 2010).

Concept and Practice of Mindfulness

The concept of mindfulness that is most prevalent in Western therapies is derived from Buddhism. The standard understanding of practicing mindfulness is the conscious performance of all activities from an attitude of pure observation. It is the moment-by-moment nonjudgmental awareness of every aspect of life itself:

> Everything is meditation in this practice, even while eating, drinking, dressing, seeing, hearing, smelling, tasting, touching, thinking. Whatever you are doing, everything should be done mindfully, dynamically, with totality, completeness, thoroughness. Then it becomes meditation, meaningful, purposeful. It is not thinking, but experiencing from moment to moment, living from moment to moment, without clinging, without condemning, without judging, without criticizing—choiceless awareness…It should be integrated into our whole life. It is actually an education in how to see, how to hear, how to smell, how to eat, how to drink, how to walk with full awareness. (Munindra in Knaster, 2010, p. 1)

Indeed, the practice of mindfulness is experiential, a bare awareness of everyday life, and not focused on the engagement in or control of one's thoughts.

Mindfulness can be systematically taught through the Buddha's teachings as presented in the Sutra on the Full Awareness of Breathing (*Ānāpānasati Sutra*) and the Sutra on the Four Foundations of Mindfulness (*Satipatthāna Sutra*). The heart of the *Ānāpānasati Sutra* contains 16 methods of fully aware breathing (Buddhadasa Bhikkhu, 1997). The first four breathing exercises focus on an awareness of the breath and the body, and by practicing these exercises we experience the oneness of the breath and body. The second set of four breathing exercises focuses on an awareness of feelings as they arise from the body or the mind, and by practicing all eight exercises we experience the unity of breath, body, and feelings. The third set of four breathing exercises focuses on the activities of the mind, and by practicing all twelve exercises we experience the unity of the breath, body, feelings, and mind. The fourth set of four breathing exercises focuses on the object of the mind. The mind cannot exist in a vacuum; thus, there needs to be something that gives rise to it. For example, if there is an attachment or aversion, it is an attachment or aversion to something. This something is the object of the mind. By practicing all sixteen breathing exercises we experience the unity of the breath, body, feelings, mind, and the objects of the mind. These sixteen exercises are often prescribed as the practice basis for fully exploring the *Satipatthāna Sutra*.

The *Satipatthāna Sutra* provides the prescription for practicing full awareness of the four foundations of mindfulness—body, feelings, mind, and the objects of the mind (Anālayo, 2003; Gunaratana, 2012). The first foundation is the body, and the practice of mindful breathing brings us back in touch with the body through inhalation and exhalation, by looking deeply at our body posture (i.e., walking, standing, sitting, and lying), and contemplation of the body itself. The second foundation is our feelings. The practice of mindful breathing enables us to recognize the feelings as pleasant, unpleasant, or neutral, and understanding their transitory nature. The third foundation is our mind or mental formations arising from our mind. Mental formations can be physical objects (e.g., flower, furniture) or various forms of emotional arousal (e.g., attachment, love, fear, anger, despair, agitation). When we are mindful of the mind, we are cognizant of every state of consciousness that arises in our daily lives. Mindful breathing enables us to calmly and deeply examine the mental formations and gain insight into the conditions that gave rise to them. The fourth foundation is the object of the mind, or our perceptions. Mindful breathing enables us to examine the nature of our perceptions, eventually leading us to see the body, feelings, mind, and objects of the mind as they are; that is, that they have no independent origination (or inherent existence) and are thus essentially empty (*shunyata*; Dalai Lama, 1991, 2006).

Definition of Mindfulness

Given the surge of mindfulness-based therapies, it may be assumed that there is a consensus on the concept and definition of mindfulness, but this is not so (Chiesa, 2013; Grossman & Van Dam, 2011; Singh, Lancioni, Wahler, Winton, & Singh, 2008). For example, the various rating scales available for its measurement present mindfulness either as a single factor (e.g., Brown & Ryan, 2003) or multiple-factor construct (e.g., Baer, Smith, Hopkins, Krietemeyer, & Toney, 2006), suggesting the definition of mindfulness differs depending on the measure used (see Bergomi, Tschacher, & Kupper, 2013; Grossman, 2008). At a descriptive level, Kabat-Zinn (1994) has described mindfulness as "paying attention in a particular way: on purpose, in the present moment and nonjudgmentally" (Kabat-Zinn, 1994, p. 4). Similarly, the practice of mindfulness has been defined as "learning to simply rest in a bare awareness of thoughts, feelings, and perceptions as they occur" (Mingyur Rinpoche, 2007, p. 43). The essence of mindfulness in these definitions is the experiencing or observation of habitual thoughts, feelings, and perceptions as the natural function of the mind. If we simply observe the natural functioning of the mind, the power of the objects of the mind slowly fade away because of our noninteraction with them. By simply observing, the mind changes the activity of the mind.

Purpose of Practicing Mindfulness

The reason one may engage in the practice of mindfulness varies with the intention of the meditation practitioner. In general terms, mindfulness practices in Eastern cultures arose from a quest for spiritual transformation and liberation. While this has also been true for many mindfulness practitioners in Western cultures, mindfulness-based therapies are based on an expectation of improved physical and mental health. As noted by Chiesa and Malinowski (2011), achieving such health benefits is the primary aim of mindfulness-based therapies in Western cultures; in Eastern cultures these are considered secondary outcomes of a spiritual practice. Instead of focusing on gaining insight into the nature of suffering, Western mindfulness-based therapies appear to be single-mindedly focused on its amelioration (Gilpin, 2008). The emerging studies on mindfulness-based therapies used with individuals with autism spectrum disorder (ASD) have included a number of meditation techniques that encourage both insight and treatment.

Inner Workings of Mindfulness

Meditation practice produces transformational changes in the practitioner (Dalai Lama, 2002). How this transformation comes about is an open research question. Various researchers have developed theories of the mechanisms involved, but supportive experimental data are limited (Shapiro, Carlson, Astin, & Freedman, 2006). We have advanced some possible explanations based on our own research and extensive experience of mindfulness meditation practices. We believe the practice of mindfulness results in unconditional acceptance of oneself and others. In the context of parents and support staff, unconditional acceptance of individuals with ASD, regardless of their challenging behaviors, enables them to build a strong alliance with these individuals. That is, being mindful enables parents and support staff to shift the focus of their attention from the challenging behaviors to seeing individuals in a more holistic way. This shift in attention changes the attitudes of parents and support staff toward the individuals, and this attitudinal transformation, rather than application of specific behavior-change techniques, facilitates the behavioral change in the individuals.

Our studies suggest that the related mindfulness concept of nonjudgmental acceptance may play a role in treatment outcome. For example, we have found that mindful staff members minimize categorizing an individual's behaviors as either positive or negative and accept them simply as behaviors. Thus, they try not to respond to challenging behaviors as negative behaviors that need to be immediately controlled or eliminated by altering environmental contingencies; instead, they assist the individuals in their care to relate and respond differently to the same situation. This change in the staff–individual interaction puts their future interactions on a different transactional pathway due to a more positive therapeutic milieu instead of programmed environmental contingencies (Sameroff, 1995).

Mindfulness produces calm attention, which enables staff to reduce escalation of situations that typically lead to or exacerbate challenging behaviors. For example, anecdotal staff reports suggest that staff members use calm attention to instill peace and calmness in both themselves and individuals during stressful situations. Similar findings have been reported with parents of children with disabilities.

Practicing mindfulness enables parents and staff to empty their minds of preconceived notions of the behavior of others they interact with, including individuals with disabilities (Suzuki, 1970). Emptying our minds in this way gives us a beginner's mind, a mind that is able to see positive possibilities where none, or only negative possibilities, were envisioned previously. With mindfulness meditation, parents and staff members develop the ability to see and use positive ways of interacting with children and adults with ASD when compared to their previously negative interactions. When the cycle of negative parent–individual and staff–individual interactions is broken, more positive outcomes arise.

We have found that when parents and staff are mindful, they may become more responsive to each moment of their interactions with the individuals in their care. Developing calm acceptance of whatever behaviors are exhibited, without attempting to impose their will on the situation, minimizes the amount of energy used and the buildup of any resistance. This effortless action, in which parents and staff are able to blend their efforts into the natural flow of life itself, is the Taoist principle of *Wu wei*. With experience and practice they are able to enter the *Wu Dao* dance, the continual giving and receiving of wisdom (Mitchell, 1988; Walker, 1992). In time, parents, staff, and individuals begin to learn from each other, resulting in many positive experiences for all.

In recent work, we have taught the basic breathing meditation to individuals with intellectual disabilities before they learn the *Meditation on the Soles of the Feet* (SoF) procedure to control their anger and aggressive behavior (e.g., Singh et al., 2012). Learning the basic breathing meditation assists the individuals to develop a disciplined approach to meditation well before they learn the SoF procedure. While the basic meditation enables them to begin a process of personal transformation, the SoF meditation provides them with an immediate means of controlling their anger and aggression. The SoF can be seen as a stabilizing meditation (Dalai Lama, 2002) that shifts an individual's focus from the anger, or emotionally arousing thought, event, or situation, to a neutral part of the body. Given that the mind cannot fully concentrate on two nonhabitual processes simultaneously (Foerde, Knowlton, & Poldrack, 2006), the SoF meditation results in the fading of the anger or emotionally arousing situation. We suspect that the SoF procedures works because it enables the individual to stop, refocus the mind from the emotionally arousing situation to the body, be in the present moment, and then make an informed response to the situation without anger.

Applications to Autism Spectrum Disorder

The use of mindfulness-based strategies in individuals with ASD is in its infancy and only four studies have been reported (Bogels, Hoogstad, van Dun, de Schutter, & Restifo, 2008; Singh, Lancioni, Manikam, et al., 2011; Singh, Lancioni, Singh, et al., 2011; Spek, van Ham, & Nyklíček, 2013). In addition, there are two studies that deal with mindfulness-based training of parents of children with autism or ASD (Ferraioli & Harris, 2013; Singh, Lancioni, Winton, Fisher et al., 2006). However, the extant research indicates that the effects obtained in this population are closely aligned with those obtained in similar studies with individuals with intellectual disabilities and their caregivers. Thus, in this chapter, the broad spectrum of mindfulness-based studies involving individuals with ASD and intellectual disabilities are used to highlight the potential of this intervention for individuals with ASD. While many of the reviewed studies involved adults as participants, the procedures used are equally applicable (with minor adjustments for cognitive status) to children and youth with ASD.

PRIORITY CONCERNS

Mindfulness-based strategies have been used with individuals with intellectual disabilities in a growing number of areas, including challenging behaviors, staff training, and parent training.

Challenging Behaviors

Challenging behaviors are a priority concern for individuals with ASD (Matson & Sturmey, 2011; Powers, Palmieri, D'Eramo, & Powers, 2011). Generally, these behaviors can be defined as "culturally abnormal behavior(s) of such intensity, frequency or duration that the physical safety of the person or others is likely to be placed in serious jeopardy, or behavior which is likely to seriously limit use of, or result in the person being denied access to, ordinary community facilities" (Emerson, 2001, p. 3). Individuals with ASD often display aggression, tantrums, property destruction, disruptive behavior, and self-injury (Singh, Lancioni, Winton, & Singh, 2011).

In terms of challenging behaviors, aggression has received considerable attention in the research literature, not only because of negative educational, vocational, and social consequences for the individual, but, more important, because it jeopardizes the individual's continuing placement and acceptance in the community. In addition, severe challenging behaviors can significantly impair the quality of life not only of the individual but also of parents, siblings, and support staff (Hastings, 2002a). Other behaviors, such as self-injury and property destruction, do not appear to be as frequent or severe in individuals who live in the community and do not produce similar negative consequences, as does aggression.

Behavioral and psychopharmacological treatments for aggression and other challenging behaviors dominate the research literature. However, treatment choices made by parents and community support staff are quite diverse. For example, there have been several surveys of treatments used by parents of children with ASD, including those for challenging behaviors. Green et al. (2006) reported data from 552 parents who responded to each of 111 treatments in terms of what they (a) currently used, (b) used previously but not presently, and (c) never used. These included the following classes of treatments: (a) medications, (b) vitamin supplements, (c) special diets, (d) medical procedures, (e) educational/therapy approaches (e.g., applied behavior analysis, speech therapy, music therapy), (f) alternative therapy/medicine (e.g., acupuncture, aromatherapy), and (g) combined programs (e.g., TEACCH, Giant Steps). Of the 111 listed treatments, 108 were being used, or had been used in the past, by one or more parents. However, as this study did not parse out what the therapies targeted, it is not possible to separate treatments for skills deficits from those for behavioral excesses, such as aggression. In another survey, Goin-Kochel, Myers, and Mackintosh (2007) reported findings from 479 parents of children with ASD. About 43% of the parents reported that their children had tried pharmacological treatments and about 32% had been on special diets. Behavioral and other interventions included applied behavior analysis, early intervention services, floor time, music therapy, occupational therapy, physical therapy, sensory integration, and speech therapy. Overall, the children were currently receiving between four and six treatments and had tried a mean of eight treatments in the past, replicating the findings of Green et al. (2006).

These and similar studies indicate that parents and support staff are searching for effective treatments. In a series of studies over the last decade, mindfulness-based procedures have been developed and tested for their effectiveness in treating aggression in individuals with developmental disabilities, including autism and ASD. Furthermore, some studies have reported teaching mindfulness practices to parents and then observing the effects of these practices on the challenging behaviors of their children with developmental disabilities or autism. Similar studies have reported on the teaching of mindfulness practices to support staff that provide care to individuals with intellectual disabilities.

MINDFULNESS-BASED INTERVENTIONS

Mindful Caregiving

Stress appears to be a constant companion of many support staff who work with individuals with intellectual disabilities. Furthermore, those working with individuals who exhibit severe challenging behaviors are at high risk for stress (Hastings, 2002b; Raczka, 2005) and staff turnover in intellectual disability services (Hatton & Emerson, 1998). Researchers have reported reducing staff stress by increasing worker control (Innstrand, Espnes, & Myletun, 2004) and personal support (Rose, Jones, & Fletcher, 1998). An added benefit of reducing staff stress is the collateral effect of increasing the quality and frequency of interactions among support staff and individuals with intellectual disabilities (e.g., Rose et al., 1998).

Staff Training

Different strategies can be used to reduce staff stress and increase the quality of staff members' work performance and their lives generally. For example, because staff generally find the challenging behaviors of individuals with intellectual disabilities to be aversive (Hartley & MacLean, 2007), training in behavior management skills may not only enable staff to better manage individuals who exhibit severe challenging behaviors, but it may also reduce staff members' stress levels and increase their job satisfaction. Other approaches have focused on strengthening the inner resources of the staff members themselves so that they can change the relationship they have with their work situation (Noone, 2013). These approaches focus not so much on changing the nature of their work situation, but rather on the way they perceive their work. Acceptance and commitment therapy (ACT) and mindfulness-based training are prime examples of these approaches.

Noone and Hastings (2009) developed a work stress intervention, the Promotion of Acceptance in Carers and Teachers (PACT), for intellectual disability services support staff. In a pilot study, 14 support staff were trained in a 1-day PACT workshop, followed by a half-day follow-up session 6 weeks later. The pre- and post-PACT workshop data showed a significant reduction in support staff psychological distress on the General Health Questionnaire-12 (GHQ-12; Doi & Minowa, 2003) even in the face of a slight increase in stress on the Staff Stressor Questionnaire (SSQ; Hatton et al., 1999). This preliminary study suggested that PACT training might enhance staff members' well-being, without affecting their experience of work-related stress.

Noone and Hastings (2010) added data from 20 additional participants to the pilot data reported in the earlier study, in an effort to undertake further outcome analyses. Results with the larger sample essentially confirmed the findings from the pilot study. That is, the support staff reported reduced psychological distress despite experiencing minimal reduction in the perceived level of workplace stress. In addition, the study indicated that reduced psychological distress was greatest for staff without a professional qualification and for those who had higher levels of stress prior to the PACT training. This study strengthens the evidence that support staff who work with individuals with intellectual disabilities may benefit from acceptance and mindfulness-based training.

Three studies have used mindfulness-based procedures with support staff that provide services to individuals with intellectual disabilities. In the first study, Singh et al. (2004) assessed the effects of mindfulness-based training for support staff on the levels of happiness in three adults with medical and physical disabilities, who functioned at the profound level of intellectual disability. Using alternating treatments embedded within a multiple-baseline design across support staff, they measured baseline levels of happiness displayed by the three adults when they were being taught leisure skills activities by six support staff. During intervention, they taught mindfulness methods to three of the six caregivers and measured the levels of happiness displayed by the three adults during the 8-week training period. Finally, they measured the three adults' levels of happiness for 16 weeks following the termination of training. Results showed that, regardless of whether happiness was initially observed to be high or low in the presence of a support staff member, the levels of happiness increased markedly when the three adults were being taught leisure skills by support staff members who were taught and practiced mindfulness, when compared to control support staff members who were not taught mindfulness. These findings suggest that increasing the mindfulness of support staff may increase levels of happiness displayed by adults with medical and physical disabilities who function at the profound level of intellectual disability.

In the second study, Singh, Lancioni, Winton, Curtis, et al. (2006) provided behavioral training to group home staff members and assessed its impact on aggressive and destructive behaviors of the residents. This study measured the number of staff interventions needed, as well as the residents' learning in terms of the number of objectives mastered to competency, under 1:2, 2:3, and 1:2 staff-resident ratios. Singh et al. provided mindfulness training to the same staff and assessed the impact of this training on the individuals under 1:2 and 1:3 staff-resident ratios. When compared to baseline, the results showed that, following behavioral training across the three group homes, staff interventions for aggression and property destruction occurred at relatively high rates under the three staff-resident ratios, but the number of interventions decreased substantially following mindfulness training under the two staff-resident ratios. Furthermore, the number of learning objectives mastered by the individuals increased from baseline to behavioral training and increased further following mindfulness training. These findings suggest that the addition of mindfulness training enhanced the ability of the group home staff to manage the behavior and learning of the individuals more effectively.

In the third study, Singh et al. (2009) assessed how training support staff in mindfulness affected the use of physical restraints for aggressive and destructive behaviors of individuals with intellectual disabilities. Twenty-three support staff working in four group homes participated in a 12-week mindfulness-training program. Results showed that, as mindfulness training progressed, the use of restraints decreased, with almost no use being recorded by the end of the study. Any use of physical restraints was correlated with new admissions and on-call staff who had not received training in mindfulness. Furthermore, use of emergency medications also decreased and staff and peer injuries were reduced to almost zero levels during the latter stages of mindfulness practice. Thus, training support staff in mindfulness may reduce physical restraints and emergency medications as interventions for aggression and property destruction.

Parent Training

Based on the notion that parent–child transactions provide an important social context for the development of adaptive and problem behaviors, Singh, Lancioni, Winton, Fisher et al. (2006) provided mindfulness-based training to the parents of young children with autism, in an effort to develop alternative transactional pathways that would lead to positive behavioral patterns in their children. They taught three parents the philosophy and practice of mindfulness in a 12-week course and assessed the outcome of the training on their children's behavior, the mothers' satisfaction with their parenting skills, and interactions with their children. When compared to baseline ratings, the mothers' mindful parenting decreased their children's aggression, noncompliance, and self-injury, and increased the mothers' satisfaction with their parenting skills and interactions with their children. These findings were replicated with parents of children with intellectual disabilities (Singh et al., 2007) and attention-deficit/hyperactivity disorder (Singh et al., 2010). Together, the data from these three studies indicate that mindful parenting increases adaptive behavior and decreases challenging behaviors in their children, in the absence of any programmed contingencies targeting these behaviors.

Ferraioli and Harris (2012) reported a small study that examined the comparative effects of mindfulness and skills-based parent training programs for parents of children with autism. Twenty-one parents were randomized into an 8-week mindfulness program ($n = 10$) or the skills program ($n = 11$), with only six and nine parents, respectively, completing the two training programs. The mindfulness training included five mindfulness skills: observing, describing events and personal responses, nonjudgmental acceptance, distancing from thoughts, and staying present. The skills training program included psychoeducation, a review of evidence-based treatments, and behavioral strategies for increasing functional behavior and for decreasing challenging behavior. Results showed that only the mindfulness group had statistically significant improvements on parental stress and global health outcomes.

In sum, an emerging literature suggests that mindfulness training of support staff and parents of individuals with ASD has positive effects on staff and parents, as well as those they provide care for. Studies show that parents who report higher levels of mindfulness have lower levels of stress and depressive symptoms (Beer, Ward, & Moar, 2012). Furthermore, psychological distress in parents is strongly correlated with the challenging behaviors of children with ASD (Davis & Carter, 2008; Estes et al., 2099). Thus, providing mindfulness training may offset the effects of poor psychological health in staff and parents who provide care for children and youth with

ASD (Blackledge & Hayes, 2006; MacDonald, Hastings, & Fitzsimons, 2010).

Mindful Support

Therapists and caregivers (i.e., support staff, parents, and teachers) can provide mindfulness-based instructions to individuals with ASD so that they can be mindful of their adaptive and challenging behaviors.

Bogels et al. (2008) compared the effects of mindfulness training against a waiting-list control condition, with 14 adolescents (mean age 14.4 years) and their parents. The adolescents had a range of primary psychiatric disorders that included attention-deficit/hyperactivity disorder, oppositional defiant disorder, conduct disorder, and ASD. Bogels et al. provided mindfulness training to the adolescents and parents in parallel, based on the eight-session MBCT protocol as described by Segal et al. (2002). In general, the mindfulness program included body scan, mindful breathing, breathing space, mindfulness of thoughts and sounds, and sitting meditation. Results showed substantial improvements in the adolescents' self-reported personal goals, internalizing and externalizing complaints, attention problems, happiness, mindful awareness, and performance on a sustained attention test. In addition, parents reported improvements in their children's goals, externalizing and attention problems, self-control, attunement to others, and withdrawal.

Two studies investigated the effects of using a stabilizing meditation procedure, *Meditation on the Soles of the Feet* (SoF; Singh, Singh, Singh, Singh, & Winton, 2011), in the self-management of aggression by adolescents with ASD. Reviews suggest that this procedure is reasonably effective for self-management of aggression, disruption, and property destruction by individuals with intellectual disabilities (Hwang & Kearney, 2013). By using SoF, an individual can divert attention from an emotionally arousing thought, event, or situation that may lead to aggressive behavior, to an emotionally neutral part of the body, the soles of the feet. The individual learns to stop, focus the mind back on the body, calm down, and then make a choice about how to react to the thought, event, or situation that triggered the emotional arousal.

The first study was with three adolescents with autism whose physical aggression included hitting, kicking, and biting others (Singh, Lancioni, Manikam et al., 2011). Following a baseline phase, the adolescents were taught to use the SoF procedure by their respective mothers. During baseline, the three adolescents' aggression averaged 14 to 20 incidents per week but with mindfulness training, incidents of aggression averaged 4.1 to 6.3 per week, and reached zero rates during the last 4 weeks of intervention. During a 3-year follow-up, incidents of aggression occurred at a rate of about 1 per year.

The second study was with three adolescents with Asperger syndrome whose physical aggression included punching, hitting, kicking, biting, slapping, destroying property, and scratching others (Singh, Lancioni, Singh et al., 2011). As in the first study, following baseline, the three adolescents were taught by their respective mothers to use SoF to control physical aggression in the family home and during community outings. Results showed that during baseline, the three adolescents' aggression ranged from 1 to 6 incidents per week. During mindfulness training, incidents of aggression ranged from 0 to 4 per week, with zero rates occurring during the last 3 weeks of intervention across all three adolescents. No incidents of aggression occurred during a 4-year follow-up.

Spek et al. (2013) compared the effects of mindfulness training against a treatment-as-usual control condition in a randomized control trial with 41 high-functioning adults with ASD and depression, anxiety and rumination, with 20 in the mindfulness group and 21 in the control group. The mindfulness training, based on the MBCT protocol (Segal et al., 2002), was delivered during nine weekly sessions of 2.5 hours each, and the participants were required to practice 40–60 minutes of meditation daily, 6 days a week. Results showed statistically significant reductions in anxiety, depression, and rumination only in the mindfulness group. Furthermore, there was a statistically significant increase in positive affect only in the mindfulness group. This study indicates that adults with ASD may be able to learn and use meditation skills to decrease psychiatric symptoms that are comorbid with ASD and to generally improve their psychological well-being.

In sum, these four studies indicate a strong likelihood that individuals with ASD can learn different meditation techniques to decrease their challenging behaviors, decrease their psychological distress, and increase their well-being. Given the small number of studies using single-subject and group designs, further well-controlled studies are needed to verify the findings reported in these studies, and to determine the boundary conditions for the effectiveness of mindfulness-based interventions in this population.

Related Interventions

Two studies have used interventions that include a mindfulness component. For example, in a study based on an adapted dialectical behavior therapy (DBT) group skills training program, Sakdalan, Shaw, and Collier (2010) reported a decrease in the level of risks, an increase in relative strengths, and general improvements in overall functioning in six adults with intellectual disabilities (mean age = 26 years, mean IQ = 57) that had forensic involvement.

Brown and Hooper (2009) reported a case study in which they provided acceptance and commitment therapy (ACT) to an 18-year-old woman who functioned in the moderate to severe range of intellectual disability. The intervention was provided during 17 individual sessions, over a 6-month period, to reduce her anxiety and obsessive thoughts. Results indicated reduced avoidance of cognitions and emotions as measured on an adapted version of the Acceptance and Action Questionnaire. Anecdotal reports indicated that she was calmer, her ruminations were shorter, and she was more socially confident.

These studies provide the beginnings of a database on adaptations of two standard interventions that include a mindfulness component and show some promise when used with individuals with intellectual disabilities. Whether this promise will be actualized remains to be demonstrated in children and youth with ASD, in studies using controlled experimental methodologies.

PRACTICE RECOMMENDATIONS

We have learned several lessons over the last 25 years that we have been teaching mindfulness practices to individuals with developmental disorders, including ASD, and their parents, support staff, and teachers. Our hope is that future therapists may benefit from these lessons, presented herein as practice recommendations.

Therapist Variable

Therapist competency is a critical factor in the outcome of any therapy. For example, in the context of cognitive-behavioral therapy, a recent review concluded that treatment outcome is positively correlated to the amount of training a therapist has received (Shafran et al., 2009). Therapist variable is also a major factor in mindfulness research; however, the emphasis is not necessarily on the mindfulness training provided by the therapist, but on the therapist's personal practice of mindfulness meditation. That is, it is important that the therapist has a personal meditation practice in daily life and embodies mindfulness (Crane, Kuyken, Hastings, Rothwell, & Williams, 2010). The literature on teaching mindfulness emphasizes the key role of the trainer's existential commitment to mindfulness as the foundation for an authentic trainer (McCown, Reibel, & Micozzi, 2010). For example, Segal, Teasdale, and Williams (2004) stressed that one of the key aspects of the success of MBCT is their emphasis on the therapist acquiring a personal mindfulness practice. In a double-blind study, Grepmair et al. (2007) reported that patients rated more positively psychotherapists-in-training who practiced 30 minutes of Zen meditation each day than those without a daily meditation practice. Furthermore, therapists are likely to dilute program integrity without a personal meditation practice (Crane et al., 2012).

In a qualitative study of the role of the trainer in MBCT courses, Van Aalderen, Breukers, Reuzel, and Speckens (2012) reported three major aspects of the trainer in an MBCT course that were considered by the trainers and the course participants to be of paramount importance: (a) the embodiment of mindfulness by the trainer, especially a nonjudgmental attitude and compassionate stance; (b) empowerment; and (c) nonreactivity, in terms of teaching the participants awareness of their own thinking patterns. Although the results were derived from small samples of trainers and participants in an MBCT course, this study underscores the importance of a personal mindfulness meditation practice by the trainers.

We believe that therapists who intend to use mindfulness-based therapies with individuals with intellectual disabilities (including ASD), or with their parents and other caregivers, should either have an existing mindfulness meditation practice or develop a disciplined practice prior to offering mindfulness-based instructions. There is currently little in the research literature to suggest just how long this practice needs to be before a therapist is deemed competent to use mindfulness-based procedures as a therapeutic modality. What is evident from psychophysiological studies is that short-term (i.e., 8 weeks) training in mindfulness meditation has a measurable effect on brain and immune function (Davidson et al., 2003), although it is unclear how long it takes for new practitioners to actually embody mindfulness.

Slow Arrival of Effects

Therapists, particularly those with a strong behavior analytic orientation, often expect to see changes within the first few weeks of implementation of a treatment plan. Indeed, it has often been assumed that if treatment effects—even if limited to subtle changes in the intensity or duration of the target behavior—are not evident within the first week or two of treatment implementation, then it is likely the intervention will either be minimally successful or not successful at all. Unlike other intervention modalities (e.g., pharmacotherapy and behavior therapy), there is often a slow arrival of effects with mindfulness-based interventions (Singh et al., 2013).

In the mindfulness-based studies with adolescents with ASD, their mothers instructed them on the SoF procedures for 5 days and then provided them with audiotaped instructions on their iPods to allow self-training (Singh, Lancioni, Manikam et al., 2011; Singh, Lancioni, Singh et al., 2011). Changes in the adolescents' target behaviors began appearing within a few days of the initiation of training, but the full effects of the training took several weeks (range = 14 to 22 weeks). In related studies with individuals with intellectual disabilities without ASD, the mindfulness practice required extensive practice before the individuals were able to consistently control the precursors of their aggressive behavior. Although the SoF procedure is relatively simple to learn, its mastery and application in real time requires a high degree of motivation and a strong commitment by the individuals. The SoF procedure requires practice until it becomes habitual for the individual to stop, focus the mind back to the present moment, calm down, and then make an informed choice about how to react to the thought, event, or situation that triggered the arousal response. Indeed, during training of the individuals, it is heavily stressed that learning the SoF procedure in the absence of application is a mere academic exercise. Therapists intending to use mindfulness-based therapies should rest in the awareness of the slow arrival of effects while personal transformation takes place in the individuals they are working with. Furthermore, they should also know

that when the transformation takes place, the effects are generally long lasting and generalize across different environments and people.

Evidence Base

The evidence base for the mindfulness-based procedures used with individuals with intellectual disabilities, including ASD, and with their parents and caregivers is limited but gradually increasing (Hwang & Kearney, 2013; Spek et al., 2013). For example, in the specific practice of the SoF mindfulness meditation, an uncontrolled case study reported outcomes for a single individual (Singh, Wahler, Adkins, & Myers, 2003) and indicated a need to test its effectiveness using controlled single-subject designs. This was achieved in a series of proof-of-concept studies across individuals with intellectual disabilities and/ or mental illness, adolescents and adults, and across hospital and community settings (Singh et al., 2013). The success of these proof-of-concept studies indicated a need to test the efficacy of the SoF procedure in a randomized control trial. This was achieved in a recent randomized controlled trial of the effectiveness of SoF to treat physical and verbal aggression when compared to a waiting-list control for individuals with intellectual disabilities (Singh et al., 2013). This study reported a robust level of statistical significance between the SoF and control groups in terms of treatment outcomes. However, replication of these findings by independent researchers is still needed because a single research group has undertaken the current line of investigations.

The evidence base for mindfulness-based training for support staff and parents is more extensive. Although somewhat different combinations of mindfulness meditations were included in various studies, when taken together, these studies show that mindfulness can be enhanced in support staff and parents (Bogels & Restifo, 2014; Singh, Lancioni, Winton, Fisher et al., 2006). The data on training support staff and parents who care for individuals with ASD are derived from studies using multiple-baseline experimental designs, group designs, and randomized control trials (Bogels et al., 2008; Singh, Lancioni, Winton, Fisher et al., 2006; Spek et al., 2013). In addition, the mothers of adolescents with autism (Singh, Lancioni, Manikam et al., 2011) and Asperger syndrome (Singh, Lancioni, Singh et al., 2011) were responsible for learning the SoF procedure and subsequently teaching it to their children. Therapists wanting to use mindfulness-based interventions should feel confident that there is a growing evidence base for the effectiveness of these procedures with individuals with ASD and their support staff and parents.

When to Use Mindfulness Procedures

The majority of intervention research and practice with children and adults with ASD is based on the creed of health maintenance organizations—treatment is provided when there is a demonstrable need. Thus, behavior supports and pharmacotherapy are provided when individuals with ASD exhibit challenging behaviors. When effective, these treatment modalities provide almost immediate relief to parents and support staff. Thus, for example, there are evidence-based behavioral methods that can be used to manage and/or treat a wide range of challenging behaviors in children and adults with ASD (see Luiselli, 2011, for a practitioner's guide). While mindfulness-based methods can be used in a similar manner, the slow arrival of effects of these procedures suggests that, unlike pharmacotherapy, they may be ineffective as an emergency treatment modality. Similarly, unlike some behavioral interventions, they may be ineffective when used as an approach for crisis management.

Therapists contemplating using mindfulness-based procedures with individuals with ASD, or training parents and support staff in this modality, should take into account specific features of this approach. First, the therapist will need a personal mindfulness meditation practice and embody mindfulness prior to using or training others to use mindfulness-based procedures. Second, most standard mindfulness-based procedures take 8 weeks of training, followed by intensive practice. Third, when these procedures are implemented, there is slow arrival of effects because there is an inherent process of self-transformation involved in mindfulness practices. Fourth, most parents and staff seek therapeutic assistance when they are overwhelmed with the challenging behaviors of individuals in their care, and are thus seeking immediate relief. This will not pertain to mindfulness-based procedures. Thus, therapists would be well advised that mindfulness-based procedures are best taught as a preventative approach— much in the manner therapists implement steps that reduce the risk of a behavior or disease from occurring rather than waiting for its occurrence to treat it. Mindfulness-based procedures are transformative and they prepare the individual, parents, and staff to

deal with issues that may arise in their lives with calm and equanimity as the solutions arise from within, as opposed to learning the application of techniques for specific disorders, diseases, and behavioral deficits and excesses. Indeed, one of the most potent findings has been that mindful parents and staff have a measurable impact on the behavior of their children and individuals they provide care to in the absence of programmed contingencies (Singh et al., 2010; Singh, Lancioni, Winton, Fisher et al., 2006).

Components of Mindfulness-Based Interventions

In the psychopharmacological and behavioral literature, there has been a continuing call for optimized treatments, that is, using the minimum number of treatments to produce the most effective outcomes. In psychopharmacology, inter- and intraclass polypharmacy is eschewed in the absence of clinical justification for intractable psychiatric conditions (Janicak, Marder, & Pavuluri, 2010). In applied behavior analysis, behavioral interventions sometimes consist of a package of behavioral procedures that prove effective in managing challenging behaviors. While this is an effective approach to managing the behavior of specific individuals, we cannot specify the degree of treatment outcome that can be accounted for by individual components, different combinations of components, or by the interactions among the components of the package of behavioral treatments. Component analyses have been used to systematically examine the relative contributions of different components and combinations of components of behavioral treatment packages (Mayer, Sulzer-Azaroff, & Wallace, 2012). Basically, this requires an examination of the effects of each component separately and in combination with others.

Mindfulness-based interventions come in packages of meditations, with each meditation focusing on specific mental conditions. It is inevitable that there will be calls for component analyses of mindfulness-based meditation practices. Therapists using or intending to use mindfulness-based practices with individuals with ASD should understand that although the practice of mindfulness is centuries old, its application to ameliorate specific conditions is relatively new. Furthermore, its use with individuals with ASD—children, adolescents, and adults—is very limited and the research data on its effectiveness are emerging, but are not fully established. Thus, calls for component analyses may be appropriate but somewhat premature. Furthermore, whether it makes sense to undertake component analyses of mindfulness-based meditations that are carefully selected to speak to different aspects of personal transformation may need to be addressed.

Outcome Variables

In applied behavior analysis, outcome variables are clearly identified and measured to show the effectiveness of behavioral interventions. How a behavior is defined often suggests how it should be measured—through direct observations, questionnaires, rating scales, or permanent products. All of these measures can be used to measure the impact of specific interventions on target behavioral deficits and excesses, diseases, or disorders.

Several methods have been used to measure the outcome of mindfulness-based interventions. The effects of mindfulness meditation has been studied on brain function in a large number of studies (Fletcher, Schoendorf, & Hayes, 2010) and, while this produces interesting data, it is unlikely to be practical in terms of how mindfulness works in the daily lives of people who are under psychological distress. Computer-based cognitive assessments have been used to measure the impact of mindfulness meditation, typically on such measures as sustained attention and working memory (Jha, Stanley, Kiyonga, Wong, & Gelfand, 2010). There are two issues with using such measures: first, they do not inform therapists of the effects of mindfulness-based interventions on clinical outcomes and, second, mindfulness cannot be equated with sustained attention or working memory.

The most popular measure of outcomes involves self-report rating scales of mindfulness (Bergomi et al., 2013). Of course, these rating scales measure what their developers consider mindfulness to be, and no two rating scales measure the same exact construct of mindfulness. Indeed, the very definition of mindfulness adopted in these rating scales differs, with some derived from cognitive psychology and others from selected aspects of Buddhist sutras as interpreted by teachers of different schools of Buddhism. Regardless of their shortcomings, mindfulness rating scales form the backbone of outcome measures for clinical interventions. The major rating scales include the *Freiburg Mindfulness Inventory* (Buchheld, Grossman, & Walach, 2001), *Mindfulness Attention Awareness Scale* (Brown & Ryan, 2003), *Kentucky Inventory of Mindfulness Skills* (Baer, Smith,

& Allen, 2004), *Five Facet Mindfulness Questionnaire* (Baer et al., 2006), *Toronto Mindfulness Scale* (Lau et al., 2006), *Cognitive and Affective Mindfulness Scale—Revised* (Feldman, Hayes, Kumar, Greeson, & Laurenceau, 2007), *Philadelphia Mindfulness Scale* (Cardaciatto, Herbert, Forman, Moitra, & Farrow, 2007), and *Southampton Mindfulness Questionnaire* (Chadwick et al., 2008). Before choosing, therapists wishing to use a rating scale as an outcome measure should study the available scales for details of what each scale purports to measure, number of items, psychometric status of the scale, and the intended population.

In clinical research, the outcome of training in mindfulness can be measured as changes in the dependent variable (e.g., pain, stress, symptoms of specific disorders) (see Didonna, 2009). Qualitative and quantitative changes in the dependent variables can be measured and used as an index of personal well-being (Grossman, Niemann, Schmidt, & Walach, 2004). Another strategy is to measure the effects of mindfulness practice on others. With regard to research in intellectual disabilities, staff trained in mindfulness meditations produces happiness in individuals with profound intellectual disability (Singh et al., 2004) and reduces the use of restraints and increases learning in adults with intellectual disability (Singh, Lancioni, Winton, Curtis et al., 2006) without direct intervention for these behaviors. Other studies show that parents trained in mindfulness meditations increase social behavior and reduce maladaptive behaviors in their children (Singh et al., 2007). Therapists wishing to assess the effects of mindfulness-based interventions on individuals with ASD have a wide range of outcome measures to choose from. The choice of the measure will depend on the clinical question being addressed.

CONCLUSIONS

There is an emerging literature on the utility of mindfulness-based interventions focused on individuals with ASD. This literature suggests mindfulness-based interventions can be used in three ways. First, individuals with ASD can learn simple mindfulness meditations, such as SoF, to respond to their arousal state in a calm manner and preempt their anger from leading to aggression. Second, they can use the same meditation to manage their aggressive behavior. Third, parents can learn mindfulness meditation for personal transformation that has spillover effects on the behavior of their children with ASD. Furthermore, mothers can learn and then teach meditation techniques to their children with ASD. Therapists wishing to use mindfulness-based interventions need to have a personal meditation practice and embody mindfulness prior to using this treatment modality. They should be aware of the slow arrival of effects with mindfulness-based interventions and that the outcome of these interventions can be measured in a variety of ways depending on the clinical issues presented by individuals with ASD. Finally, it is critical to understand that, however promising, mindfulness is not a magic bullet therapy and it may not prove useful or applicable to all individuals with ASD or to their parents and support staff.

REFERENCES

Anālayo. (2003). *Satipatthāna: The direct path to realization.* Birmingham, UK: Windhorse.

Baer, R. A., Smith, G. T., & Allen, K. B. (2004). Assessment of mindfulness by self-report: The Kentucky Inventory of Mindfulness Skills. *Assessment, 11,* 191–206.

Baer, R. A., Smith, G. T., Hopkins, J., Krietemeyer, J., & Toney, L. (2006). Using self-report assessment methods to explore facets of mindfulness. *Assessment, 13,* 27–45.

Beer, M., Ward, L., & Moar, K. (2012). The relationship between mindful parenting and distress in parents of children with an autism spectrum disorder. *Mindfulness, 4*(2), 102–112.

Bergomi, C., Tschacher, W., & Kupper, Z. (2013). The assessment of mindfulness with self-report measures: Existing scales and open issues. *Mindfulness, 4*(3), 191–202.

Blackledge, J. T., & Hayes, S. C. (2006). Using acceptance and commitment training in the support of parents of children diagnosed with autism. *Child and Family Behavior Therapy, 28,* 1–18.

Bogels, S., Hoogstad, B., van Dun, L., de Schutter, S., & Restifo, K. (2008). Mindfulness training for adolescents with externalizing disorders and their parents. *Behavioral and Cognitive Therapy, 36,* 193–209.

Bogels, S., & Restifo, K. (2014). *Mindful parenting: A guide for mental health practitioners.* New York, NY: Springer.

Bowen, S., Chawla, N., & Marlatt, G. A. (2010). *Mindfulness-based relapse prevention for addictive behaviors: A clinician's guide.* New York, NY: Guilford Press.

Brown, F. J., & Hooper, S. (2009). Acceptance and commitment therapy (ACT) with a learning disabled young person experiencing anxious and obsessive thoughts. *Journal of Intellectual Disabilities, 13,* 195–201.

Brown, K. W., & Ryan, R. M. (2003). The benefits of being present: Mindfulness and its role in psychological well-being. *Journal of Personality and Social Psychology, 84,* 822–848.

Buchheld, N., Grossman, P., & Walach, H. (2001). Measuring mindfulness in insight meditation and meditation-based psychotherapy: The development of the Freiburg Mindfulness Inventory (FMI). *Journal of Meditation and Meditation Research, 1,* 11–34.

Buddhadasa Bhikkhu (1997). *Mindfulness with breathing: A manual for serious beginners.* Boston, MA: Wisdom Publications.

Cardaciatto, L., Herbert, J. D., Forman, E. M., Moitra, E., & Farrow, V. (2007). The assessment of present-moment awareness and acceptance: The Philadelphia Mindfulness Scale. *Assessment, 15,* 204–223.

Chadwick, P., Hember, M., Symes, J., Peters, E., Kuipers, E., & Dagnan, D. (2008). Responding mindfully to unpleasant thoughts and images: Reliability and validity of the Southampton Mindfulness Questionnaire. *British Journal of Clinical Psychology, 47,* 451–455.

Chiesa, A. (2013). The difficulty of defining mindfulness: Current thought and critical issues. *Mindfulness, 4,* 255–268.

Chiesa, A., & Malinowski, P. (2011). Mindfulness-based approaches: Are they all the same? *Journal of Clinical Psychology, 67,* 404–424.

Crane, R. S., Kuyken, W., Hastings, R. P., Rothwell, N., & Williams, J. M. G. (2010). Training teachers to deliver mindfulness-based interventions: Learning from the UK experience. *Mindfulness, 1,* 74–86.

Crane, R. S., Kuyken, W., Williams, J. M. G., Hastings, R. P., Cooper, L., & Fennell, M. J. (2012). Competence in teaching mindfulness-based courses: Concepts, development and assessment. *Mindfulness, 3,* 76–84.

Dalai Lama. (1991). *The path to bliss.* Ithaca, NY: Snow Lion.

Dalai Lama. (2002). *How to practice: The way to a meaningful life.* New York, NY: Atria Books.

Dalai Lama. (2006). *How to see yourself as you really are.* New York, NY: Atria Books.

Davidson, R. J., Kabat-Zinn, J., Schumacher, J., Rosenkranz, M., Muller, D., Santorelli, S. F.,... Sheridan, J. F. (2003). Alterations in brain and immune function produced by mindfulness meditation. *Psychosomatic Medicine, 65,* 564–570.

Davis, N. O., & Carter, A. S. (2008). Parenting stress in mothers and fathers of toddlers with autism spectrum disorders: Associations with child characteristics. *Journal of Autism and Developmental Disorders, 38,* 1278–1291.

Didonna, F. (2009). *Clinical handbook of mindfulness.* New York, NY: Springer.

Doi, Y., & Minowa, M. (2003). Factor structure of the 12-item General Health Questionnaire in the Japanese general adult population. *Psychiatry and Clinical Neurosciences, 57,* 379–383.

Emerson, E. (2001). *Challenging behavior: Analysis and intervention in people with severe intellectual disabilities* (2nd ed.). Cambridge, UK: Cambridge University Press.

Estes, A., Mumson, J., Dawson, G., Koehler, E., Zhou, X-H., & Abbott, R. (2009). Parenting stress and psychological functioning among mothers of preschool children with autism and developmental delay. *Autism*, 13, 375–387.

Feldman, G. C., Hayes, A. M., Kumar, S. M., Greeson, J. G., & Laurenceau, J. P. (2007). Mindfulness and emotion regulation: The development and initial validation of the cognitive and affective mindfulness scale-revised (CAMS-R). *Journal of Psychopathology and Behavioral Assessment*, 29, 177–190.

Ferraioli, S. J., & Harris, S. L. (2013). Comparative effects of mindfulness and skills-based parent training programs for parents of children with autism: Feasibility and preliminary outcome data. *Mindfulness*, 4, 89–101.

Fletcher, L. B., Schoendorff, B., & Hayes, S. C. (2010). Searching for mindfulness in the brain: A process-oriented approach to examining the neural correlates of mindfulness. *Mindfulness*, 1, 41–63.

Foerde, K., Knowlton, B. J., & Poldrack, R. A. (2006). Modulation of competing memory systems by distraction. *Proceedings of the National Academy of Sciences USA*, 103, 11778–11783.

Gilpin, R. (2008). The use of Theravada Buddhist practices and perspectives in mindfulness-based cognitive therapy. *Contemporary Buddhism*, 9, 227–251.

Goin-Kochel, R. P., Myers, B. J., & Mackintosh, V. H. (2007). Parental reports on the use of treatments and therapies for children with autism spectrum disorders. *Research in Autism Spectrum Disorders*, 1, 195–209.

Green, V. A., Pituch, K. A., Itchon, J., Choi, A., O'Reilly, M., & Sigafoos, J. (2006). Internet survey of treatments used by parents of children with autism. *Research in Developmental Disabilities*, 27, 70–84.

Grepmair, L., Mitterlehner, F., Loew, T., Bachler, E., Rother, W., & Nickel, M. (2007). Promoting mindfulness in psychotherapists in training influences the treatment results of their patients: A randomized, double-blind, controlled study. *Psychotherapy and Psychosomatics*, 76, 332–338.

Grossman, P. (2008). On measuring mindfulness in psychosomatic and psychological research. *Journal of Psychosomatic Research*, 64, 405–408.

Grossman, P., Niemann, L., Schmidt, S. & Walach, H. (2004). Mindfulness-based stress reduction and health benefits: a meta-analysis. *Journal of Psychosomatic Research*, 57, 35–43.

Grossman, P., & Van Dam, N. T. (2011). Mindfulness, by any other name...: Trials and tribulations of Sati in western psychology and science. *Contemporary Buddhism*, 12, 219–239.

Gunaratana, B. (2012). *The four foundations of mindfulness in plain English*. Boston, MA: Wisdom Publications.

Hartley, S. L., & MacLean, W. E. (2007). Staff-averse challenging behaviour in older adults with intellectual disabilities. *Journal of Applied Research in Intellectual Disabilities*, 20, 519–528.

Hastings, R. P. (2002a). Parental stress and behaviour problems in children with developmental disability. *Journal of Intellectual and Developmental Disability*, 27, 149–160.

Hastings, R. P. (2002b). Do challenging behaviors affect staff psychological well-being? Issues of causality and mechanism. *American Journal on Mental Retardation*, 107, 455–467.

Hatton, C., & Emerson, E. (1998). Organizational predictors of actual staff turnover in a service for people with multiple disabilities. *Journal of Applied Research in Intellectual Disabilities*, 11, 166–171.

Hatton, C., Rivers, M., Mason, H., Mason, L., Kiernan, C., Emerson, E.,... Reeves, D. (1999). Staff stressors and staff outcomes in services for adults with intellectual disabilities: The Staff Stressor Questionnaire. *Research in Developmental Disabilities*, 20, 269–285.

Hayes, S. C., Strosahl, K. D., & Wilson, K. G. (1999). *Acceptance and commitment therapy*. New York, NY: Guilford Press.

Hwang, Y-S., & Kearney, P. (2013). A systematic review of mindfulness intervention for individuals with developmental disabilities: Long-term practice and long lasting effects. *Research in Developmental Disabilities*, 34, 314–326.

Innstrand, S. T., Espnes, G. A., & Mykletun, R. (2004). Job stress, burnout and job satisfaction: An intervention study for staff working with people with intellectual disabilities. *Journal of Applied Research in Intellectual Disabilities*, 17, 119–126.

Janicak, P. G., Marder, S. R., & Pavuluri, M. N. (2010). *Principles and practice of psychopharmacotherapy* (5th ed.). Philadelphia, PA: Lippincott Williams & Wilkins.

Jha, A. P., Stanley, E. Z., Kiyonaga, A., Wong, L., & Gelfand, L. (2010). Examining the protective effects of mindfulness training on working memory capacity and affective experience. *Emotion*, 10, 54–64.

Kabat-Zinn, J. (1990). *Full catastrophe living: Using the wisdom of your body and mind to face stress, pain, and illness*. New York, NY: Delta Books.

Kabat-Zinn, J. (1994). *Wherever you go, there you are*. New York, NY: Hyperion.

Knaster, M. (2010). *Living this life fully: Stories and teachings of Munindra*. Boston, MA: Shambhala.

Lau, M., Bishop, S., Segal, Z., Buis, T., Anderson, N., Carlson, L.,... Devins, G. (2006). The Toronto Mindfulness Scale: Development and validation. *Journal of Clinical Psychology*, 62, 1445–1467.

Linehan, M. M. (1993). *Cognitive behavioral treatment of borderline personality disorder*. New York, NY: Guilford Press.

Luiselli, J. K. (2011). *Teaching and behavior support for children and adults with autism spectrum disorder*. New York, NY: Oxford University Press.

MacDonald, E. E., Hastings, R. P., & Fitzsimons, E. (2010). Psychological acceptance mediates the impact of the behaviour problems of children with intellectual disability on fathers' psychological adjustment. *Journal of Applied Research in Intellectual Disabilities, 23*, 27–37.

Matson, J. L., & Sturmey, P. (2011). *International handbook of autism and pervasive developmental disorders.* New York, NY: Springer.

Mayer, G. R., Sulzer-Azaroff, B., & Wallace, M. (2012). *Behavior analysis for lasting change* (2nd ed.). Cornwall-on-Hudson, NY: Sloan.

McCown, D., Reibel, D., & Micozzi, M. S. (2010). *Teaching mindfulness: A practical guide for clinicians and educators.* New York, NY: Springer.

Mingyur Rinpoche, Y. (2007). *The joy of living: Unlocking the secret and science of happiness.* New York, NY: Three Rivers Press.

Mitchell, S. (1988). *Tao Te Ching.* San Francisco, CA: Harper Collins.

Noone, S. J. (2013). Supporting care staff using mindfulness–and acceptance-based approaches. In J. L. Taylor, W. R. Lindsay, R. Hastings, & C. Hatton (Eds.), *Psychological therapies for adults with intellectual disabilities* (pp. 207–221). Chichester, UK: John Wiley.

Noone, S. J., & Hastings, R. P. (2009). Building psychological resilience in support staff caring for people with intellectual disabilities: Pilot evaluation of an acceptance-based intervention. *Journal of Intellectual Disabilities, 13*, 43–53.

Noone, S. J., & Hastings, R. P. (2010). Using acceptance and mindfulness-based workshops with support staff caring for adults with intellectual disabilities. *Mindfulness, 1*, 67–73.

Powers, M. D., Palmieri, M. J., D'Eramo, K. S., & Powers, K. M. (2011). Evidenced-based treatment of behavioral excesses and deficits for individuals with autism spectrum disorders. In B. Reichow, B., Doehring, P., Cicchetti, D. V., & Volkmar, F. R. (Eds.), *Evidence-based practices and treatments for children with autism* (pp. 55–92). New York, NY: Springer.

Raczka, R. (2005). A focus group enquiry into stress experienced by staff working with people with challenging behaviours. *Journal of Intellectual Disabilities, 9*, 167–177.

Rose, J., Jones, F., & Fletcher, B. (1998). The impact of a stress management programme on staff well-being and performance at work. *Work and Stress, 12*, 112–124.

Sakdalan, J. A., Shaw, J., & Collier, V. (2010). Staying in the here-and-now: A pilot study on the use of dialectical behavior therapy group skills training for forensic clients with intellectual disability. *Journal of Intellectual Disability Research, 54*, 568–572.

Sameroff, A. J. (1995). General systems theories and developmental psychopathology. In D. Cicchetti & D. J. Cohen (Eds.), *Developmental psychopathology.*

Vol. 1: Theory and methods (pp. 659–695). New York, NY: Wiley.

Segal, Z. V., Teasdale, J. D., & Williams, J. M. G. (2004). Mindfulness-Based Cognitive Therapy: Theoretical rational and empirical status. In S. C. Hayes, V. M. Follette, & M. Linehan (Eds.), *Mindfulness and acceptance: Expanding the cognitive-behavioral tradition* (pp. 45–65). New York, NY: Guilford Press.

Segal, Z. V., Williams, J. M. G., & Teasdale, J. D. (2002). *Mindfulness-based cognitive therapy for depression: A new approach to preventing relapse.* New York, NY: Guilford Press.

Shafran, R., Clark, D. M., Fairburn, C. G., Arntz, A., Barlow, D. H., Ehlers, A.,...Wilson, G. T. (2009). Mind the gap: Improving the dissemination of CBT. *Behavior Research and Therapy, 47*, 902–909.

Shapiro, S. L., Carlson, L. E., Astin, J. A., & Freedman, B. (2006). Mechanisms of mindfulness. *Journal of Clinical Psychology, 62*, 373–386.

Singh, N. N., Lancioni, G. E., Karazsia, B. T., Winton, A. S. W., Myers, R. E., Singh, A. N. A.,...Singh, J. (2013). Mindfulness-based treatment of aggression in individuals with intellectual disabilities: A waiting-list control study. *Mindfulness, 4*, 148–157.

Singh, N. N., Lancioni, G. E., Manikam, R. Winton, A. S. W., Singh, A. N. A., Singh, J. & Singh, A. D. A. (2011). A mindfulness-based strategy for self-management of aggressive behavior in adolescents with autism. *Research in Autism Spectrum Disorders, 5*, 1153–1158.

Singh, N. N., Lancioni, G. E., Singh, A. D. A., Winton, A. S. W., Singh, A. N. A., & Singh, J. (2011). Adolescents with Asperger syndrome can use a mindfulness-based strategy to control their aggressive behavior. *Research in Autism Spectrum Disorders, 5*, 1103–1109.

Singh, N. N., Lancioni, G. E., Wahler, R. G., Winton, A. S. W., & Singh, J. (2008). Mindfulness approaches in cognitive behavior therapy. *Behavioural and Cognitive Psychotherapy, 36*, 659–666.

Singh, N. N., Lancioni, G. E., Winton, A. S. W., Curtis, W. J., Wahler, R. G., Sabaawi, M.,...McAleavey, K. (2006). Mindful staff increase learning and reduce aggression by adults with developmental disabilities. *Research in Developmental Disabilities, 27*, 545–558.

Singh, N. N., Lancioni, G. E., Winton, A. S. W., Fisher, B. C., Wahler, R. G., McAleavey, K.,...Sabaawi, M. (2006). Mindful parenting decreases aggression, noncompliance and self-injury in children with autism. *Journal of Emotional and Behavioral Disorders, 14*, 169–177.

Singh, N. N., Lancioni, G. E., Winton, A. S. W., Singh, A. D. A., Singh, A. N., & Singh, J. (2013). Mindfulness-based approaches. In J. L. Taylor, W. R. Lindsay, R. Hastings, & C. Hatton (Eds.), *Psychological therapies for adults with intellectual disabilities* (pp. 253–266). Chichester, UK: John Wiley.

Singh, N. N., Lancioni, G. E., Winton, A. S. W., Singh, A. N., Adkins, A. D., & Singh, J. (2009). Mindful staff can reduce the use of physical restraints when providing care to individuals with intellectual disabilities. *Journal of Applied Research in Intellectual Disabilities*, 22, 194–202.

Singh, N. N., Lancioni, G. E., Winton, A. S. W., & Singh, J. (2011). Aggression, tantrums, and other externally driven challenging behaviors. In J. L. Matson & P. Sturmey (Eds.), *International handbook of autism and pervasive developmental disorders* (pp. 413–435). New York, NY: Springer.

Singh, N. N., Lancioni, G. E., Winton, A. S. W., Singh, J., Curtis, W. J., Wahler, R. G., & McAleavey, K. M. (2007). Mindful parenting decreases aggression and increases social behavior in children with developmental disabilities. *Behavior Modification, 31,* 749–771.

Singh, N. N., Lancioni, G. E., Winton, A. S. W., Wahler, R. G., Singh, J., & Sage, M. (2004). Mindful caregiving increases happiness among individuals with profound multiple disabilities. *Research in Developmental Disabilities, 25,* 207–218.

Singh, N. N., Singh, A. N., Lancioni, G. E., Singh, J., Winton, A. S. W., & Adkins, A. D. (2010). Mindfulness training for parents and their children with ADHD increases the children's compliance. *Journal of Child and Family Studies, 19,* 157–166.

Singh, N. N., Singh, J., Singh, A. D. A., Singh, A. N. A., & Winton, A. S. W. (2011). *Meditation on the soles of the feet for anger management: A trainer's manual.* Raleigh, NC: Fernleaf.

Singh, N. N., Wahler, R. G., Adkins, A. D., & Myers, R. E. (2003). Soles of the feet: A mindfulness-based self-control intervention for aggression by an individual with mild mental retardation and mental illness. *Research in Developmental Disabilities, 24,* 158–169.

Spek, A. A., van Ham, N. C., & Nyklíček, I. (2013). Mindfulness-based therapy in adults with an autism spectrum disorder: A randomized controlled trial. *Research in Developmental Disabilities, 34,* 246–253.

Suzuki, S. (1970). *Zen mind, beginner's mind.* New York: Weatherhill.

Van Aalderen, J. R., Breukers, W. J., Reuzel, R. P. B., & Speckens, A. E. M. (2012). The role of the trainer in mindfulness-based approaches: A qualitative study. *Mindfulness.* doi: 10.1007/s12671-012-0162-x.

Walker, B. (1992). *Hua Hu Ching: The unknown teachings of Lao Tzu.* San Francisco, CA: Harper Collins.

Williams, J. M. G., & Kabat-Zinn, J. (2011). Mindfulness: Diverse perspectives on its meaning, origins, and multiple applications at the intersection of science and dharma. *Contemporary Buddhism, 12,* 1–18.

15

Cognitive-Behavioral Therapy

ROBERT R. SELLES, DANIELLE UNG, JOSH NADEAU,
AND ERIC A. STORCH

Characterized by deficits in social and/or communication skills and the presence of repetitive/stereotyped behaviors and interests, youth with autism spectrum disorder (ASD) are a clinically heterogeneous group experiencing a wide range of impairment in school, home, family, and social functioning (American Psychiatric Association, 2000; Bellini, 2004; Chamberlain, Kasari, & Rotheram-Fuller, 2007). Recent epidemiological studies have estimated that ASD, which encompasses the diagnoses of autistic disorder, Asperger syndrome, and pervasive developmental disorder–not otherwise specified, is on the rise and is present in as many as 1 in 81 youth in the United States (Centers for Disease Control and Prevention, 2012) and 1 out of 150 children worldwide (Fombonne, 2009). In addition to symptoms and deficits specific to ASD, nearly 75% of youth with ASD present with at least one comorbid condition, while nearly 50% present with two or more comorbid conditions (Brereton, Tonge, & Einfeld, 2006; Gjervik, Eldevik, Fjaeran-Granum, & Sponheim, 2011; Leyfer et al., 2006; Simonoff et al., 2008). Appearing at significantly higher rates in youth with ASD when compared to typically developing children (Gadow, DeVincent, Pomeroy, & Azizian, 2005; Kim et al., 2000), non-ASD psychiatric conditions present additional difficulties as well as further exacerbation of core ASD symptoms/impairments (de Bruin, Ferdinand, Meester, de Nijs, & Verheij, 2007; Joshi et al., 2010; Leyfer et al., 2006).

Assessment of comorbid disorders in youth with ASD is often complicated, due in part to the cognitive and language impairments inherent in youth with ASD that make reliable and valid interviews difficult to obtain (Leyfer et al., 2006; Simonoff et al., 2008). Youth with ASD may struggle to accurately report their mental states and daily life experiences, and often cannot successfully separate difficulties associated with core features of ASD from those attributable to comorbid psychiatric disorders (Leyfer et al., 2006). This is particularly salient to treatment specificity and outcome, as correctly delineated symptoms allow for improved intervention targeting, thereby reducing overall impairment associated with comorbid conditions.

Similar to the difficulties discussed with respect to assessment, a number of barriers exist to the successful treatment of comorbid problems in youth with ASD (e.g., limited insight, attention difficulties, low motivation). Despite these obstacles, effective treatment of comorbid disorders in youth with ASD is essential, as impairments associated with them are highly disruptive to family, school, and social functioning (Bellini, 2004; Kim et al., 2000; Matson & Nebel-Schwalm, 2007; Scarpa & Reyes, 2011; see White et al., 2009, for a review). This chapter will explore two particularly common co-occurring problems in youth with ASD, namely anxiety and anger, and how cognitive-behavioral therapy (CBT) has been modified and investigated as a possible treatment for both. Finally, recommendations for delivering treatment while addressing common barriers faced by clinicians will be provided.

RELEVANT CO-OCCURRING SYMPTOM DOMAINS

Anxiety

Anxiety disorders are among the most common psychiatric conditions diagnosed in typically developing children (Costello, Mustillo, Erkanli, Keeler, & Angold, 2003; Steinhausen, Metzke, Meier, & Kannenberg, 1998). In addition to anxiety-specific symptoms, anxiety disorders may also lead to increased irritability, restlessness, sleep disturbance, disruptive behavior, physical complaints, and inattentiveness in typically developing children and youth with ASD (Bellini, 2004; Evans, Canavera, Kleinpeter, Maccubbin, & Taga; 2005; Farrugia & Hudson, 2006; Weisbrot, Gadow, DeVincent, & Pomeroy, 2005).

Complaints of anxiety and the presence of an anxiety disorder are more prevalent in youth with ASD than in typically developing children (e.g., Farrugia & Hudson, 2006; Giliot, Furniss, & Walter, 2001; Weisbrot et al., 2005), with as many as 80% of youth with ASD meeting diagnostic criteria for at least one comorbid anxiety diagnosis (Joshi et al., 2010; Simonoff et al., 2008; Sukhodolsky et al., 2008; van Steensel, Bogels, & Perrin, 2011). Presenting with similar symptoms and severity levels seen in typically developing youth (e.g., Lewin, Wood, Gunderson, Murphy, & Storch, 2011), common comorbid anxiety disorders reported in children and adolescents with ASD include specific phobia (26%–57%), social phobia (13%–40%), separation anxiety disorder'(SAD; 9%–38%), obsessive-compulsive disorder (OCD; 17%–37%), generalized anxiety disorder (GAD; 15%–35%), and panic disorder (2%–5%; Leyfer et al., 2006; Simonoff et al., 2008; van Steensel et al., 2011; see White et al., 2009, for a review).

Youth with ASD may be more prone to anxiety disorders for several reasons, including the high prevalence rate of sensory sensitivity (Ben-Sasson et al., 2008; Green et al., 2011) and the presence of social, cognitive, and communication deficits that impair their ability to understand and respond to their environment in a socially acceptable manner (Scarpa & Reyes, 2011). For example, Bellini (2004) found that youth with ASD, particularly those considered high functioning, experienced greater distress in social situations than typically developing children perhaps due to an awareness of their social deficits combined with a continued desire for peer approval. Furthermore, although repetitive behaviors and restrictive interests can often be pleasurable for youth with ASD, they can also function as a mechanism to reduce stress and/or anxiety (Attwood, 2003; Baron-Cohen, 1989; Kim et al., 2000; Klin et al., 2007; Zandt, Prior, & Kyrios, 2007). In particular, Spiker, Lin, Van Dyke, and Wood (2011) found that in youth with ASD, engagement in certain restricted interests and repetitive behaviors (i.e., symbolical enactment, attachment to objects) were associated with higher reported levels of anxiety symptoms as compared to engagement in other types of restricted interests (facts/verbal memory). Consequently, the assessment and treatment of anxiety in youth with ASD is necessary to improve their well-being and overall functioning.

Anger

In previous and recent literature, the construct of anger has been defined as "a subjective, negatively felt state associated with cognitive deficits and distortions and maladaptive behaviors" (Sukhodolsky, Kassinove, & Gorman, 2004, p. 249). The expression of anger may take on various forms (e.g., social withdrawal, physical aggression) and may be present in varying degrees (e.g., annoyance, rage; Martin, Watson, & Wan, 2000; Sukhodolsky et al., 2004). The degree to which anger is expressed and felt may be closely associated with the cognitive ability of the individual to understand and interpret his or her environment, as well as the ability to communicate his or her emotions to others (Sukhodolsky et al., 2004). This is particularly relevant to youth with ASD, whose developmental deficits often make it difficult to understand, interpret, and respond to their emotions and the emotion of others (Scarpa & Reyes, 2011).

In youth with ASD, anger may be expressed through self-inflicting behaviors (e.g., hand biting, head banging), temper tantrums, increased aggression, and noncompliance similar to that of typically developing youth (Nicholas et al., 2008). In some cases, anger may be specifically linked to the presence of common externalizing disorders such as conduct disorder and oppositional defiant disorder (Gjervik et al., 2011; Green, Gilchrist, Burton, & Cox, 2000; Joshi et al., 2010; Simonoff et al., 2008). The exact prevalence rate of anger and frustration in youth with ASD is unknown; however, when compared to neurotypical children and adolescents, youth with ASD show significantly greater levels of anger-based symptoms ($d = 0.71$; Adamek et al., 2011; Nicholas et al., 2008). It may be that disruptions in regular routines or the inability to communicate their wants/needs make youth with ASD more prone to angry outbursts; however, the exact source of their anger/frustration is unknown.

CONSEQUENCES OF AND CONSIDERATIONS FOR CO-OCCURRING SYMPTOM DOMAINS

Impact of Co-occurring Symptoms

Youth and adults with ASD and comorbid psychiatric disorders display higher levels of repetitive behaviors, asocial behavior, and behavior problems (e.g., hitting, kicking, protracted screaming), and they are at greater risk for health problems (e.g., difficulty with sleep, more frequent gastrointestinal problems) than youth and adults with only an ASD diagnosis (Adamek et al., 2011; Kim et al., 2000; Kring, Greenberg, & Seltzer, 2008). In particular, increased hospitalizations and occurrences of medical illness have been associated with increases in anxiety severity for youth with ASD (Gadow, DeVincent, & Schneider, 2008). Specific domains of impairment that may be further exacerbated by the presence of comorbid disorders include functioning in school, home life, and social relationships (Bellini, 2004; Kim et al., 2000; Muris et al., 1998; Sukhodolsky et al., 2008). Furthermore, behavior problems are profound contributors to parental stress, depression, and family instability (Davis & Carter, 2008; Hastings, 2002; Lounds, Seltzer, Greenberg, & Shattuck, 2007; Montes & Halterman, 2007; Tomanik, Harris, & Hawkins, 2004). Symptoms associated with comorbid disorders can also compound functional impairments such as life skills, ability to work, and ability to be independent (Bellini, 2004).

Clinically significant levels of anxiety can exacerbate core autism symptoms (Sze & Wood, 2007) and compound social impairments inherent in youth with ASD, resulting in heightened avoidance of social situations and further isolation (White et al., 2009), and putting them at increased risk for peer rejection, depression, and loneliness (Attwood, 2003; Bauminger & Kasari, 2000; Kim et al., 2000; Storch, Larson et al., 2012; Tantam, 2003). Similarly, anger in youth with ASD may exacerbate the difficulties associated with initiating and maintaining social relationships (Scarpa & Reyes, 2011).

Importance of Addressing Co-occurring Symptoms

Comorbid psychiatric disorders can impede treatment progress if not targeted and properly treated (Joshi et al., 2010; Wood et al., 2009). As a result, addressing comorbid psychiatric disorders in youth with ASD has several important clinical implications. First, accurate diagnosis of comorbid conditions can facilitate appropriate treatment approach and enhance treatment efficacy (Joshi et al., 2010), particularly considering that specific treatment(s) leads to improved functioning when compared to nonspecific treatment (Leyfer et al., 2006). Second,

treating these comorbid conditions can improve or eliminate interfering factors such as low insight, motivation, and disruptive behaviors, thereby allowing clinicians to focus on core autism symptoms that often are masked by comorbid conditions. Third, a relationship exists between the presence/severity of comorbid psychiatric disorders and the severity of ASD symptoms (Kanne, Abbacchi, & Constantino, 2009; Kelly et al., 2008; Matson & Nebel-Schwalm, 2007), and as a result, treatment of comorbid diagnoses may also improve overall severity/functioning. Regardless of these implications, symptoms of comorbid disorders represent a pressing concern for parents of youth with ASD (Mills & Wing, 2005) and warrant intervention.

Autism Spectrum Disorder–Specific Barriers to Treatment

Due to the unique clinical presentation of youth with ASD, CBT-based approaches for anger and anxiety in typically developing populations cannot be assumed to work as designed in this population. Common characteristics of ASD, such as communicative, social, and cognitive deficits, emotion regulation deficits, and inflexible adherence to rules and structure, present unique treatment barriers (Leyfer et al., 2006; Simonoff et al., 2008; Wood et al., 2009). Youth with ASD may struggle to accurately report their mental states and daily life experiences, and to separate difficulties associated with core features of autism or comorbid psychiatric disorders (Leyfer et al., 2006). In addition, cognitive deficits such as limited insight (Storch et al., in press), lack of theory of mind, attention difficulties, and restricted interests (Wood et al., 2009) may reduce the efficacy of treatment. Youth with ASD may be unwilling or unmotivated to engage in treatment because they do not believe a problem exists, are uncomfortable with any changes to their routine, or are unable to understand how therapy will help. As a result, many treatments have evidenced poor generalization and maintenance of gains within this population, indicating the need for adapted forms of intervention (see Warren et al., 2011 for a review).

Considering Cognitive-Behavioral Therapy

The presence and resulting impairment of anger and anxiety in youth with ASD are clear. In typically developing populations, CBT is a treatment approach with substantial evidence for the treatment of anxiety and anger (see Abramowitz,

Whiteside, & Deacon, 2005; Cartwright-Hatton, Roberts, Chitsabesan, Fothergill, & Harrington, 2004; In-Albon & Schneider, 2007; Sukhodolsky et al., 2004 for reviews). In light of this, investigators have become interested in how CBT may translate to youth with ASD, and whether the treatment of co-occurring symptom deficits may also produce more generalized ASD improvements.

The following section first presents an overview of the CBT approach, followed by methods and empirical support of CBT for anxiety in typically developing youth, as well as in youth with ASD. Next, empirical evidence of CBT for anger in typically developing youth and youth with ASD is discussed. The chapter concludes with treatment recommendations for targeting these disorders in youth with ASD based on the currently available evidence.

TREATMENT FROM A COGNITIVE-BEHAVIORAL APPROACH

Initially developed for the treatment of depression, CBT approaches have now been developed and employed for many psychiatric conditions (see Butler, Chapman, Forman, & Beck, 2006 for a review). Cognitive-behavioral therapy is used to describe brief, structured treatment methods that attempt to disengage cognitive or behavioral factors that may contribute to, or maintain the presence of, symptoms (Anderson & Morris, 2006; Leahy & Holland, 2000). Cognitive components utilize recognition, reality testing, and restructuring tasks to target distorted thoughts, assumptions, and schemas, while behavioral components include exposure to anxiety-evoking stimuli, as well as behavioral management techniques such as reward and reinforcement systems. Cognitive-behavioral therapy may involve considerably different components across disorders and may place varying degrees of emphasis on cognitive or behavioral treatment components. The following sections outline CBT approaches for anxiety and anger in typically developing as well as ASD youth.

COGNITIVE-BEHAVIORAL THERAPY FOR ANXIETY

Typically Developing Youth

Cognitive-behavioral therapy is a well-established first-line treatment for anxiety in typically developing youth (Abramowitz et al., 2005; Cartwright-Hatton et al., 2004; In-Albon & Schneider, 2007). Some

differences exist between various treatment manuals (e.g., *Coping Cat*; Kendall & Hedtke, 2006; *Building Confidence*; Wood & McLeod, 2008), as well as between the treatment of specific anxiety disorders (e.g., OCD vs. GAD); however, CBT treatments for anxiety typically follow the same basic treatment principles such as including exposure as a core component. In addition, to address developmental barriers to treatment (e.g., poor insight and homework compliance) and high levels of family accommodation (Storch et al., 2007a), the inclusion of family members in treatment is highly recommended and has been associated with enhanced treatment outcomes (Kendall & Choudhury, 2003; Storch et al., 2007b; Wood, Piacentini, Southam-Gerow, Chu, & Sigman, 2006).

Cognitive-behavioral therapy typically begins with a psychoeducational component in which key aspects of the treatment approach are explained and taught by the therapist to the patient and the patient's family. The child learns about the nature of his or her disorder and factors that contribute to its continued maintenance. Further, a detailed explanation regarding the framework of CBT, its general course and requirements, and its efficacy is presented. Psychoeducation provides an opportunity to build rapport and address important considerations associated with positive treatment outcomes, such as expectancy of change, treatment completion, homework compliance, and motivation for treatment (Steketee et al., 2011; Westra, Dozios, & Marcus, 2007).

A key component of CBT for anxiety disorders is behavioral exposures to anxiety-provoking triggers. Behavioral theory suggests that within an anxious individual, fear has developed as a conditioned response to previously neutral stimuli, resulting in anxious thoughts and problematic active behavior (e.g., avoidance, compulsions). In practice, the patient and the therapist work to develop a fear hierarchy in which situations or stimuli are ranked according to the level of distress they arouse in the patient. This hierarchy then serves as an exposure schedule. Patients are exposed to distressing stimuli of gradually increasing intensity, while being prevented from engaging in their prototypical response (e.g., compulsions, avoidance), allowing them to naturally habituate to anxiety and reduce/eliminate the relationship between the stimulus and the negative response. In addition to exposures, cognitive therapy tasks such as emotion recognition and cognitive restructuring are employed so that children can better recognize and combat anxiogenic emotions and thought patterns.

Translating to Autism Spectrum Disorder

While preliminary case studies (e.g., Lehmkuhl, Storch, Bodfish, & Geffken, 2008; Reaven & Hepburn, 2003) and pilot studies (e.g., Ooi et al., 2008; Reaven et al., 2009) support the use of CBT in treating anxiety in youth with ASD, this chapter will focus on the five randomized controlled trials completed to date. Recognizing the barriers to treatment and specific needs of youth with ASD, investigation into the efficacy of CBT in this population has not attempted to replicate CBT protocols with ASD youth. Instead, CBT frameworks have been modified and expanded in an attempt to maximize potential treatment engagement and response. While this is likely a key component to the success of the translation of CBT to ASD, no consistent use or evaluation of treatment protocols has been employed. Therefore, little is known about what modules or components are particularly associated with treatment outcomes, and definitive conclusions regarding their various efficacies are problematic. As a result, this chapter will present the specific methods, treatment approaches, modifications, and results of the five randomized trials conducted to date, in an effort to inform the reader about various approaches and resulting evidence for CBT-based approaches as a whole.

Sofronoff, Attwood, and Hinton (2005)

Sofronoff et al. (2005) published the first randomized controlled trial of a CBT-based treatment for youth with ASD. Seventy-one children between the ages of 9 and 12 years ($M = 10.62$, $SD = 1.11$, 12.7% female) were randomized to one of three conditions: a child-only intervention; a child and parent intervention; or a waitlist control. The CBT protocol employed was brief, consisting of six, 2-hour sessions focused on exploration and restoration of various emotions (e.g., happiness, anxiety, nervousness) and the development of an anxiety management program. In addition, elements appealing to youth with Asperger syndrome were included, such as exploration of social tools, the introduction of visual aids (*Social Stories*; Gray, 1998), and the use of appealing treatment metaphors. Examining the

comparative improvement of the three experimental groups, Sofronoff et al. (2005) found a significant group by time interaction, with the child-only and child-parent groups demonstrating significant improvements in anxiety over time when compared to waitlist ($d = 0.96$) and the most robust treatment gains occurring between posttreatment and 6-week follow-up. In addition, participants randomized to the child-parent group demonstrated significantly greater improvements than even the child-only group, confirming patterns of increased treatment response associated with family involvement seen in CBT for typically developing youth (e.g., Storch et al., 2007b).

Chalfant, Rapee, and Carroll (2007)

Chalfant et al. (2007) examined a family-based CBT protocol versus waitlist control with 47 high-functioning ASD youth between the ages of 8 and 13 years ($M = 10.80$, $SD = 1.35$, 34.3% female). The CBT protocol used was based on the *Cool Kids* CBT program (Lyneham, Abbot, Wignall, & Rapee, 2003), which includes the general components of CBT for typically developing youth (see earlier). In order to better accommodate youth with ASD, the CBT-treatment was translated from the standard 12-week approach to a 9-week core treatment component followed by three monthly booster sessions. Additionally, visual and structural aids were incorporated, and therapy focused on more concrete therapeutic exercises (e.g., relaxation and exposure) with reduced emphasis on cognitive components. Parents learned similar anxiety recognition and management tasks for use with their children, in a group format apart from their children. No modules targeting core autism symptoms were employed. At posttreatment, 71.4% ($n = 20$) of individuals who received CBT had demonstrated remission of their primary anxiety disorder, compared to 0% of those randomized to waitlist control (Chalfant et al., 2007). Individuals who received CBT had significantly larger improvements on self- and parent-reported anxiety. Significantly larger improvements for CBT were also observed in a teacher-reported measure of anxiety, suggesting that CBT may generalize beyond clinic and home settings ($\eta^2 = 0.39$; Chalfant et al., 2007).

Wood and Colleagues (2009)

Wood et al. (2009a) randomly assigned 40 children between the ages of 7 and 11 years ($M = 9.20$, $SD = 1.49$, 32.5% female) to either a 16-session family-based CBT protocol or a waitlist control. Wood and colleagues employed a modified version of a standard CBT program used in typically developing youth (*Building Confidence*; Wood & McLeod, 2008), expanding the typical 12-week protocol over 16 weeks. Following an individualized, modular approach, this expansion allowed for the addition of nine conditional treatment modules specific to ASD symptoms and treatment barriers, without reducing the number of sessions devoted to traditional CBT for anxiety elements (e.g., behavioral exposures). Several additions targeted friendship, social skills, and social isolation using on-site exposure, social coaching, and the development of a peer mentor, as well as mentee, for the child. In addition to children and parents' involvement, relevant school personnel met with the therapist to learn social intervention techniques and monitor progress. Other modules focused on the development of age-appropriate self-care, such as hygiene and organization. To increase motivation and attention, and reinforce desired behaviors, Wood and colleagues used a complex reward system, consisting of daily and long-term incentives. A child's restricted interests and/or stereotypies were incorporated into treatment and used as illustrations for therapeutic concepts and rewards. Later in therapy, a suppression approach for interests and stereotypies was introduced, in which children were taught to restrain from engaging in or discussing these activities for increasing lengths of time.

At posttreatment, 76.5% (*n* = 13) of children in the treatment condition were rated as treatment responders with 52.9% (*n* = 9) reporting diagnostic remission of their anxiety disorder (Wood et al., 2009). In contrast, 8.7% (*n* = 2) were rated as responders or experienced clinical remission in the waitlist condition. Compared to waitlist control, the treatment condition also demonstrated large between-group effects for reductions in clinician-rated anxiety severity (*d* = 2.46) and parent-rated anxiety (*d* = 1.23). Additionally, for the 10 children who returned at 3 months for follow-up assessment, treatment gains appeared to be well maintained with 90% (*n* = 9) maintaining response status and 80% (*n* = 8) free of an anxiety diagnosis. With particularly robust gains in social communication, the modified CBT protocol was also associated with significant decreases in parent-rated autism symptom severity (*d* = 0.77; Wood et al., 2009b). Additionally, reports by parents indicated participants required less assistance and care on a daily

basis and had demonstrated improvements in living/self-care skills over the course of treatment (Drahota, Wood, Sze, & Van Dyke, 2011).

Storch, Arnold, and colleagues (2013) replicated the protocol of Wood et al. (2009a) in comparison to a treatment as usual control (TAU) in a sample of 45 children between the ages of 7 and 11 years (*M* = 8.89, *SD* = 1.34, 20% female). Similar to Wood et al. (2009), results supported CBT with 75% (*n* = 18) of participants randomized to immediate treatment demonstrating response and 38% (*n* = 9) achieving clinical remission of primary anxiety diagnosis, compared to 14% (*n* = 3) response and 5% (*n* = 1) remission for those randomized to the TAU arm. In addition to anxiety improvement, treatment was associated with improvements in parent-rated autism symptom severity (*d* = 0.62), particularly social communication (*d* = 0.62) and social mannerisms (*d* = 0.58).

Reaven, Blakeley-Smith, Culhane-Shelburne, and Hepburn (2012)

Reaven et al. (2012) employed a group treatment structure in a controlled trial of CBT for anxiety in youth with ASD. Fifty youth between the ages of 7 and 14 years (*M* = 10.45, *SD* = 1.74, 4.0% female) were randomized to either a TAU control group or a 12-session multifamily group treatment. Although the CBT anxiety components were drawn from empirically supported programs used in typically developing youth (e.g., *Coping Cat*; Kendall & Hedtke, 2006), the treatment protocol (*Facing Your Fears*; Reaven et al., 2011) was developed specifically for youth with ASD. Each group consisted of three to six children accompanied by their parents and was led by a clinical psychologist aided by two cotherapists. Sessions included a variety of full-group activities, children-together and parent-together activities, and family-specific activities. In order to maximize attention and participation of youth with ASD, the treatment program employed a number of additions and modifications, including a reinforcement system for in-session behavior, provision of visual structure (e.g., written examples, video modeling), and predictability of routine. Of those randomized to CBT, 50% (*n* = 10) demonstrated clinically meaningful improvement compared to 8.7% (*n* = 2) in the TAU condition (*d* = 1.03). In addition, treatment was associated with significant reductions in clinician severity ratings of anxiety diagnoses and reductions in the overall number of anxiety disorders. Parent and child reports also appeared to demonstrate that treatment was well maintained at 3 and 6 months following treatment end.

COGNITIVE-BEHAVIORAL THERAPY TREATMENT FOR ANGER AND RELATED BEHAVIORS

Typically Developing Youth

Although not a diagnosable disorder, as a behavior domain that results in considerable impairment, anger has demanded methods for clinical intervention. Common in disruptive behavior disorders (e.g., oppositional defiant disorder), a number of empirically supported treatment approaches for these disorders (e.g., parent–child interaction therapy) may include anger as a target symptom. While such treatments may be effective for anger management, the wide range of underlying theories across treatments makes a cogent discussion of "treatment for anger" impossible. Even when examining cognitive-behavioral treatment approaches, the protocols used are relatively inconsistent (Sukhodolsky et al., 2004). In light of this, results from a meta-analysis suggest that, in general, CBT-based approaches for anger are efficacious; however, approaches that employ primarily behavioral techniques (i.e., skills development and multimodal) are associated with larger treatment effects ($d = 0.74$ and $d = 0.79$, respectively) than more cognitive-focused treatments (i.e., affective education, $d = 0.36$; problem solving, $d = 0.67$; Sukhodolsky et al., 2004).

Translating to Autism Spectrum Disorder

To date, one randomized controlled trial (Sofronoff, Attwood, Hinton, & Levin, 2007) and one pilot study (Scarpa & Reyes, 2011) have investigated the potential of a CBT-based treatment for anger in youth with ASD. While not directly modeled after a preexisting neurotypical treatment protocol for anger, both studies investigated the same multimodal-type treatment protocol, first in 10- to 14-year-olds (Sofronoff et al., 2007), followed by a modified version for 5- to 7-year-olds (Scarpa & Reyes, 2011).

Sofronoff, Attwood, Hinton, and Levin (2007)

Sofronoff and colleagues (2007) examined the efficacy of CBT for anger in 45 youth with Asperger syndrome aged 10–14 years (M = 10.78, SD = 1.00, 4.4% female). The treatment consisted of six, 2-hour

group sessions that focused on emotion understanding and recognition (happiness, relaxation, and anger), as well as the introduction to behavioral (e.g., appropriate cathartic strategies, relaxation), social (e.g., reassurance and affection, solitude), and cognitive (e.g., reality testing) tools for emotion management. In addition, the treatment employed visual aids (*Social Stories*; Gray, 1998) and treatment metaphors appealing to youth with Asperger syndrome. Participants randomized to the treatment condition were able to produce significantly more anger management strategies than the waitlist condition at posttreatment ($d = 0.67$), had a significantly larger reduction in parent-reported anger episodes over time than the waitlist condition ($d = 1.18$), and demonstrated significant reductions in parent-rated anger severity over time ($d = 1.37$). Further, parents reported higher levels of confidence in their own, as well as their child's, ability to manage anger at posttreatment. The majority of improvements also appeared to be well maintained at 6-week follow-up.

Scarpa and Reyes (2011)

Scarpa and Reyes (2011) attempted to translate the treatment protocol and simultaneously target both anger and anxiety in a sample of eleven 5- to 7-year-olds (18% female). Children were randomized to either a 9-week group treatment or to a waitlist control group. Although treatment was derived from previously evaluated treatments for anxiety (Sofronoff et al., 2005) and anger (Sofronoff et al., 2007), it was modified to better suit the development level of young children. Primary outcomes suggested that the treatment was associated with a decrease in duration of outbursts ($d = 0.46$), as well as increased parental confidence of their ($d = 0.63$) and their child's anger management ($d = 0.89$).

EVIDENCE INTO PRACTICE: GUIDING FACTORS/CONSIDERATIONS

Although there are multiple well-designed studies providing support for the utility and effectiveness of CBT to address anger control and anxiety symptoms in neurotypical youth (see Abramowitz et al., 2005; Cartwright-Hatton et al., 2004; In-Albon & Schneider, 2007; Sukhodolsky et al., 2004 for reviews), there are issues that make it difficult to extend these findings to youth with ASD and specific comorbid conditions. While some of these issues are related to technical and/or design limitations of particular studies (e.g., using ASD as exclusionary criteria, lack of assays for core ASD symptoms), others are linked to societal conceptualizations of ASD and their etiology.

From Bleuler's (1950) description of a child's willful withdrawal into fantasy, Kanner (1943) emphasized autism as a skills deficit in recognition and use of external social cues. However, Kanner attributed these deficits to a lack of familial warmth, an idea that gained traction during the late 1940s and 1950s. In this conceptualization, the notion of treating ASD meant removal of children to foster care. Bettelheim (1967) further shifted this attribution to neglectful mothers, an assumption which altered the relationship between help-seeking parents and treatment providers. Interventions remained focused upon transferring children from parental care to institutional confinement and experimental treatments, including untested pharmacotherapy, electric shock therapy, and aversive behavioral conditioning.

It is ironic that the first reports of positive treatment response among children with ASD were made during this period of misinformed and poorly structured intervention efforts. The first behavioral-based treatments were used (Lovaas, Koegel, Simmons, & Long, 1973) to address disruptive and/or dangerous behaviors in children with ASD and included analysis of behavior function(s), task analysis, and shaping techniques. This treatment approach remains effective for building social skills and managing inappropriate behaviors in children with ASD (Matson & Smith, 2008; Sofronoff & Beaumont, 2009).

A fundamental difficulty in using CBT for higher functioning children with ASD is that the entry-level emotional and behavioral skills required for CBT are those most commonly impaired among children with ASD diagnoses (Brereton et al., 2006; Cohen & Volkmar, 1997; Myers, Plauche-Johnson, & Council on Children with Disabilities, 2007). In fact, the magnitude of deficits in these skills is an effective predictor of CBT response for children (Kendall et al., 1997). Bearing such deficits in mind, examination of the CBT elements for neurotypical youth can provide much-needed guidance as to where modifications are warranted and what such changes might include. Cognitive-behavioral therapy for anxiety disorders (Kendall et al., 1997; Wood et al., 2006) includes emotional identification, cognitive restructuring, exposure therapy, contingency management, and problem solving. However, it should be noted that CBT protocols for various presenting

concerns contain most or all of these elements (Anderson & Morris, 2006). Therefore, any modification to CBT for children with ASD will primarily be related to the previously mentioned skill deficits, rather than to the presenting comorbid condition (Paxton & Estay, 2007; Shapiro, 2009).

As a result, the few available studies of CBT for children with ASD and comorbid conditions utilize protocols similar to CBT for neurotypical youth; however, there is a more intensive focus upon foundational skill building to address deficits in cognitive, social, and emotional functioning (Wood et al., 2009a). The remainder of this chapter will examine in more detail the specific modifications of CBT used to treat comorbid anxiety and anger symptoms among children with ASDs.

EVIDENCE INTO PRACTICE: COGNITIVE MODIFICATIONS OF COGNITIVE-BEHAVIORAL THERAPY IN AUTISM SPECTRUM DISORDER

In order to better justify recommendations for specific modifications to and/or accommodations within existing treatment protocols for children with ASD and comorbid anxiety or anger, it is helpful to consider the traditional component structure of CBT. A more detailed examination of the methods used in cognitive therapy will assist in illuminating areas for potential modification to address the needs of youth with ASD and comorbid anxiety and anger symptoms. Traditional cognitive methods include the use of Socratic questioning to promote guided discovery, examining the evidence, examining advantages and disadvantages, identifying cognitive errors, completing thought change records, generating rational alternatives, guided imagery, role-play scenarios, and rehearsal (Cashin, 2008). In addition to these components, tailoring of CBT for treatment of specific disorders (e.g., anxiety or anger) typically also will include psychoeducation, emotional identification, reality testing, and thought distortion identification and restructuring (Steketee et al., 2011).

Examination of those studies finding success in treatment of comorbid anxiety and/or anger symptoms among youth with ASD reveals a significant reduction of reliance upon wholly cognitive tasks. Commonly present, cognitive deficits often limit the ability of youth with ASD to engage in activities similar to direct cognitive restructuring and can create barriers for cognitive therapy. As a result, cognitive restructuring tasks should be adjusted to include more concrete terminology and activities; note that the child's understanding of *why* cognitive restructuring works becomes less important when compared to the child's understanding of *when* and *how* to engage in the cognitive tasks themselves. Additionally, reducing the cognitive loading on the child can be addressed through the use of information transmission and retention techniques, such as acronyms to remember the sequencing of various conceptual components, or tailoring cognitive activities to fit the child's individual interests. Similarly, clinicians should adjust goal-setting activities to reflect the difficulty children with cognitive deficits experience with setting and maintaining long-term goals.

With respect to developmental considerations, changes can be made to the specific language used in therapy. More specifically, the terms used in providing psychoeducation about anxiety or anger should be easily understood at the child's developmental level. This is usually accomplished through conceptualization of anxiety or anger as a separate, external entity (e.g., "What is your anxiety telling you to do right now?"). This idea also applies to emotional assessment, through techniques such as the use of cartoon facial expressions instead of numeric ratings for emotional intensity. Similarly, at lower developmental levels, the language used should avoid abstract language in favor of more concrete terminology and ideas. For example, emotional identification techniques for younger children (or for children and adolescents with significant cognitive limitations) will rely upon concrete observations (e.g., facial expressions, gestures, etc.) rather than upon cognitive exercises commonly used to determine potential setting events and/or triggers.

With respect to individualization, the format and specific techniques used in therapy should be tailored to each child's individual pattern of deficits and relative strengths. The treatment metaphors and examples, as well as specific activities used to deliver skill-building curricula, can be altered as necessary to avoid or work around skill deficits. Similarly, these treatment components can also be modified to take advantage of individual strengths. As specific examples, the activities used for affective education can make use of experiences from the child's everyday life, particularly if such information is sought from the caregiver(s) early in treatment. Additionally, children with ASD commonly display restricted

sets of interest. It is imperative that treating clinicians expand their thinking to recognize such areas of heightened communication as nontraditional avenues for delivery of treatment, rather than simply as diagnostic markers.

Applied examples of these modifications can be found in the studies previously discussed. The notion of treatment conceptualization metaphors and language friendly to youth with Asperger syndrome was a major modification utilized by Sofronoff and colleagues (2005, 2007). Chalfant et al. (2007) relied upon a significant de-emphasis of cognitive treatment components where possible and developmental scaling of such techniques when they were considered vital to treatment. Treatment delivery has been altered to increase structure of transitions and sequencing (Reaven et al., 2012), as well as to utilize visual sequencing and scheduling techniques (Reaven et al., 2012; Sofronoff et al., 2007). Parental psychoeducation has been built into the session time line (Scarpa & Reyes, 2011). Verbal and written instruction to introduce various skills has been augmented with live and video modeling (Reaven et al., 2012). Treatment duration has been expanded to allow for inclusion of additional ASD-specific skill instruction (Wood et al., 2009a), while individual session time has been shortened to better accommodate developmental variations in attentional resources (Scarpa & Reyes, 2011).

EVIDENCE INTO PRACTICE: BEHAVIORAL MODIFICATIONS OF COGNITIVE-BEHAVIORAL THERAPY IN AUTISM SPECTRUM DISORDER

As with cognitive methods, understanding the potential for modifications relevant to youth with ASD and comorbid anxiety and/or anger symptoms is aided by closer examination of behavioral CBT methods. Traditional behavioral methods include activity and/or pleasant event scheduling, graded task/homework assignments, exposure with response prevention, relaxation/breathing training, coping cards, rehearsal or application of learned cognitive routines, and behavioral management via classical and operant conditioning techniques (Cashin, 2008). With respect to the treatment of anxiety, effective CBT relies heavily upon the utilization of anxiety/fear hierarchy, associated exposure activities with response prevention, and behavioral reinforcement/reward techniques (Steketee et al., 2011).

In the studies reporting success in treatment of anxiety/anger symptoms among youth with ASD, there is a consistent intensification of the behavioral focus of treatment. Note that this is simply an inversion of reducing cognitive loading, as skills that cannot be taught in CBT through cognitive techniques must therefore be introduced and built using behavioral components. Therefore, it can be seen that techniques such as exposure, social coaching, behavioral reinforcement, and reward systems achieve a higher level of importance to overall treatment. In addition to these common techniques, the previously mentioned shift from abstract to concrete terminology and examples can further be enhanced through an increase in practice of behavioral routines associated with newly introduced skills.

In terms of developmental considerations, another commonly utilized behavioral modification relates to matching activity duration and contingency management to the developmental level of the child in question. For example, when the child's attentional resources are significantly limited, the use of frequent breaks can increase their level of participation, as can shortening the latency between display of desired behavior(s) and delivery of positive reinforcement. A last point in this area relates to caregiver involvement. Although parental participation is a tenet of most child-focused treatments, it acquires additional importance when the developmental level of the child is such that he or she requires significant amounts of adult supervision and/or prompting to engage in newly taught skills and behaviors outside of the session environment.

Examination of previously discussed studies provides exemplars of behavioral modifications. Visual modeling of exposures and relaxation techniques were heavily emphasized (Chalfant et al., 2007; Reaven et al., 2012; Sofronoff et al., 2007). Social skill-building and coaching (Sofronoff et al., 2005; Wood et al., 2009a) and disruptive behavior reduction and behavioral management techniques (Chalfant et al., 2007; Reaven et al., 2012; Wood et al., 2009a) were utilized. Sequencing and transitioning between various behavioral activities was accomplished through more concrete and individually tailored cues (Reaven et al., 2012; Sofronoff et al., 2005). The specific activities utilized in treatment were individualized to the personal preferences (Wood et al., 2009a) and developmental profiles (Scarpa & Reyes, 2011) of the child. Parents and caregivers were included in behavioral treatment

components through the use of dedicated session activities (Wood et al., 2009a) and homework routines (Chalfant et al., 2007). Finally, duration of treatment was expanded to allow for increased rehearsal of behavioral skills in applied settings (Chalfant et al., 2007), while individual session times were shortened to accommodate developmental differences in attentional resources (Scarpa & Reyes, 2011).

EVIDENCE INTO PRACTICE: ADDITIONAL GUIDANCE ON MODIFICATION OF COGNITIVE-BEHAVIORAL THERAPY

Beyond the modification of specific cognitive and behavioral techniques to accommodate cognitive limitations and increase reliance on behavioral learning and rehearsal, there are a number of subtle, though important, points from the cited studies that deserve additional consideration. First, the majority of these studies were not designed with the reduction of core ASD symptoms in mind; rather, the overriding consideration was alleviation of problematic comorbid symptoms whether anxiety or anger. This point is somewhat counterintuitive, as traditional views on CBT (Cashin, 2008) place more importance on primary diagnoses than on comorbid conditions.

A second, related, point of importance rests on the existing ASD-related symptoms (e.g., repetitive behaviors, restricted interests). More specifically, if the aim of treatment is not reduction and/or elimination of diagnostic markers associated with ASD, then such symptoms could instead be seen as a potential avenue for delivery of treatment aimed at reducing comorbid anxiety symptoms and/or behavioral dysregulation. Maintaining the focus of treatment on comorbid symptoms among youth with ASD allows for considerable latitude in designing treatment delivery methods that can actually make use of—or at the very least profit from a lack of barriers due to—such diagnostic markers.

The last point relates to the potential for modified CBT to reduce the perceived severity of core ASD symptoms. The protocol developed by Wood et al. (2009a) was found to correlate with significant decreases in parent-rated severity of core autism symptoms associated with communicative deficits (Storch, Arnold, et al., 2013; Wood et al., 2009b), as well as with decreases in levels of required care (Drahota, Wood, Sze, & Van Dyke, 2011). This point is instrumental in furthering understanding of effective treatment design for youth with ASD, as it represents the first large-scale observation wherein building of cognitive skills commonly deficient in children with ASD was shown to increase the effectiveness of treatment with respect to reduction of anxiety symptoms.

CONCLUSIONS

Considering the large portion of youth with ASD who meet diagnostic criteria for comorbid conditions (Brereton et al., 2006; Gjervik et al., 2011; Leyfer et al., 2006; Nicholas et al., 2008; Simonoff et al., 2008) and the considerable impact these disorders and their symptoms have on the functioning of these youth (Kim et al., 2000; Muris et al., 1998; Scarpa & Reyes, 2011; Sukhodolsky et al., 2008), the need for effective treatment of comorbid disorders in this population is clear. With a strong empirical basis within neurotypical youth (e.g., In-Albon & Schneider, 2007; Sukhodolsky et al., 2004), CBT has been investigated as a potential method of intervention for anger and anxiety, with preliminary results supporting its efficacy (e.g., Sofronoff et al., 2007; Wood et al., 2009a). While promising, each trial of CBT for anger or anxiety in youth with ASD employed its own unique protocol, which makes further systematic investigation and replication imperative before CBT can be deemed effective for youth with ASD and comorbid conditions (see Selles & Storch, 2012, for a review). Despite this, the current evidence broadly suggests that interventions employing traditional CBT protocols modified to address ASD-specific skill deficits and symptoms can be efficacious in reducing comorbid anger and anxiety, and potentially reduce the severity of specific core autism symptoms.

REFERENCES

Abramowitz, J. S., Whiteside, S. P., & Deacon, B. J. (2005). The effectiveness of treatment for pediatric obsessive compulsive disorder: A meta-analysis. *Behavior Therapy, 36*, 55–63.

Adamek, L., Nichols, S., Tetenbaum, S. P., Bregman, J., Ponzio, C. A., & Carr, E. G. (2011). Individual temperament and problem behavior in children with autism spectrum disorders. *Focus on Autism and Other Developmental Disabilities, 26*(3), 173–183.

American Psychiatric Association. (2000). *Diagnostic and statistical manual of mental disorders* (4th ed.). Washington, DC: American Psychiatric Press.

Anderson, S., & Morris, J. (2006). Cognitive behaviour therapy for people with Asperger syndrome. *Behavioural and Cognitive Psychotherapy, 34*, 293–303.

Attwood, T. (2003). Frameworks for behavioral interventions. *Child and Adolescent Psychiatric Clinics of North America, 12*(1), 65–86, vi.

Baron-Cohen, S. (1989). Do autistic children have obsessions and compulsions? *British Journal of Clinical Psychology, 28*(3), 193–200.

Bauminger, N., & Kasari, C. (2000). Loneliness and friendship in high-functioning children with autism. *Child Development, 71*(2), 447–456.

Bellini, S. (2004). Social skill deficits and anxiety in high-functioning adolescents with autism spectrum disorders. *Focus on Autism and Other Developmental Disabilities, 19*, 78–86.

Ben-Sasson, A., Cermak, S. A., Orsmond, G. I., Tager-Flusberg, H., Kadlec, M. B., & Carter, A. S. (2008). Sensory clusters of toddlers with autism spectrum disorders: Differences in affective symptoms. *Journal of Child Psychology and Psychiatry, 49*(8), 817–825.

Bettelheim, B. (1967). *The empty fortress: Infantile autism and the birth of the self.* New York, NY: Free Press.

Bleuler, E. (1950). *Dementia praecox, or the group of schizophrenias.* (J. Zincs, Trans.). New York, NY: International Universities Press. (Original work published 1911).

Brereton, A. V., Tonge, B. J., & Einfeld, S. L. (2006). Psychopathology in children and adolescents with autism compared to young people with intellectual disability. *Journal of Autism and Developmental Disorders, 36*(7), 863–870.

Butler, A. C., Chapman, J. E., Forman, E. M., & Beck, A. T. (2006). The empirical status of cognitive-behavioral therapy: A review of meta-analyses. *Clinical Psychology Review, 26*(1), 17–31. doi: 10.1016/j.cpr.2005.07.003.

Cartwright-Hatton, S., Roberts, C., Chitsabesan, P., Fothergill, C., & Harrington, R. (2004). Systematic review of the efficacy of cognitive behaviour therapies for childhood and adolescent anxiety disorders. *British Journal of Clinical Psychology, 43*(4), 421–436.

Cashin, A. (2008). Narrative therapy: A psychotherapeutic approach in the treatment of adolescents with Asperger's disorder. *Journal of Child and Adolescent Psychiatric Nursing, 21*(1), 48–56.

Centers for Disease Control and Prevention. (2012). Prevalence of autism spectrum disorders–autism and developmental disabilities monitoring network, 14 sites, United States, 2002. *MMWR Surveillance Summaries, 61*(3), 1–24.

Chalfant, A. M., Rapee, R., & Carroll, L. (2007). Treating anxiety disorders in children with high functioning autism spectrum disorders: A controlled trial. *Journal of Autism and Developmental Disorders, 37*(10), 1842–1857.

Chamberlain, B., Kasari, C., & Rotheram-Fuller, E. (2007). Involvement or isolation? The social networks of children with autism in regular classrooms. *Journal of Autism and Developmental Disorders, 37*(2), 230–242.

Cohen, D. J., & Volkmar, F. (1997). Conceptualization of autism and intervention practices: International perspectives. In D. J. Cohen & F. R. Volkmar (Eds.), *Handbook of autism and pervasive developmental disorders* (pp. 947–950). New York, NY: Wiley.

Costello, E. J., Mustillo, S., Erkanli, A., Keeler, G., & Angold, A. (2003). Prevalence and development of psychiatric disorders in childhood and adolescence. *Archives of General Psychiatry, 60*(8), 837–844.

Davis, N. O., & Carter, A. S. (2008). Parenting stress in mothers and fathers of toddlers with autism spectrum disorders: Associations with child characteristics. *Journal of Autism and Developmental Disorders, 38*(7), 1278–1291.

de Bruin, E. I., Ferdinand, R. F., Meester, S., de Nijs, P. F., & Verheij, F. (2007). High rates of psychiatric co-morbidity in PDD-NOS. *Journal of Autism and Developmental Disorders, 37*(5), 877–886.

Drahota, A., Wood, J. J., Sze, K. M., & Van Dyke, M. (2011). Effects of cognitive behavioral therapy on daily living skills in children with high-functioning autism and concurrent anxiety disorders. *Journal of Autism and Developmental Disorders, 41*(3), 257–265.

Evans, D. W., Canavera, K., Kleinpeter, F. L., Maccubbin, E., & Taga, K. (2005). The fears, phobias and anxieties of children with autism spectrum disorders and Down syndrome: Comparisons with developmentally and chronologically age matched children. *Child Psychology and Human Development, 36*, 3–26.

Farrugia, S., & Hudson, J. (2006). Anxiety in adolescents with Asperger syndrome: Negative thoughts, behavioral problems, and life interference. *Focus on Autism and Other Developmental Disabilities, 21*, 25–35.

Fombonne, E. (2009). Epidemiology of pervasive developmental disorders. *Pediatric Research, 65*(6), 591–598.

Gadow, K. D., DeVincent, C., & Schneider, J. (2008). Predictors of psychiatric symptoms in children with an autism spectrum disorder. *Journal of Autism and Developmental Disorders, 38*(9), 1710–1720.

Gadow, K. D., DeVincent, C. J., Pomeroy, J., & Azizian, A. (2005). Comparison of DSM-IV symptoms in elementary school-age children with PDD versus clinic and community samples. *Autism, 9*(4), 392–415. doi: 10.1177/1362361305056079.

Gillott, A., Furniss, F., & Walter, A. (2001). Anxiety in high-functioning children with autism. *Autism, 5*(3), 277–286.

Gjervik, E., Eldevik, S., Fjaeran-Granum, T., & Sponheim, E. (2011). Kiddie-SADS reveals high rates of DSM-IV disorders in children and adolescents with autism spectrum disorders. *Journal of Autism and Developmental Disorders, 41*, 761–769.

Gray, C. (1998). Social stories and comic strip conversations with students with Asperger syndrome and high functioning autism. In E. Schopler, G. B. Mesibov & L.

J. Kunce (Eds.), *Asperger syndrome or high functioning autism* (pp. 167-198). New York, NY: Plenum Press.

Green, J., Gilchrist, A., Burton, D., & Cox, A. (2000). Social and psychiatric functioning in adolescents with Asperger syndrome compared with conduct disorder. *Journal of Autism and Developmental Disorders, 30*(4), 279–293.

Green, S. A., Ben-Sasson, A., Soto, T. W., & Carter, A. S. (2011). Anxiety and sensory over-responsivity in toddlers with autism spectrum disorders: Bidirectional effects across time. *Journal of Autism and Developmental Disorders, 42*(6), 1112–1119.

Hastings, R. P. (2002). Parental stress and behaviour problems of children with developmental disability. *Journal of Intellectual and Developmental Disabilities, 18*, 149–160.

In-Albon, T., & Schneider, S. (2007). Psychotherapy of childhood anxiety disorders: A meta-analysis. *Psychotherapy and Psychosomatics, 76*(1), 15–24.

Joshi, G., Petty, C., Wozniak, J., Henin, A., Fried, R., Galdo, M.,...Biederman, J. (2010). The heavy burden of psychiatric comorbidity in youth with autism spectrum disorders: A large comparative study of a psychiatrically referred population. *Journal of Autism and Developmental Disorders, 40*, 1361–1370.

Kanne, S. M., Abbacchi, A. M., & Constantino, J. N. (2009). Multi-informant ratings of psychiatric symptom severity in children with autism spectrum disorders: The importance of environmental context. *Journal of Autism and Developmental Disorders, 39*(6), 856–864.

Kanner, L. (1943). Autistic disturbances of affective contact. *The Nervous Child, 2*, 217–250.

Kelly, A. B., Garnett, M. S., Attwood, T., & Peterson, C. (2008). Autism spectrum symptomatology in children: The impact of family and peer relationships. *Journal of Abnormal Child Psychology, 36*(7), 1069–1081.

Kendall, P. C., & Choudhury, M. S. (2003). Children and adolescents in cognitive–behavioral therapy: Some past efforts and current advances, and the challenges in our future. *Cognitive Therapy and Research, 27*(1), 89–104.

Kendall, P. C., Flannery-Schroeder, E., Panichelli-Mindel, S. M., Southam-Gerow, M., Henin, A., & Warman, M. (1997). Therapy for youths with anxiety disorders: A second randomized clinical trial. *Journal of Consulting and Clinical Psychology, 65*(3), 366–380.

Kendall, P. C., & Hedtke, K. (2006). *Coping cat workbook* (2nd ed). Ardmore, PA: Workbook Publishing.

Kim, J. A., Szatmari, P., Bryson, S. E., Streiner, D. L., & Wilson, F. J. (2000). The prevalence of anxiety and mood problems among children with autism and Asperger syndrome. *Autism, 4*(2), 117.

Klin, A., Saulnier, C. A., Sparrow, S. S., Cicchetti, D. V., Volkmar, F. R., & Lord, C. (2007). Social and communication abilities and disabilities in higher functioning individuals with autism spectrum disorders: The Vineland and the ADOS. *Journal of Autism and Developmental Disorders, 37*(4), 748–759.

Kring, S. R., Greenberg, J. S., & Seltzer, M. M. (2008). Adolescents and adults with autism with and without co-morbid psychiatric disorders: Differences in maternal well-being. *Journal of Mental Health Research in Intellectual Disabilities, 1*(2), 53–74.

Leahy, R. L., & Holland, S. J. (2000). *Treatment plans and interventions for depression and anxiety disorders.* New York, NY Guilford Press.

Lehmkuhl, H. D., Storch, E. A., Bodfish, J. W., & Geffken, G. R. (2008). Brief report: Exposure and response prevention for obsessive compulsive disorder in a 12-year-old with autism. *Journal of Autism and Developmental Disorders, 38*(5), 977–981.

Lewin, A. B., Wood, J. J., Gunderson, S., Murphy, T. K., & Storch, E. A. (2011). Phenomenology of comorbid autism spectrum and obsessive-compulsive disorders among children. *Journal of Developmental and Physical Disabilities, 23*(6), 543–553.

Leyfer, O. T., Folstein, S. E., Bacalman, S., Davis, N. O., Dinh, E., Morgan, J.,...Lainhart, J. E. (2006). Comorbid psychiatric disorders in children with autism: Interview development and rates of disorders. *Journal of Autism and Developmental Disorders, 36*(7), 849–861.

Lounds, J., Seltzer, M. M., Greenberg, J. S., & Shattuck, P. T. (2007). Transition and change in adolescents and young adults with autism: Longitudinal effects on maternal well-being. *American Journal on Mental Retardation, 112*(6), 401–417.

Lovaas, O. I., Koegel, R., Simmons, J. Q., & Long, J. S. (1973). Some generalization and follow-up measures on autistic children in behavior therapy. *Journal of Applied Behavioral Analysis, 6*(1), 131–165.

Lyneham, H. J., Abbott, M. J., Wignall, A., & Rapee, R. M. (2003). *The Cool Kids family program—therapist manual.* Sydney, Australia: Macquarie University.

Martin, R., Watson, D., & Wan, C. K. (2000). A three-factor model of trait anger: Dimensions of affect, behavior, and cognition. *Journal of Personality, 68*(5), 869–897.

Matson, J. L., & Nebel-Schwalm, M. S. (2007). Comorbid psychopathology with autism spectrum disorder in children: An overview. *Research in Developmental Disabilities, 28*(4), 341–352.

Matson, J. L., & Smith, K. R. M. (2008). Current status of intensive behavioural interventions for young children with autism and PDD-NOS. *Research in Autism Spectrum Disorders, 2,* 60-74.

Mills, R., & Wing, L. (2005). *Researching interventions in ASD and priorities for research: Surveying the membership of the NAS.* London, UK: National Autistic Society.

Montes, G., & Halterman, J. S. (2007). Psychological functioning and coping among mothers of children with autism: a population-based study. *Pediatrics, 119*(5), 1040–1046.

Muris, P., Steerneman, P., Merckelbach, H., Holdrinet, I., & Meesters, C. (1998). Comorbid anxiety symptoms in children with pervasive developmental disorders. *Journal of Anxiety Disorders, 12*(4), 387–393.

Myers, S. M., Plauche-Johnson, C., & Council on Children with Disabilities. (2007). Management of children with autism spectrum disorders. *Pediatrics, 120*(5), 1162–1182.

Nicholas, J. S., Charles, J. M., Carpenter, L. A., King, L. B., Jenner, W., & Spratt, E. G. (2008). Prevalence and characteristics of children with autism-spectrum disorders. *Annals of Epidemiology, 18*(2), 130–136.

Ooi, Y. P., Lam, C. M., Sung, M., Tan, W. T., Goh, T. J., Fung, D. S.,...Chua, A. (2008). Effects of cognitive-behavioural therapy on anxiety for children with high-functioning autistic spectrum disorders. *Singapore Medical Journal, 49*(3), 215–220.

Paxton, K., & Estay, I. A. (2007). *Counselling people on the autism spectrum: A practical manual.* London, UK: Jessica Kingsley.

Reaven, J., Blakeley-Smith, A., Culhane-Shelburne, K., & Hepburn, S. (2012). Group cognitive behavior therapy for children with high-functioning autism spectrum disorders and anxiety: A randomized trial. *Journal of Child Psychology and Psychiatry, 53*(4), 410–419.

Reaven, J., Blakeley-Smith, A., Nichols, S., Dasari, M., Flanigan, E., & Hepburn, S. (2009). Cognitive-behavioral group treatment for anxiety symptoms in children with high-functioning autism spectrum disorders: A pilot study. *Focus on Autism and Other Developmental Disabilities, 24*(1), 27-37.

Reaven, J., Blakeley-Smith, A., Nichols, S., & Hepburn, S. (2011). *Facing your fears: Group therapy for managing anxiety in children with high-functioning autism spectrum disorders.* Baltimore, MD: Paul H. Brookes.

Reaven, J., & Hepburn, S. (2003). Cognitive-behavioral treatment of obsessive-compulsive disorder in a child with Asperger syndrome: A case report. *Autism, 7*(2), 145–164.

Scarpa, A., & Reyes, N. M. (2011). Improving emotion regulation with CBT in young children with high functioning autism spectrum disorders: A pilot study. *Behavioural and Cognitive Psychotherapy, 39*(4), 495–500.

Selles, R. R., & Storch, E. A. (2012). Translation of anxiety treatment to youth with autism spectrum disorders. *Journal of Child and Family Studies.*

Shapiro, T. (2009). Psychotherapy for autism. *Journal of Infant, Child and Adolescent Psychotherapy, 8*(1), 22-31.

Simonoff, E., Pickles, A., Charman, T., Chandler, S., Loucas, T., & Baird, G. (2008). Psychiatric disorders in children with autism spectrum disorders: Prevalence, comorbidity, and associated factors in a population-derived sample. *Journal of the American Academy of Child and Adolescent Psychiatry, 47*(8), 921–929.

Sofronoff, K., Attwood, T., & Hinton, S. (2005). A randomised controlled trial of a CBT intervention for anxiety in children with Asperger syndrome. *Journal of Child Psychology and Psychiatry, 46*(11), 1152–1160.

Sofronoff, K., Attwood, T., Hinton, S., & Levin, I. (2007). A randomized controlled trial of a cognitive behavioural intervention for anger management in children diagnosed with Asperger syndrome. *Journal of Autism and Developmental Disorders, 37*(7), 1203–1214.

Sofronoff, K., & Beaumont, R. (2009). The challenges of working with young people diagnosed with Asperger syndrome. In D. McKay & E. A. Storch (Eds.), *Cognitive-behavior therapy for children: Treating complex and refractory cases* (pp.421-433). New York, NY: Springer.

Spiker, M. A., Lin, C. E., Van Dyke, M., & Wood, J. J. (2011). Restricted interests and anxiety in children with autism. *Autism, 16*(3), 306–320.

Steinhausen, H. C., Metzke, C. W., Meier, M., & Kannenberg, R. (1998). Prevalence of child and adolescent psychiatric disorders: The Zurich Epidemiological Study. *Acta Psychiatrica Scandinavica, 98*(4), 262–271.

Steketee, G., Siev, J., Fama, J. M., Keshaviah, A., Chosak, A., & Wilhelm, S. (2011). Predictors of treatment outcome in modular cognitive therapy for obsessive-compulsive disorder. *Depression and Anxiety, 28*(4), 333–341.

Storch, E. A., Arnold, E. B., Lewin, A. B., Nadeau, J., Jones, A. M., De Nadai, A. S.,...Murphy, T. K. (2013). The effect of cognitive-behavioral therapy versus treatment as usual for anxiety in children with autism spectrum disorders: A randomized, controlled trial. *Journal of the American Academy of Child & Adolescent Psychiatry, 52*(2), 132-142.

Storch, E. A., Geffken, G. R., Merlo, L. J., Jacob, M. L., Murphy, T. K., Goodman, W. K.,...Grabill, K. (2007a). Family accommodation in pediatric obsessive-compulsive disorder. *Journal of Clinical Child and Adolescent Psychology, 36*(2), 207–216.

Storch, E. A., Geffken, G. R., Merlo, L. J., Mann, G., Duke, D., Munson, M.,...Goodman, W. K. (2007b). Family-based cognitive-behavioral therapy for pediatric obsessive-compulsive disorder: Comparison of intensive and weekly approaches. *Journal of the American Academy of Child and Adolescent Psychiatry, 46*(4), 469–478.

Storch, E. A., Larson, M. J., Ehrenreich-May, J., Arnold, E. B., Jones, A. M., Renno, P.,...Wood, J. J. (2012). Peer victimization in youth with autism spectrum disorders and co-occurring anxiety: Relations with psychopathology and loneliness. *Journal of*

Developmental and Physical Disabilities. doi:10.1007/ s10882-012-9290-4.

Sukhodolsky, D. G., Kassinove, H., & Gorman, B. S. (2004). Cognitive-behavioral therapy for anger in children and adolescents: A meta-analysis. *Aggression and Violent Behavior, 9*(3), 247–269.

Sukhodolsky, D. G., Scahill, L., Gadow, K. D., Arnold, L. E., Aman, M. G., McDougle, C. J.,...Vitiello, B. (2008). Parent-rated anxiety symptoms in children with pervasive developmental disorders: Frequency and association with core autism symptoms and cognitive functioning. *Journal of Abnormal Child Psychology, 36*(1), 117–128.

Sze, K. M., & Wood, J. J. (2007). Cognitive behavioral treatment of comorbid anxiety disorders and social difficulties in children with high-functioning autism: A case report. *Journal of Contemporary Psychotherapy, 37*, 133–143.

Tantam, D. (2003). The challenge of adolescents and adults with Asperger syndrome. *Child and Adolescent Psychiatric Clinics of North America, 12*(1), 143–163, vii-viii.

Tomanik, S., Harris, G. E., & Hawkins, J. (2004). The relationship between behaviors exhibited by children with autism and maternal stress. *Journal of Intellectual and Developmental Disabilities, 29*, 16–26.

van Steensel, F. J., Bogels, S. M., & Perrin, S. (2011). Anxiety disorders in children and adolescents with autistic spectrum disorders: A meta-analysis. *Clinical Child and Family Psychology Review, 14*(3), 302–317.

Warren, Z., Veenstra-VanderWeele, J., Stone, W., Bruzek, J. L., Nahmias, A. S., Foss-Feig, J. H.,...McPheeters, M. L. (2011). *Therapies for children with autism spectrum disorders. [Comparative Effectiveness Review, 2011/08/12 ed., Vol. 26].* Rockville, MD: Agency for Healthcare Research and Quality.

Weisbrot, D. M., Gadow, K. D., DeVincent, C. J., & Pomeroy, J. (2005). The presentation of anxiety in children with pervasive developmental disorders. *Journal Child Adolescent Psychopharmacology, 15*(3), 477–496.

Westra, H. A., Dozois, D. J., & Marcus, M. (2007). Expectancy, homework compliance, and initial change in cognitive-behavioral therapy for anxiety. *Journal of Counseling and Clinical Psychology, 75*(3), 363–373.

White, S. W., Oswald, D., Ollendick, T., & Scahill, L. (2009). Anxiety in children and adolescents with autism spectrum disorders. *Clinical Psychology Review, 29*(3), 216–229.

Wood, J. J., Drahota, A., Sze, K., Har, K., Chiu, A., & Langer, D. A. (2009). Cognitive behavioral therapy for anxiety in children with autism spectrum disorders: A randomized, controlled trial. *Journal of Child Psychology and Psychiatry, 50*(3), 224–234.

Wood, J. J., Drahota, A., Sze, K., Van Dyke, M., Decker, K., Fujii, C.,...Spiker, M. (2009). Brief report: Effects of cognitive behavioral therapy on parent-reported autism symptoms in school-age children with high-functioning autism. *Journal of Autism and Developmental Disorders, 39*(11), 1608–1612.

Wood, J. J., & McLeod, B. (2008). *Child anxiety disorders: A treatment manual for practitioners.* New York, NY: Norton.

Wood, J. J., Piacentini, J. C., Southam-Gerow, M., Chu, B. C., & Sigman, M. (2006). Family cognitive behavioral therapy for child anxiety disorders. *Journal of the American Academy of Child and Adolescent Psychiatry, 45*(3), 314–321.

Zandt, F., Prior, M., & Kyrios, M. (2007). Repetitive behaviour in children with high functioning autism and obsessive compulsive disorder. *Journal of Autism and Developmental Disorders, 37*(2), 251–259.

16

Behavioral Family Intervention

ADEL C. NAJDOWSKI AND EVELYN R. GOULD

Several decades of research support the inclusion of parents and family members as a key component of successful treatment programs for children with autism spectrum disorder (ASD) (National Autism Center, 2009; National Research Council, 2001). Parent training (also referred to as parent education) broadly refers to interventions or programs designed to develop parent behaviors that will promote positive developmental outcomes in their children. Behavioral parent training is a particularly effective and well-researched intervention for parents of children with ASD (Brookman-Frazee, Stahmer, Baker-Ericzén, & Tsai, 2006; Burrell & Borrego, 2011). As well as contributing to a child's overall and ongoing progress, training parents to be educators or behavior change agents is a potentially cost-effective model of service delivery (e.g., Cordisco, Strain, & Depew, 1988; Cunningham, 1985; McClannahan, Krantz, & McGee, 1982; Sanders & Glynn, 1981; Symon, 2001). Research has shown that children with ASD receiving *intensive* treatment based on the principles of applied behavior analysis (ABA) show significantly greater gains than those receiving less intensive treatment (Eldevik, Eikeseth, Jahr, & Smith, 2006; Granpeesheh, Dixon, Tarbox, Kaplan, & Wilke, 2009; Lovaas, 1987). Because young children with ASD likely spend most of their waking hours at home with their parents, ABA services will likely be maximally effective when parents are involved in implementing ABA interventions (Matson, Mahan, & Matson, 2009). By training parents to be educators, clinicians can immediately increase the number of opportunities for learning a child can access throughout his or her daily life since parents can potentially provide "around-the-clock intervention" for children in a way that service providers, professionals, and teachers cannot (McConachie & Diggle, 2007; Symon, 2001). Parent training may also help ensure consistency of program implementation and provide greater potential for maintenance and generalization of treatment gains (Brookman-Frazee, Vismara, Drahota, Stahmer, & Openden, 2009; Kaiser & Hancock, 2003; McConachie & Diggle, 2007; National Research Council, 2001; Symon, 2001).

Indeed, research suggests that in addition to increasing child skills and reducing challenging behavior, parent training can produce other benefits, such as increased family access to social and leisure activities (Feldman & Werner, 2002; Koegel, Bimbela, & Schreibman, 1996), improved quality of parent–child interactions (Koegel et al., 1996), increased feelings of parental competency, and decrease in stress (Ingersoll & Wainer, 2011; Koegel et al., 1996; Moes, 1995; Symon, 2001). Koegel and colleagues (1996) found that parents appeared happier, more interested, less stressed, and experienced more positive interactions with their child following pivotal response training (PRT) in the home. Feldman and Werner (2002) also found that, compared to a waitlist comparison group, parents receiving a behavioral skills training program reported less stress, fewer depressive symptoms, higher self-efficacy, and improved family quality of life up to 5 years after discharge. Parent training may thus "buffer" against parental stress and mental health issues that can interfere with child outcomes, by not only ensuring ongoing progress and improving overall child outcomes (Osborne, McHugh, Saunders, & Reed, 2008) but by improving the overall quality of life for the family as a whole (Symon, 2001).

Overall, parent training is an essential part of ABA intervention programs (Reid & Fitch, 2011). This chapter aims to provide a summary of behavioral parent training literature from the past 20 years and to equip students and practitioners with practice recommendations based on current research. In addition, we discuss areas of future research.

RESEARCH FINDINGS

Mothers and fathers have been trained to address many skills and challenging behaviors in their children in various settings, using different training formats and procedures. What follows is a review of parent training research, including (a) behaviors that have been addressed in children and interventions taught to parents; (b) characteristics of the trainer and the trainees; (c) training settings, intensity, and length; (d) training formats (e.g., self-directed, group versus individual, etc.) and procedures; (e) outcomes; and (f) social validity and adherence. Practice recommendations centered around these research findings will be reserved for a later section of the chapter specific to this topic.

Behavior Addressed

Intensive (on average around 25 to 40 hours per week) behavioral intervention has been repeatedly demonstrated to be an effective intervention for children with ASD (for reviews and metanalyses, see Eldevik et al., 2009; Peters-Scheffer, Didden, Korzilius, & Sturmey, 2011; Reichow & Wolery, 2009; Rogers & Vismara, 2008) and, indeed, we suggest that the demand for intensive behavioral intervention far exceeds the supply of professionals able to deliver the intervention. In addition to the lack of services to cope with the growing need, many families who do have services in their area are unsuccessful securing funding and cannot afford it. One possible solution to this problem has been for parents (and oftentimes their team of paraprofessionals) to be trained as therapists in their children's intervention programs. Multiple studies investigating this model have demonstrated gains in adaptive, language, and intellectual functioning (e.g., Bibby, Eikeseth, Martin, Mudford, & Reeves, 2002; Sheinkopf & Siegel, 1998; Smith, Buch, & Gamby, 2000; Smith, Groen, & Wynn, 2000). However, beyond the reporting of short-term gains, little is known about long-term improvements and effects of this type of intervention on core ASD deficit areas (Warren et al., 2011). Further, it appears that parent-managed programs may not bring about gains as large as those achieved by professionals (Bibby et al., 2002).

In addition to training parents to be managers of their children's intensive behavioral intervention programs, parents of children and youth with ASD have been trained to use procedures both to teach specific new skills (skill acquisition) and/or to eliminate challenging behavior in their children.

In terms of skill acquisition, parents have learned to implement (a) discrete trial teaching (DTT; e.g., Crockett, Fleming, Doepke, & Stevens, 2007; Lafasakis & Sturmey, 2007; Ward-Horner & Sturmey, 2008; Young, Boris, Thomson, Martin, & Yu, 2012); (b) techniques for teaching language such as the picture exchange communication system (PECS; e.g., Chaabane, Alber-Morgan, & DeBar, 2009); and (c) naturalistic procedures such as incidental teaching (e.g., Charlop-Christy & Carpenter, 2000), modified incidental teaching (e.g., Charlop-Christy & Carpenter, 2000), enhanced mileu teaching (e.g., Kaiser, Hancock, & Nietfeld, 2000), natural language paradigm (e.g., Gillett & LeBlanc, 2007; Laski, Charlop, & Schreibman, 1988), and pivotal response treatment (PRT; e.g., Baker-Ericzén, Stahmer, & Burns, 2007; Coolican, Smith, & Bryson, 2010; Koegel, Symon, & Koegel, 2002; Nefdt, Koegel, Singer, & Gerber, 2010; Randolph, Stichter, Schmidt, & O'Connor, 2011; Symon, 2005). Likewise, parents have been trained to implement procedures for increasing their children's self-help skills such as (a) following an activity schedule (e.g., Krantz, MacDuff, & McClannahan, 1993), (b) community skills (e.g., shopping, ordering food, and giving a cloth to a dry cleaner; Tekin-Iftar, 2008), (c) domestic skills (e.g., sweeping, putting toys away, and using the telephone; Cavkaytar & Pollard, 2009), (d) toileting (e.g., Kroeger & Sorensen, 2010), and (e) other self-care skills (e.g., tooth brushing, washing hands, and putting shoes on; Cavkaytar & Pollard, 2009). Finally, parents have also been trained to implement procedures to increase social and play skills, for example, (a) reciprocal imitation training (RIT) for increasing object and gesture imitation during play (e.g., Ingersoll & Gergans, 2006), (b) script fading for promoting vocal initiations during play (e.g., Reagon & Higbee, 2009), and (c) techniques that included components of both DTT and PRT for targeting joint attention (Rocha, Schreibman, & Stahmer, 2007).

As for assessment of and intervention for challenging behavior, parents have been trained to implement procedures during experimental functional analysis (e.g., Arndorfer, Miltenberger, Woster, Rortvedt, & Gaffaney, 1994; Moes & Frea, 2002; Najdowski, Wallace, Doney, & Ghezzi, 2003;

Najdowski et al., 2008) and treat challenging behavior by implementing functional communication training (FCT) alone (e.g., Arndorfer et al., 1994; Moes & Frea, 2002) as well as combined with milieu teaching (e.g., Mancil, Conroy, & Haydon, 2009). For more specific challenging behaviors, for example, parents have learned to implement response blocking for object mouthing (e.g., Tarbox, Wallace, & Tarbox, 2002) and various procedures for noncompliance, including errorless compliance training (e.g., Ducharme & Drain, 2004), guided compliance (e.g., Miles & Wilder, 2009; Smith & Lerman, 1999), and high-probability instructional sequences (e.g., Smith & Lerman, 1999). They have also been trained in behavioral strategies for treating sleep difficulties (e.g., Reed et al., 2009; Weiskop, Richdale, & Matthews, 2005) as well as feeding problems by implementing (a) differential reinforcement of alternative behavior (DRA) combined with escape extinction (EE; e.g., Anderson & McMillan, 2001; McCartney, Anderson, English, & Horner, 2005; Mueller et al., 2003; Najdowski et al., 2003, 2010), (b) a variation of EE termed nonremoval of the meal (e.g., Tarbox, Schiff, & Najdowski, 2010), (c) the Premack principle (e.g., O'Reilly & Lancioni, 2001), (d) noncontingent reinforcement (NCR; e.g., Mueller et al., 2003), (e) contingent attention (e.g., Werle, Murphy, & Budd, 1993, 1998), (f) time-out (e.g., Werle et al., 1993), (g) corrective feedback (e.g., Werle et al., 1993), and (h) stimulus fading by increasing bite requirements (e.g., McCartney et al., 2005; Najdowski et al., 2003, 2010) or portion sizes (e.g., Galensky, Miltenberger, Stricker, & Garlinghouse, 2001).

There are also a handful of branded parent training programs that appear promising. For example, there is some support for Project ImPACT, which teaches parents to implement a blend of developmental and naturalistic behavioral intervention procedures for improving their children's language, social, and play skills (Ingersoll & Dvortcsak, 2006; Ingersoll & Wainer, 2011). *Stepping Stones Triple P* (SSTP; Plant & Sanders, 2007; Whittingham, Sofronoff, Sheffield, & Sanders, 2009), *Incredible Years Parent Training* (IYPT; McIntyre, 2008), and *Parent-Child Interaction Therapy* (PCIT; Solomon, Ono, Timmer, & Goodlin-Jones, 2008), all programs for teaching parents to manage their children's challenging behavior, have also been effective. Additionally, CARD eLearning™, a Web-based program, has been shown to effectively train parents in academic knowledge of

principles and procedures of ABA related to delivering 1:1 intensive behavioral intervention to children with ASD (Jang et al., 2012).

Trainer and Trainee Characteristics
Research has focused more on the content and methods of training, rather than on who provides (Brookman-Frazee et al., 2006) and receives the training. However, this topic is important and has been addressed in a few cases.

Trainer Characteristics
Little is known about what trainer characteristics might contribute to better outcomes. For example, trainer delivery style, rapport-building skills, and methods for delivering feedback are but a few research questions lacking in this area. Likewise, little to no research has addressed what level of knowledge trainers should have to achieve best outcomes. However, one study by Ingersoll and Wainer (2011) provides some insight on this subject matter. In this study, teachers were trained during a 2-day workshop on the intervention strategies and methods for parent training and later delivered parent training. Results found that parents improved their implementation of strategies, but there was still room for additional improvement. It is possible that using teachers with only 2 days of training was the reason that parents did not show more improvement in their skills; however, this variable was not studied. More research is needed in order to determine who can effectively train parents and what trainer characteristics lead to optimal outcomes.

Training Audience
There is also limited research about the influence of trainee characteristics on outcomes. Notably, most parent training studies have trained mothers instead of fathers (Schultz, Schmidt, & Stichter, 2011). Currently there is not enough research to suggest whether it matters whether mothers versus fathers are trained to implement interventions with their children. One study conducted by Neef (1995) successfully trained 26 (20 mothers and 6 fathers) parents to teach various skills to their children, while another study by Seung, Ashwell, Elder, and Valcante (2006), albeit a retrospective analysis, suggested that it might be necessary to modify programs to accommodate fathers and increase paternal involvement (e.g., offer more flexible scheduling and settings for training sessions). More research in this area is

warranted before professionals can draw conclusions about training mothers versus fathers.

It is possible that culture, socioeconomic status, and other family variables may influence training outcomes. Currently there is little to no research for parents of children with ASD, a gap that will likely hinder success (Forehand & Kotchick, 1996, 2002).

Setting, Intensity, and Length of Training

Unlike the lack of research on trainer and trainee characteristics, many studies demonstrate that parent training can be effective in multiple settings. However, much is still unknown about the optimal intensity and length of training.

Training Setting

Research has shown that parents can be trained successfully in clinic (e.g., Ingersoll & Gergans, 2006; Koegel et al., 2002; Laski et al., 1988) and home settings (e.g., Anderson & McMillan, 2001; Moes & Frea, 2002; Najdowski et al., 2003, 2010; Reagon & Higbee, 2009; Smith & Lerman, 1999; Tarbox et al., 2010). In some cases, intensive short-term training in a clinic setting has been used as an option for families living in geographically remote areas without access to specialized services and generalization to the home setting has been found (e.g., Koegel et al., 2002; Symon, 2005). In other cases, parents have been trained both in the home and clinic successfully (e.g., Weiskop et al., 2005). For example, some studies have first trained parents to implement an intervention in the clinic and then followed up with training in the home (e.g., McCartney et al., 2005). There is no research to suggest that one training setting is particularly better than another; however, there are advantages and disadvantages to each setting that will be addressed later in the practice recommendations of this chapter.

Intensity and Length of Training

Length, the span of time over which training occurs, and frequency, how often training occurs, varies considerably between programs. While some literature provides this information, it is inconclusive (Schultz et al., 2011). For example, delivery could vary from only 1 hour per week conducted across multiple weeks (e.g., Baker-Ericzén et al., 2007; Stahmer & Gist, 2001) to 25 hours condensed into 1 week (e.g., Koegel et al., 2002). Similarly, the duration could range from less than 1 week (e.g., Koegel et al., 2002;

Symon, 2005) to 1 year (e.g., Moes & Frea, 2002). Unfortunately, current evidence cannot suggest the optimal intensity or length of training (Schultz et al., 2011).

Training Formats

How training is delivered is equally as important as the content, trainer/trainee characteristics, settings, intensities, and lengths of parent training programs. Due to the growing number of children with ASD (now 1 in 88; Autism and Developmental Disabilities Monitoring Network, 2012) and the significant needs of this population, there is also an urgent need for the development of cost-effective and efficient models of treatment delivery that can provide services to as many families as possible, including those in geographically remote areas. Without the development of new models of delivery, providers will struggle to meet this growing need (Symon, 2005).

There are several potential alternatives to the traditional one-to-one, clinician-directed model, including self-directed programs, distance training via Web tools, group delivered programs, "three-tier" models (starting with least intrusive training formats first), and a "train the trainer" model (i.e., pyramidal training).

Self-Directed

To meet the growing need for training, self-directed training products for parents of children with ASD are now popular, including books, DVDs, online programs (e.g., CARD eLearning™, Skills®, Rethink Autism, etc.), and other technology solutions. Such programs require little or no contact between a professional and the parent, and thus may be a useful option for families who are on long waiting lists or living in remote areas. Although not many of these alternatives have been formally evaluated, a few studies are noteworthy. For example, Jang and colleagues (2012) successfully used the CARD eLearning™ program to train parents in academic knowledge of principles and procedures of ABA. Nefdt and colleagues (2010) successfully trained parents to implement PRT procedures using an interactive 2-hour DVD with an accompanying manual; however, only 27 of the 34 (79.4%) parents completed the program, suggesting clinicians may need to consider whether such programs may be less likely to be completed. While some studies support the use of self-directed methods, there is also research suggesting that, in some cases, self-directed programs may be ineffective or much less effective than in-person training strategies. For example, Young and colleagues (2012) found only weak effects for two out of five parents completing a self-directed package on DTT.

Although the efficacy of self-directed formats for parent training is still unclear, this modality of treatment (especially technology-based versions) is likely to increase in future years because using technology may decrease time, effort, and cost. Therefore, more research is needed to determine what components of a self-directed training program will lead to better results. It may be that technology-based programs that incorporate more interactive components are more effective by giving trainees rapid feedback. It is also possible that self-directed programs will be successful with certain parents but not with others.

Group Versus Individual

Parent training is most often clinician directed in a group or individual format, or through a combination of both. The vast majority of programs in the literature have effectively used an individual, one-to-one approach (Schultz et al., 2011), while other studies have shown positive outcomes via group combined with one-on-one training (e.g., Ducharme & Drain, 2004; Ingersoll & Dvortcsak, 2006; Ingersoll & Wainer, 2011; Plant & Sanders, 2007) and group-only training (e.g., McIntyre, 2008; Whittingham et al., 2009). Currently, it is unclear whether a group or individual format is superior, or which components of group-based intervention are most important. In short, we do not know what the best practices are when working with families of children specifically diagnosed with ASD (Schultz et al., 2011; Steiner, Koegel, Koegel, & Ence, 2012). However, there are some obvious advantages and disadvantages that are associated with each option that will be discussed in the practice recommendations of this chapter.

Three-Tier Model

The three-tier model (McIntyre & Phaneuf, 2008) is also clinician directed and similar to a least-to-most prompting procedure by progressing from the least intensive support (self-directed training) to group-based training (more intensive), to individualized, one-on-one training (most intensive treatment). Families are assessed and then progress through each level according to their specific needs. For example, some parents might skip the primary (self-directed) or secondary level (group training) and go straight to the tertiary level (individual training), or they may only progress as far as level two (group) if individual training is deemed unnecessary. More research on the three-tier model is needed before the efficacy, effectiveness, and cost-efficiency of it can be determined for families of children with ASD.

Pyramidal Model

In most parent training programs, parents are viewed as trainees who learn procedures from experienced trainers. Although uncommon in the ASD parent training literature, some studies have evaluated pyramidal training or a "train-the-trainer" model. This model measures the extent to which trained parents are able to train other care providers (e.g., family members or other professionals) in the learned techniques. Symon (2005) demonstrated that parents who were trained to implement PRT for teaching social communication in a week-long program were later able to successfully train other care providers. In addition to the parent-trained care providers demonstrating competency in implementing techniques, the children's social communication improved.

One major advantage of the pyramidal training model is its "spread of effect" (Symon, 2005). That is, more parents can be trained without having to attend the original training program. In another study, Neef (1995) not only demonstrated that trained parents (referred to as tier 1) could train other parents (tier 2) to teach various skills to their children, but that tier 2 parents could train tier 3 parents, making the spread of effect even larger. There are many additional potential benefits of the pyramidal model, including enhancement of cost efficiency, a support network among parents, and maintenance of the skills learned by parents who become trainers (Bruder & Bricker, 1985). The pyramidal approach provides a particularly promising option for families living in geographically distant areas, allowing families who are trained to potentially train others local to them.

Training Procedures

The procedures for training parents to implement techniques are equally as important as many of the variables discussed earlier. A large sample of the parent training literature has involved multicomponent training packages, typically including three or more of the following: (a) didactic training in which parents are provided instructional information through either verbal or written (e.g., handouts, PowerPoint presentations, manuals, etc.) modalities; (b) modeling, wherein trainers show parents how to implement the procedures (either live or via video modeling); (c) rehearsal, wherein parents role-play implementing procedures with a trainer or practice directly with their children; and (d) feedback, wherein parents are provided with positive feedback for correct implementation and corrective feedback for incorrect implementation.

Only a few studies have evaluated individual components of training packages. Written instructions alone are usually ineffective and sometimes included to demonstrate baseline performance (e.g., Lerman, Swiezy, Perkins-Parks, & Roane, 2000; Mueller et al., 2003). Studies evaluating written instruction combined with verbal instruction have produced mixed results. For example, Mueller and colleagues (2003) found verbal and written instructions to be as effective as packages containing three or more components, whereas Lerman and colleagues (2000) found that all parents receiving verbal and written instructions demonstrated accuracy but only on some skills and that feedback was needed to learn remaining skills. Erbas (2010) also found that written and verbal instructions combined with feedback was better than written and verbal instructions alone in training mothers of children with developmental disabilities but not necessarily ASD.

While it is clear that multicomponent training packages are effective in training parents to deliver intervention both for skill acquisition and for managing challenging behavior, there is not enough research at this point to draw conclusions about the components that promote success. Although speculative, it is possible that effectiveness of different instructional methods might depend on the type of skill being taught (Lerman et al., 2000). There are many other potential variables that could contribute to the effectiveness of different methods, including but not limited to, whether parents have had previous training, complexity of the protocol being learned, and parent motivation, stress, depression, income, education, and reading levels. For example, future research may find that more training components are necessary for families with less education or who are under a great deal of stress. Future research should not only attempt to determine which training methods are necessary to increase efficiency of training but also which variables are associated with the success or failure of particular methods. One model for identifying the required and sufficient components of

training may be to use the easiest and least expensive method first (e.g., written instructions) followed by evaluating the parent's performance and then adding supplemental instruction only for incorrectly implemented procedures, thereby allowing the trainer to focus efforts where needed (Lerman et al., 2000).

Training Outcomes

Although there has been some research centered around the logistics of parent training such as setting, intensity, length, format, and procedures, the main dependent variables are changes in parent (i.e., procedural integrity) and child behavior (i.e., response to the intervention) and whether these changes generalize and maintain.

Procedural Integrity

Measuring procedural integrity indicates whether parents applied procedures as intended. A high degree of integrity may contribute to an intervention's effectiveness (Chaabane et al., 2009; Randolph et al., 2011). Unfortunately, many studies have not collected procedural integrity data, instead focusing on child response to parent-implemented interventions (Schultz et al., 2011). When procedural integrity has been evaluated, measurement methods have included coding parent behavior during direct observation (e.g., Moes & Frea, 2002; Najdowski et al., 2003; Stewart, Carr, & LeBlanc, 2007) and/or measurement of parent procedural integrity via videotaped sessions (e.g., Najdowski et al., 2010). In the studies that have reported these data, procedural integrity has been high (e.g., Chaabane et al., 2009; Mancil et al., 2009; Miles & Wilder, 2009; Najdowski et al., 2003, 2010; Smith & Lerman, 1999; Stewart et al., 2007).

Generalization and Maintenance

Even if training equips parents with new skills, there is no guarantee that these skills will generalize to novel situations and be maintained later. Few studies include complete information about generalization and maintenance (Meadan, Ostrosky, Zaghlawan, & Yu, 2009), but when reported, results have been positive for parent and/or child behaviors.

Generalization across settings and stimuli has been observed for both parent behavior (e.g., Crockett et al., 2007; Ingersoll & Gergans, 2006; Kaiser et al., 2000; Koegel et al., 2002; Lafasakis & Sturmey, 2007; Laski et al., 1988; Miles & Wilder, 2009; Symon, 2005; Ward-Horner & Sturmey,

2008) and child behavior (e.g., Chaabane et al., 2009; Ducharme & Drain, 2004; Ingersoll & Gergans, 2006; Mancil et al., 2009; Moes & Frea, 2002; Najdowski et al., 2010; Reagon & Higbee, 2009; Tekin-Iftar, 2008). However, limited generalization has also been reported in some cases (e.g., Kaiser et al., 2000; Rocha et al., 2007).

Other research reveals maintenance of parent procedural implementation (e.g., Coolican et al., 2010; Koegel et al., 2002; Najdowski et al., 2010; Plant & Sanders, 2007; Symon, 2005) and child behavior change (e.g., Ducharme & Drain, 2004; Krantz et al., 1993; Mancil et al., 2009; McCartney et al., 2005; Moes & Frea, 2002; Plant & Sanders, 2007; Tarbox et al., 2010; Tekin-Iftar, 2008) from several weeks to 1 year post training, although, in some cases both parent (e.g., Ingersoll & Gergans, 2006; Kaiser et al., 2000; Randolph et al., 2011; Rocha et al., 2007) and child responses (e.g., Ingersoll & Gergans, 2006; Kaiser et al., 2000; Randolph et al., 2011; Reagon & Higbee, 2009; Rocha et al., 2007; Weiskop et al., 2005) were maintained at lower levels than during treatment. Thus, research suggests that generalization and maintenance are sometimes but not always outcomes of parent training.

Social Validity and Adherence
Social validity and treatment adherence are two other areas that have been researched and presented in the parent training literature. Social validity refers to acceptance and satisfaction of the intervention by parents, and adherence concerns their compliance with programmed procedures.

Social Validity
Many studies have not included measurement of social validity and/or have included only limited measures (parent satisfaction). There are also often methodological weaknesses in how acceptability is evaluated (Reid & Fitch, 2011). In the studies that have evaluated social validity, parents generally reported that they were satisfied with the training they received (e.g., Ingersoll & Dvortcsak, 2006; Ingersoll & Gergans, 2006; Ingersoll & Wainer, 2011; Kaiser et al., 2000; Kroeger & Sorensen, 2010; Mancil et al., 2009; McCartney et al., 2005; Najdowski et al., 2010; Reed et al., 2009; Smith & Lerman, 1999; Weiskop et al., 2005; Whittingham et al., 2009). In one study, confidence ratings indicated that parents appeared more confident during parent–child interactions following training (Nefdt et al., 2010).

Adherence
Practitioners conducting parent training often experience compliance issues that can interfere with program effectiveness if not addressed (Schreibman, Dufek, & Cunningham, 2011). Despite being an apparently common problem encountered by trainers, there has been little research examining the contingencies involved and methods for improving parental adherence (Allen & Warzak, 2000). In fact, the studies we describe next have not necessarily involved children with ASD.

Strategies to increase adherence within parent training studies include making training contingent on submitting data (Mira, 1970) or completing assignments (O'Dell, Blackwell, Larcen, & Hogan, 1977); providing tangible reinforcement such as gift cards for completing requirements (Reed et al., 2009); and implementing a response cost contract involving loss of monetary deposits for missing meetings, failing to collect data, and children not achieving behavioral goals (Aragona, Cassady, & Drabman, 1975). However, because these procedures were often one component of a parent training program and outcome was not measured in isolation, the effects on adherence are not known.

Only a few studies have measured child outcomes in relation to parental adherence. Muir and Milan (1982) demonstrated that delivering lottery tickets (to be used toward winning prizes) to parents contingent upon their children making progress produced greater child gains than routine practices. Csapo (1979) found that both training parents in self-management of their carrying out of the protocol and/or providing social reinforcement to parents produced greater improvement in child behavior than when these strategies were not used. Additionally, when both of these strategies were combined, there were even greater improvements.

PRACTICE RECOMMENDATIONS
We have shown that parents are capable of being trained (using various training procedures) to implement behavioral techniques for changing their children's behavior, sometimes producing generalization and maintenance. However, there are many considerations for designing an effective parent training program. If trainers are aware of potential factors that might influence training outcomes, they can

incorporate modifications and additional supports to boost effects (Forehand & Kotchick, 2002).

Buy-in and Adherence

It is beyond the scope of this chapter to provide a behavioral analysis of the contingencies involved in adherence (see Allen & Warzak, 2000), but buy-in and adherence will continue to be common themes in the remaining sections. As outlined earlier, preliminary findings of studies implementing contingencies to increase adherence appear promising, suggesting that trainers might want to use these strategies with parents.

In addition to implementing contingencies to increase adherence, trainers should also carefully consider variables that compromise buy-in (McIntyre & Phaneuf, 2008) while implementing adaptations, additional support strategies, and/or accommodations to enable families to adopt positive behavior management practices in their home and community. We note that a collaborative and supportive trainer–parent relationship may play an important role in parent training outcome, particularly with respect to parental compliance. Thus, trainers should aim to combine confident behavioral training skills with rapport-building skills such as warmth, empathy, and humor (Forehand & Kotchick, 2002). Even after addressing rapport building, there may be other challenges parents face that will affect their adherence to procedures. For example, single parents, low-income parents, and parents of lower educational status may be more likely to struggle with compliance issues (Breiner & Beck, 1984). Such families are likely to have less time and resources, are more isolated, and lack social support. Given such difficulties, trainers may need to help address a family's broader needs in order to be successful, which might include involving or developing other sources of support. Until their basic needs are being met or accommodated, it is unlikely that parents will fully participate and benefit from training (Forehand & Kotchick, 2002).

Behavior Addressed

In the beginning stages of designing a parent training program for a family, trainers must gather information about the child and collaborate with the parents to determine both child and family goals. Once goals are established, trainers can collaborate with the parents in selecting relevant interventions.

Child Variables, Target Behaviors, and Goals

There are various child variables that may potentially affect what target behaviors will be addressed and what goals will be set for the child. For example, the child's age, level of functioning, and severity of the problem might mediate or moderate treatment outcomes. Logically, it is possible that parent training will be easier or results may occur more quickly if the child is younger, has received behavioral intervention in the past, and/or is a fast learner or high functioning. Likewise, individuals with more severe or chronic behavior problems could potentially require more intensive intervention and parent support.

It will be critical to consult closely with parents to identify their needs, priorities, and other important variables prior to designing and implementing a training program (Santarelli, Koegel, Casas, & Koegel, 2001; Steiner et al., 2012). Note, too, that collaboration may reduce parental stress and improve buy-in. The trainer should ask the child's parents what they want their child to learn or what challenging behavior they want to eliminate, as well as where and when the challenging moments with their child occur. Trainers will also need to assess parent expectations about training and intervention. Unrealistic expectations or perceptions on the part of the parents may interfere with adherence (Forehand & Kotchick, 2002).

Interventions to Teach Parents

Ensuring good contextual fit should be an important part of designing parent training programs (Albin, Lucyshyn, Horner, & Flannery, 1996; Moes & Frea, 2002). Moes and Frea (2002) found parents rated the sustainability of intervention higher and greater gains were made when family context was addressed in the parent training planning phases. Trainers should aim for ongoing collaboration with families that results in programs that are (a) responsive to the values and goals of the parents; (b) utilizes the experience, knowledge, and skills that parents bring; and (c) is compatible with the family's typical routines and daily activities (Albin et al., 1996). When presenting options to parents, trainers should establish whether parents are comfortable with procedures and are likely to adhere to them, and whether procedures will fit into the family's lifestyle and culture. Designing a program compatible with the family's daily life will ensure higher procedural integrity, be truly meaningful for families (Moes & Frea, 2002), and ensure good contextual fit.

When determining parent training interventions, those with more empirical support are obviously preferred. Interestingly, a few comparison studies have investigated which interventions lead to better outcomes when implemented by parents. Charlop-Christy and Carpenter (2000) found that parent-implemented modified incidental teaching resulted in better acquisition of target phrases in child participants than incidental teaching and discrete trial teaching. In two other comparison studies, Yoder and Stone (2006) found that PECS was more successful in increasing spoken communication in child participants than responsive education and prelinguistic milieu teaching (RPMT) when implemented by parents, and Smith and Lerman (1999) found that child compliance was higher for parents with guided compliance than high-probability instructional sequences.

In addition to choosing empirically supported interventions, trainers should select parenting skills and child behavior change that will be supported by real-life contingencies. Naturalistic teaching methods may be well suited for achieving such goals because they are easy to individualize and fit into family routines, possibly resulting in lower levels of parent stress. Naturalistic methods also create multiple learning opportunities throughout a child's day and possibly promote generalization. Finally, they may hasten treatment gains and produce less problem behavior compared to a more structured "drill practice program" (Koegel, Koegel, & Surratt, 1992).

Trainer and Trainee Characteristics

Trainer Characteristics

Typically, clinicians are not taught how to be trainers; rather they are trained to design interventions and to implement ABA techniques with children (Brookman-Frazee et al., 2006; Reid & Fitch, 2011). Unfortunately, being skilled in implementing interventions oneself does not necessarily mean one will be able to train someone else to implement the same procedures (McGimsey, Greene, & Lutzker, 1995; Parsons & Reid, 1995). Thus, as well as being knowledgeable behavior analysts, trainers must acquire other skills such as delivering reinforcement and providing corrective feedback in ways that motivate parents. Effective trainers, as noted previously, should also emphasize collaborative approaches to developing programs and have well-developed rapport-building and empathy skills (Brookman-Frazee, 2004).

Training Audience

When creating a program with good contextual fit, trainers should determine whether both parents can be trained for promoting consistency and generalization across people. In other cases, it may be difficult to schedule training sessions with both parents due to work schedules (Santarelli et al., 2001). In this situation, it might be better to train the nonworking parent who is also, by default, the parent with whom the child spends more time. In order to promote consistency, trainers should identify whether there are other family members living in the household that should also be trained (Santarelli et al., 2001).

Once the persons who will be trained have been identified, the trainer should consider differences in parental approaches, educational backgrounds, and other cultural variables. For example, it is possible that different strategies may be needed when working with fathers versus mothers (Steiner et al., 2012). Notably, we advise that training manuals and behavior intervention plans should be at a reading level accessible to parents and that training is delivered using jargon-free language that will be understood.

Historically, culture and ethnicity has been largely ignored in the conceptualization of parenting (Forehand & Kotchick, 1996) and most intervention programs have been developed with White families, making it unclear how well parent training programs generalize to other ethnic backgrounds. Currently, there is no research addressing the influence of culture on training success for parents of children with ASD. Some researchers have suggested that ignoring these factors may hinder success (Forehand & Kotchick, 1996, 2002). Trainers should be aware of and sensitive to the particular cultural attitudes and parenting practices of a family before embarking on developing a training program for them (Forehand & Kotchick, 2002), and in addition, trainers should acknowledge when their own cultural biases and assumptions might become a barrier to effective training (Santarelli et al., 2001). A flexible, individualized approach is important (Johnson et al., 2007); trainers can work with families to overcome barriers, for example, by ensuring families have access to a trainer who speaks their language, among many other things.

Setting, Intensity, and Length of Training

Trainers will need to work with families to determine the best training setting as well as the treatment intensity (number of hours for a given time period) and length of training (number of days, weeks, or months). Research does not provide us with hard fast rules for these variables; what is effective will likely be determined by a variety of factors.

Training Setting

It is currently unclear whether training in the clinic versus the home is superior. Thus, the trainer must consider the advantages and disadvantages to each setting option and make a decision about the training setting on an individual basis. Clinic-based training has the advantage of offering a more controlled environment (fewer distractions) for establishing new skills (Brookman-Frazee et al., 2006). Plus, studies have shown that training in the clinic can generalize to home environments (e.g., Ingersoll & Gergans, 2006; Kaiser et al., 2000).

However, home-based parent training offers the advantage of more closely matching the child's "real world" and thus may result in more rapid skill acquisition and better generalization of treatment gains both for parents and children (e.g., Charlop & Trasowech, 1991; Koegel, 2000; Laski et al., 1988). Another advantage of in-home training is that it might potentially improve attendance rates, especially for families that do not own a motor vehicle and cannot afford public transportation (Santarelli et al., 2001). Furthermore, some skills, such as toilet training, may be better suited for home training.

Intensity and Length

Although there currently is not any research to suggest optional intensity and/or length of training, it is plausible that different intensities and lengths of treatment will be successful under different conditions. Some relevant factors in this regard are assessing parent and family needs, selecting a training method, and setting short- as well as long-term goals. To determine the family's needs, trainers should consult with the family to determine how much time and energy they have to devote to the training, especially if they work full time or have other children and extracurricular activities requiring attention. If the family will participate in individual training instead of group training, trainers also have the ability to be more accommodating. Trainers should keep in mind that flexibility when scheduling training sessions and/or reducing the time commitment required by parents might also increase parental adherence (Ingersoll & Dvortcsak, 2006).

Training Formats and Procedures

Group Versus Individual Training Formats

Since it is currently not clear whether the group or individual training format is superior, trainers need to individualize the training format on a case-by-case basis as it is likely some families will benefit more than others from individual versus group training. There are a number of advantages of each for trainers to consider.

One advantage of a one-to-one training approach allows a high degree of individualization. Training can be scheduled around each family's particular routines, content can be tailored to meet specific needs of the family, and training can be done in a variety of settings, which may aid generalization of skills (e.g., Najdowski et al., 2003; Steiner et al., 2012). Individual parent training formats also allow for a greater focus on providing practice with feedback, which has been shown to facilitate learning (Ingersoll & Dvortcsak, 2006; Kaiser & Hancock, 2003). Some parents may not only show a greater benefit from more intensive individual training, but attendance for individual training formats may also be higher than for group sessions because they are easier to fit around a family's schedule (Chadwick, Momčilović, Rossiter, Stumbles, & Taylor, 2001).

However, group-based training may offer a more cost-effective and time-efficient way to deliver services (Brookman-Frazee et al., 2006), as more families can benefit from training within a short period of time. Group formats, usually involving 8 to 12 parents (McIntyre & Phaneuf, 2008), may also provide a cost-effective format for delivering training to families in remote areas (Brookman-Frazee et al., 2006). In addition to the clear economic advantages, group training may facilitate mutual support among parents and decrease parent stress (McIntyre & Phaneuf, 2008; Singer, Ethridge, & Aldana, 2007).

Training Procedures

Along with determining whether parents will be trained in groups or individually, trainers should determine what procedures will be used to train parents. We know from research that multicomponent treatment packages consisting of three or more components (e.g., didactic training, modeling, rehearsal, and feedback) are effective, but little is known about what specific components are necessary. However, it appears that written instruction alone is inadequate (e.g., Mueller et al., 2003) and that feedback plays an important role (e.g., Lerman et al., 2000). In choosing procedures efficiently, the trainer will likely want to use as few procedures as necessary to get the desired results. Yet it is reasonable to assume that the training procedures should at least include feedback and something more than written instructions (unless it is a manualized self-directed program).

Training Outcomes

Once the logistics of parent training have been determined, as in, the setting, intensity, length, format, and procedures, it is important to put in place measurement of and procedures for ensuring optimal outcomes with respect to parent and child behavior change.

Procedural Integrity

While no studies have specifically set out to identify the relationship between parent procedural integrity and child outcomes, presumably, high procedural integrity will contribute to the effectiveness of the intervention the parent is implementing (assuming it is already an empirically supported treatment). Given this, it is important to measure and train parents to high levels of procedural integrity, and it is critical that trainees receive supervision that includes continuous monitoring of performance (Johnson et al., 2007). In the event that procedural integrity is inadequate, the trainer will need to make adjustments to the training protocol or provide more training to increase procedural integrity to acceptable levels.

It is equally important to measure the child's response to treatment to ensure that the efforts of parents are resulting in desired behavior change in the child. If the parent's procedural integrity is high but the child's behavior is not improving, perhaps the intervention that the parent is using is ineffective and changes need to be made to the procedures the parent is using with the child.

Generalization and Maintenance

To promote generalization and maintenance of parent and child behavior change, trainers must implement strategies such as programming multiple exemplars (e.g., Crocket et al., 2007; Najdowski et al., 2010), training in multiple settings (e.g., Tekin-Iftar, 2008), and teaching parents problem-solving skills (Steibel, 1999). We refer readers to Stokes and Baer (1977) for a detailed discussion about facilitating generalization.

To promote maintenance, trainers should choose functional skills (for both parent and child) that will continue to be supported by reinforcement contingencies present in the natural home environment. Additionally, follow-up or on-the-job supervision with feedback may be needed to ensure procedural integrity and maintenance of parent skills. Although there is no specific research focusing on parents, effective results have been reported for teachers and care staff working with children with ASD (Brackett, Reid, & Green, 2007; DiGennaro-Reed, Codding, Catania, & Maguire, 2010; Parsons & Reid, 1995; Petscher & Bailey, 2006). One method for increasing maintenance of parent behavior that has been evaluated is training spouses to give one another feedback on their performances (Harris, Peterson, Filliben, & Glassberg, 1998). This method was found to improve or sustain performance for five of six parent participants for up to 6 months. Additionally, see Cooper, Heron, and Heward (2007) for some guiding principles that may further enhance generalization and maintenance strategies.

Alternative strategies must be considered if generalization and maintenance are not achieved. For example, if the child's behavior is improving, but generalization is not occurring, then various strategies for obtaining generalization will need to be employed. If the parent is implementing procedures with high integrity but there is weak generalization to novel situations, the trainer should implement strategies that can be adapted accordingly. The trainer should also measure maintenance of parent and child behavior for as long as is necessary to ensure meaningful and long-lasting results. If during follow-up, the trainer finds that procedural integrity has decreased or that child behavior has worsened, the trainer will likely want to provide booster parent training sessions.

Social Validity and Parent Stress

We previously shared strategies for increasing social validity and decreasing parent stress. Stress or other mental health issues and lack of social support may impede parents' ability to benefit from parent training programs (Osborne et al., 2008; Symon, 2001). Parents of children with ASD report feeling in deep crisis, unsupported, and frustrated (Weiss & Lunsky, 2010). As a result, it is understandable that parents may struggle to stay committed to treatment programs and comply with treatment protocols, considering all the difficult thoughts and feelings they are struggling with, as well as constant life stressors (Snyder, Lambert, & Twohig, 2011).

Although behavior management training or problem-focused training may significantly reduce parent stress, in some circumstances, it may *increase* stress (Koegel, 2000) or be insufficient to increase parent adjustment in cases where behavior problems or stressors are chronic (Weiss & Lunsky, 2010). For example, since asking parents to set aside specific time to work with their child may increase stress levels, trainers should design programs that fit into the family's daily routine (Koegel, 2000). Trainers should also identify additional sources of support for families, and strategies or accommodations that will promote training effectiveness. Parents may first or concurrently need peer or social support, counseling, respite care, and legal advice, to name a few. Lack of social support appears to be a significant issue for parents of children with ASD, and there is some research to support that parents who are concurrently enrolled in a support group are more likely to master the techniques they are trained to implement (Stahmer & Gist, 2001).

Parent training outcomes might also be improved by incorporating acceptance commitment therapy (ACT) into treatment packages. ACT is a scientifically based approach, rooted in ABA, and potentially useful to parents of children with ASD where problems are chronic, stressful, and not easily corrected through normal problem-solving strategies (Blackledge & Hayes, 2006; Grindle, Kovshoff, Hastings, & Remington, 2009). ACT is based on the concepts of mindfulness and values and emphasizes acceptance of unpleasant emotions, diffusion from difficult thoughts (such as unhelpful verbal rules regarding their child and their parenting), clarification of personal values and corresponding goals, and enhancement of effective action toward those values and goals. ACT may help parents adjust to the difficulties in raising a child with ASD, increase positive parenting interactions, and potentially decrease child behavior problems (Blackledge & Hayes, 2006; Singh et al., 2006, 2007). ACT could help parents cope more effectively with difficult feelings and thoughts, thus enabling them to make better parenting choices from moment to moment (including increasing their use of effective behavior management strategies), helping them stay committed to their child's treatment program, increasing compliance with treatment protocols, and improving family interactions and relationships.

CONCLUSION

With the rapid rise in ASD, more and more families require professional guidance and training. The need for evidence-based and cost-effective models of service delivery that can reach as many families as possible has never been so great. Parent training is a critical component of effective interventions for children with ASD (Reid & Fitch, 2011) involving different teaching formats, modes of service delivery, settings, intensities/lengths of training, content areas, and techniques. However, there is similarity between core training programs that have been effective in teaching parents new skills (Reid & Fitch, 2011). Most behavioral parent training programs focus on teaching parents evidence-based procedures for dealing with the core symptoms of ASD (e.g., social communication deficits) and challenging behaviors (e.g., noncompliance and aggression) using multiple training procedures (e.g., didactic, modeling, rehearsal, and feedback) that have been repeatedly demonstrated to result in parent and child improvements.

Trainers must be accountable by using strategies which ensure that both parents implement procedures with high procedural integrity and promote generalization and maintenance of parent and child behavior change. Individualization of training packages is essential if practitioners are to ensure parents are able to stay committed to programs and continue to utilize taught skills and ensure long-term positive outcomes for their children and family as a whole. Thus, trainers should also collaborate closely with families to identify any potential variables that could affect training outcomes, including but not limited to parent stress or mental health issues, parent expectations, cultural and socioeconomic factors, and family structure (McConachie & Diggle, 2007).

REFERENCES

Albin, R. W., Lucyshyn, J. M., Horner, R. H., & Flannery, K. B. (1996). Contextual fit for behavioral support plans: A model for "goodness of fit." In L. K. Koegel, R. L. Koegel, & G. Dunlap (Eds.), *Positive behavioral support: Including people with difficult behaviors in the community* (pp. 81–98). Baltimore, MD: Paul H. Brookes.

Allen, K. D., & Warzak, W. J. (2000). The problem of parental nonadherence in clinical behavior analysis: Effective treatment is not enough. *Journal of Applied Behavior Analysis, 33,* 73–391.

Anderson, C. M., & McMillan, K. (2001). Parental use of escape extinction and differential reinforcement to treat food selectivity. *Journal of Applied Behavior Analysis, 34,* 511–515.

Aragona, J., Cassady, J., & Drabman, R. S. (1975). Treating overweight children through parental training and contingency contracting. *Journal of Applied Behavior Analysis, 8,* 269–278.

Arndorfer, R. E., Miltenberger, R. G., Woster, S. H., Rortvedt, A. K., & Gaffaney, T. (1994). Home-based descriptive and experimental analysis of problem behaviors in children. *Topics in Early Childhood Special Education, 14,* 64–87.

Autism and Developmental Disabilities Monitoring Network. (2012). Prevalence of autism spectrum disorders – Autism and Developmental Disabilities Monitoring Network, 14 sites, United States, 2008. *Surveillance Summaries, 61,* 1–19.

Baker-Ericzén, M. J., Stahmer, A. C., & Burns, A. (2007). Child demographics associated with outcomes in a community-based pivotal response training program. *Journal of Positive Behavior Interventions, 9,* 52–60.

Bibby, P., Eikeseth, S., Martin, N. T., Mudford, O. C., & Reeves, D. (2002). Progress and outcomes for children with autism receiving parent-managed intensive interventions. *Research in Developmental Disabilities, 23,* 81–104.

Blackledge, J. T., & Hayes, S. C. (2006). Using acceptance and commitment training in the support of parents of children diagnosed with autism. *Child and Family Behavior Therapy, 28,* 1–18.

Brackett, L., Reid, D. H., & Green, C. W. (2007). Effects of reactivity to observations on staff performance. *Journal of Applied Behavior Analysis, 40,* 191–195.

Breiner, J., & Beck, S. (1984). Parents as change agents in the management of their developmentally delayed children's noncompliant behaviors: A critical review. *Applied Research in Mental Retardation, 5,* 259–278.

Brookman-Frazee, L. (2004). Using parent/clinician partnerships in parent education programs for children with autism. *Journal of Positive Behavior Interventions, 6,* 195–213.

Brookman-Frazee, L., Stahmer, A., Baker-Ericzén, M. J., & Tsai, K. (2006). Parenting interventions for children with autism spectrum and disruptive behavior disorders: Opportunities for cross-fertilization. *Clinical Child and Family Psychology Review, 9,* 181–200.

Brookman-Frazee, L., Vismara, L., Drahota, A., Stahmer, A., & Openden, D. (2009). Parent training interventions for children with autism spectrum disorders. In J. L. Matson (Ed.), *Applied behavior analysis for children with autism spectrum disorders* (pp. 237–257). New York, NY: Springer.

Bruder, M. B., & Bricker, D. (1985). Parents as teachers of their children and other parents. *Journal of the Division for Early Childhood, 9,* 136–150.

Burrell, T. L., & Borrego, J. (2011). Parents' involvement in ASD treatment: What is their role? *Cognitive and Behavioral Practice, 19,* 423–432.

Cavkaytar, A., & Pollard, E. (2009). Effectiveness of parent and therapist collaboration program (PTCP) for teaching self-care and domestic skills to individuals with autism. *Education and Training in Developmental Disabilities, 44,* 381–395.

Chaabane, D. B. B., Alber-Morgan, S. R., & DeBar, R. M. (2009). The effects of parent Implemented PECS training on improvisation of mands by children with autism. *Journal of Applied Behavior Analysis, 42,* 671–677.

Chadwick, O., Momčilović, N., Rossiter, R., Stumbles, E., & Taylor, E. (2001). A randomized trial of brief individual versus group parent training for behaviour problems in children with severe learning disabilities. *Behavioural and Cognitive Psychotherapy, 29,* 151–167.

Charlop, M. H., & Trasowech, J. E. (1991). Increasing autistic children's daily spontaneous speech. *Journal of Applied Behavior Analysis, 24,* 747–761.

Charlop-Christy, M. H., & Carpenter, M. H. (2000). Modified incidental teaching sessions: A procedure for parents to increase spontaneous speech in their children with autism. *Journal of Positive Behavior Interventions, 2,* 98–112.

Coolican, J., Smith, I. M., & Bryson, S. E. (2010). Brief parent training in pivotal response treatment for preschoolers with autism. *Journal of Child Psychology and Psychiatry, 51,* 1321–1330.

Cooper, J. O., Heron, T. E., & Heward, W. L. (2007). *Applied behavior analysis* (2nd ed.). Upper Saddle River, NJ: Merrill/Prentice Hall.

Cordisco, L. K., Strain, P. S., & Depew, N. (1988). Assessment for generalization of parenting skills in home settings. *Journal of the Association for Persons with Severe Handicaps, 13,* 202–210.

Crockett, J. L., Fleming, R. K., Doepke, K. J., & Stevens, J. S. (2007). Parent training: Acquisition and generalization of discrete trials teaching skills with parents of children with autism. *Research in Developmental Disabilities, 28,* 23–36.

Csapo, M. (1979). The effect of self-recording and social reinforcement components of parent training programs. *Journal of Experimental Child Psychology, 27,* 479–488.

Cunningham, C. (1985). Training and education approaches for parents of children with special needs. *British Journal of Medical Psychology, 58,* 285–305.

DiGennaro-Reed, F. D., Codding, R., Catania, C. N., & Maguire, H. (2010). Effects of video modeling on treatment integrity of behavioral interventions. *Journal of Applied Behavior Analysis, 43,* 291–295.

Ducharme, J. M., & Drain, T. L. (2004). Errorless academic compliance training: Improving generalized cooperation with parental requests in children with autism. *Journal of the American Academy of Child and Adolescent Psychiatry, 43,* 163–171.

Eldevik, S., Eikeseth, S., Jahr, E., & Smith, T. (2006). Effects of low-intensity behavioral treatment for children with autism and mental retardation. *Journal of Autism and Developmental Disorders, 36,* 211–224.

Eldevik, S., Hastings, R. P., Hughes, J. C., Jahr, E., Eikeseth, S., & Cross, S. (2009). Meta–analysis of early intensive behavioral intervention for children with autism. *Journal of Clinical Child and Adolescent Psychology, 38*, 439–450.

Erbas, D. (2010). A collaborative approach to implement positive behavior support plans for children with problem behaviors: A comparison of consultation versus consultation and feedback approach. *Education and Training in Autism and Developmental Disabilities, 45*, 94–106.

Feldman, M. A., & Werner, S. E. (2002). Collateral effects of behavioral parent training on families of children with developmental disabilities and behavior disorders. *Behavioral Interventions, 17*, 75–83.

Forehand, R., & Kotchick, B. A. (1996). Cultural diversity: Awake-up call for parent training. *Behavior Therapy, 27*, 187–206.

Forehand, R., & Kotchick, B. A. (2002). Behavioral parent training: Current challenges and potential solutions. *Journal of Child and Family Studies, 11*, 377–384.

Galensky, T. L., Miltenberger, R. G., Stricker, J. M., & Garlinghouse, M. A. (2001). Functional assessment and treatment of mealtime behavior problems. *Journal of Positive Behavioral Interventions, 4*, 211–224.

Gillett, J. N., & LeBlanc, L. A. (2007). Parent-implemented natural language paradigm to increase language and play in children with autism. *Research in Autism Spectrum Disorders, 1*, 247–255.

Granpeesheh, D., Dixon, D. R., Tarbox, J., Kaplan, A. M., & Wilke, A. E. (2009). The effects of age and treatment intensity on behavioral intervention outcomes for children with autism spectrum disorders. *Research in Autism Spectrum Disorders, 3*, 1014–1022.

Grindle, C. F., Kovshoff, H., Hastings, R. P., & Remington, B. (2009). Parents' experiences of home-based applied behavior analysis programs for young children with autism. *Journal of Autism and Developmental Disorders, 39*, 42–56.

Harris, T. A., Peterson, S. L., Filliben, T. L., & Glassberg, M. (1998). Evaluating a more cost efficient alternative to providing in-home feedback to parents: The use of spousal feedback. *Journal of Applied Behavior Analysis, 31*, 131–134.

Ingersoll, B., & Dvortcsak, A. (2006). Including parent training in the early childhood special education curriculum for children with autism spectrum disorders. *Journal of Positive Behavior Interventions, 8*, 79–87.

Ingersoll, B., & Gergans, S. (2006). The effect of a parent-implemented imitation intervention on spontaneous imitation skills in young children with autism. *Research in Developmental Disabilities, 28*, 163–175.

Ingersoll, B. R., & Wainer, A. L. (2011). Pilot study of a school-based parent training program for preschoolers with ASD. *Autism*, 434–438.

Jang, J., Dixon, D. R., Tarbox, J., Granpeesheh, D., Kornack, J., & de Nocker, Y. (2012). Randomized trial of an eLearning program for training family members of children with autism in the principles and procedures of applied behavior analysis. *Research in Autism Spectrum Disorders, 6*, 852–856.

Johnson, C. R., Handen, B. L., Butter, E., Wagner, A., Mulick, J., Sukhodolsky, D. G., ... Smith, T. (2007). Development of a parent training program for children with pervasive developmental disorders. *Behavioral Interventions, 22*, 201–221.

Kaiser, A. P., & Hancock, T. B. (2003). Teaching parents new skills to support their young children's development. *Infants and Young Children, 16*, 9–21.

Kaiser, A. P., Hancock, T. B., & Nietfeld, J. P. (2000). The effects of parent-implemented enhanced milieu teaching on the social communication of children who have autism. *Early Education and Development, 11*, 423–446.

Koegel, L. K. (2000). Interventions to facilitate communication in autism. *Journal of Autism and Developmental Disorders, 30*, 383–391.

Koegel, R. L., Bimbela, A., & Schreibman, L. (1996). Collateral effects of parent training on family interactions. *Journal of Autism and Developmental Disorders, 26*, 347–359.

Koegel, R. L., Koegel, L. K., & Surratt, A. (1992). Language intervention and disruptive behavior in preschool children with autism. *Journal of Autism and Developmental Disorders, 22*, 141–153.

Koegel, R. L., Symon, J. B., & Koegel, L. K. (2002). Parent education for families of children with autism living in geographically distant areas. *Journal of Positive Behavior Interventions, 4*, 88–103.

Krantz, P. J., MacDuff, M. T., & McClannahan, L. E. (1993). Programming participation in family activities for children with autism: Parents' use of photographic activity schedules. *Journal of Applied Behavior Analysis, 26*, 137–138.

Kroeger, K., & Sorensen, R. (2010). A parent training model for toilet training children with autism. *Journal of Intellectual Disability Research, 54*, 556–567.

Lafasakis, M., & Sturmey, P. (2007). Training parent implementation of discrete-trial teaching: Effects on generalization of parent teaching and child correct responding. *Journal of Applied Behavior Analysis, 40*, 685–689.

Laski, K. E., Charlop, M. H., & Schreibman, L. (1988). Training parents to use the natural language paradigm to increase their autistic children's speech. *Journal of Applied Behavior Analysis, 21*, 391–400.

Lerman, D. C., Swiezy, N., Perkins-Parks, S., & Roane, H. S. (2000). Skill acquisition in parents of children with developmental disabilities: Interaction between skill type and instructional format. *Research in Developmental Disabilities, 21*, 183–196.

Lovaas, I. O. (1987). Behavioral treatment and normal educational and intellectual functioning in young autistic children. *Journal of Consulting and Clinical Psychology, 55*, 3–9.

Mancil, G. R., Conroy, M. A., & Haydon, T. F. (2009). Effects of a modified milieu therapy intervention on the social communicative behaviors of young children with autism spectrum disorders. *Journal of Autism and Developmental Disorders, 39,* 149–163.

Matson, M. L., Mahan, S., & Matson, J. L. (2009). Parent training: A review of methods for children with autism spectrum disorders. *Research in Autism Spectrum Disorders, 3,* 868–875.

McCartney, E. J., Anderson, C. M, English, C. L., & Horner, R. H. (2005). Effect of brief clinic based training on the ability of caregivers to implement escape extinction. *Journal of Positive Behavior Interventions, 7,* 18–32.

McClannahan, L. E., Krantz, P. J., & McGee, G. G. (1982). Parents as therapists for autistic children: A model for effective parent training. *Analysis and Intervention in Developmental Disabilities, 2,* 223–252.

McConachie, H., & Diggle, T. (2007). Parent implemented early intervention for young children with autism spectrum disorder: A systematic review. *Journal of Evaluation in Clinical Practice, 13,* 120–129.

McGimsey, J. F., Greene, B. F., & Lutzker, J. R. (1995). Competence in aspects of behavioral treatment and consultation: Implications for service delivery and graduate training. *Journal of Applied Behavior Analysis, 28,* 301–315.

McIntyre, L. L. (2008). Parent training for young children with developmental disabilities: Randomized controlled trial. *American Journal on Mental Retardation, 113,* 356–368.

McIntyre, L. L., & Phaneuf, L. K. (2008). A three-tier model of parent education in early childhood: Applying a problem-solving model. *Topics in Early Childhood Special Education, 27,* 214–222.

Meadan, H., Ostrosky, M. M., Zaghlawan, H. Y., & Yu, S. (2009). Promoting the social and communicative behavior of young children with autism spectrum disorders: A review of parent-implemented intervention studies. *Topics in Early Childhood Special Education, 29,* 90–104.

Miles, N. I., & Wilder, D. A. (2009). The effects of behavioral skills training on caregiver implementation of guided compliance. *Journal of Applied Behavior Analysis, 42,* 405–410.

Mira, M. (1970). Results of a behavior modification training program for parents and teachers. *Behaviour Research and Therapy, 8,* 309–311.

Moes, D. (1995). Parent education and parenting stress. In R. L. Koegel & L. K. Koegel (Eds.), *Teaching children with autism: Strategies for initiating positive interactions and improving learning opportunities* (pp. 79–94). Baltimore, MD: Paul H. Brookes.

Moes, D. R., & Frea, W. D. (2002). Contextualized behavioral support in early intervention for children with autism and their families. *Journal of Autism and Developmental Disorders, 32,* 519–533.

Mueller, M. M., Piazza, C. C., Moore, J. W., Kelley, M. E., Bethke, S. A., Pruett, A. E., ... Layer, S. A. (2003). Training parents to implement pediatric feeding protocols. *Journal of Applied Behavior Analysis, 36,* 545–562.

Muir, K. A., & Milan, M. A. (1982). Parent reinforcement for child achievement: The use of a lottery to maximize parent training effects. *Journal of Applied Behavior Analysis, 15,* 455–460.

Najdowski, A. C., Wallace, M. D., Doney, J. K., & Ghezzi, P. M. (2003). Parental assessment and treatment of food selectivity in natural settings. *Journal of Applied Behavior Analysis, 36,* 383–386.

Najdowski, A. C., Wallace, M. D., Penrod, B., Tarbox, J., Reagon, K., & Higbee, T. S. (2008). Caregiver-conducted experimental functional analyses of inappropriate mealtime behavior. *Journal of Applied Behavior Analysis, 41,* 459–465.

Najdowski, A. C., Wallace, M. D., Reagon, K., Penrod, B., Higbee, T. S., & Tarbox, J. (2010). Utilizing a home-based parent training approach in the treatment of food selectivity. *Behavioral Interventions, 25,* 89–107.

National Autism Center. (2009). *National standards report: The National Standards Project – Addressing the need for evidence-based practice guidelines for autism spectrum disorders.* Randolph, MA: Author.

National Research Council. (2001). *Educating children with autism. Committee on educational interventions for children with autism.* Catherine Lord & James McGee (Eds.), Division of behavioral and social sciences and education. Washington, DC: National Academy Press.

Neef, N. A. (1995). Pyramidal parent training by peers. *Journal of Applied Behavior Analysis, 283,* 333–337.

Nefdt, N., Koegel, R., Singer, G., & Gerber, M. (2010). The use of a self-directed learning program to provide introductory training in pivotal response treatment to parents of children with autism. *Journal of Positive Behavior Interventions, 12,* 23–32.

O'Dell, S. L., Blackwell, L. J., Larcen, S. W., & Hogan, J. L. (1977). Competency-based training for severely behaviorally handicapped children and their parents. *Journal of Autism and Childhood Schizophrenia, 7,* 231–242.

O'Reilly, M. F., & Lancioni, G. E. (2001). Treating food refusal in a child with Williams syndrome using the parent as therapist in the home setting. *Journal of Intellectual Disability Records, 45,* 41–46.

Osborne, L. A., McHugh, L., Saunders, J., & Reed, P. (2008). Parenting stress reduces the effectiveness of early teaching interventions for autistic spectrum disorders. *Journal of Autism and Developmental Disorders, 38,* 1092–1103.

Parsons, M. B., & Reid, D. H. (1995). Training residential supervisors to provide feedback for maintaining staff teaching skills with people who have severe disabilities. *Journal of Applied Behavior Analysis, 28,* 317–322.

Peters-Scheffer, N., Didden, R., Korzilius, H., & Sturmey, P. (2011). A meta-analytic study on the effectiveness of comprehensive ABA-based early intervention programs for children with autism spectrum disorders. *Research in Autism Spectrum Disorders, 5,* 60–69.

Petscher, E. S., & Bailey, J. S. (2006). Effects of training, prompting, and self-monitoring on staff behavior in a classroom for students with disabilities. *Journal of Applied Behavior Analysis, 39,* 215–226.

Plant, K. M., & Sanders, M. R. (2007). Reducing problem behavior during care-giving in families of preschool-aged children with developmental disabilities. *Research in Developmental Disabilities, 28,* 362–385.

Randolph, J. K., Stichter, J. P., Schmidt, C. T., & O'Connor, K. V. (2011). Fidelity and effectiveness of PRT implemented by caregivers without college degrees. *Focus Autism Other Developmental Disabilities, 26,* 230–238.

Reagon, K. A., & Higbee, T. S. (2009). Parent-implemented script fading to promote play-based verbal initiations in children with autism. *Journal of Applied Behavior Analysis, 42,* 659–664.

Reed, H. E., McGrew, S. G., Artibee, K., Surdkya, K., Goldman, S. E., Frank, K., ... Malow, B. A. (2009). Parent-based sleep education workshops in autism. *Journal of Child Neurology, 24,* 936–945.

Reichow, B., & Wolery, M. (2009). Comprehensive synthesis of early intensive behavioral interventions for young children with autism based on the UCLA young autism project model. *Journal of Autism and Developmental Disorders, 39,* 23–41.

Reid, D. H., & Fitch, W. H. (2011). Training staff and parents: Evidence-based approaches. In J. L. Matson & P. Sturmey (Eds.), *International handbook of autism and pervasive developmental disorders* (pp. 509–519). New York, NY: Springer.

Rocha, M. L., Schreibman, L., & Stahmer, A. C. (2007). Effectiveness of training parents to teach joint attention in children with autism. *Journal of Early Intervention, 29,* 154–172.

Rogers, S. J., & Vismara, L. A. (2008). Evidence-based comprehensive treatments for early autism. *Journal of Clinical Child and Adolescent Psychology, 37,* 8–38.

Sanders, M. R., & Glynn, T. (1981). Training parents in behavioral self-management: An analysis of generalization and management. *Journal of Applied Behavior Analysis, 14,* 223–237.

Santarelli, G., Koegel, R. L., Casas, J. M., & Koegel, L. K. (2001). Culturally diverse families participating in behavior therapy parent education programs for children with developmental disabilities. *Journal of Positive Behavior Interventions, 3,* 120–123.

Schreibman, L., Dufek, S., & Cunningham, A. B. (2011). Identifying moderators of treatment outcome for children with autism. In J. L. Matson & P. Sturmey (Eds.), *International handbook of autism and pervasive developmental disorders* (pp. 295–305). New York, NY: Springer.

Schultz, T. R., Schmidt, C. T., & Stichter, J. P. (2011). A review of parent education programs for parents of children with autism spectrum disorders. *Focus on Autism and Other Developmental Disabilities, 26,* 96–104.

Seung, H. K., Ashwell, S., Elder, J. H., & Valcante, G. (2006). Verbal communication outcomes in children with autism after in-home father training. *Journal of Intellectual Disability Research, 50,* 139–150.

Sheinkopf, S. J., & Siegel, B. (1998). Home-based behavioral treatment of young children with autism. *Journal of Autism and Developmental Disorders, 28,* 15–23.

Singer, G. H. S., Ethridge, B. L., & Aldana, S. I. (2007). Primary and secondary effects of parenting and stress management interventions for parents of children with developmental disabilities: A meta-analysis. *Mental Retardation and Developmental Disabilities Research Reviews, 13,* 357–369.

Singh, N. N., Lancioni, G. E., Winton, A. S. W., Fisher, B. C., Wahler, R. G., Mcaleavey, K., ... Sabaawi, M. (2006). Mindful parenting decreases aggression, noncompliance, and self-injury in children with autism. *Journal of Emotional and Behavioral Disorders, 14,* 169–177.

Singh, N. N., Lancioni, G. E., Winton, A. S. W., Singh, J., Curtis, J. W., Wahler, R. G., & McAleavey, K. M. (2007). Mindful parenting decreases aggression and increases social behavior in children with developmental disabilities. *Behavior Modification, 31,* 749–771.

Smith, M. R., & Lerman, D. C. (1999). A preliminary comparison of guided compliance and high-probability instructional sequences as treatment for noncompliance in children with developmental disabilities. *Research in Developmental Disabilities, 20,* 183–195.

Smith, T., Buch, G. A., & Gamby, T. E. (2000). Parent-directed, intensive early intervention for children with pervasive developmental disorder. *Research in Developmental Disabilities, 21,* 297–309.

Smith, T., Groen, A. D., & Wynn, J. W. (2000). Randomized trial of intensive early intervention for children with pervasive developmental disorder. *American Journal on Mental Retardation, 105,* 269–285.

Snyder, K., Lambert, J., & Twohig, M. P. (2011). Defusion: A behavior-analytic strategy for addressing private events. *Behavior Analysis in Practice, 4,* 4–13.

Solomon, M., Ono, M., Timmer, S., & Goodlin-Jones, B. (2008). The effectiveness of parent–child interaction therapy for families of children on the autism spectrum. *Journal of Autism and Developmental Disorders, 38,* 1767–1776.

Stahmer, A. C., & Gist, K. (2001). The effects of an accelerated parent education program on technique mastery and child outcome. *Journal of Positive Behavior Interventions, 3,* 75–82.

Steiner, A. M., Koegel, L. K., Koegel, R. L., & Ence, W. A. (2012). Issues and theoretical constructs regarding parent education for autism spectrum disorders. *Journal of Autism and Developmental Disorders, 42,* 1218–1227.

Stewart, K. K., Carr, J. E., & LeBlanc, L. A. (2007). Evaluation of family-implemented behavioral skills training for teaching social skills to a child with asperger's disorder. *Clinical Case Studies, 6*, 252–262.

Stiebel, D. (1999). Promoting augmentative communication during daily routines: A parent problem-solving intervention. *Journal of Positive Behavior Interventions, 1*, 159–169.

Stokes, T. E., & Baer, D. M. (1977). An implicit technology of generalization. *Journal of Applied Behavior Analysis, 10*, 349–367.

Symon, J. B. (2001). Parent education for autism: Issues in providing services at a distance. *Journal of Positive Behavior Interventions, 3*, 160–174.

Symon, J. B. (2005). Expanding interventions for children with autism: Parents as trainers. *Journal of Positive Behavior Interventions, 7*, 159–173.

Tarbox, J., Schiff, A., & Najdowski, A. C. (2010). Parent-implemented procedural modification of escape extinction in the treatment of food selectivity in a young child with autism. *Education and Treatment of Children, 33*, 223–234.

Tarbox, J., Wallace, M. D., & Tarbox, R. S. F. (2002). Successful generalized parent training and failed schedule thinning of response blocking for automatically maintained object mouthing. *Behavioral Interventions, 17*, 169–178.

Tekin-Iftar, E. (2008). Parent-delivered community-based instruction with simultaneous prompting for teaching community skills to children with developmental disabilities. *Education and Training in Developmental Disabilities, 43*, 249–265.

Ward-Horner, J., & Sturmey, P. (2008). The effects of general-case training and behavioral skills training on the generalization of parents' use of discrete-trial teaching, child correct responses, and child maladaptive behavior. *Behavioral Interventions, 23*, 271–284.

Warren, Z., McPheeters, M. L., Sathe, N., Foss-Feig, J. H., Glasser, A., & Veenstra–VanderWeele, J. (2011). A systematic review of early intensive intervention for autism spectrum disorders. *Pediatrics, 127*, 1303–1311.

Weiskop, S., Richdale, A., & Matthews, J. (2005). Behavioural treatment to reduce sleep problems in children with autism or fragile X syndrome. *Developmental Medicine and Child Neurology, 47*, 94–104.

Weiss, J., & Lunsky, Y. (2010). Service utilization patterns in parents of youth and adults with intellectual disability who experienced behavioral crisis. *Journal of Mental Health Research in Intellectual Disabilities, 3*, 145–163.

Werle, M. A., Murphy, T. B., & Budd, K. S. (1993). Treating chronic food refusal in young children: Home-based parent training. *Journal of Applied Behavior Analysis, 26*, 421–433.

Werle, M. A., Murphy, T. B., & Budd, K. S. (1998). Broadening the parameters of investigation in treating young children's chronic food refusal. *Behavior Therapy, 29*, 87–105.

Whittingham, K., Sofronoff, K., Sheffield, J., & Sanders, M. R. (2009). Stepping stones triple P: An RCT of a parenting program with parents of a child diagnosed with an autism spectrum disorder. *Journal of Abnormal Child Psychology, 37*, 469–480.

Yoder, P., & Stone, W. L. (2006). A randomized comparison of the effect of two prelinguistic communication interventions on the acquisition of spoken communication in preschoolers with ASD. *Journal of Speech, Language, and Hearing Research, 49*, 698–711.

Young, K. L., Boris, A. L., Thomson, K. M., Martin, G. L., & Yu, C. T. (2012). Evaluation of a self-instructional package on discrete-trials teaching to parents of children with autism. *Research in Autism Spectrum Disorders, 6*, 1321–1330.

COMMENTARY

Conclusions and Future Directions

JAMES K. LUISELLI

The chapters in this book addressed many diagnostic, assessment, intervention, and research concerns among children and youth with ASD. Clearly, there have been noteworthy advances and innovations in practice and scientific inquiry. Moving forward, there will be additional developments, refinements, and controversies about the types of services and expected outcomes in the ASD population. My purpose in this concluding chapter is to briefly consider some of the areas that were emphasized by chapter authors and set the tone for future directions.

DIAGNOSTIC ASSESSMENT

The appearance of the *DSM-5* in 2013 will affect the numbers of children and youth that are diagnosed with ASD. If, as some preliminary research suggests, the new *DSM-5* diagnostic criteria reduces prevalence of ASD, then current service options may dwindle or be modified in ways that decrease effectiveness. Though the diagnostic landscape subsequent to *DSM-5* is uncertain, the effects of modified criteria on screening, assessing, and servicing children and youth with ASD should be a priority for practitioners and researchers alike.

Acknowledging the critical importance of early ASD detection and diagnosis, several chapters highlighted the need for developing reliable and valid assessment instruments that are easily implemented and interpreted. For example, pediatricians are frequently the first professional contact for parents who are concerned about developmental delays in their young children. Screening and assessment tools must be sensitive enough to identify cognitive and behavioral presentation that triggers referral for formal diagnostic evaluation. This process of detecting,

evaluating, and confirming an ASD diagnosis is evolving but still requires standardization and comprehensive field testing within clinics, hospitals, and similar child service settings.

Similarly, there should be more discussion about explaining diagnostic results to parents. The vulnerability of families during the early stages of diagnosis is well recognized but there are few guidelines for presenting and interpreting assessment findings. Furthermore, some parents may require personal counseling to help them adjust after learning about their child's diagnosis. Perhaps the greatest challenge to professionals is advising families about making treatment choices from the overwhelming alternatives that confront them. More than ever, families of children and youth with ASD should be acquainted with and guided toward evidence-based methods that will put them on the road to maximally successful outcomes.

One additional issue, also referenced in several of the chapters, is comorbidity among children and youth with ASD. There is still controversy about how *DSM* diagnostic criteria, which are derived from a normative population, apply to people who have developmental disabilities. In many cases children and youth with ASD are unable to meet diagnostic criteria for conditions such as obsessive-compulsive disorder (OCD) and generalized anxiety disorder (GAD) because they cannot self-report or do not have sufficient awareness about the problem (e.g., "I know this is irrational but I can't seem to stop."). Several authors noted that children and youth with ASD may indeed have comorbid features which are expressed differently from people in the general population. Thus, further work is necessary to validate assessment instruments that will clarify differential diagnosis and properly recognize treatable conditions.

MEASUREMENT

Multiple outcome and process measures are required to properly evaluate educational and intervention plans with children and youth who have ASD. Most commonly, practitioners measure skill acquisition and challenging behaviors to verify the effectiveness of instructional and behavior support plans respectively. However these measures alone are not sufficient—instead there are other "quality of life" indices which should be included. For example, are children, youth, parents, and care-providers satisfied with the professional services they receive? Were the interventions and training procedures acceptable to them? These and similar questions represent objectives of social validity assessment which documents how well stakeholders value the work that was done with them. Having this information enables professionals to design plans that fit the needs and limitations of interventionists.

Personal happiness is another quality of life indication that deserves routine measurement. Too often educational and intervention procedures are implemented without directly assessing the emotional impact on the people served. Some measures of personal happiness would be smiling, laughing, verbal comments (e.g., "I like that."), and similar observable behaviors. Such measurement could be conducted in the context of instructional, social-interactive, and leisure activities, thereby ensuring that learning and development objectives are being achieved in the most positive and personally satisfying way.

Finally, process measurement refers to service provision quantification such as the number of hours spent training teachers at a school and the frequency of home-based consultation visits with a family. With process measures professionals and service programs can gauge desired outcomes relative to "what is needed." That is, service organizations should know how much time, money, and resources are required to produce quality programs for children and youth with ASD in their schools, homes, community agencies, clinics, and specialized centers. Analyses of these data provide support and advocacy for programmatic recommendations.

INTERVENTION

As detailed in this book, children and youth with ASD have benefited greatly from decades of innovative research that produced effective intervention procedures for teaching skills, reducing challenging behaviors, and improving quality of life. Furthermore, research-to-practice translation has been expedited by conducting studies under natural conditions. I note that research advances have not only identified evidence-based and empirically supported methods but additionally, the conceptual bases and comparative effectiveness of established and promising procedures.

Virtually all of the chapters devoted to intervention discussed integrity assessment. To reiterate, we can only draw valid conclusions about the effects of intervention procedures by documenting that care-providers implemented those procedures accurately. Accordingly, intervention integrity assessment must be integrated within instructional and behavior support plans. How often to conduct this assessment and what methods are necessary to improve implementation and maintain procedural fidelity long-term are just some of the research foci that will guide future practice.

Consistent with the goal of fortifying intervention integrity, professionals must continue to evaluate procedures for training care-providers. The most successful training is applied in vivo according to a competency-based model that teaches people requisite skills. Competency-based training must also be adaptable to the learning needs of recipient care-providers much like programs are individualized for children and youth with ASD. It is unlikely, for example, that all training methods will be equally effective with every therapist, teacher, and parent. Similarly, cultural and language differences among care-providers must be factored into the objectives and composition of training programs.

Alternative and augmentative communication (AAC) will continue to play a vital role in educational programs, in part because of the language needs of children and youth with ASD, but also as a consequence of the rapid evolution of general consumer level hardware and communication software. Notably, the availability of various hand-held media devices and programmatic applications has hastened a new era of AAC practice that surely will become more sophisticated in the coming years. Advancement in this area will depend on the results of systematic research, currently at a nascent stage, in order to validate hardware and software systems that are truly effective and can be used proficiently in the "real world." Future research should also include comparative analyses of different portable devices and applications, social validation of user satisfaction, and ancillary positive outcomes such as expanded social networks and fewer challenging behaviors among communication users.

Recent years have revealed new developments for intervening with and supporting children and youth with ASD. For example, the chapter about cognitive-behavioral therapy (CBT) illustrated methods and techniques that previously were not considered as legitimate therapeutic choices for people with language and intellectual limitations. We now know that having ASD does not preclude a person from receiving CBT to overcome problems like OCD, GAD, and specific phobia. Likewise, mindfulness caregiving and support represents a novel but empirically tested approach within the professional community. On one hand, mindfulness-based strategies have been evaluated as intervention for challenging behaviors displayed by children and youth with ASD. Another approach is using mindfulness principles and practices to train parents and direct-care providers. There also appears to be heightened interest in self-management training to enhance learning, reduce challenging behaviors, expand personal autonomy, and lessen the supervisory demands of care-providers.

Many purported ASD treatments are disseminated to the professional and lay public via the Internet, popular books, and workshops. Because much of this information is not research supported, relies on testimonials, and often includes unfounded pronouncements, researchers have opportunity to study the purported effects of poorly validated intervention methods that have gained acceptance by practitioners and parents. I highlight, among many, sensory-integration therapy, elimination diets, nutritional supplementation, animal therapies, and EEG biofeedback. It is the responsibility of ASD professionals to advance rigorous inquiry and dissemination efforts that counter pseudoscience and the unfortunate effects of "fad treatments."

INDEX